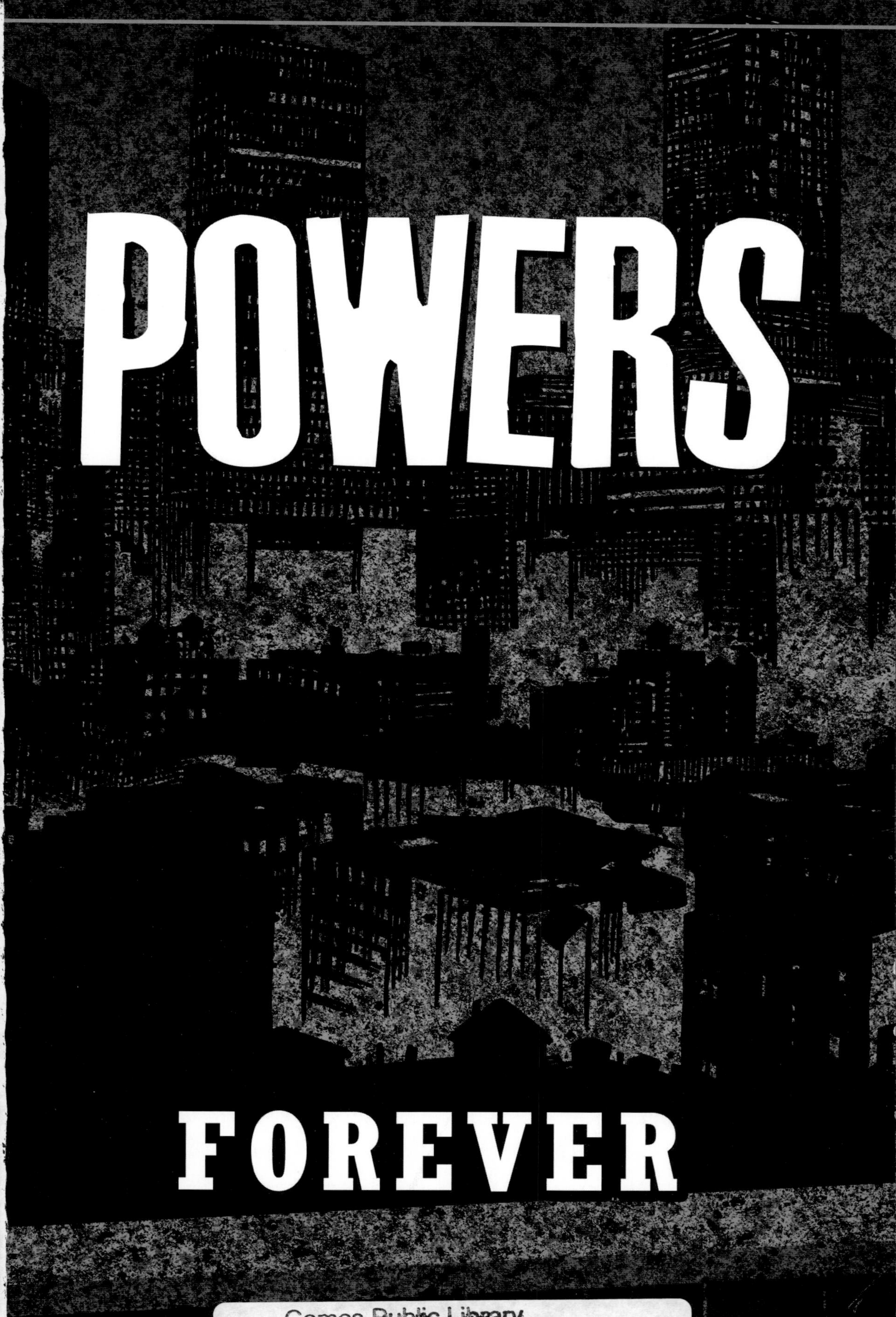
POWERS
FOREVER

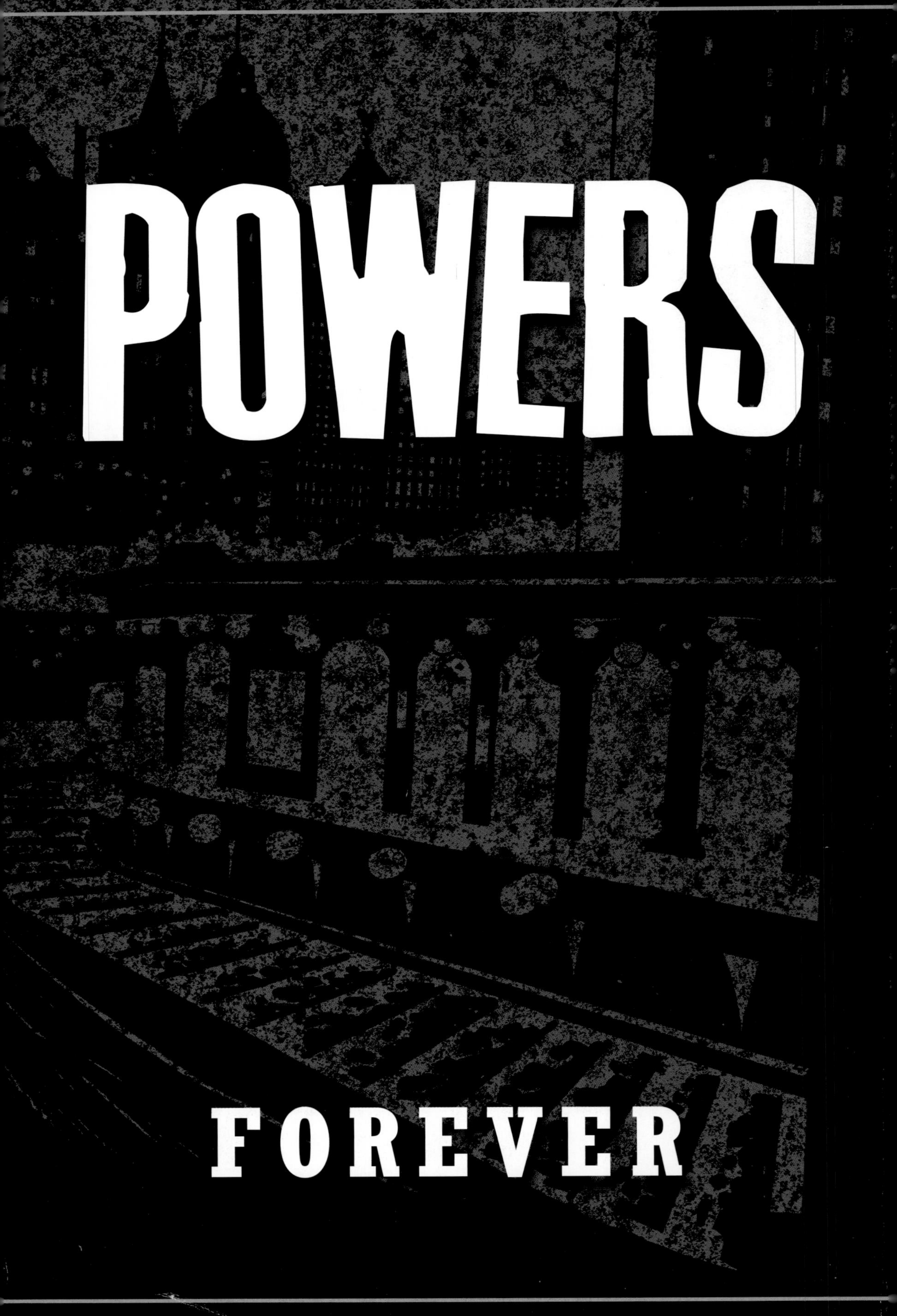

# POWERS

## FOREVER

Created and Produced by

# BRIAN
# MICHAEL
# BENDIS
# &
# MICHAEL
# AVON
# OEMING

Color Art: **PETE PANTAZIS**
Letters: **KEN BRUZENAK**
Editors: **K.C. McCRORY**
**& JAMIE S. RICH**
WITH
**JAMES LUCAS JONES**

Collection Editor: **JENNIFER GRÜNWALD**
Book Design: **PATRICK McGRATH**
Cover Design: **TIM DANIEL**
Business Affairs: **ALISA BENDIS**

**Previously:**

**Detectives Christian Walker and Deena Pilgrim work out of the special homicide unit in charge of cases that involve Powers.**

**Walker has been off the force for almost a year due to his scandalous interview in the press about the federal corruption in law enforcement.**

**POWERS VOL. 7: FOREVER.** Contains material originally published in magazine form as POWERS VOL. 1 #31-37. First printing 2012. ISBN# 978-0-7851-6019-9. Published by MARVEL WORLDWIDE, INC., a subsidiary of MARVEL ENTERTAINMENT, LLC. OFFICE OF PUBLICATION: 135 West 50th Street, New York, NY 10020.  $24.99 per copy in the U.S. and $27.99 in Canada (GST #R127032852); Canadian Agreement #40668537. **Printed in the U.S.A.**

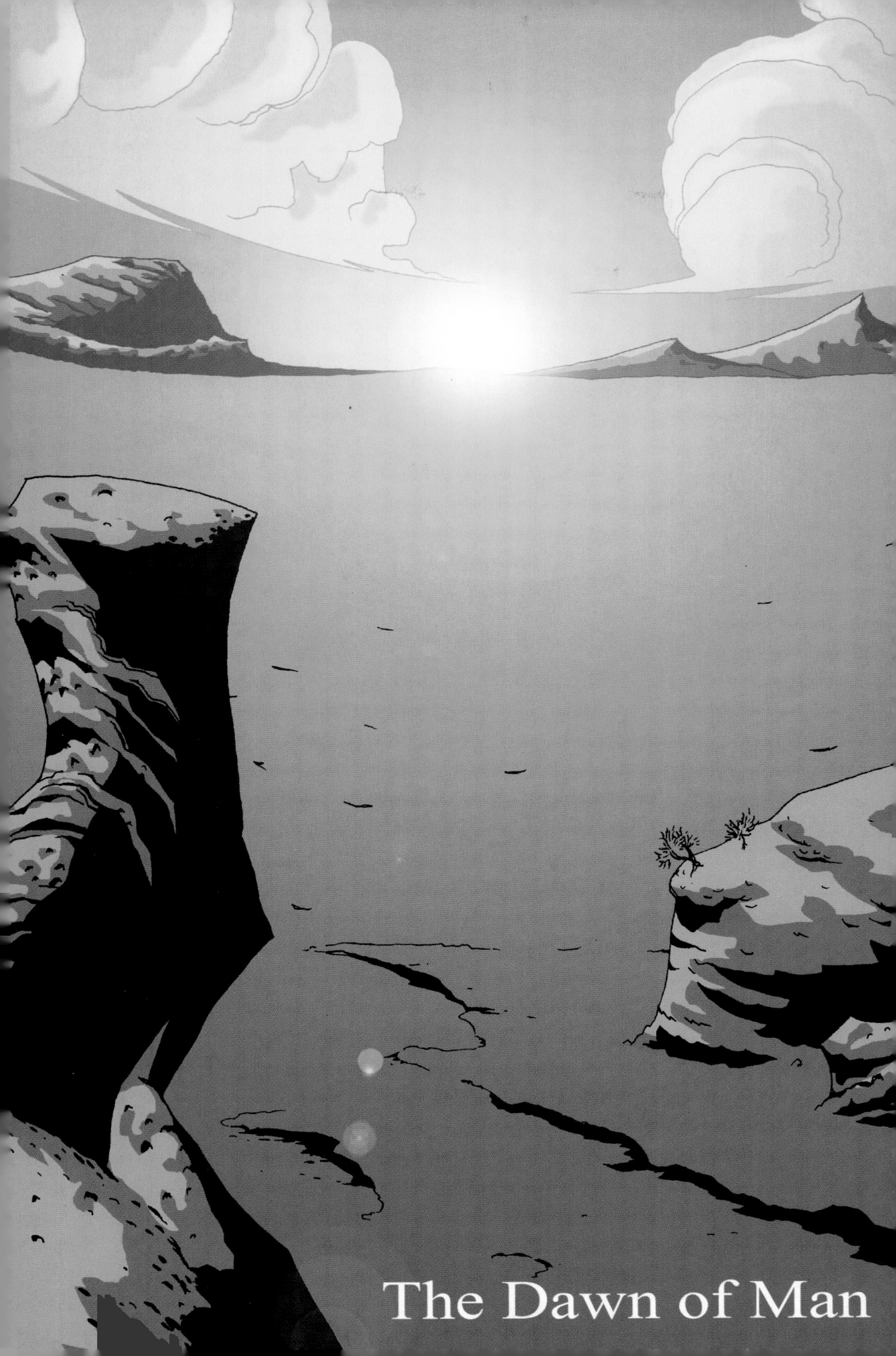
The Dawn of Man

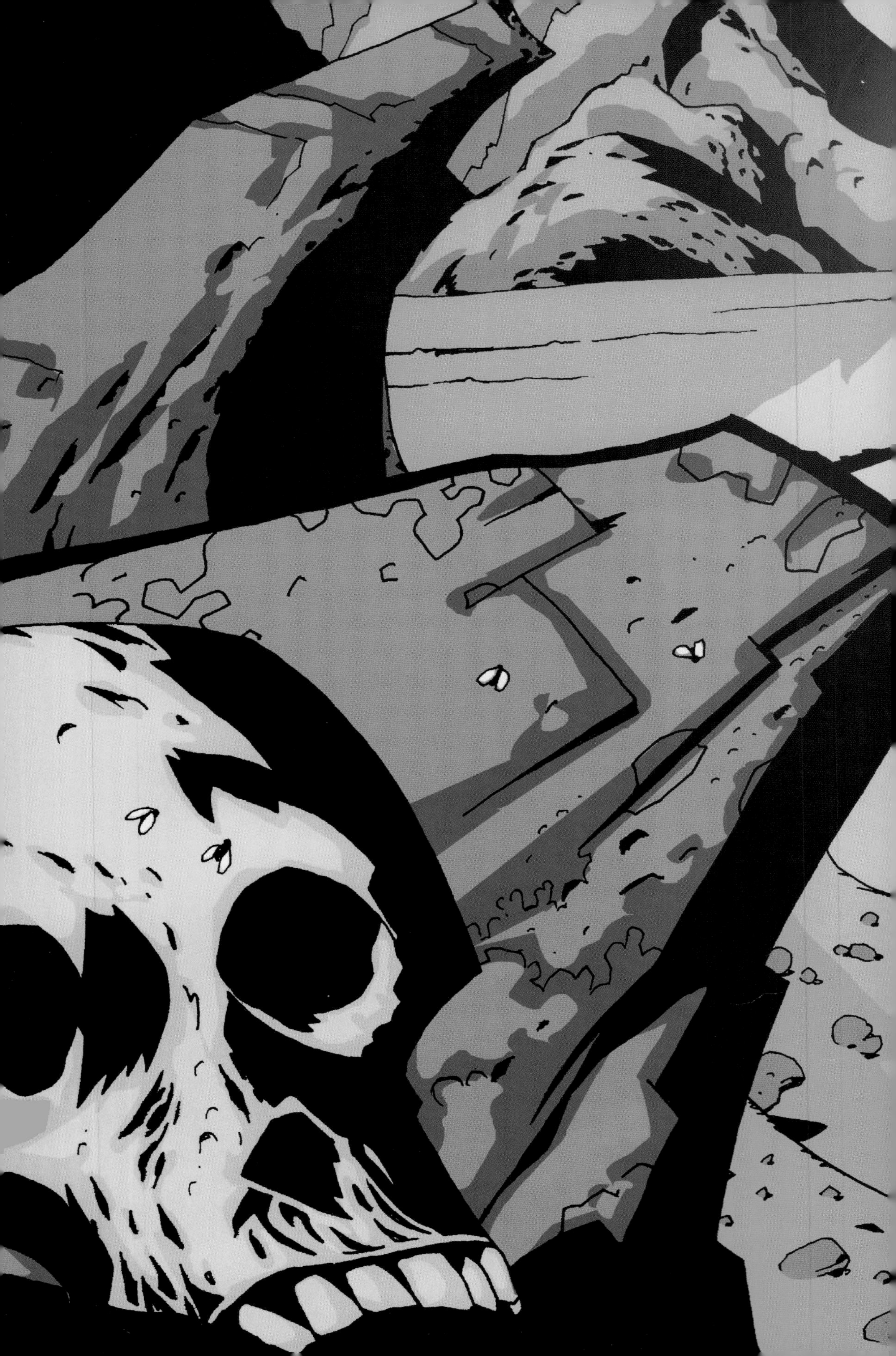

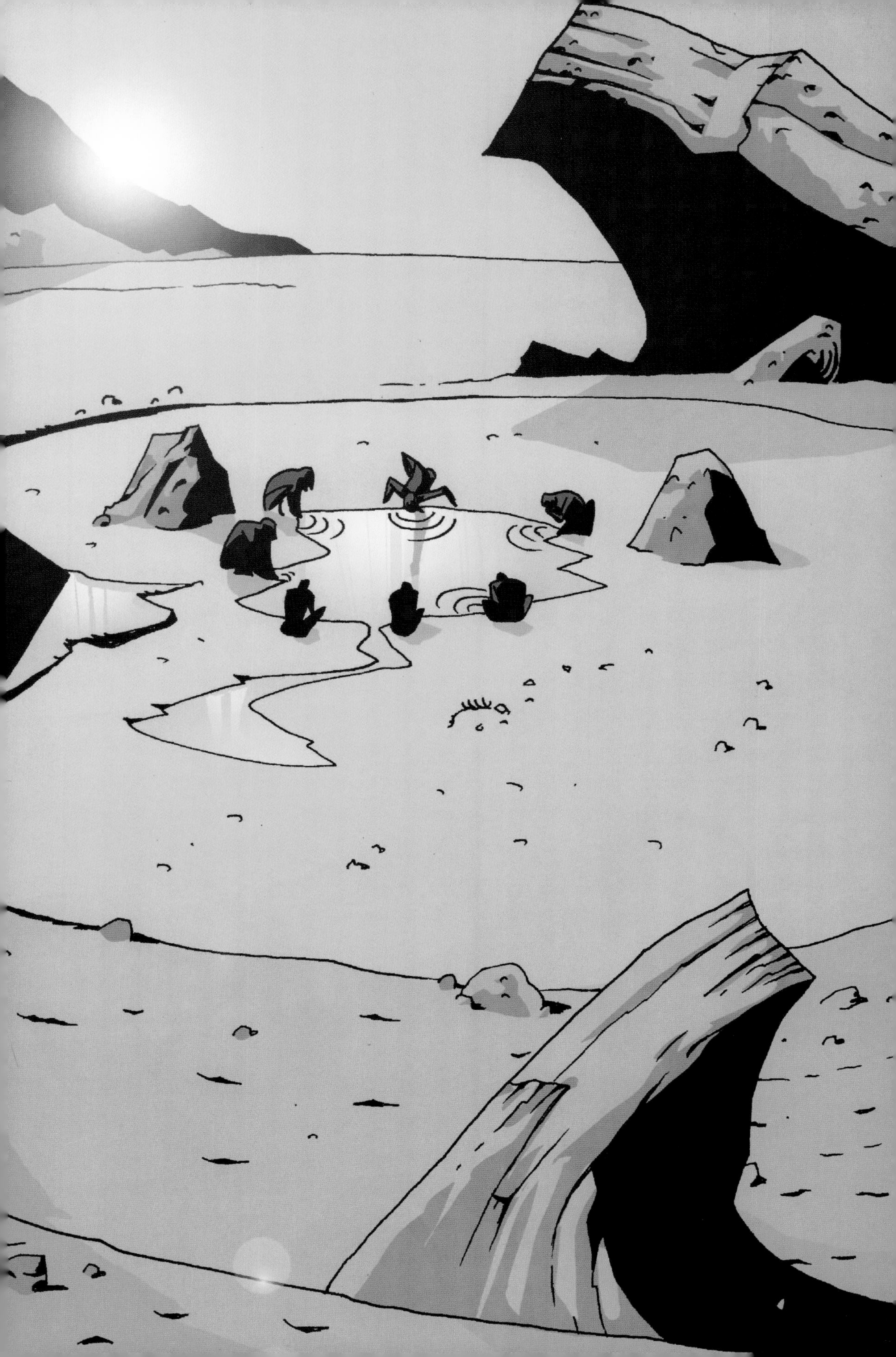

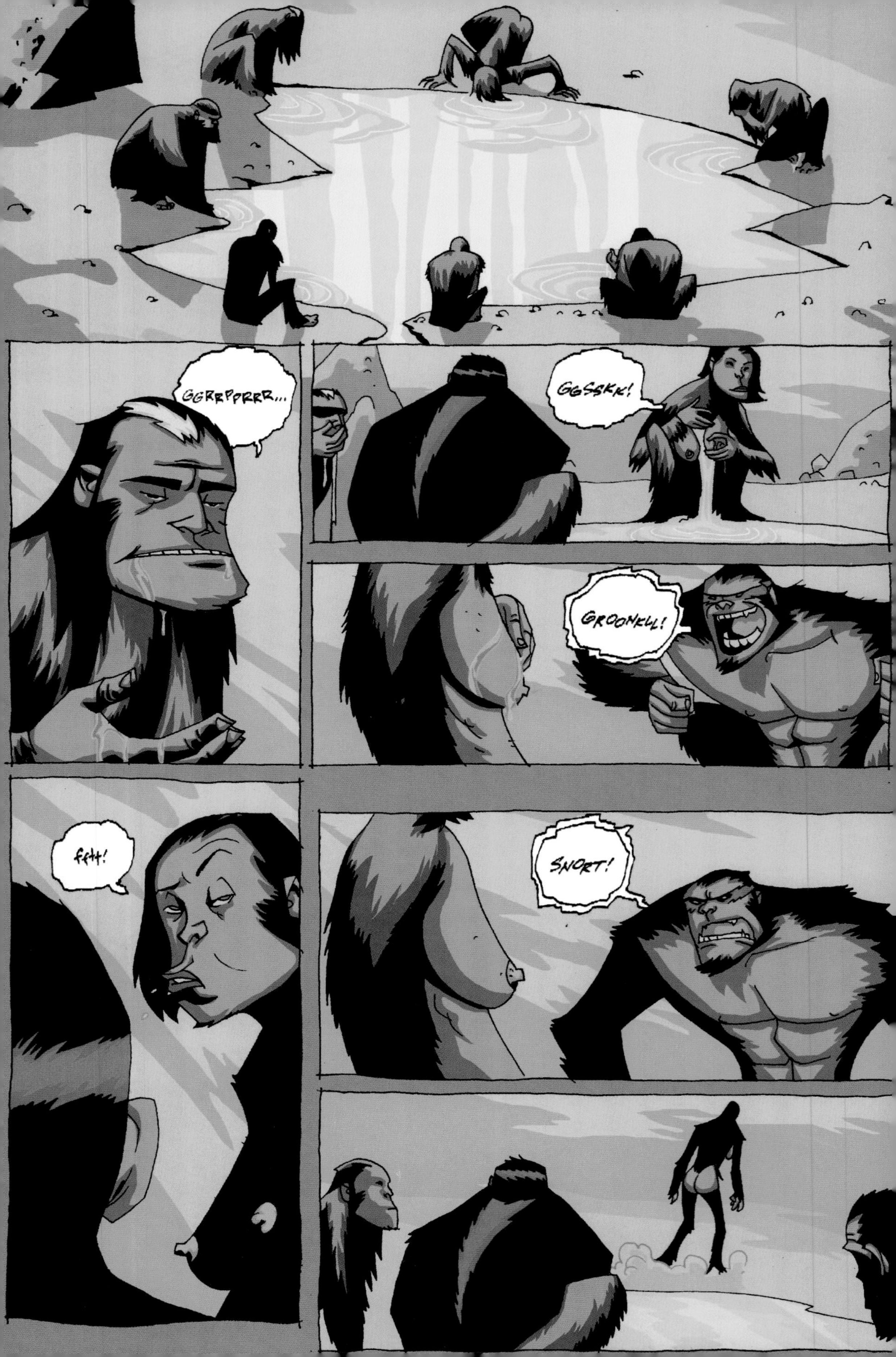
GGRRPPRRR...
GGSSKK!
GROONKUL!
FFTT!
SNORT!

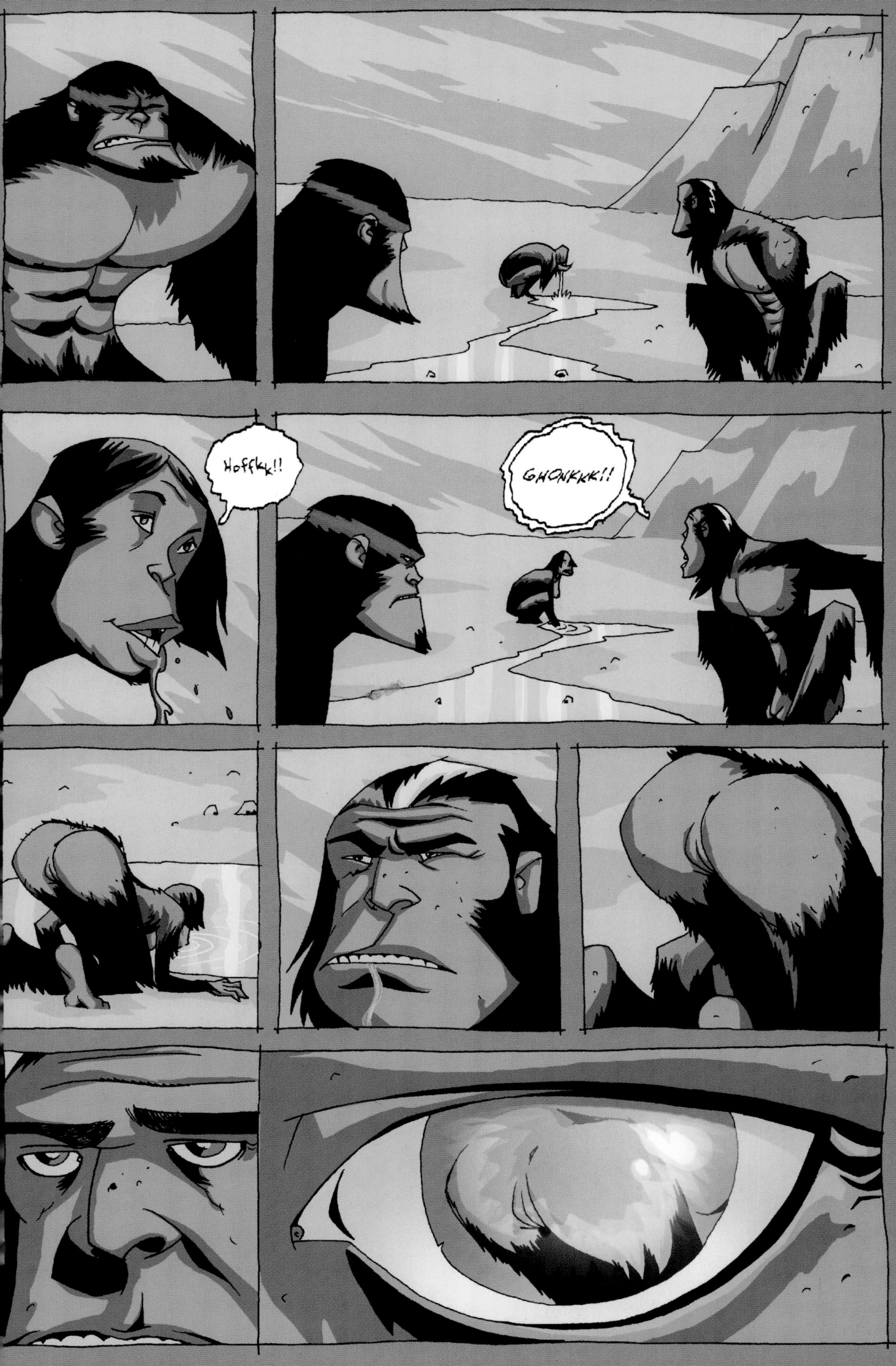
Hoffkk!!
GHONKKK!!

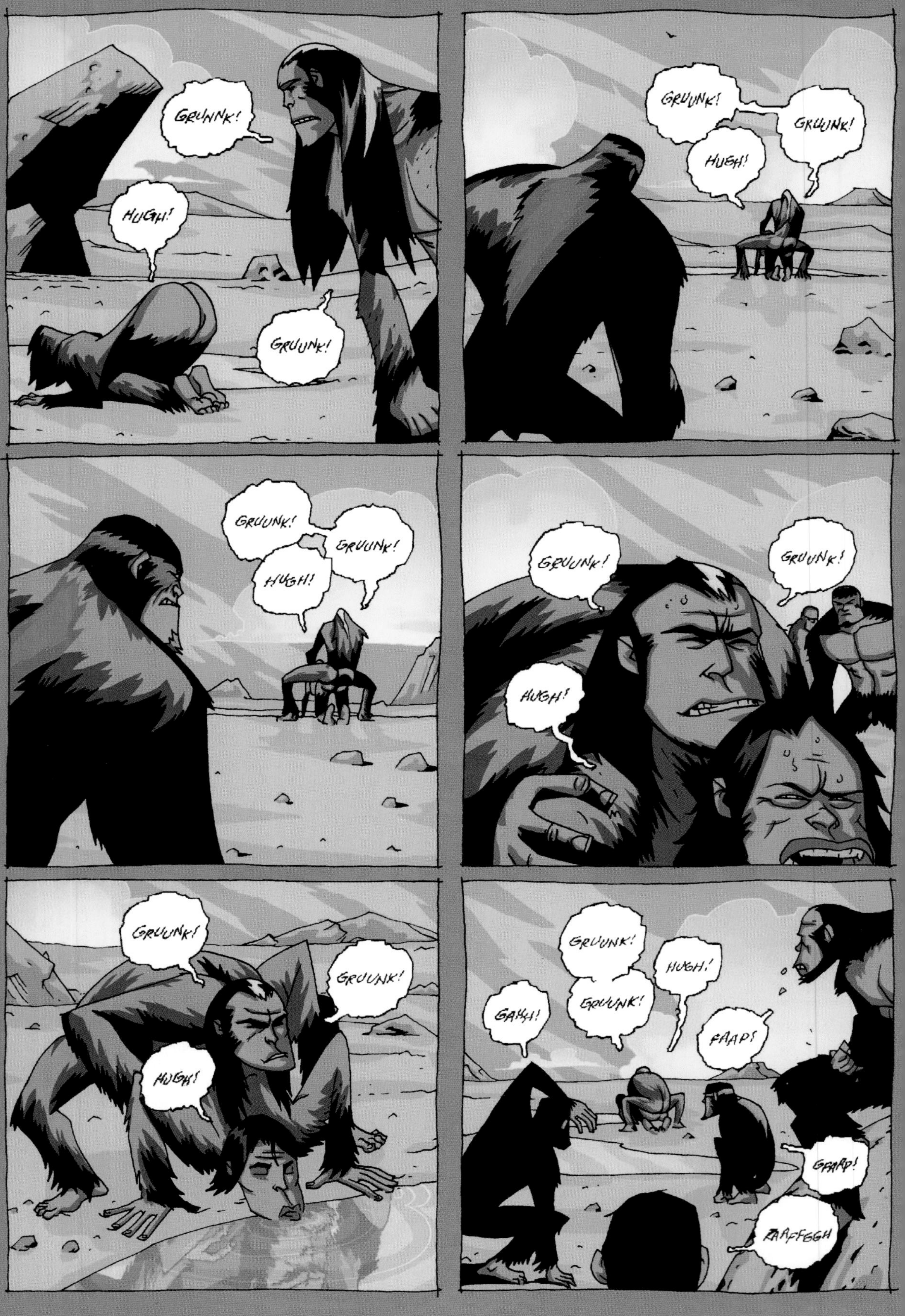

GRUNNK!
HUGH!
GRUUNK!
GRUUNK!
GRUUNK!
HUGH!
GRUUNK!
GRUUNK!
HUGH!
GRUUNK!
GRUUNK!
HUGH!
GRUUNK!
GRUUNK!
HUGH!
GRUUNK!
HUGH!
GRUUNK!
GAHH!
FAAP!
GFARP!
ZARFFGGH

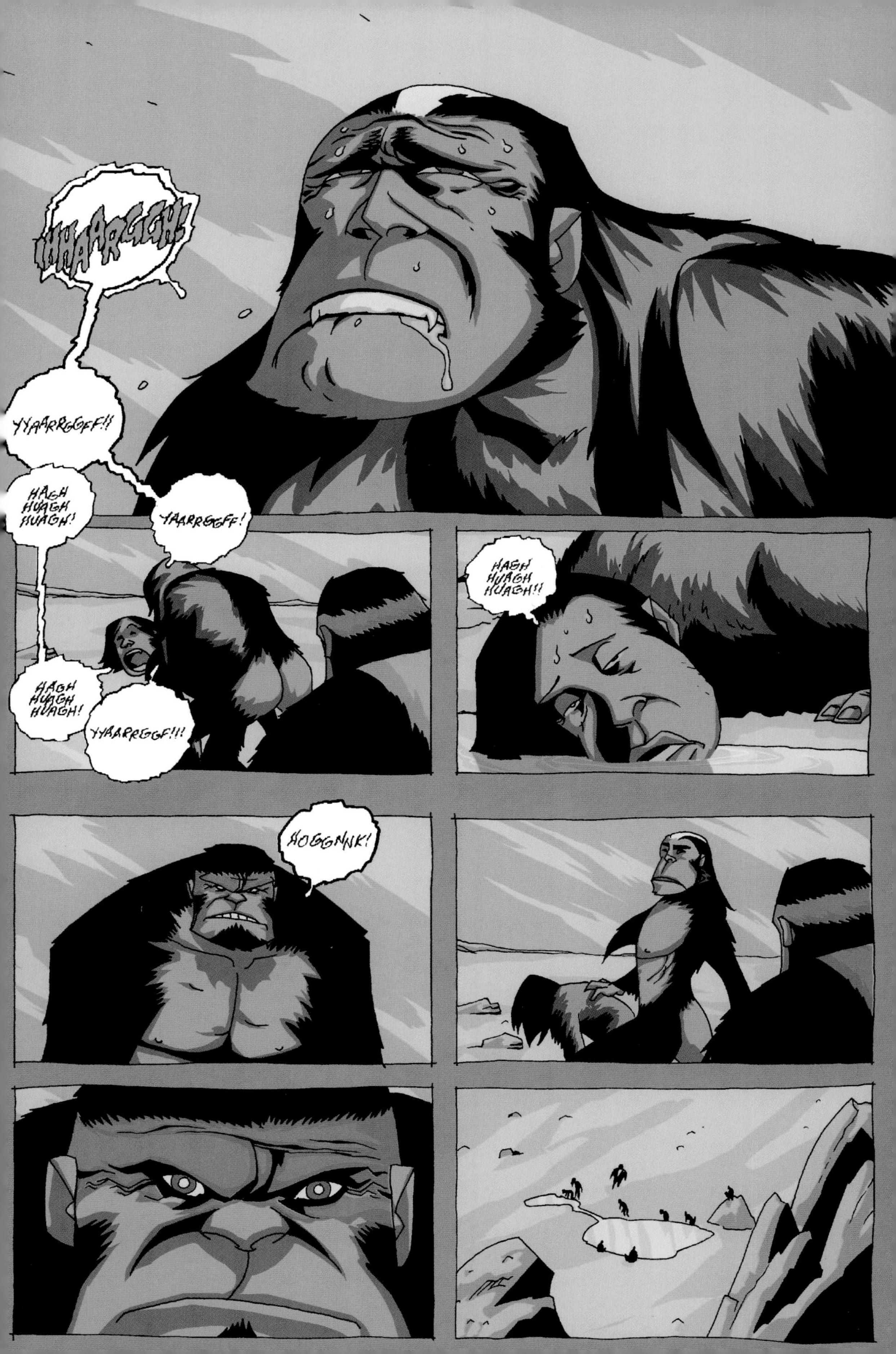
HHAARGGH!
YYAARRGGFF!!
HAGH HUAGH HUAGH!
YAARRGGFF!
HAGH HUAGH HUAGH!!
HAGH HUAGH HUAGH!
YYAARRGGF!!!
HOGGNNK!

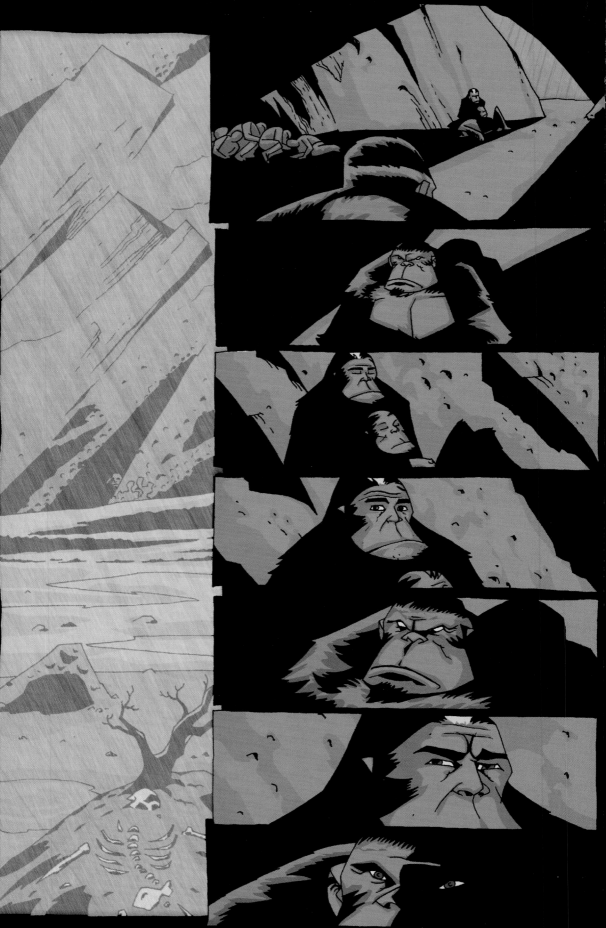

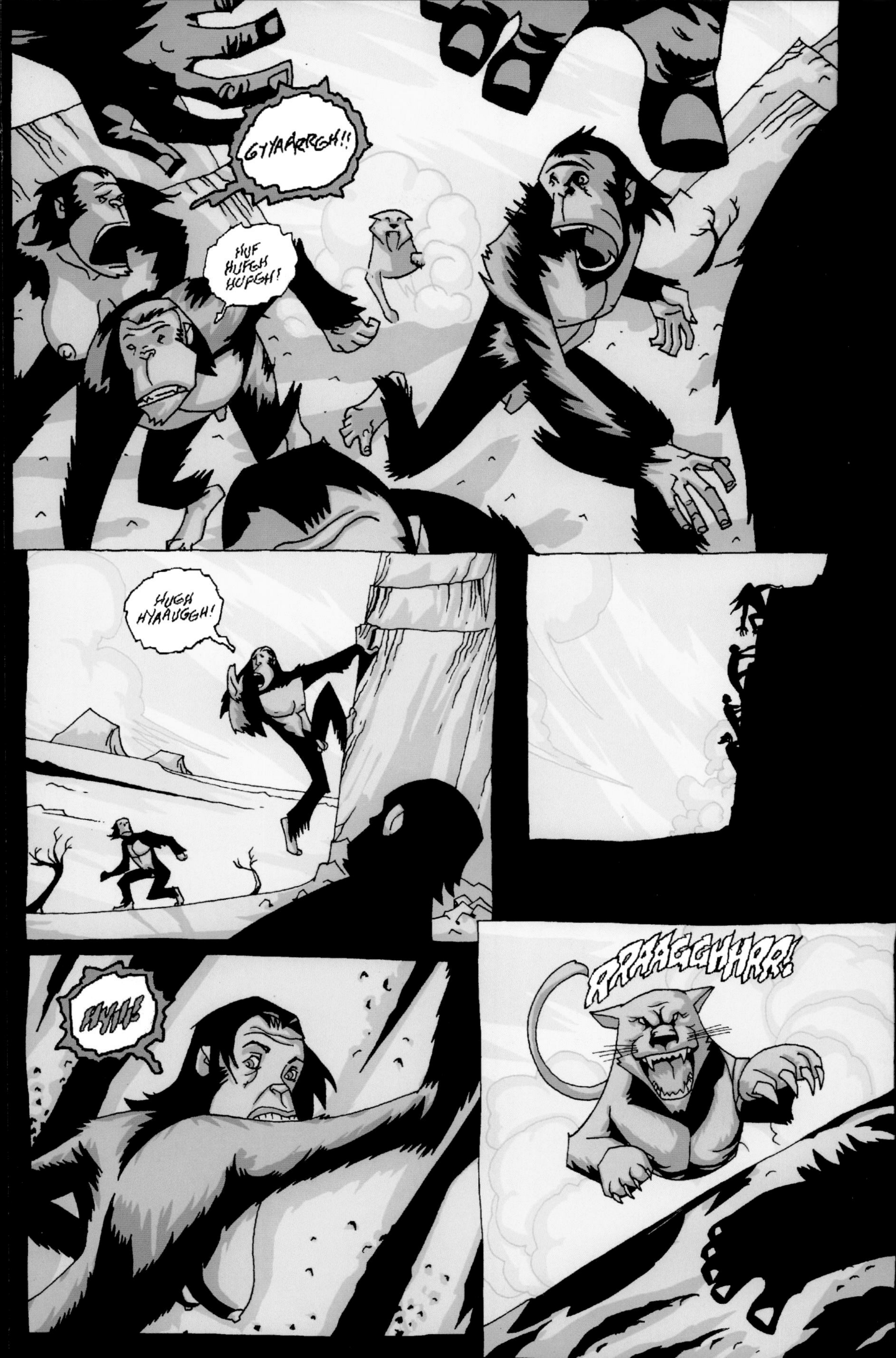
GYAARRGH!!
HUF HUFGH HUFGH!
HUGH HYAAUGH!
RAAAGGHHRR!

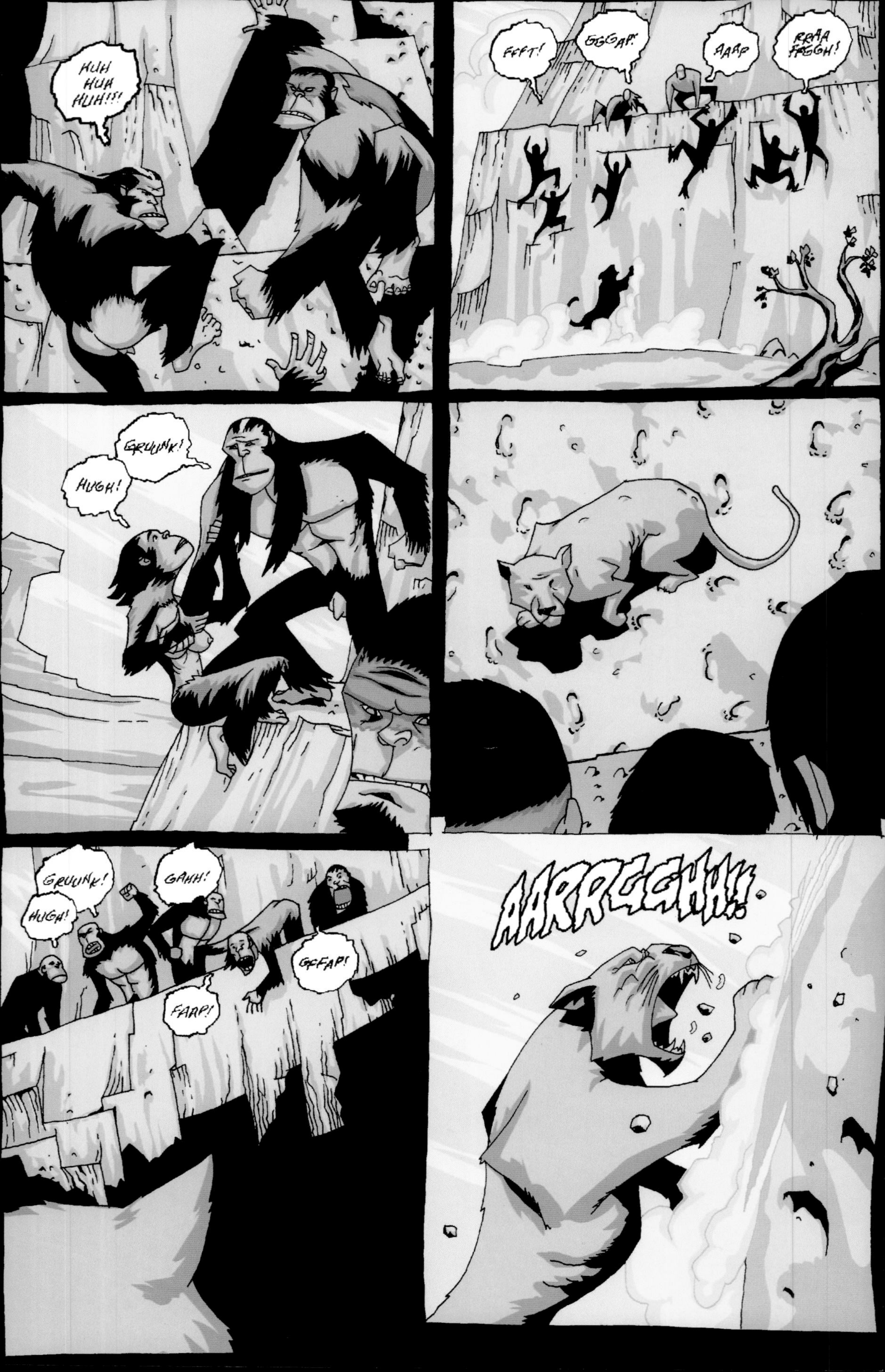
HUH HUH HUH!!!
FFFT!
GGGAP!
AAAP
RRAA FFFGH!
GRUUNK!
HUGH!
GRUUNK!
HUGH!
GAHH!
GFFAP!
FARP!
AARRGGHH!!

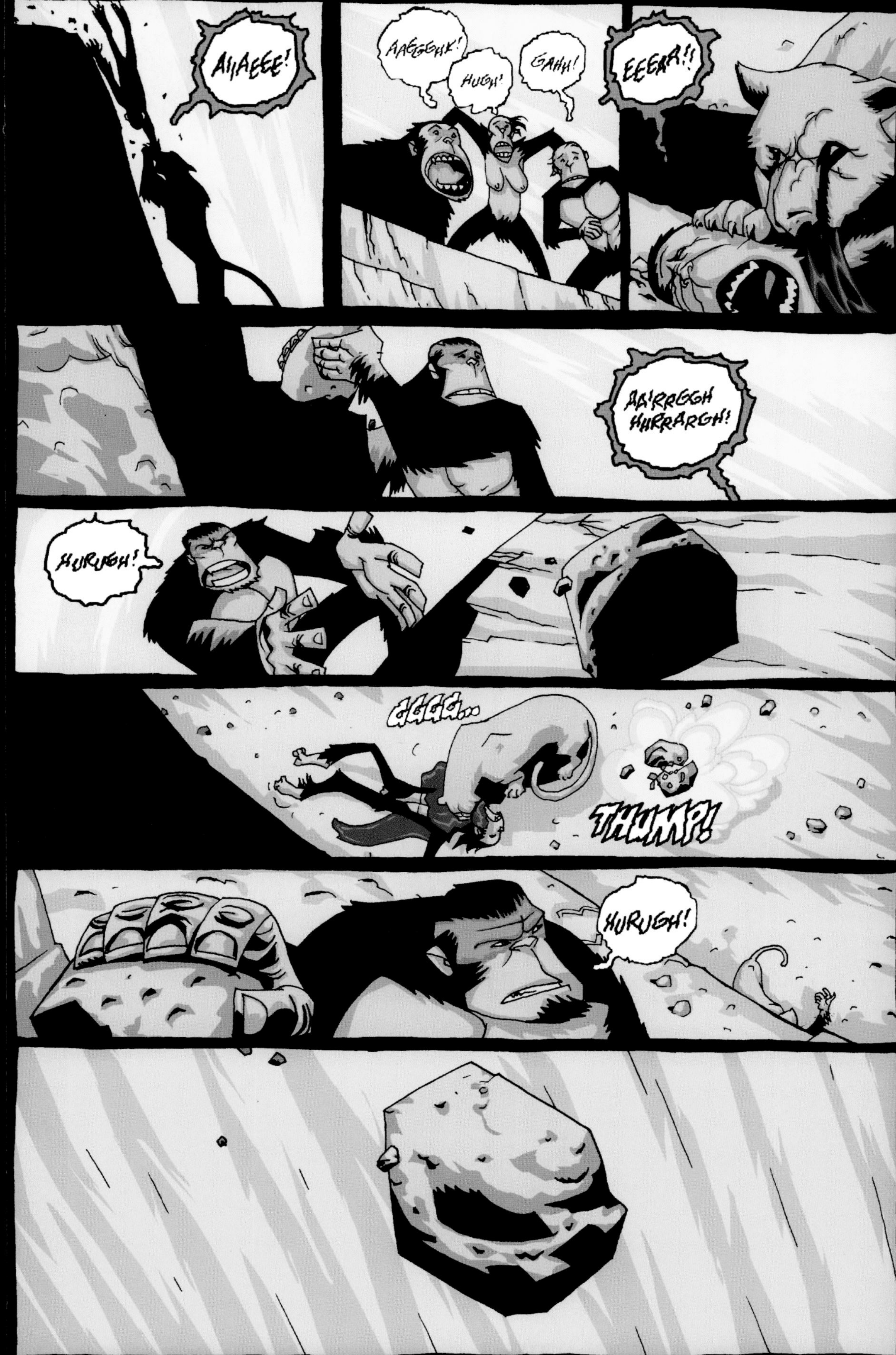

AIIAEEE!
AAEGGHK!
HUGH!
GAHH!
EEEAA!!
AA'RRGGH HRRARGH!
HURUGH!
GGGG...
THUMP!
HURUGH!

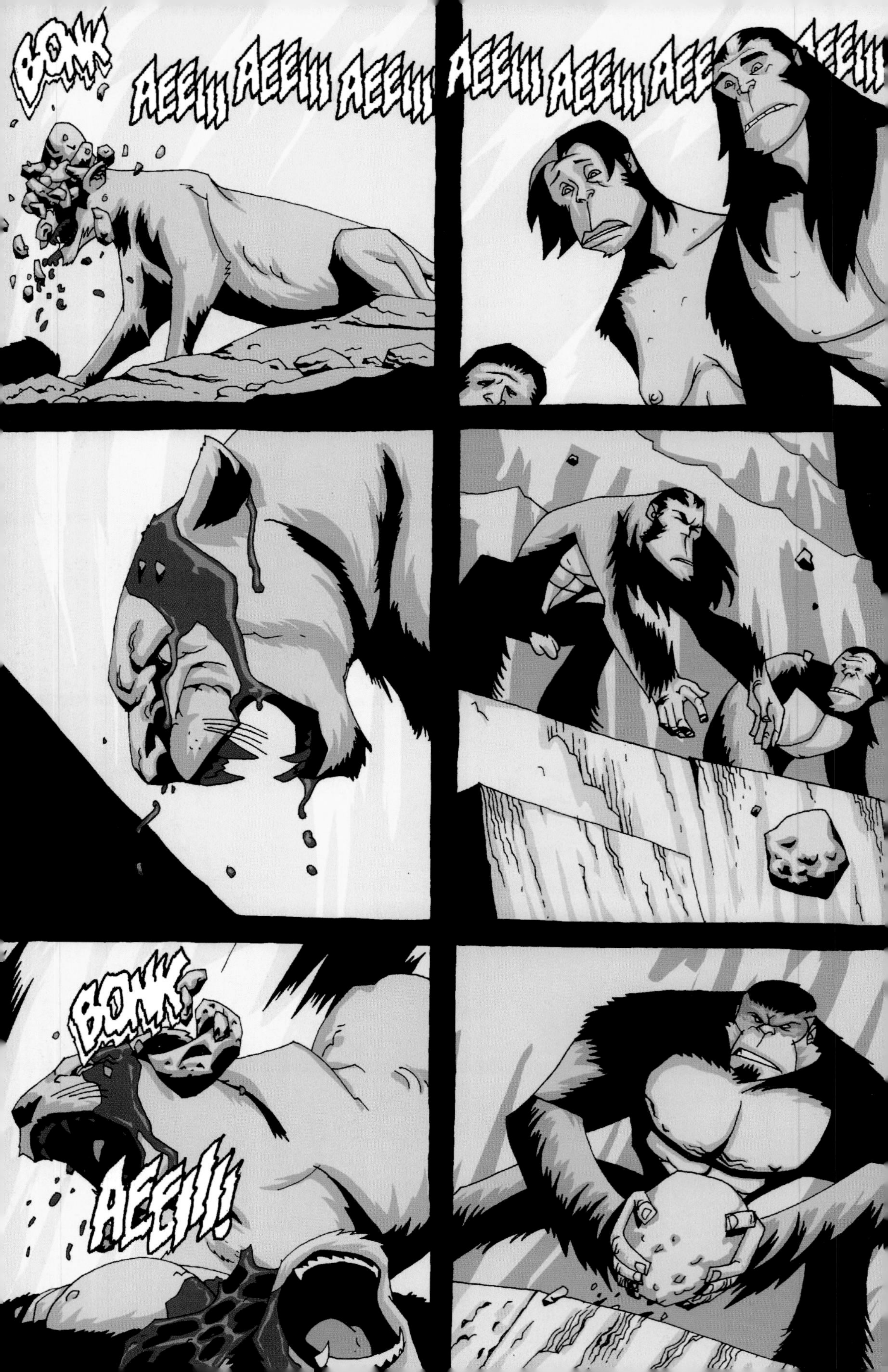
BONK
AEE!!! AEE!!! AEE!!! AEE!!! AEE!!! AEE!!! AEE!!!
BONK
AEE!!!

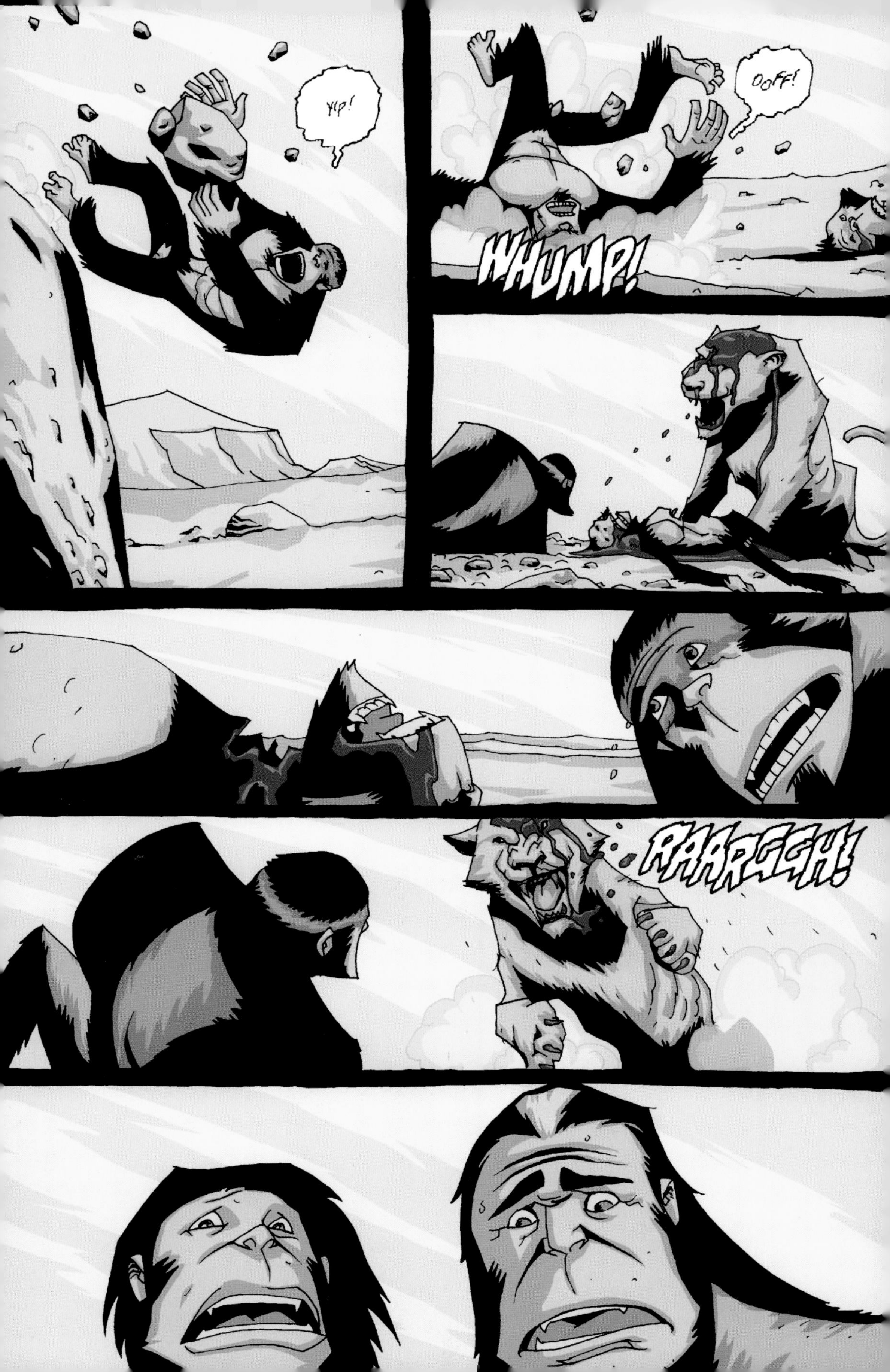
YIP!
OOFF!
WHUMP!
RAARGGH!

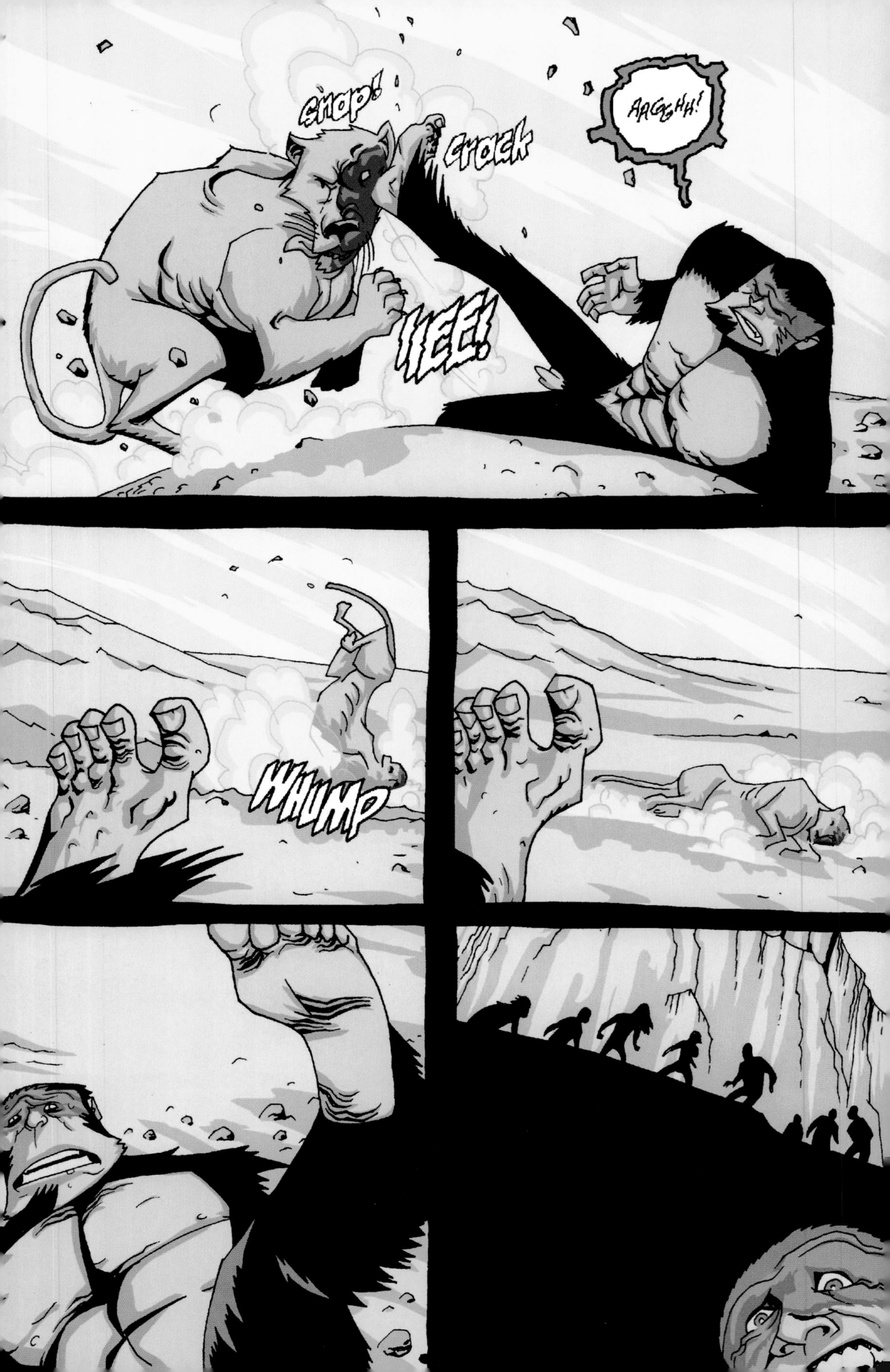
Snap!
Crack
AARGGHH!
IIEE!
WHUMP

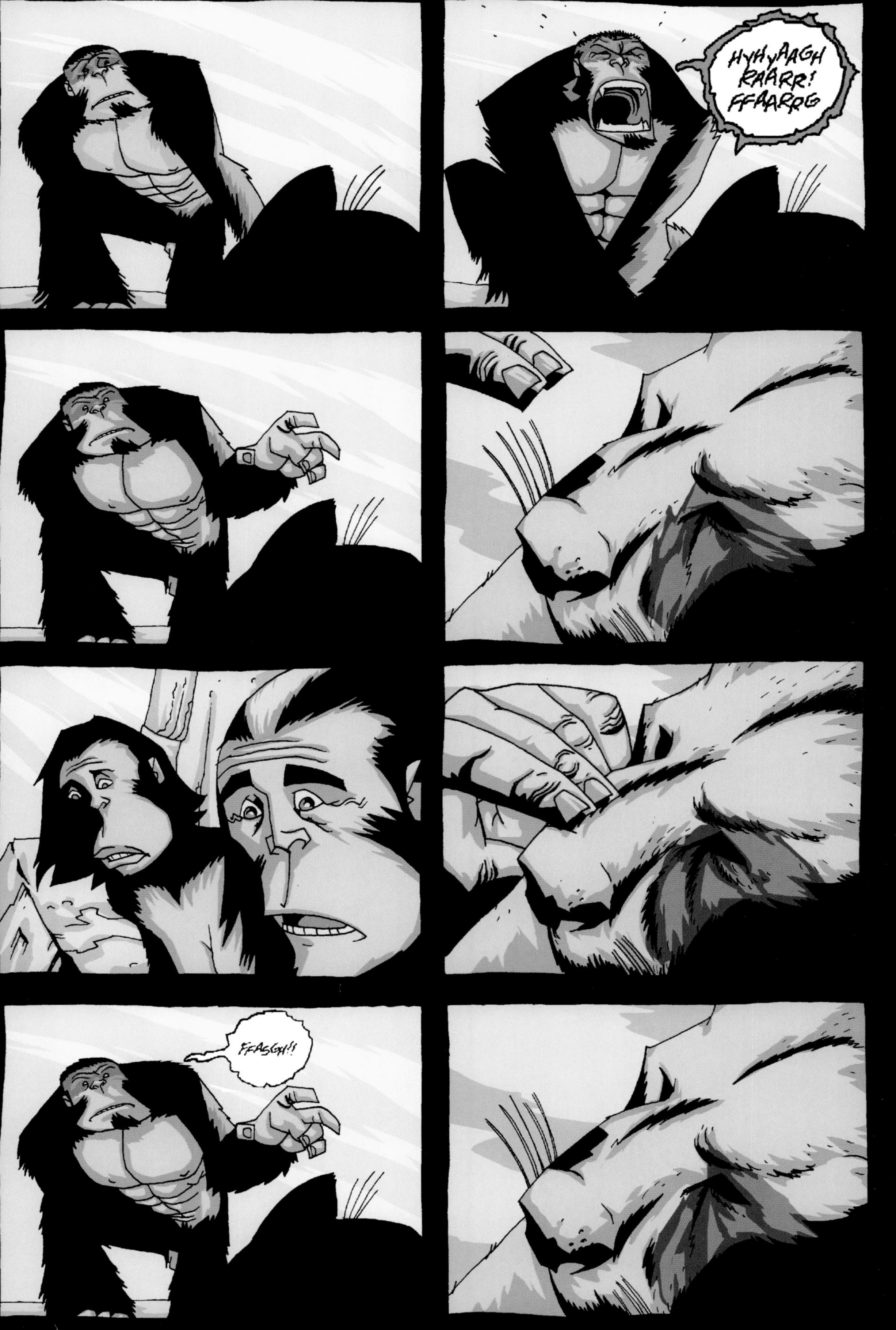
HYHYAAGH RAARR! FFAARRG
FFASGH!!

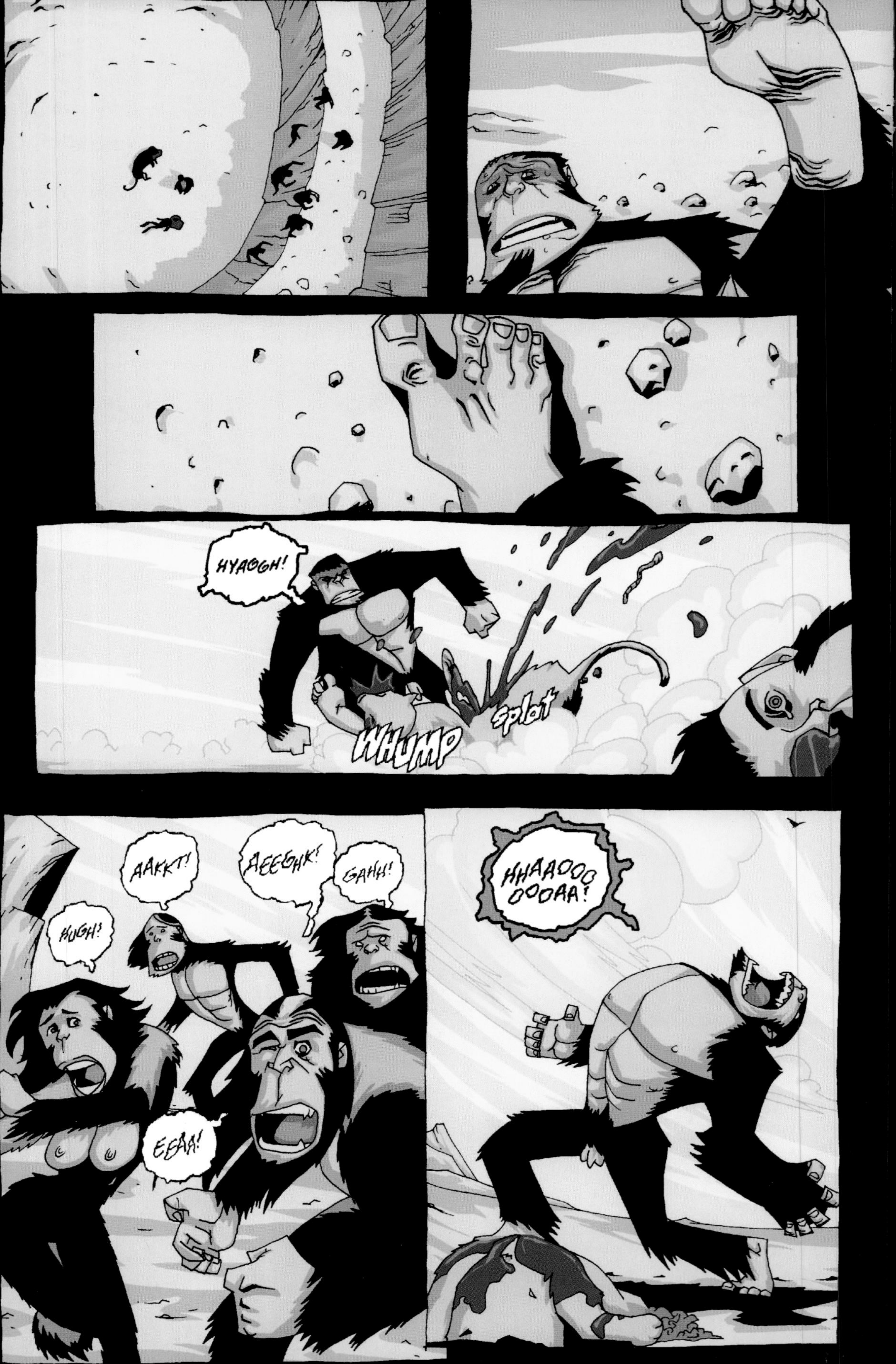
HYAOGH!
WHUMP
splot
HUGH!
AAKKT!
AEEGHK!
GAHH!
EEAA!
HHAAOOO OOOAA!

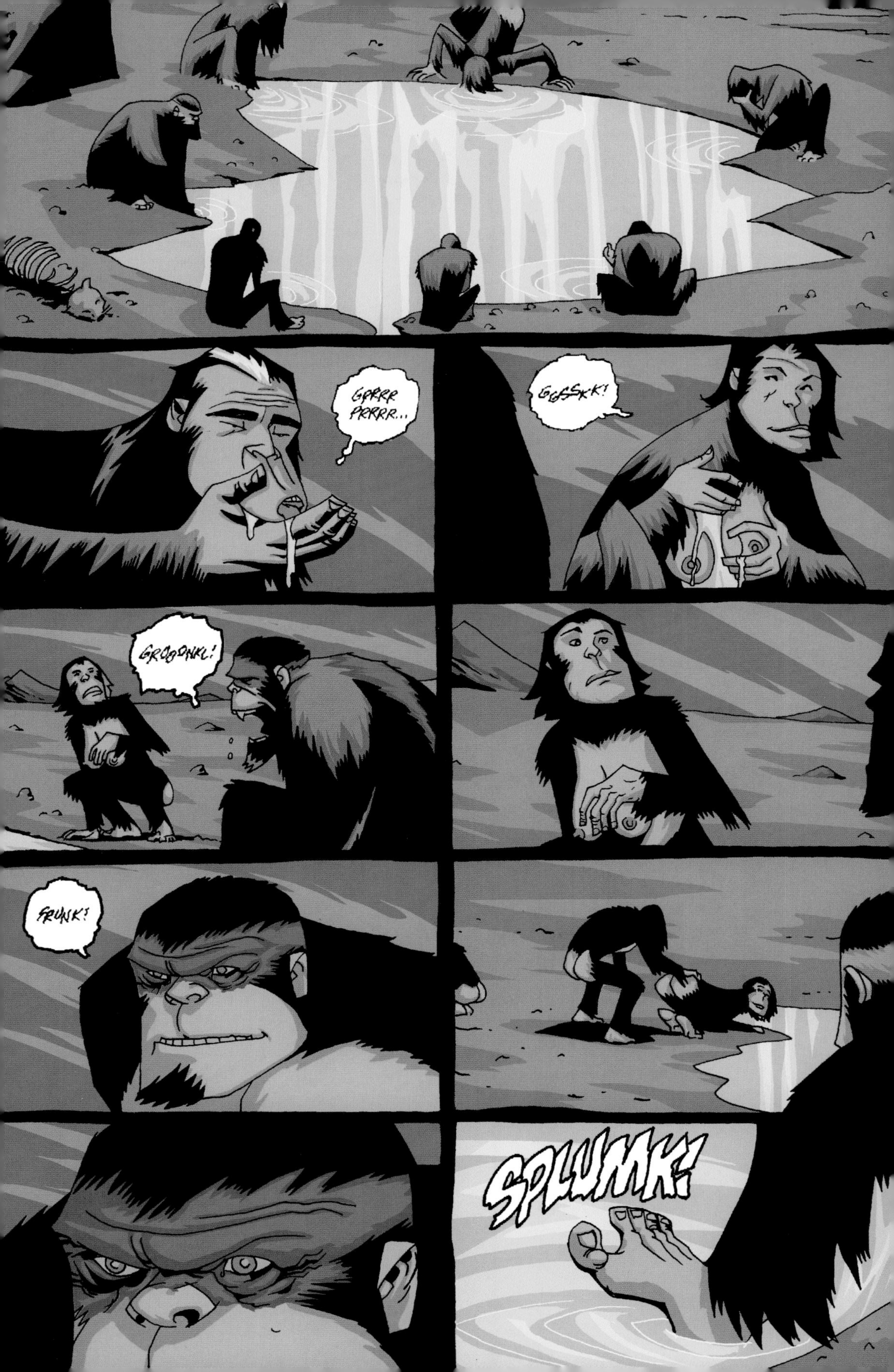
GRRRR PRRRR...
GGSSK-K!
GROOONK!
FRUNK!
SPLUMK!

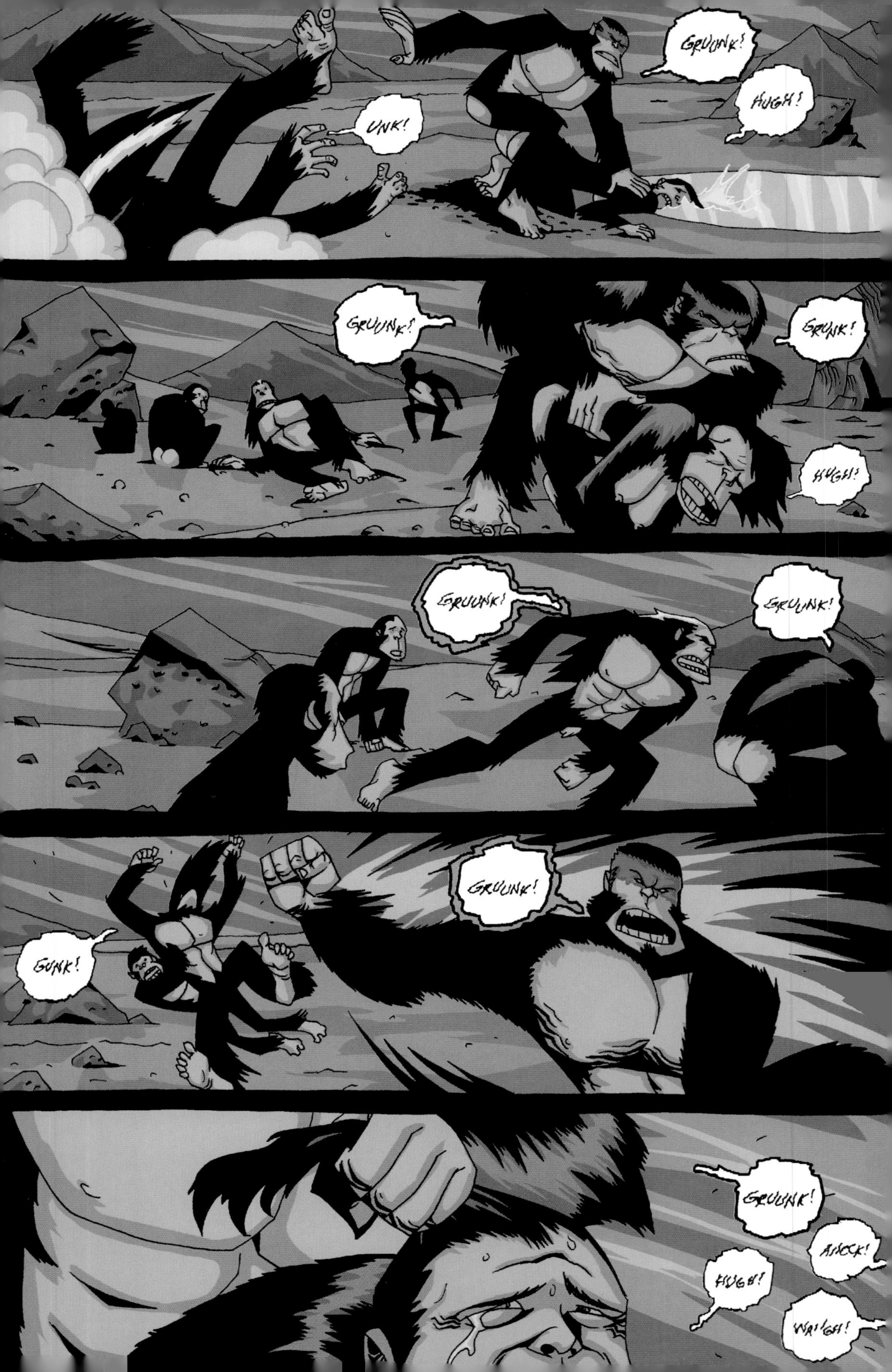
UNK!
GRUUNK!
HUGH!
GRUUNK!
GRUNK!
HUGH!
GRUUNK!
GRUUNK!
GRUUNK!
GUNK!
GRUUNK!
ANCCK!
HUGH!
WAUGH!

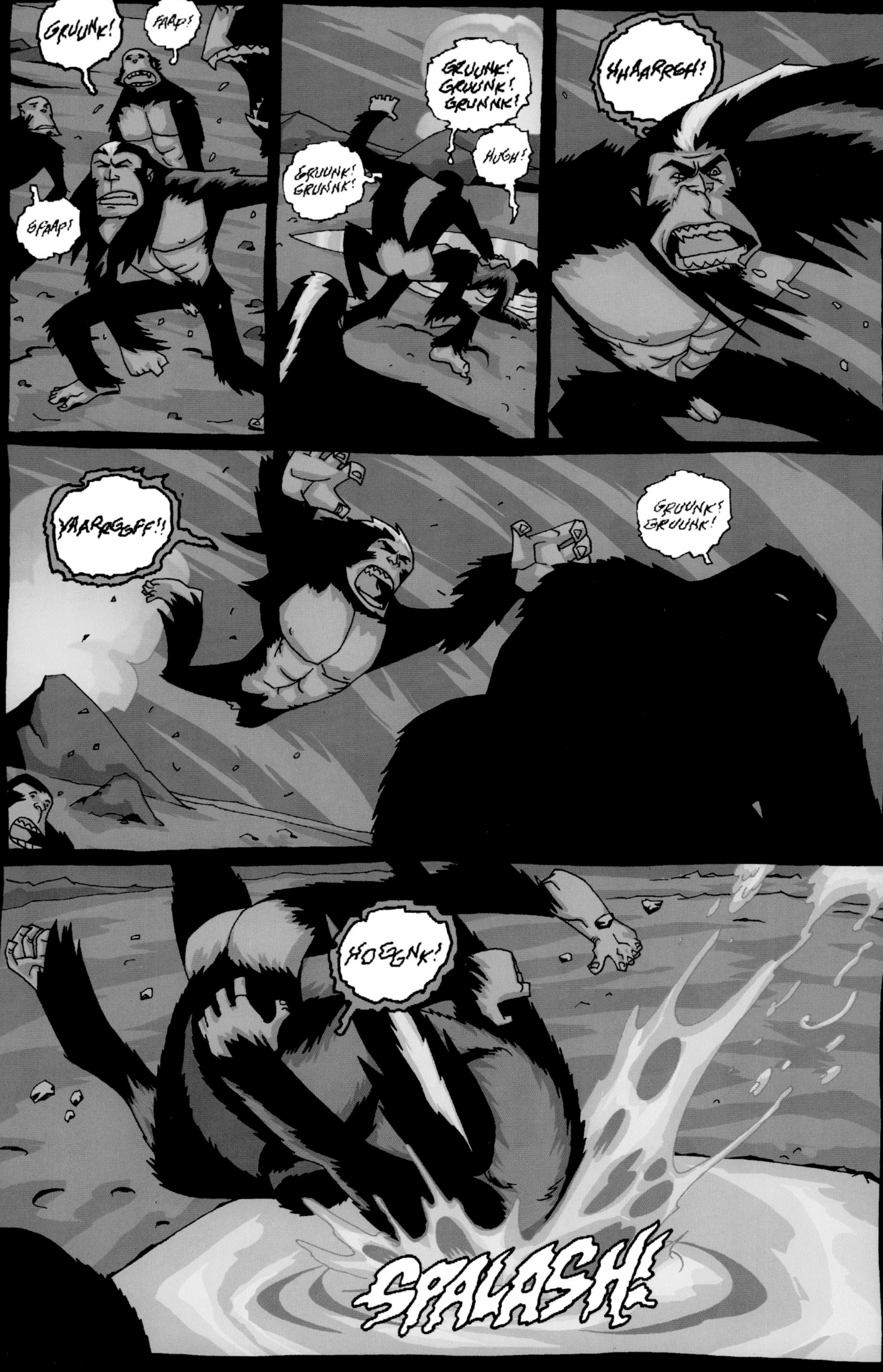
GRUUNK!
FRAP!
GFAAP!
GRUUNK! GRUUNK! GRUNNK!
GRUUNK! GRUNNK!
HUGH!
HHAARRGH!
YAARRGOFF!!
GRUUNK! GRUUNK!
HOGGNK!
SPALASH!

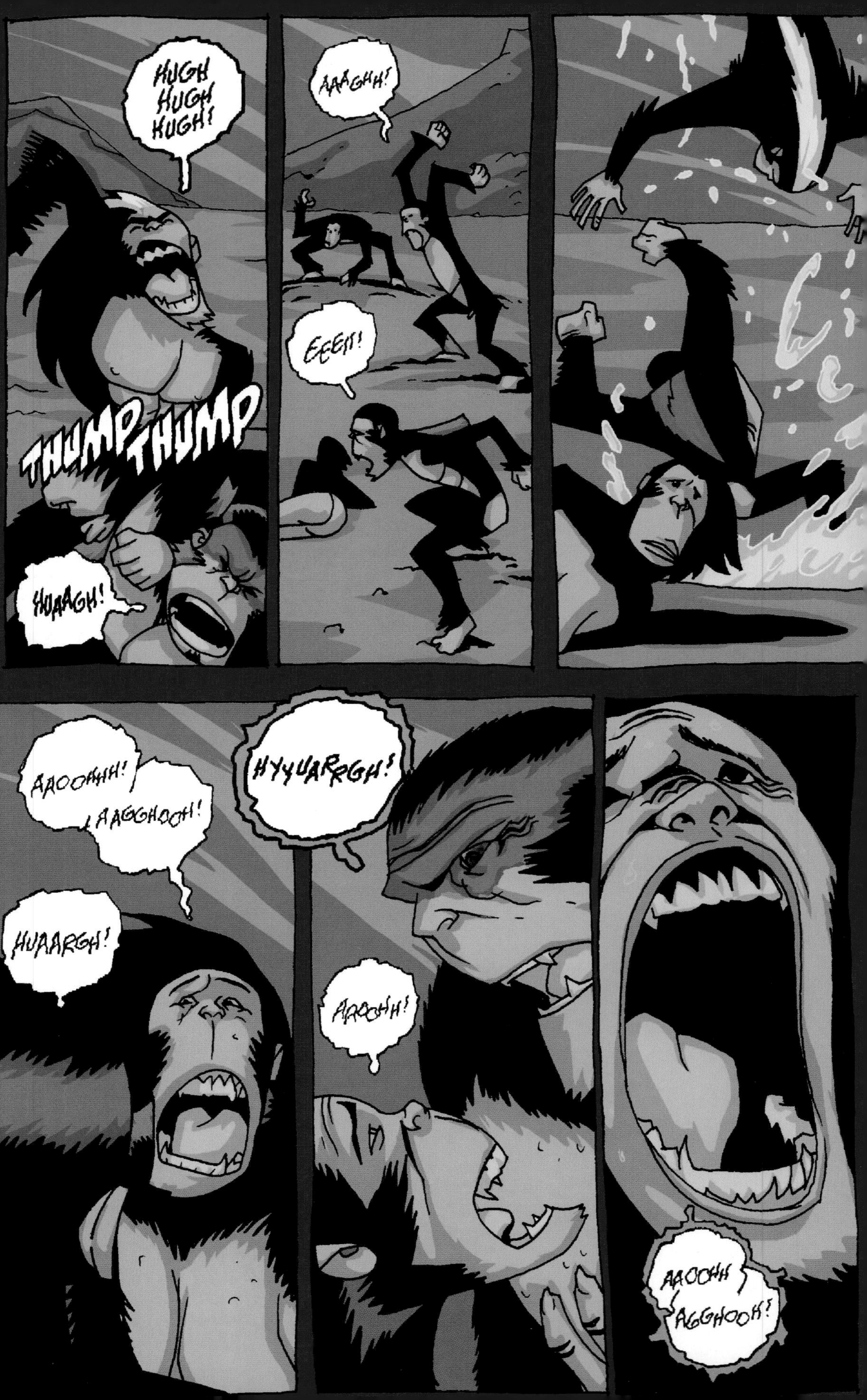
HUGH HUGH HUGH!
THUMP THUMP
HUAAGH!
AAAGHH!
EEEII!
AAOOHHH!
AAGGHOOH!
HUAARGH!
HYYUARRGH!
AAOOHH!
AAOOHH AGGHOOH!

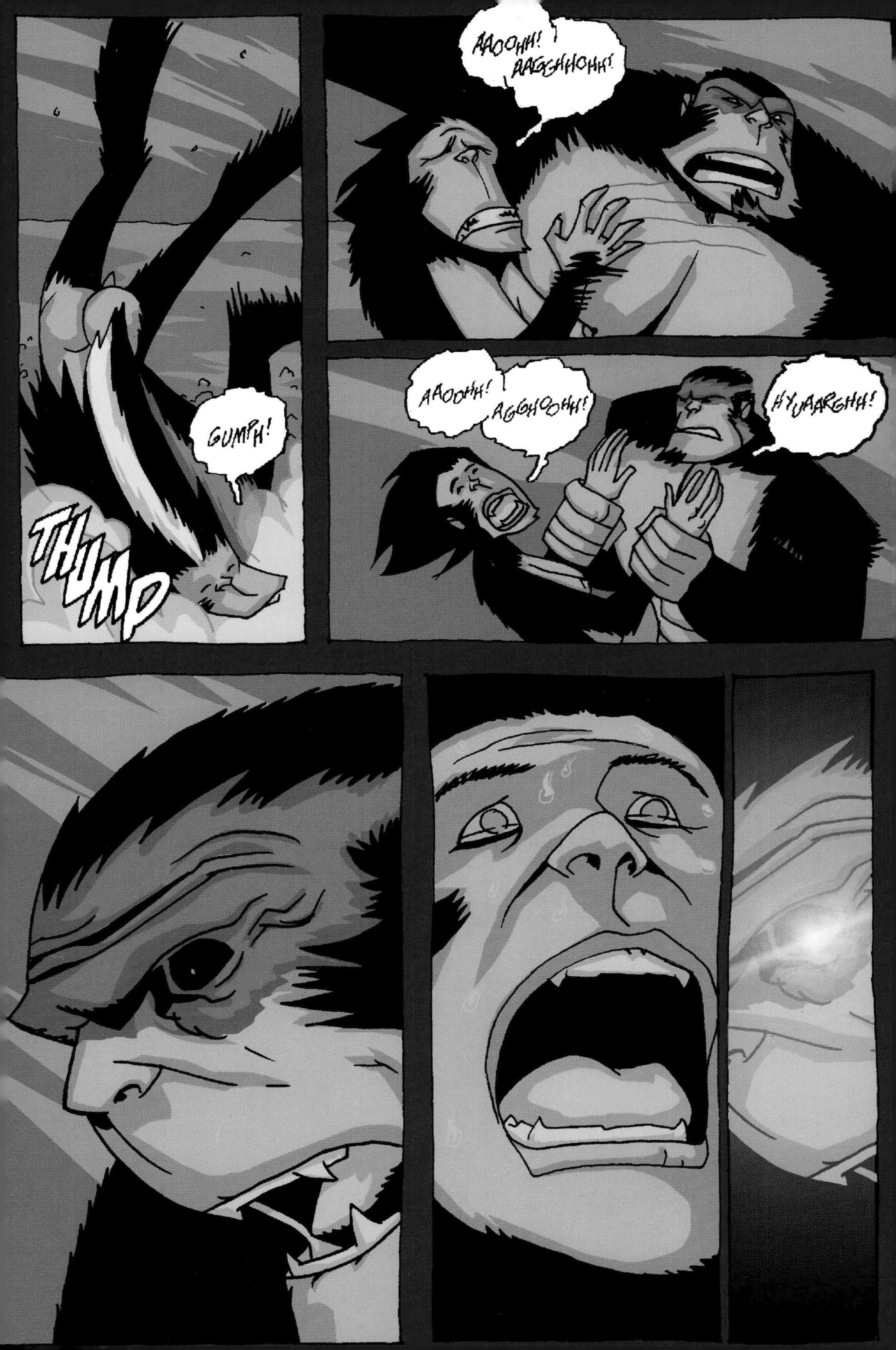
GUMPH!
THUMP
AAOOHH!
AAGGHHOHH!
AAOOHH!
AGGHOOHH!
HYUAARGHH!

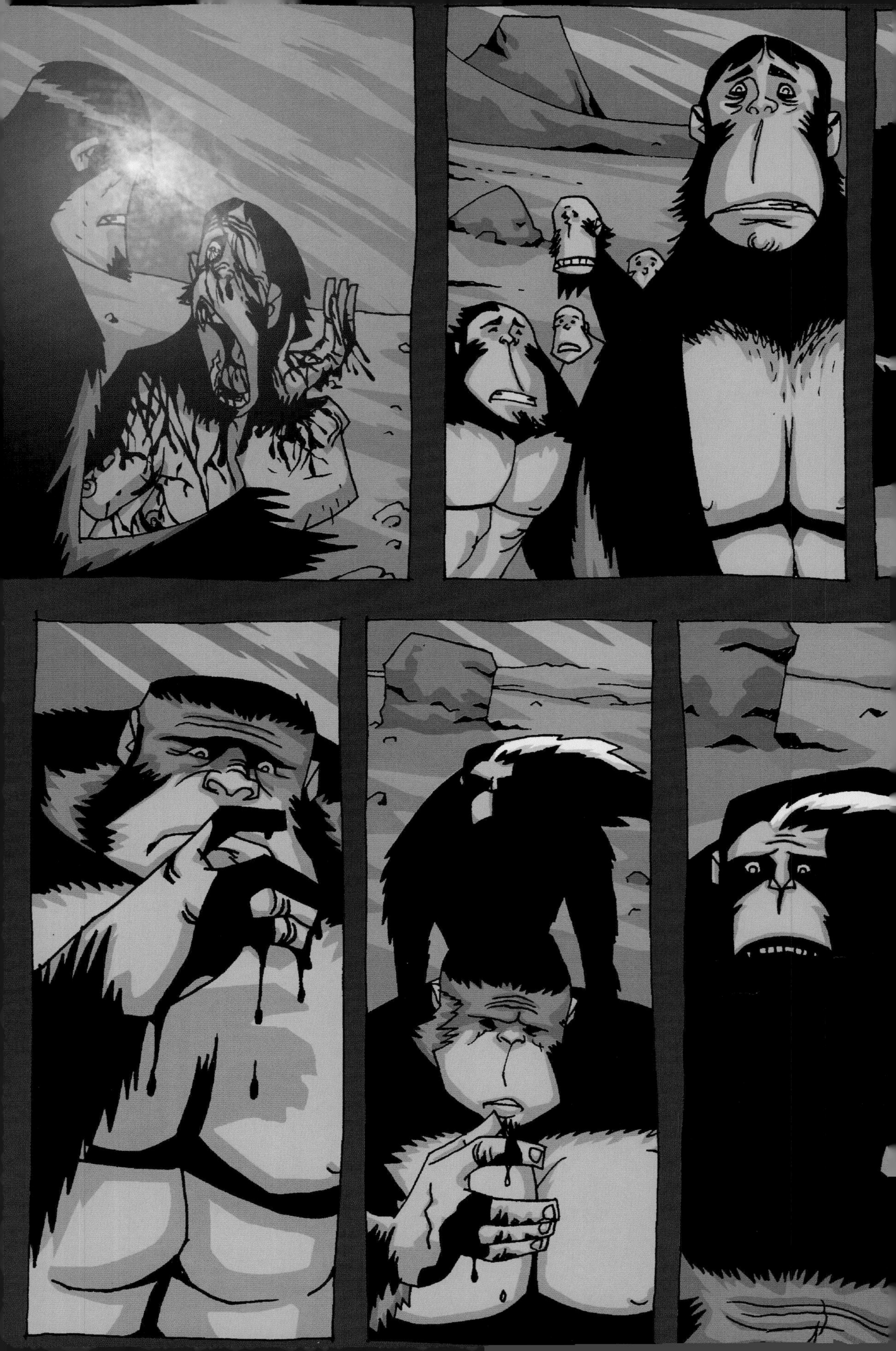

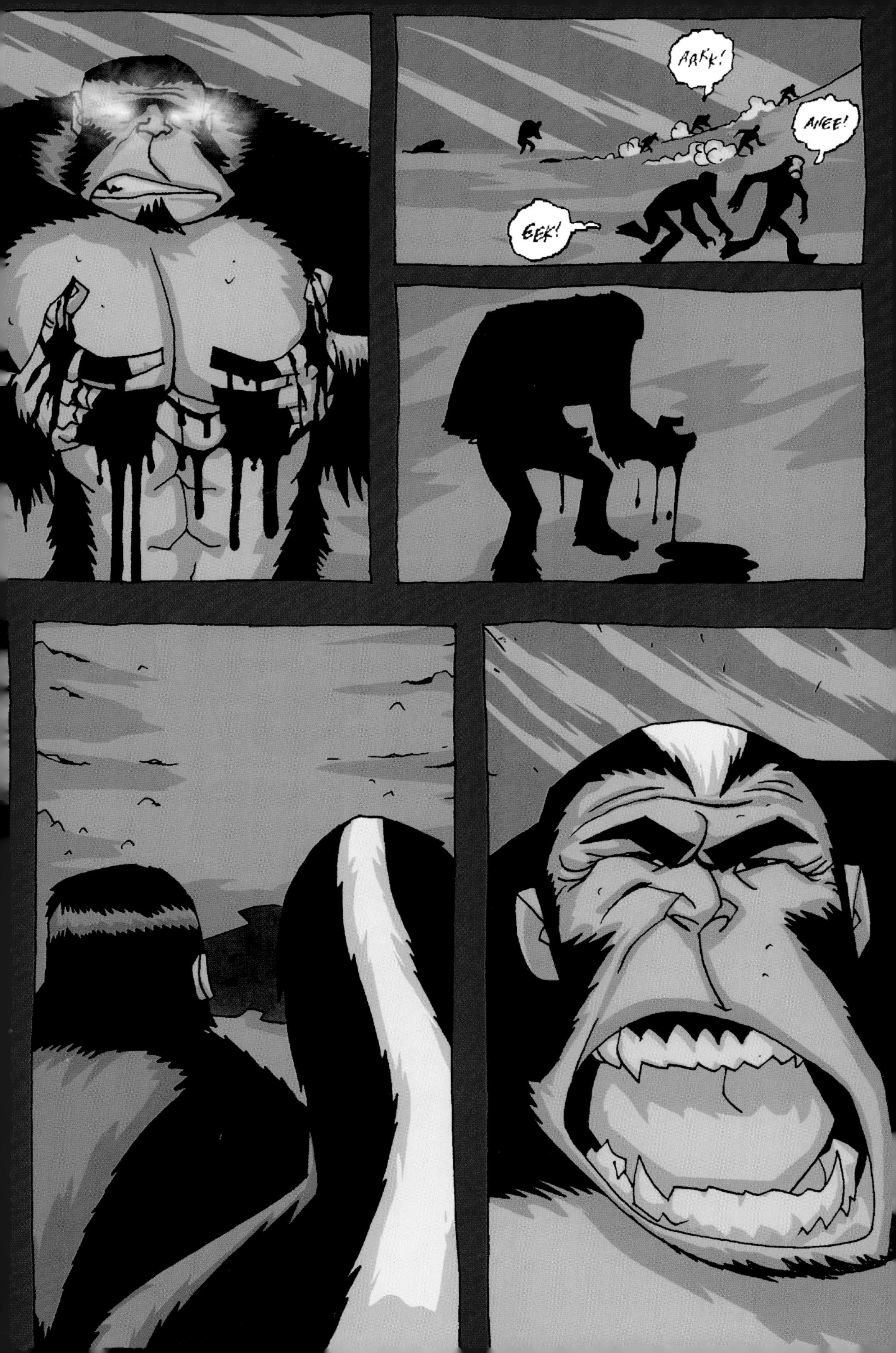
AAKK!
ANEE!
EEK!

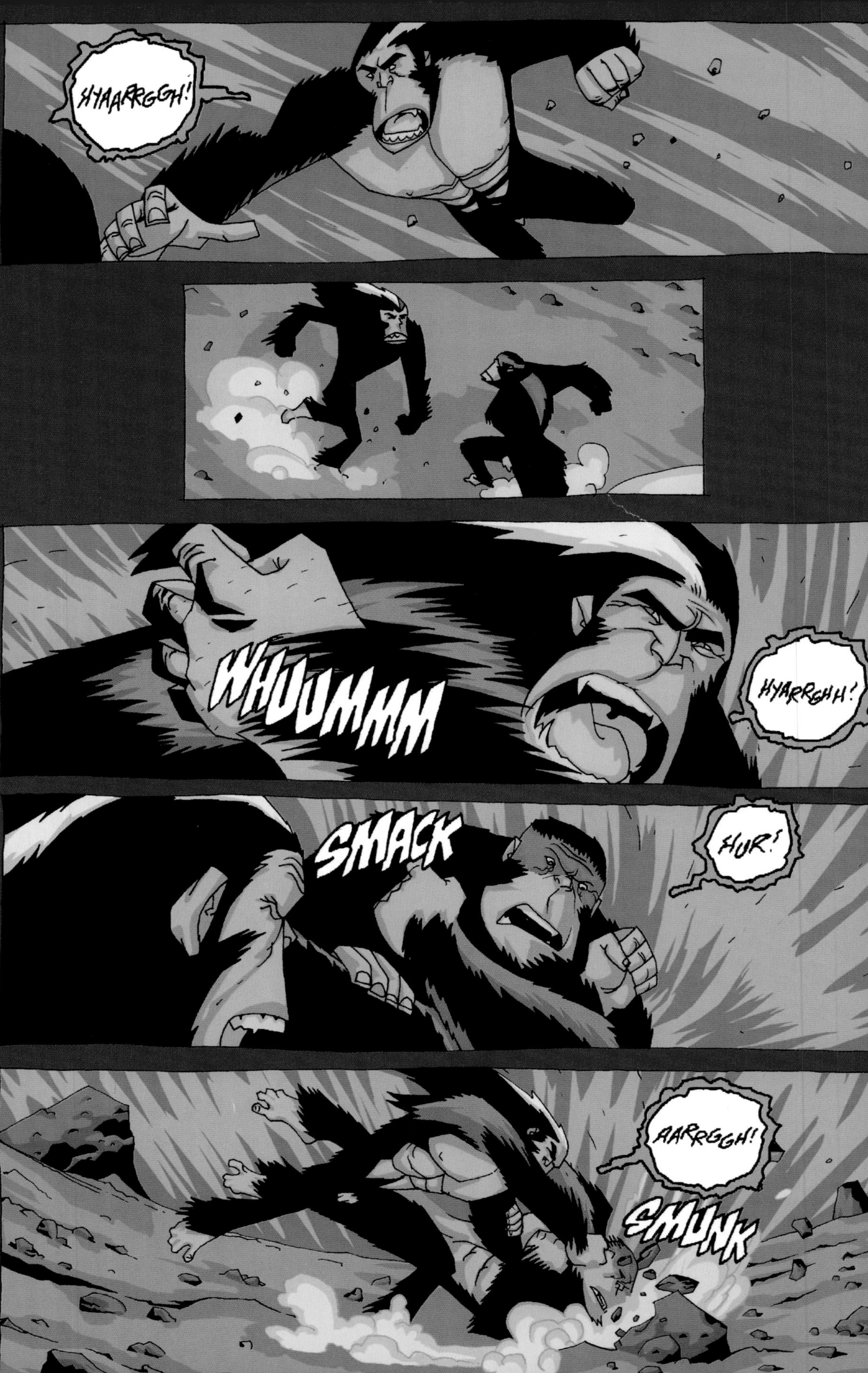
HYAARRGGH!
WHUUMMM
HYARRGHH!
SMACK
HUR!
AARRGGH!
SMUNK

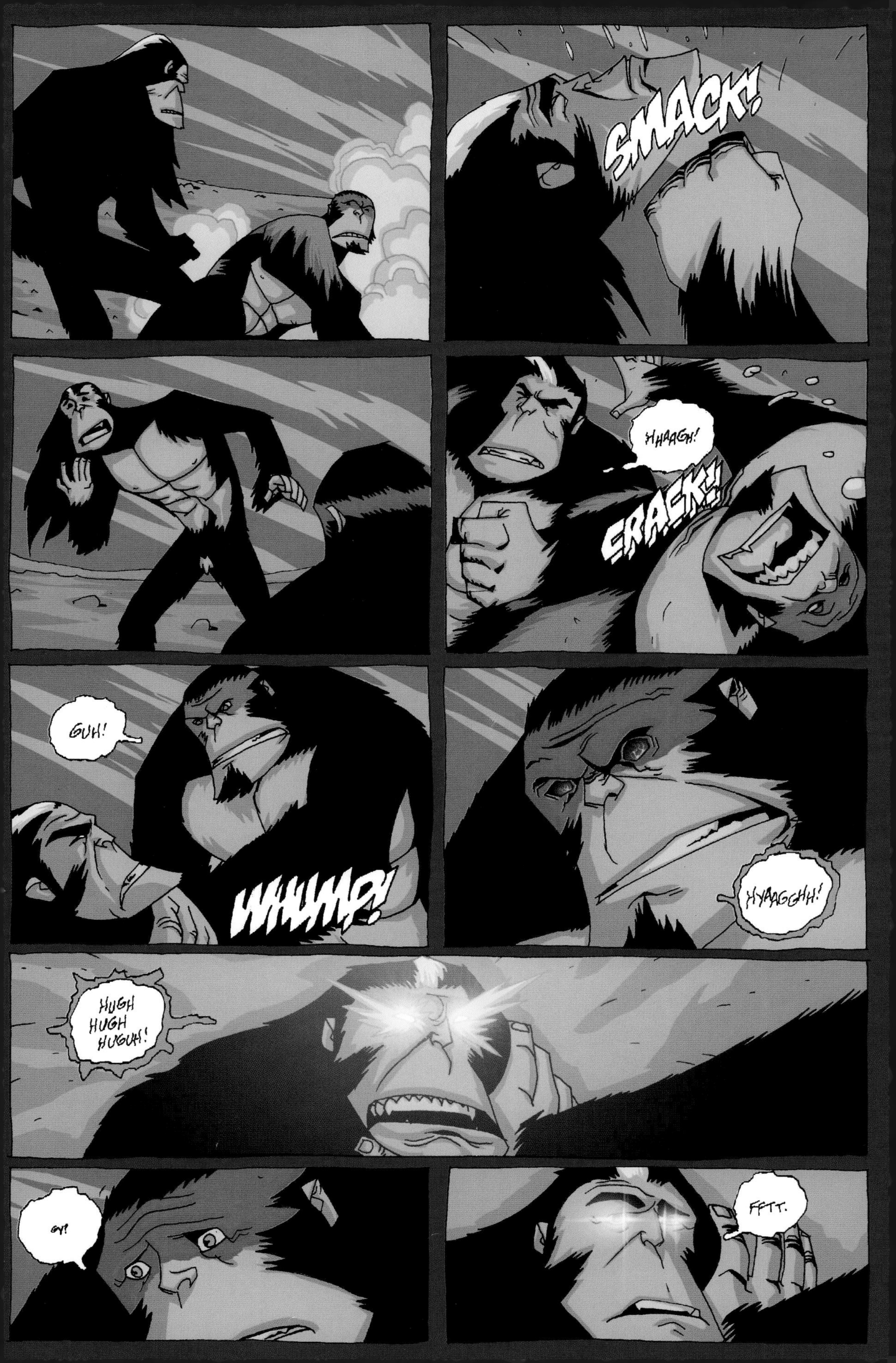
SMACK!
HHAAGH!
CRACK!
GUH!
WHUMP!
HYAAGGHH!
HUGH HUGH HUGUH!
GY?
FFTT.

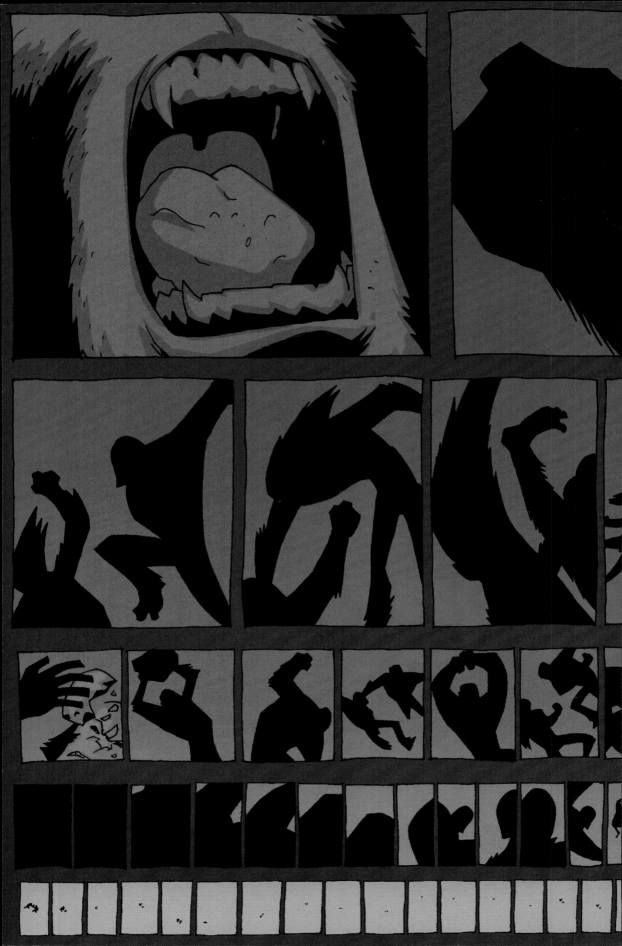

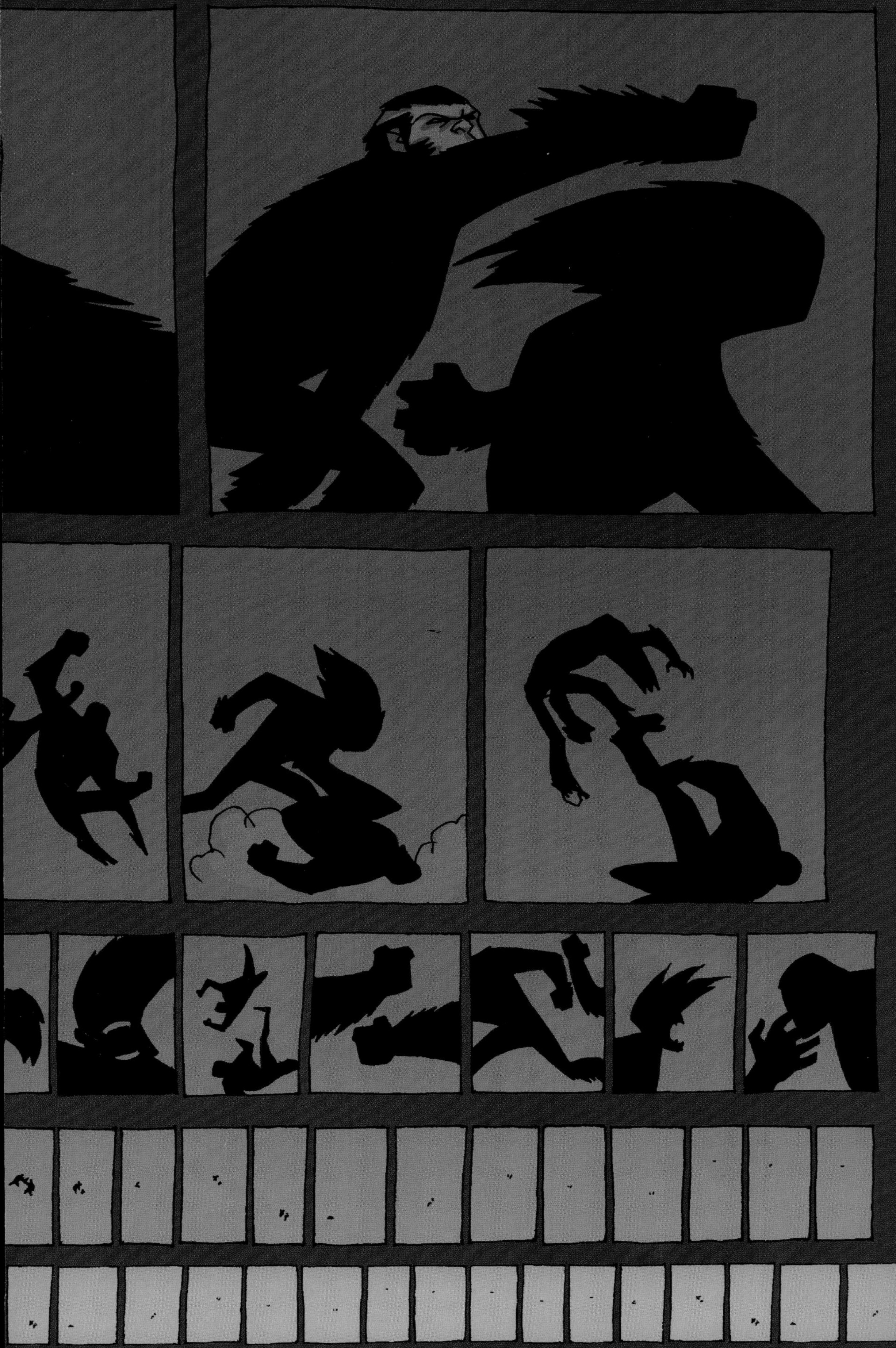

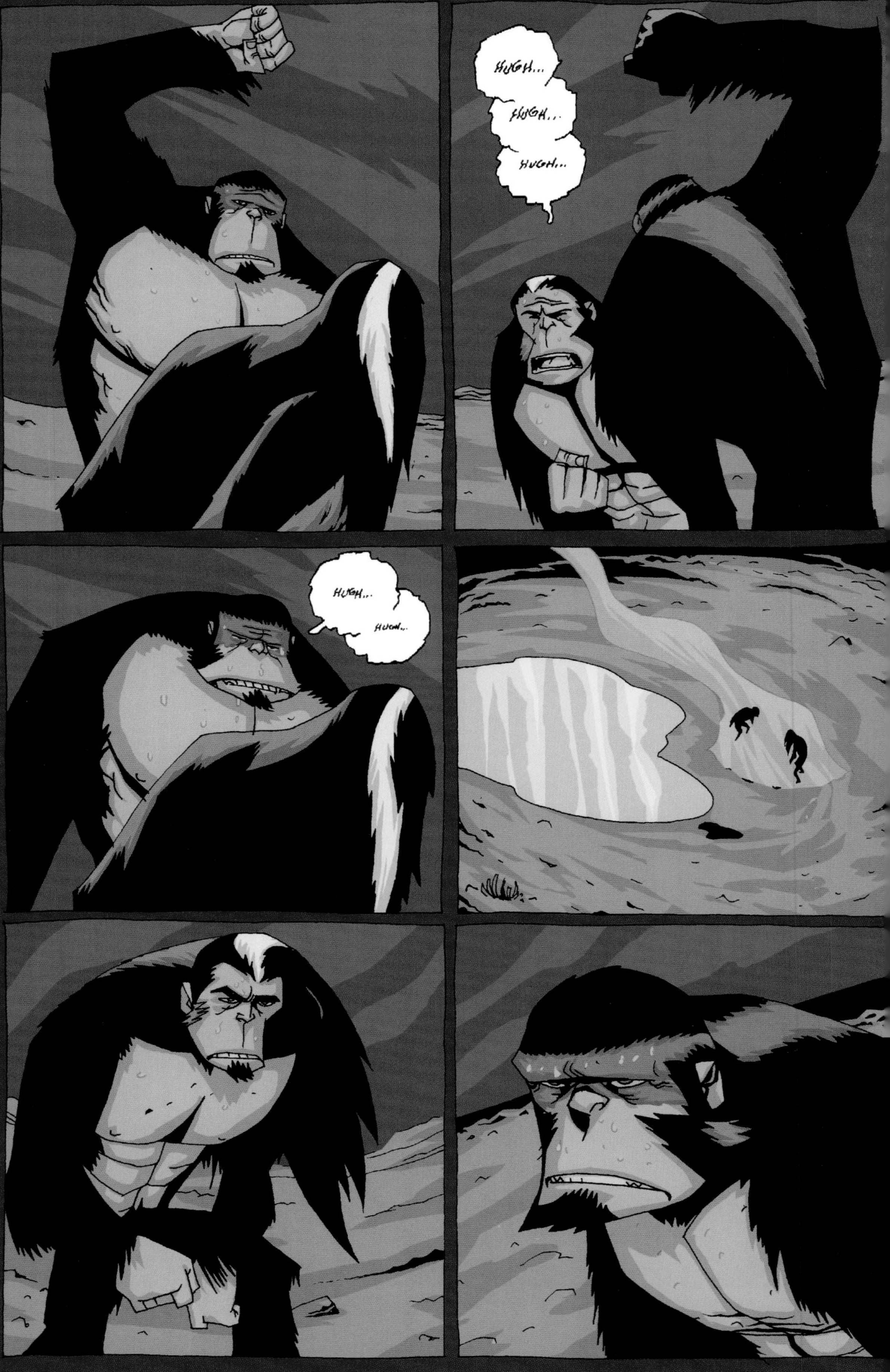
HUGH...
HUGH...
HUGH...
HUGH...
HUGH...

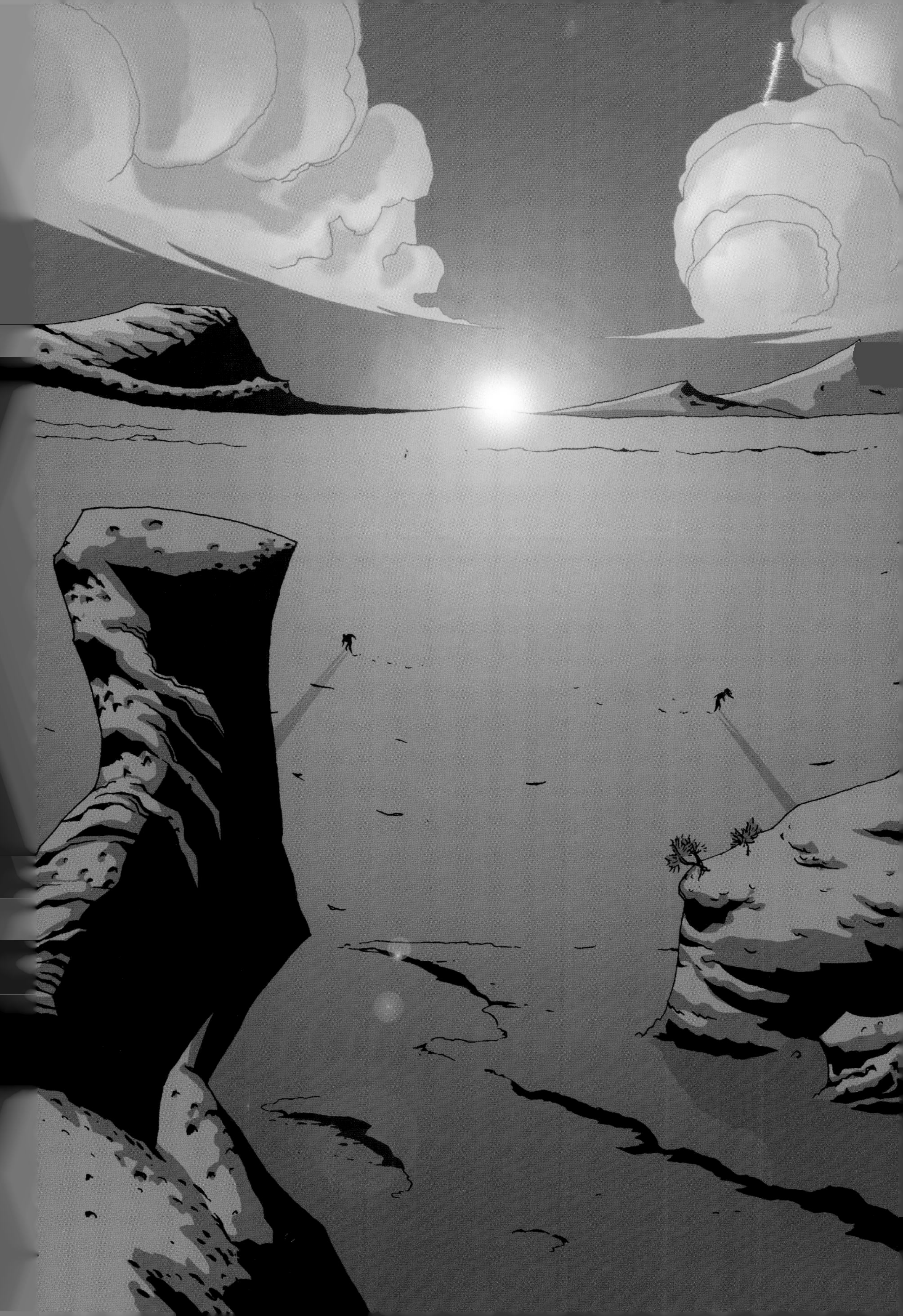

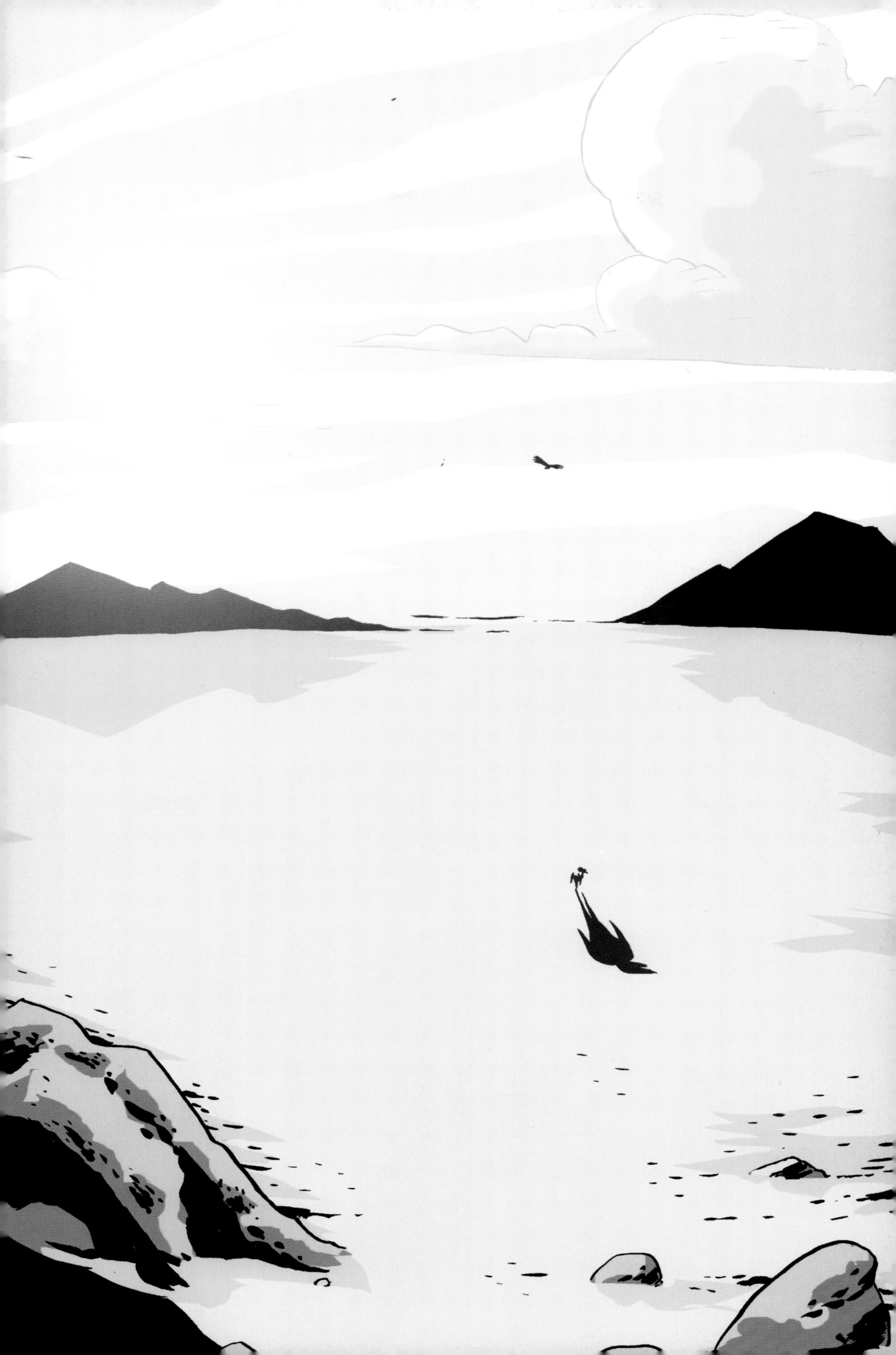

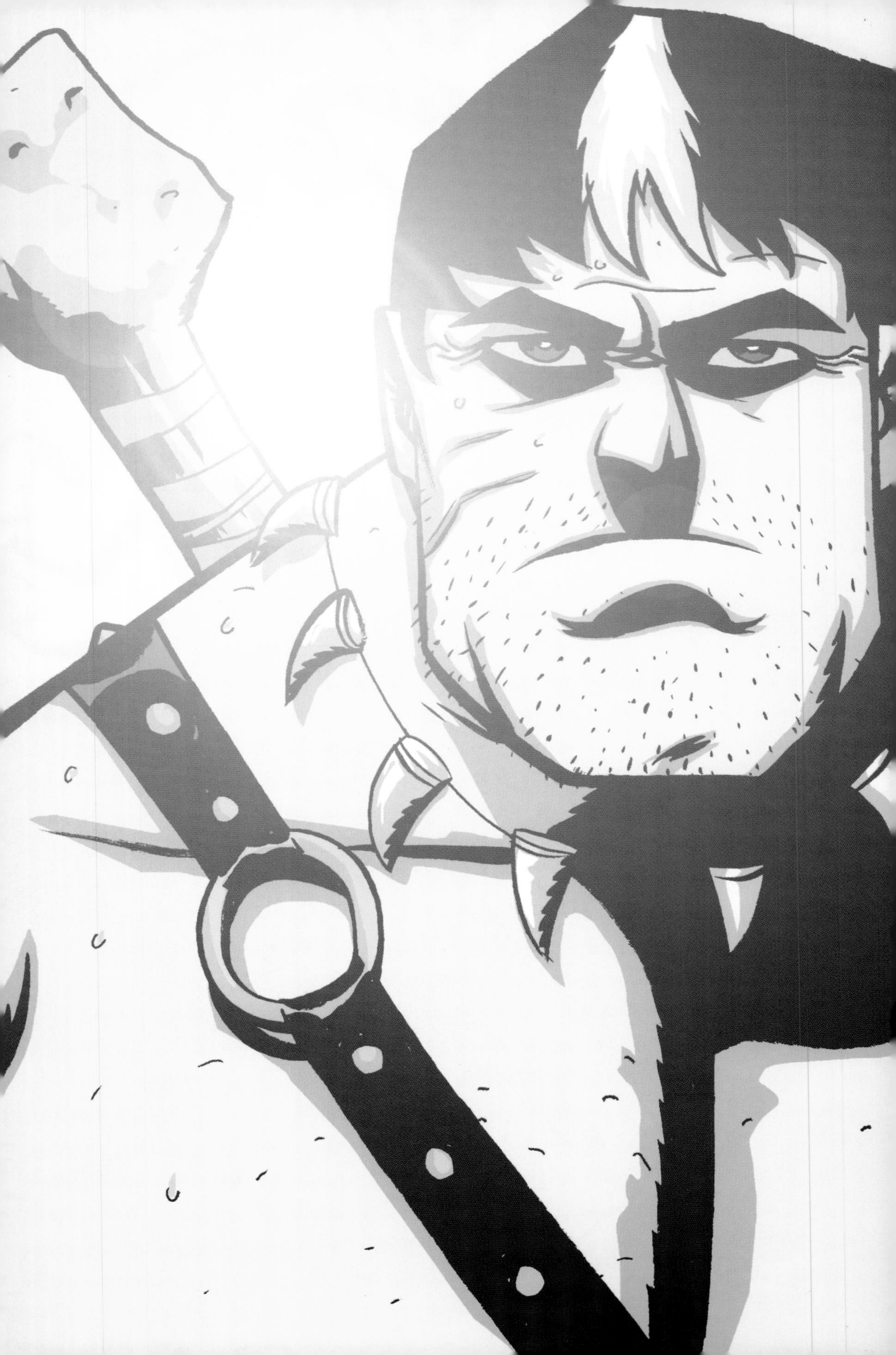

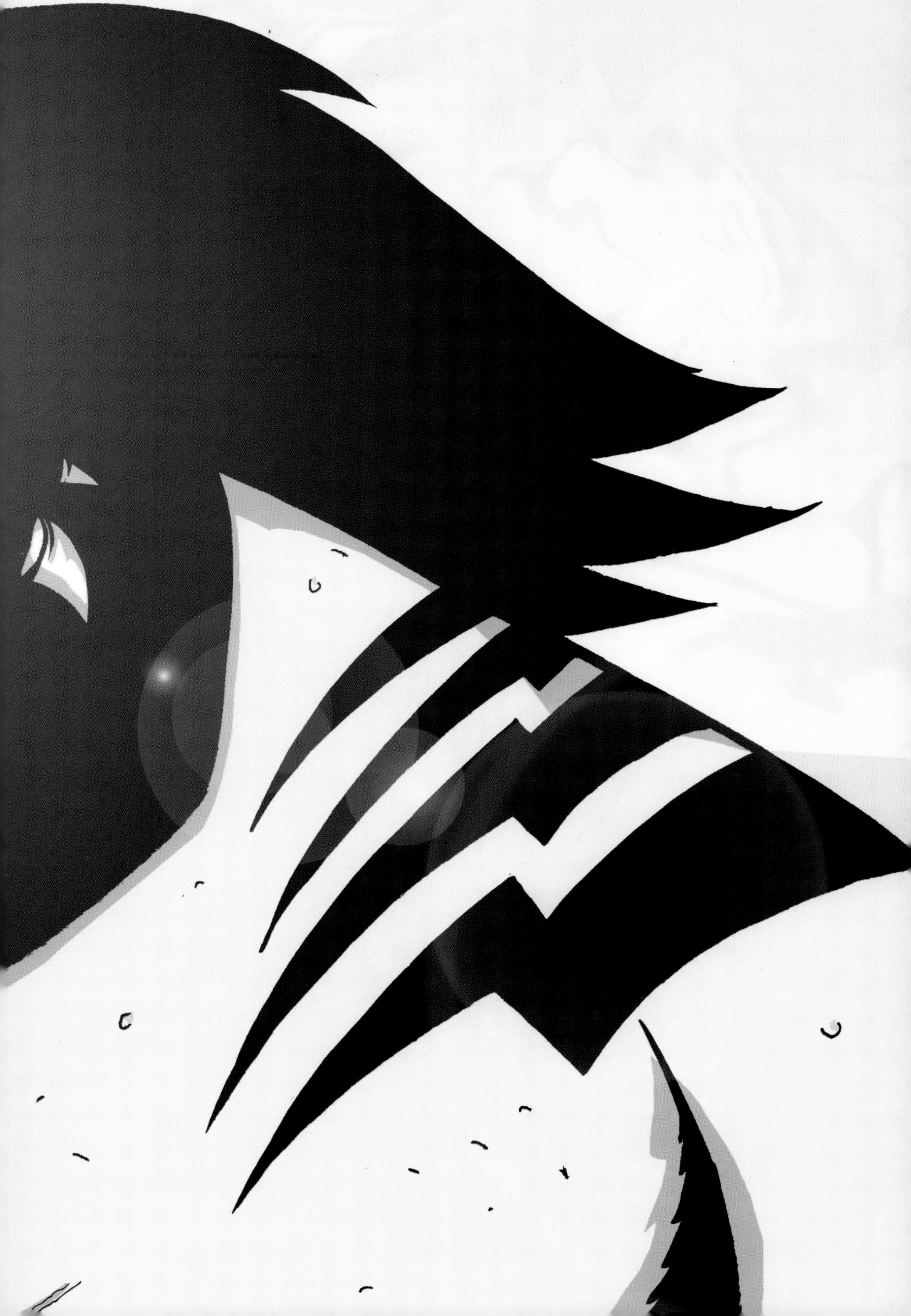

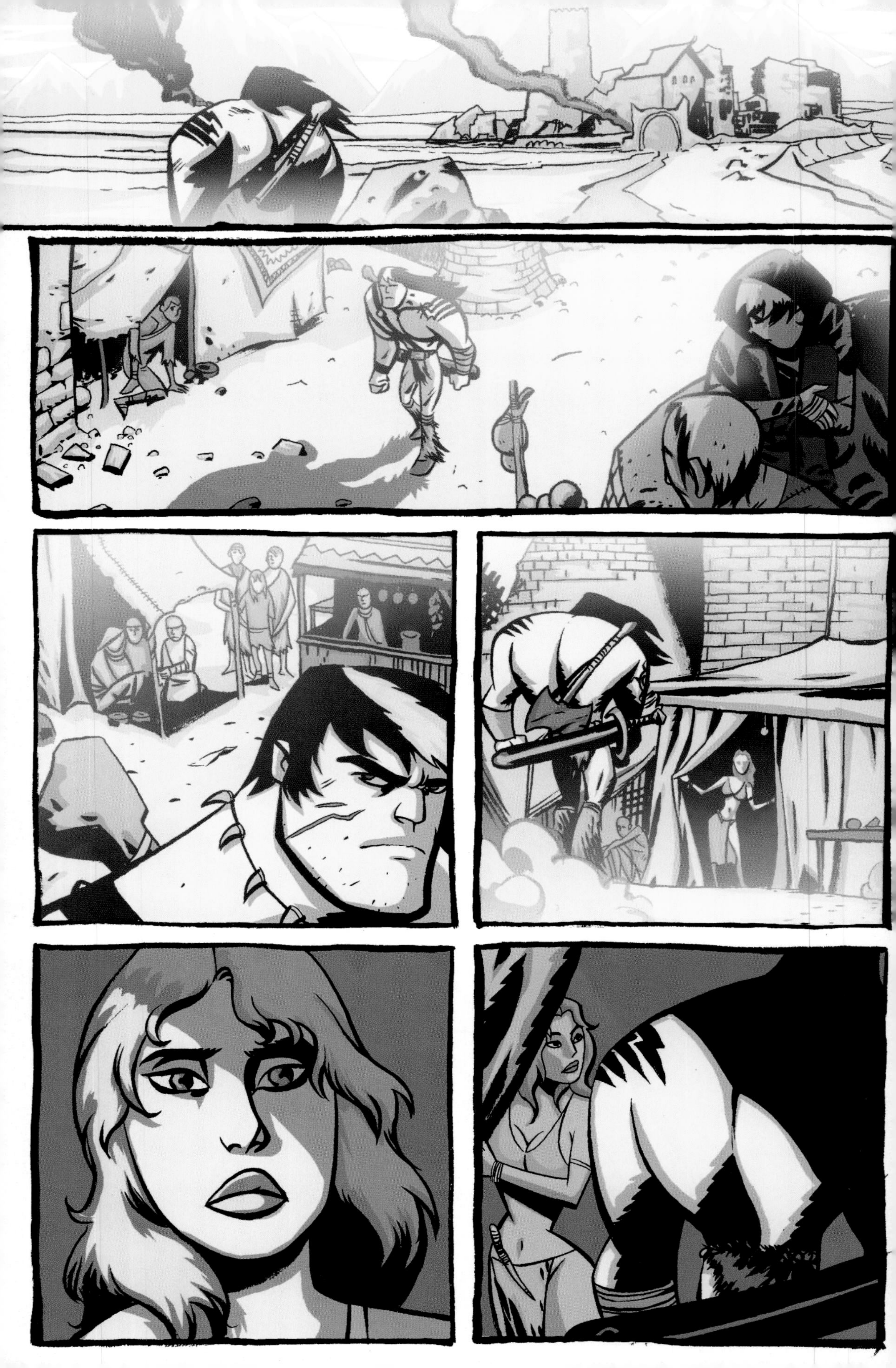

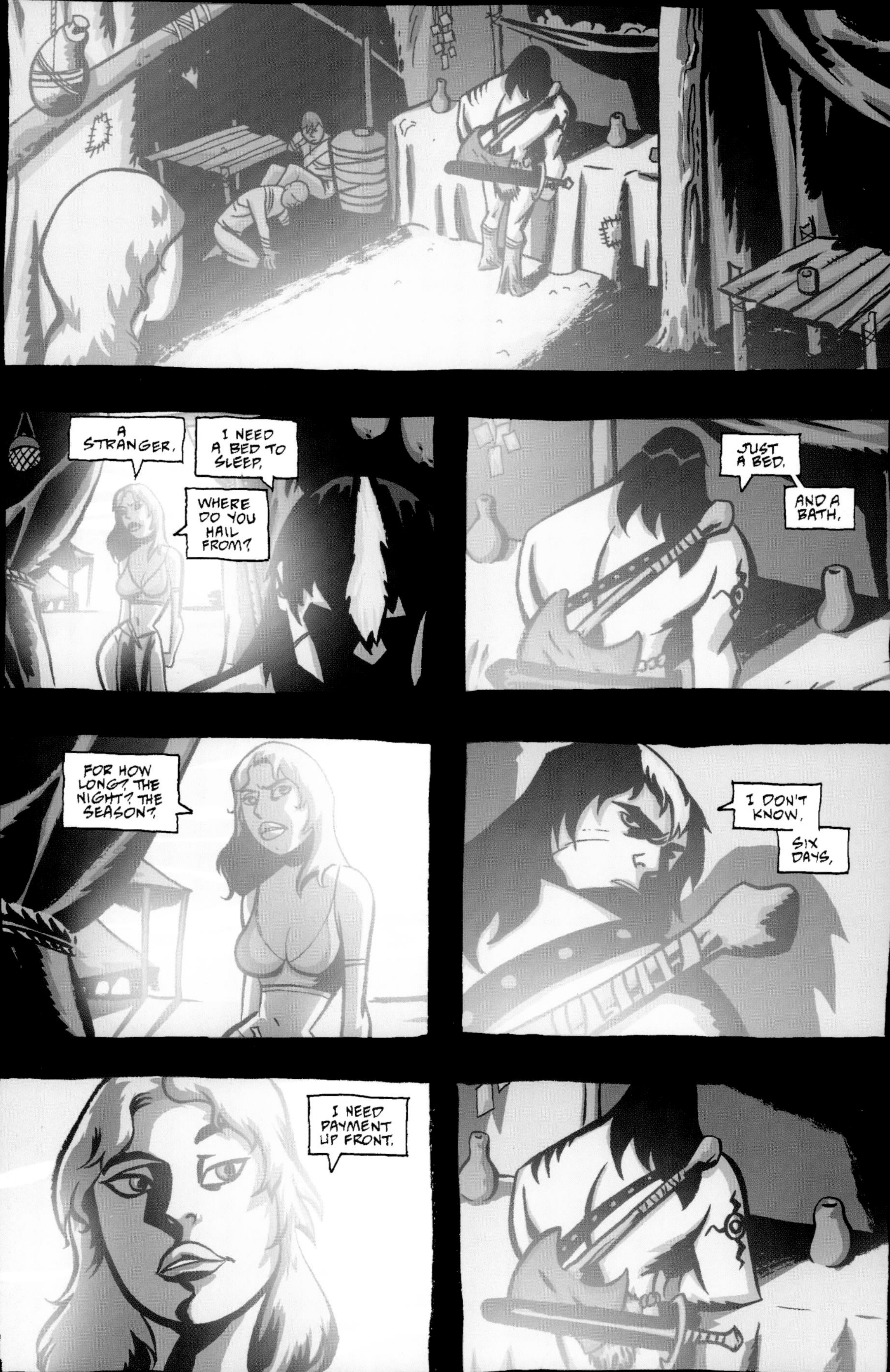

A STRANGER.
I NEED A BED TO SLEEP.
WHERE DO YOU HAIL FROM?
JUST A BED.
AND A BATH.
FOR HOW LONG? THE NIGHT? THE SEASON?
I DON'T KNOW.
SIX DAYS.
I NEED PAYMENT UP FRONT.

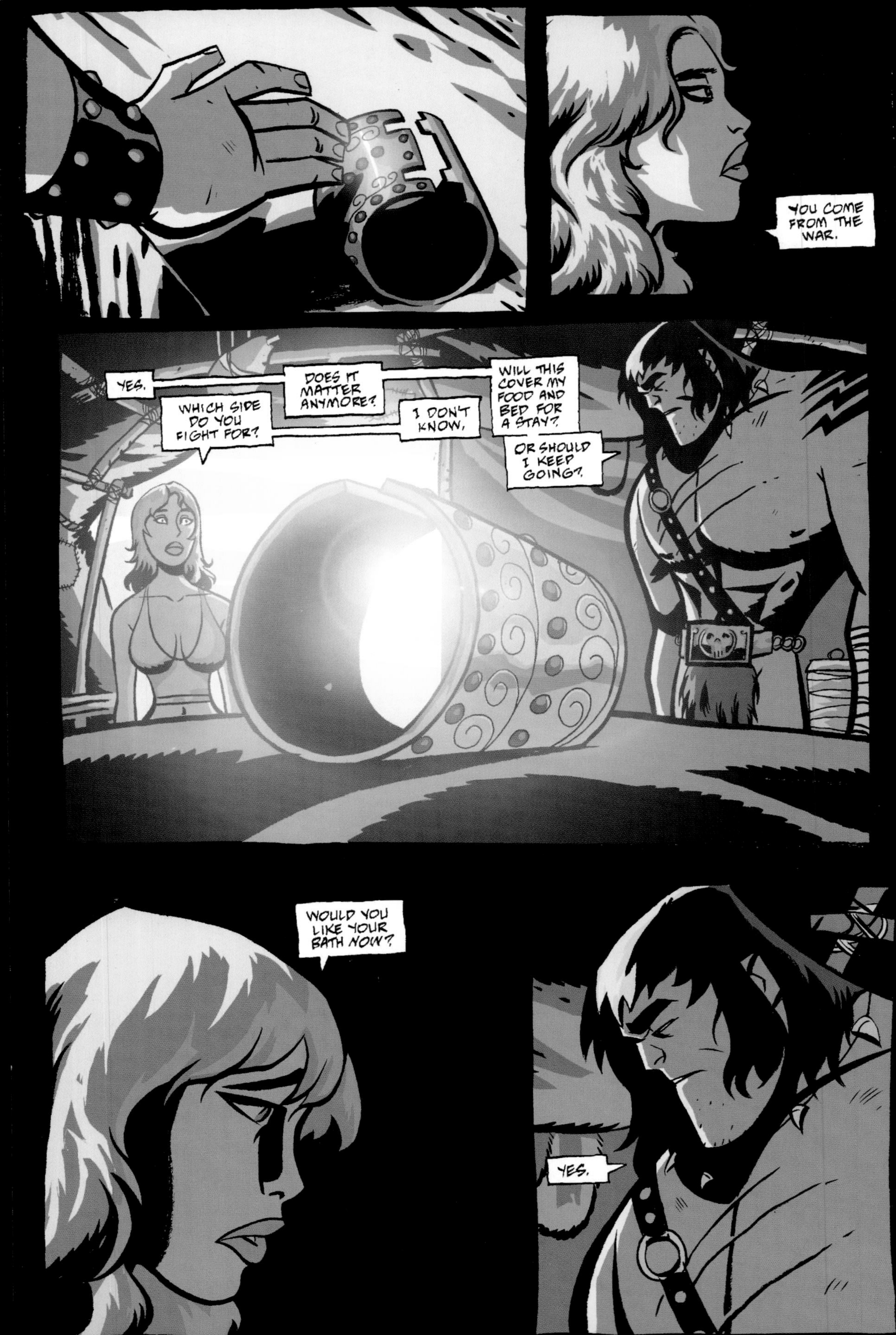
YOU COME FROM THE WAR.
YES.
WHICH SIDE DO YOU FIGHT FOR?
DOES IT MATTER ANYMORE?
I DON'T KNOW,
WILL THIS COVER MY FOOD AND BED FOR A STAY?
OR SHOULD I KEEP GOING?
WOULD YOU LIKE YOUR BATH NOW?
YES.

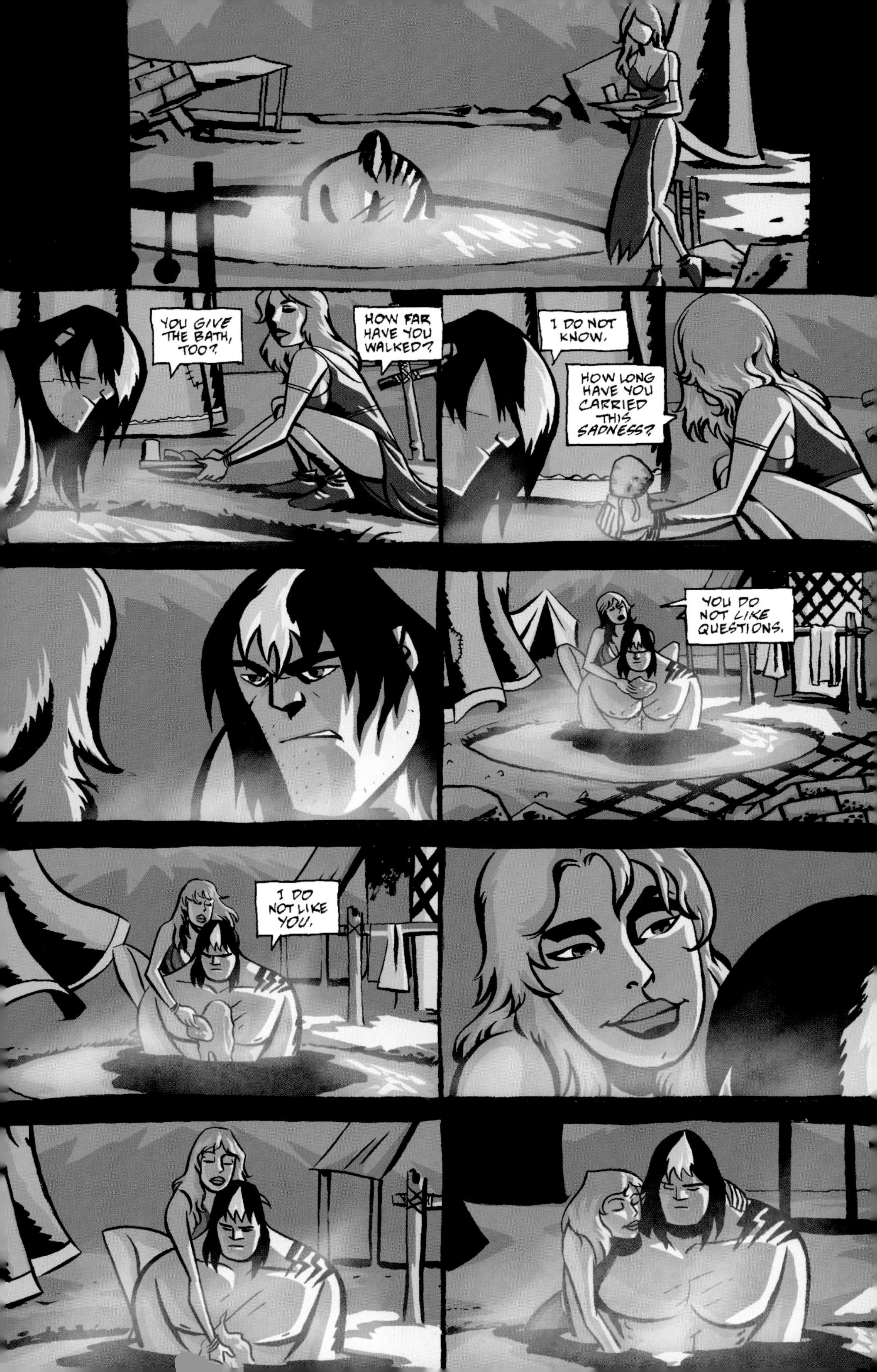
YOU GIVE THE BATH, TOO?
HOW FAR HAVE YOU WALKED?
I DO NOT KNOW.
HOW LONG HAVE YOU CARRIED THIS SADNESS?
YOU DO NOT LIKE QUESTIONS.
I DO NOT LIKE YOU.

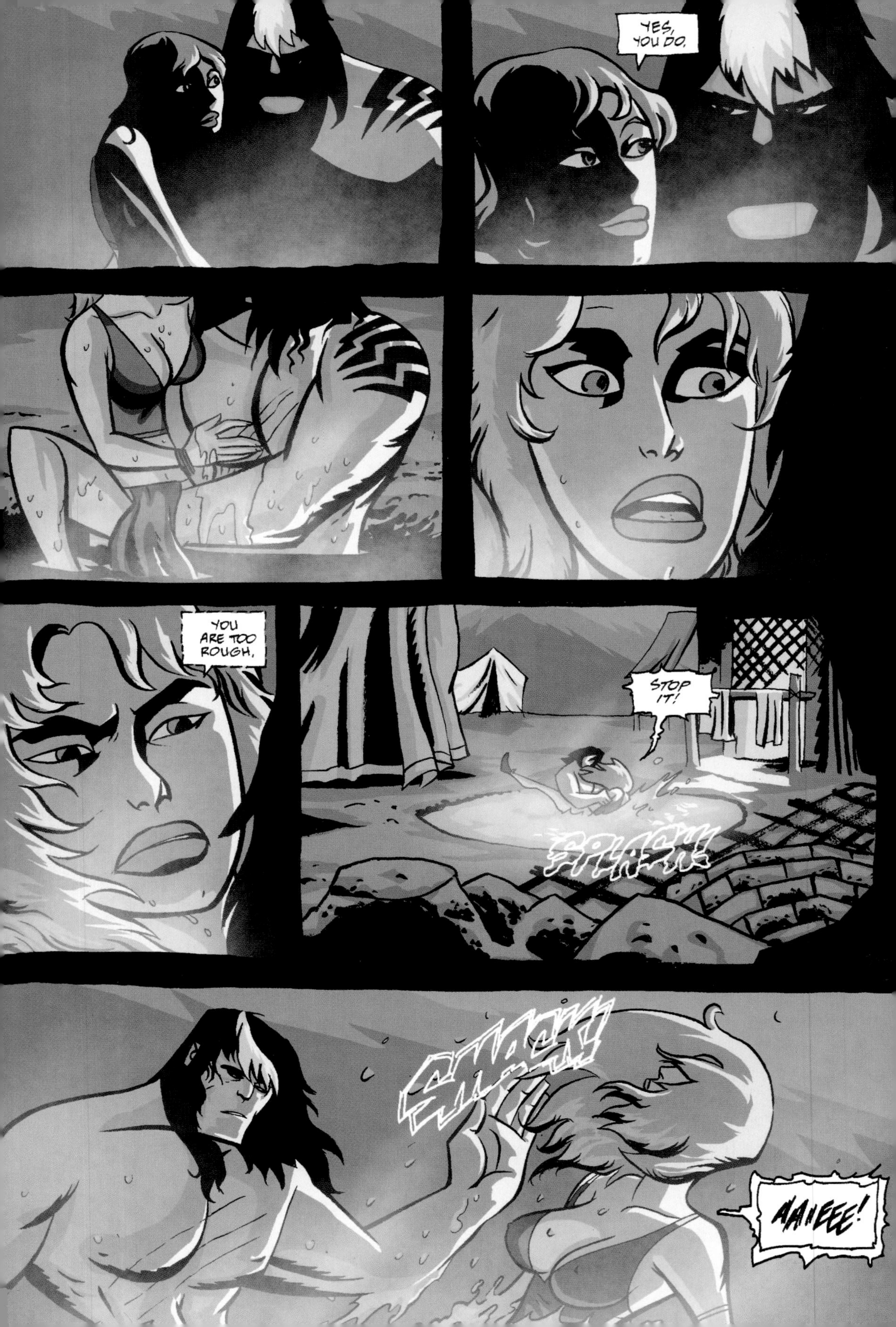
YES, YOU DO.
YOU ARE TOO ROUGH.
STOP IT!
SPLASH!
SMACK!
AAIEEE!

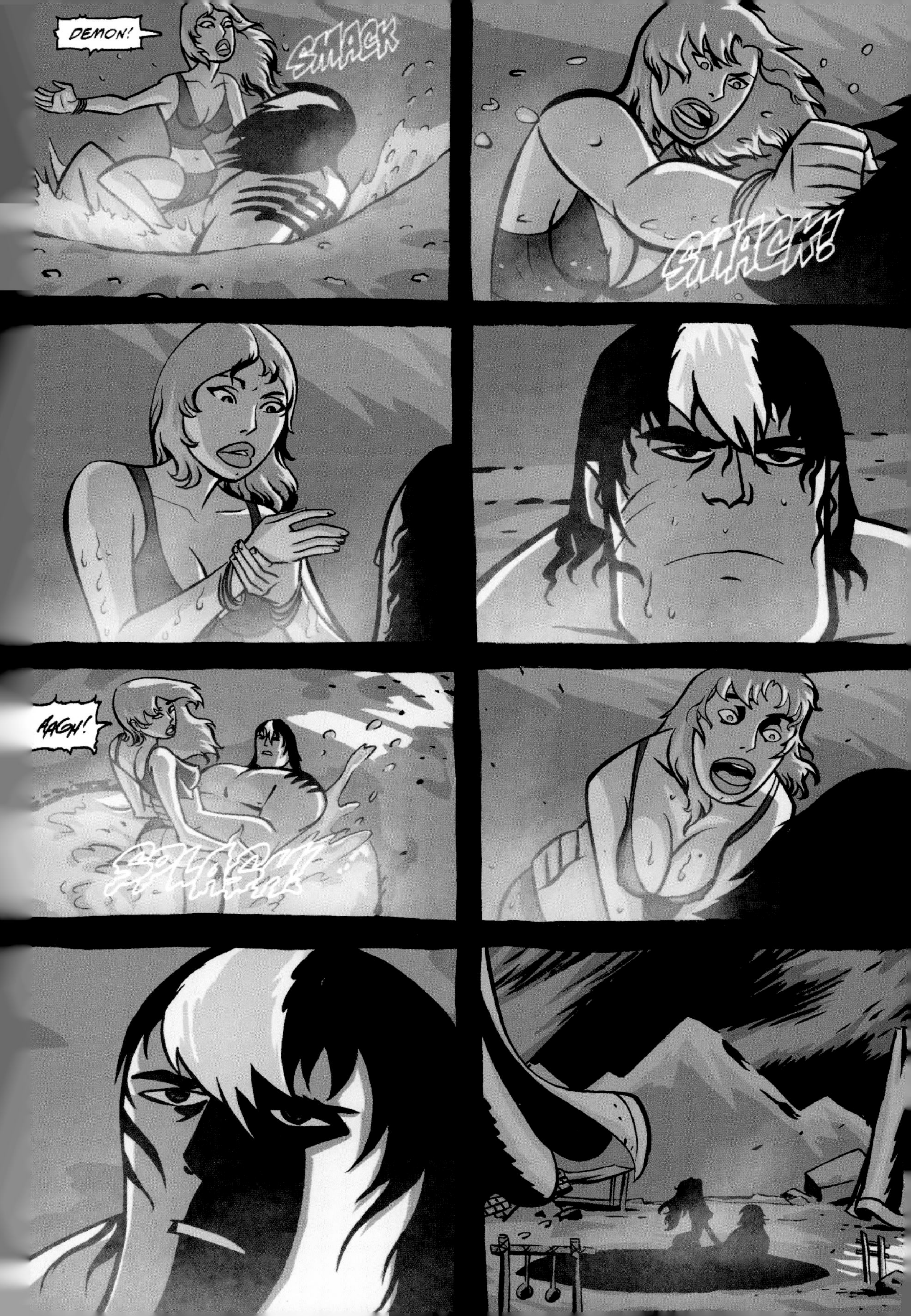
DEMON!
SMACK
SMACK!
AAGH!

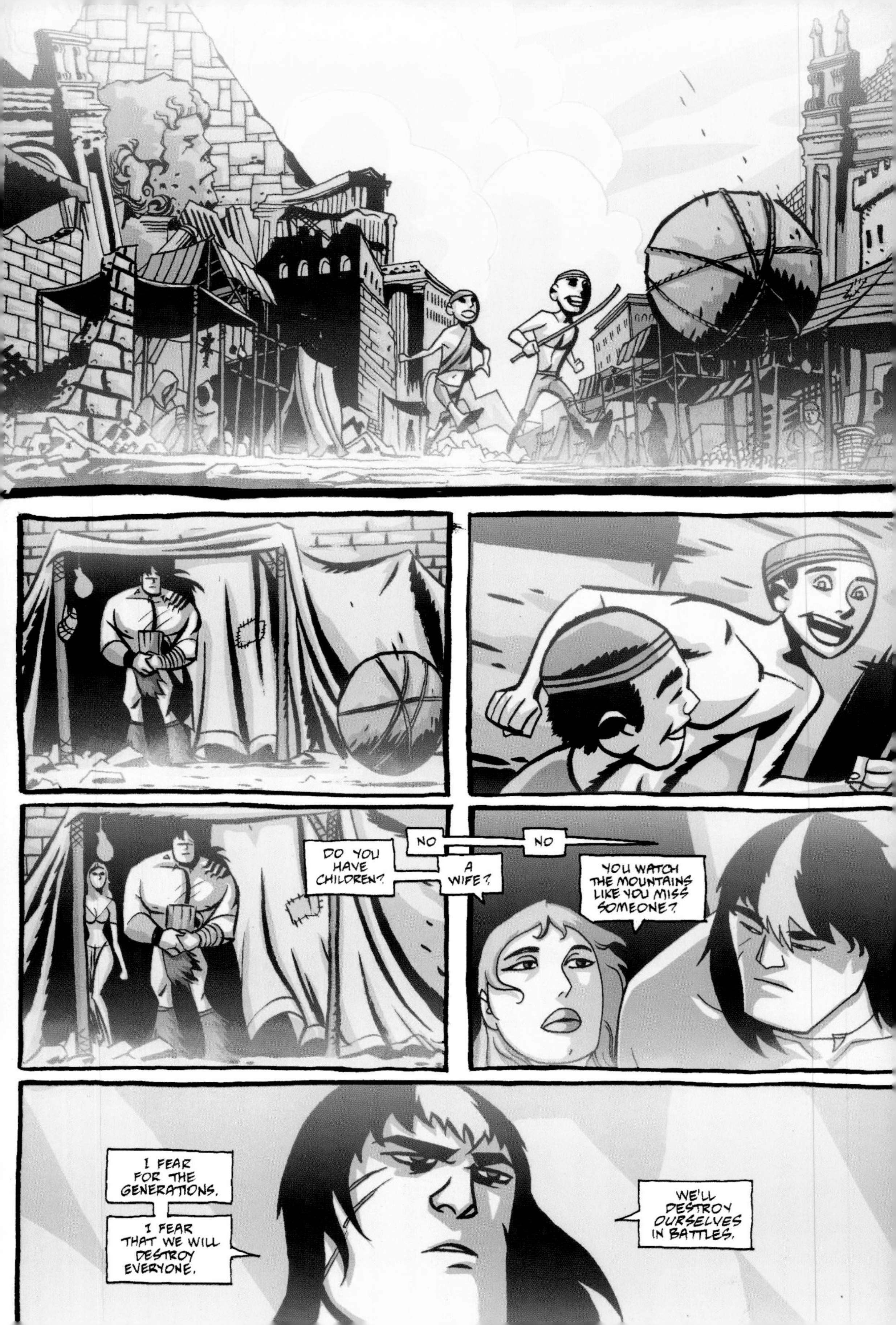
DO YOU HAVE CHILDREN?
NO
A WIFE?
NO
YOU WATCH THE MOUNTAINS LIKE YOU MISS SOMEONE?
I FEAR FOR THE GENERATIONS.
I FEAR THAT WE WILL DESTROY EVERYONE.
WE'LL DESTROY OURSELVES IN BATTLES.

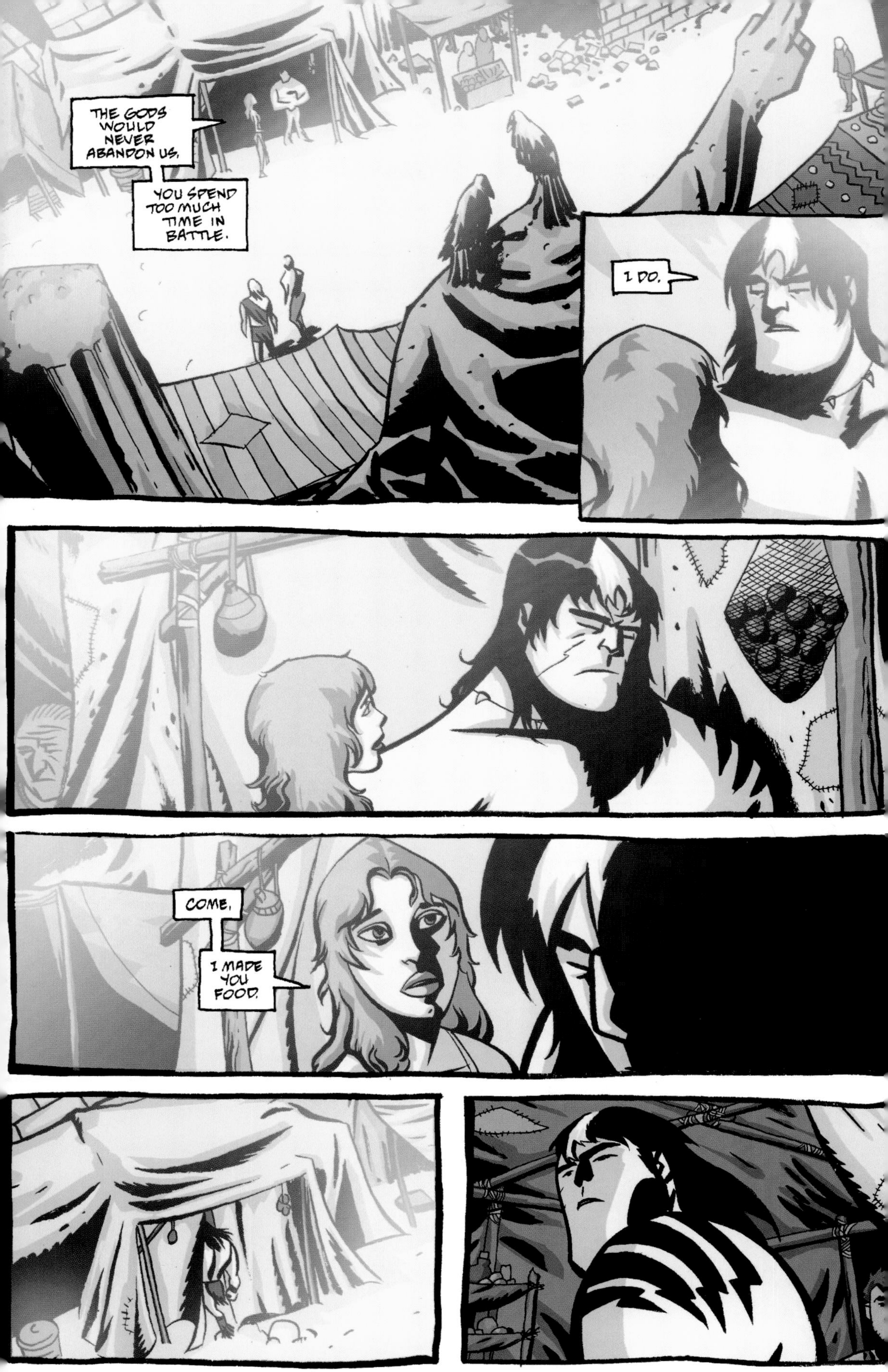
THE GODS WOULD NEVER ABANDON US.
YOU SPEND TOO MUCH TIME IN BATTLE.
I DO.
COME.
I MADE YOU FOOD.

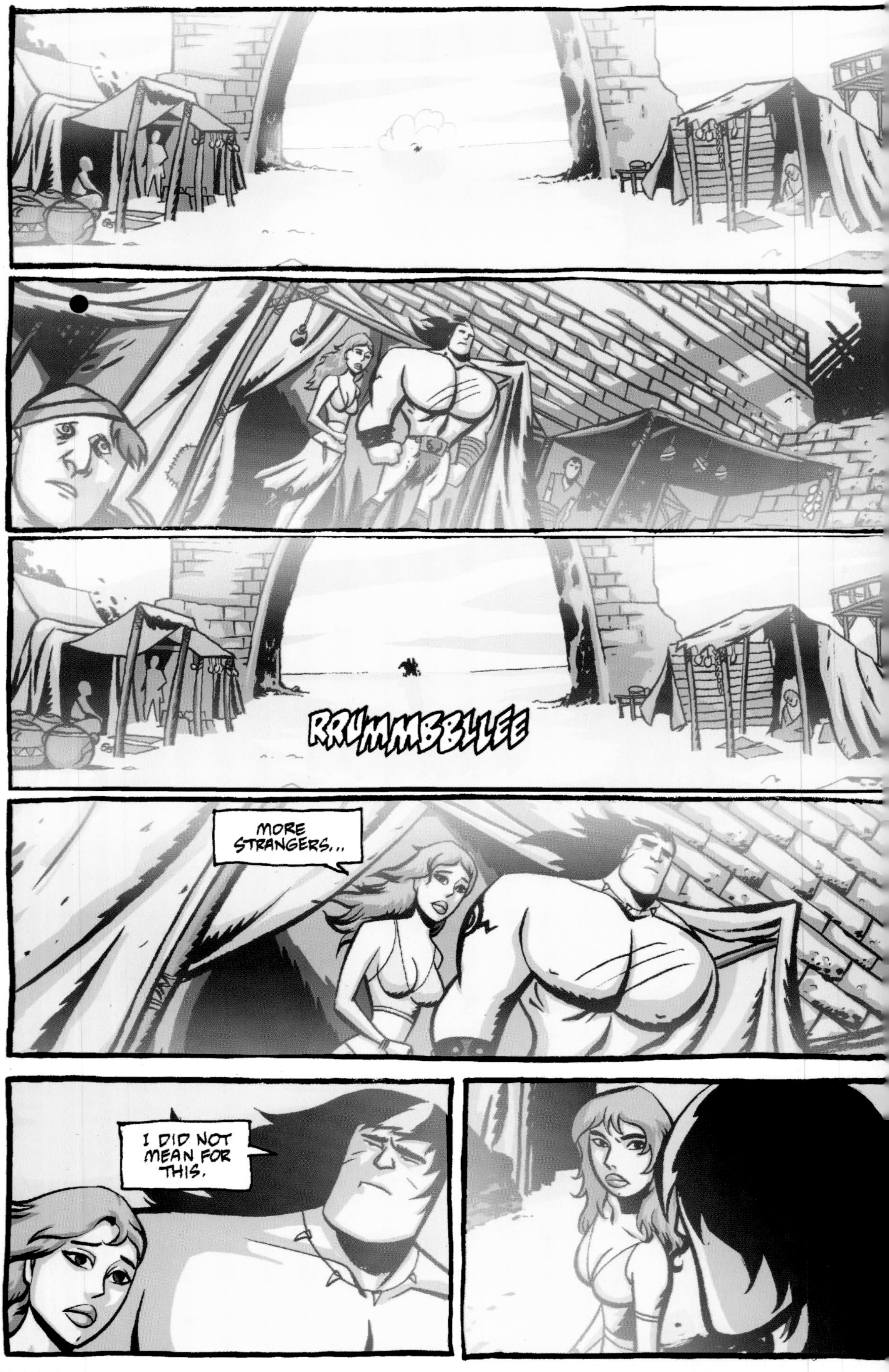
RRUMMBBLLEE
MORE STRANGERS...
I DID NOT MEAN FOR THIS.

RRUUMMMMMMBBBBLLLLLEEEEE

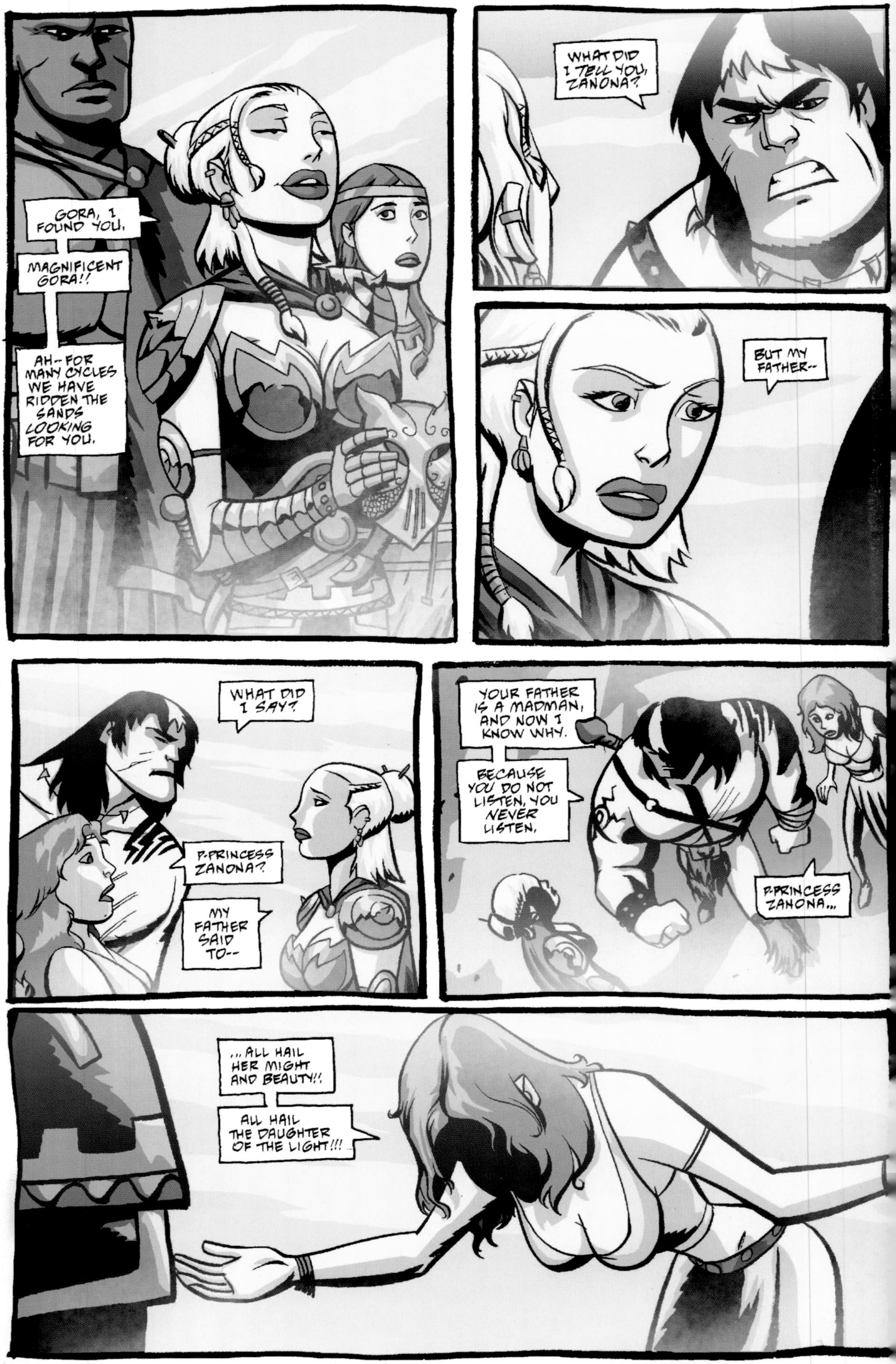
GORA, I FOUND YOU.
MAGNIFICENT GORA!!
AH-- FOR MANY CYCLES WE HAVE RIDDEN THE SANDS LOOKING FOR YOU.
WHAT DID I TELL YOU, ZANONA?
BUT MY FATHER--
WHAT DID I SAY?
P-PRINCESS ZANONA?
MY FATHER SAID TO--
YOUR FATHER IS A MADMAN, AND NOW I KNOW WHY.
BECAUSE YOU DO NOT LISTEN. YOU NEVER LISTEN.
P-PRINCESS ZANONA...
...ALL HAIL HER MIGHT AND BEAUTY!!
ALL HAIL THE DAUGHTER OF THE LIGHT!!!

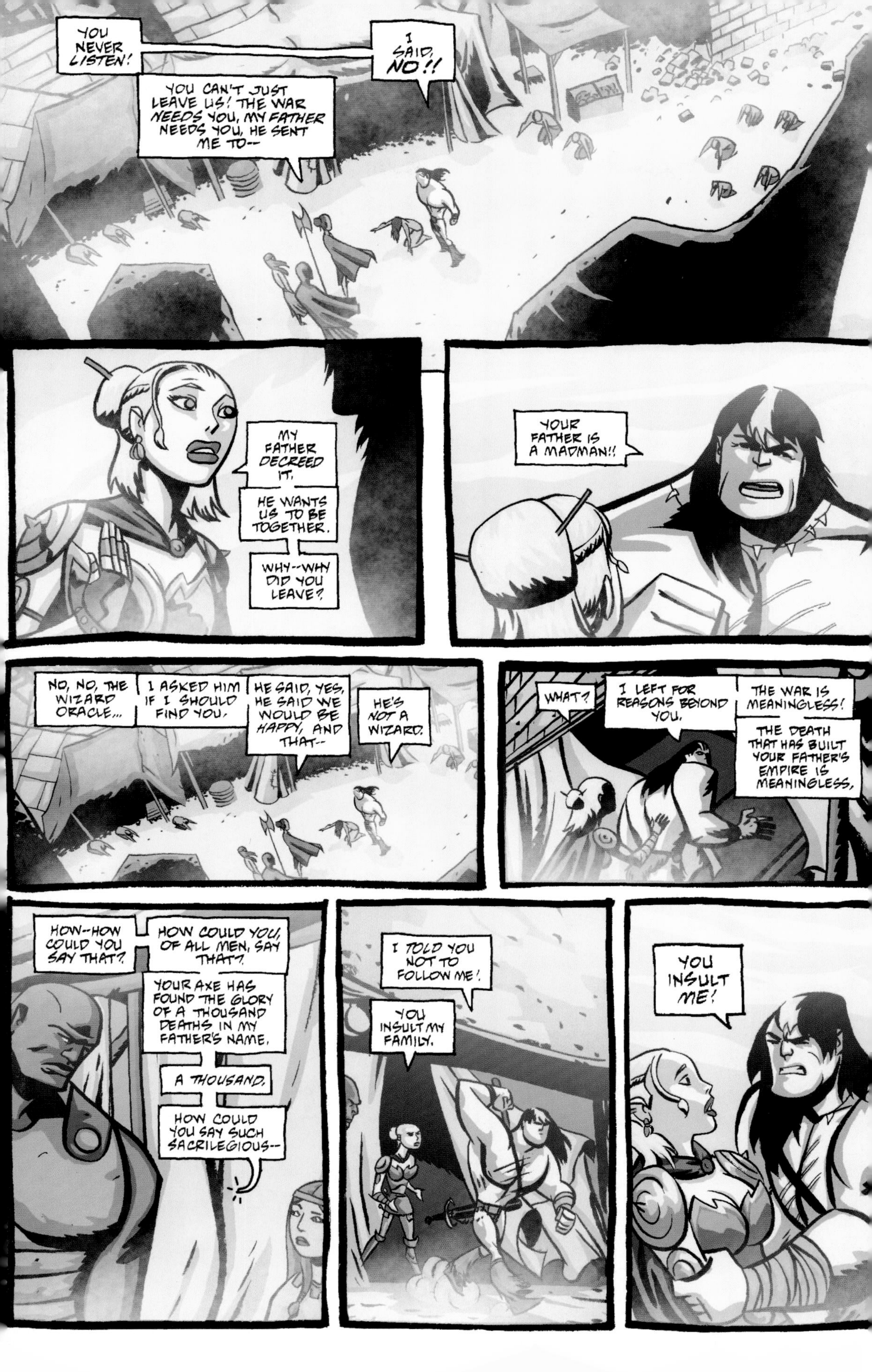
YOU NEVER LISTEN!
I SAID, NO!!
YOU CAN'T JUST LEAVE US! THE WAR NEEDS YOU, MY FATHER NEEDS YOU, HE SENT ME TO--
MY FATHER DECREED IT.
HE WANTS US TO BE TOGETHER.
WHY--WHY DID YOU LEAVE?
YOUR FATHER IS A MADMAN!!
NO, NO, THE WIZARD ORACLE...
I ASKED HIM IF I SHOULD FIND YOU.
HE SAID, YES, HE SAID WE WOULD BE HAPPY, AND THAT--
HE'S NOT A WIZARD.
WHAT?
I LEFT FOR REASONS BEYOND YOU.
THE WAR IS MEANINGLESS!
THE DEATH THAT HAS BUILT YOUR FATHER'S EMPIRE IS MEANINGLESS.
HOW--HOW COULD YOU SAY THAT?
HOW COULD YOU, OF ALL MEN, SAY THAT?
YOUR AXE HAS FOUND THE GLORY OF A THOUSAND DEATHS IN MY FATHER'S NAME.
A THOUSAND.
HOW COULD YOU SAY SUCH SACRILEGIOUS--
I TOLD YOU NOT TO FOLLOW ME!
YOU INSULT MY FAMILY.
YOU INSULT ME!

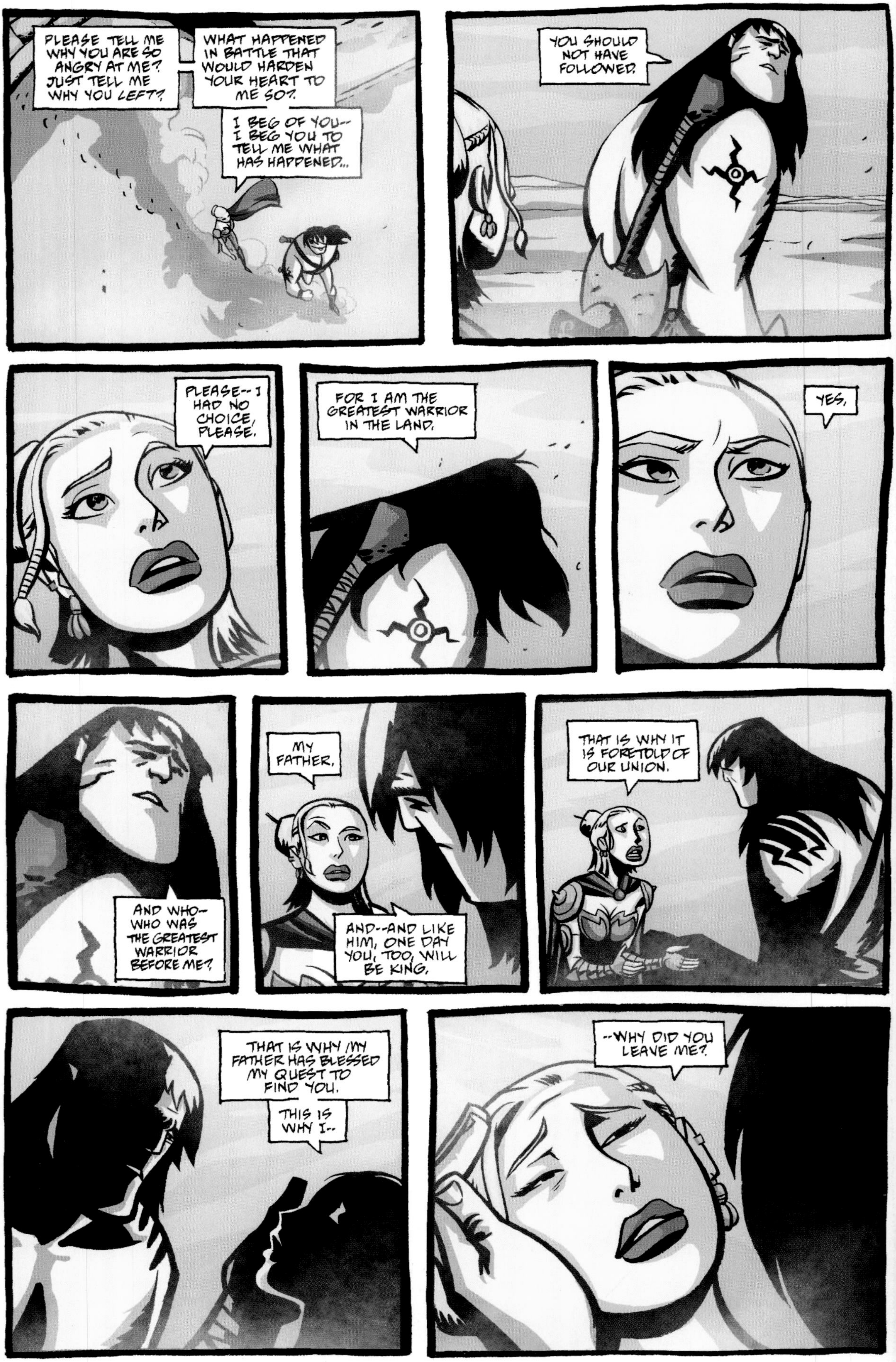
PLEASE TELL ME WHY YOU ARE SO ANGRY AT ME? JUST TELL ME WHY YOU LEFT?
WHAT HAPPENED IN BATTLE THAT WOULD HARDEN YOUR HEART TO ME SO?
I BEG OF YOU-- I BEG YOU TO TELL ME WHAT HAS HAPPENED...
YOU SHOULD NOT HAVE FOLLOWED.
PLEASE-- I HAD NO CHOICE, PLEASE.
FOR I AM THE GREATEST WARRIOR IN THE LAND.
YES.
AND WHO-- WHO WAS THE GREATEST WARRIOR BEFORE ME?
MY FATHER.
AND--AND LIKE HIM, ONE DAY YOU, TOO, WILL BE KING.
THAT IS WHY IT IS FORETOLD OF OUR UNION.
THAT IS WHY MY FATHER HAS BLESSED MY QUEST TO FIND YOU.
THIS IS WHY I--
--WHY DID YOU LEAVE ME?

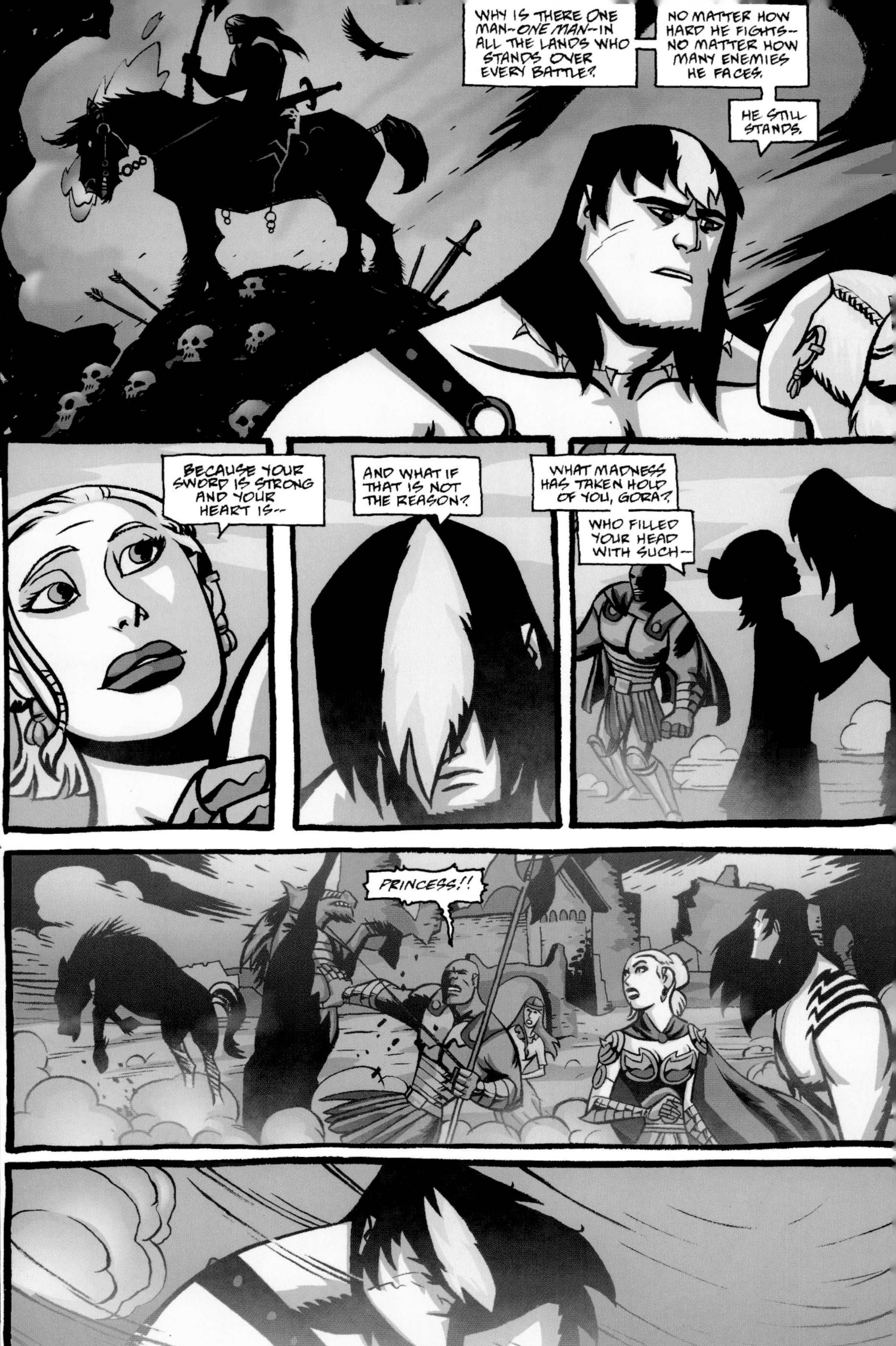

WHY IS THERE ONE MAN--ONE MAN--IN ALL THE LANDS WHO STANDS OVER EVERY BATTLE?
NO MATTER HOW HARD HE FIGHTS-- NO MATTER HOW MANY ENEMIES HE FACES,
HE STILL STANDS.
BECAUSE YOUR SWORD IS STRONG AND YOUR HEART IS--
AND WHAT IF THAT IS NOT THE REASON?
WHAT MADNESS HAS TAKEN HOLD OF YOU, GORA?
WHO FILLED YOUR HEAD WITH SUCH--
PRINCESS!!

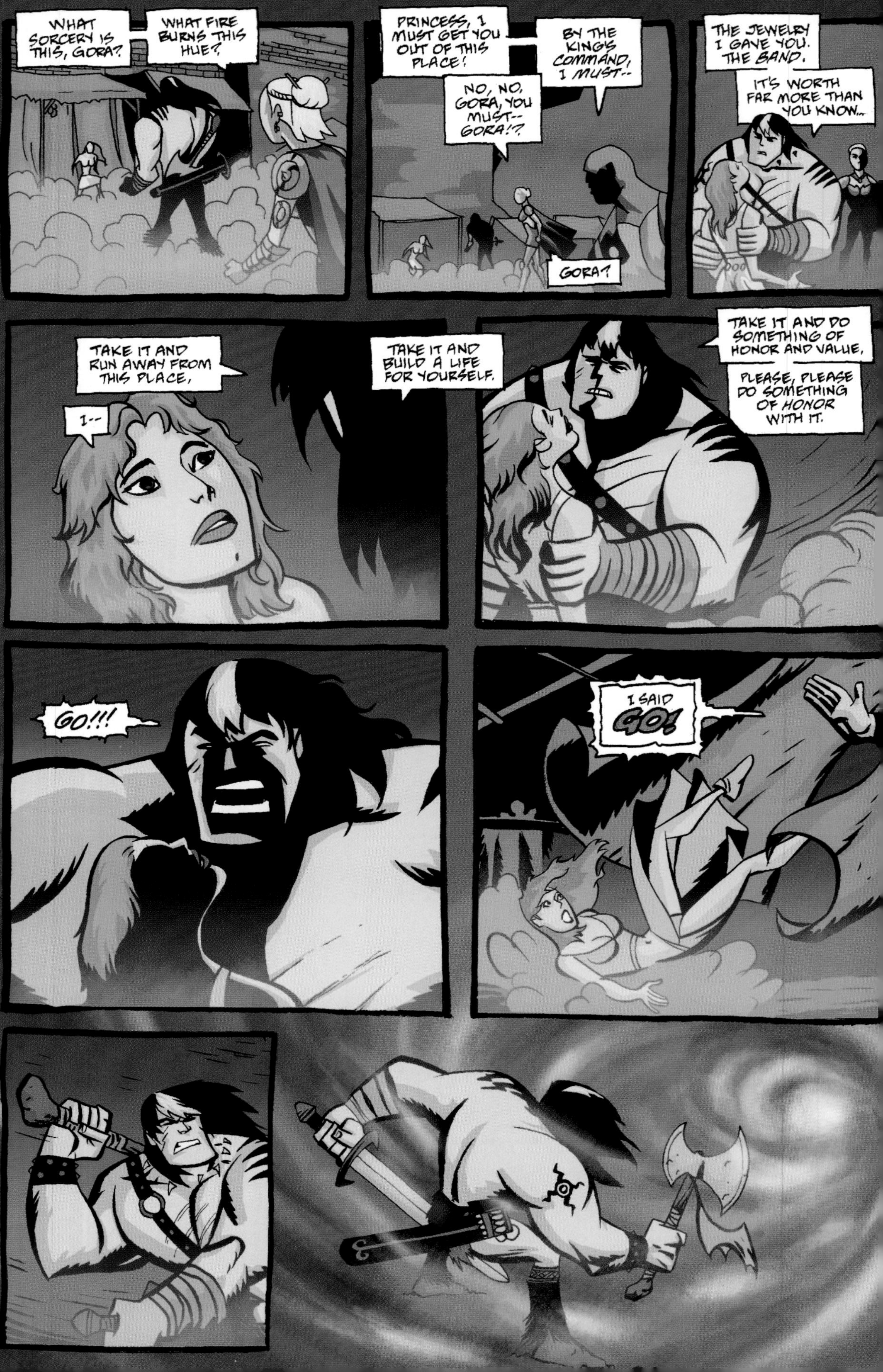
WHAT SORCERY IS THIS, GORA?
WHAT FIRE BURNS THIS HUE?
PRINCESS, I MUST GET YOU OUT OF THIS PLACE!
BY THE KING'S COMMAND, I MUST--
NO, NO, GORA, YOU MUST-- GORA!?
GORA?
THE JEWELRY I GAVE YOU. THE BAND.
IT'S WORTH FAR MORE THAN YOU KNOW...
TAKE IT AND RUN AWAY FROM THIS PLACE,
I--
TAKE IT AND BUILD A LIFE FOR YOURSELF.
TAKE IT AND DO SOMETHING OF HONOR AND VALUE.
PLEASE, PLEASE DO SOMETHING OF HONOR WITH IT.
GO!!!
I SAID GO!

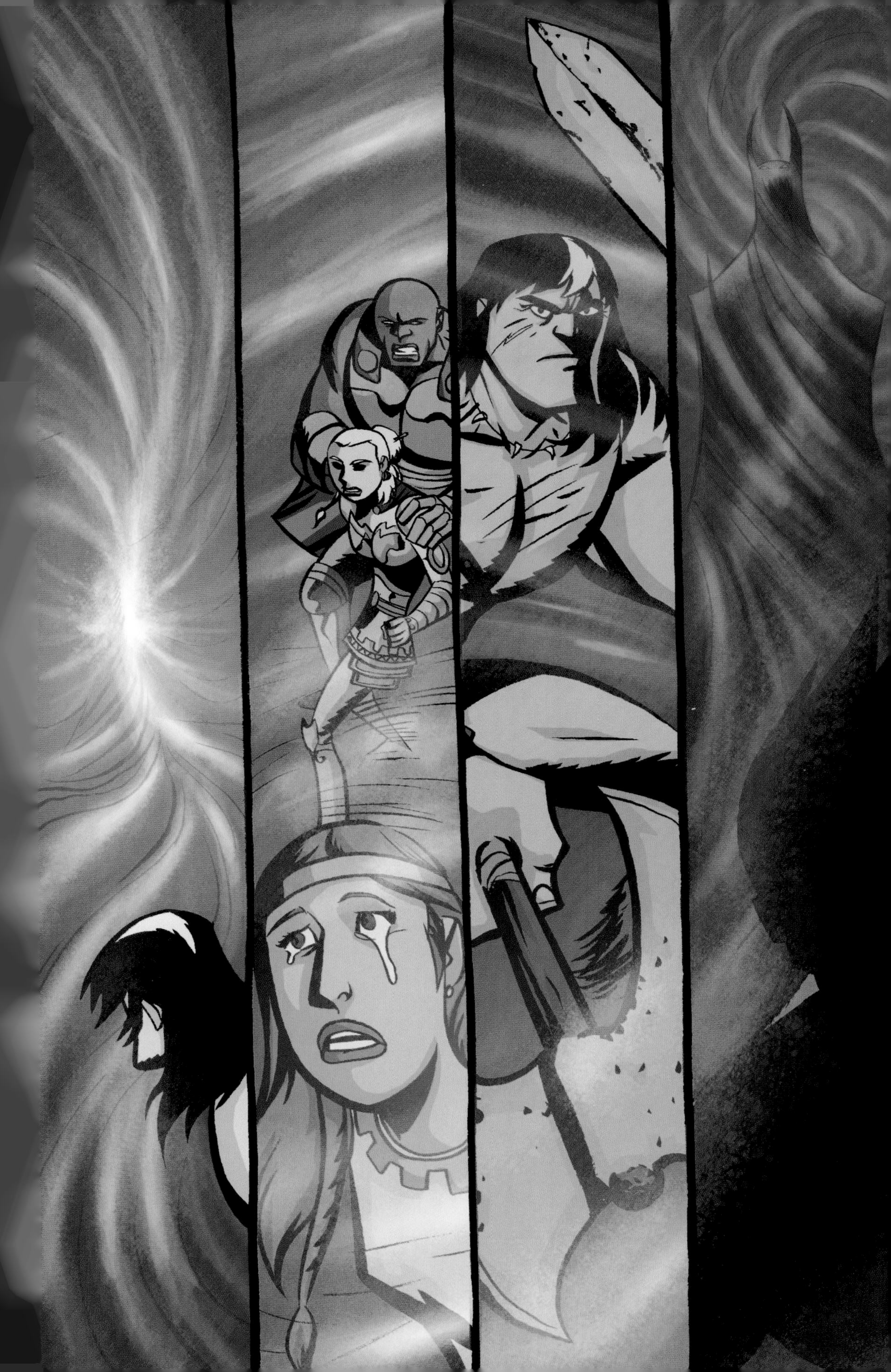

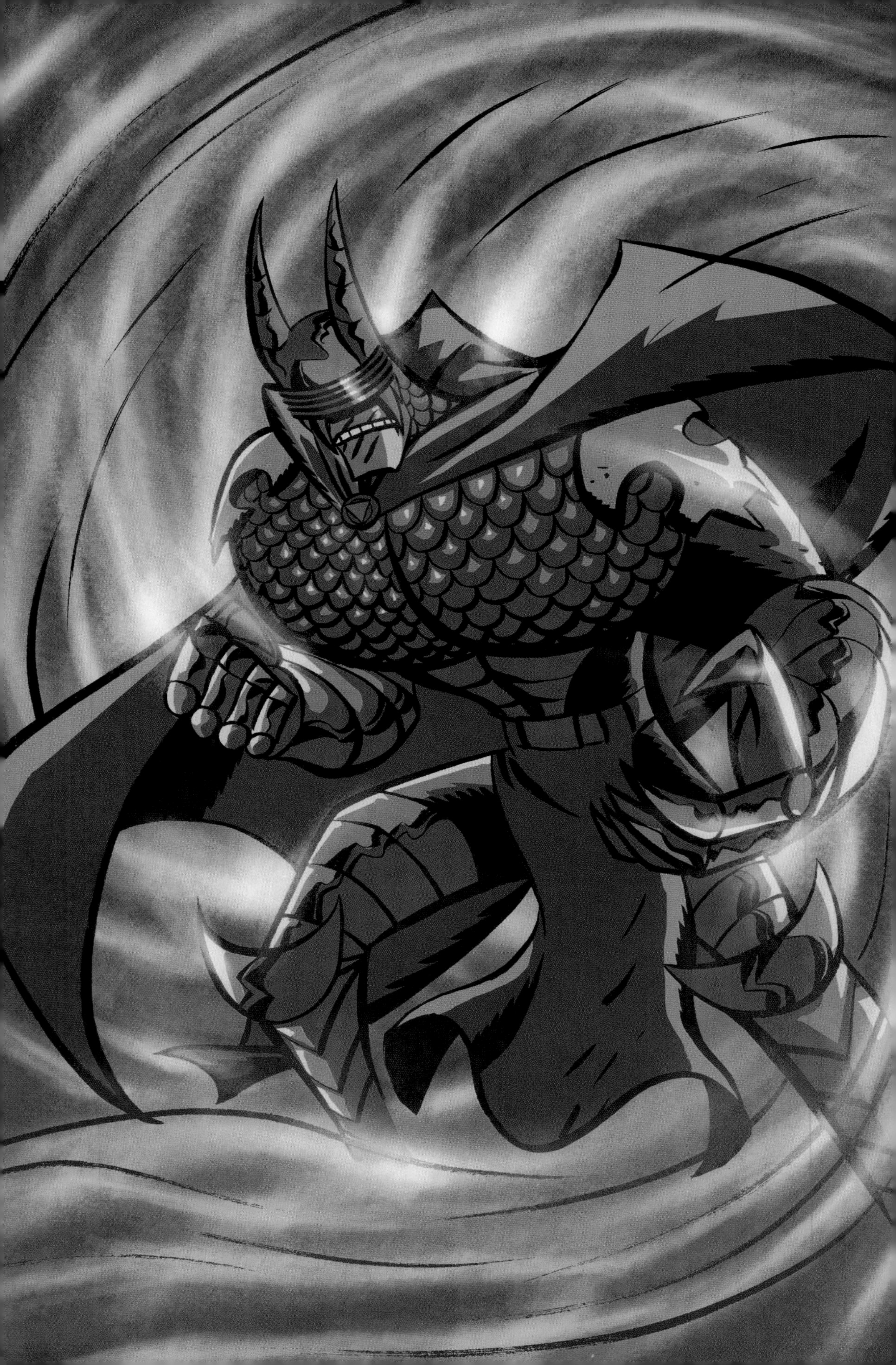

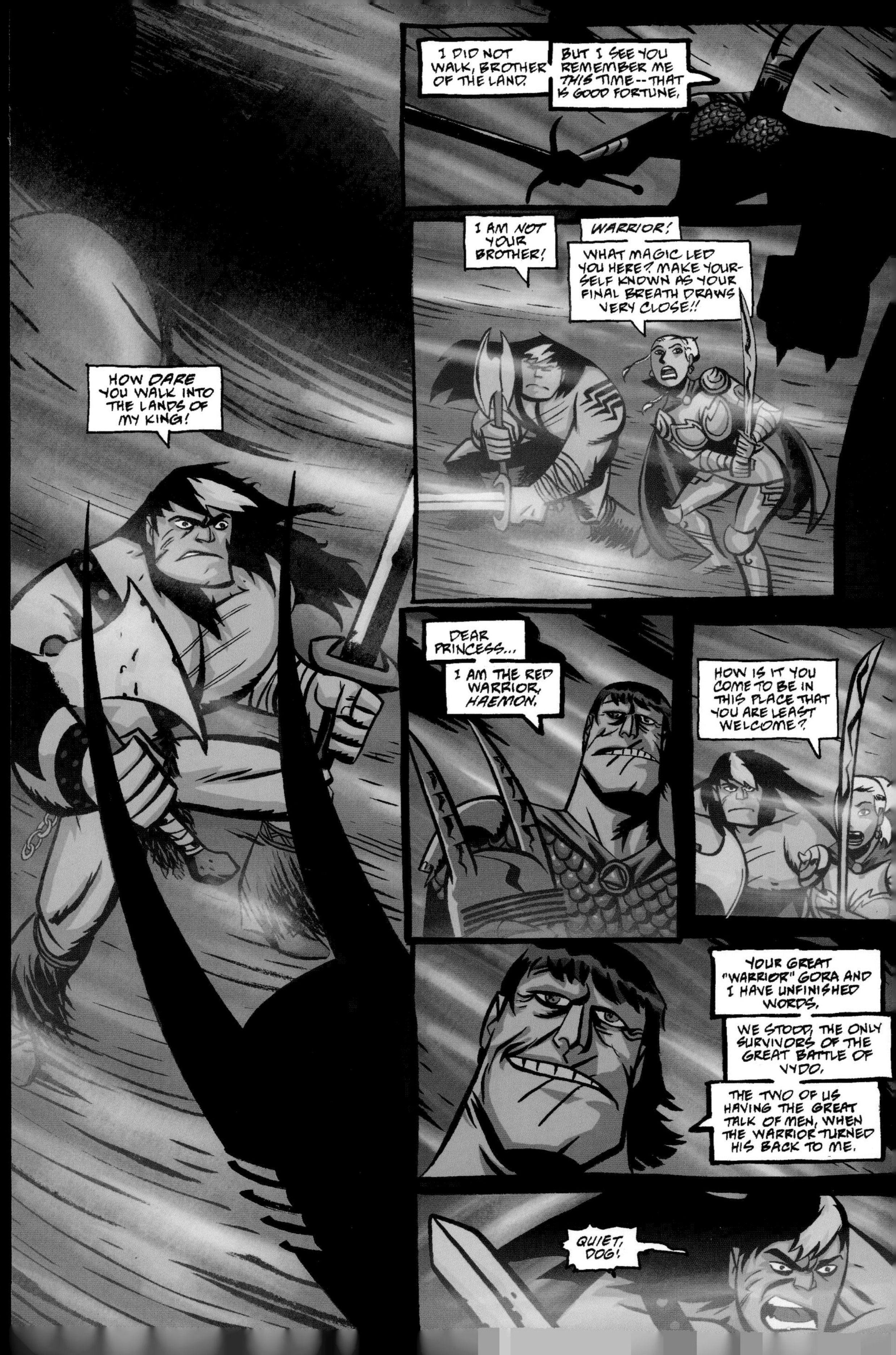
I DID NOT WALK, BROTHER OF THE LAND.
BUT I SEE YOU REMEMBER ME THIS TIME -- THAT IS GOOD FORTUNE.
HOW DARE YOU WALK INTO THE LANDS OF MY KING!
I AM NOT YOUR BROTHER!
WARRIOR!
WHAT MAGIC LED YOU HERE? MAKE YOURSELF KNOWN AS YOUR FINAL BREATH DRAWS VERY CLOSE!!
DEAR PRINCESS...
I AM THE RED WARRIOR, HAEMON.
HOW IS IT YOU COME TO BE IN THIS PLACE THAT YOU ARE LEAST WELCOME?
YOUR GREAT "WARRIOR" GORA AND I HAVE UNFINISHED WORDS.
WE STOOD, THE ONLY SURVIVORS OF THE GREAT BATTLE OF VYDO.
THE TWO OF US HAVING THE GREAT TALK OF MEN, WHEN THE WARRIOR TURNED HIS BACK TO ME.
QUIET, DOG!

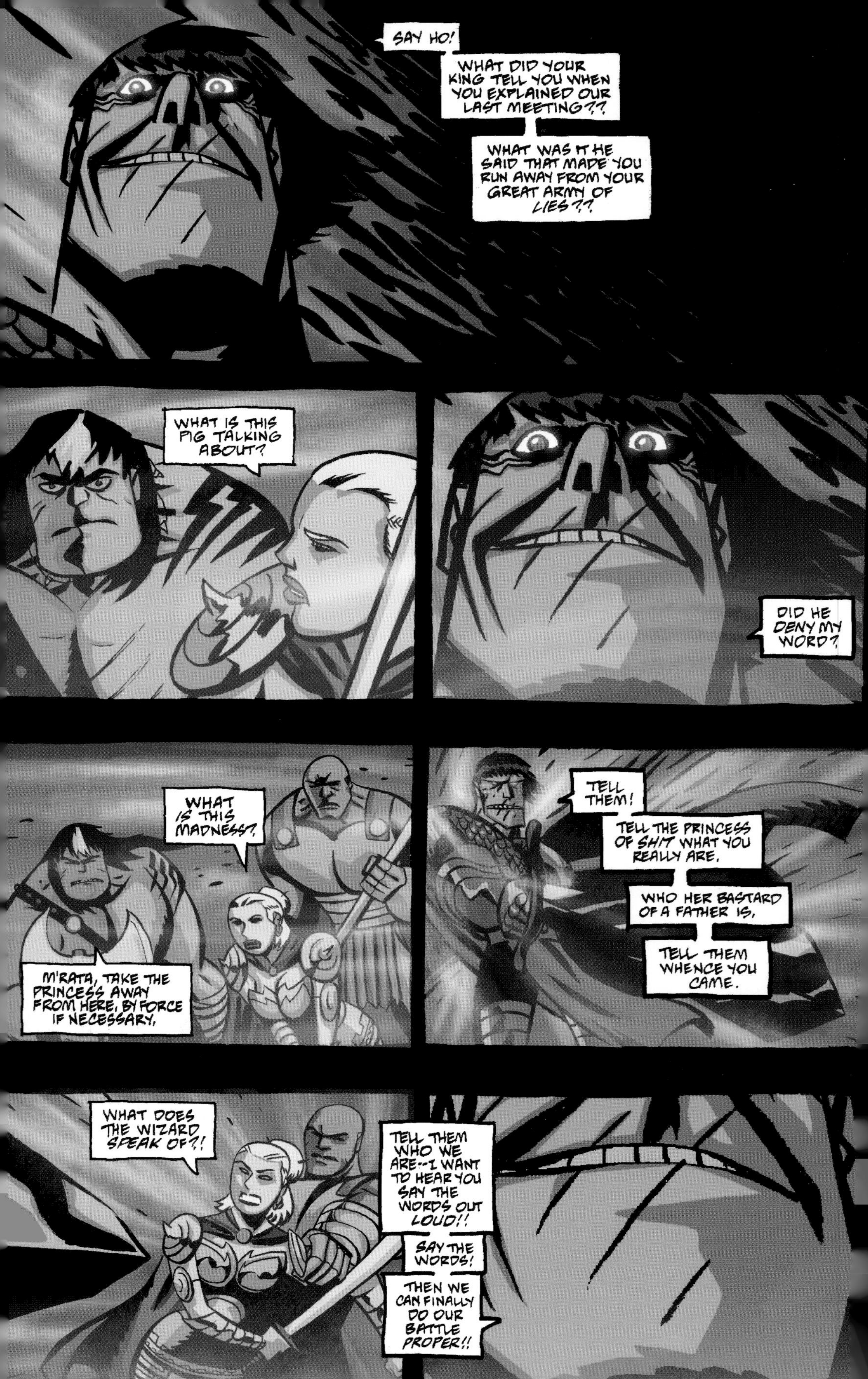
SAY HO!
WHAT DID YOUR KING TELL YOU WHEN YOU EXPLAINED OUR LAST MEETING??
WHAT WAS IT HE SAID THAT MADE YOU RUN AWAY FROM YOUR GREAT ARMY OF LIES??
WHAT IS THIS PIG TALKING ABOUT?
DID HE DENY MY WORD?
WHAT IS THIS MADNESS?
M'RATA, TAKE THE PRINCESS AWAY FROM HERE, BY FORCE IF NECESSARY.
TELL THEM!
TELL THE PRINCESS OF SH!T WHAT YOU REALLY ARE.
WHO HER BASTARD OF A FATHER IS.
TELL THEM WHENCE YOU CAME.
WHAT DOES THE WIZARD SPEAK OF?!
TELL THEM WHO WE ARE--I WANT TO HEAR YOU SAY THE WORDS OUT LOUD!!
SAY THE WORDS!
THEN WE CAN FINALLY DO OUR BATTLE PROPER!!

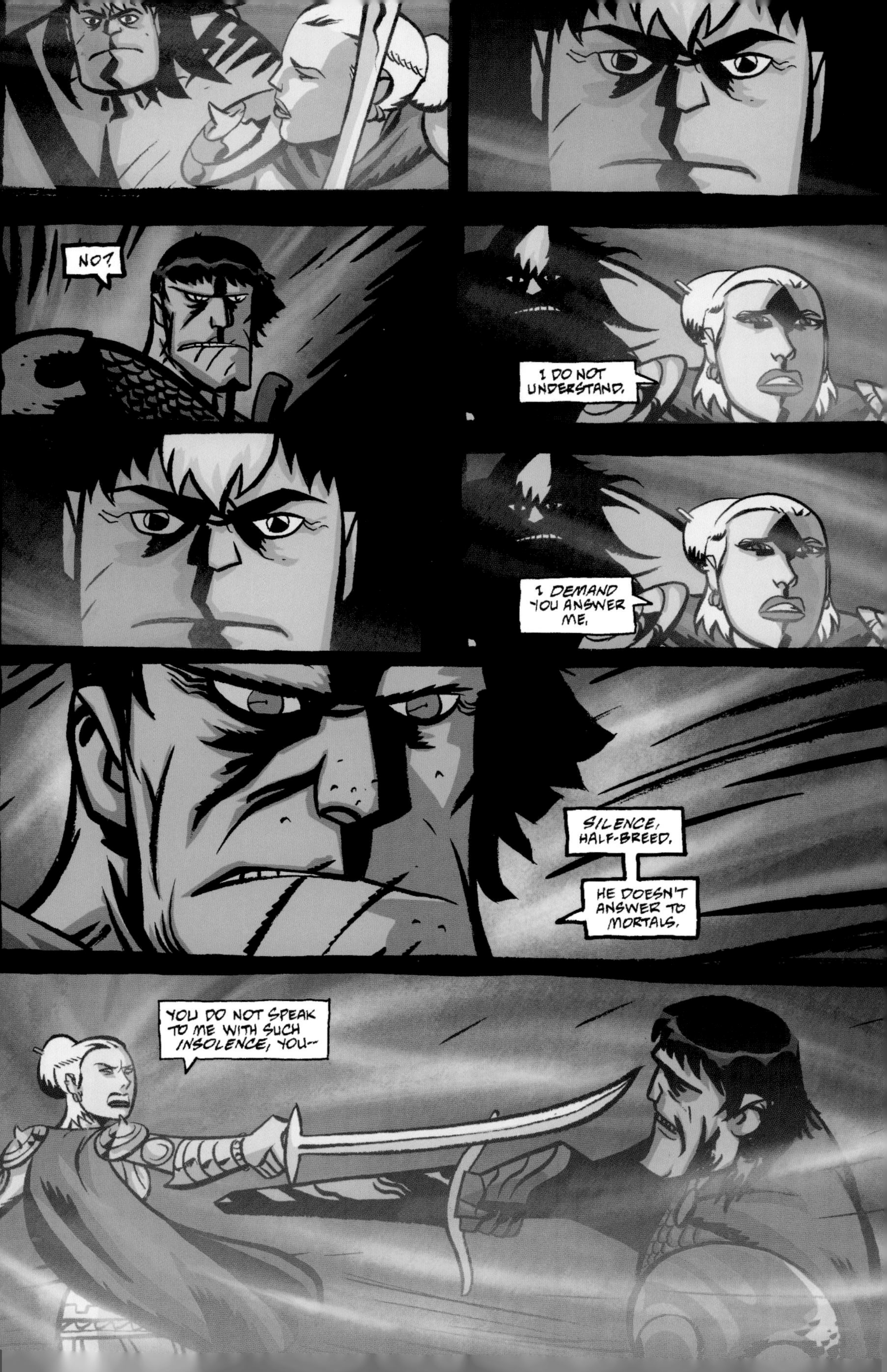

NO?
I DO NOT UNDERSTAND.
I DEMAND YOU ANSWER ME.
SILENCE, HALF-BREED.
HE DOESN'T ANSWER TO MORTALS.
YOU DO NOT SPEAK TO ME WITH SUCH INSOLENCE, YOU--

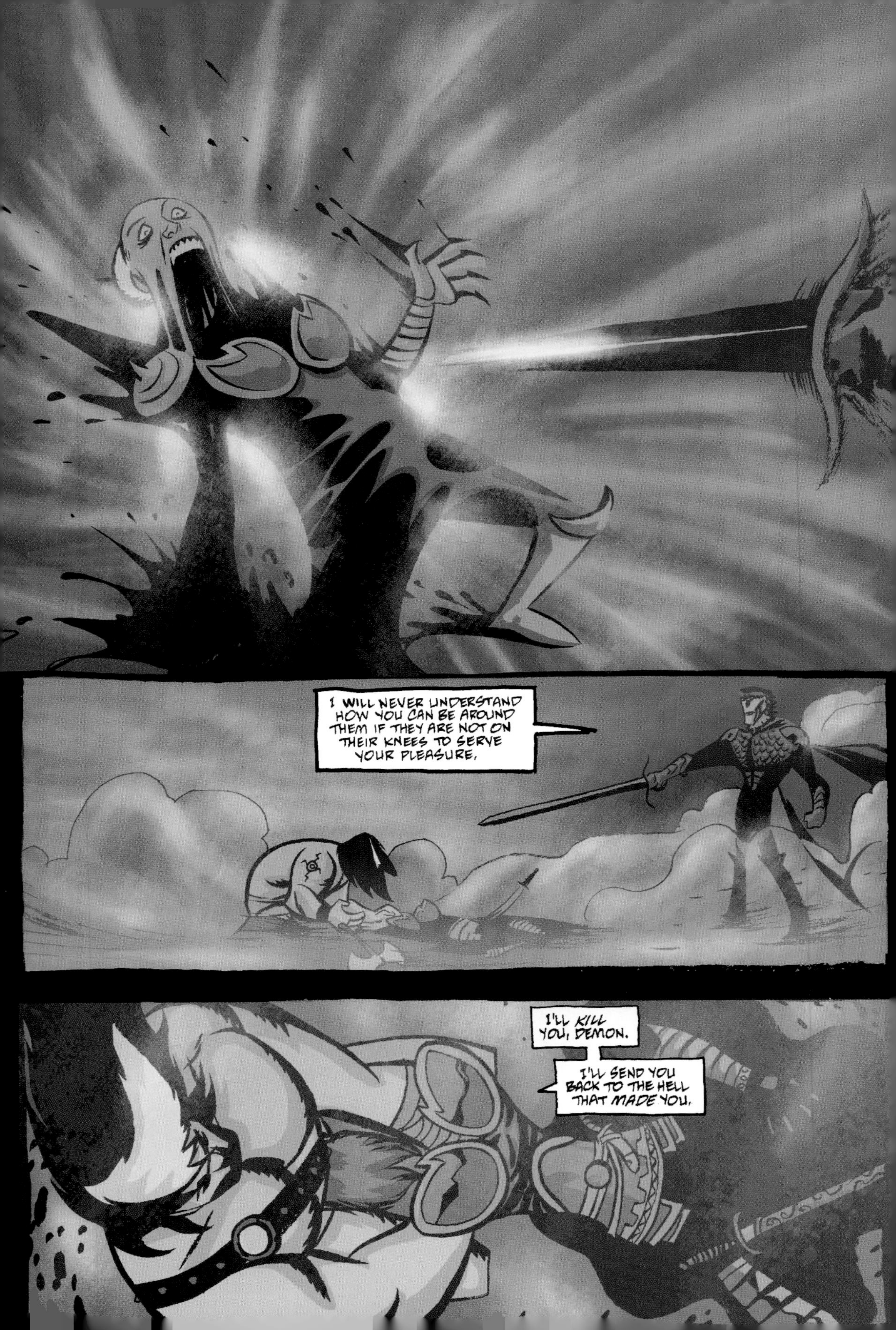
I WILL NEVER UNDERSTAND HOW YOU CAN BE AROUND THEM IF THEY ARE NOT ON THEIR KNEES TO SERVE YOUR PLEASURE.
I'LL *KILL* YOU, DEMON.
I'LL SEND YOU BACK TO THE HELL THAT *MADE* YOU.

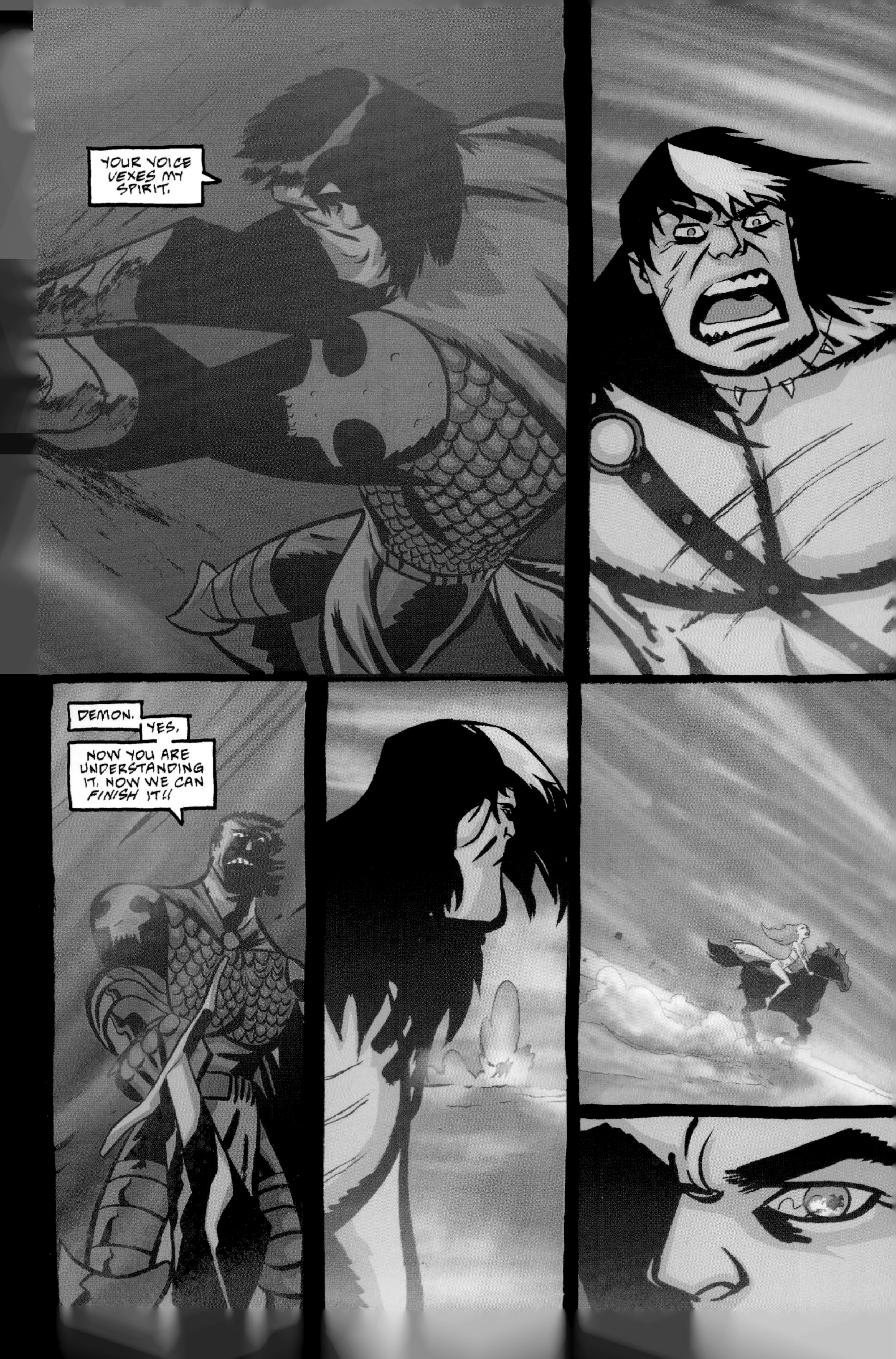
YOUR VOICE VEXES MY SPIRIT.
DEMON.
YES,
NOW YOU ARE UNDERSTANDING IT. NOW WE CAN *FINISH* IT!!

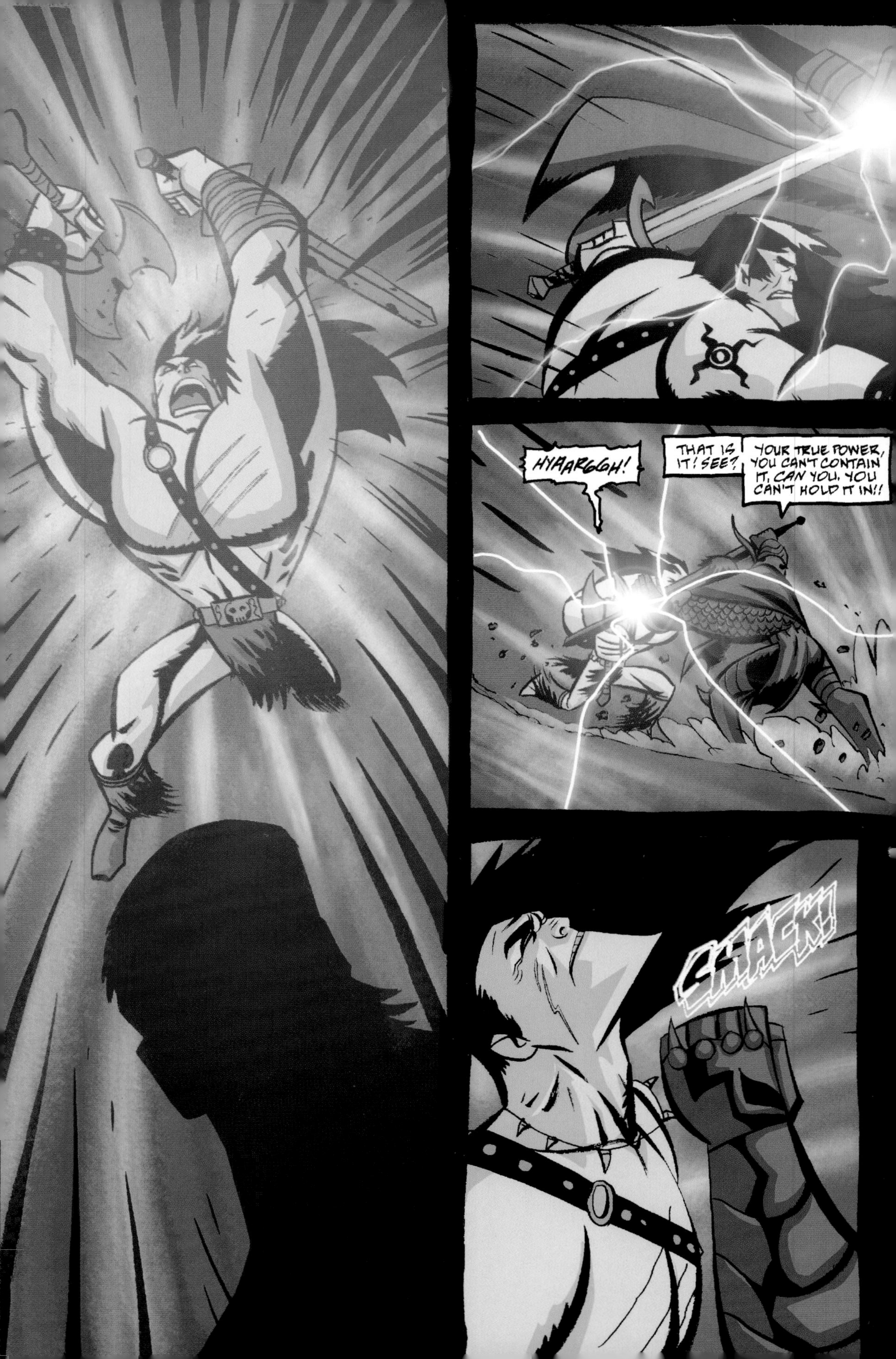
HYAARGGH!
THAT IS IT! SEE?
YOUR TRUE POWER, YOU CAN'T CONTAIN IT, CAN YOU. YOU CAN'T HOLD IT IN!!
SMACK!

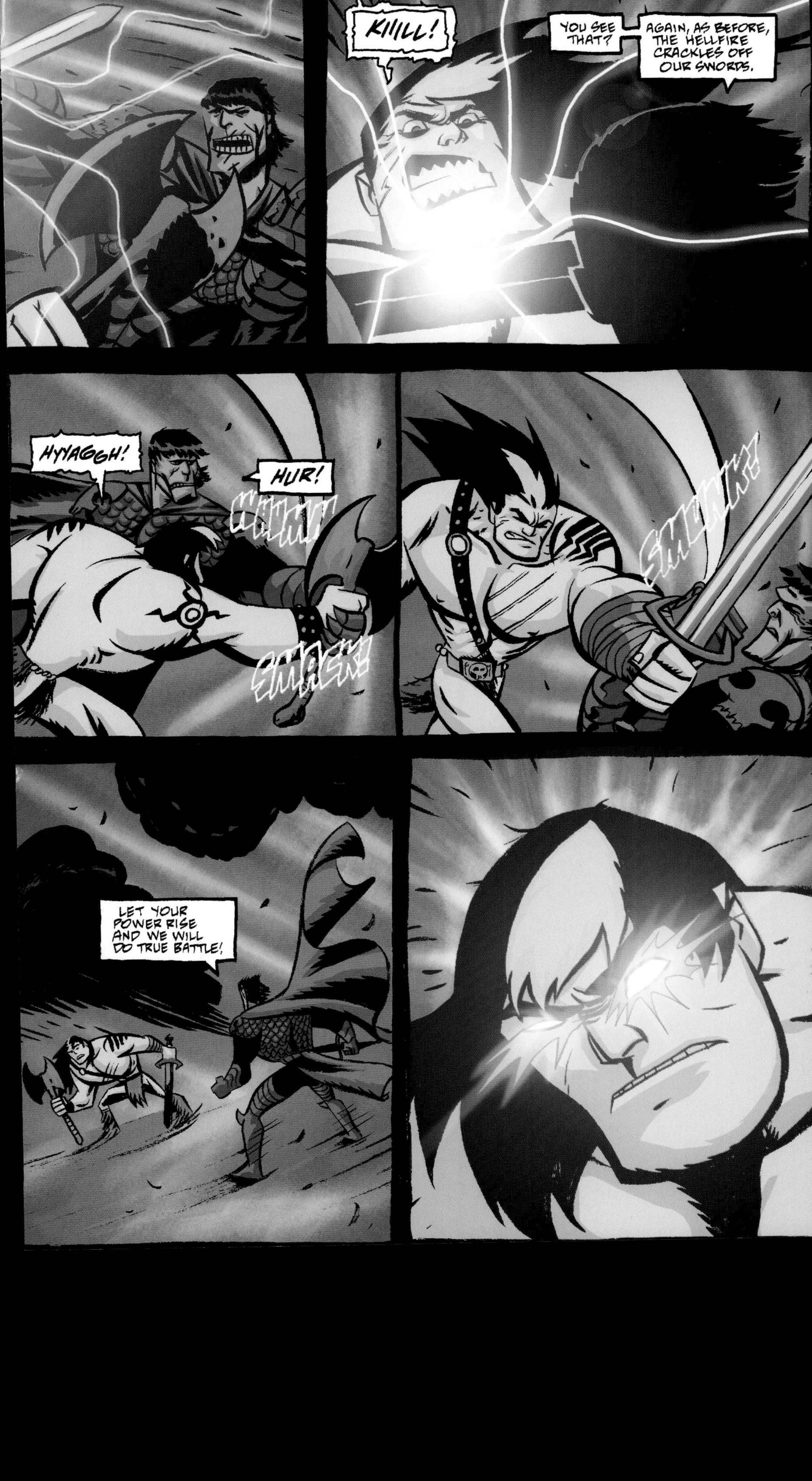
KIIILL!
YOU SEE THAT?
AGAIN, AS BEFORE, THE HELLFIRE CRACKLES OFF OUR SWORDS.
HYYAGGH!
HUR!
SMASH!
LET YOUR POWER RISE AND WE WILL DO TRUE BATTLE!

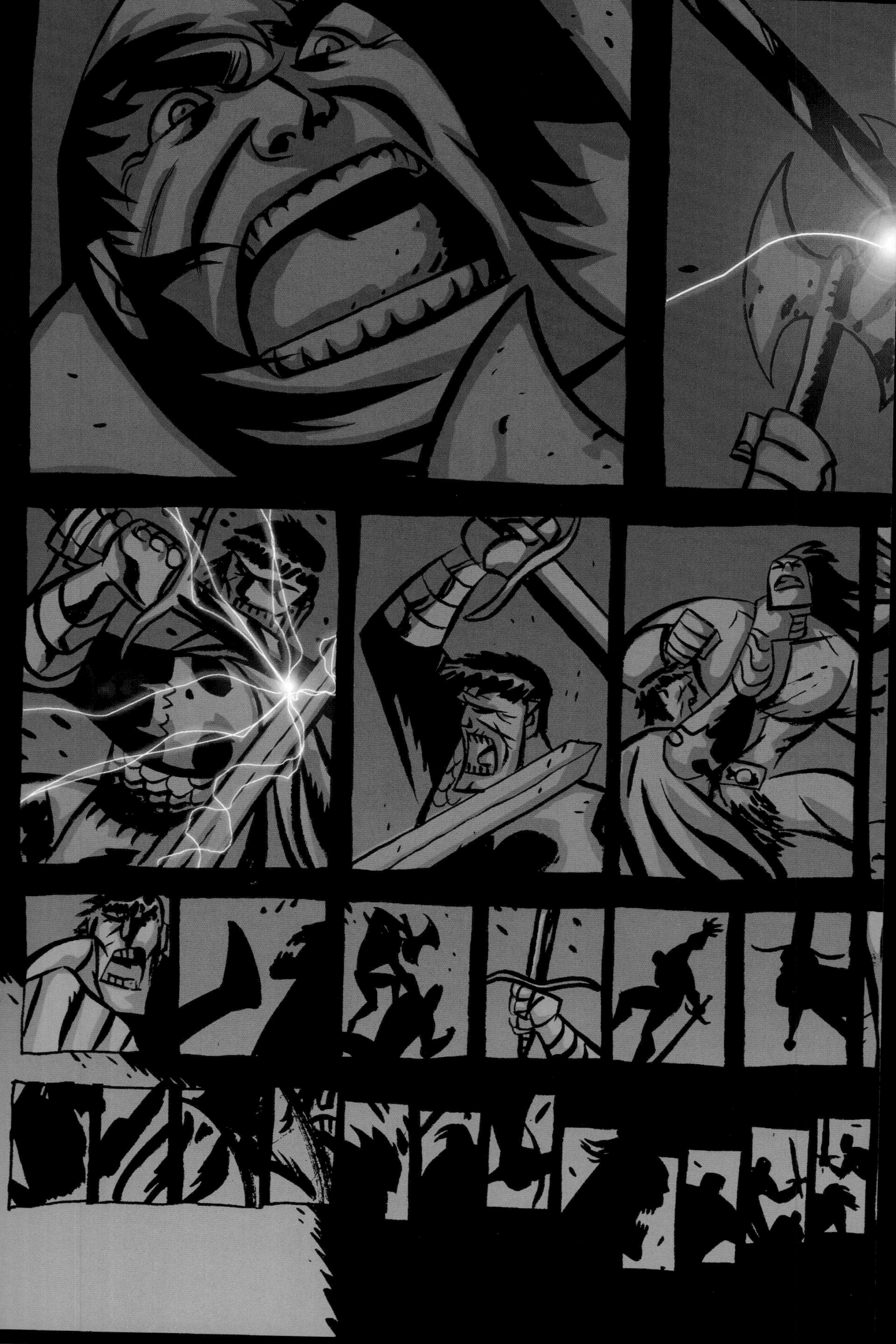

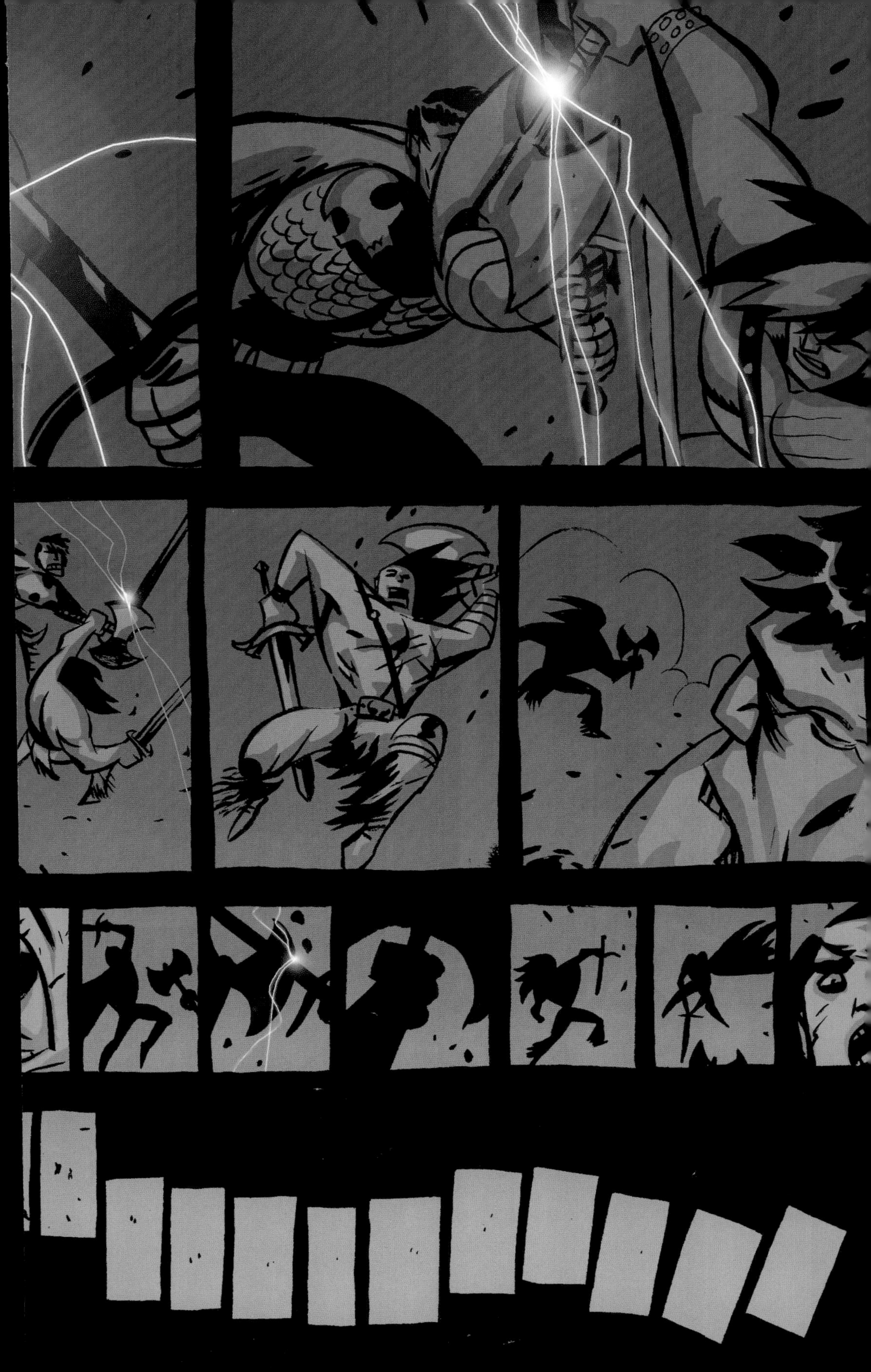

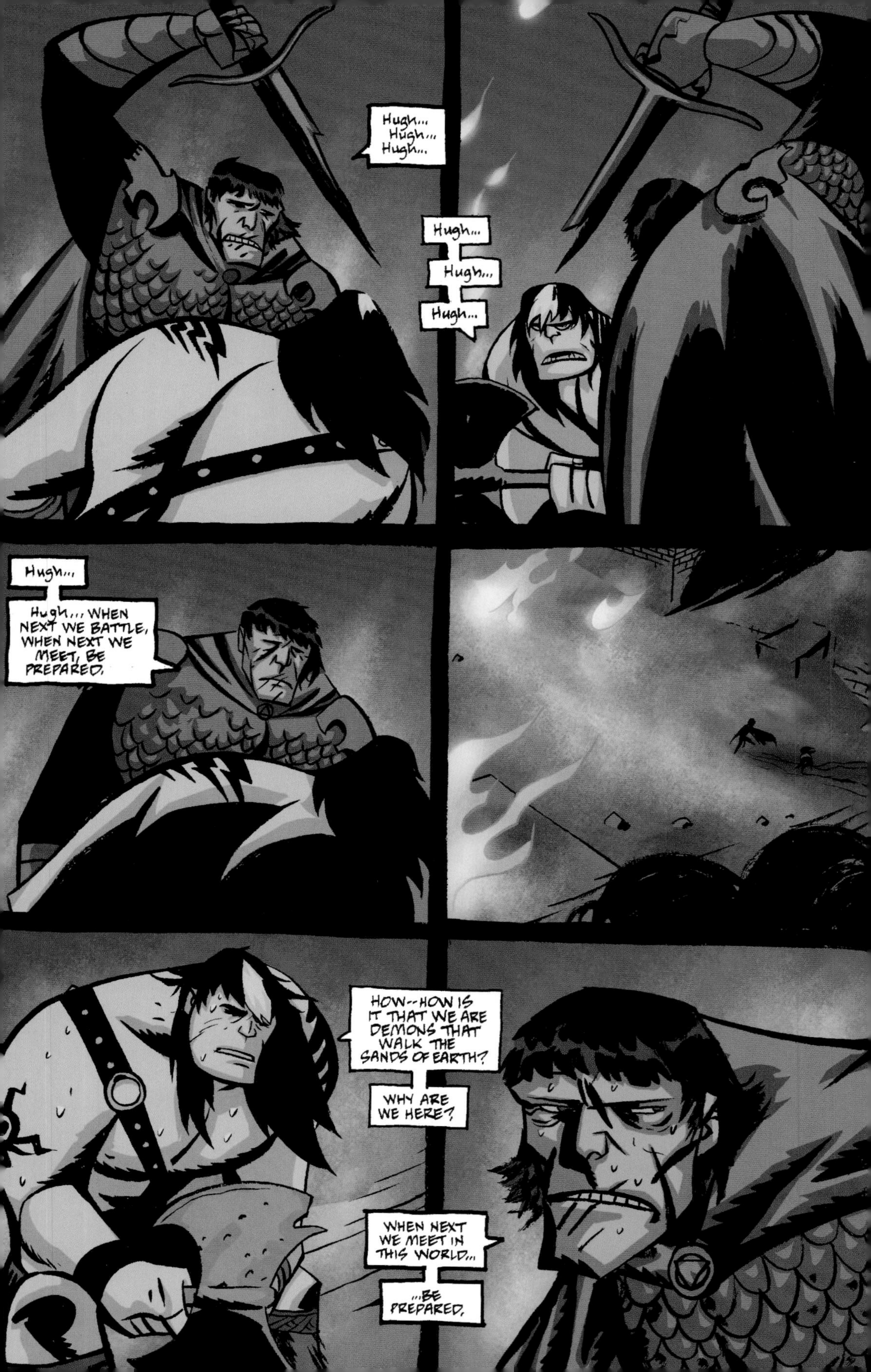

Hugh... Hugh... Hugh...
Hugh...
Hugh...
Hugh...
Hugh...
Hugh... WHEN NEXT WE BATTLE, WHEN NEXT WE MEET, BE PREPARED.
HOW--HOW IS IT THAT WE ARE DEMONS THAT WALK THE SANDS OF EARTH?
WHY ARE WE HERE?
WHEN NEXT WE MEET IN THIS WORLD...
...BE PREPARED.

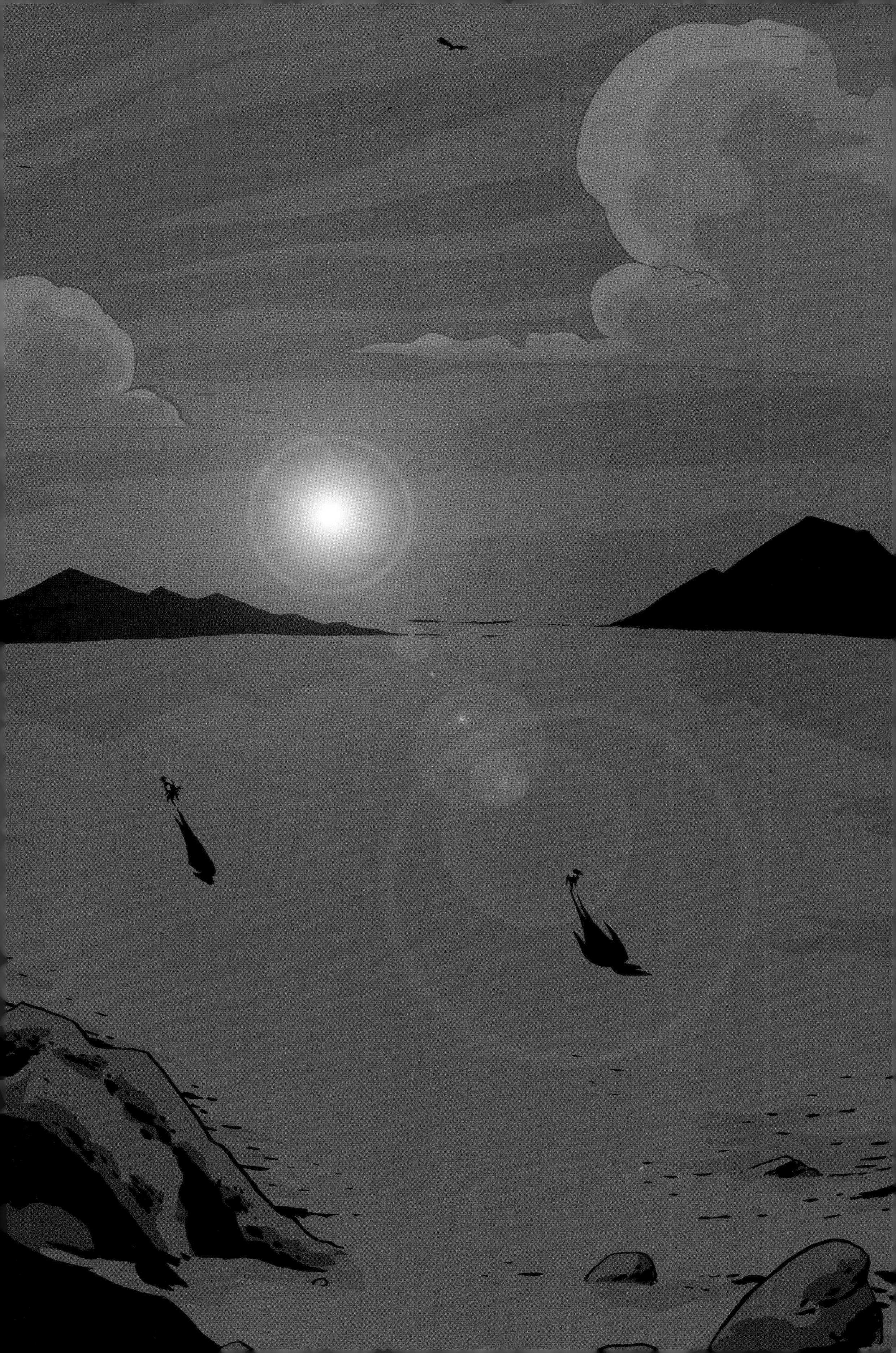

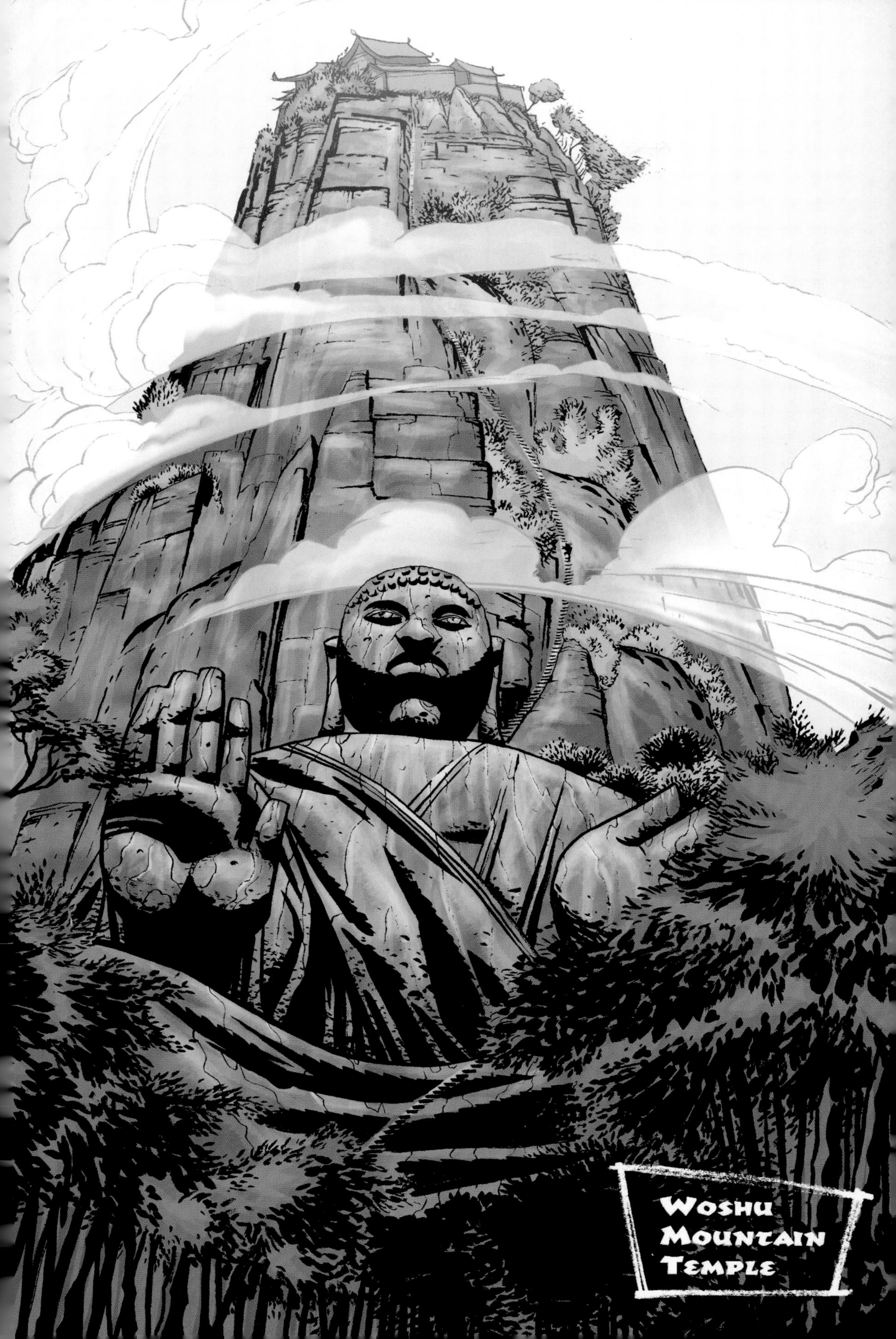
WOSHU
MOUNTAIN
TEMPLE

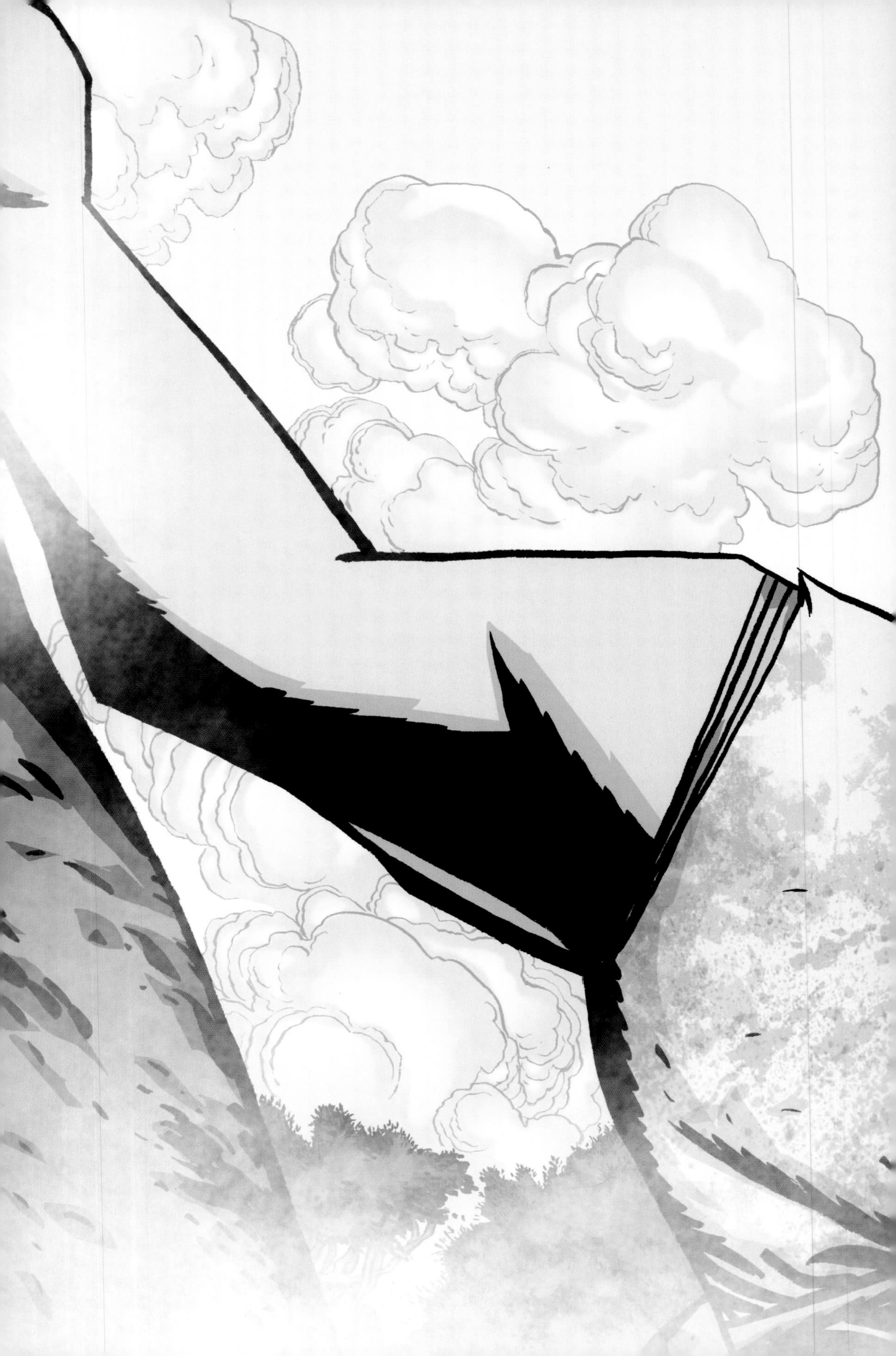

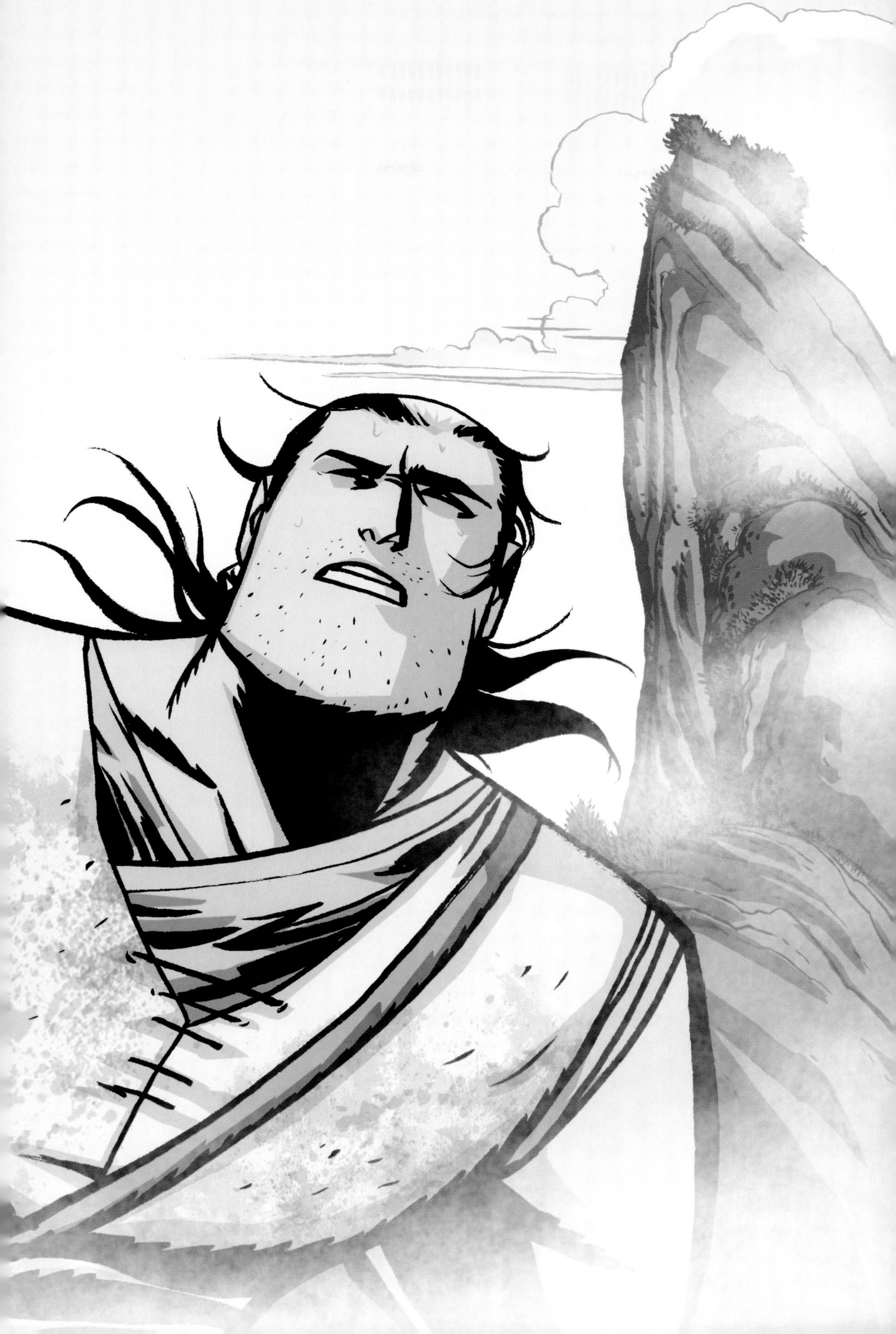

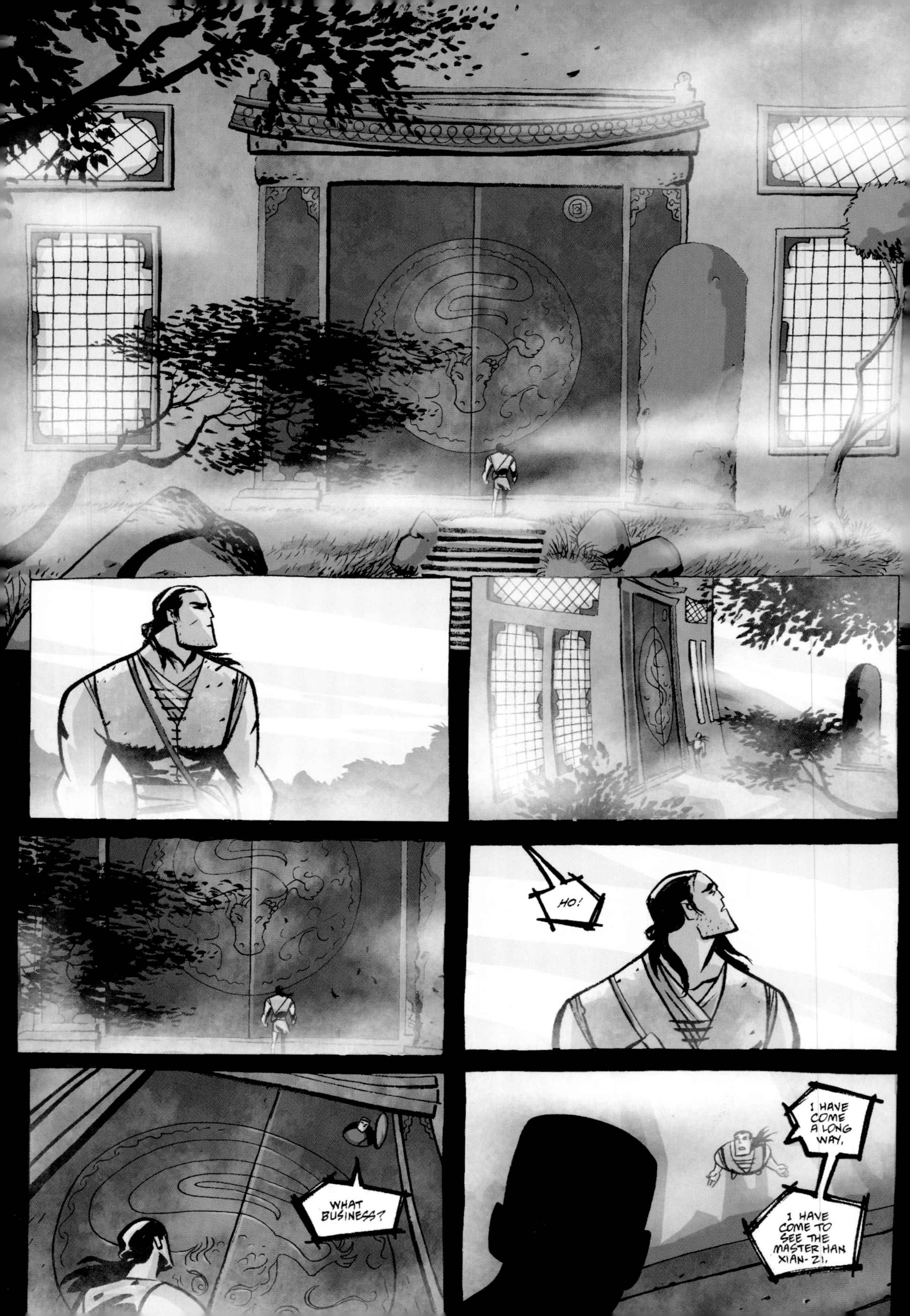
HO!
WHAT BUSINESS?
I HAVE COME A LONG WAY.
I HAVE COME TO SEE THE MASTER HAN XIAN-ZI.

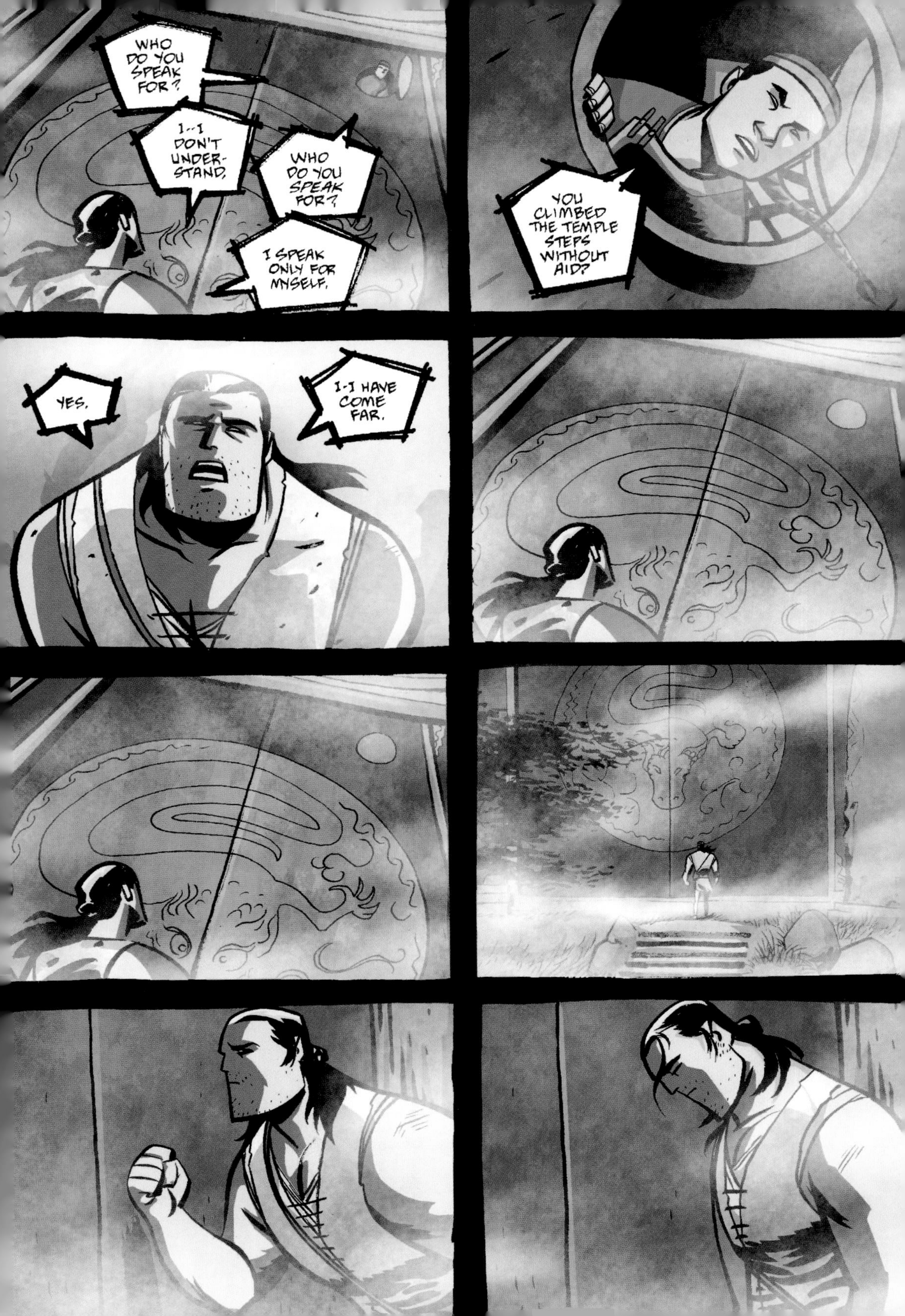
WHO DO YOU SPEAK FOR?
I--I DON'T UNDERSTAND.
WHO DO YOU SPEAK FOR?
I SPEAK ONLY FOR MYSELF.
YOU CLIMBED THE TEMPLE STEPS WITHOUT AID?
YES.
I-I HAVE COME FAR.

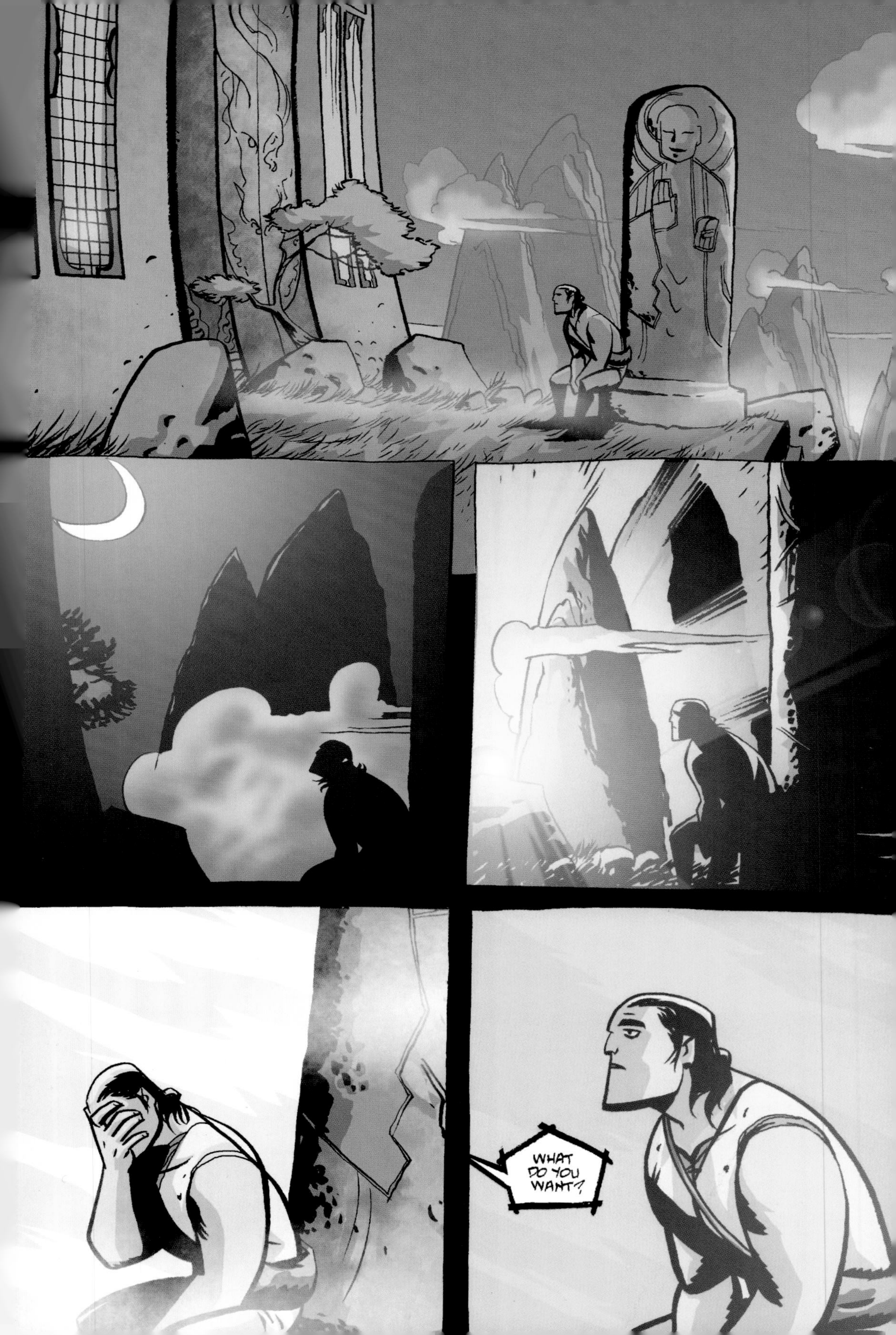
WHAT DO YOU WANT?

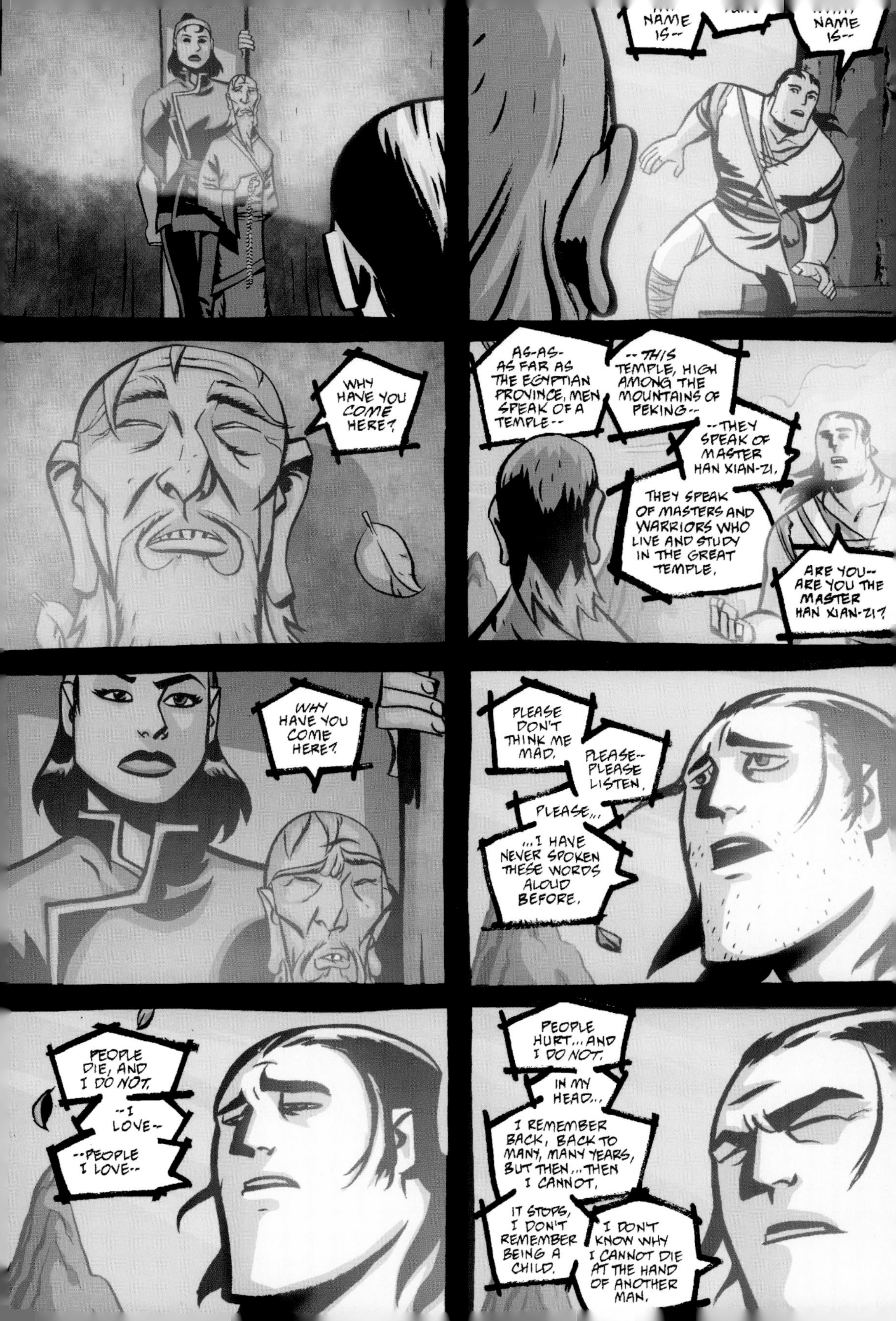
NAME IS--
NAME IS--
WHY HAVE YOU COME HERE?
AS-AS- AS FAR AS THE EGYPTIAN PROVINCE, MEN SPEAK OF A TEMPLE--
--THIS TEMPLE, HIGH AMONG THE MOUNTAINS OF PEKING--
--THEY SPEAK OF MASTER HAN XIAN-ZI.
THEY SPEAK OF MASTERS AND WARRIORS WHO LIVE AND STUDY IN THE GREAT TEMPLE.
ARE YOU-- ARE YOU THE MASTER HAN XIAN-ZI?
WHY HAVE YOU COME HERE?
PLEASE DON'T THINK ME MAD.
PLEASE-- PLEASE LISTEN.
PLEASE...
...I HAVE NEVER SPOKEN THESE WORDS ALOUD BEFORE.
PEOPLE DIE, AND I DO NOT.
--I LOVE--
--PEOPLE I LOVE--
PEOPLE HURT... AND I DO NOT.
IN MY HEAD...
I REMEMBER BACK, BACK TO MANY, MANY YEARS, BUT THEN... THEN I CANNOT.
IT STOPS. I DON'T REMEMBER BEING A CHILD.
I DON'T KNOW WHY I CANNOT DIE AT THE HAND OF ANOTHER MAN.

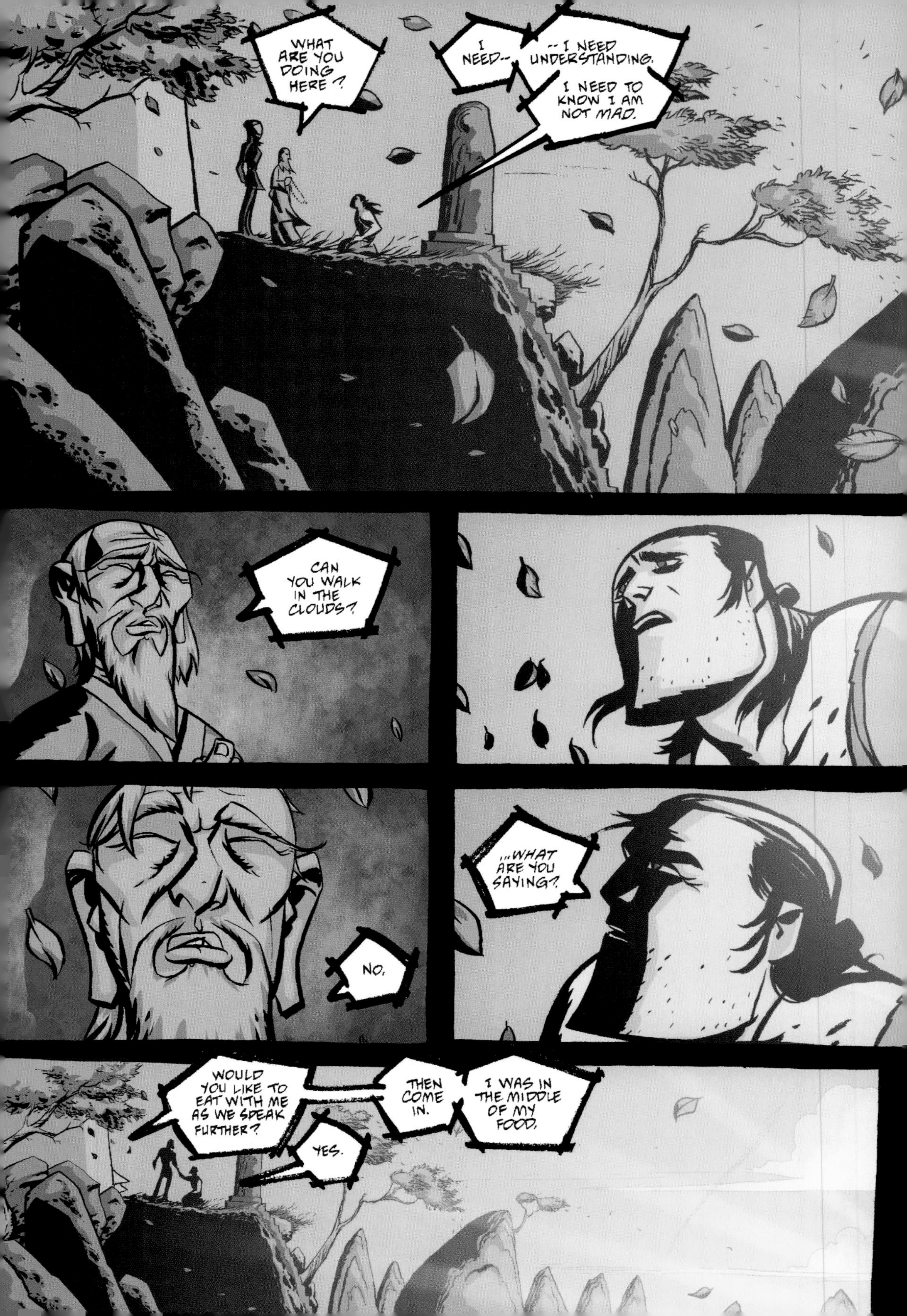
WHAT ARE YOU DOING HERE ?
I NEED--
--I NEED UNDERSTANDING.
I NEED TO KNOW I AM NOT MAD.
CAN YOU WALK IN THE CLOUDS?
...WHAT ARE YOU SAYING?
NO.
WOULD YOU LIKE TO EAT WITH ME AS WE SPEAK FURTHER?
YES.
THEN COME IN.
I WAS IN THE MIDDLE OF MY FOOD.

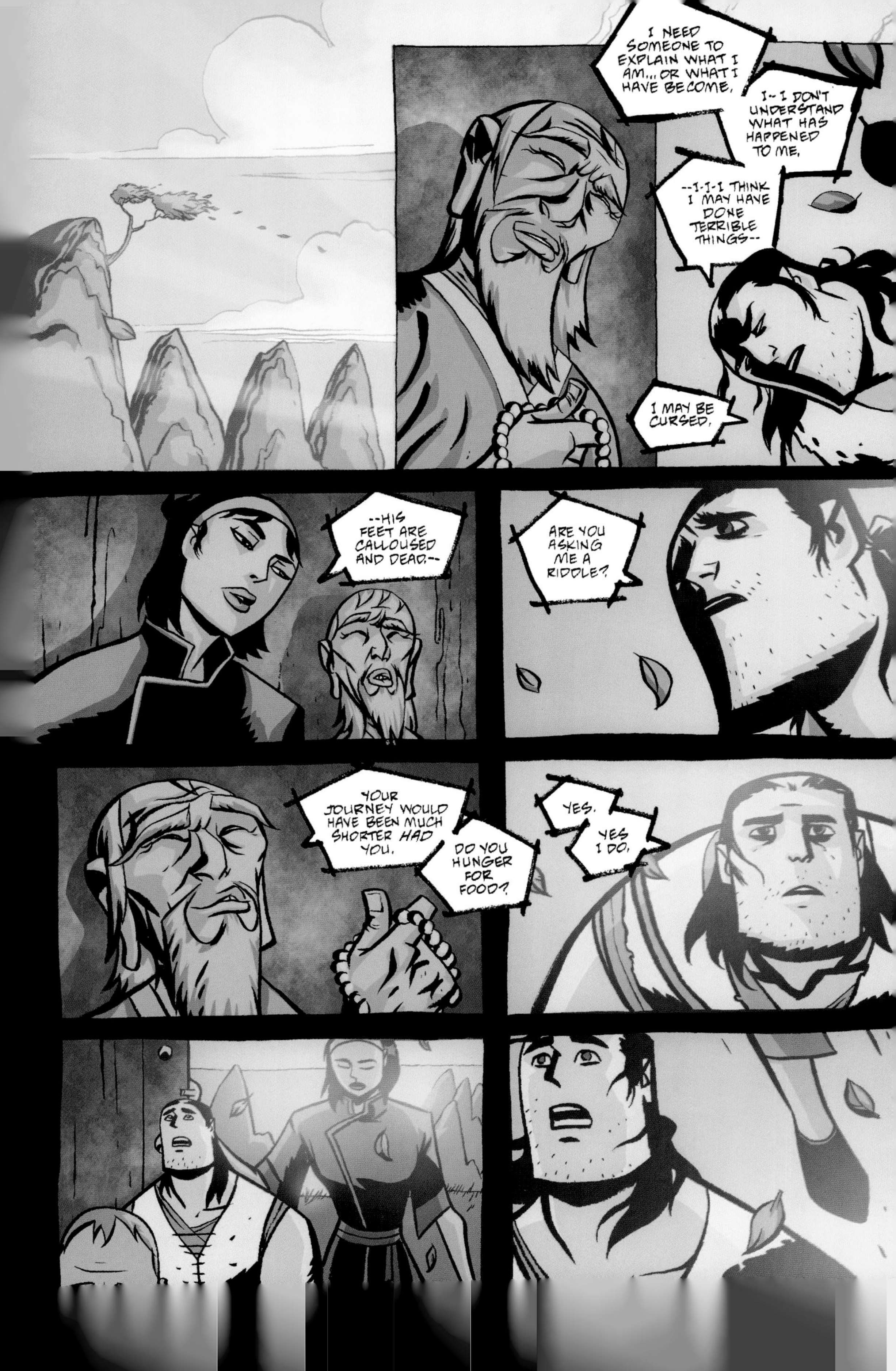
I NEED SOMEONE TO EXPLAIN WHAT I AM... OR WHAT I HAVE BECOME.
I-- I DON'T UNDERSTAND WHAT HAS HAPPENED TO ME.
--I-I-I THINK I MAY HAVE DONE TERRIBLE THINGS--
I MAY BE CURSED.
--HIS FEET ARE CALLOUSED AND DEAD.--
ARE YOU ASKING ME A RIDDLE?
YOUR JOURNEY WOULD HAVE BEEN MUCH SHORTER HAD YOU.
DO YOU HUNGER FOR FOOD?
YES.
YES I DO.

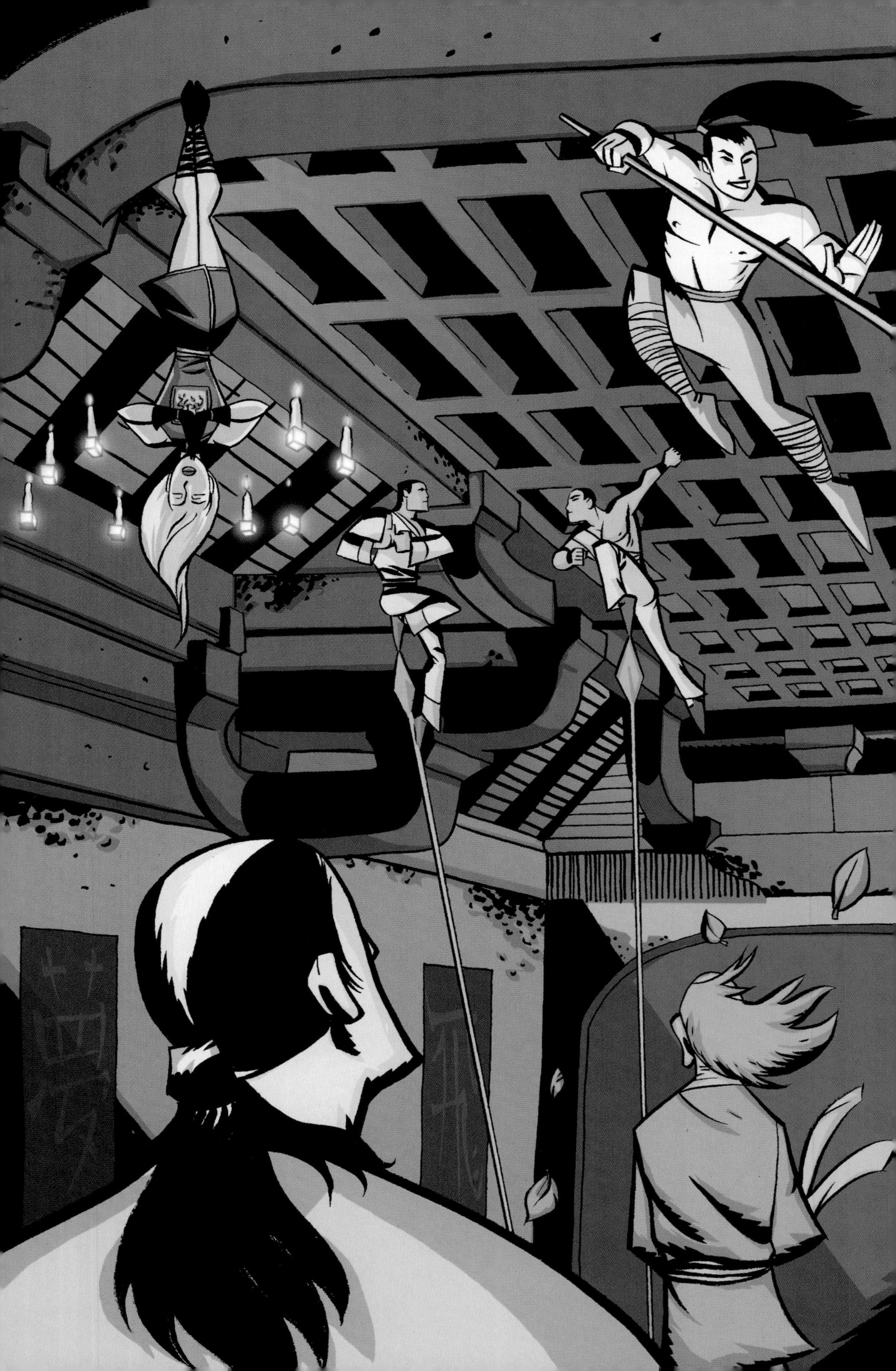

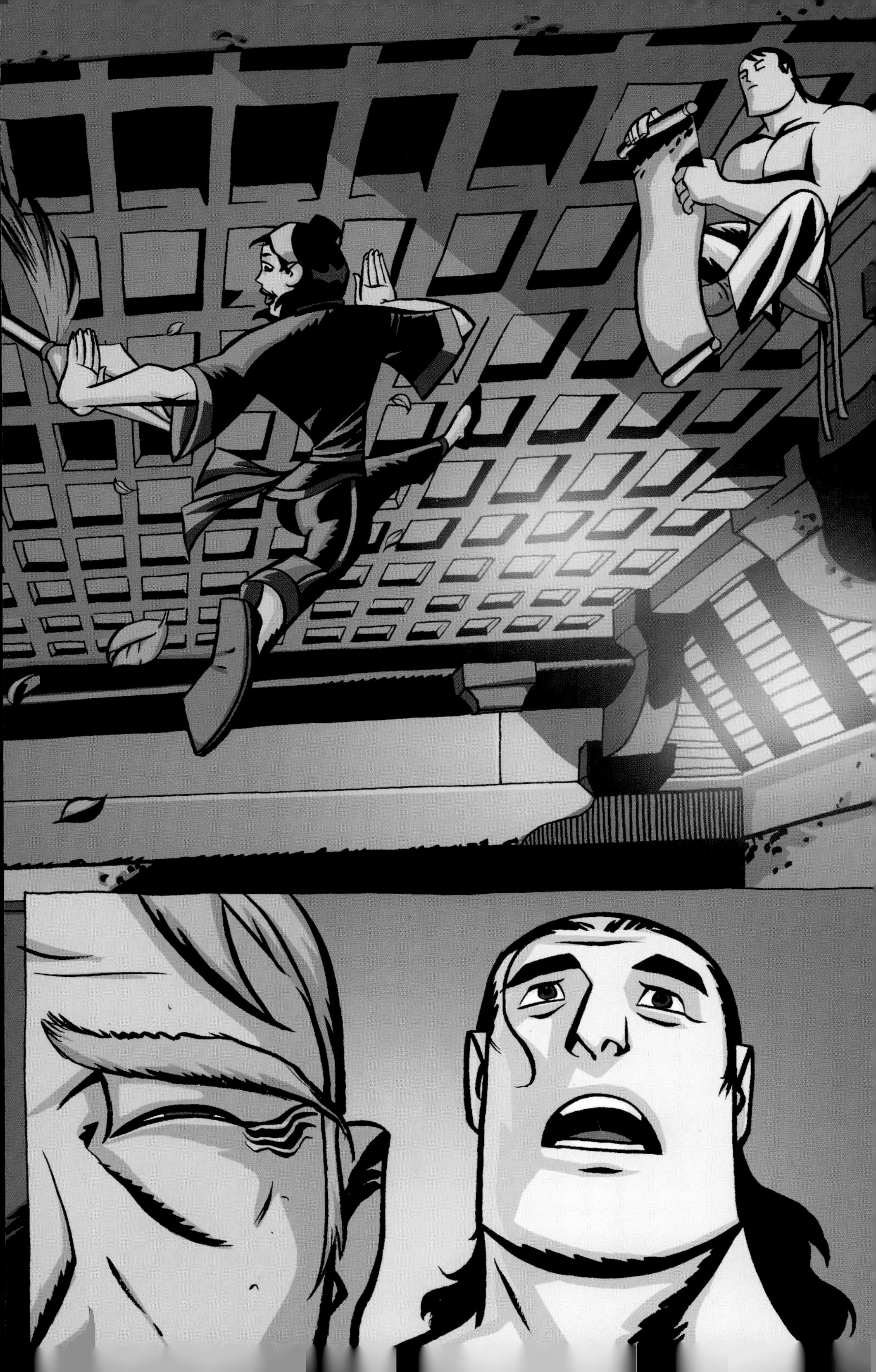

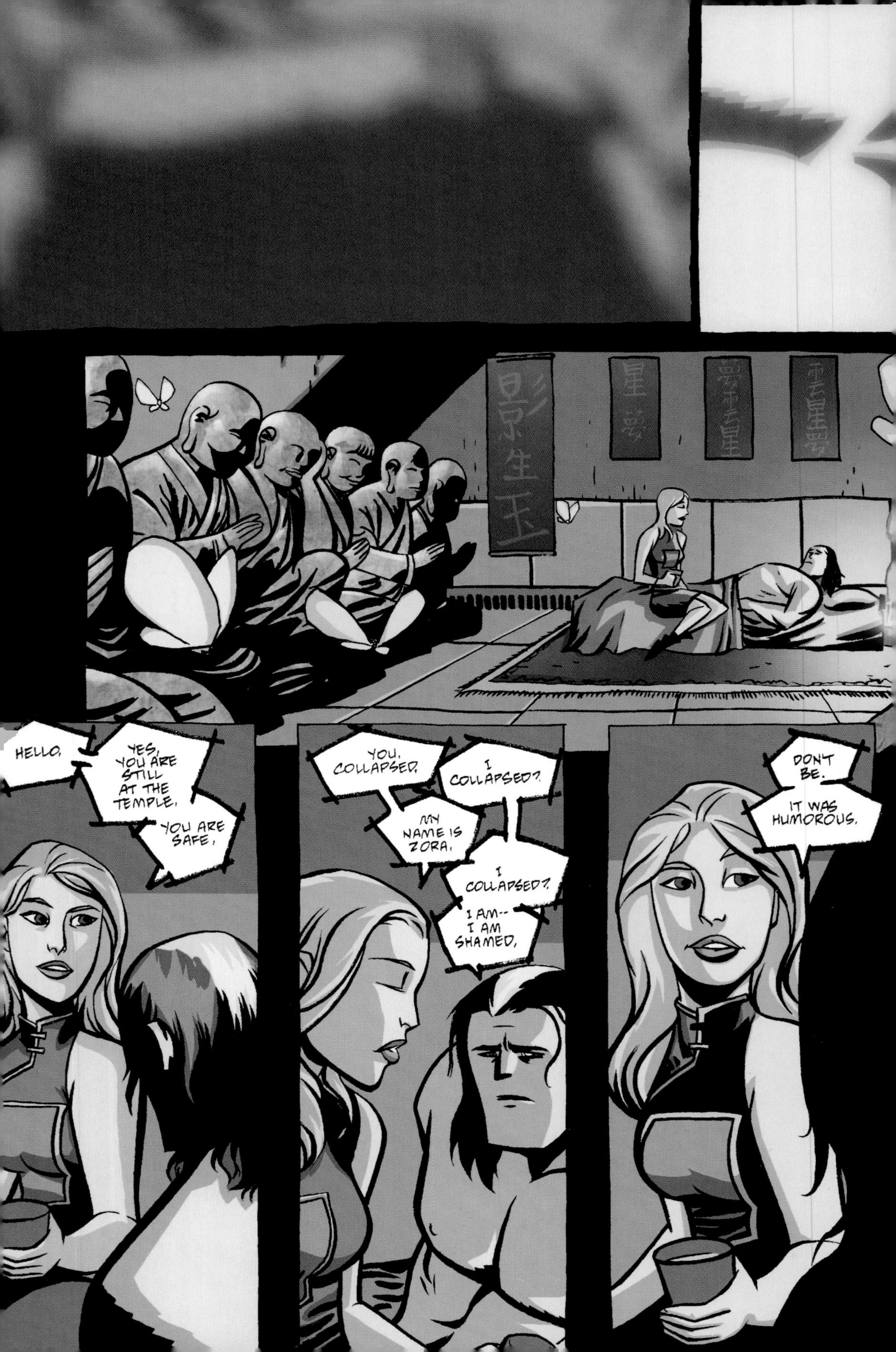
HELLO.
YES, YOU ARE STILL AT THE TEMPLE.
YOU ARE SAFE.
YOU COLLAPSED.
I COLLAPSED?
MY NAME IS ZORA.
I COLLAPSED?
I AM-- I AM SHAMED.
DON'T BE.
IT WAS HUMOROUS.

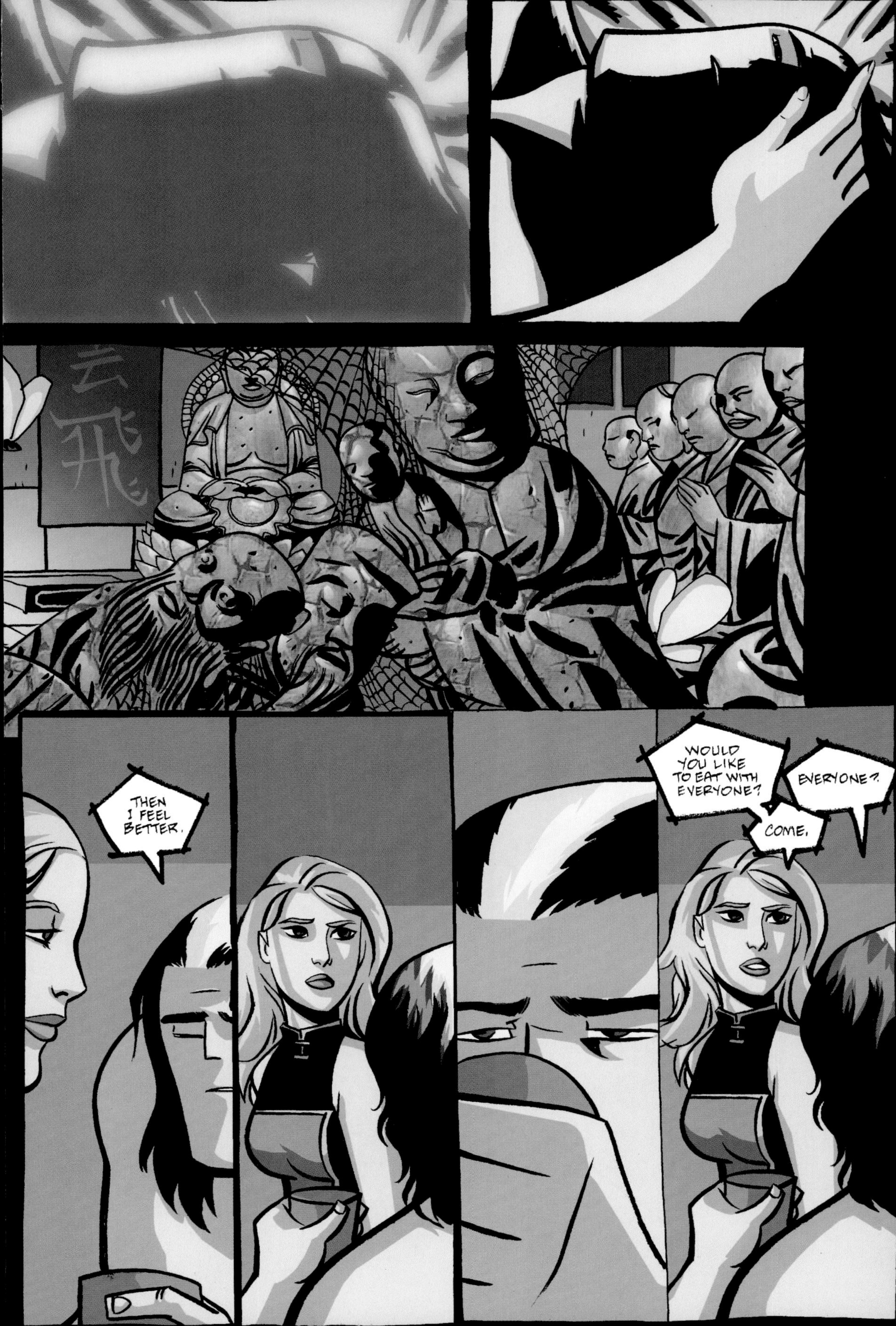
THEN I FEEL BETTER.
WOULD YOU LIKE TO EAT WITH EVERYONE?
EVERYONE?
COME.

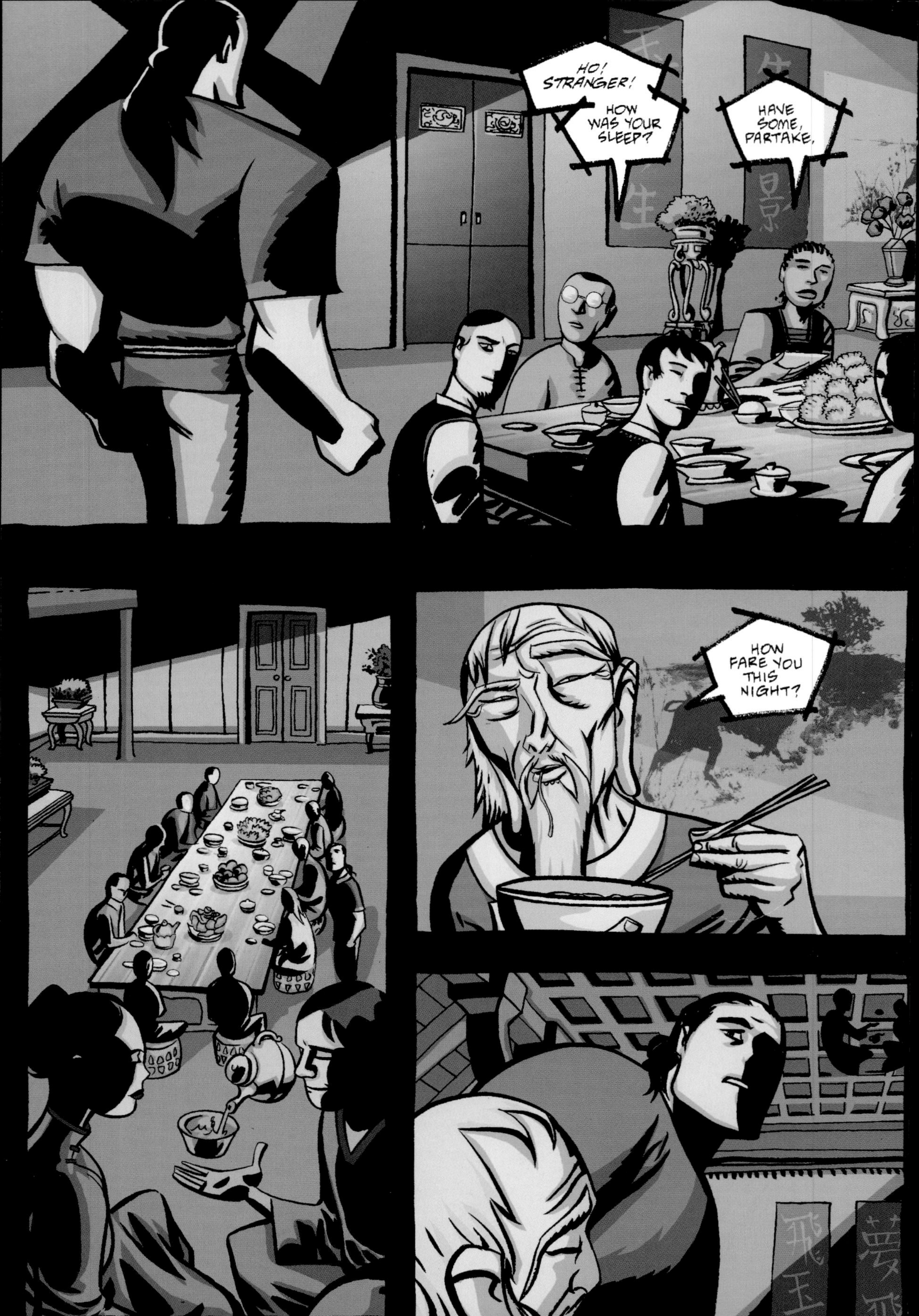
HO! STRANGER!
HOW WAS YOUR SLEEP?
HAVE SOME, PARTAKE,
HOW FARE YOU THIS NIGHT?

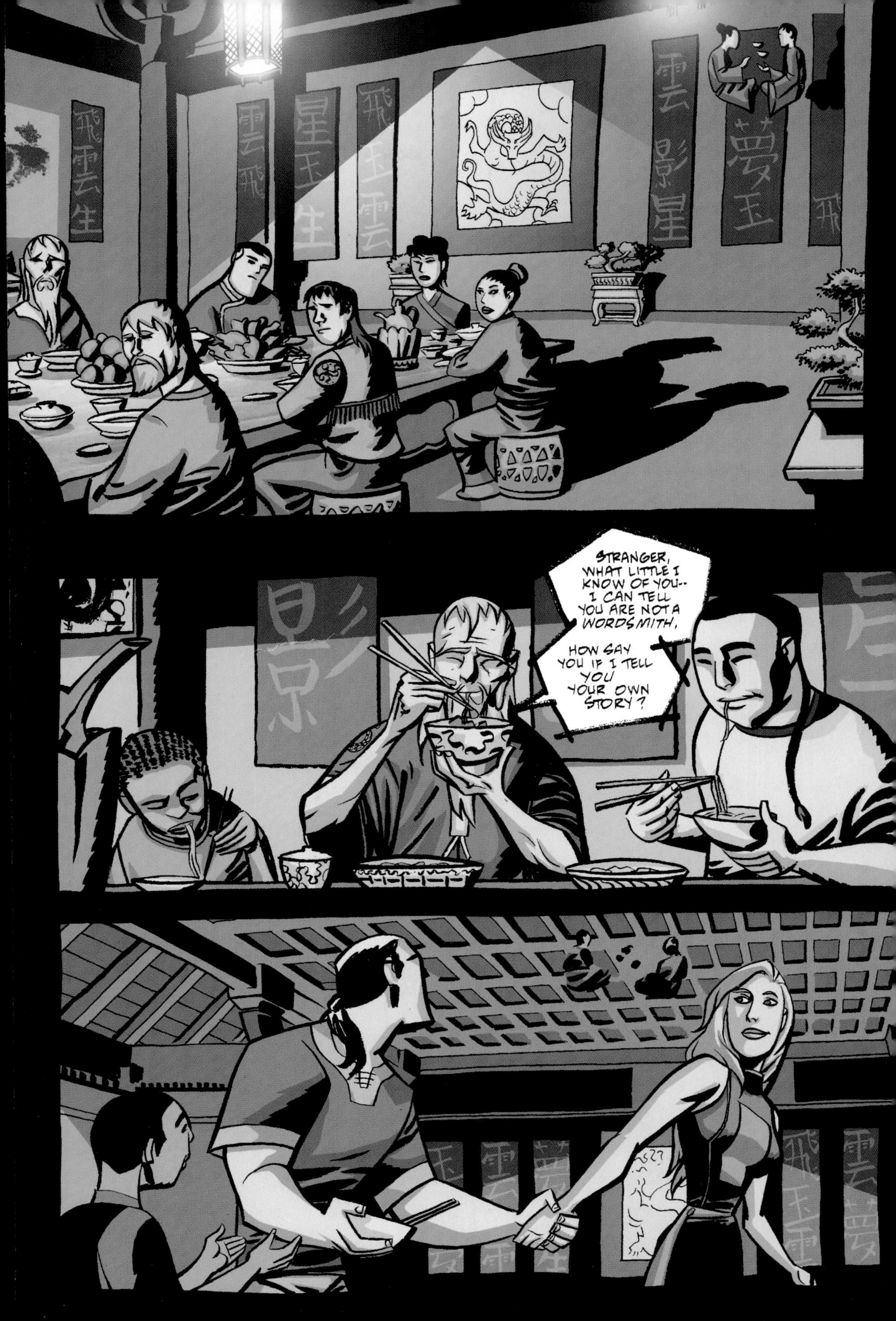
STRANGER, WHAT LITTLE I KNOW OF YOU-- I CAN TELL YOU ARE NOT A WORDSMITH.
HOW SAY YOU IF I TELL YOU YOUR OWN STORY?

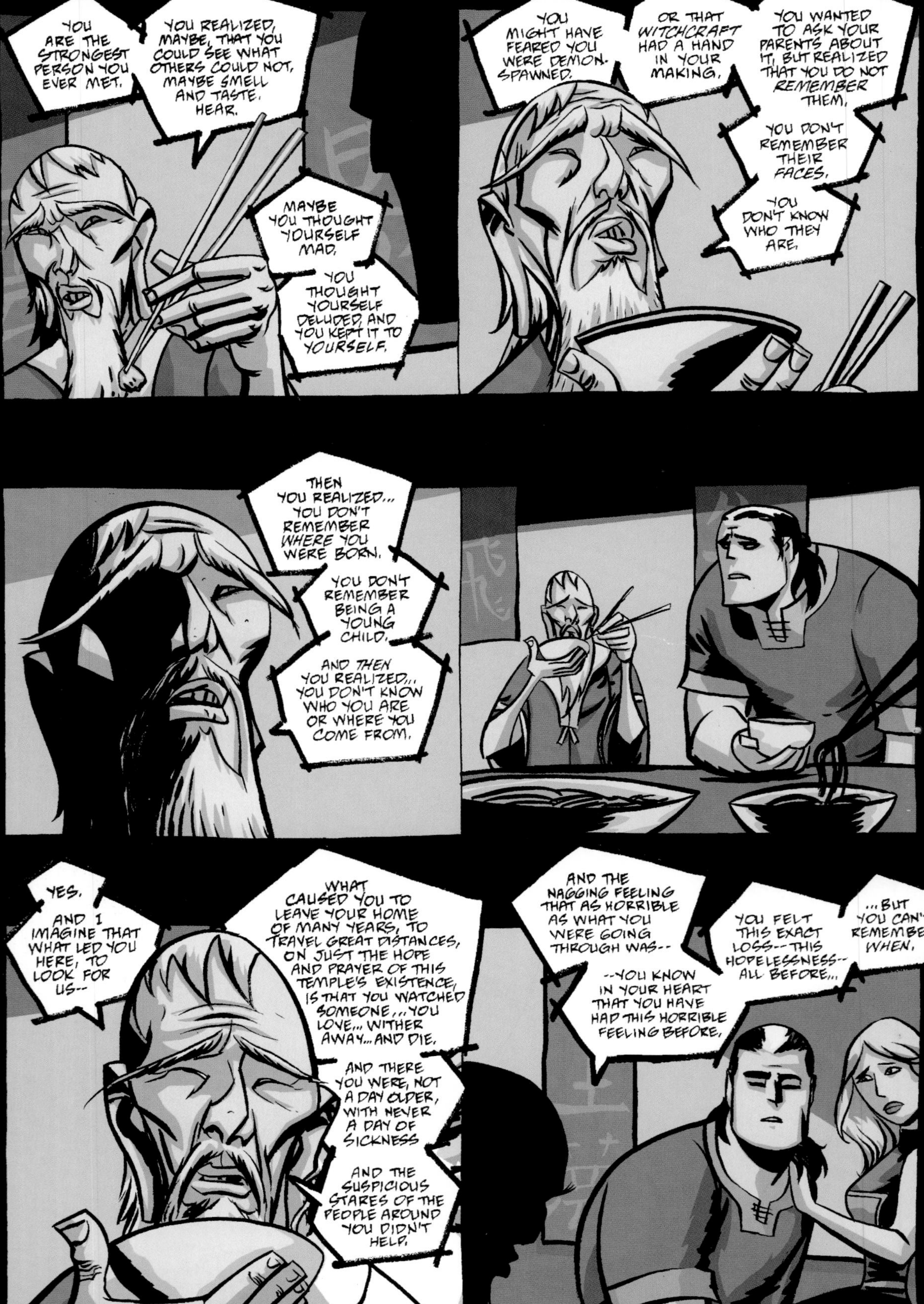
YOU ARE THE STRONGEST PERSON YOU EVER MET.
YOU REALIZED, MAYBE, THAT YOU COULD SEE WHAT OTHERS COULD NOT, MAYBE SMELL AND TASTE. HEAR.
MAYBE YOU THOUGHT YOURSELF MAD.
YOU THOUGHT YOURSELF DELUDED, AND YOU KEPT IT TO YOURSELF.
YOU MIGHT HAVE FEARED YOU WERE DEMON-SPAWNED.
OR THAT WITCHCRAFT HAD A HAND IN YOUR MAKING.
YOU WANTED TO ASK YOUR PARENTS ABOUT IT, BUT REALIZED THAT YOU DO NOT REMEMBER THEM.
YOU DON'T REMEMBER THEIR FACES.
YOU DON'T KNOW WHO THEY ARE.
THEN YOU REALIZED... YOU DON'T REMEMBER WHERE YOU WERE BORN.
YOU DON'T REMEMBER BEING A YOUNG CHILD.
AND THEN YOU REALIZED... YOU DON'T KNOW WHO YOU ARE OR WHERE YOU COME FROM.
YES.
AND I IMAGINE THAT WHAT LED YOU HERE, TO LOOK FOR US--
WHAT CAUSED YOU TO LEAVE YOUR HOME OF MANY YEARS, TO TRAVEL GREAT DISTANCES, ON JUST THE HOPE AND PRAYER OF THIS TEMPLE'S EXISTENCE, IS THAT YOU WATCHED SOMEONE... YOU LOVE... WITHER AWAY... AND DIE.
AND THERE YOU WERE, NOT A DAY OLDER, WITH NEVER A DAY OF SICKNESS
AND THE SUSPICIOUS STARES OF THE PEOPLE AROUND YOU DIDN'T HELP.
AND THE NAGGING FEELING THAT AS HORRIBLE AS WHAT YOU WERE GOING THROUGH WAS--
--YOU KNOW IN YOUR HEART THAT YOU HAVE HAD THIS HORRIBLE FEELING BEFORE.
YOU FELT THIS EXACT LOSS--THIS HOPELESSNESS--ALL BEFORE...
...BUT YOU CAN'T REMEMBER WHEN.

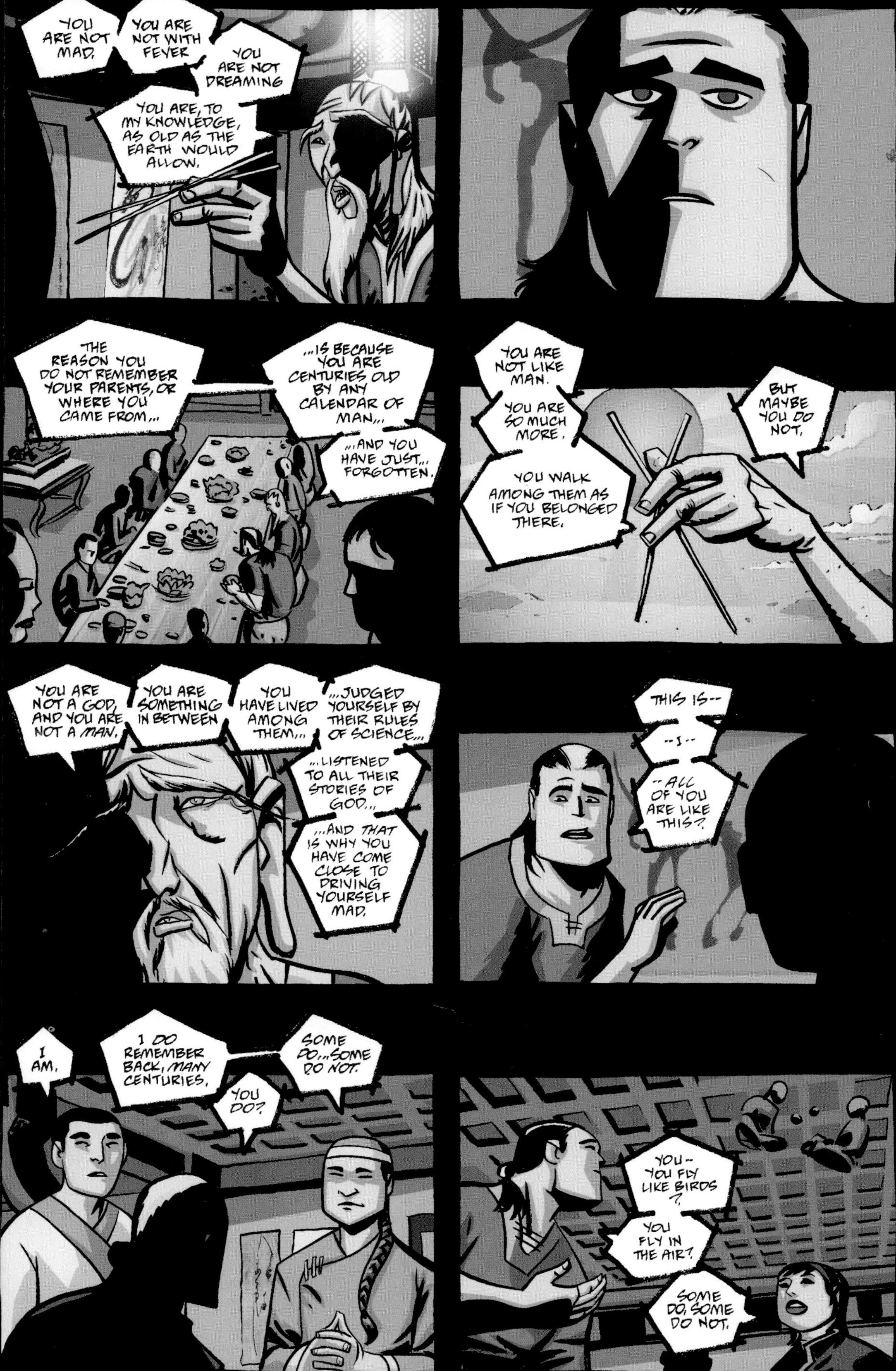
YOU ARE NOT MAD.
YOU ARE NOT WITH FEVER
YOU ARE NOT DREAMING
YOU ARE, TO MY KNOWLEDGE, AS OLD AS THE EARTH WOULD ALLOW.
THE REASON YOU DO NOT REMEMBER YOUR PARENTS, OR WHERE YOU CAME FROM...
...IS BECAUSE YOU ARE CENTURIES OLD BY ANY CALENDAR OF MAN...
...AND YOU HAVE JUST... FORGOTTEN.
YOU ARE NOT LIKE MAN.
YOU ARE SO MUCH MORE.
YOU WALK AMONG THEM AS IF YOU BELONGED THERE.
BUT MAYBE YOU DO NOT.
YOU ARE NOT A GOD, AND YOU ARE NOT A MAN.
YOU ARE SOMETHING IN BETWEEN
YOU HAVE LIVED AMONG THEM...
...JUDGED YOURSELF BY THEIR RULES OF SCIENCE...
...LISTENED TO ALL THEIR STORIES OF GOD...
...AND THAT IS WHY YOU HAVE COME CLOSE TO DRIVING YOURSELF MAD.
THIS IS--
--I--
--ALL OF YOU ARE LIKE THIS?
I AM.
I DO REMEMBER BACK, MANY CENTURIES.
YOU DO?
SOME DO... SOME DO NOT.
YOU-- YOU FLY LIKE BIRDS?
YOU FLY IN THE AIR?
SOME DO, SOME DO NOT.

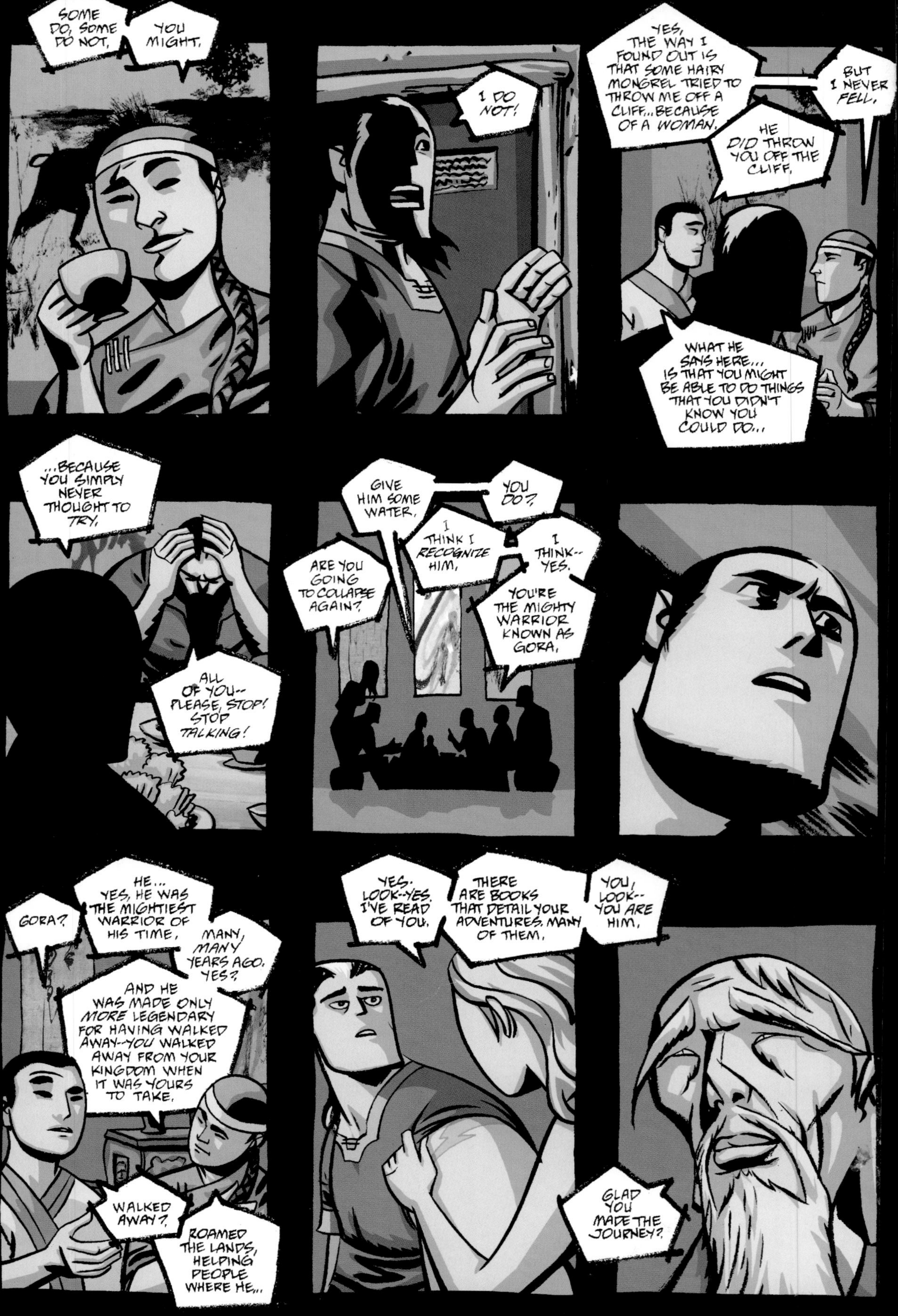
SOME DO, SOME DO NOT.
YOU MIGHT.
I DO NOT!
YES, THE WAY I FOUND OUT IS THAT SOME HAIRY MONGREL TRIED TO THROW ME OFF A CLIFF... BECAUSE OF A WOMAN.
BUT I NEVER FELL.
HE DID THROW YOU OFF THE CLIFF.
WHAT HE SAYS HERE... IS THAT YOU MIGHT BE ABLE TO DO THINGS THAT YOU DIDN'T KNOW YOU COULD DO...
...BECAUSE YOU SIMPLY NEVER THOUGHT TO TRY.
ALL OF YOU-- PLEASE, STOP! STOP TALKING!
GIVE HIM SOME WATER.
YOU DO?
I THINK I RECOGNIZE HIM.
I THINK-- YES.
ARE YOU GOING TO COLLAPSE AGAIN?
YOU'RE THE MIGHTY WARRIOR KNOWN AS GORA.
GORA?
HE... YES, HE WAS THE MIGHTIEST WARRIOR OF HIS TIME.
MANY, MANY YEARS AGO. YES?
AND HE WAS MADE ONLY MORE LEGENDARY FOR HAVING WALKED AWAY--YOU WALKED AWAY FROM YOUR KINGDOM WHEN IT WAS YOURS TO TAKE.
WALKED AWAY?
ROAMED THE LANDS, HELPING PEOPLE WHERE HE...
YES. LOOK--YES. I'VE READ OF YOU.
THERE ARE BOOKS THAT DETAIL YOUR ADVENTURES. MANY OF THEM.
YOU, LOOK-- YOU ARE HIM.
GLAD YOU MADE THE JOURNEY?

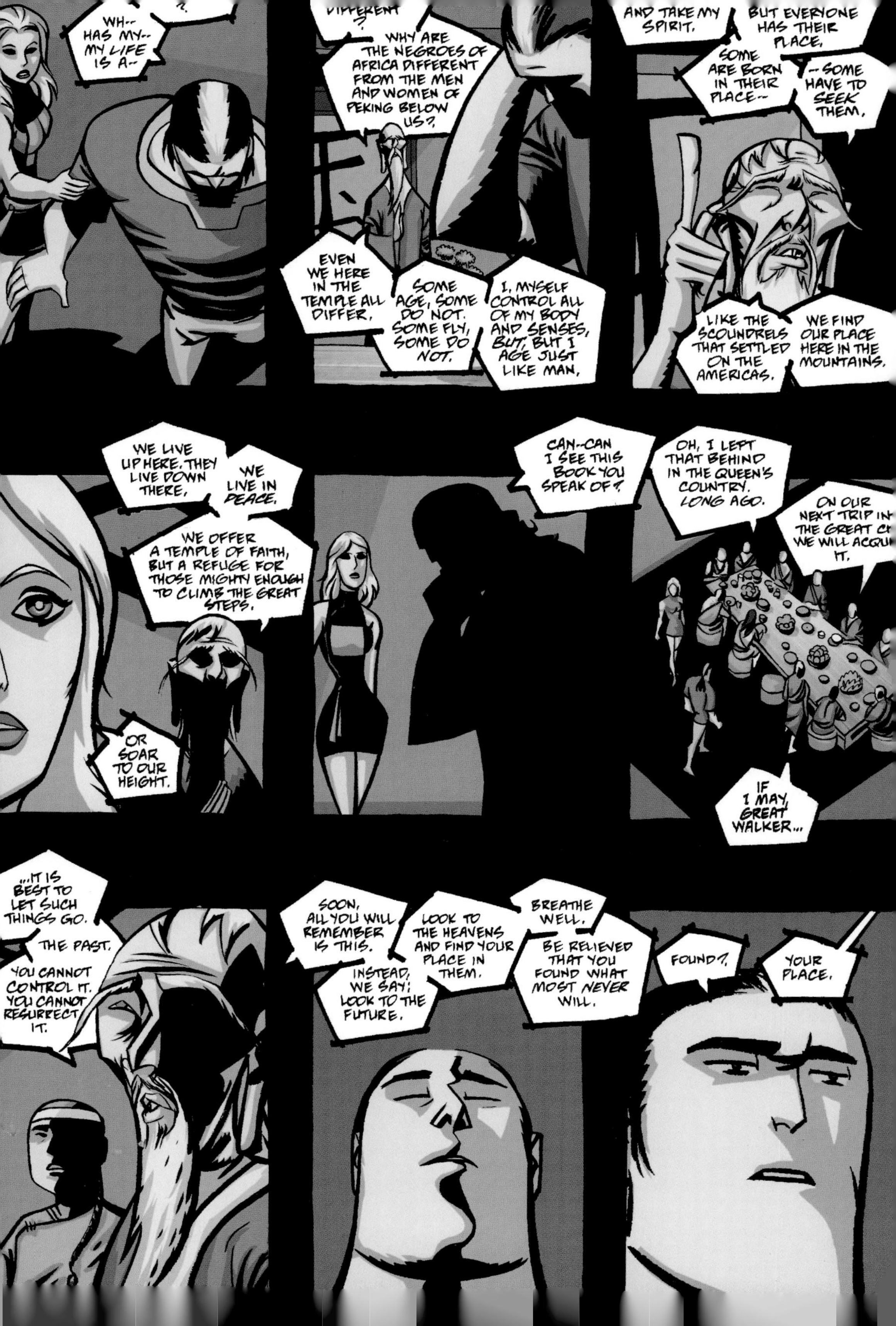
WH-- HAS MY-- MY LIFE IS A--
DIFFERENT ?
WHY ARE THE NEGROES OF AFRICA DIFFERENT FROM THE MEN AND WOMEN OF PEKING BELOW US?
EVEN WE HERE IN THE TEMPLE ALL DIFFER.
SOME AGE, SOME DO NOT. SOME FLY, SOME DO NOT.
I, MYSELF CONTROL ALL OF MY BODY AND SENSES, BUT, BUT I AGE JUST LIKE MAN.
AND TAKE MY SPIRIT.
BUT EVERYONE HAS THEIR PLACE.
SOME ARE BORN IN THEIR PLACE--
--SOME HAVE TO SEEK THEM.
LIKE THE SCOUNDRELS THAT SETTLED ON THE AMERICAS.
WE FIND OUR PLACE HERE IN THE MOUNTAINS.
WE LIVE UP HERE. THEY LIVE DOWN THERE.
WE LIVE IN PEACE.
WE OFFER A TEMPLE OF FAITH, BUT A REFUGE FOR THOSE MIGHTY ENOUGH TO CLIMB THE GREAT STEPS.
OR SOAR TO OUR HEIGHT.
CAN--CAN I SEE THIS BOOK YOU SPEAK OF?
OH, I LEFT THAT BEHIND IN THE QUEEN'S COUNTRY. LONG AGO.
ON OUR NEXT TRIP IN THE GREAT C WE WILL ACQU IT.
IF I MAY, GREAT WALKER...
...IT IS BEST TO LET SUCH THINGS GO.
THE PAST.
YOU CANNOT CONTROL IT. YOU CANNOT RESURRECT IT.
SOON, ALL YOU WILL REMEMBER IS THIS.
INSTEAD, WE SAY: LOOK TO THE FUTURE.
LOOK TO THE HEAVENS AND FIND YOUR PLACE IN THEM.
BREATHE WELL.
BE RELIEVED THAT YOU FOUND WHAT MOST NEVER WILL.
FOUND?
YOUR PLACE.

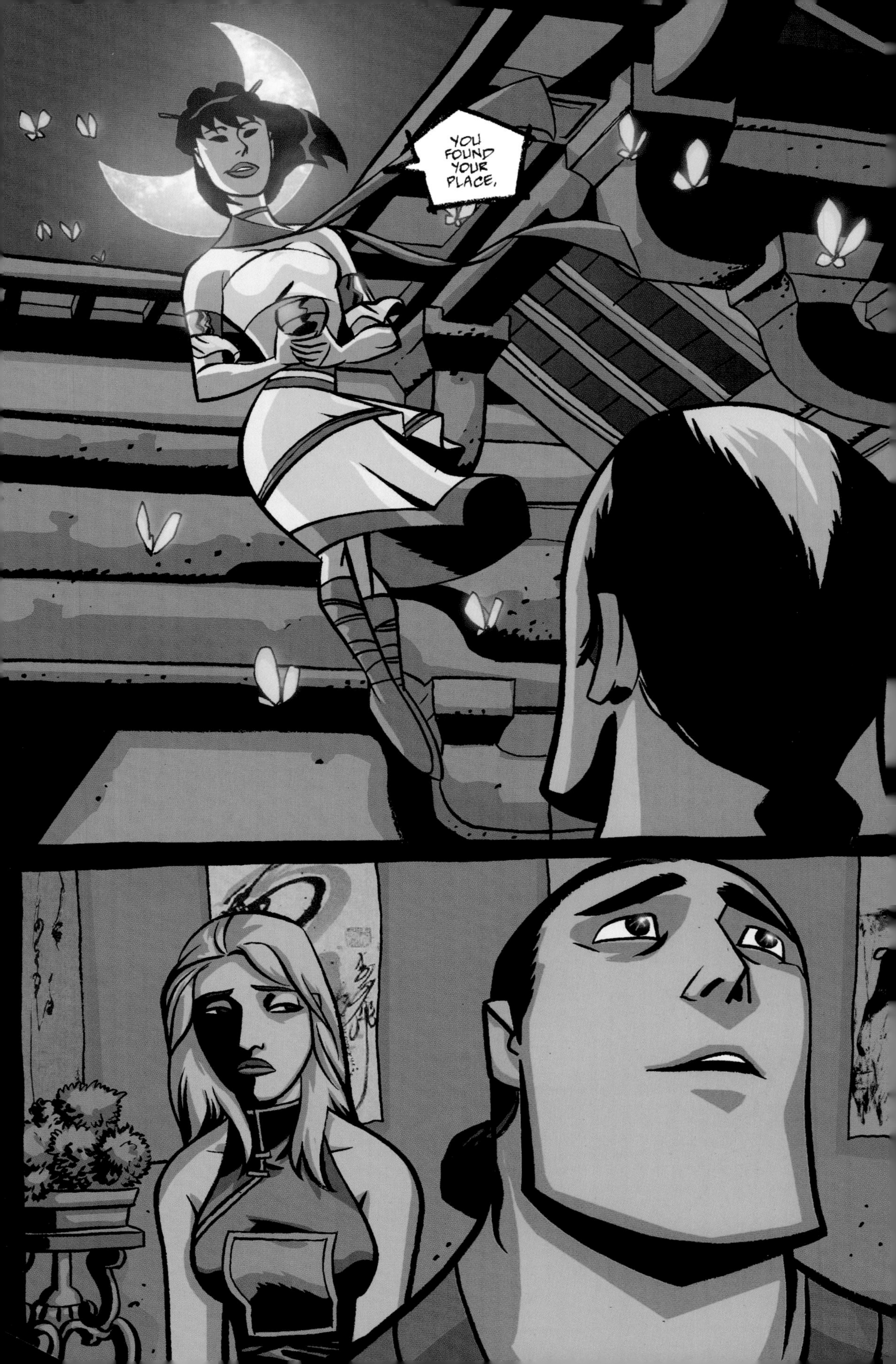
YOU FOUND YOUR PLACE,

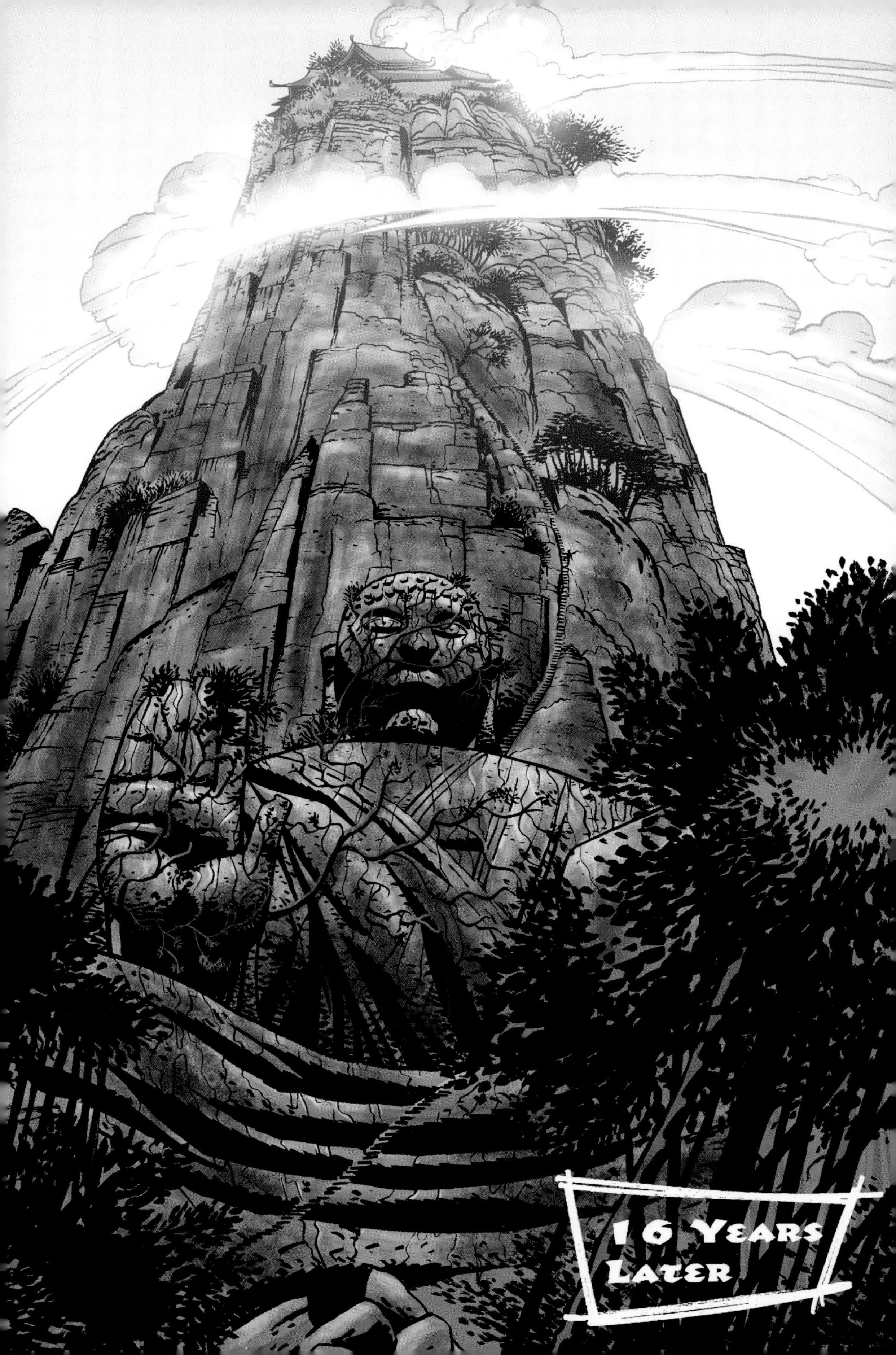
16 Years
Later

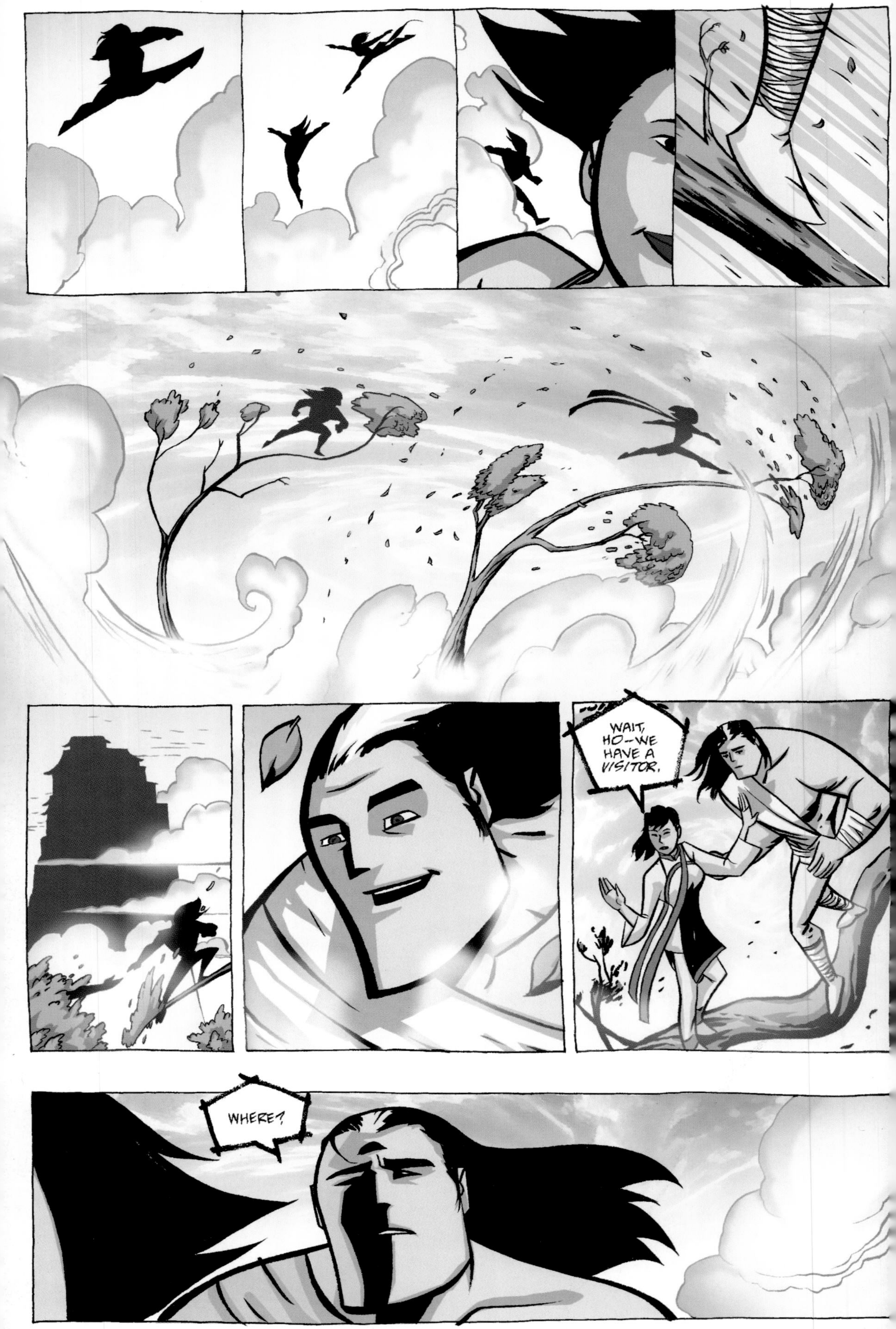
WAIT, HO--WE HAVE A VISITOR.
WHERE?

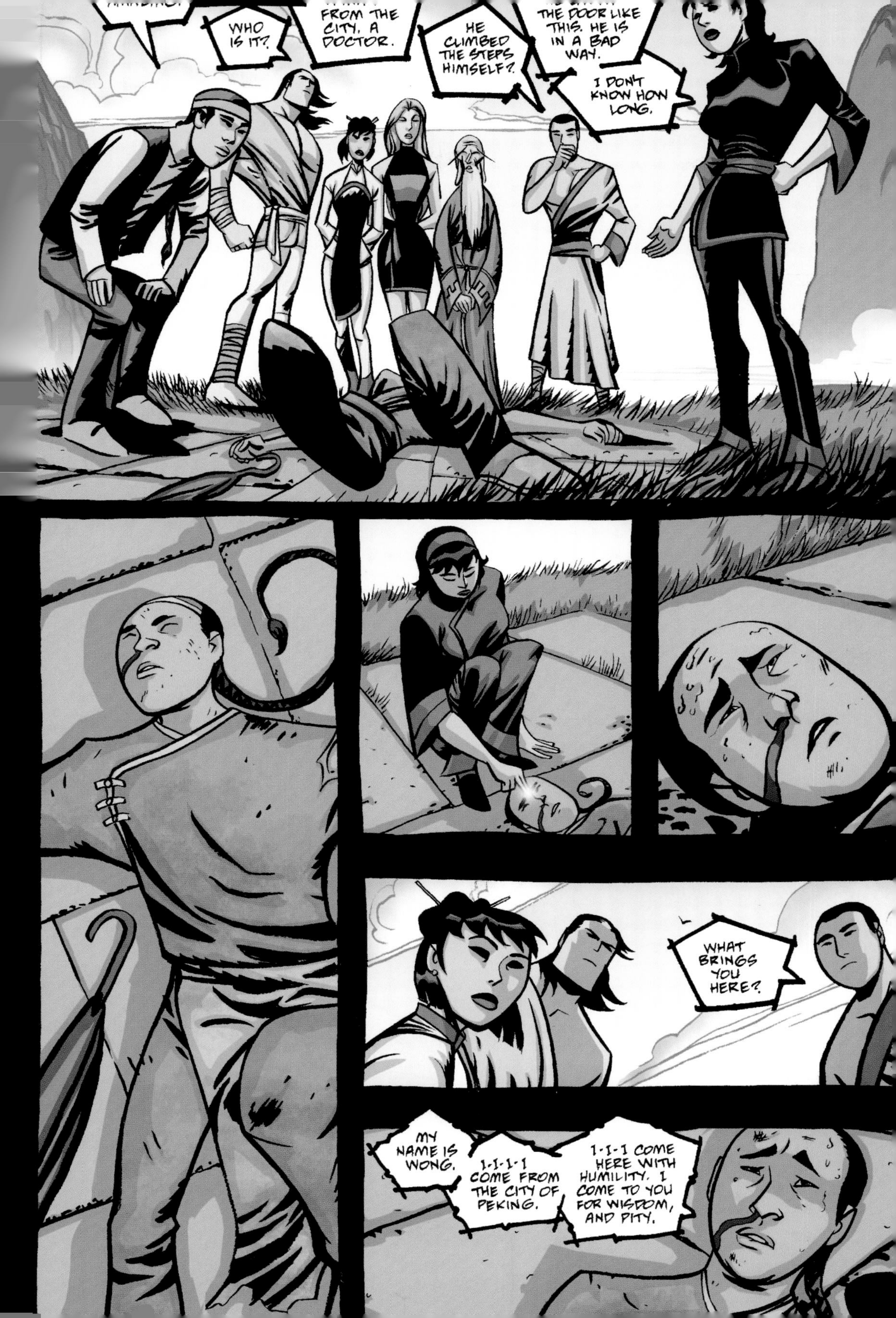
WHO IS IT?
FROM THE CITY, A DOCTOR.
HE CLIMBED THE STEPS HIMSELF?
THE DOOR LIKE THIS. HE IS IN A BAD WAY.
I DON'T KNOW HOW LONG.
WHAT BRINGS YOU HERE?
MY NAME IS WONG.
I-I-I-I COME FROM THE CITY OF PEKING.
I-I-I COME HERE WITH HUMILITY. I COME TO YOU FOR WISDOM, AND PITY.

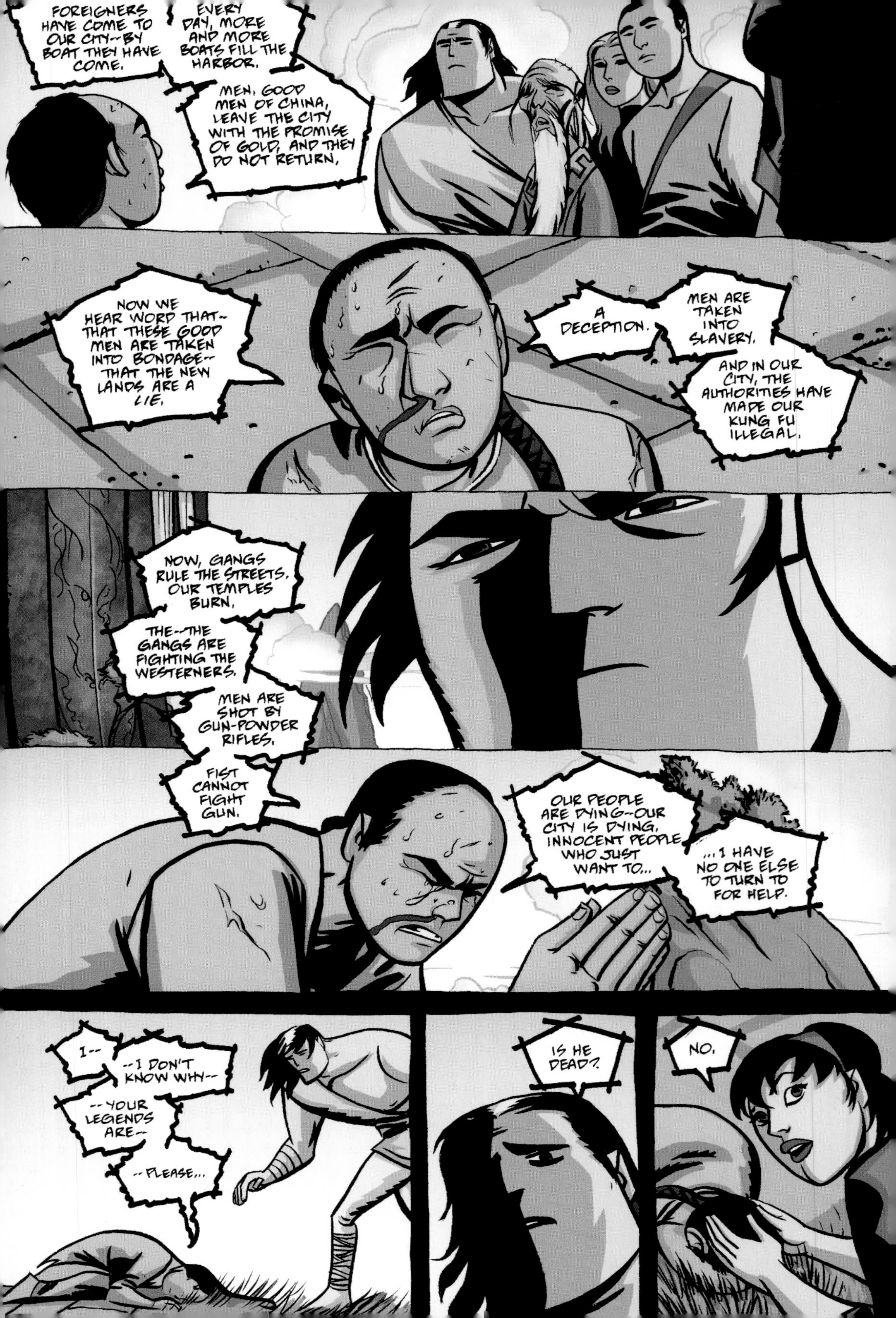
FOREIGNERS HAVE COME TO OUR CITY--BY BOAT THEY HAVE COME.
EVERY DAY, MORE AND MORE BOATS FILL THE HARBOR.
MEN, GOOD MEN OF CHINA, LEAVE THE CITY WITH THE PROMISE OF GOLD, AND THEY DO NOT RETURN.
NOW WE HEAR WORD THAT--THAT THESE GOOD MEN ARE TAKEN INTO BONDAGE--THAT THE NEW LANDS ARE A LIE.
A DECEPTION.
MEN ARE TAKEN INTO SLAVERY.
AND IN OUR CITY, THE AUTHORITIES HAVE MADE OUR KUNG FU ILLEGAL.
NOW, GANGS RULE THE STREETS. OUR TEMPLES BURN.
THE--THE GANGS ARE FIGHTING THE WESTERNERS.
MEN ARE SHOT BY GUN-POWDER RIFLES.
FIST CANNOT FIGHT GUN.
OUR PEOPLE ARE DYING--OUR CITY IS DYING. INNOCENT PEOPLE WHO JUST WANT TO...
...I HAVE NO ONE ELSE TO TURN TO FOR HELP.
I--
--I DON'T KNOW WHY--
--YOUR LEGENDS ARE--
--PLEASE...
IS HE DEAD?
NO.

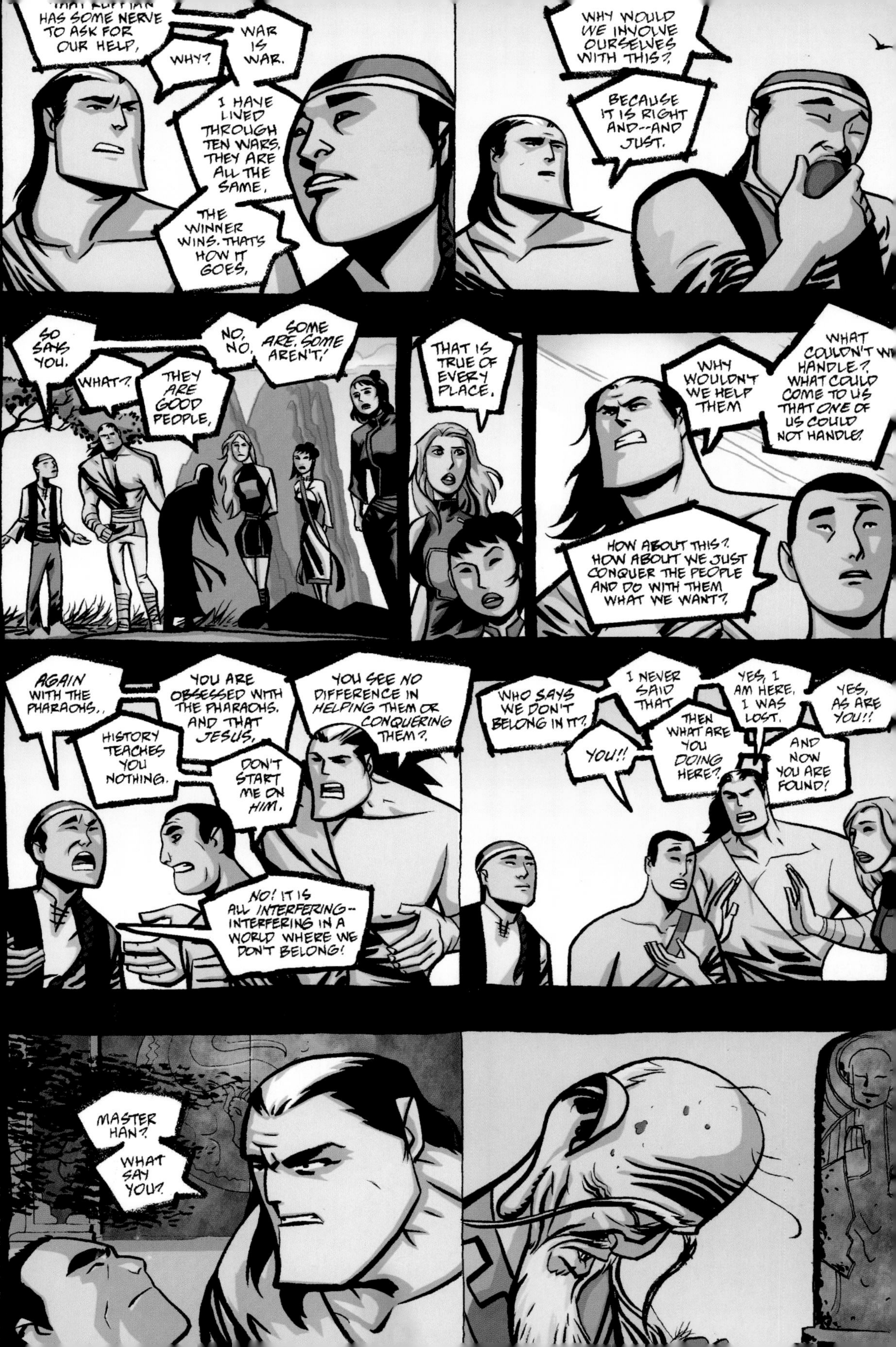
HAS SOME NERVE TO ASK FOR OUR HELP.
WHY?
WAR IS WAR.
I HAVE LIVED THROUGH TEN WARS. THEY ARE ALL THE SAME.
THE WINNER WINS. THAT'S HOW IT GOES.
WHY WOULD WE INVOLVE OURSELVES WITH THIS?
BECAUSE IT IS RIGHT AND--AND JUST.
SO SAYS YOU.
WHAT?
THEY ARE GOOD PEOPLE.
NO, NO.
SOME ARE. SOME AREN'T.
THAT IS TRUE OF EVERY PLACE.
WHY WOULDN'T WE HELP THEM
WHAT COULDN'T W
HANDLE? WHAT COULD COME TO US THAT ONE OF US COULD NOT HANDLE?
HOW ABOUT THIS? HOW ABOUT WE JUST CONQUER THE PEOPLE AND DO WITH THEM WHAT WE WANT?
AGAIN WITH THE PHARAOHS..
HISTORY TEACHES YOU NOTHING.
YOU ARE OBSESSED WITH THE PHARAOHS. AND THAT JESUS.
DON'T START ME ON HIM.
YOU SEE NO DIFFERENCE IN HELPING THEM OR CONQUERING THEM?
NO! IT IS ALL INTERFERING-- INTERFERING IN A WORLD WHERE WE DON'T BELONG!
WHO SAYS WE DON'T BELONG IN IT?
YOU!!
I NEVER SAID THAT
THEN WHAT ARE YOU DOING HERE?
YES, I AM HERE. I WAS LOST.
YES, AS ARE YOU!!
AND NOW YOU ARE FOUND!
MASTER HAN?
WHAT SAY YOU?

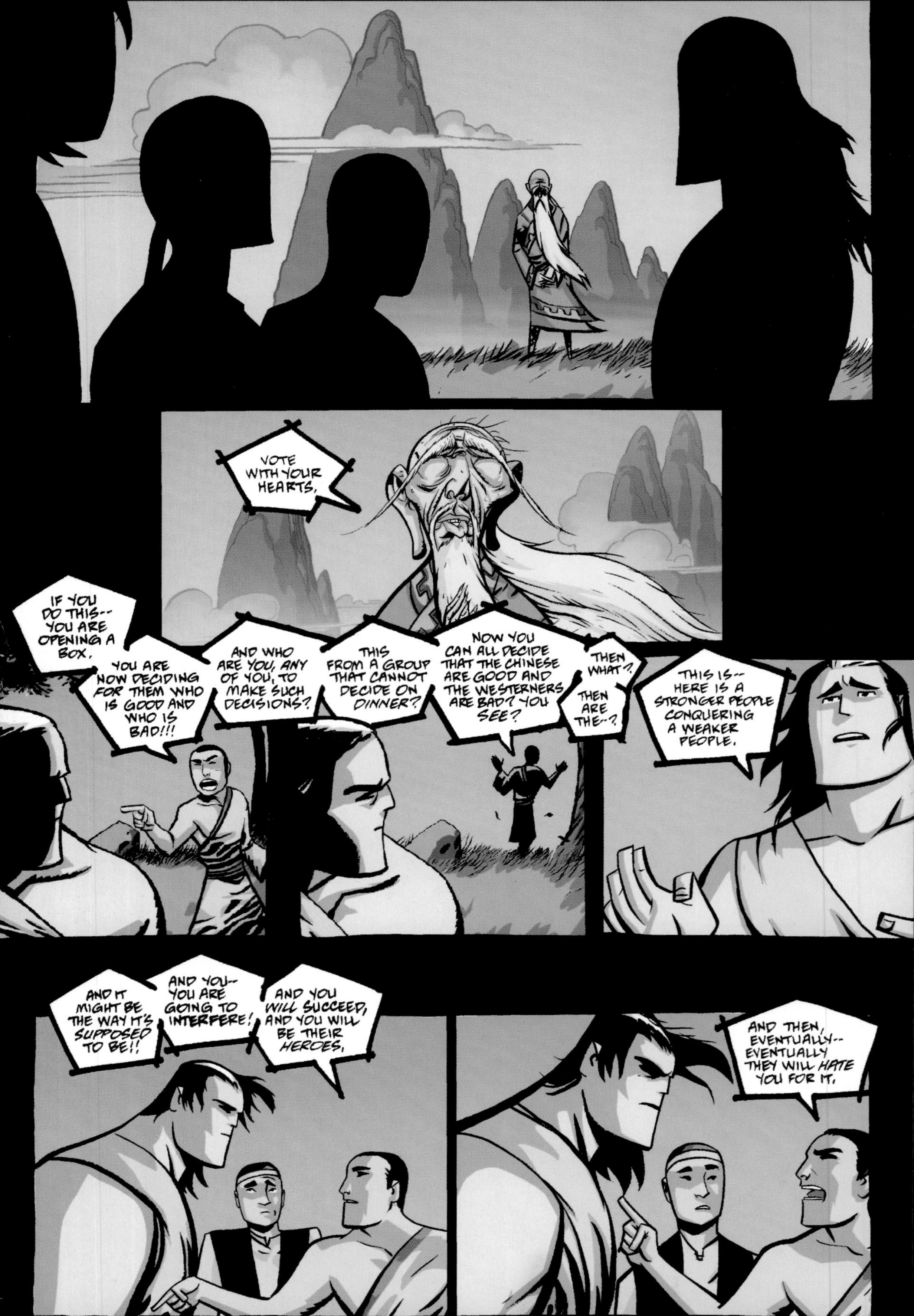
VOTE WITH YOUR HEARTS.
IF YOU DO THIS-- YOU ARE OPENING A BOX.
YOU ARE NOW DECIDING FOR THEM WHO IS GOOD AND WHO IS BAD!!!
AND WHO ARE YOU, ANY OF YOU, TO MAKE SUCH DECISIONS?
THIS FROM A GROUP THAT CANNOT DECIDE ON DINNER?
NOW YOU CAN ALL DECIDE THAT THE CHINESE ARE GOOD AND THE WESTERNERS ARE BAD? YOU SEE?
THEN WHAT?
THEN ARE THE--?
THIS IS-- HERE IS A STRONGER PEOPLE CONQUERING A WEAKER PEOPLE.
AND IT MIGHT BE THE WAY IT'S SUPPOSED TO BE!!
AND YOU-- YOU ARE GOING TO INTERFERE!
AND YOU WILL SUCCEED, AND YOU WILL BE THEIR HEROES.
AND THEN, EVENTUALLY-- EVENTUALLY THEY WILL HATE YOU FOR IT.

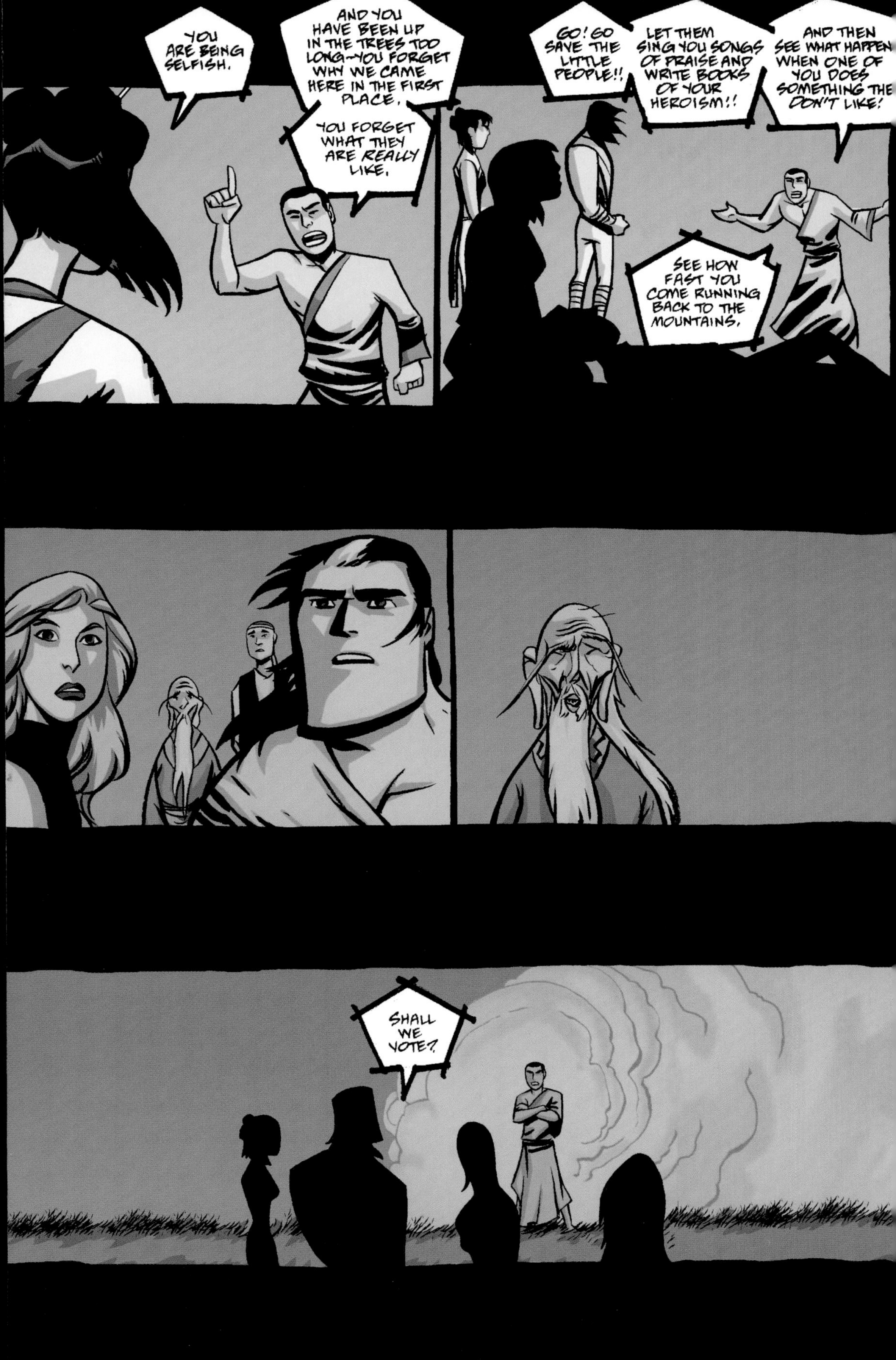
YOU ARE BEING SELFISH.
AND YOU HAVE BEEN UP IN THE TREES TOO LONG--YOU FORGET WHY WE CAME HERE IN THE FIRST PLACE.
YOU FORGET WHAT THEY ARE *REALLY* LIKE.
GO! GO SAVE THE LITTLE PEOPLE!!
LET THEM SING YOU SONGS OF PRAISE AND WRITE BOOKS OF YOUR HEROISM!!
AND THEN SEE WHAT HAPPEN WHEN ONE OF YOU DOES SOMETHING THE *DON'T* LIKE!
SEE HOW FAST YOU COME RUNNING BACK TO THE MOUNTAINS.
SHALL WE VOTE?

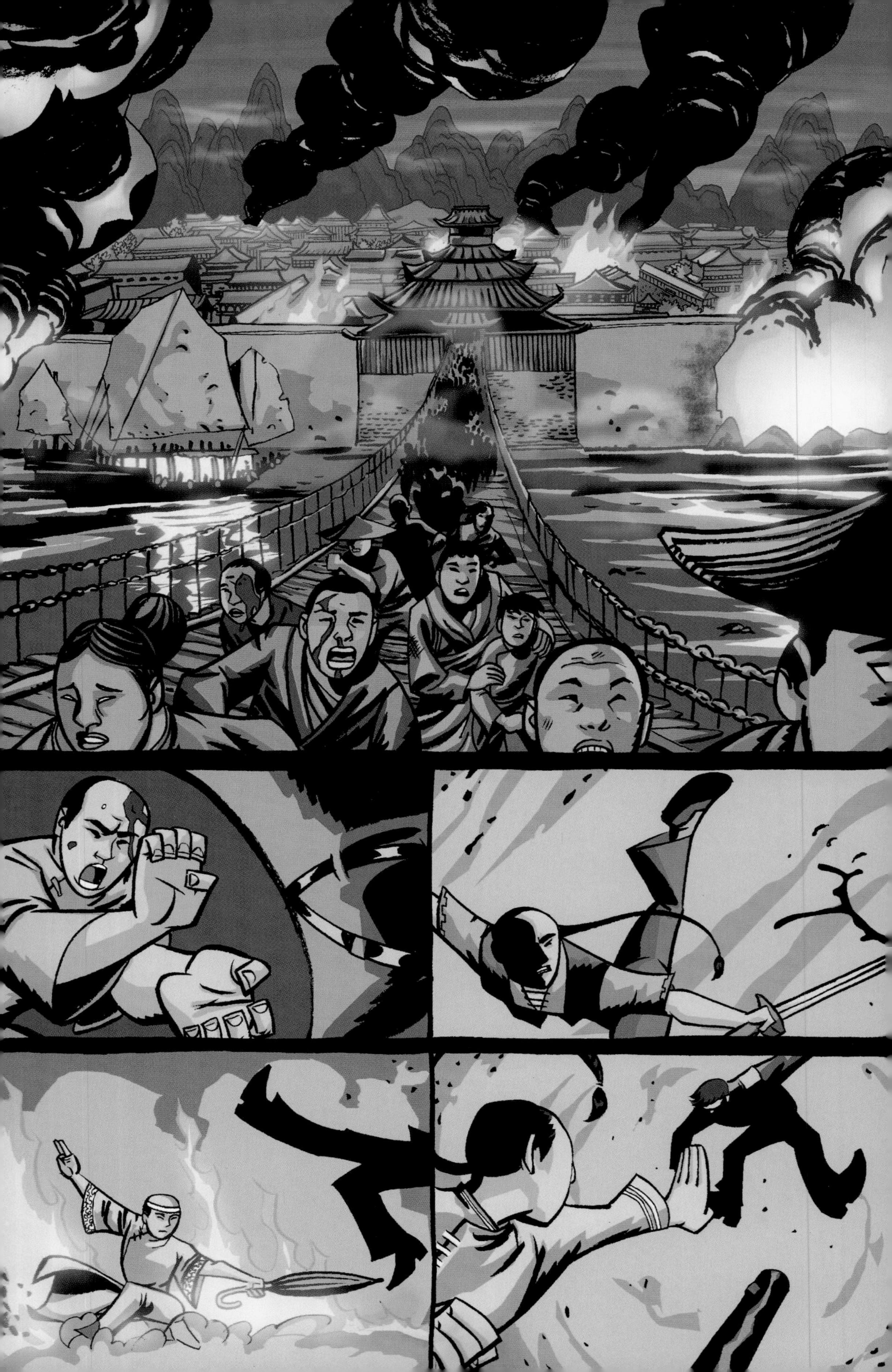

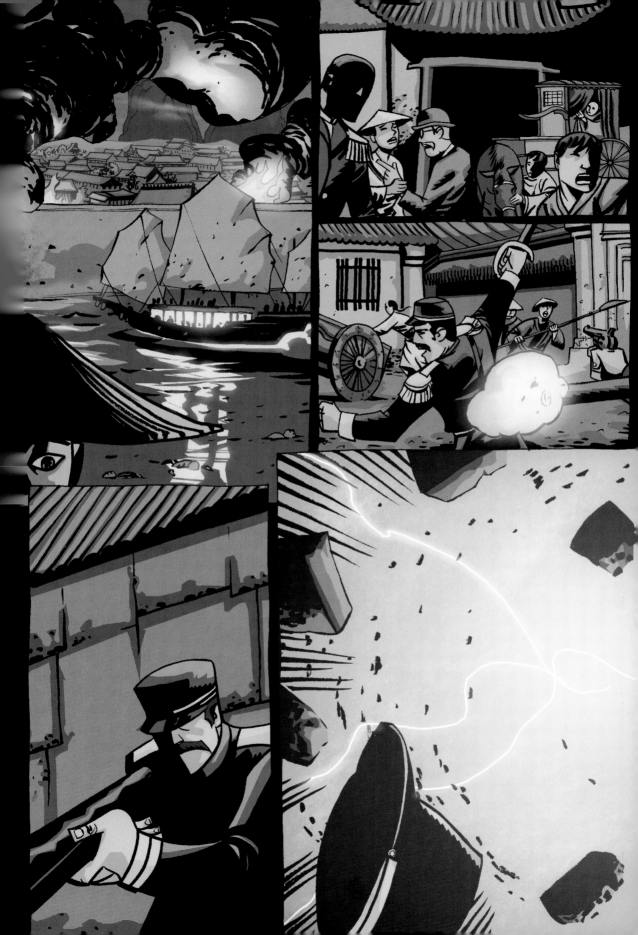

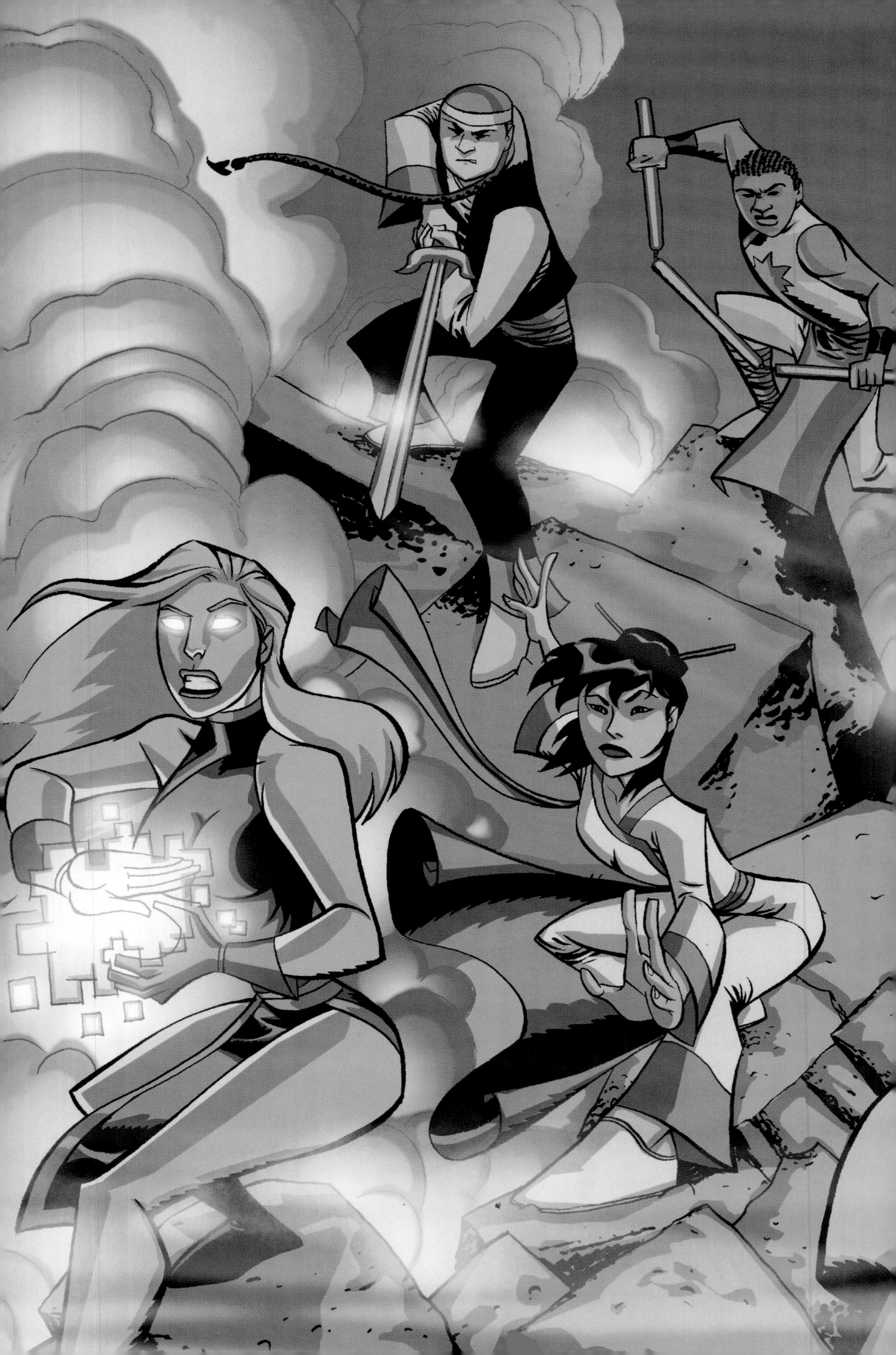

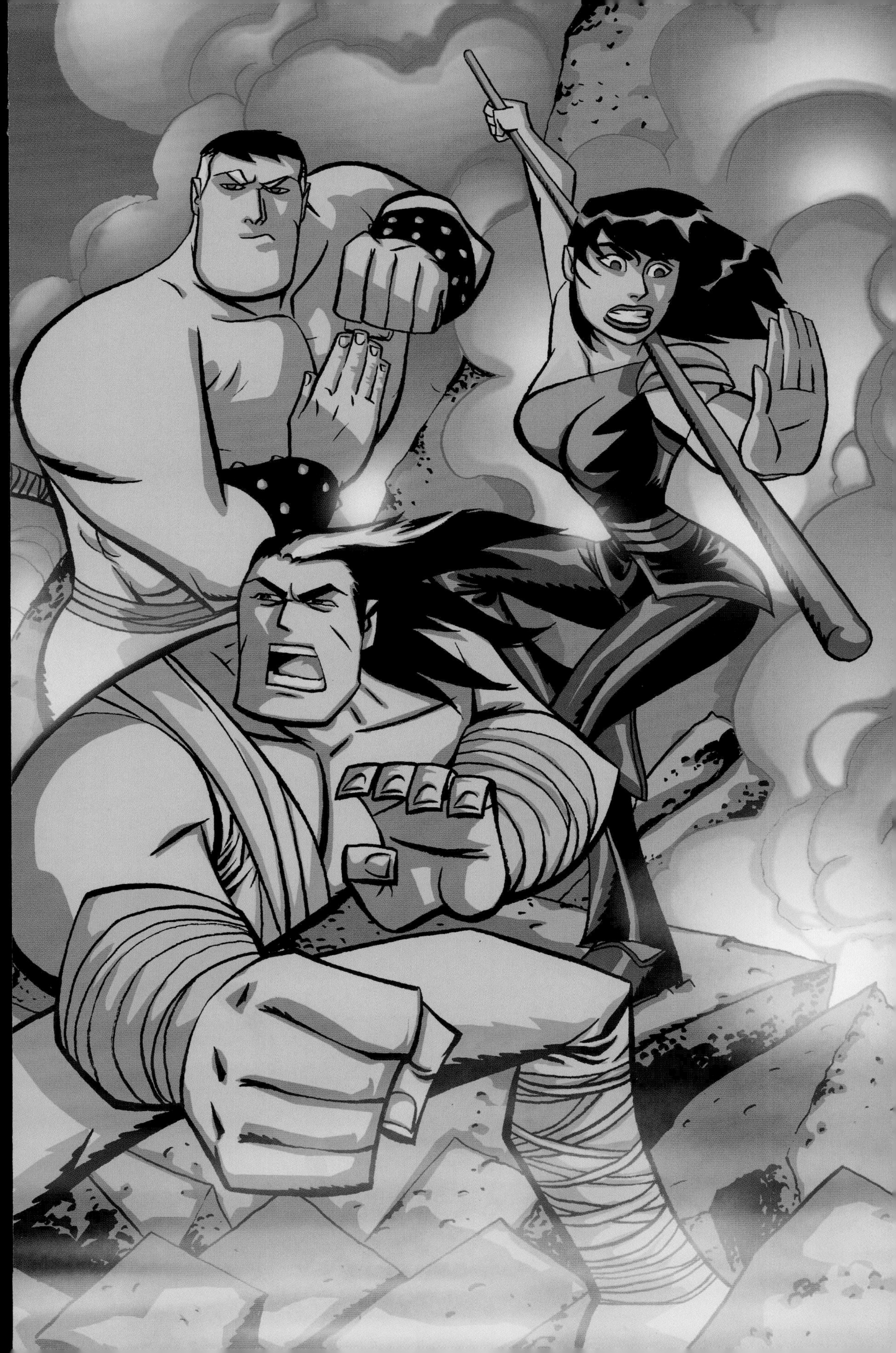

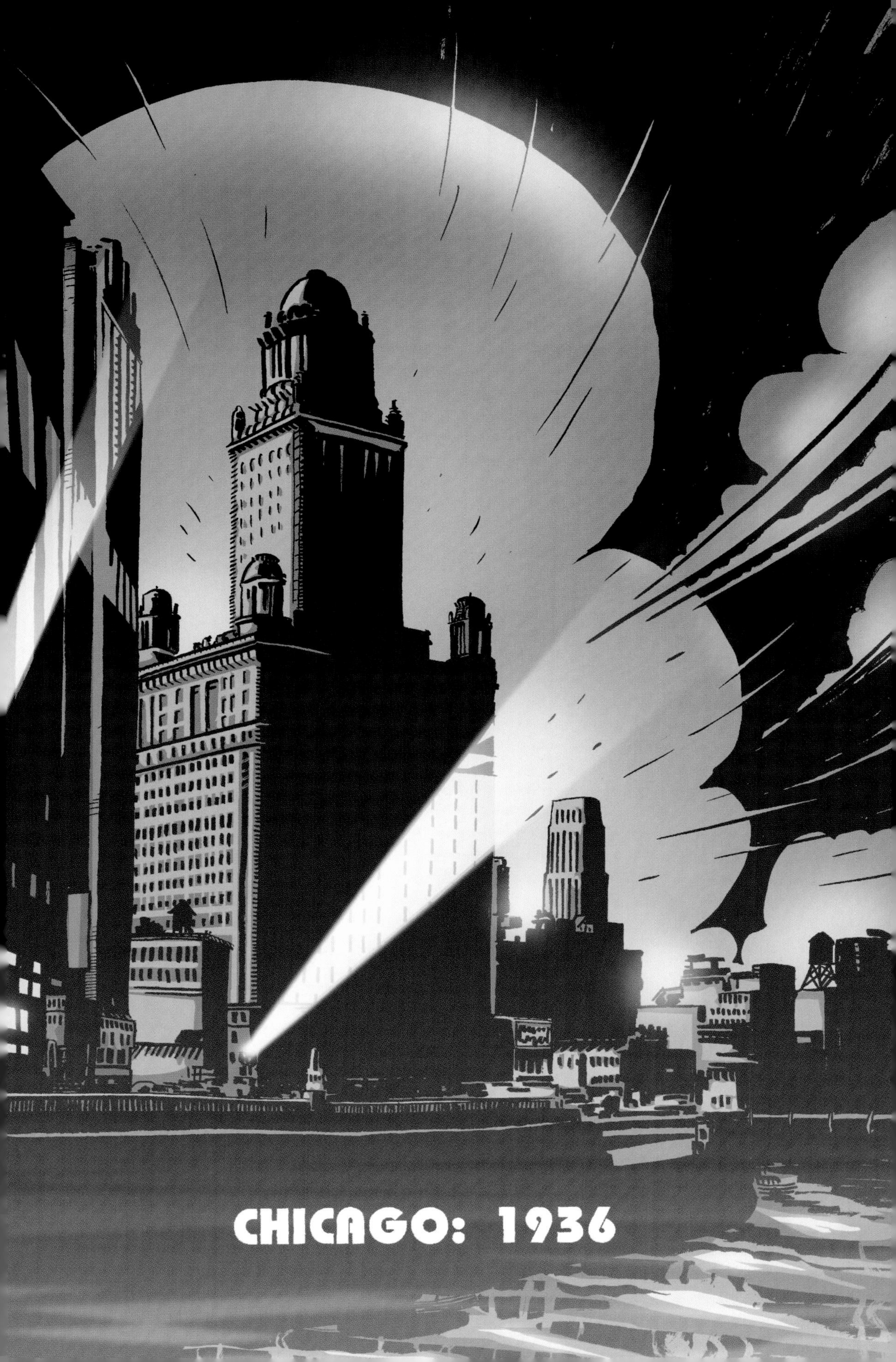
CHICAGO: 1936

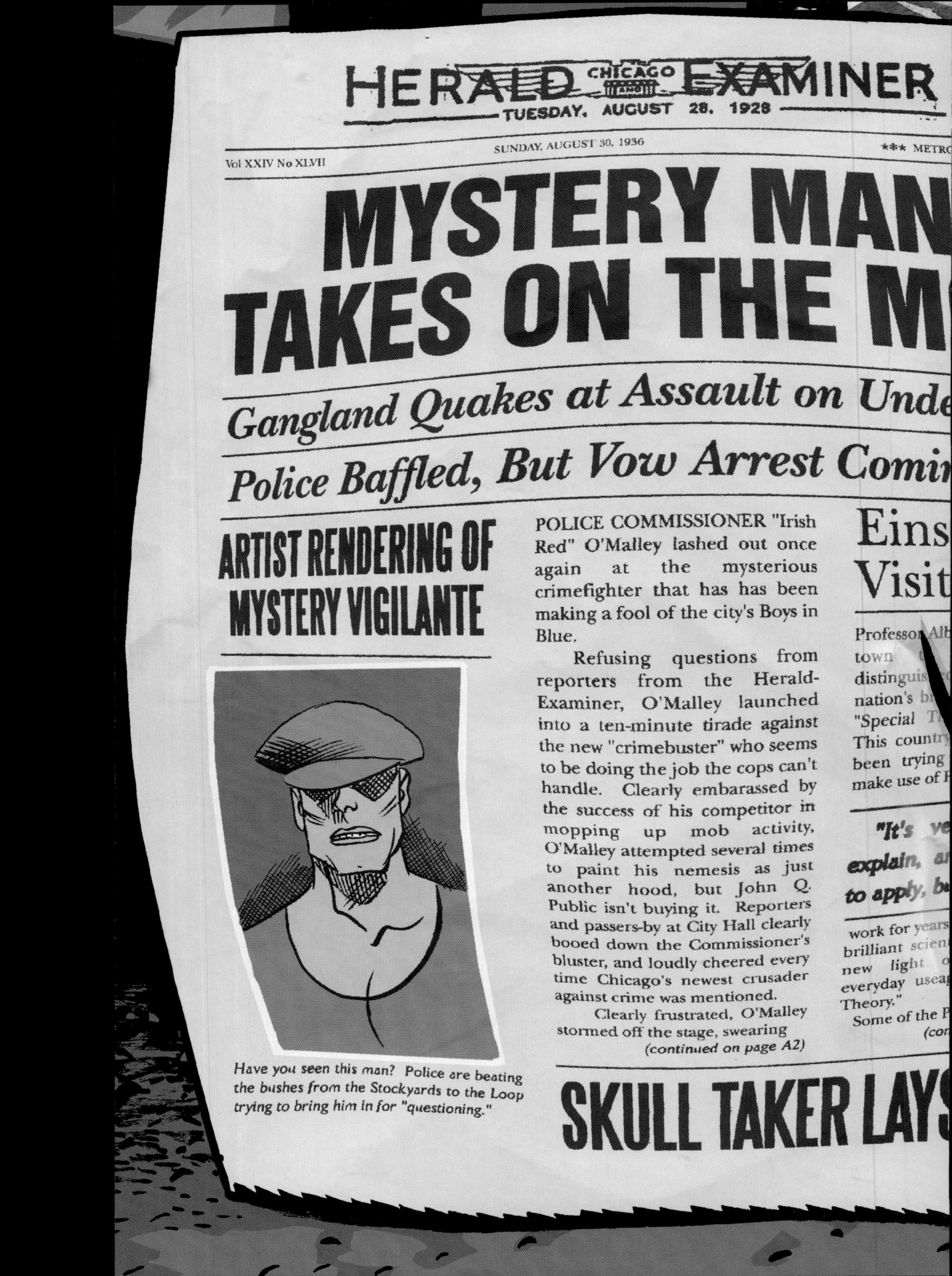

HERALD CHICAGO AND EXAMINER
TUESDAY, AUGUST 28, 1928

SUNDAY, AUGUST 30, 1936

Vol XXIV No XLVII

*** METRO

# MYSTERY MAN TAKES ON THE M

## Gangland Quakes at Assault on Unde

## Police Baffled, But Vow Arrest Comi

### ARTIST RENDERING OF MYSTERY VIGILANTE

*Have you seen this man? Police are beating the bushes from the Stockyards to the Loop trying to bring him in for "questioning."*

POLICE COMMISSIONER "Irish Red" O'Malley lashed out once again at the mysterious crimefighter that has has been making a fool of the city's Boys in Blue.

Refusing questions from reporters from the Herald-Examiner, O'Malley launched into a ten-minute tirade against the new "crimebuster" who seems to be doing the job the cops can't handle. Clearly embarassed by the success of his competitor in mopping up mob activity, O'Malley attempted several times to paint his nemesis as just another hood, but John Q. Public isn't buying it. Reporters and passers-by at City Hall clearly booed down the Commissioner's bluster, and loudly cheered every time Chicago's newest crusader against crime was mentioned.

Clearly frustrated, O'Malley stormed off the stage, swearing

(continued on page A2)

### Eins Visit

Professor Alb town t distinguis nation's b "Special T This country been trying make use of F

"It's ve explain, a to apply, b

work for years brilliant scien new light o everyday useag Theory."

Some of the F

(co

# SKULL TAKER LAYS

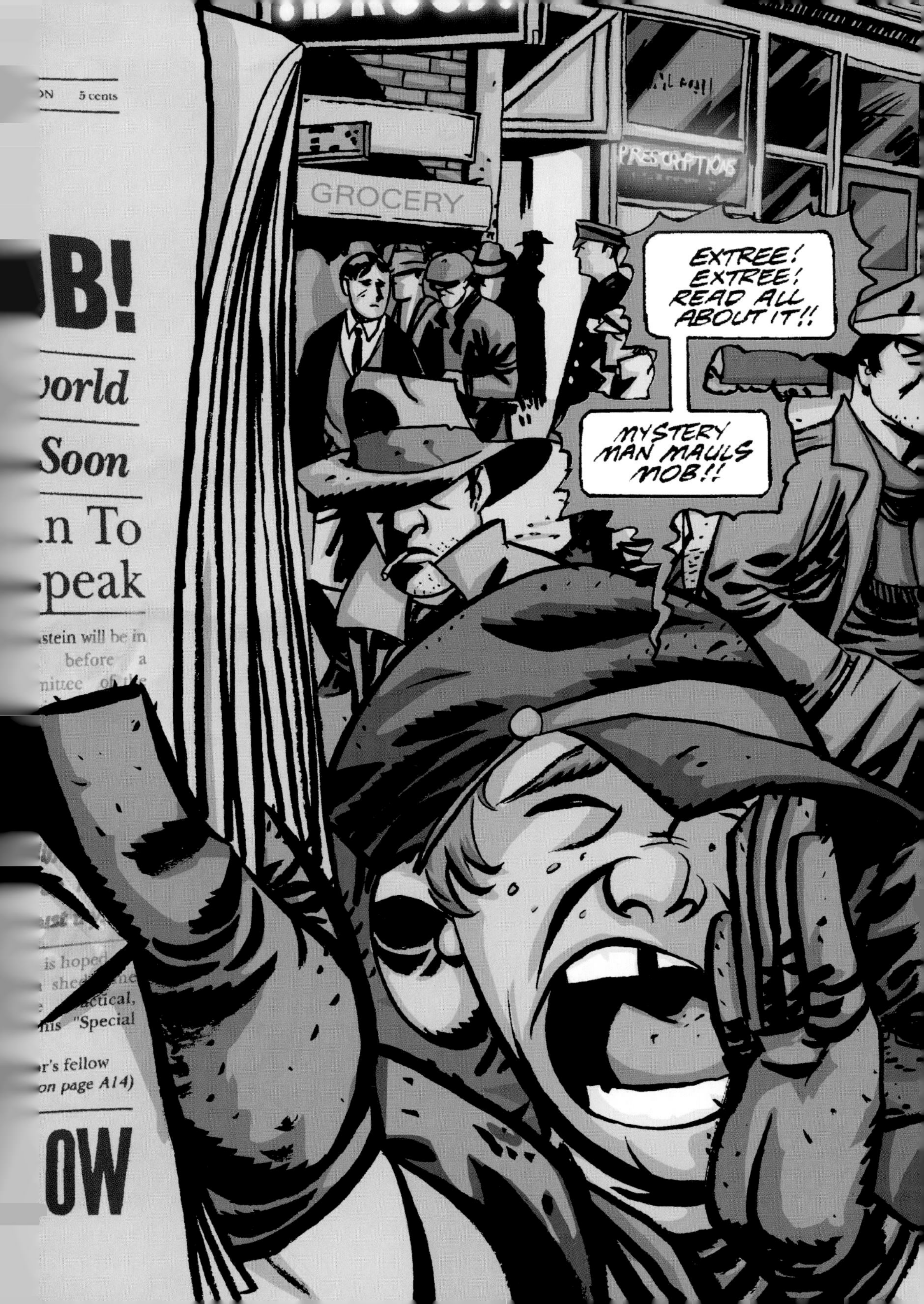
5 cents
B!
world
Soon
n To
peak
stein will be in
before a
nittee of the
is hoped
'Special
r's fellow
on page A14)
OW
GROCERY
PRESCRIPTIONS
EXTREE! EXTREE! READ ALL ABOUT IT!!
MYSTERY MAN MAULS MOB!!

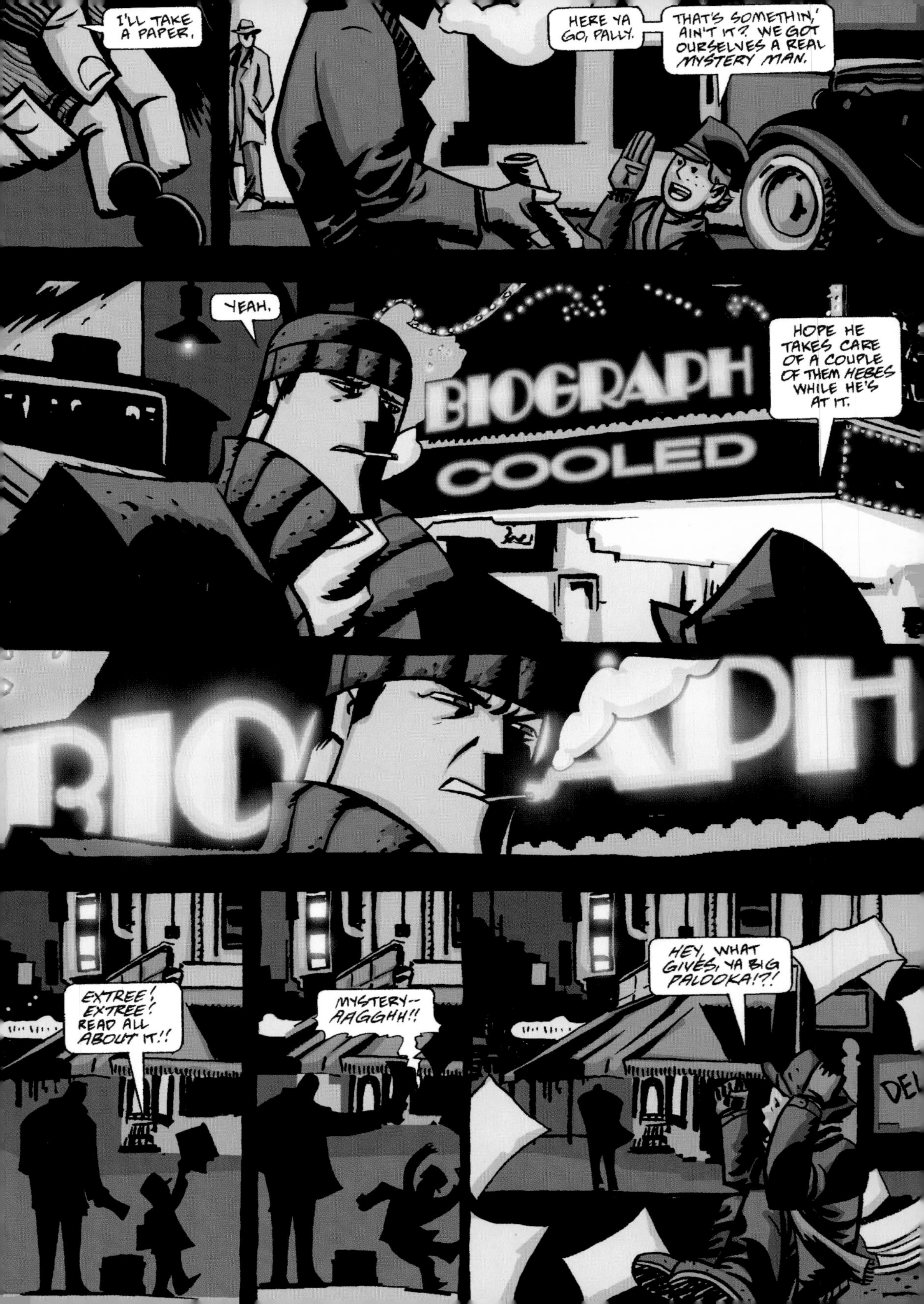

I'LL TAKE A PAPER.
HERE YA GO, PALLY.
THAT'S SOMETHIN', AIN'T IT? WE GOT OURSELVES A REAL MYSTERY MAN.
YEAH.
HOPE HE TAKES CARE OF A COUPLE OF THEM HEBES WHILE HE'S AT IT.
BIOGRAPH
COOLED
EXTREE! EXTREE! READ ALL ABOUT IT!!
MYSTERY-- AAGGHH!!
HEY, WHAT GIVES, YA BIG PALOOKA!?!

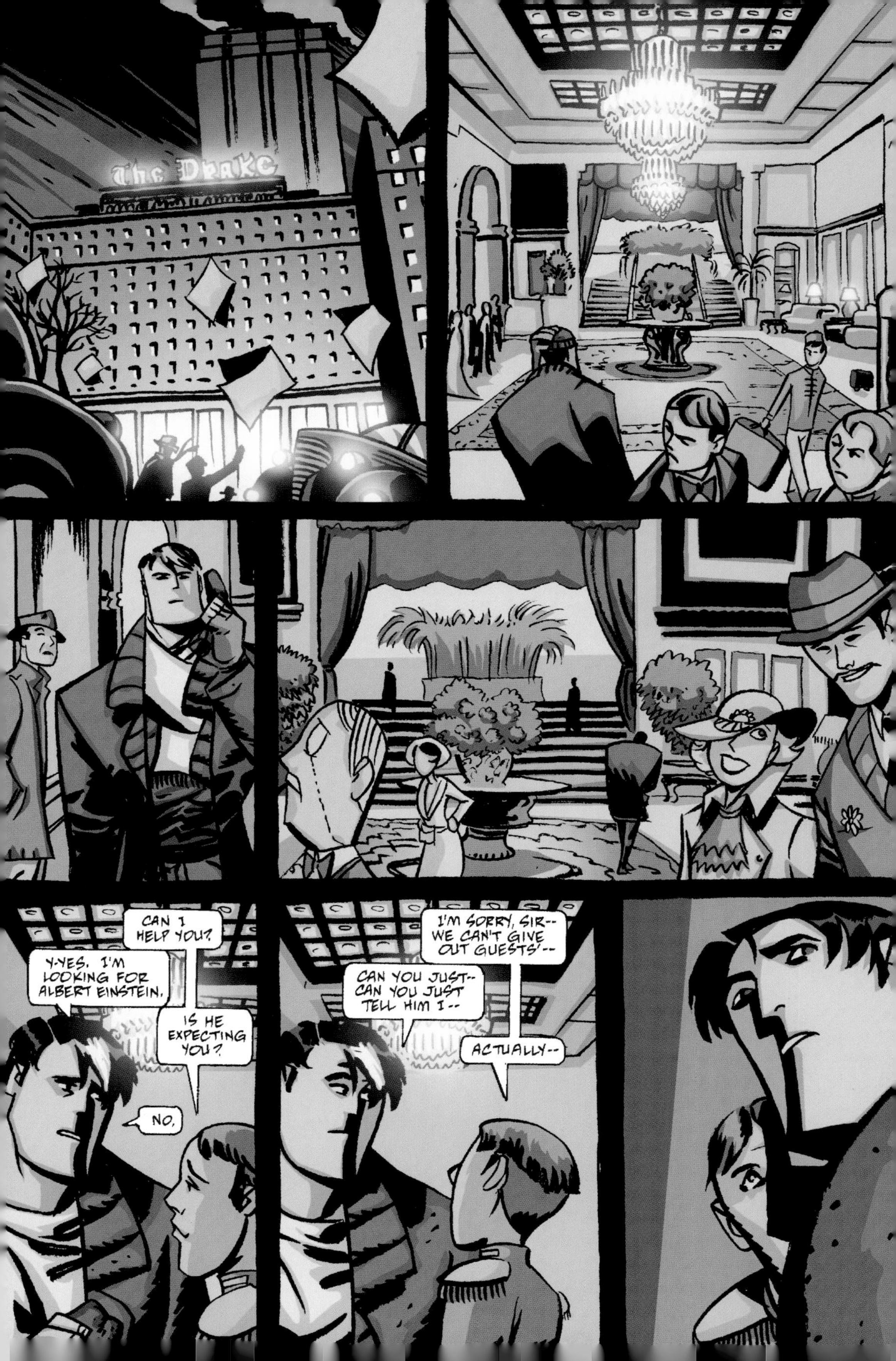
THE DRAKE
CAN I HELP YOU?
Y-YES. I'M LOOKING FOR ALBERT EINSTEIN.
IS HE EXPECTING YOU?
NO.
I'M SORRY, SIR-- WE CAN'T GIVE OUT GUESTS'--
CAN YOU JUST-- CAN YOU JUST TELL HIM I --
ACTUALLY--

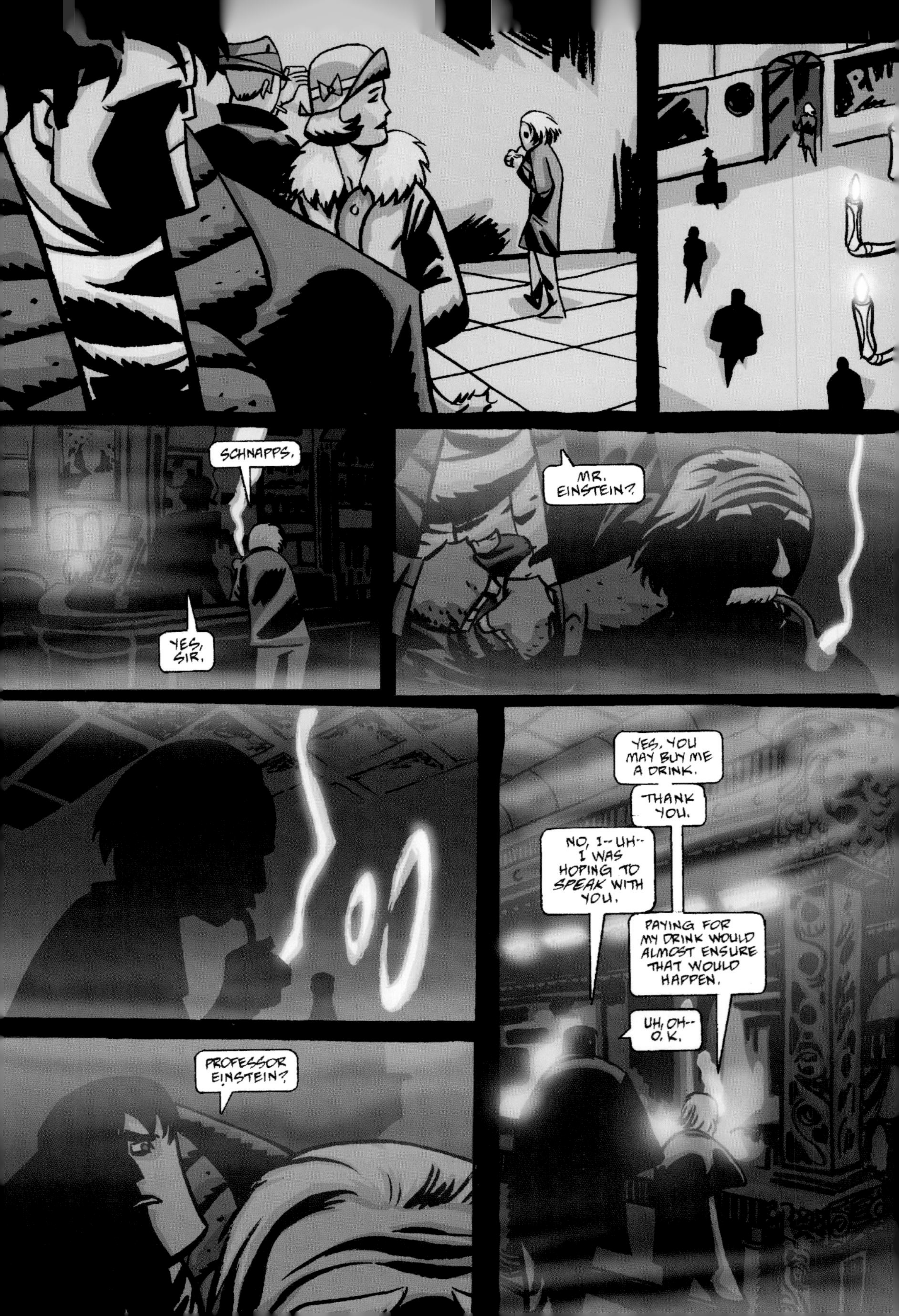
SCHNAPPS.
YES, SIR.
MR. EINSTEIN?
PROFESSOR EINSTEIN?
YES, YOU MAY BUY ME A DRINK.
THANK YOU.
NO, I-- UH-- I WAS HOPING TO *SPEAK* WITH YOU.
PAYING FOR MY DRINK WOULD ALMOST ENSURE THAT WOULD HAPPEN.
UH, OH-- O.K.

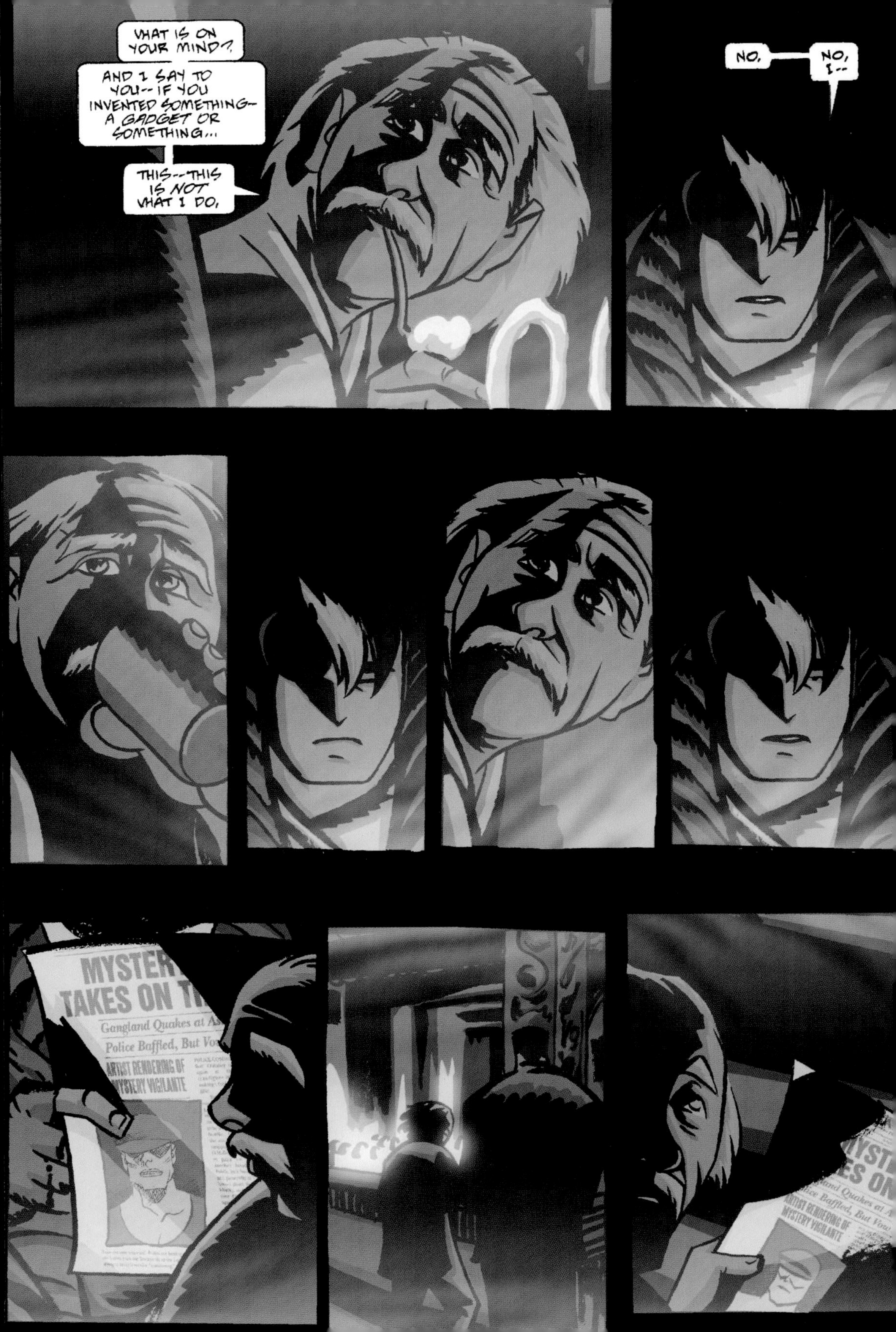
WHAT IS ON YOUR MIND?
AND I SAY TO YOU-- IF YOU INVENTED SOMETHING-- A GADGET OR SOMETHING...
THIS--THIS IS NOT WHAT I DO.
NO,
NO, I--
MYSTER
TAKES ON TH
Gangland Quakes at A
Police Baffled, But Vo
ARTIST RENDERING OF MYSTERY VIGILANTE
MYSTER
ES ON
Gangland Quakes at A
Police Baffled, But Vo
ARTIST RENDERING OF MYSTERY VIGILANTE

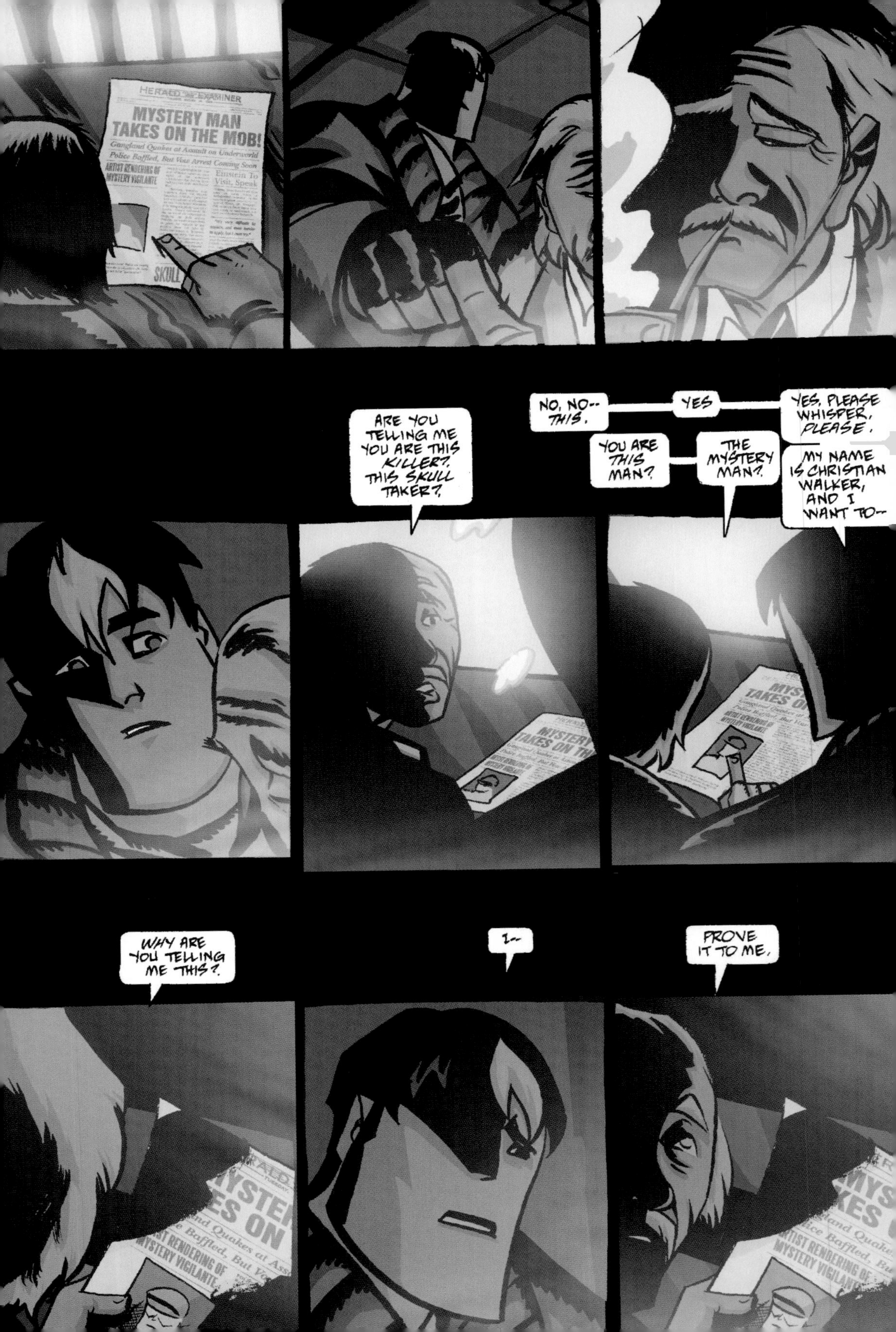
HERALD EXAMINER
MYSTERY MAN TAKES ON THE MOB!
Gangland Quakes at Assault on Underworld
Police Baffled, But Vows Arrest Coming Soon
ARTIST RENDERING OF MYSTERY VIGILANTE
Einstein To Visit, Speak
SKULL
ARE YOU TELLING ME YOU ARE THIS KILLER? THIS SKULL TAKER?
NO, NO-- THIS.
YOU ARE THIS MAN?
THE MYSTERY MAN?
YES
YES, PLEASE WHISPER, PLEASE.
MY NAME IS CHRISTIAN WALKER, AND I WANT TO--
WHY ARE YOU TELLING ME THIS?
I--
PROVE IT TO ME.

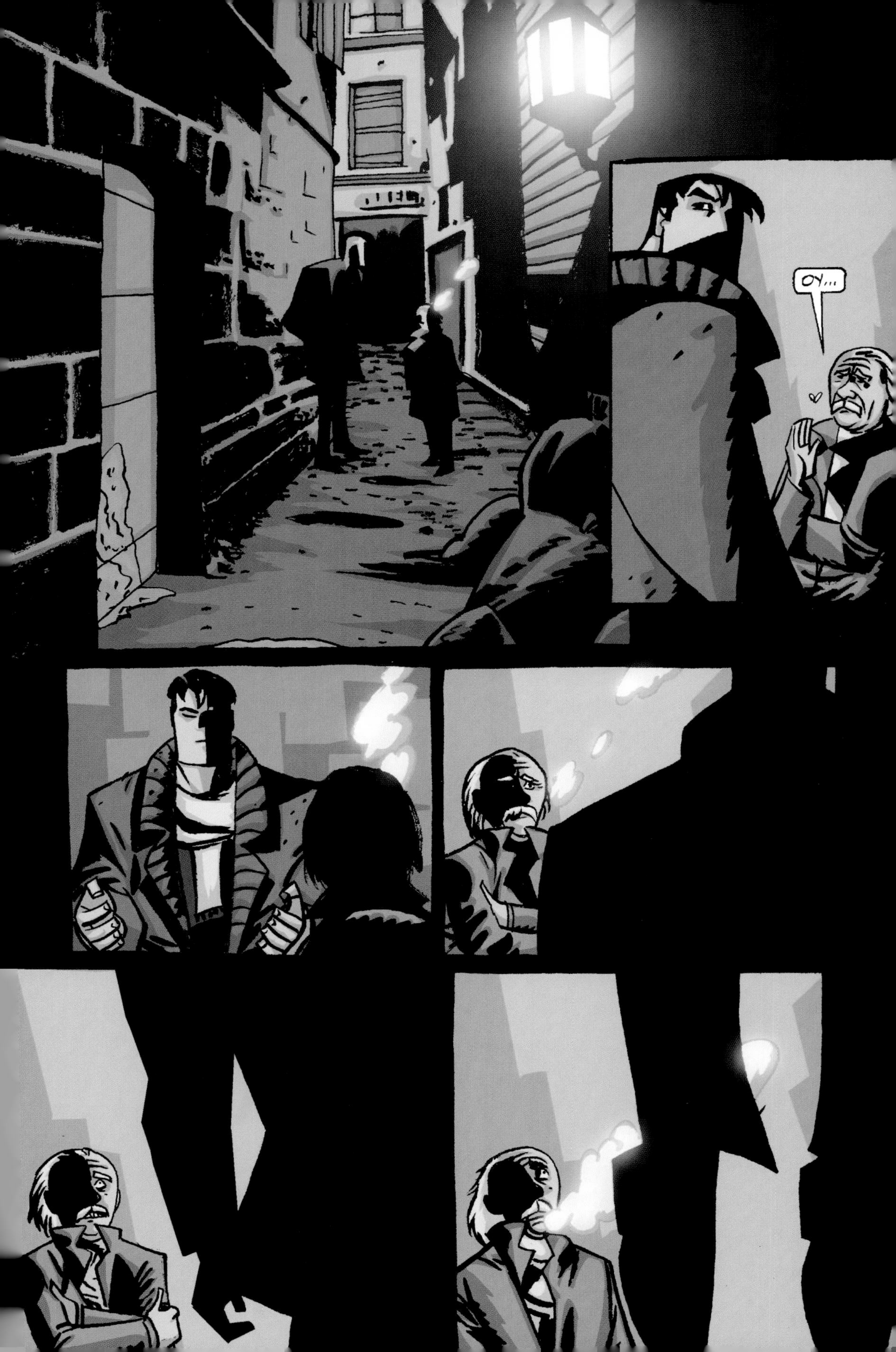
OY...

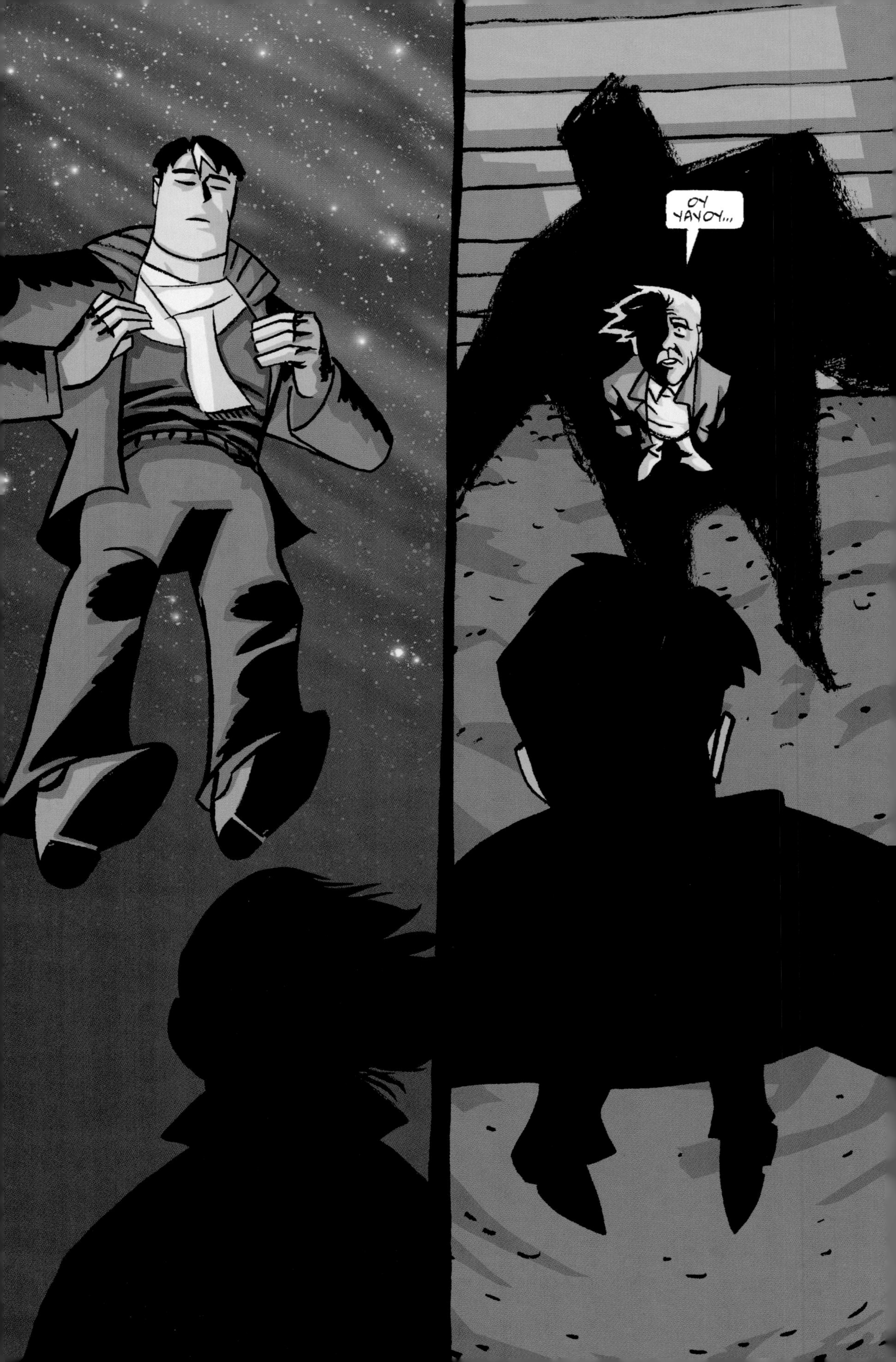
OY YAVOY...

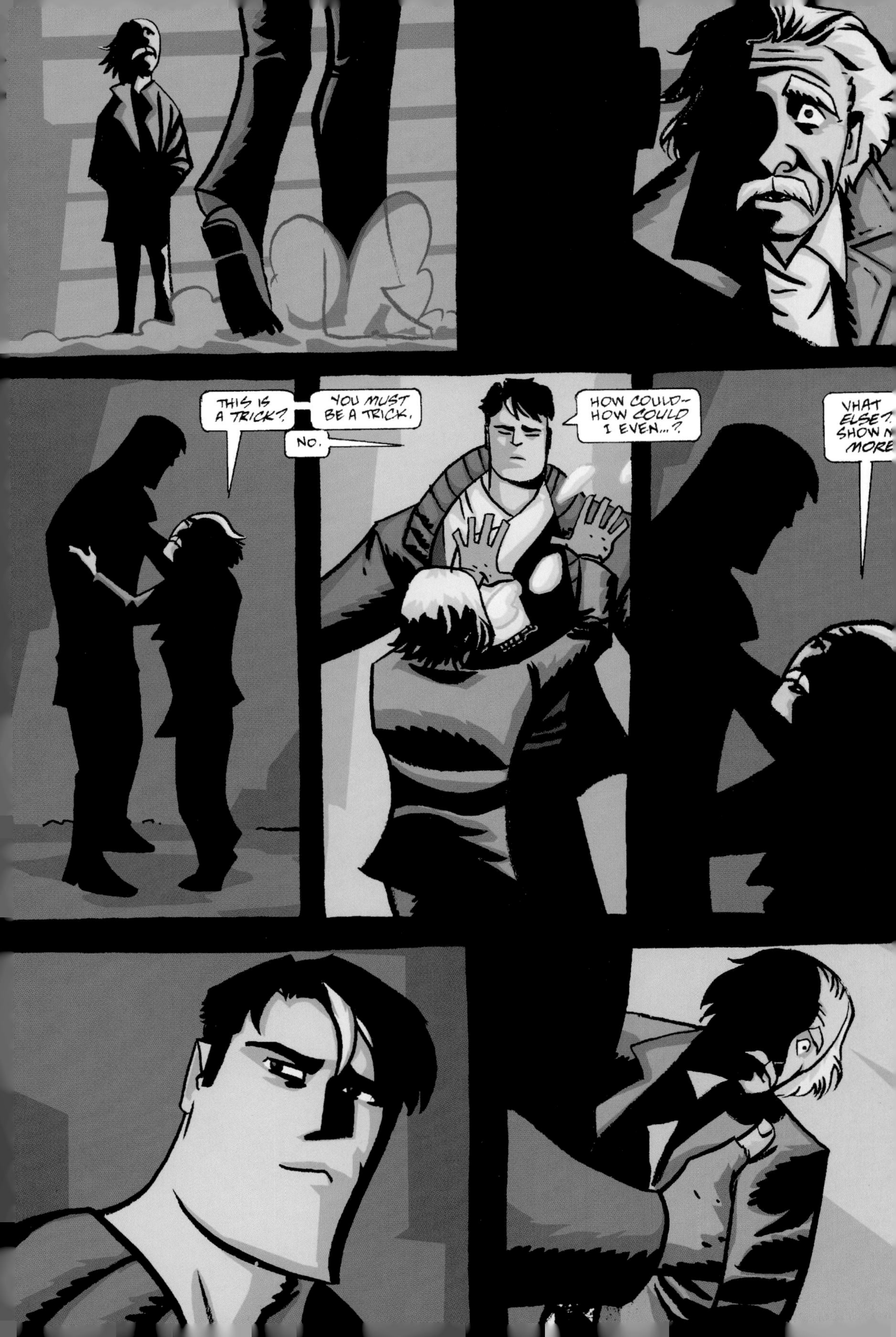
THIS IS A TRICK?
YOU MUST BE A TRICK.
NO.
HOW COULD— HOW COULD I EVEN...?
VHAT ELSE? SHOW
MORE

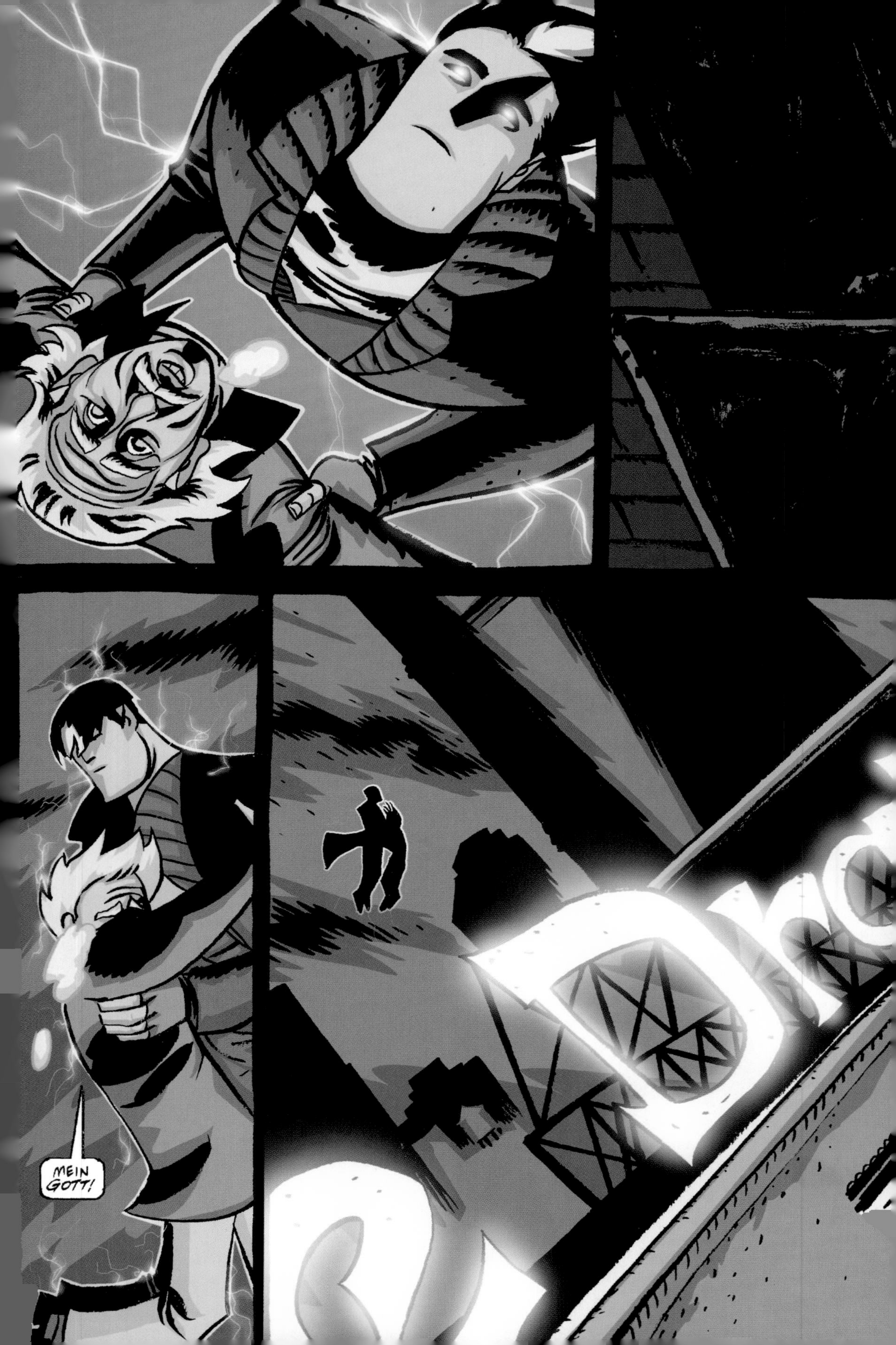
MEIN GOTT!

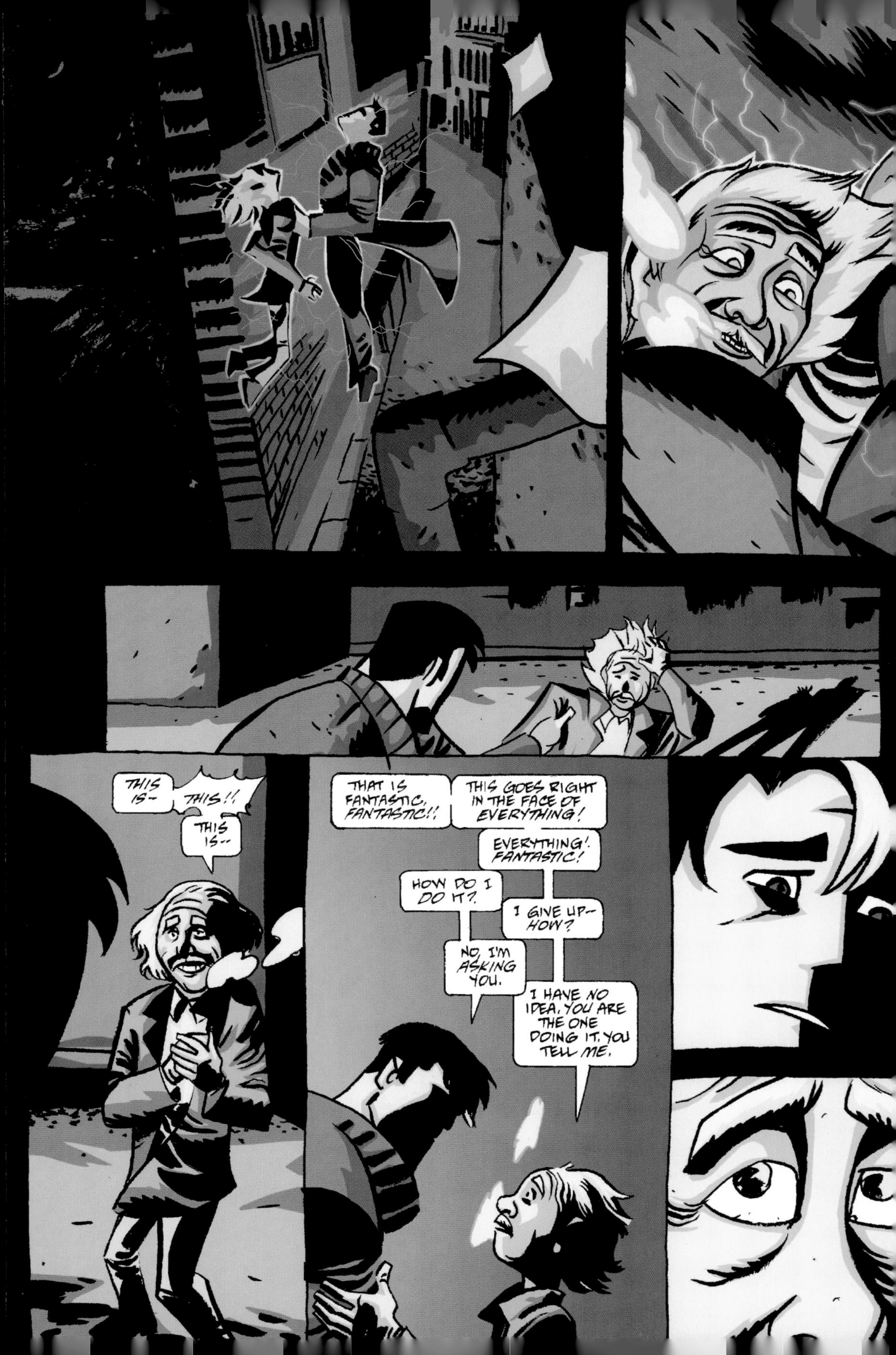
THIS IS--
THIS!!
THIS IS--
THAT IS FANTASTIC, FANTASTIC!!
THIS GOES RIGHT IN THE FACE OF EVERYTHING!
EVERYTHING! FANTASTIC!
HOW DO I DO IT?
I GIVE UP-- HOW?
NO, I'M ASKING YOU.
I HAVE NO IDEA. YOU ARE THE ONE DOING IT. YOU TELL ME.

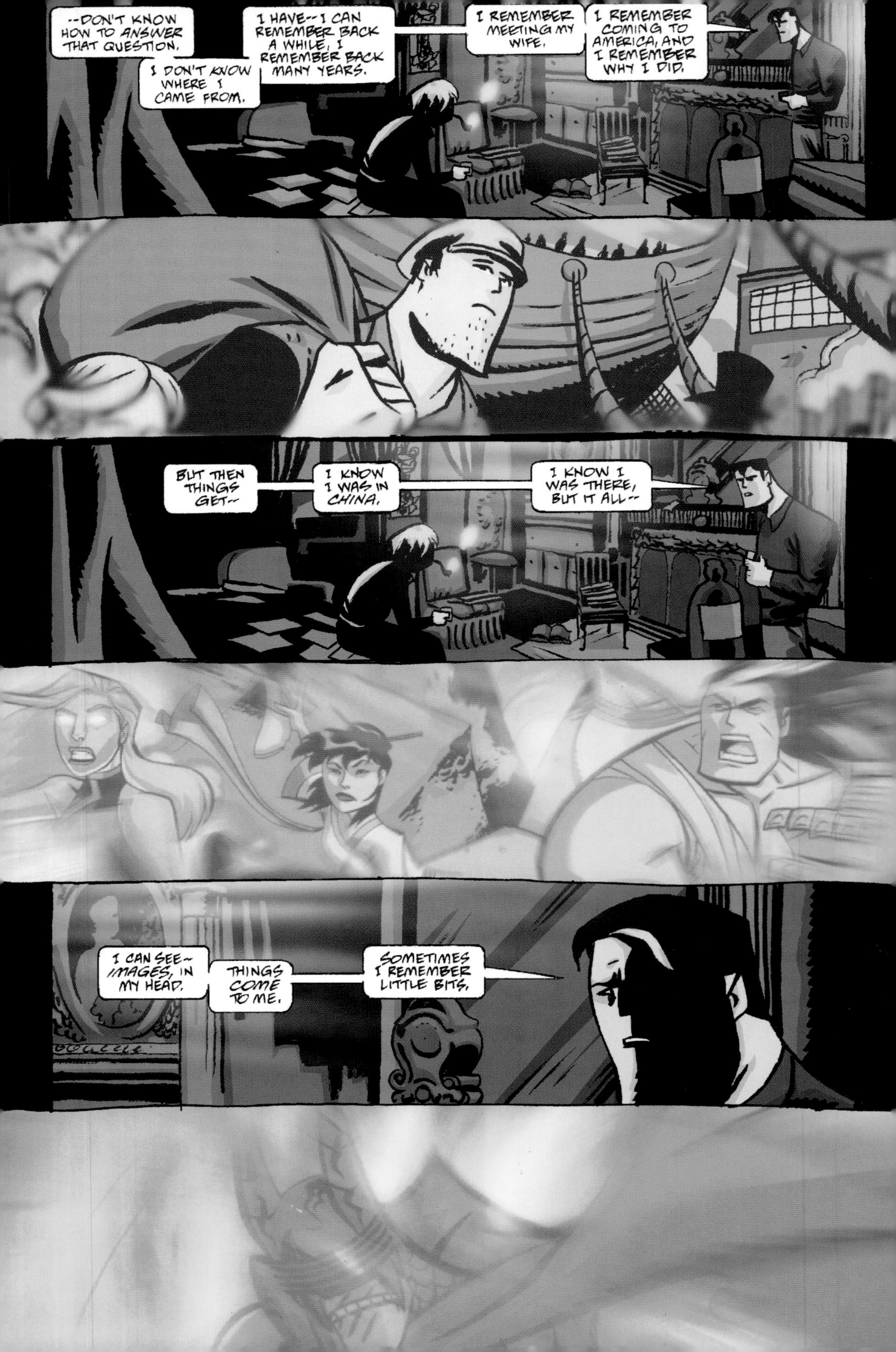
--DON'T KNOW HOW TO ANSWER THAT QUESTION.
I DON'T KNOW WHERE I CAME FROM.
I HAVE--I CAN REMEMBER BACK A WHILE, I REMEMBER BACK MANY YEARS.
I REMEMBER MEETING MY WIFE.
I REMEMBER COMING TO AMERICA, AND I REMEMBER WHY I DID.
BUT THEN THINGS GET--
I KNOW I WAS IN CHINA.
I KNOW I WAS THERE, BUT IT ALL--
I CAN SEE-- IMAGES, IN MY HEAD.
THINGS COME TO ME.
SOMETIMES I REMEMBER LITTLE BITS.

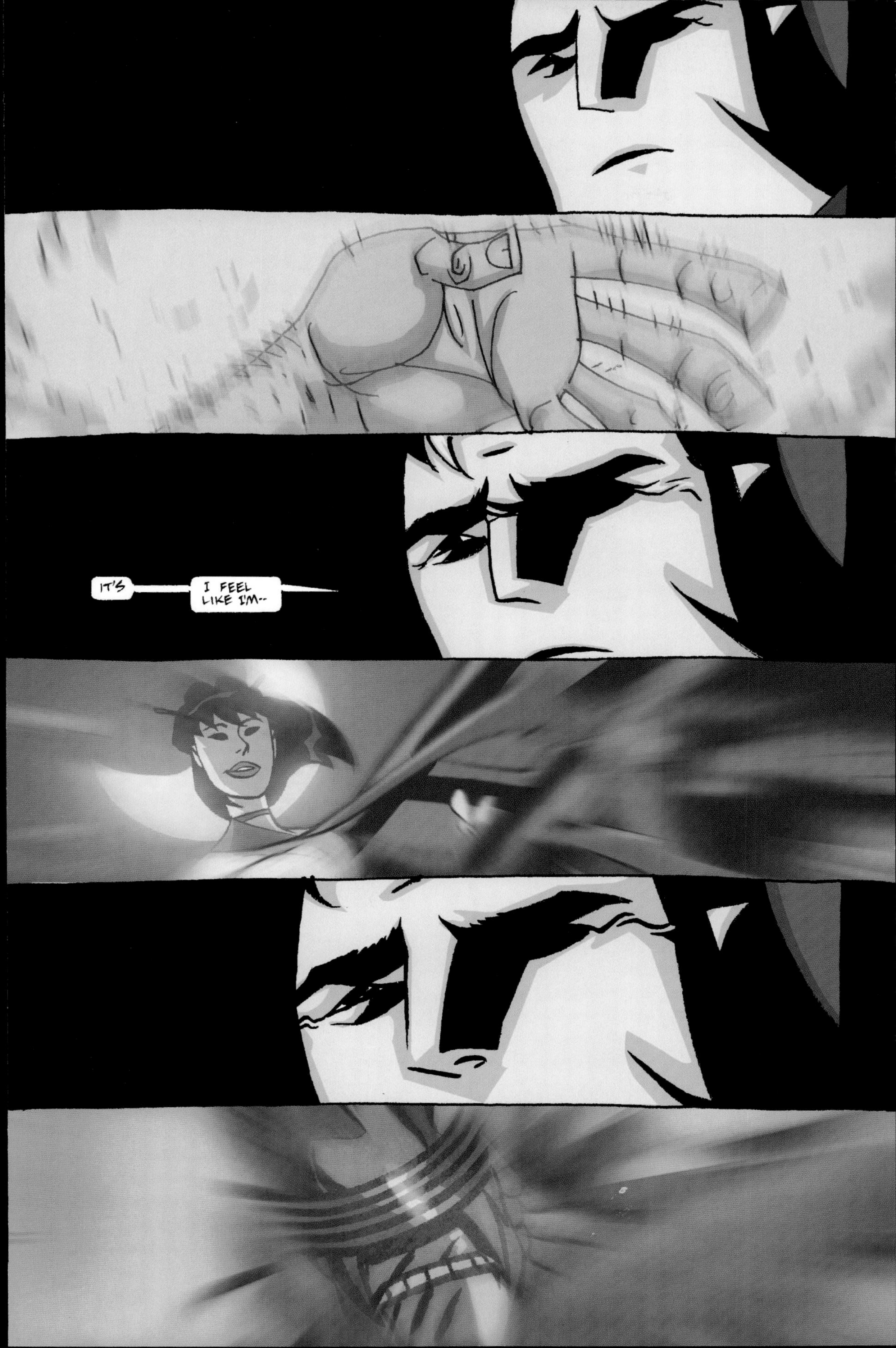
IT'S
I FEEL LIKE I'M--

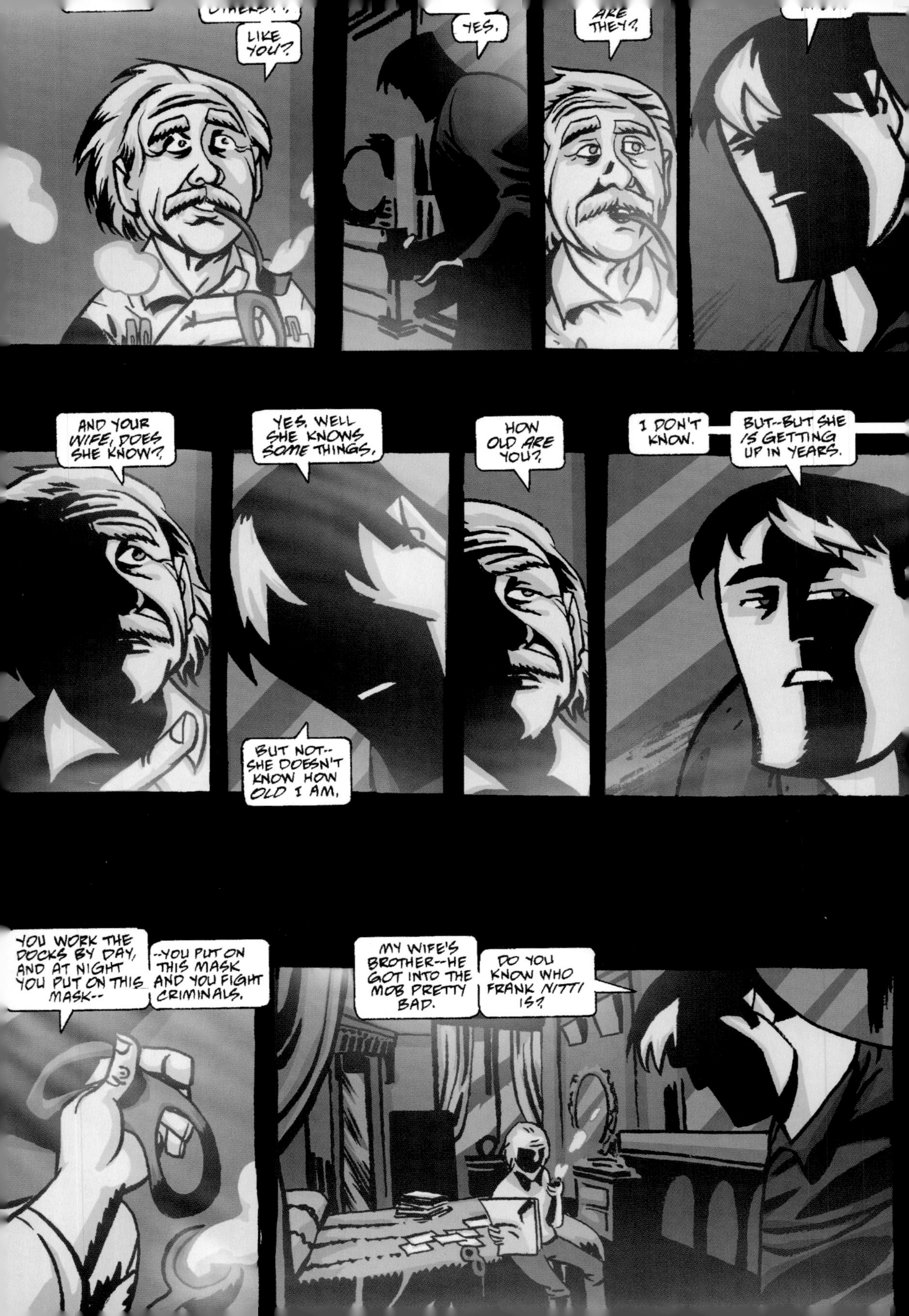

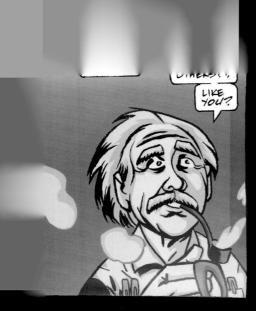

LIKE YOU?
YES.
ARE THEY?
AND YOUR WIFE, DOES SHE KNOW?
YES. WELL SHE KNOWS SOME THINGS.
BUT NOT--SHE DOESN'T KNOW HOW OLD I AM.
HOW OLD ARE YOU?
I DON'T KNOW.
BUT--BUT SHE IS GETTING UP IN YEARS.
YOU WORK THE DOCKS BY DAY, AND AT NIGHT YOU PUT ON THIS MASK--
--YOU PUT ON THIS MASK AND YOU FIGHT CRIMINALS.
MY WIFE'S BROTHER--HE GOT INTO THE MOB PRETTY BAD.
DO YOU KNOW WHO FRANK NITTI IS?

I THINK--I WAS IN CHINA WITH SOME OF THEM.

MANY, MANY YEARS YEARS AGO I WAS IN CHINA.

AND I--I LEFT. I WENT TO LONDON.

AND I WENT ALONE.

GOD, I CAN'T REMEMBER WHY I LEFT.

AND YOU SAY YOU JUST--YOU WORK THE DOCKS ALL DAY.

YOU HAVE A WIFE?

YES-- ROSALITA.

WE'VE BEEN TOGETHER FOR QUITE A WHILE, AND SHE IS GETTING OLDER, AND--

--AND IT'S GOING TO BE SOMETHING WE HAVE TO DISCUSS SOON, IT'S--

--SHE'S SICK A LOT.

SHE AGES-- AND YOU DO NOT.

THAT--Y THAT'S O THE REA I CAME TALK T

NO.

PIECE OF GARBAGE TOOK OVER FOR AL CAPONE AFTER THEY PUT HIM AWAY.

I KNOW THIS AL CAPONE PERSON.

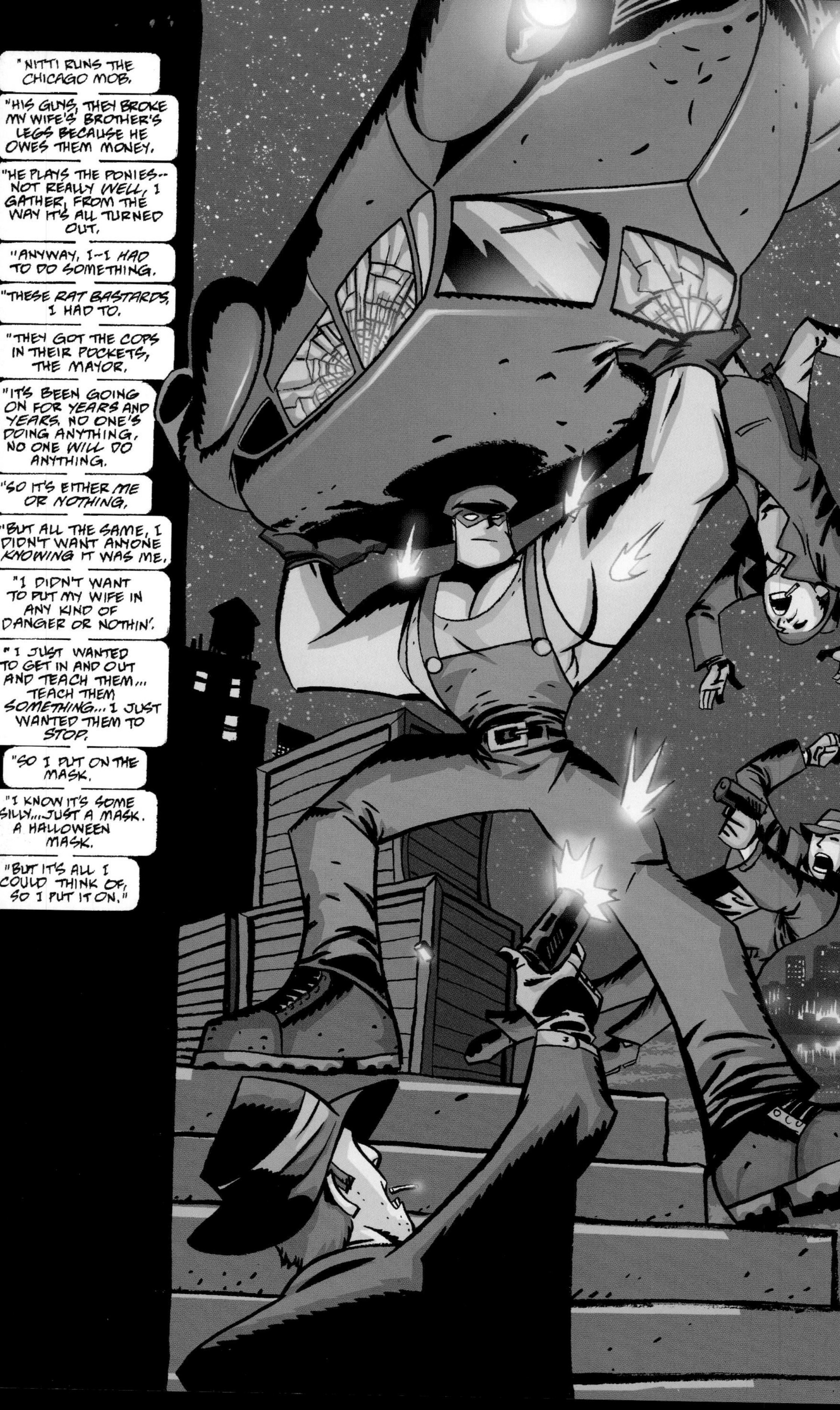
"NITTI RUNS THE CHICAGO MOB.
"HIS GUNS, THEY BROKE MY WIFE'S BROTHER'S LEGS BECAUSE HE OWES THEM MONEY.
"HE PLAYS THE PONIES-- NOT REALLY WELL, I GATHER, FROM THE WAY IT'S ALL TURNED OUT.
"ANYWAY, I--I HAD TO DO SOMETHING.
"THESE RAT BASTARDS, I HAD TO.
"THEY GOT THE COPS IN THEIR POCKETS, THE MAYOR.
"IT'S BEEN GOING ON FOR YEARS AND YEARS. NO ONE'S DOING ANYTHING, NO ONE WILL DO ANYTHING.
"SO IT'S EITHER ME OR NOTHING.
"BUT ALL THE SAME, I DIDN'T WANT ANYONE KNOWING IT WAS ME.
"I DIDN'T WANT TO PUT MY WIFE IN ANY KIND OF DANGER OR NOTHIN'.
"I JUST WANTED TO GET IN AND OUT AND TEACH THEM... TEACH THEM SOMETHING... I JUST WANTED THEM TO STOP.
"SO I PUT ON THE MASK.
"I KNOW IT'S SOME SILLY... JUST A MASK. A HALLOWEEN MASK.
"BUT IT'S ALL I COULD THINK OF, SO I PUT IT ON."

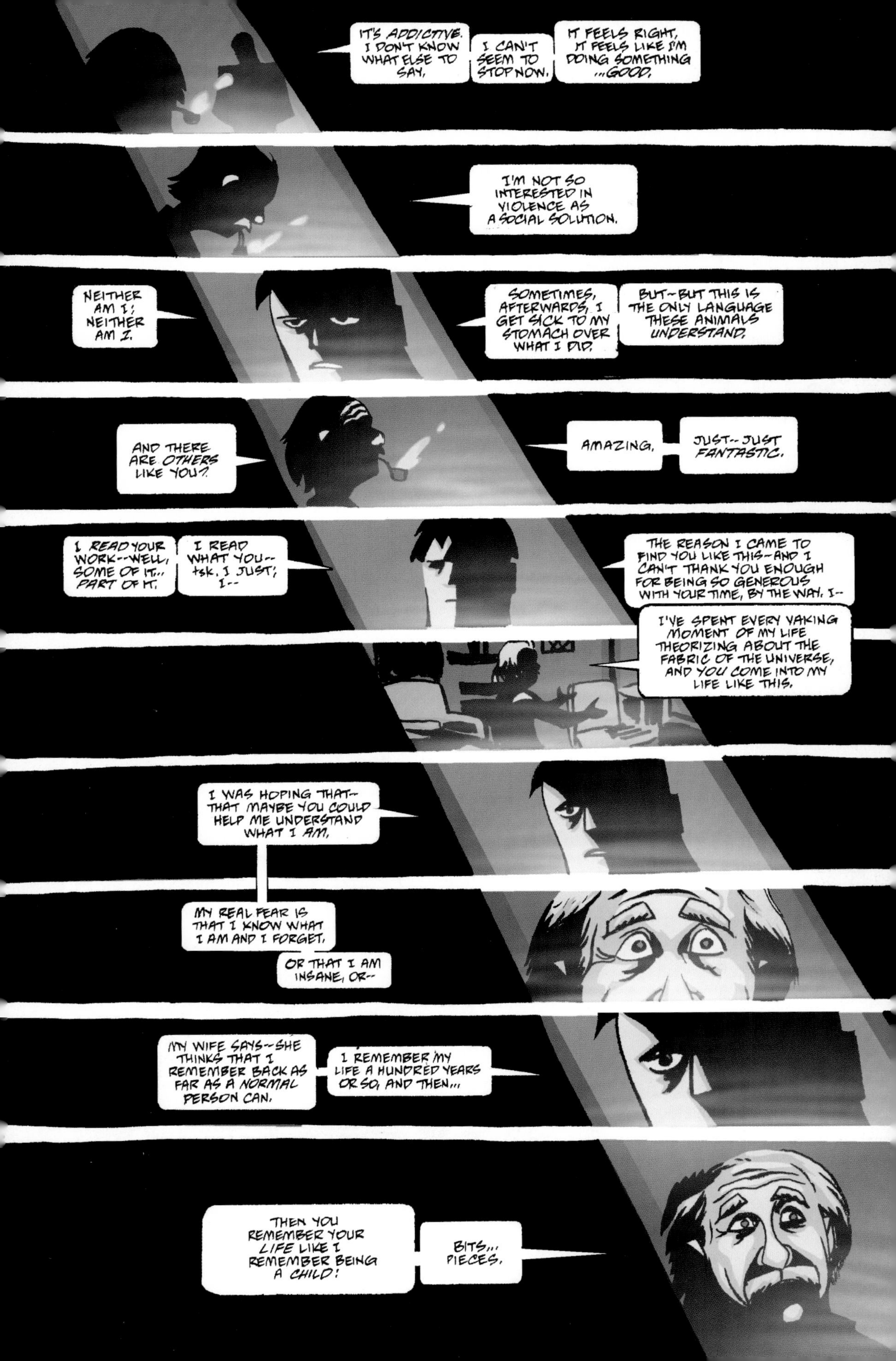
IT'S ADDICTIVE. I DON'T KNOW WHAT ELSE TO SAY.
I CAN'T SEEM TO STOP NOW.
IT FEELS RIGHT, IT FEELS LIKE I'M DOING SOMETHING ...GOOD.
I'M NOT SO INTERESTED IN VIOLENCE AS A SOCIAL SOLUTION.
NEITHER AM I; NEITHER AM I.
SOMETIMES, AFTERWARDS, I GET SICK TO MY STOMACH OVER WHAT I DID.
BUT--BUT THIS IS THE ONLY LANGUAGE THESE ANIMALS UNDERSTAND.
AND THERE ARE OTHERS LIKE YOU?
AMAZING.
JUST--JUST FANTASTIC.
I READ YOUR WORK--WELL, SOME OF IT... PART OF IT.
I READ WHAT YOU-- tsk. I JUST; I--
THE REASON I CAME TO FIND YOU LIKE THIS--AND I CAN'T THANK YOU ENOUGH FOR BEING SO GENEROUS WITH YOUR TIME, BY THE WAY. I--
I'VE SPENT EVERY WAKING MOMENT OF MY LIFE THEORIZING ABOUT THE FABRIC OF THE UNIVERSE, AND YOU COME INTO MY LIFE LIKE THIS.
I WAS HOPING THAT--THAT MAYBE YOU COULD HELP ME UNDERSTAND WHAT I AM.
MY REAL FEAR IS THAT I KNOW WHAT I AM AND I FORGET.
OR THAT I AM INSANE, OR--
MY WIFE SAYS--SHE THINKS THAT I REMEMBER BACK AS FAR AS A NORMAL PERSON CAN.
I REMEMBER MY LIFE A HUNDRED YEARS OR SO, AND THEN...
THEN YOU REMEMBER YOUR LIFE LIKE I REMEMBER BEING A CHILD!
BITS... PIECES.

YES!!! YES, EXACTLY.

I'M EMBARRASSED BY THIS, YOU KNOW.

IT'S--TO THINK THAT I CAN DO ALL THIS, AND I FORGOT HOW AND WHY--

THAT SEEMS-- I MEAN, WHY CAN I FLY?

HOW IN GOD'S EARTH CAN I FLY??

GOD'S EARTH-- INTERESTING VORDS YOU CHOOSE.

LISTEN TO ME.

I HAVE A FRIEND-- AN ACQUAINTANCE--

AND LIKE SO MANY OF MY ACQUAINTANCES--ZEY TRY TO SAY THINGS TO ME ZEY SINK WOULD IMPRESS ME.

THIS ONE ACQUAINTANCE SAID TO ME, "MAN LEARNED TO WALK UPRIGHT. HE LEARNED TO RUN ON HIS TWO LEGS--

"AND THEN WHAT?"

THIS ACQUAINTANCE SAID, "MAN STOOD UP-- HE STOOD UPRIGHT-- AND SAID, 'THIS IS FINE!'"

BUT, YOU-- YOU KEEP GOING.

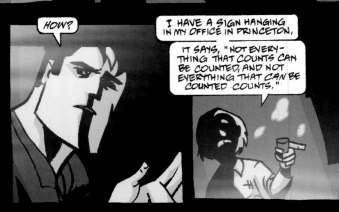

HOW?

I HAVE A SIGN HANGING IN MY OFFICE IN PRINCETON.

IT SAYS, "NOT EVERY- THING THAT COUNTS CAN BE COUNTED, AND NOT EVERYTHING THAT CAN BE COUNTED COUNTS."

WHAT DOES THAT MEAN?

NOT EVERYTHING THAT COUNTS CAN BE COUNTED... AND NOT EVERYTHING THAT CAN BE COUNTED... COUNTS.

(I'M FORGETTING WHY I CAME TO SEE YOU.)

I GET THAT A LOT.

--I NEED TO KNOW WHY!!

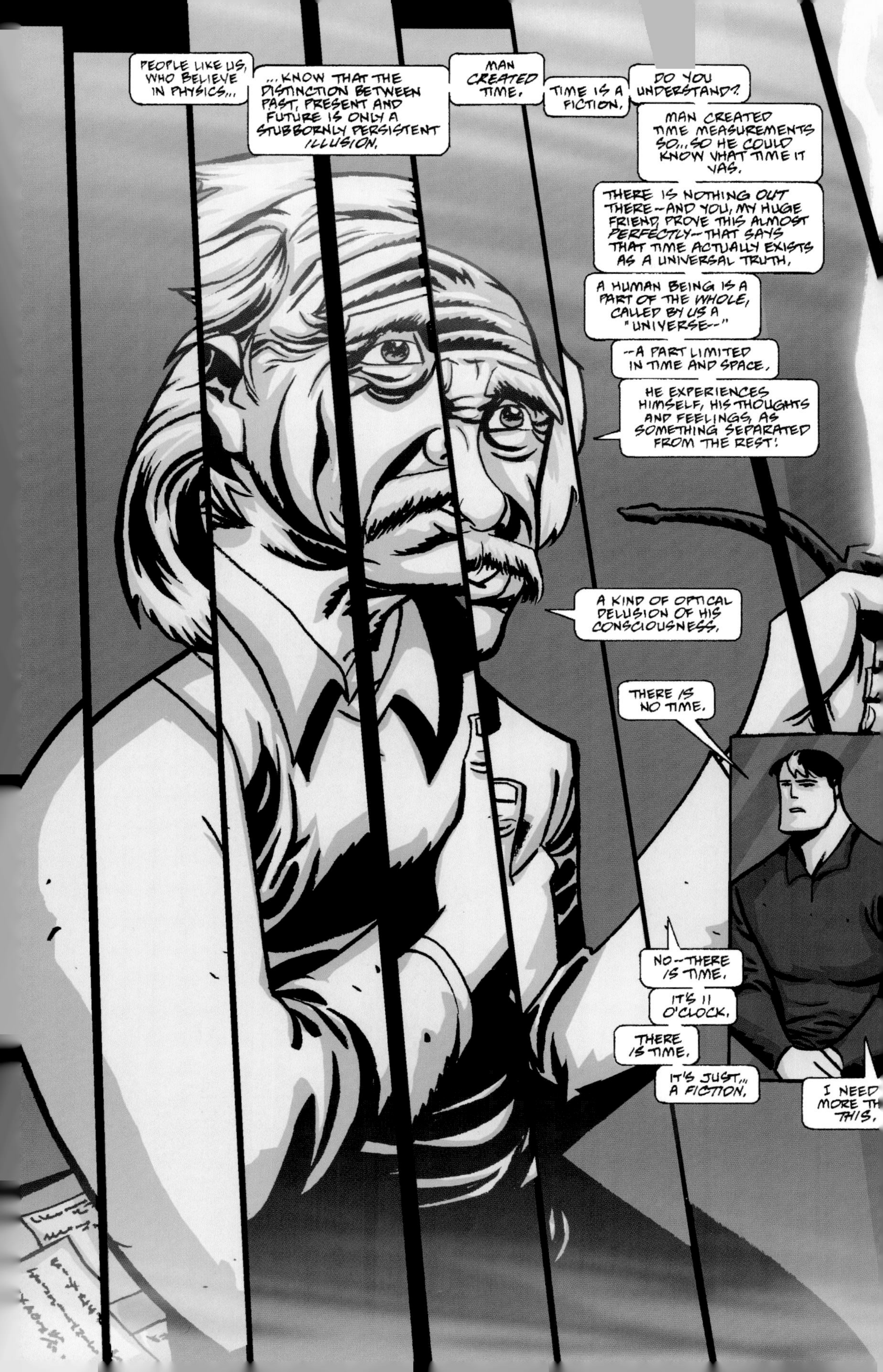
PEOPLE LIKE US, WHO BELIEVE IN PHYSICS...
...KNOW THAT THE DISTINCTION BETWEEN PAST, PRESENT AND FUTURE IS ONLY A STUBBORNLY PERSISTENT ILLUSION.
MAN CREATED TIME.
TIME IS A FICTION.
DO YOU UNDERSTAND?
MAN CREATED TIME MEASUREMENTS SO...SO HE COULD KNOW VHAT TIME IT VAS.
THERE IS NOTHING OUT THERE--AND YOU, MY HUGE FRIEND PROVE THIS ALMOST PERFECTLY--THAT SAYS THAT TIME ACTUALLY EXISTS AS A UNIVERSAL TRUTH.
A HUMAN BEING IS A PART OF THE WHOLE, CALLED BY US A "UNIVERSE--"
--A PART LIMITED IN TIME AND SPACE.
HE EXPERIENCES HIMSELF, HIS THOUGHTS AND FEELINGS, AS SOMETHING SEPARATED FROM THE REST!
A KIND OF OPTICAL DELUSION OF HIS CONSCIOUSNESS.
THERE IS NO TIME.
NO--THERE IS TIME.
IT'S 11 O'CLOCK.
THERE IS TIME.
IT'S JUST... A FICTION.
I NEED MORE TH THIS.

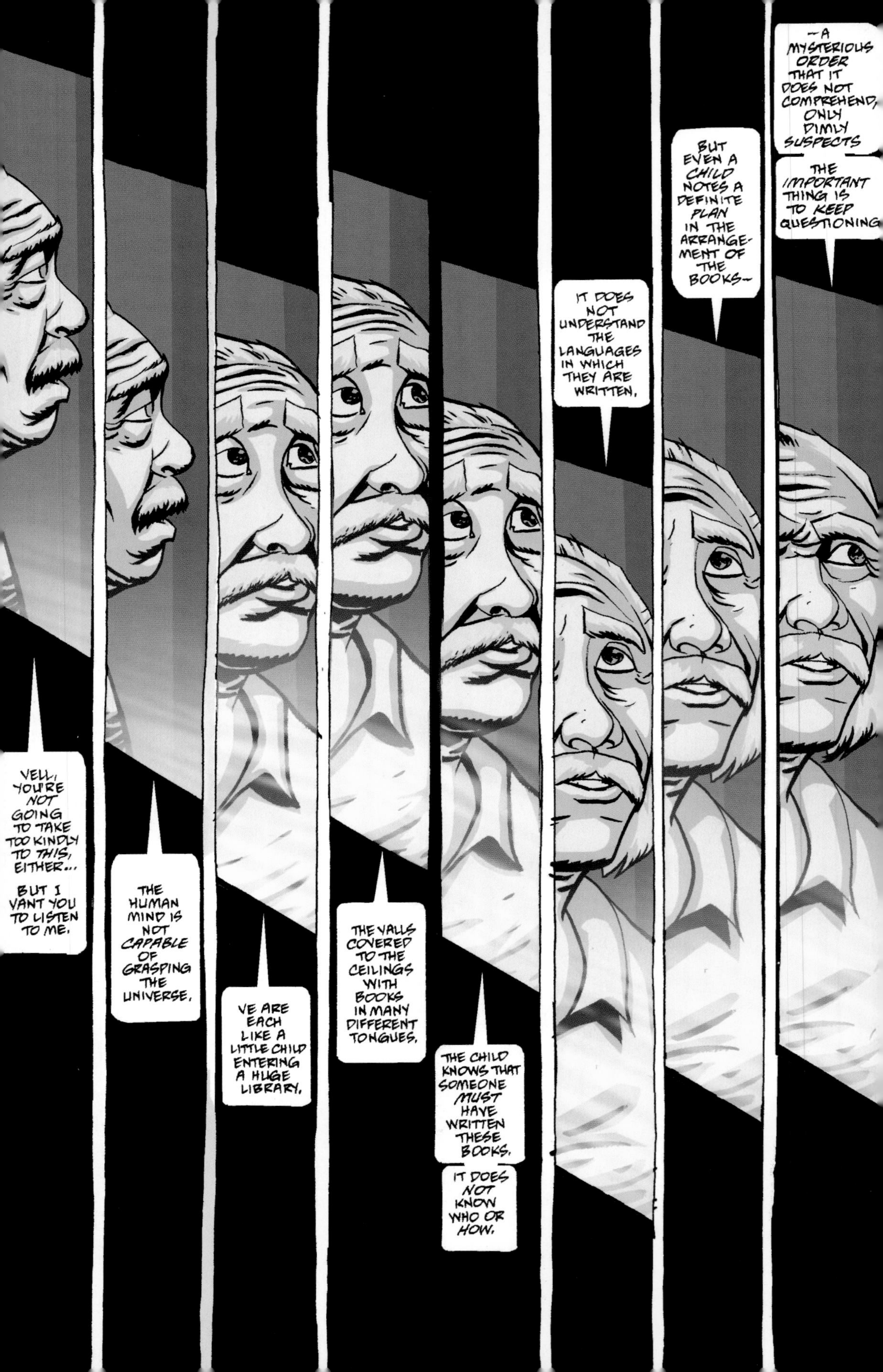
VELL, YOU'RE NOT GOING TO TAKE TOO KINDLY TO THIS, EITHER...
BUT I VANT YOU TO LISTEN TO ME.
THE HUMAN MIND IS NOT CAPABLE OF GRASPING THE UNIVERSE.
VE ARE EACH LIKE A LITTLE CHILD ENTERING A HUGE LIBRARY.
THE VALLS COVERED TO THE CEILINGS WITH BOOKS IN MANY DIFFERENT TONGUES.
THE CHILD KNOWS THAT SOMEONE MUST HAVE WRITTEN THESE BOOKS.
IT DOES NOT KNOW WHO OR HOW.
IT DOES NOT UNDERSTAND THE LANGUAGES IN WHICH THEY ARE WRITTEN.
BUT EVEN A CHILD NOTES A DEFINITE PLAN IN THE ARRANGEMENT OF THE BOOKS--
--A MYSTERIOUS ORDER THAT IT DOES NOT COMPREHEND, ONLY DIMLY SUSPECTS
THE IMPORTANT THING IS TO KEEP QUESTIONING

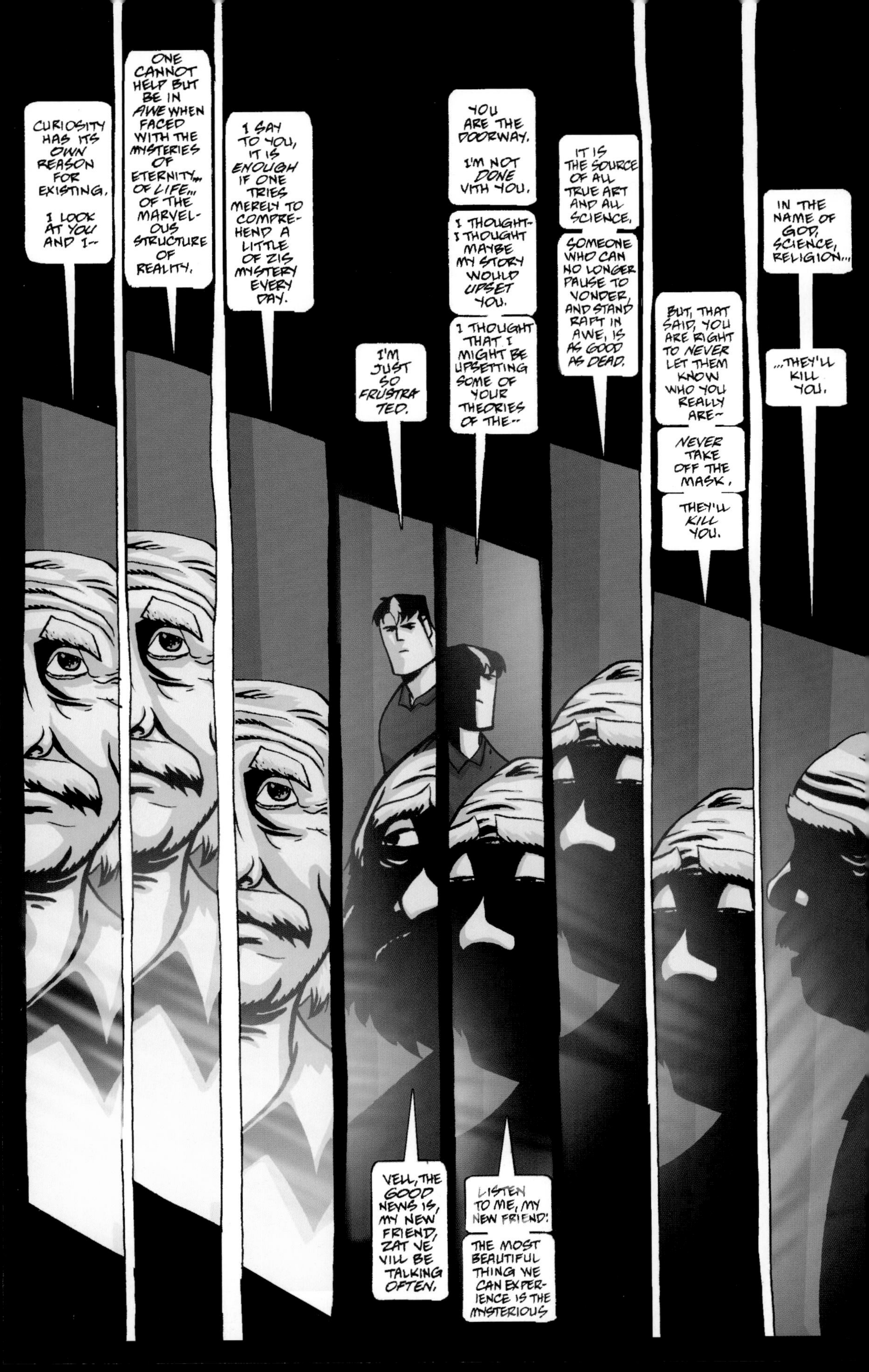
CURIOSITY HAS ITS OWN REASON FOR EXISTING.
I LOOK AT YOU AND I--
ONE CANNOT HELP BUT BE IN AWE WHEN FACED WITH THE MYSTERIES OF ETERNITY... OF LIFE... OF THE MARVELOUS STRUCTURE OF REALITY.
I SAY TO YOU, IT IS ENOUGH IF ONE TRIES MERELY TO COMPREHEND A LITTLE OF ZIS MYSTERY EVERY DAY.
I'M JUST SO FRUSTRATED.
VELL, THE GOOD NEWS IS, MY NEW FRIEND, ZAT VE VILL BE TALKING OFTEN.
YOU ARE THE DOORWAY.
I'M NOT DONE VITH YOU.
I THOUGHT-- I THOUGHT MAYBE MY STORY WOULD UPSET YOU.
I THOUGHT THAT I MIGHT BE UPSETTING SOME OF YOUR THEORIES OF THE--
LISTEN TO ME, MY NEW FRIEND!
THE MOST BEAUTIFUL THING WE CAN EXPERIENCE IS THE MYSTERIOUS
IT IS THE SOURCE OF ALL TRUE ART AND ALL SCIENCE.
SOMEONE WHO CAN NO LONGER PAUSE TO VONDER, AND STAND RAPT IN AWE, IS AS GOOD AS DEAD.
BUT, THAT SAID, YOU ARE RIGHT TO NEVER LET THEM KNOW WHO YOU REALLY ARE--
NEVER TAKE OFF THE MASK.
THEY'LL KILL YOU.
IN THE NAME OF GOD, SCIENCE, RELIGION...
...THEY'LL KILL YOU.

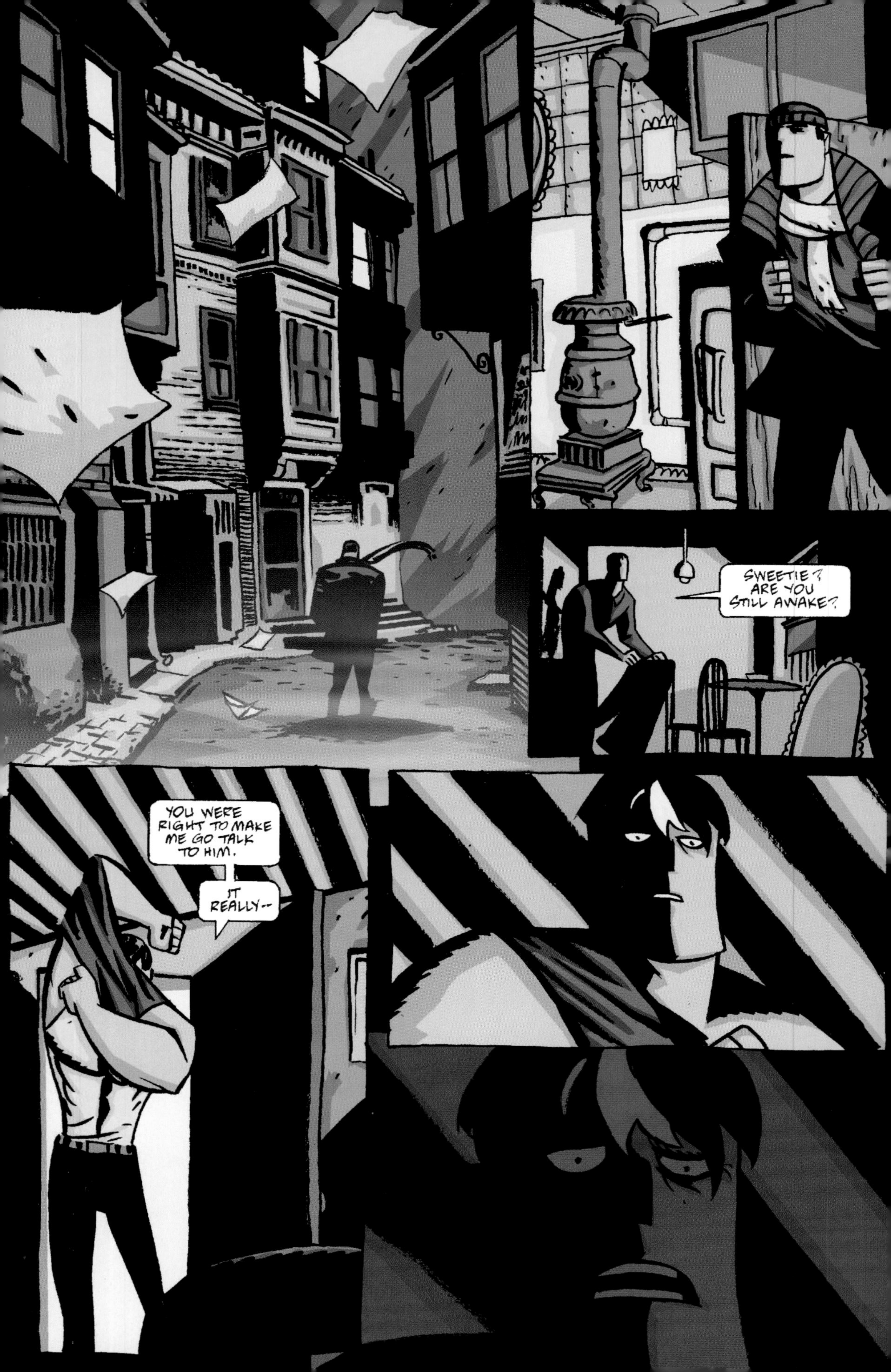
SWEETIE? ARE YOU STILL AWAKE?
YOU WERE RIGHT TO MAKE ME GO TALK TO HIM.
IT REALLY--

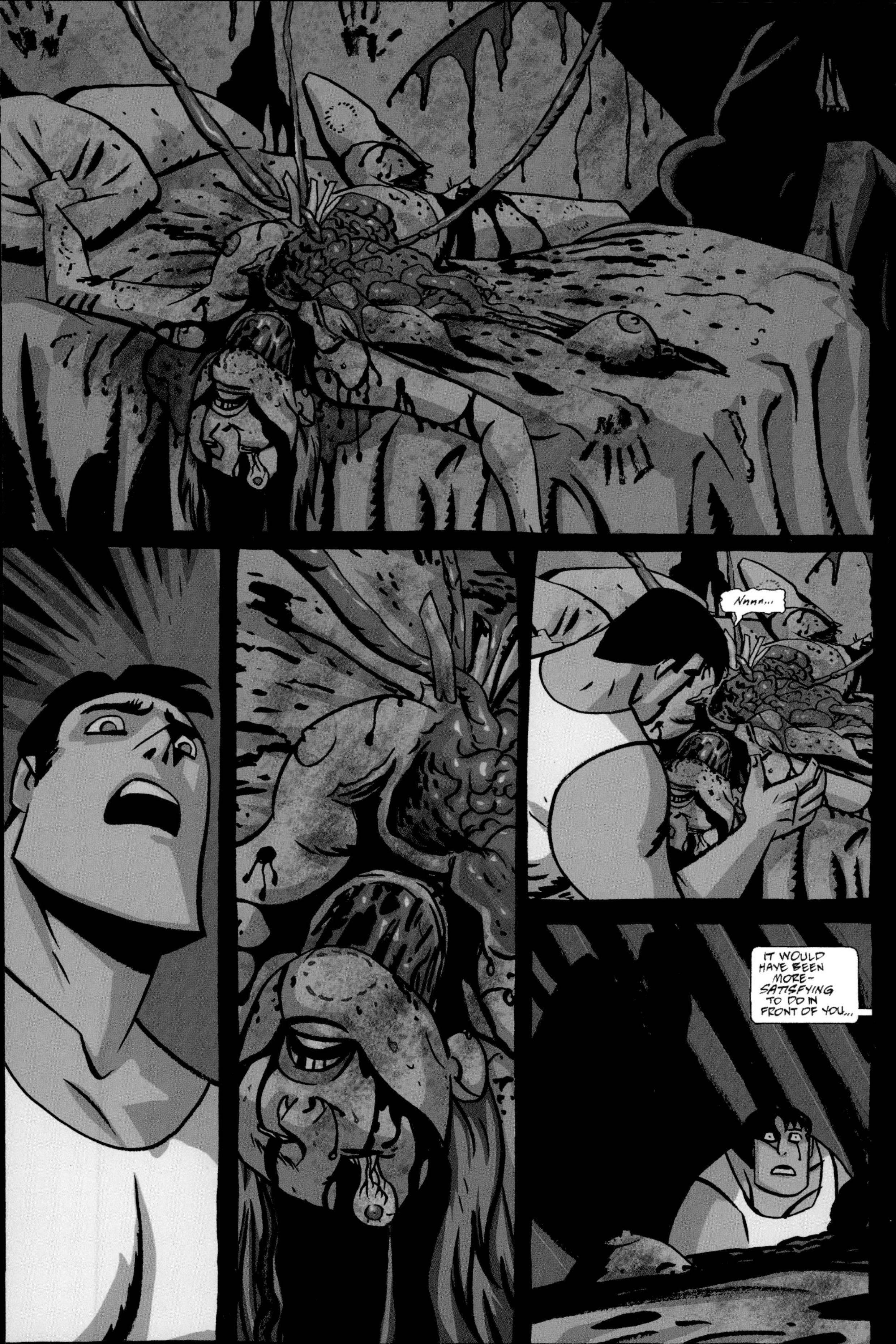
Nnnn...
IT WOULD HAVE BEEN MORE-SATISFYING TO DO IN FRONT OF YOU...

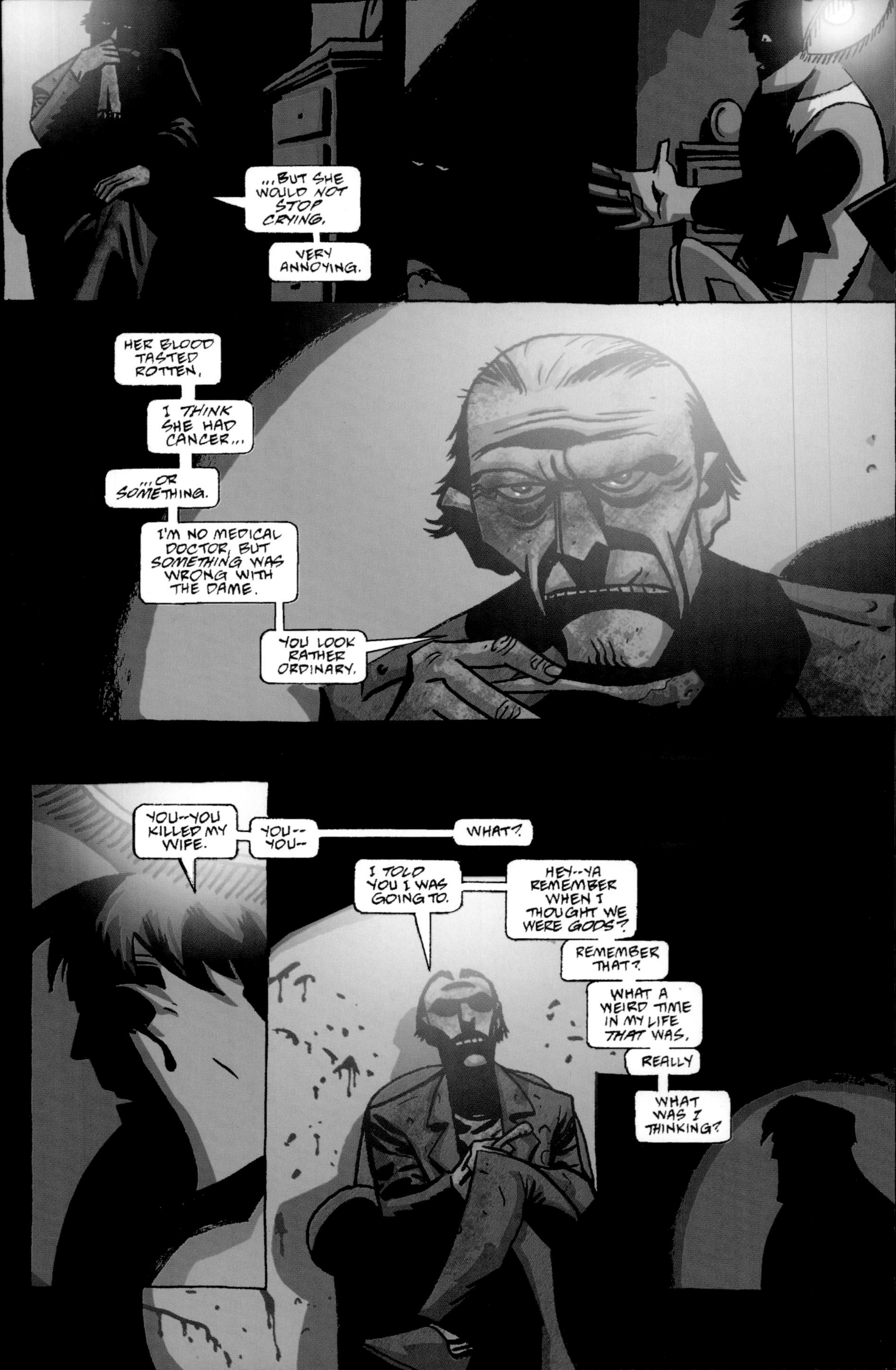
...BUT SHE WOULD NOT STOP CRYING.
VERY ANNOYING.
HER BLOOD TASTED ROTTEN.
I THINK SHE HAD CANCER...
...OR SOMETHING.
I'M NO MEDICAL DOCTOR, BUT SOMETHING WAS WRONG WITH THE DAME.
YOU LOOK RATHER ORDINARY.
YOU--YOU KILLED MY WIFE.
YOU-- YOU--
WHAT?
I TOLD YOU I WAS GOING TO.
HEY--YA REMEMBER WHEN I THOUGHT WE WERE GODS?
REMEMBER THAT?
WHAT A WEIRD TIME IN MY LIFE THAT WAS.
REALLY
WHAT WAS I THINKING?

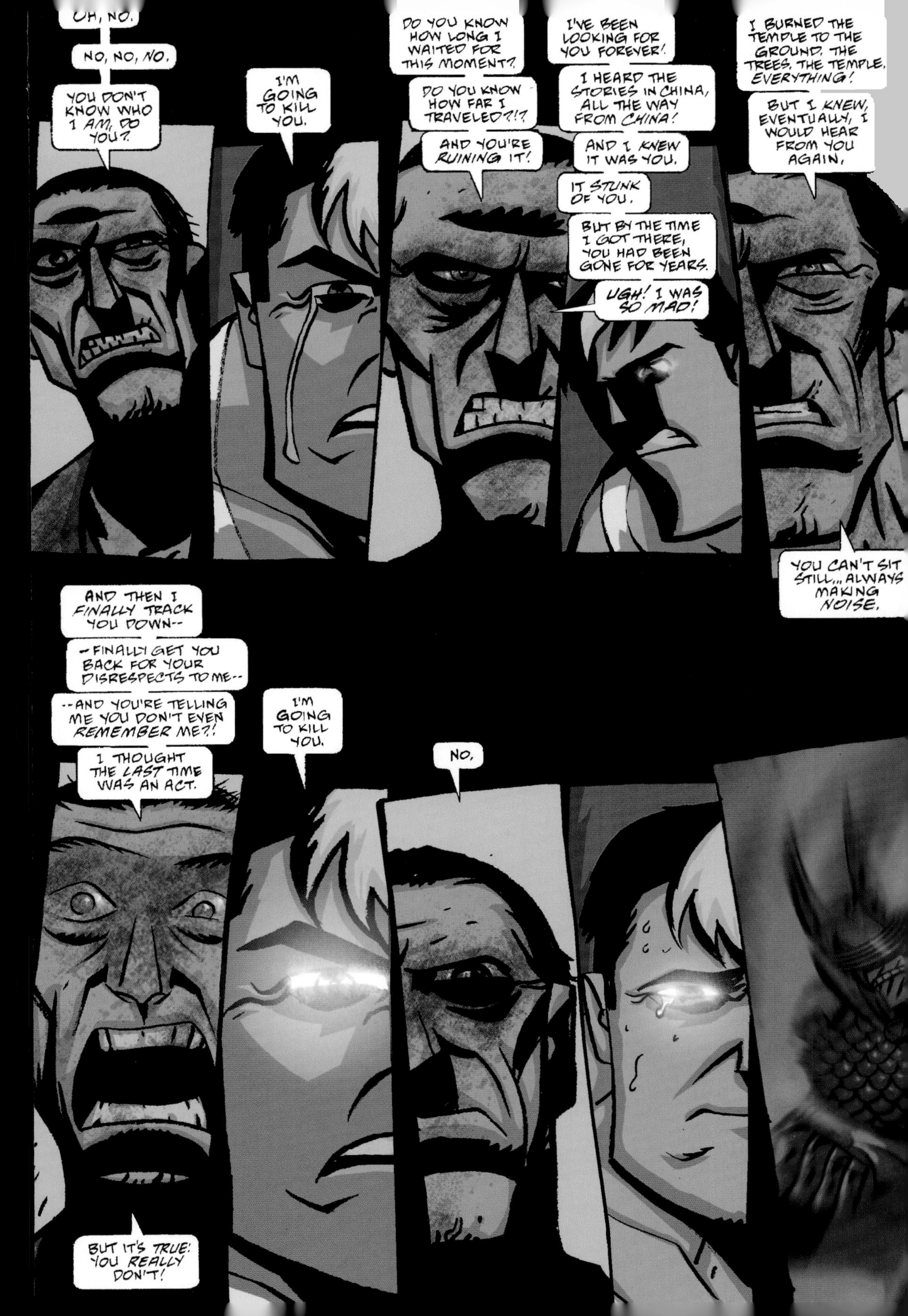
OH, NO.
NO, NO, NO.
YOU DON'T KNOW WHO I AM, DO YOU?
I'M GOING TO KILL YOU.
DO YOU KNOW HOW LONG I WAITED FOR THIS MOMENT?
DO YOU KNOW HOW FAR I TRAVELED?!?
AND YOU'RE RUINING IT!
I'VE BEEN LOOKING FOR YOU FOREVER!
I HEARD THE STORIES IN CHINA, ALL THE WAY FROM CHINA!
AND I KNEW IT WAS YOU.
IT STUNK OF YOU.
BUT BY THE TIME I GOT THERE, YOU HAD BEEN GONE FOR YEARS.
UGH! I WAS SO MAD!
I BURNED THE TEMPLE TO THE GROUND. THE TREES. THE TEMPLE. EVERYTHING!
BUT I KNEW, EVENTUALLY, I WOULD HEAR FROM YOU AGAIN.
YOU CAN'T SIT STILL... ALWAYS MAKING NOISE.
AND THEN I FINALLY TRACK YOU DOWN--
--FINALLY GET YOU BACK FOR YOUR DISRESPECTS TO ME--
--AND YOU'RE TELLING ME YOU DON'T EVEN REMEMBER ME?!
I THOUGHT THE LAST TIME WAS AN ACT.
I'M GOING TO KILL YOU.
NO.
BUT IT'S TRUE! YOU REALLY DON'T!

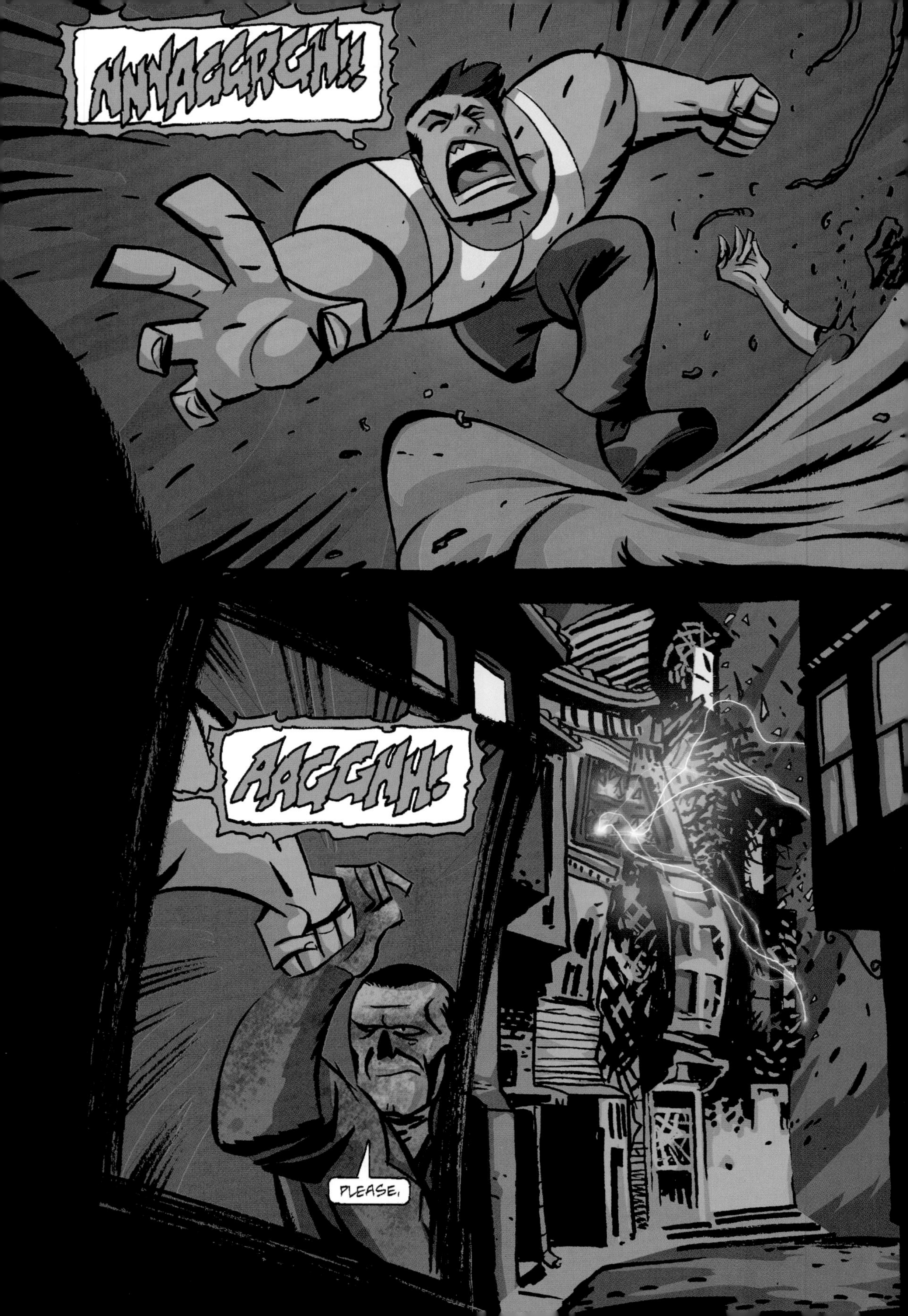
NNYAGGRGH!!
AAGGHH!
PLEASE.

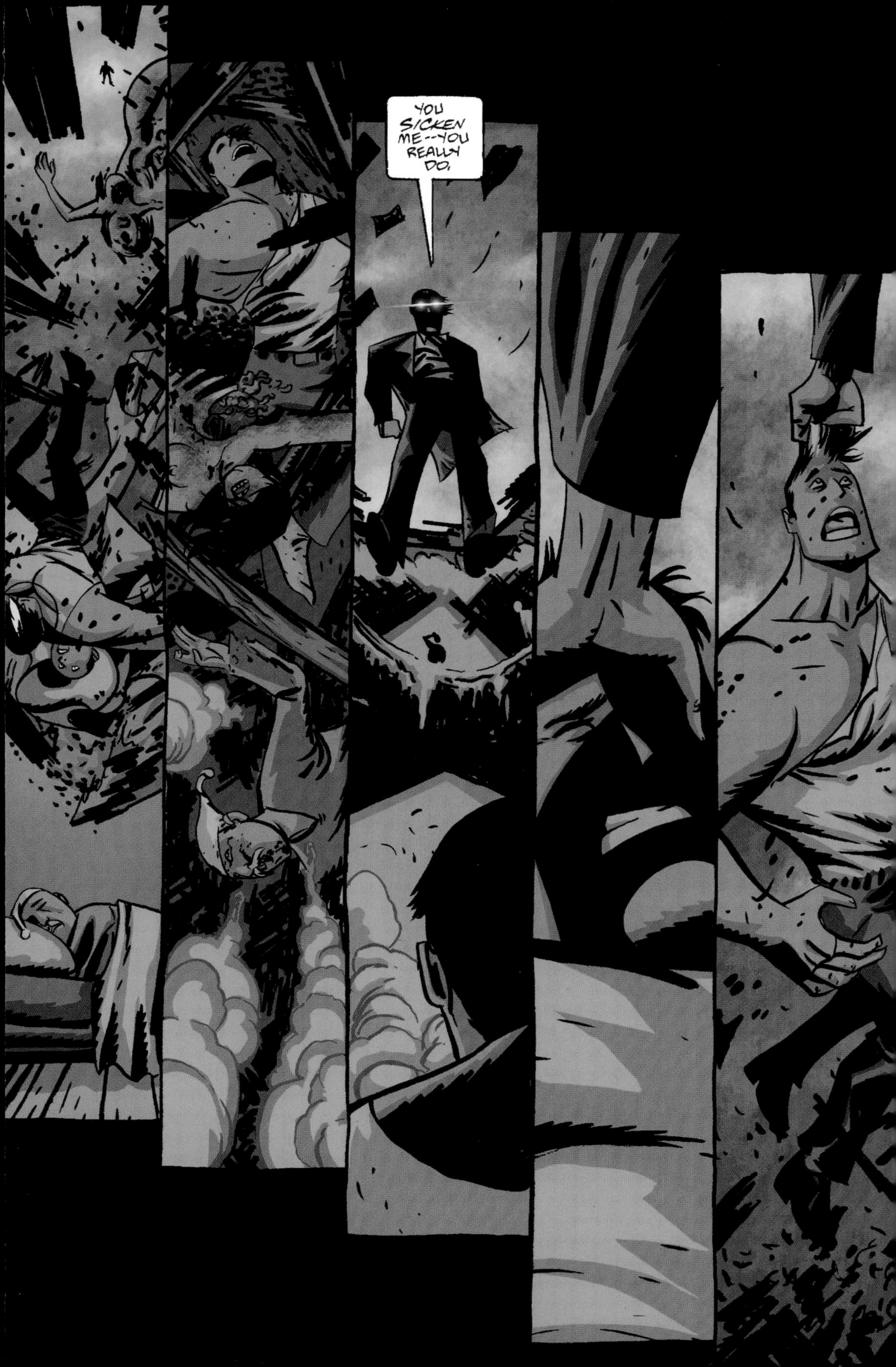
YOU SICKEN ME--YOU REALLY DO.

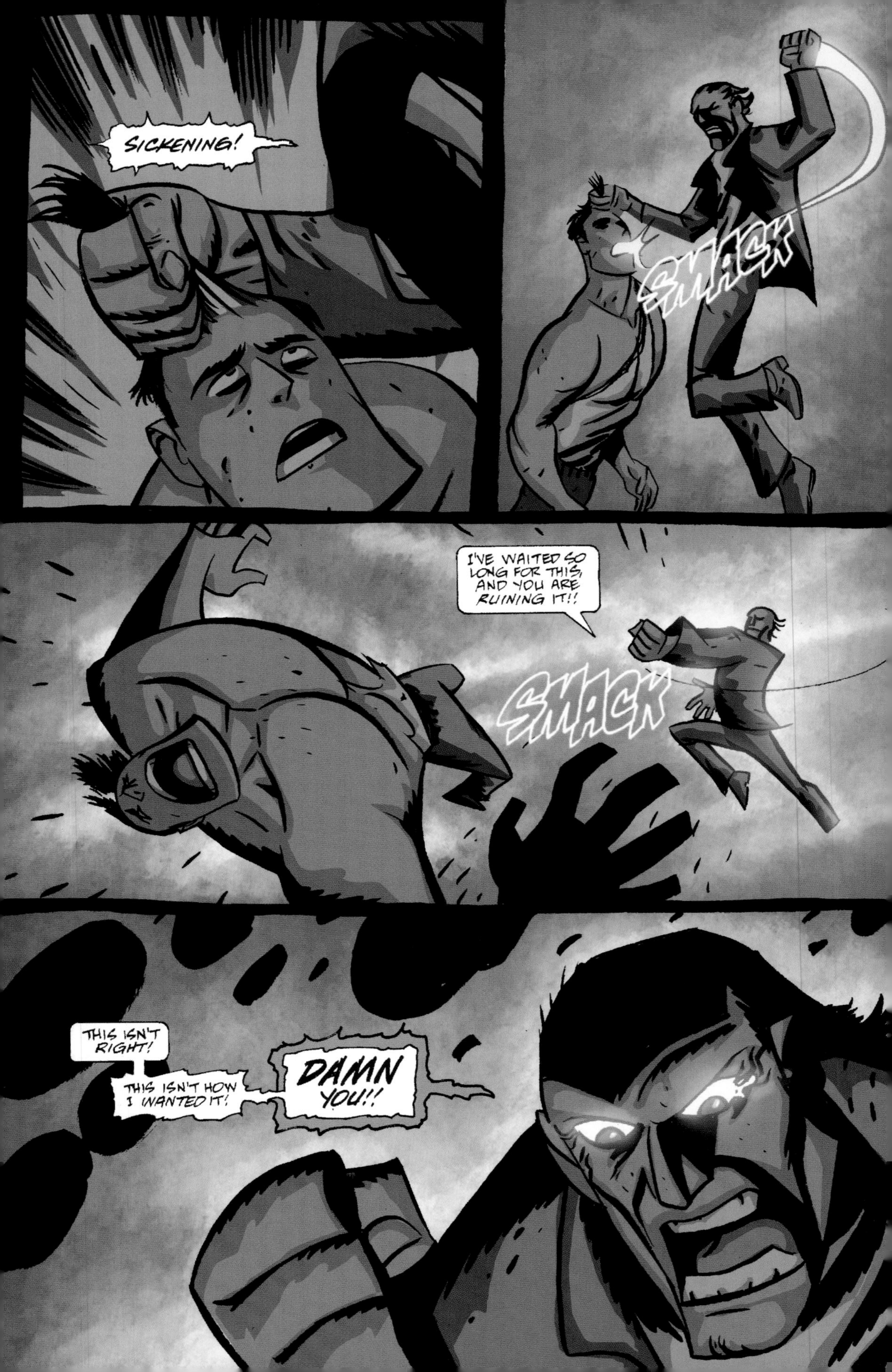
SICKENING!
SMACK
I'VE WAITED SO LONG FOR THIS, AND YOU ARE RUINING IT!!
SMACK
THIS ISN'T RIGHT!
THIS ISN'T HOW I WANTED IT!
DAMN YOU!!

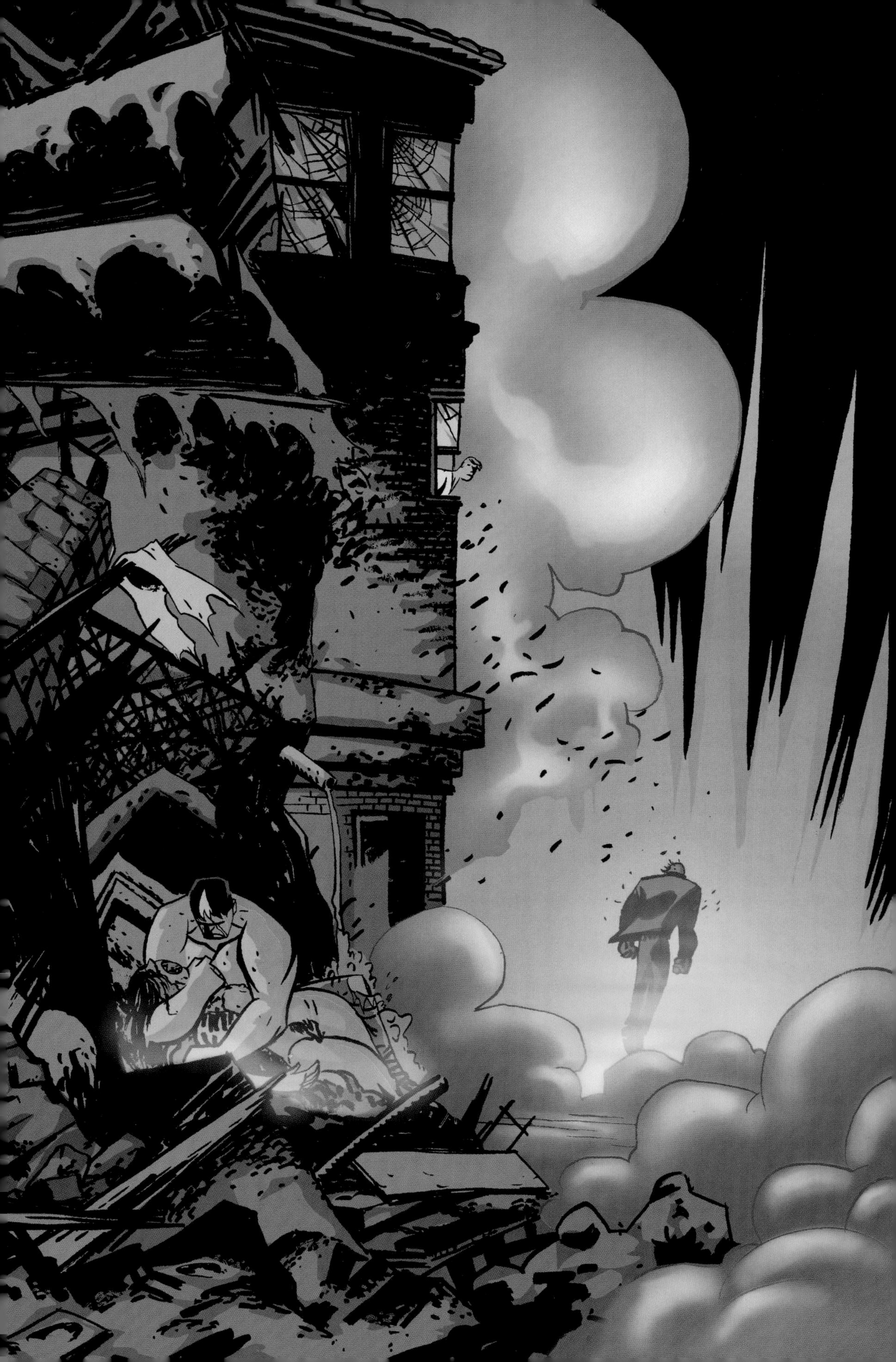

# 1986

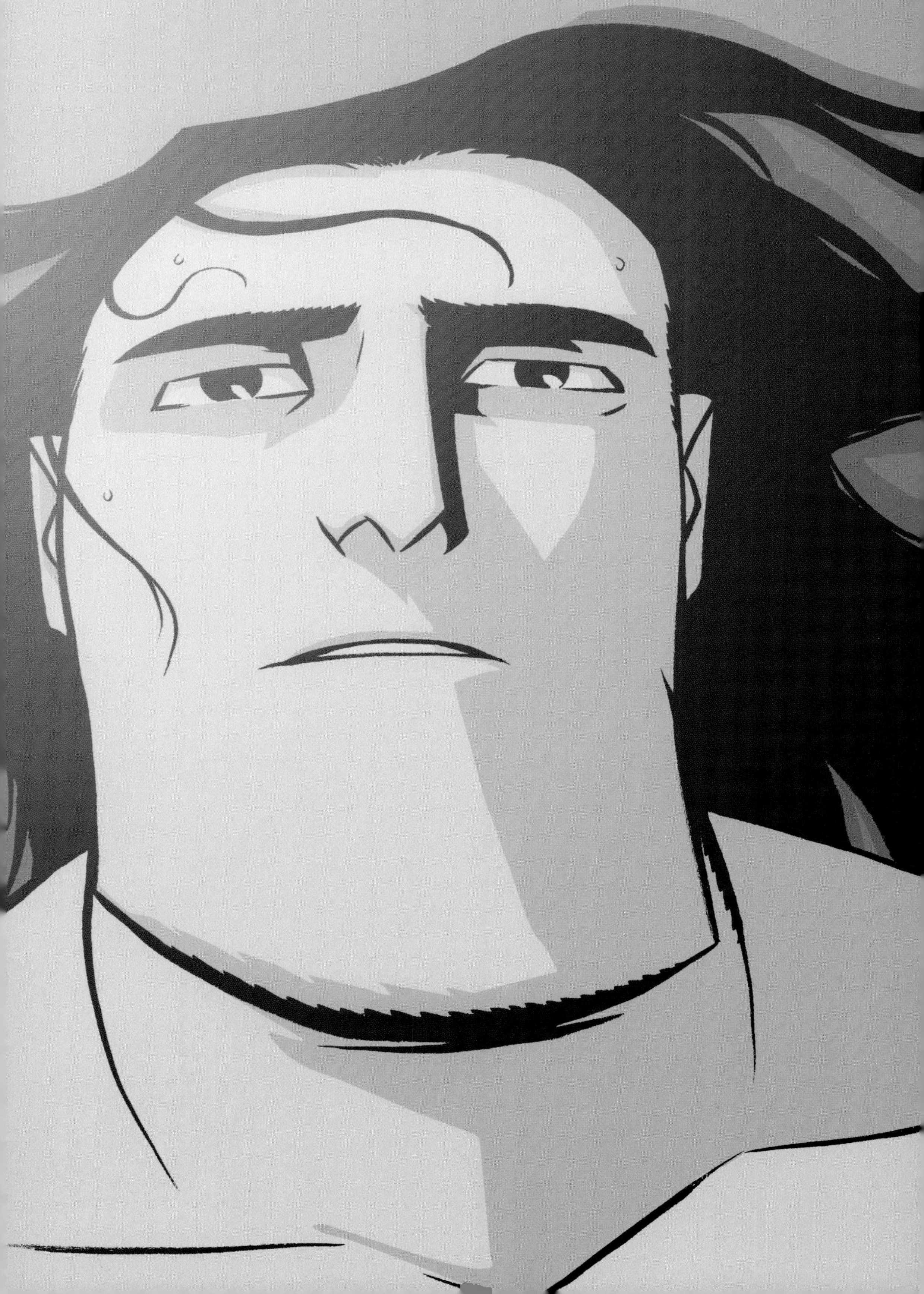

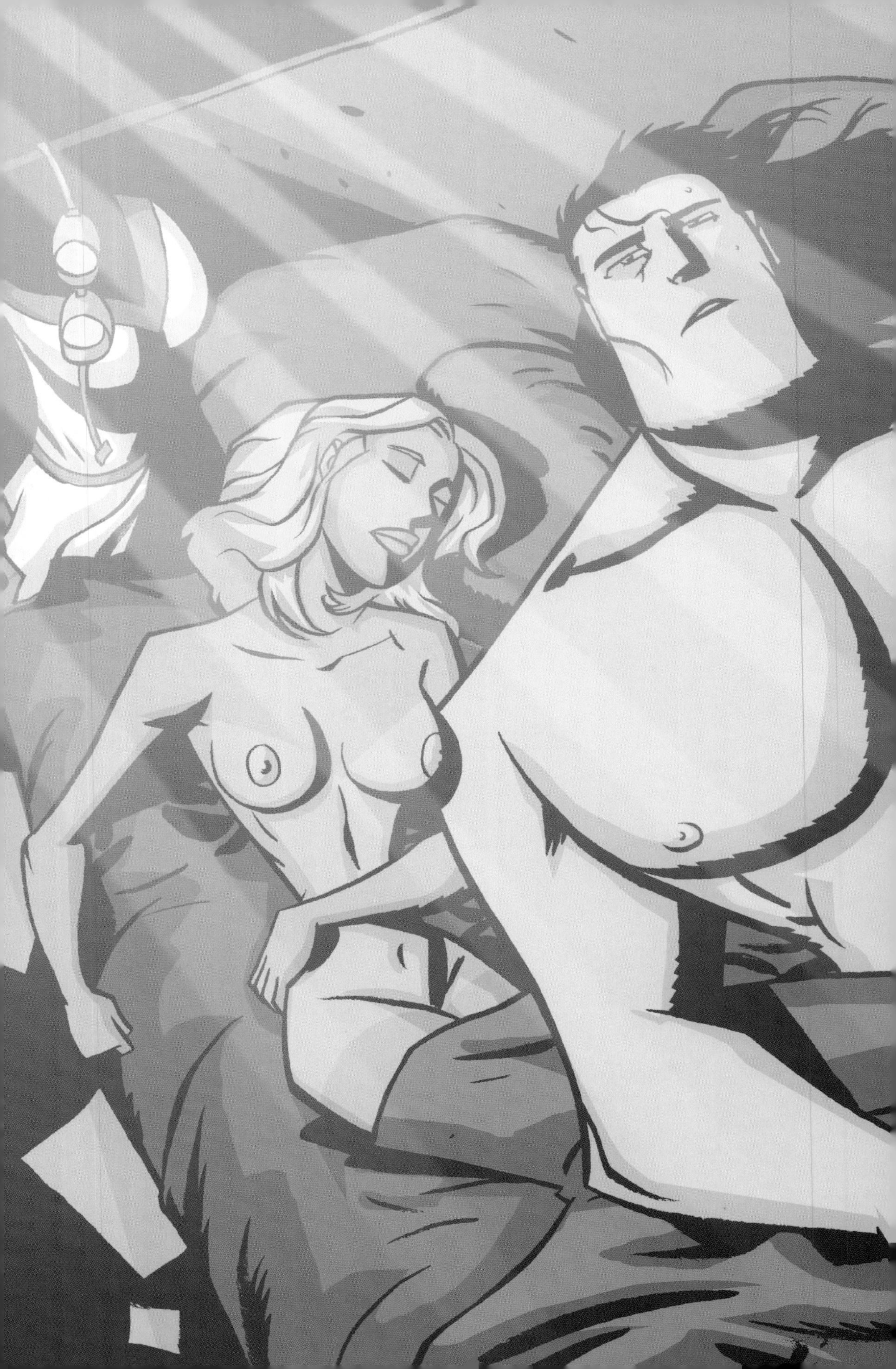

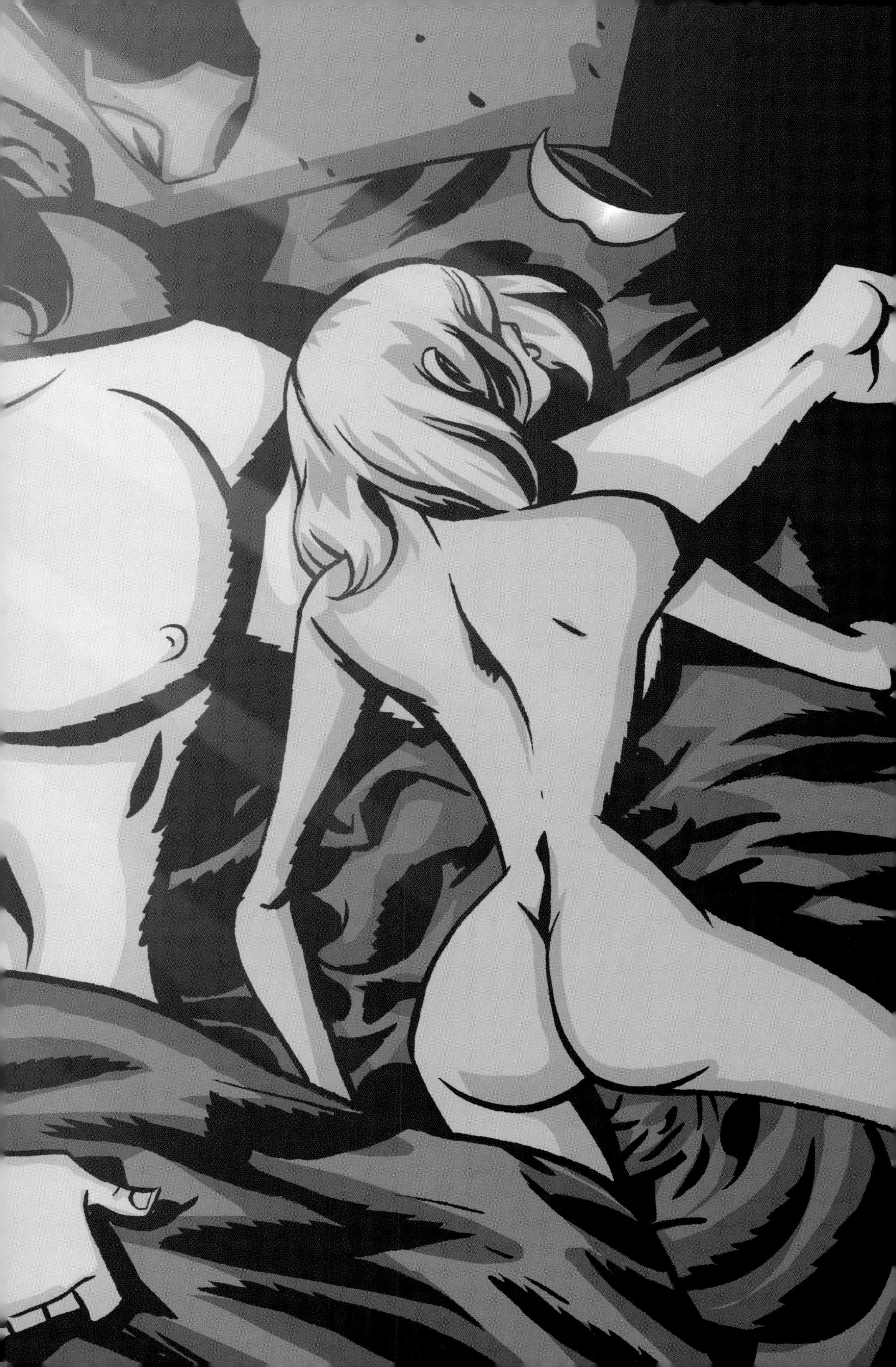

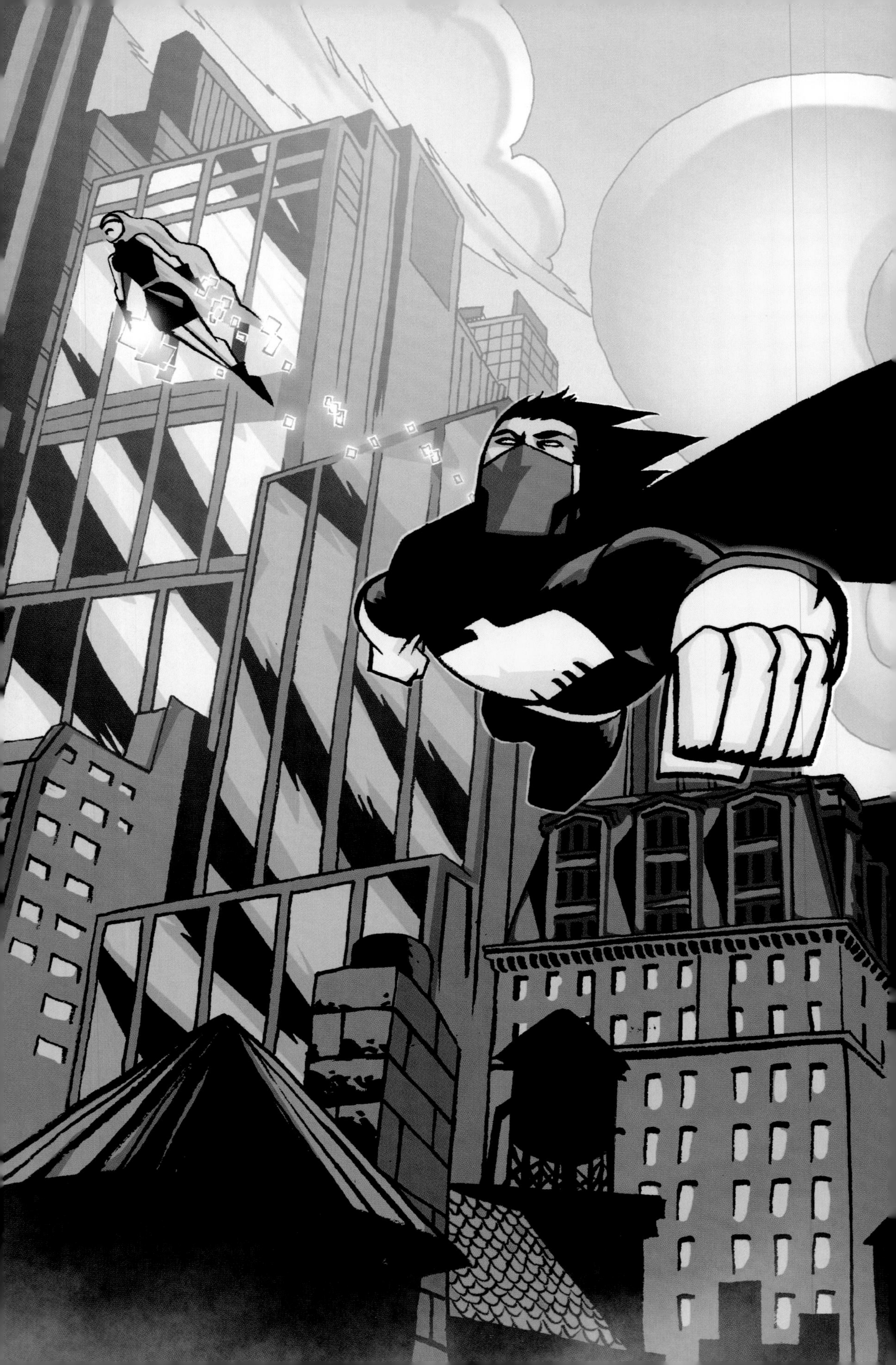

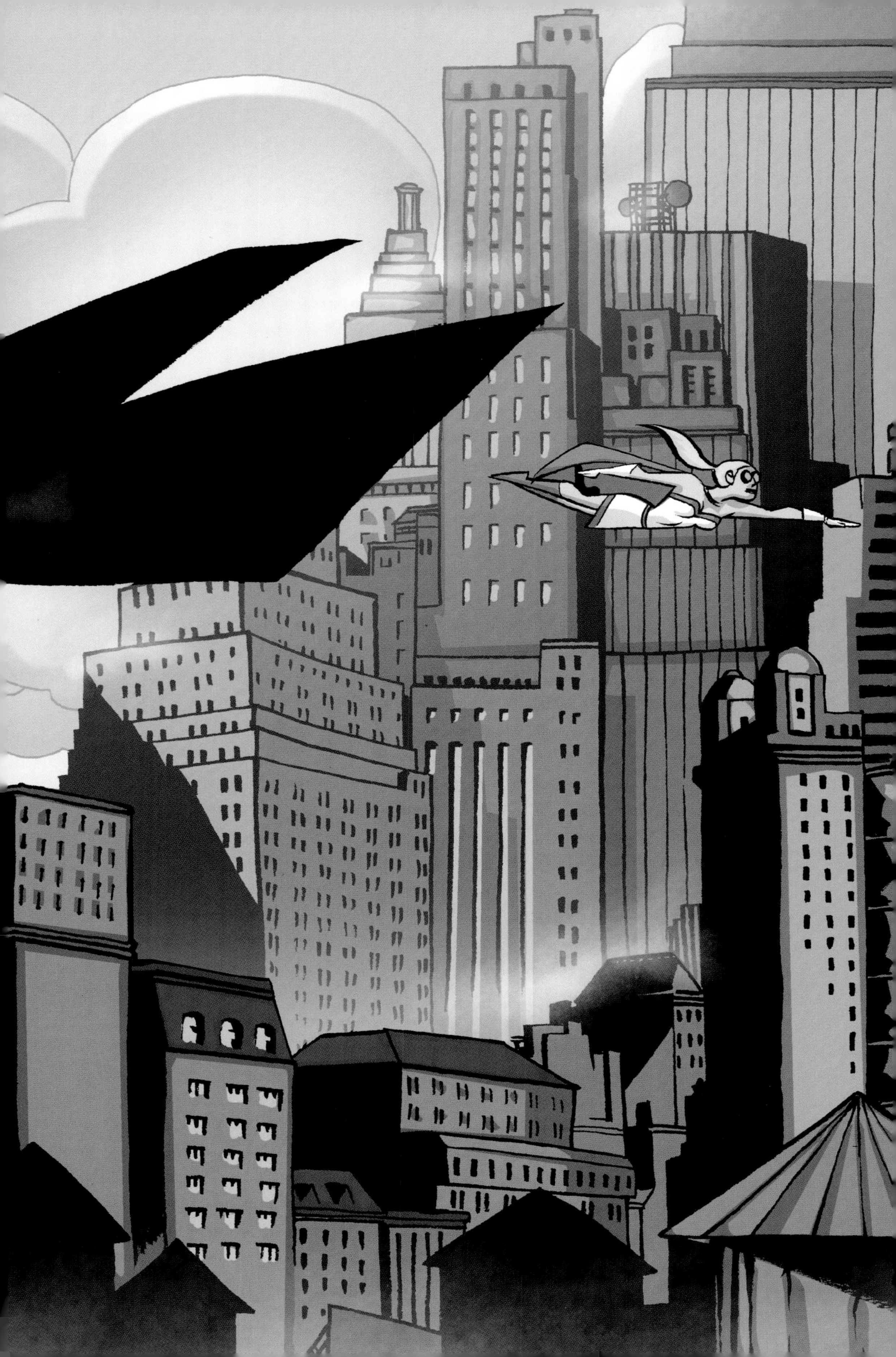

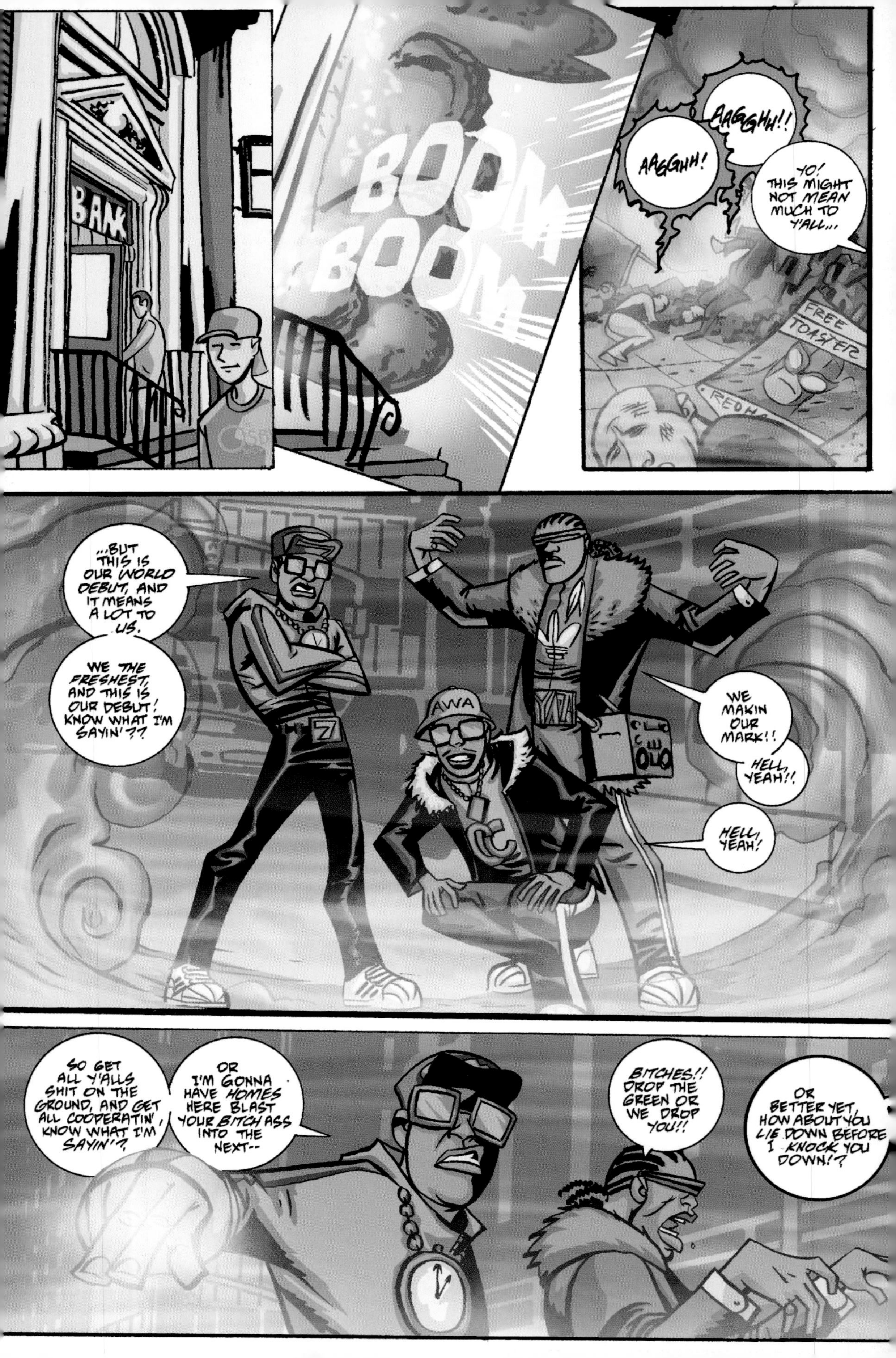
BANK
BOOM BOOM
AAGGHH!
AAGGHH!!
YO! THIS MIGHT NOT MEAN MUCH TO Y'ALL...
FREE TOASTER
...BUT THIS IS OUR WORLD DEBUT, AND IT MEANS A LOT TO US.
WE THE FRESHEST, AND THIS IS OUR DEBUT! KNOW WHAT I'M SAYIN'??
WE MAKIN OUR MARK!!
HELL, YEAH!!
HELL, YEAH!
SO GET ALL Y'ALLS SHIT ON THE GROUND, AND GET ALL COOPERATIN', KNOW WHAT I'M SAYIN'?
OR I'M GONNA HAVE HOMES HERE BLAST YOUR BITCH ASS INTO THE NEXT--
BITCHES!! DROP THE GREEN OR WE DROP YOU!!
OR BETTER YET, HOW ABOUT YOU LIE DOWN BEFORE I KNOCK YOU DOWN!?

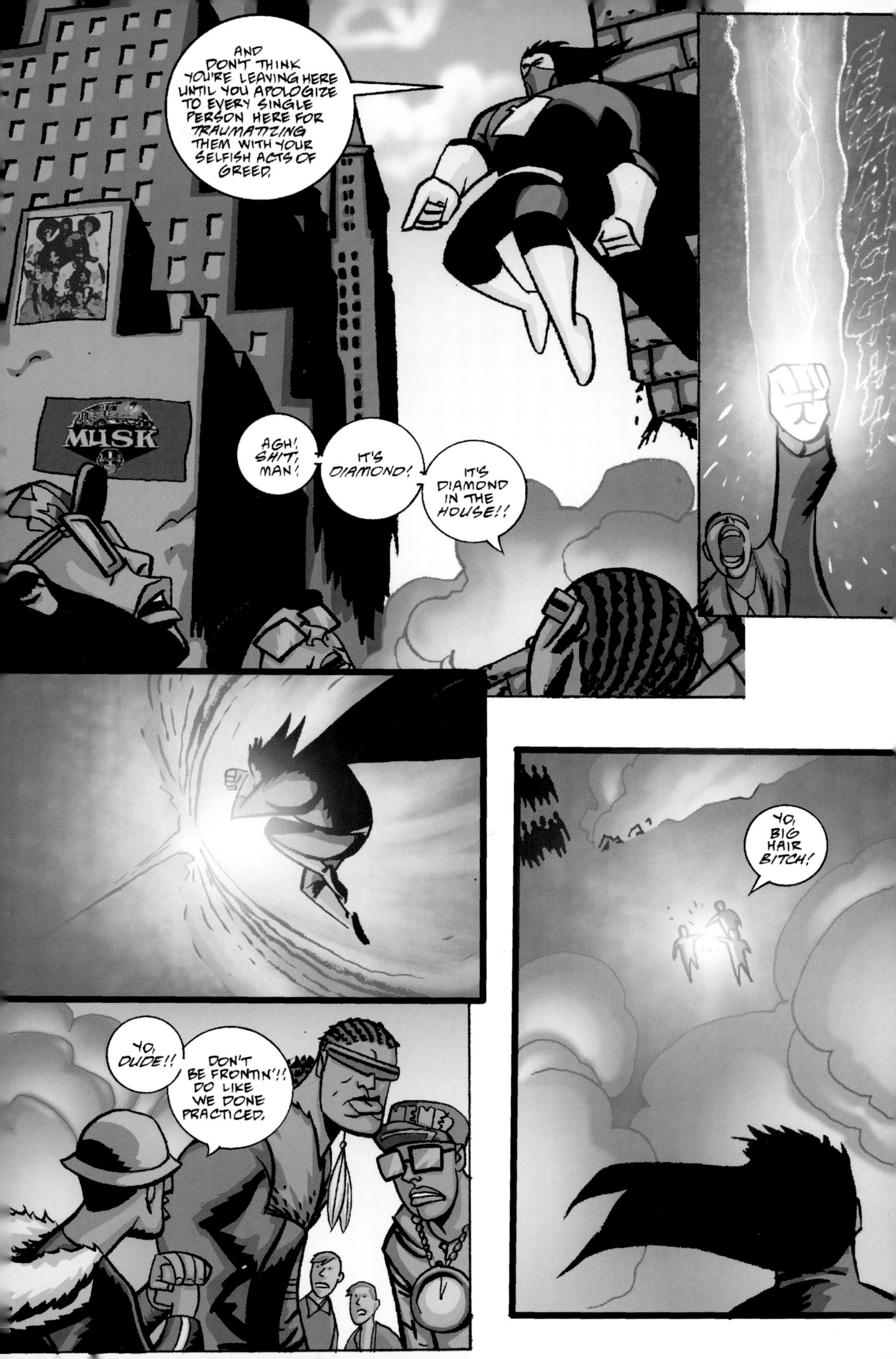
AND DON'T THINK YOU'RE LEAVING HERE UNTIL YOU APOLOGIZE TO EVERY SINGLE PERSON HERE FOR TRAUMATIZING THEM WITH YOUR SELFISH ACTS OF GREED.
MUSK
AGH! SHIT, MAN!
IT'S DIAMOND!
IT'S DIAMOND IN THE HOUSE!!
YO, BIG HAIR BITCH!
YO, DUDE!!
DON'T BE FRONTIN'!! DO LIKE WE DONE PRACTICED.

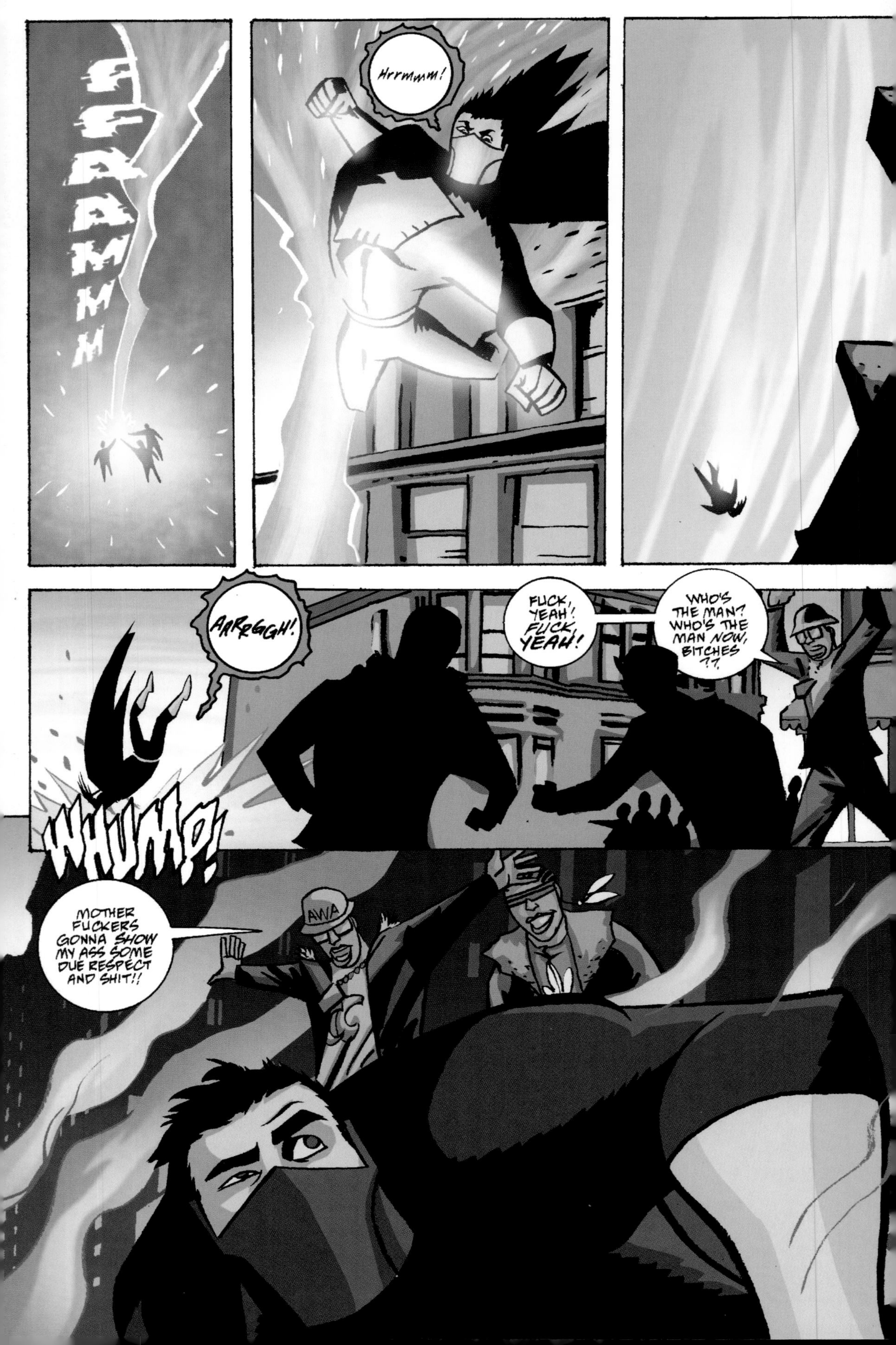
SKRAMMM
Hrrmmm!
ARRRGGH!
FUCK, YEAH! FUCK YEAH!
WHO'S THE MAN? WHO'S THE MAN NOW, BITCHES??
WHUMP!
AWA
MOTHER FUCKERS GONNA SHOW MY ASS SOME DUE RESPECT AND SHIT!!

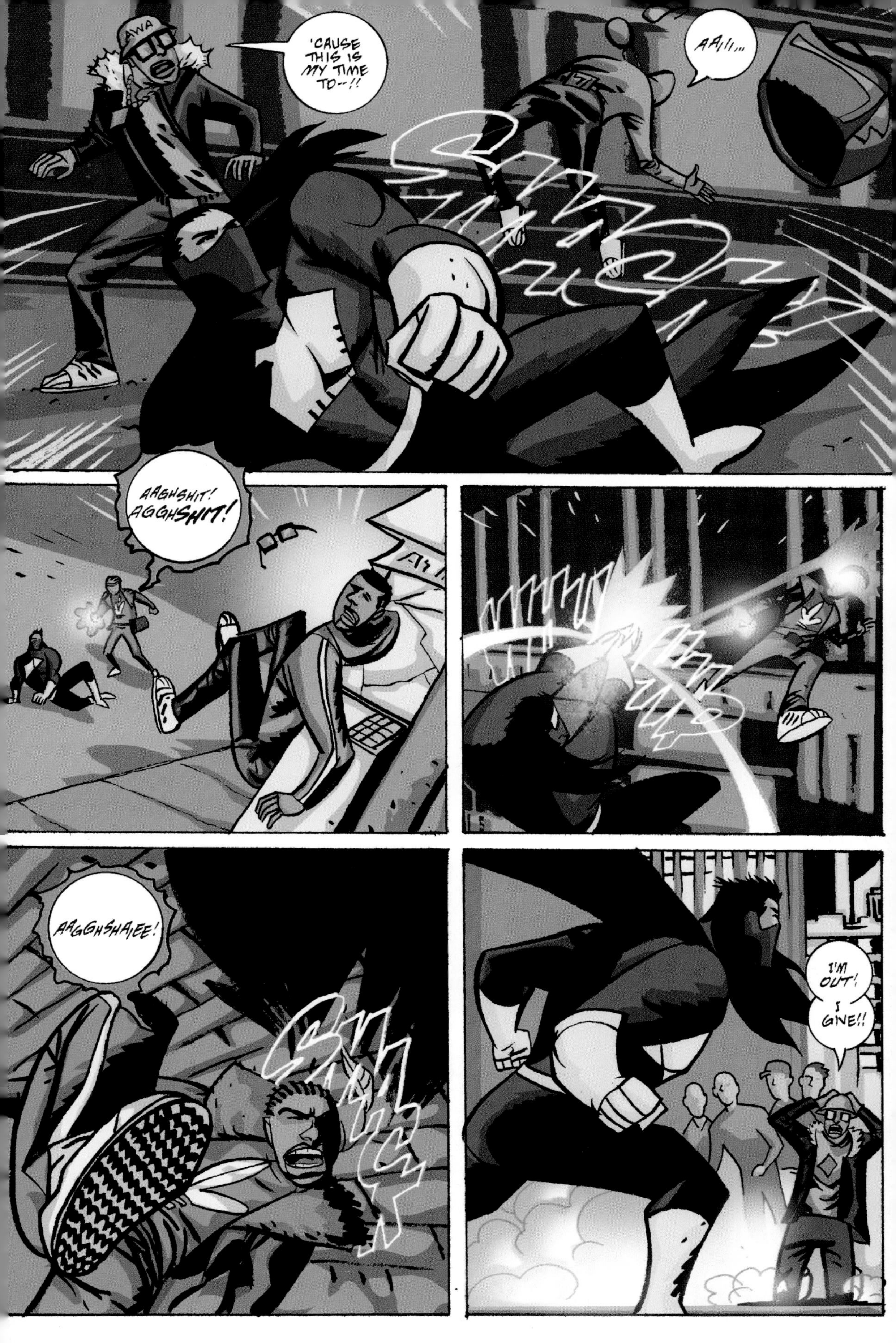
'CAUSE THIS IS MY TIME TO--!!
AAIII...
AARGHSHIT! AGGHSHIT!
AARGHSHAIEE!
I'M OUT!
I GIVE!!

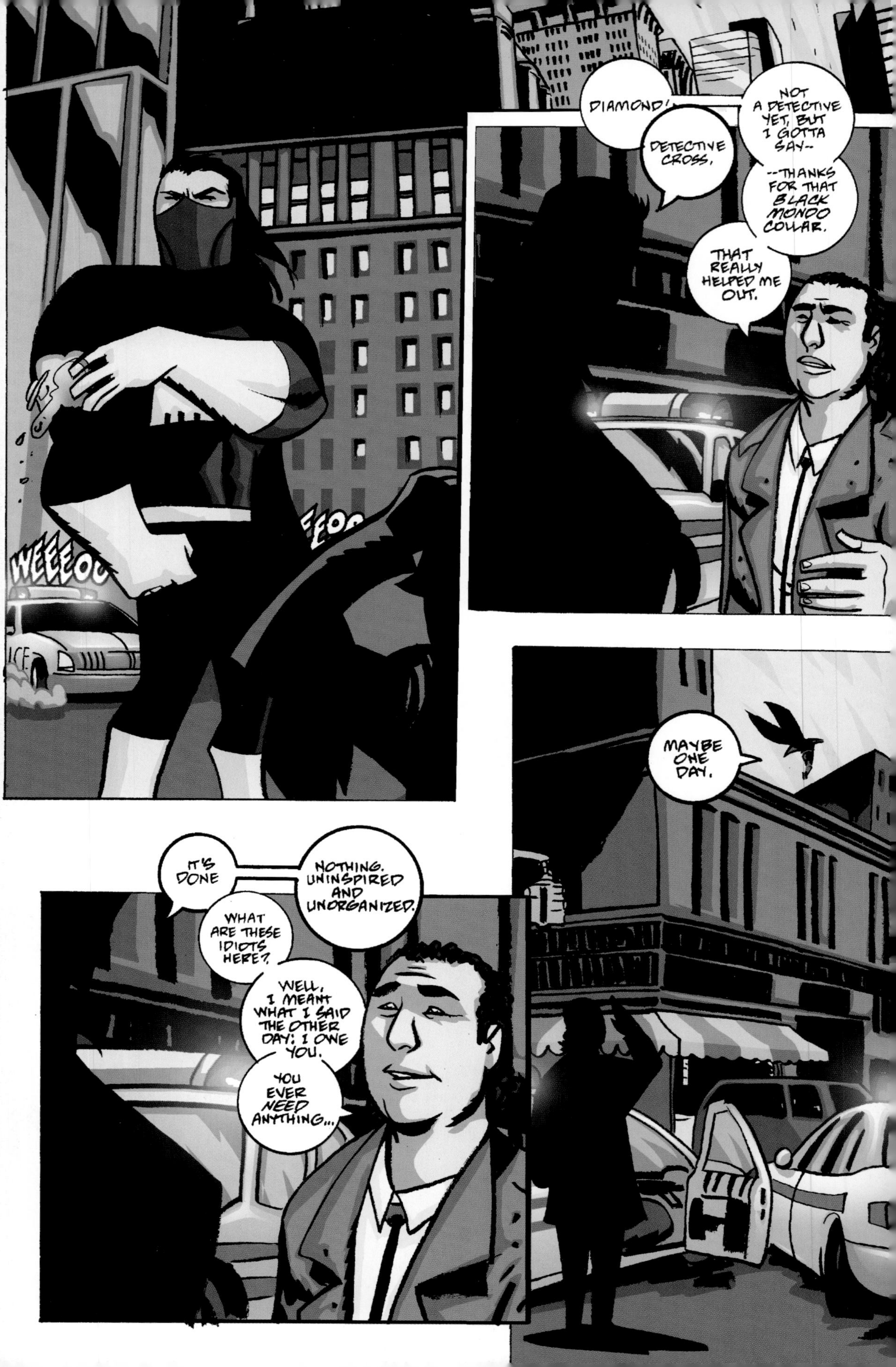
WEEEOO
EEOO
DIAMOND!
DETECTIVE CROSS.
NOT A DETECTIVE YET, BUT I GOTTA SAY--
--THANKS FOR THAT BLACK MONDO COLLAR.
THAT REALLY HELPED ME OUT.
IT'S DONE
NOTHING. UNINSPIRED AND UNORGANIZED.
WHAT ARE THESE IDIOTS HERE?
WELL, I MEANT WHAT I SAID THE OTHER DAY: I OWE YOU.
YOU EVER NEED ANYTHING...
MAYBE ONE DAY.

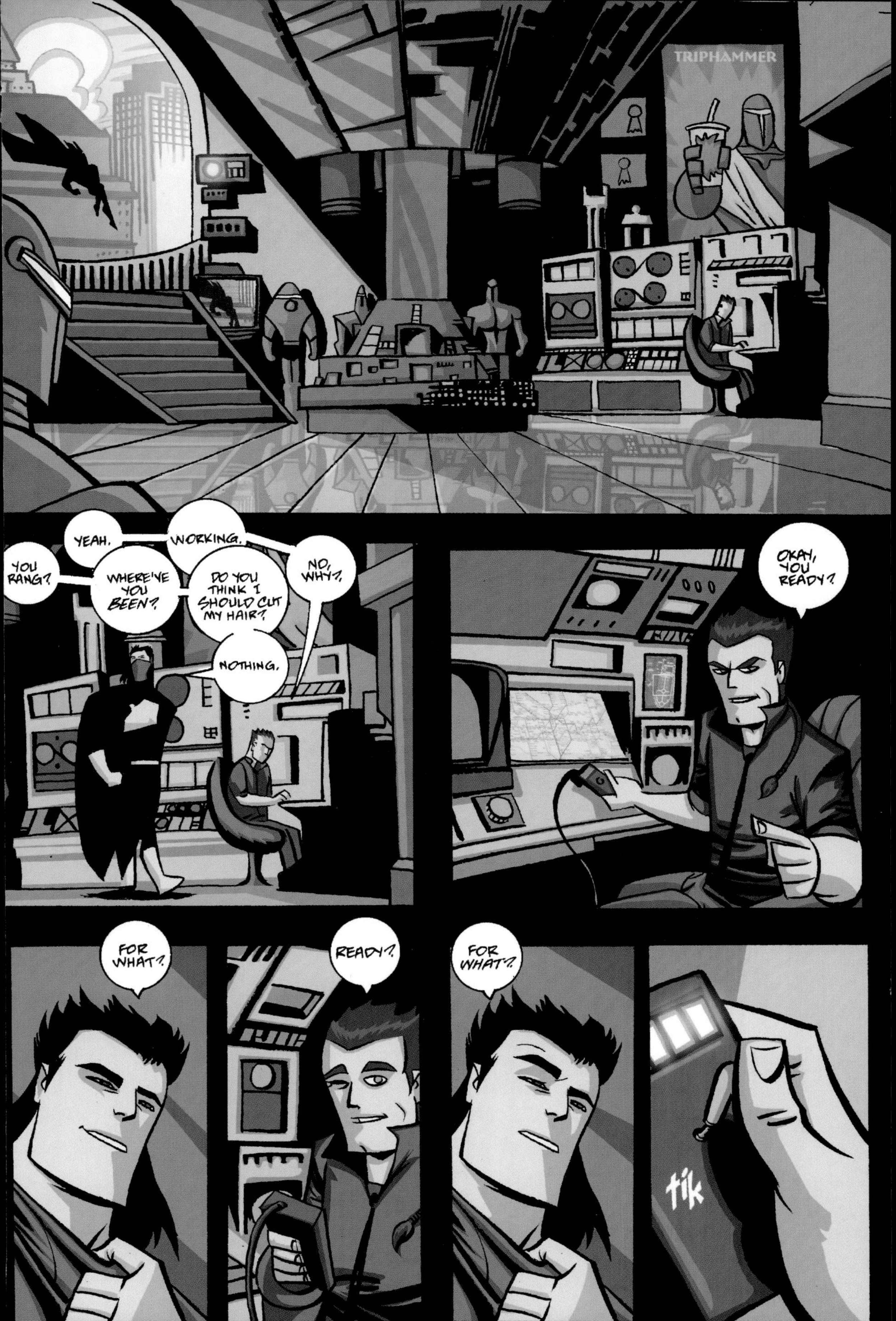
TRIPHAMMER
YOU RANG?
YEAH.
WHERE'VE YOU BEEN?
WORKING.
DO YOU THINK I SHOULD CUT MY HAIR?
NO, WHY?
NOTHING.
OKAY, YOU READY?
FOR WHAT?
READY?
FOR WHAT?
tik

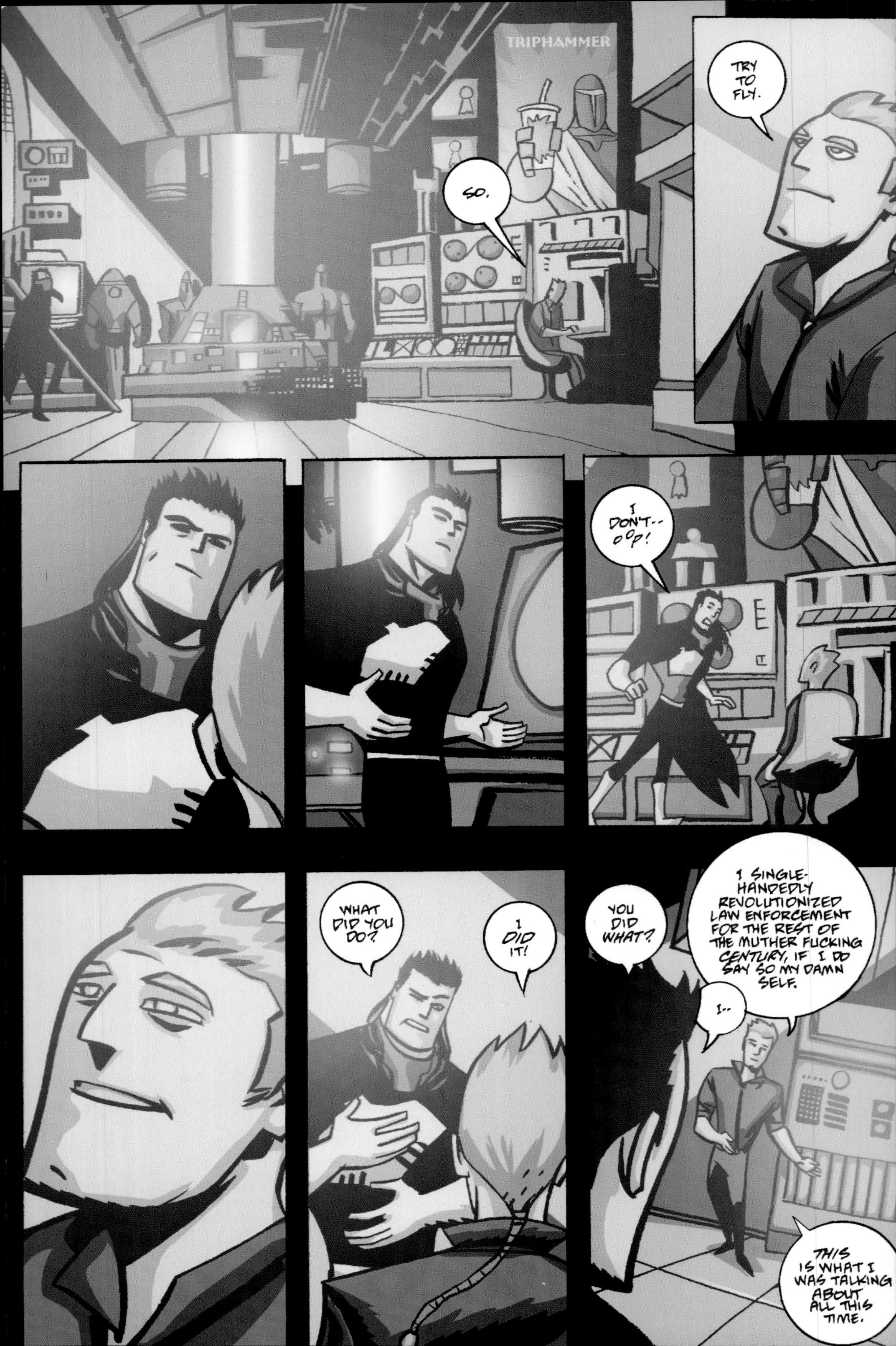
TRIPHAMMER
TRY TO FLY.
SO.
I DON'T-- OOP!
WHAT DID YOU DO?
I DID IT!
YOU DID WHAT?
I SINGLE-HANDEDLY REVOLUTIONIZED LAW ENFORCEMENT FOR THE REST OF THE MUTHER FUCKING CENTURY, IF I DO SAY SO MY DAMN SELF.
I..
THIS IS WHAT I WAS TALKING ABOUT ALL THIS TIME.

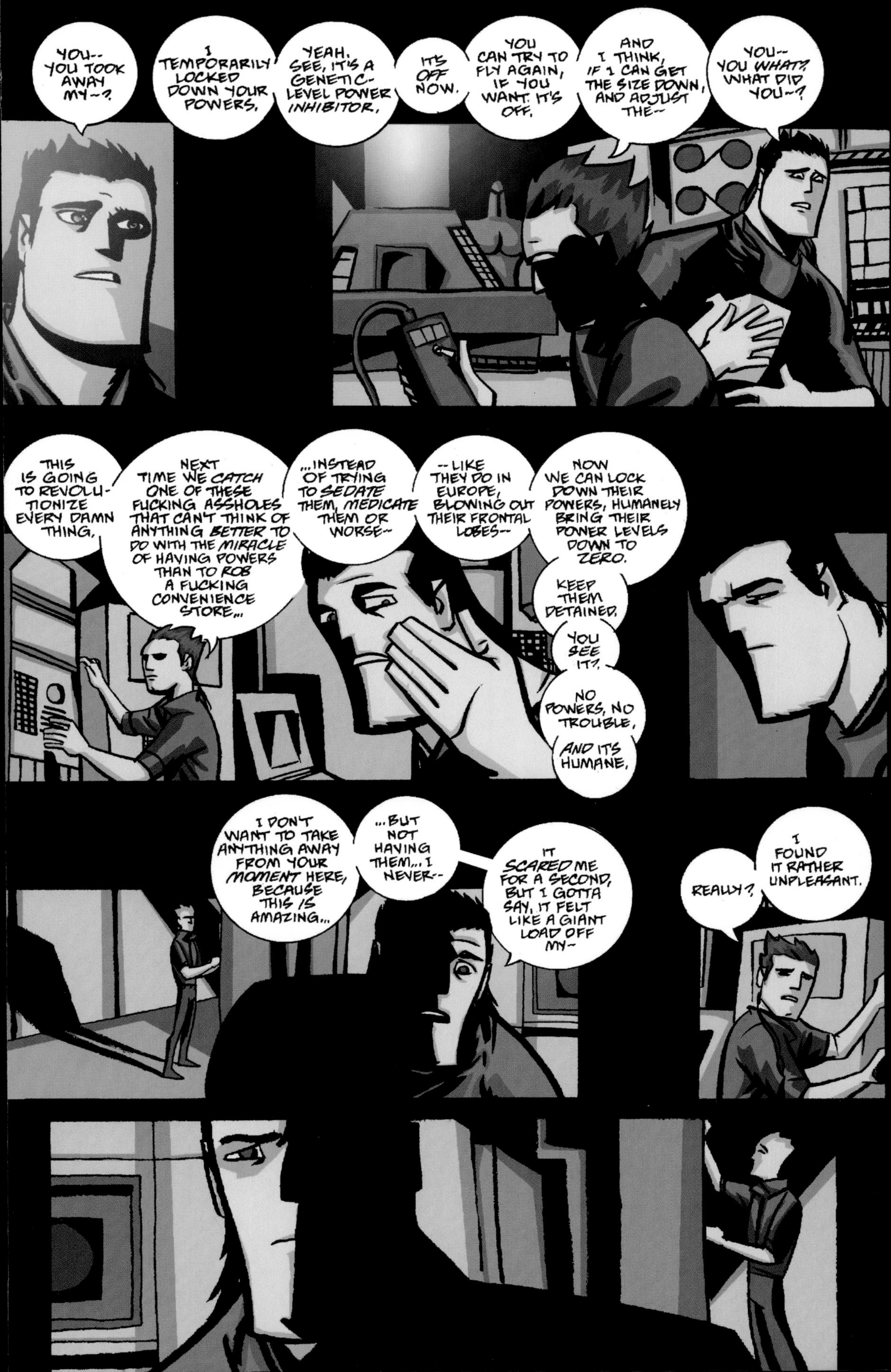
YOU-- YOU TOOK AWAY MY--?
I TEMPORARILY LOCKED DOWN YOUR POWERS.
YEAH. SEE, IT'S A GENETIC-LEVEL POWER INHIBITOR.
IT'S OFF NOW.
YOU CAN TRY TO FLY AGAIN, IF YOU WANT. IT'S OFF.
AND I THINK, IF I CAN GET THE SIZE DOWN, AND ADJUST THE--
YOU-- YOU WHAT? WHAT DID YOU--?
THIS IS GOING TO REVOLUTIONIZE EVERY DAMN THING.
NEXT TIME WE CATCH ONE OF THESE FUCKING ASSHOLES THAT CAN'T THINK OF ANYTHING BETTER TO DO WITH THE MIRACLE OF HAVING POWERS THAN TO ROB A FUCKING CONVENIENCE STORE...
...INSTEAD OF TRYING TO SEDATE THEM, MEDICATE THEM OR WORSE--
--LIKE THEY DO IN EUROPE, BLOWING OUT THEIR FRONTAL LOBES--
NOW WE CAN LOCK DOWN THEIR POWERS, HUMANELY BRING THEIR POWER LEVELS DOWN TO ZERO.
KEEP THEM DETAINED.
YOU SEE IT?
NO POWERS, NO TROUBLE.
AND IT'S HUMANE.
I DON'T WANT TO TAKE ANYTHING AWAY FROM YOUR MOMENT HERE, BECAUSE THIS IS AMAZING...
...BUT NOT HAVING THEM... I NEVER--
IT SCARED ME FOR A SECOND, BUT I GOTTA SAY, IT FELT LIKE A GIANT LOAD OFF MY--
I FOUND IT RATHER UNPLEASANT.
REALLY?

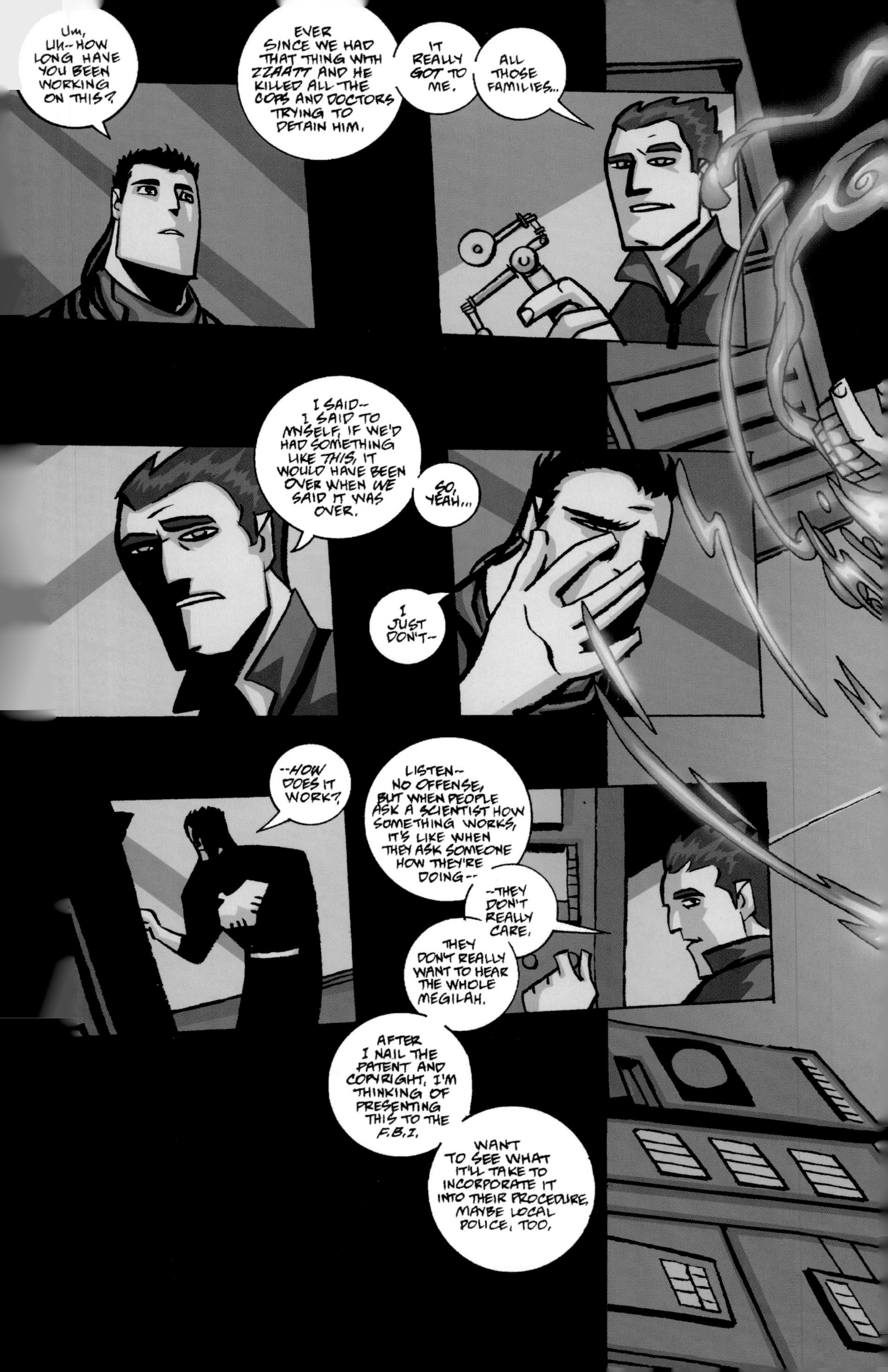
UM, UH--HOW LONG HAVE YOU BEEN WORKING ON THIS?
EVER SINCE WE HAD THAT THING WITH ZZAATT AND HE KILLED ALL THE COPS AND DOCTORS TRYING TO DETAIN HIM.
IT REALLY GOT TO ME.
ALL THOSE FAMILIES...
I SAID-- I SAID TO MYSELF, IF WE'D HAD SOMETHING LIKE THIS, IT WOULD HAVE BEEN OVER WHEN WE SAID IT WAS OVER.
SO, YEAH...
I JUST DON'T--
--HOW DOES IT WORK?
LISTEN-- NO OFFENSE, BUT WHEN PEOPLE ASK A SCIENTIST HOW SOMETHING WORKS, IT'S LIKE WHEN THEY ASK SOMEONE HOW THEY'RE DOING--
--THEY DON'T REALLY CARE.
THEY DON'T REALLY WANT TO HEAR THE WHOLE MEGILAH.
AFTER I NAIL THE PATENT AND COPYRIGHT, I'M THINKING OF PRESENTING THIS TO THE F.B.I.
WANT TO SEE WHAT IT'LL TAKE TO INCORPORATE IT INTO THEIR PROCEDURE. MAYBE LOCAL POLICE, TOO.

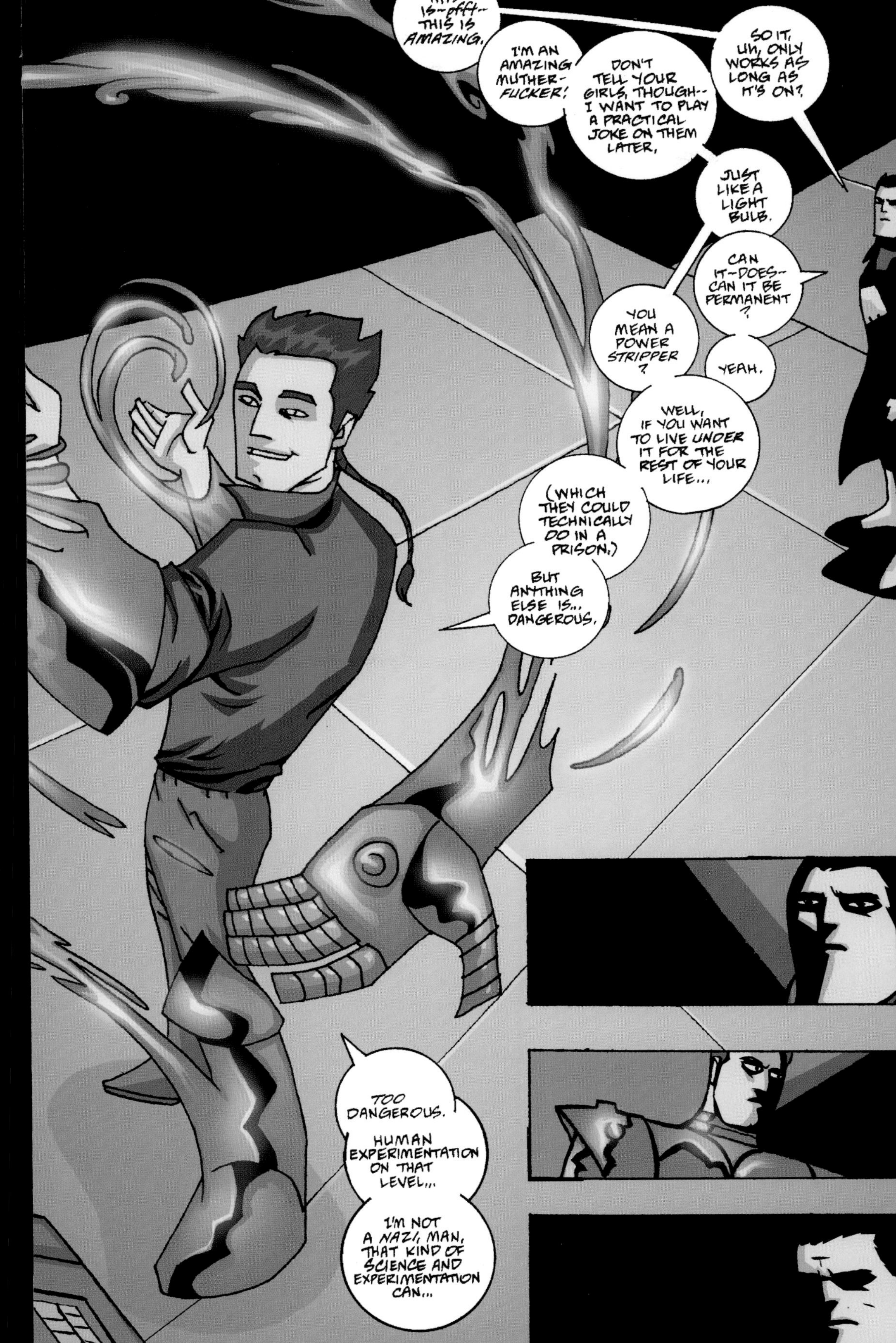
IS--PFFT-- THIS IS AMAZING.
I'M AN AMAZING MUTHER-FUCKER!
DON'T TELL YOUR GIRLS, THOUGH-- I WANT TO PLAY A PRACTICAL JOKE ON THEM LATER.
SO IT, UH, ONLY WORKS AS LONG AS IT'S ON?
JUST LIKE A LIGHT BULB.
CAN IT--DOES-- CAN IT BE PERMANENT?
YOU MEAN A POWER STRIPPER?
YEAH.
WELL, IF YOU WANT TO LIVE UNDER IT FOR THE REST OF YOUR LIFE...
(WHICH THEY COULD TECHNICALLY DO IN A PRISON.)
BUT ANYTHING ELSE IS... DANGEROUS.
TOO DANGEROUS.
HUMAN EXPERIMENTATION ON THAT LEVEL...
I'M NOT A NAZI, MAN. THAT KIND OF SCIENCE AND EXPERIMENTATION CAN...

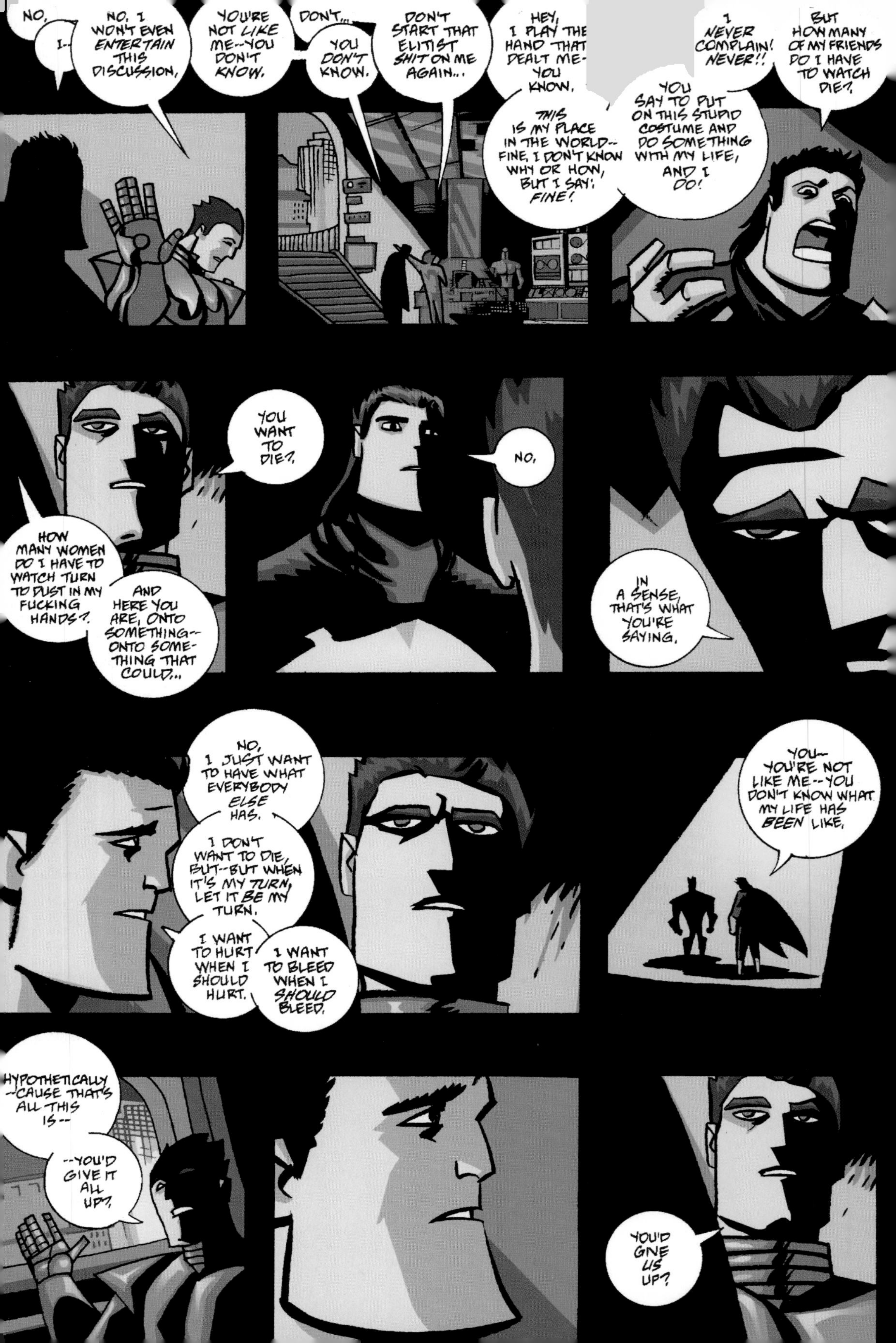
NO,
I--
NO, I WON'T EVEN ENTERTAIN THIS DISCUSSION,
YOU'RE NOT LIKE ME--YOU DON'T KNOW.
DON'T...
YOU DON'T KNOW.
DON'T START THAT ELITIST SHIT ON ME AGAIN...
HEY, I PLAY THE HAND THAT DEALT ME-- YOU KNOW.
THIS IS MY PLACE IN THE WORLD-- FINE, I DON'T KNOW WHY OR HOW, BUT I SAY: FINE!
YOU SAY TO PUT ON THIS STUPID COSTUME AND DO SOMETHING WITH MY LIFE, AND I DO!
I NEVER COMPLAIN! NEVER!!
BUT HOW MANY OF MY FRIENDS DO I HAVE TO WATCH DIE?
HOW MANY WOMEN DO I HAVE TO WATCH TURN TO DUST IN MY FUCKING HANDS?
AND HERE YOU ARE, ONTO SOMETHING-- ONTO SOMETHING THAT COULD...
YOU WANT TO DIE?
NO.
IN A SENSE, THAT'S WHAT YOU'RE SAYING.
NO, I JUST WANT TO HAVE WHAT EVERYBODY ELSE HAS.
I DON'T WANT TO DIE, BUT--BUT WHEN IT'S MY TURN, LET IT BE MY TURN.
I WANT TO HURT WHEN I SHOULD HURT.
I WANT TO BLEED WHEN I SHOULD BLEED.
YOU-- YOU'RE NOT LIKE ME--YOU DON'T KNOW WHAT MY LIFE HAS BEEN LIKE.
HYPOTHETICALLY --CAUSE THAT'S ALL THIS IS--
--YOU'D GIVE IT ALL UP?
YOU'D GIVE US UP?

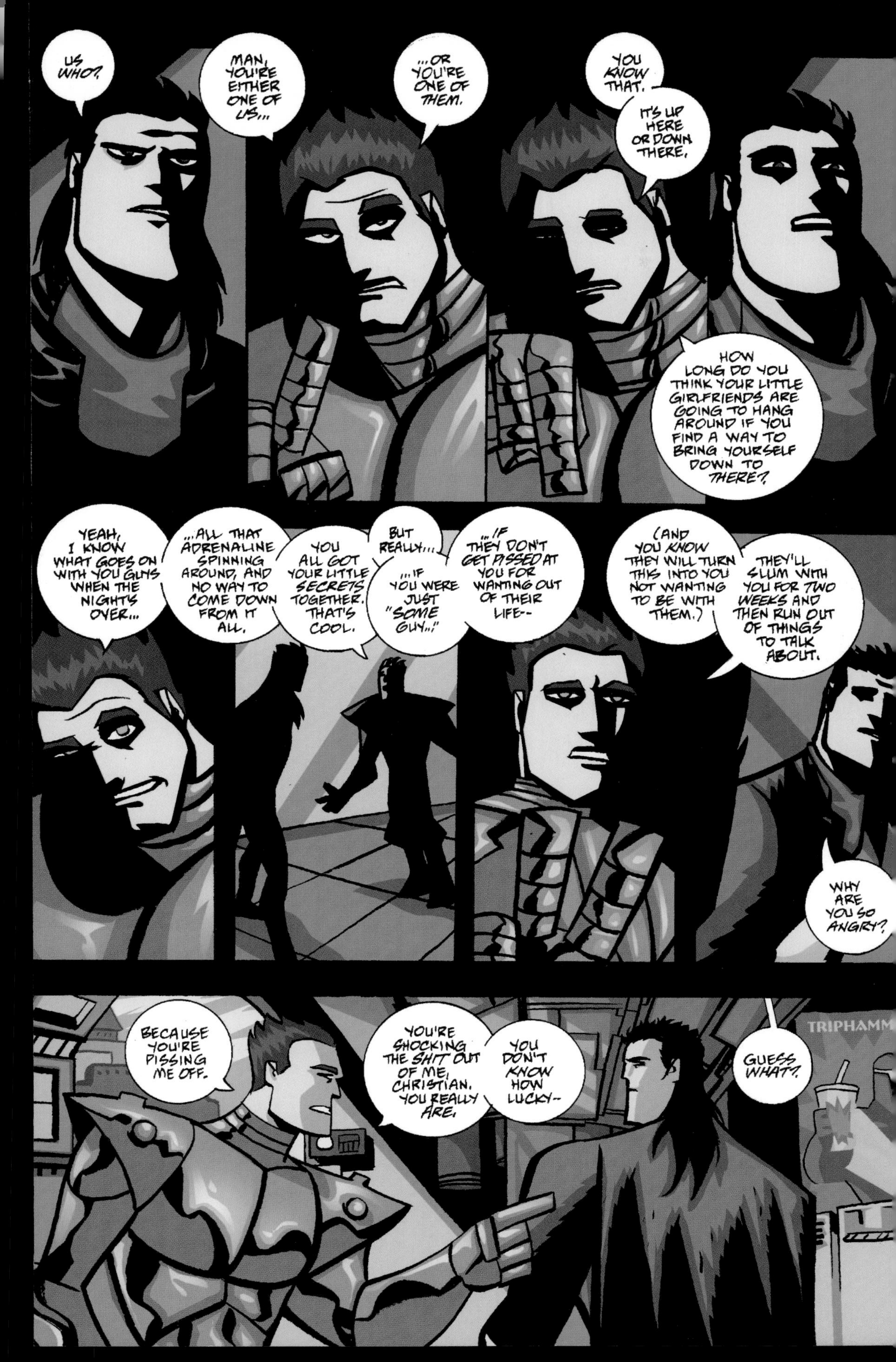
US WHO?
MAN, YOU'RE EITHER ONE OF US...
...OR YOU'RE ONE OF THEM.
YOU KNOW THAT.
IT'S UP HERE OR DOWN THERE.
HOW LONG DO YOU THINK YOUR LITTLE GIRLFRIENDS ARE GOING TO HANG AROUND IF YOU FIND A WAY TO BRING YOURSELF DOWN TO THERE?
YEAH, I KNOW WHAT GOES ON WITH YOU GUYS WHEN THE NIGHT'S OVER...
...ALL THAT ADRENALINE SPINNING AROUND, AND NO WAY TO COME DOWN FROM IT ALL.
YOU ALL GOT YOUR LITTLE SECRETS TOGETHER. THAT'S COOL.
BUT REALLY...
...IF YOU WERE JUST "SOME GUY..."
...IF THEY DON'T GET PISSED AT YOU FOR WANTING OUT OF THEIR LIFE--
(AND YOU KNOW THEY WILL TURN THIS INTO YOU NOT WANTING TO BE WITH THEM.)
THEY'LL SLUM WITH YOU FOR TWO WEEKS AND THEN RUN OUT OF THINGS TO TALK ABOUT.
WHY ARE YOU SO ANGRY?
BECAUSE YOU'RE PISSING ME OFF.
YOU'RE SHOCKING THE SHIT OUT OF ME, CHRISTIAN. YOU REALLY ARE.
YOU DON'T KNOW HOW LUCKY--
GUESS WHAT?
TRIPHAMM

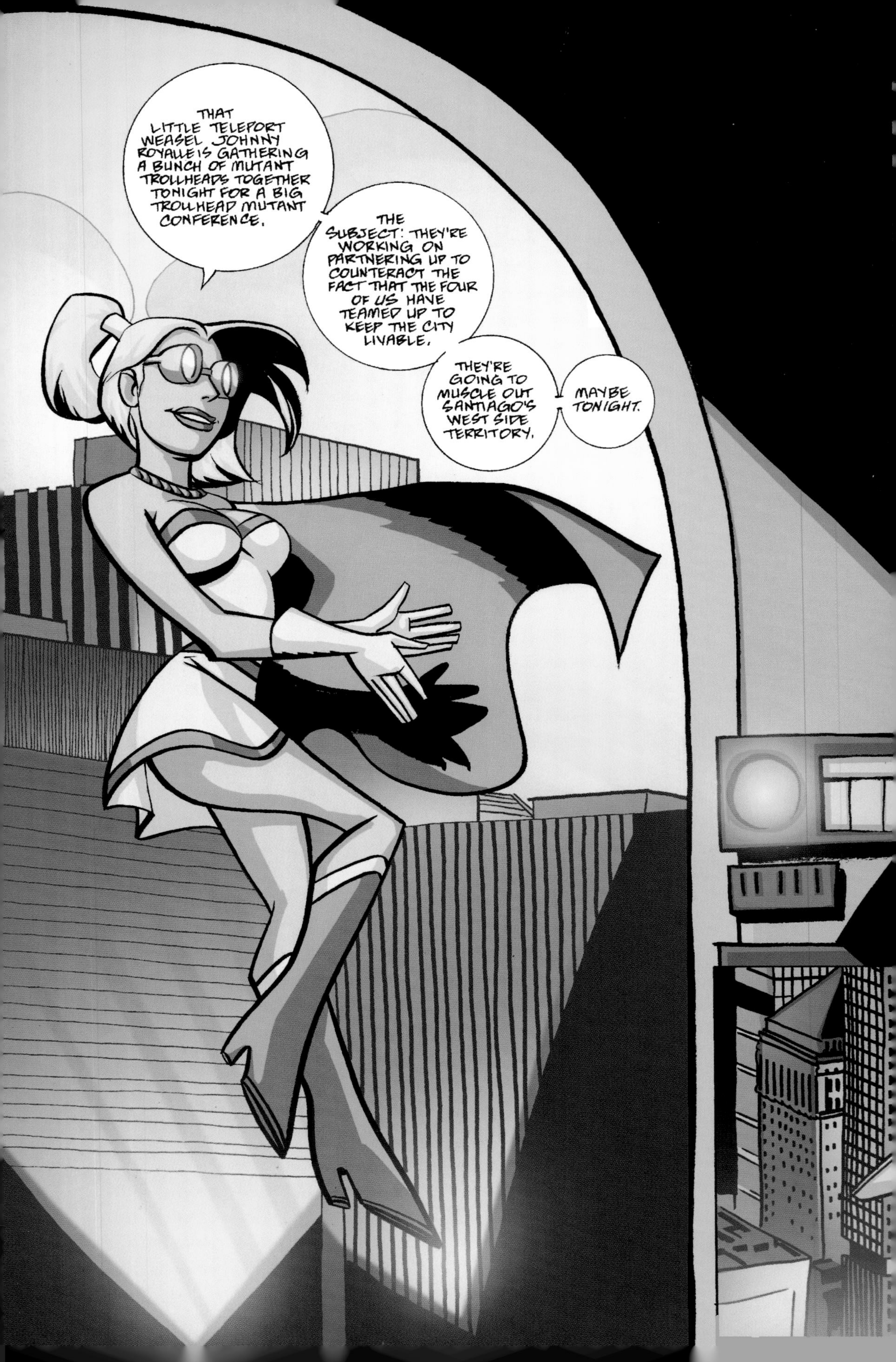
THAT LITTLE TELEPORT WEASEL JOHNNY ROYALLE IS GATHERING A BUNCH OF MUTANT TROLLHEADS TOGETHER TONIGHT FOR A BIG TROLLHEAD MUTANT CONFERENCE.
THE SUBJECT: THEY'RE WORKING ON PARTNERING UP TO COUNTERACT THE FACT THAT THE FOUR OF US HAVE TEAMED UP TO KEEP THE CITY LIVABLE.
THEY'RE GOING TO MUSCLE OUT SANTIAGO'S WEST SIDE TERRITORY.
MAYBE *TONIGHT.*

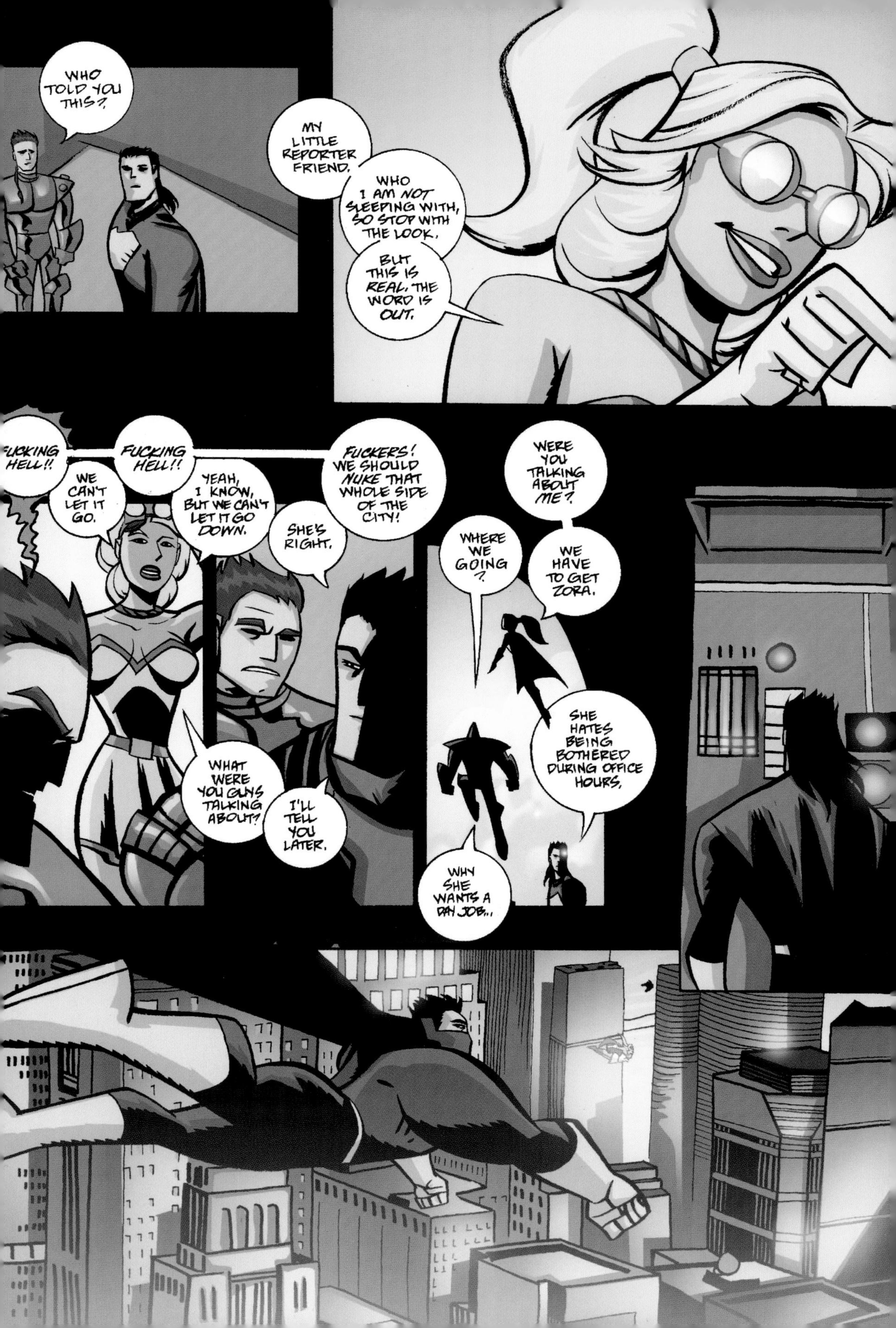
WHO TOLD YOU THIS?
MY LITTLE REPORTER FRIEND.
WHO I AM NOT SLEEPING WITH, SO STOP WITH THE LOOK.
BUT THIS IS REAL. THE WORD IS OUT.
FUCKING HELL!!
FUCKING HELL!!
WE CAN'T LET IT GO.
YEAH, I KNOW, BUT WE CAN'T LET IT GO DOWN.
FUCKERS! WE SHOULD NUKE THAT WHOLE SIDE OF THE CITY!
SHE'S RIGHT.
WHAT WERE YOU GUYS TALKING ABOUT?
I'LL TELL YOU LATER.
WERE YOU TALKING ABOUT ME?
WHERE WE GOING?
WE HAVE TO GET ZORA.
SHE HATES BEING BOTHERED DURING OFFICE HOURS.
WHY SHE WANTS A DAY JOB...

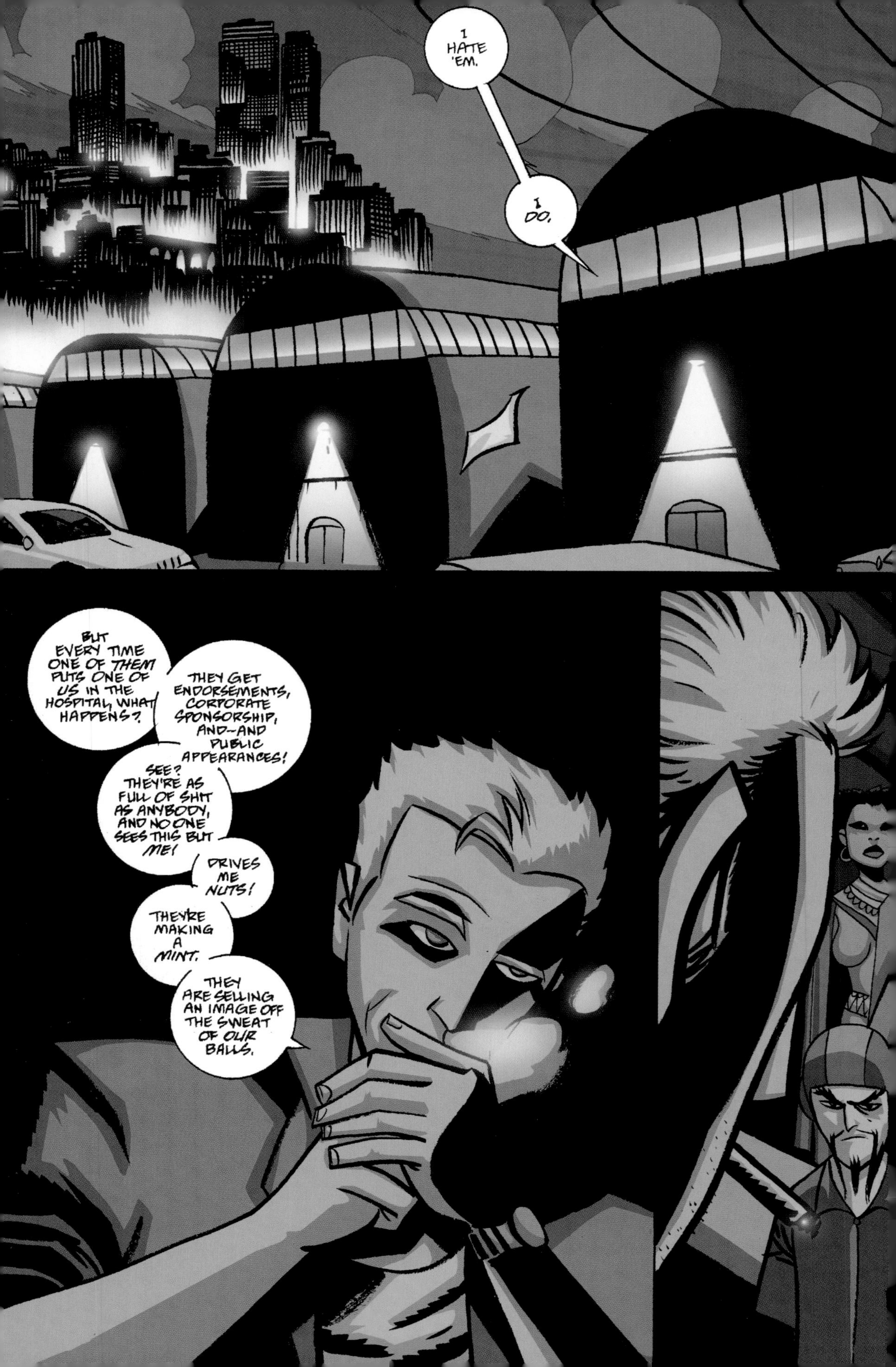
I HATE 'EM.
I DO.
BUT EVERY TIME ONE OF THEM PUTS ONE OF US IN THE HOSPITAL, WHAT HAPPENS?
THEY GET ENDORSEMENTS, CORPORATE SPONSORSHIP, AND--AND PUBLIC APPEARANCES!
SEE? THEY'RE AS FULL OF SHIT AS ANYBODY, AND NO ONE SEES THIS BUT ME!
DRIVES ME NUTS!
THEY'RE MAKING A MINT.
THEY ARE SELLING AN IMAGE OFF THE SWEAT OF OUR BALLS.

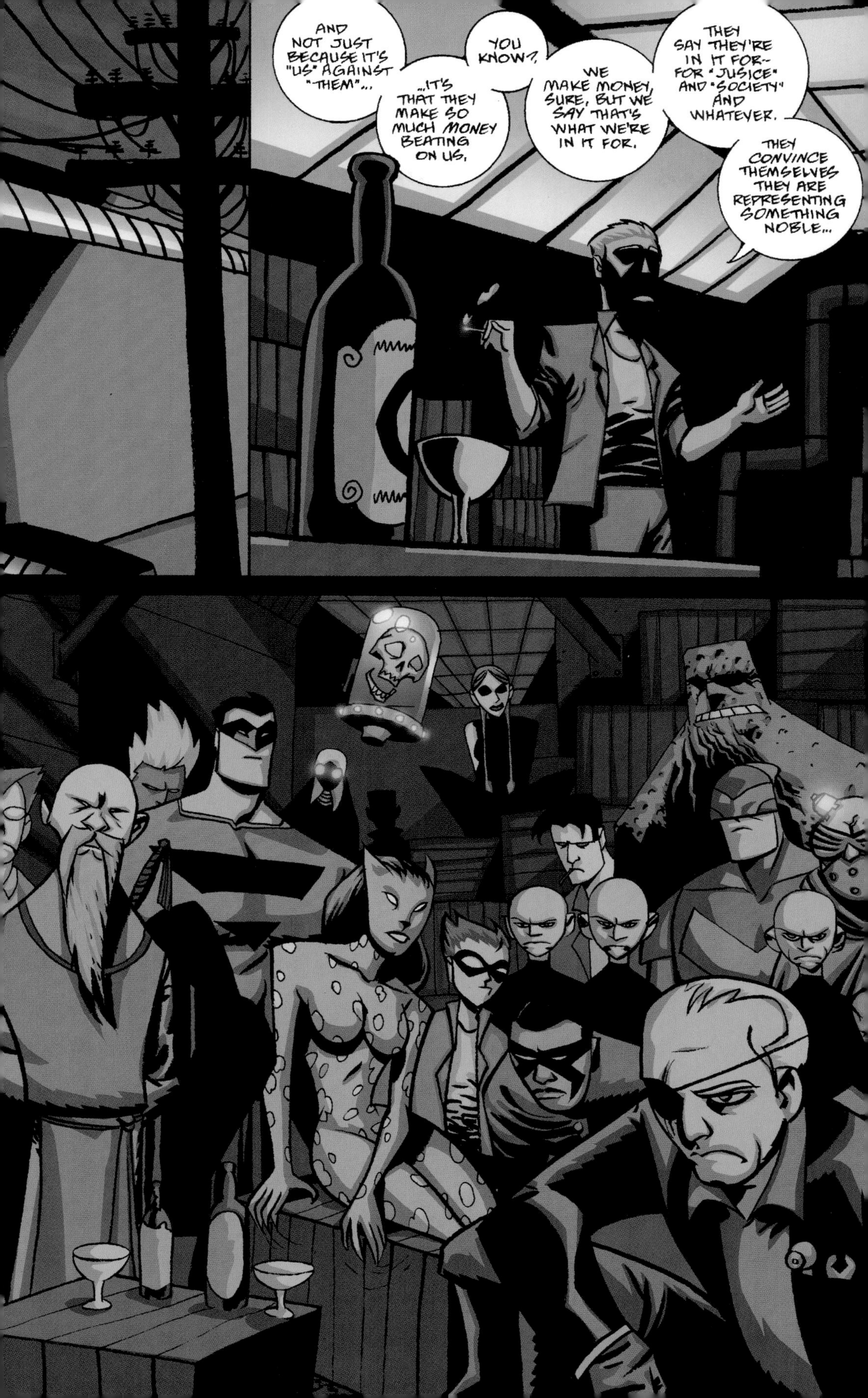
AND NOT JUST BECAUSE IT'S "US" AGAINST "THEM"...
...IT'S THAT THEY MAKE SO MUCH MONEY BEATING ON US.
YOU KNOW?
WE MAKE MONEY, SURE, BUT WE SAY THAT'S WHAT WE'RE IN IT FOR.
THEY SAY THEY'RE IN IT FOR-- FOR "JUSICE" AND "SOCIETY" AND WHATEVER.
THEY CONVINCE THEMSELVES THEY ARE REPRESENTING SOMETHING NOBLE...

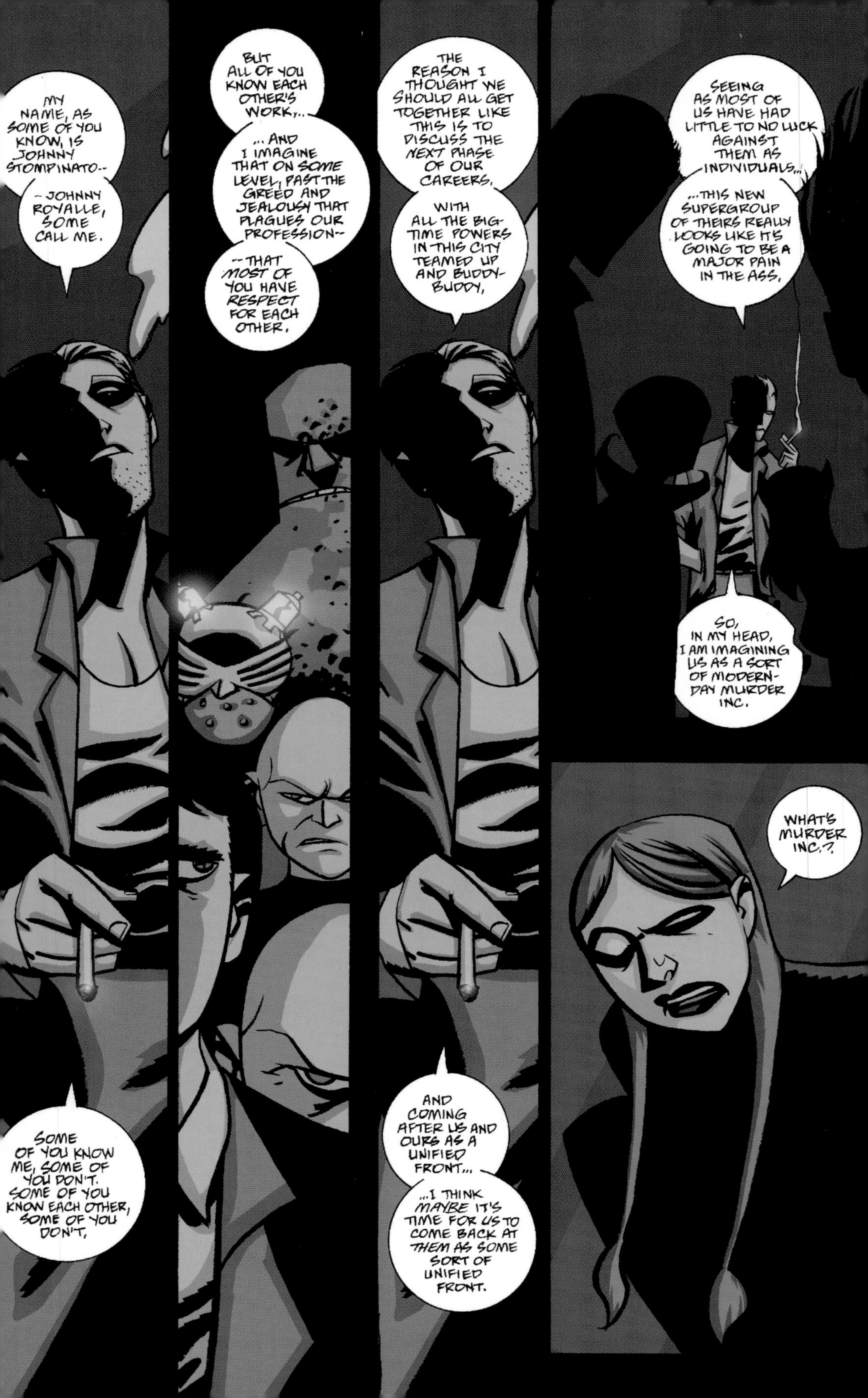
MY NAME, AS SOME OF YOU KNOW, IS JOHNNY STOMPINATO--
--JOHNNY ROYALLE, SOME CALL ME.
SOME OF YOU KNOW ME, SOME OF YOU DON'T. SOME OF YOU KNOW EACH OTHER, SOME OF YOU DON'T,
BUT ALL OF YOU KNOW EACH OTHER'S WORK...
...AND I IMAGINE THAT ON SOME LEVEL, PAST THE GREED AND JEALOUSY THAT PLAGUES OUR PROFESSION--
--THAT MOST OF YOU HAVE RESPECT FOR EACH OTHER.
THE REASON I THOUGHT WE SHOULD ALL GET TOGETHER LIKE THIS IS TO DISCUSS THE NEXT PHASE OF OUR CAREERS.
WITH ALL THE BIG-TIME POWERS IN THIS CITY TEAMED UP AND BUDDY-BUDDY,
AND COMING AFTER US AND OURS AS A UNIFIED FRONT...
...I THINK MAYBE IT'S TIME FOR US TO COME BACK AT THEM AS SOME SORT OF UNIFIED FRONT.
SEEING AS MOST OF US HAVE HAD LITTLE TO NO LUCK AGAINST THEM AS INDIVIDUALS...
...THIS NEW SUPERGROUP OF THEIRS REALLY LOOKS LIKE IT'S GOING TO BE A MAJOR PAIN IN THE ASS.
SO, IN MY HEAD, I AM IMAGINING US AS A SORT OF MODERN-DAY MURDER INC.
WHAT'S MURDER INC.?

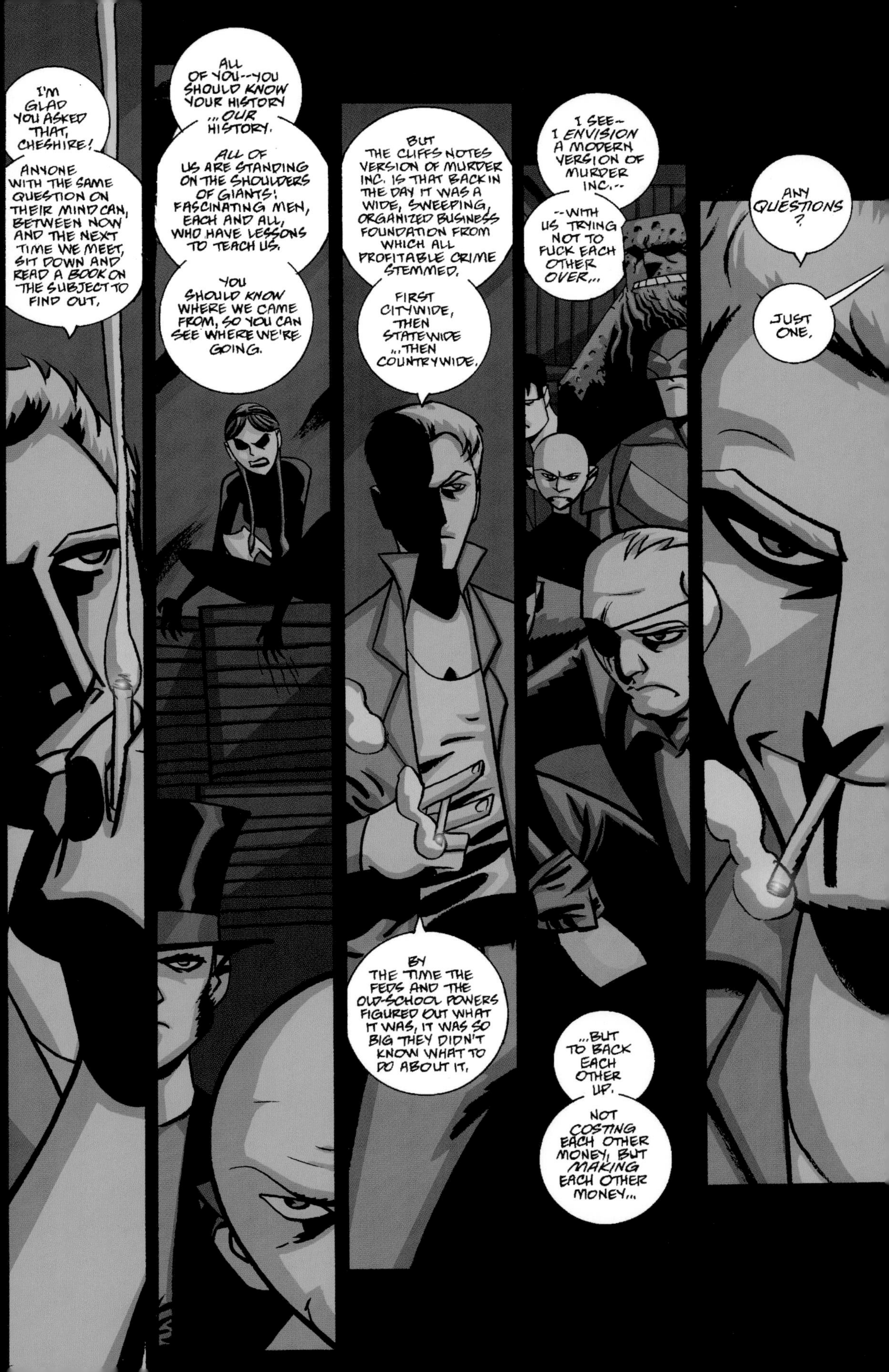
I'M GLAD YOU ASKED THAT, CHESHIRE!
ANYONE WITH THE SAME QUESTION ON THEIR MIND CAN, BETWEEN NOW AND THE NEXT TIME WE MEET, SIT DOWN AND READ A BOOK ON THE SUBJECT TO FIND OUT.
ALL OF YOU--YOU SHOULD KNOW YOUR HISTORY ...OUR HISTORY.
ALL OF US ARE STANDING ON THE SHOULDERS OF GIANTS: FASCINATING MEN, EACH AND ALL, WHO HAVE LESSONS TO TEACH US.
YOU SHOULD KNOW WHERE WE CAME FROM, SO YOU CAN SEE WHERE WE'RE GOING.
BUT THE CLIFFS NOTES VERSION OF MURDER INC. IS THAT BACK IN THE DAY IT WAS A WIDE, SWEEPING, ORGANIZED BUSINESS FOUNDATION FROM WHICH ALL PROFITABLE CRIME STEMMED.
FIRST CITYWIDE, THEN STATEWIDE ...THEN COUNTRYWIDE.
BY THE TIME THE FEDS AND THE OLD-SCHOOL POWERS FIGURED OUT WHAT IT WAS, IT WAS SO BIG THEY DIDN'T KNOW WHAT TO DO ABOUT IT.
I SEE-- I ENVISION A MODERN VERSION OF MURDER INC.--
--WITH US TRYING NOT TO FUCK EACH OTHER OVER...
...BUT TO BACK EACH OTHER UP.
NOT COSTING EACH OTHER MONEY, BUT MAKING EACH OTHER MONEY...
ANY QUESTIONS?
JUST ONE.

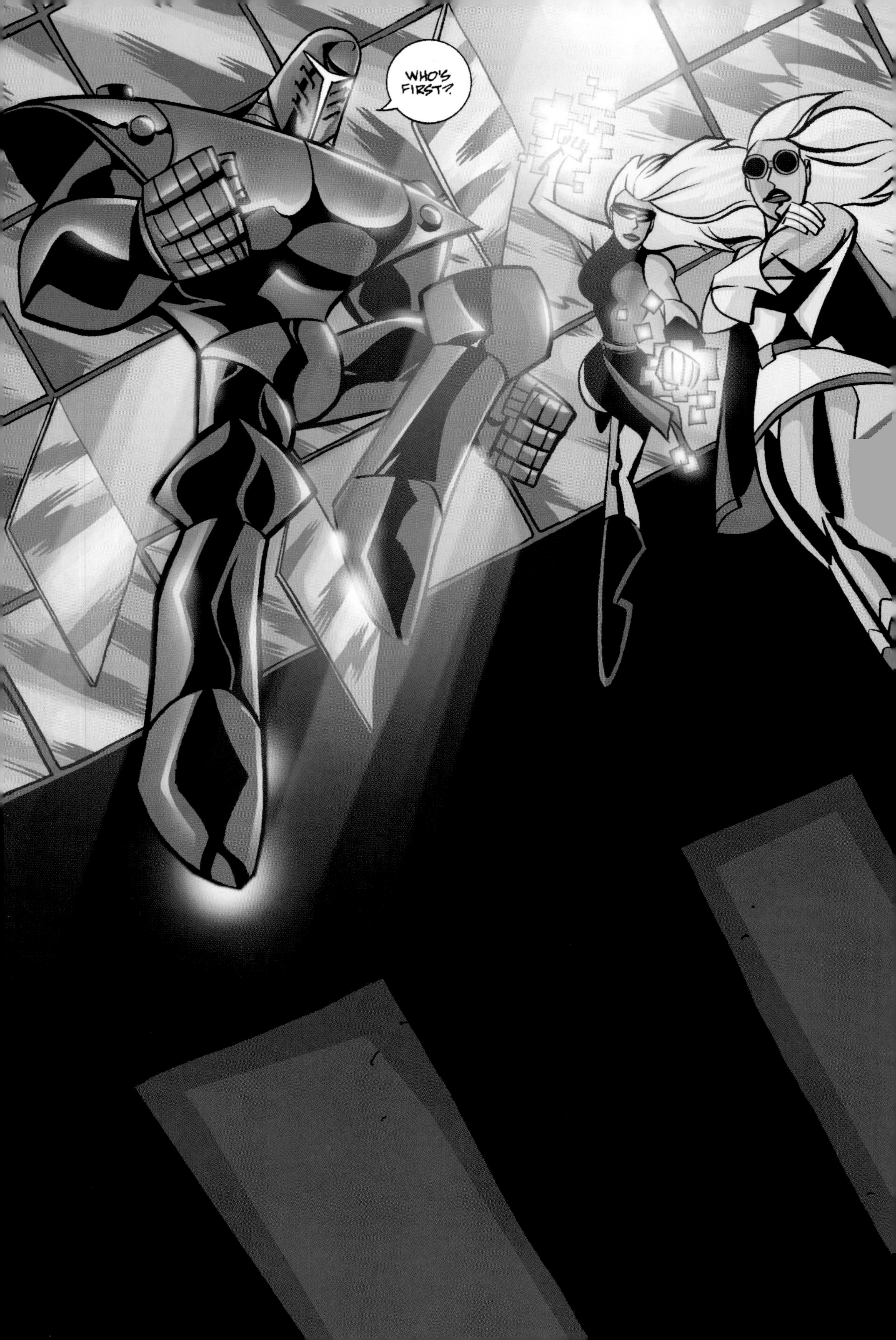
WHO'S FIRST?

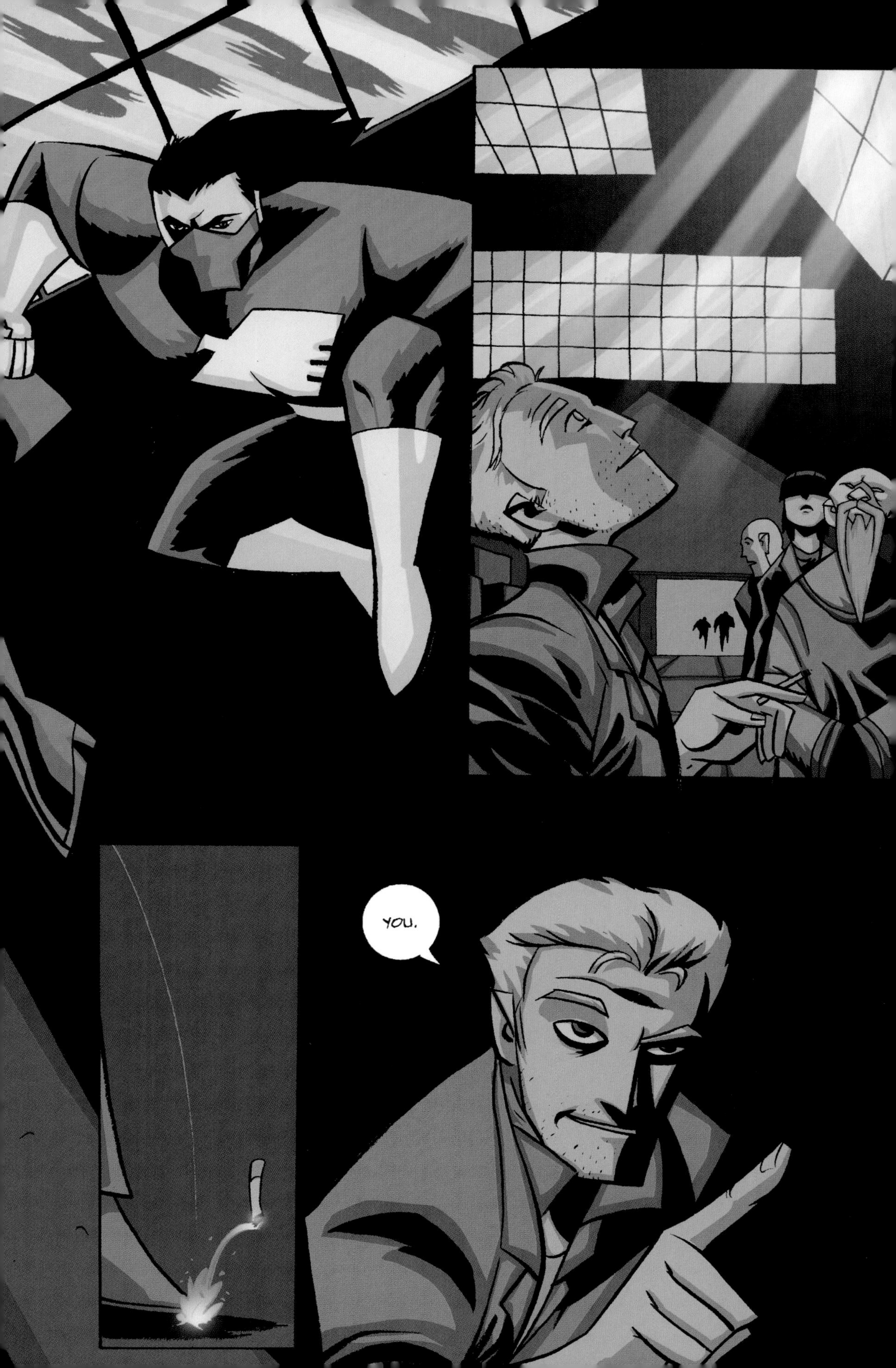
YOU.

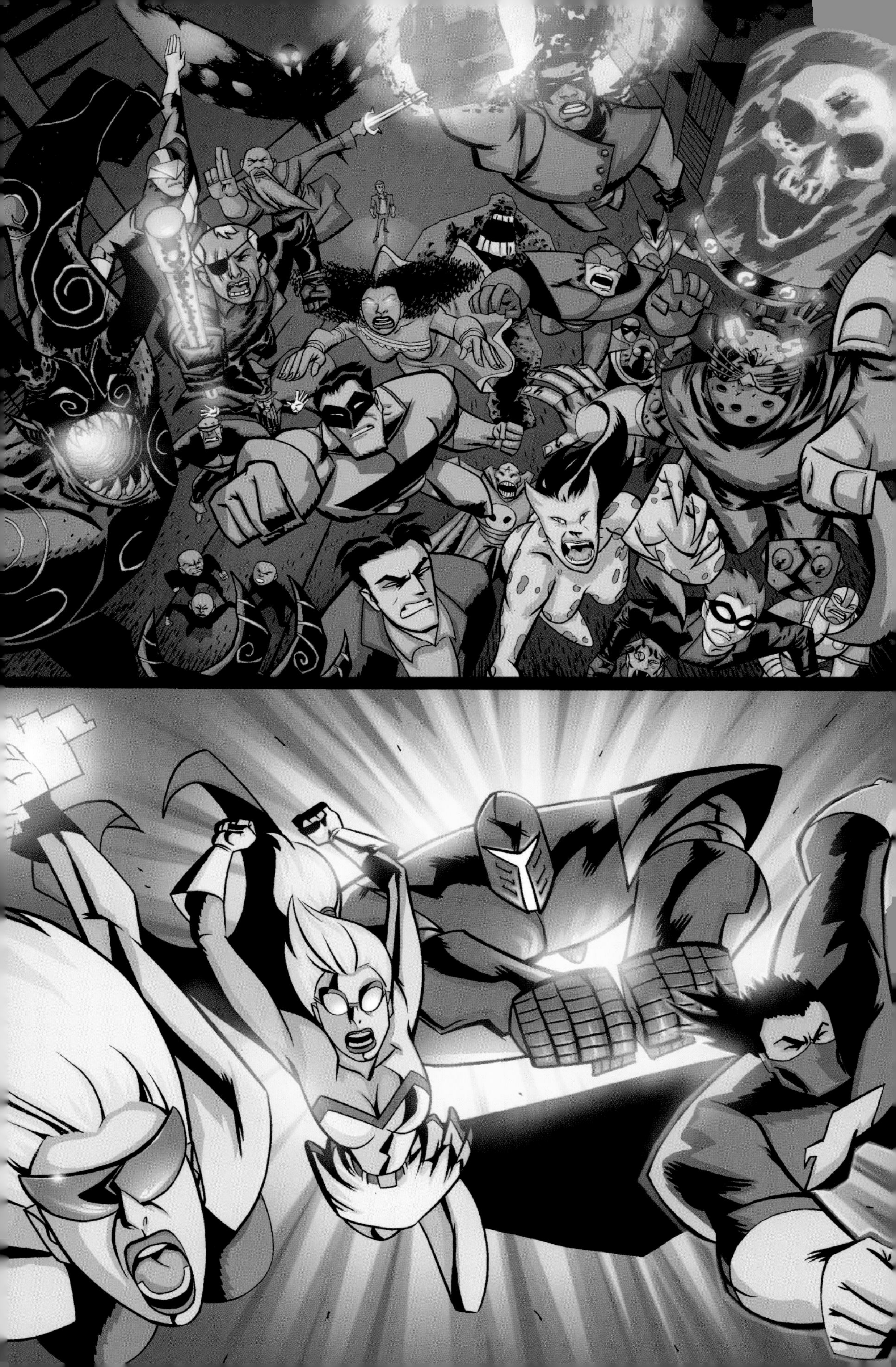

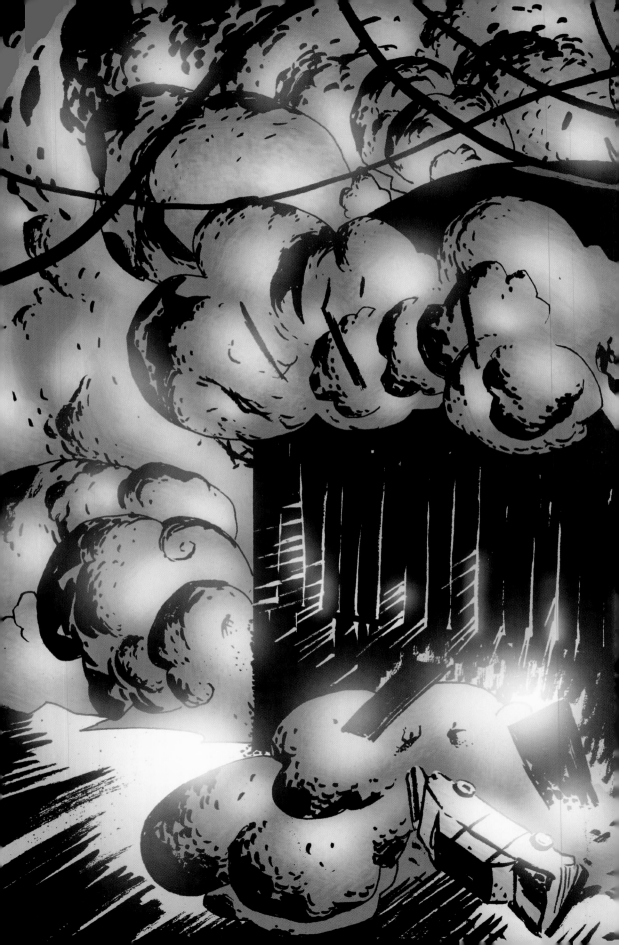

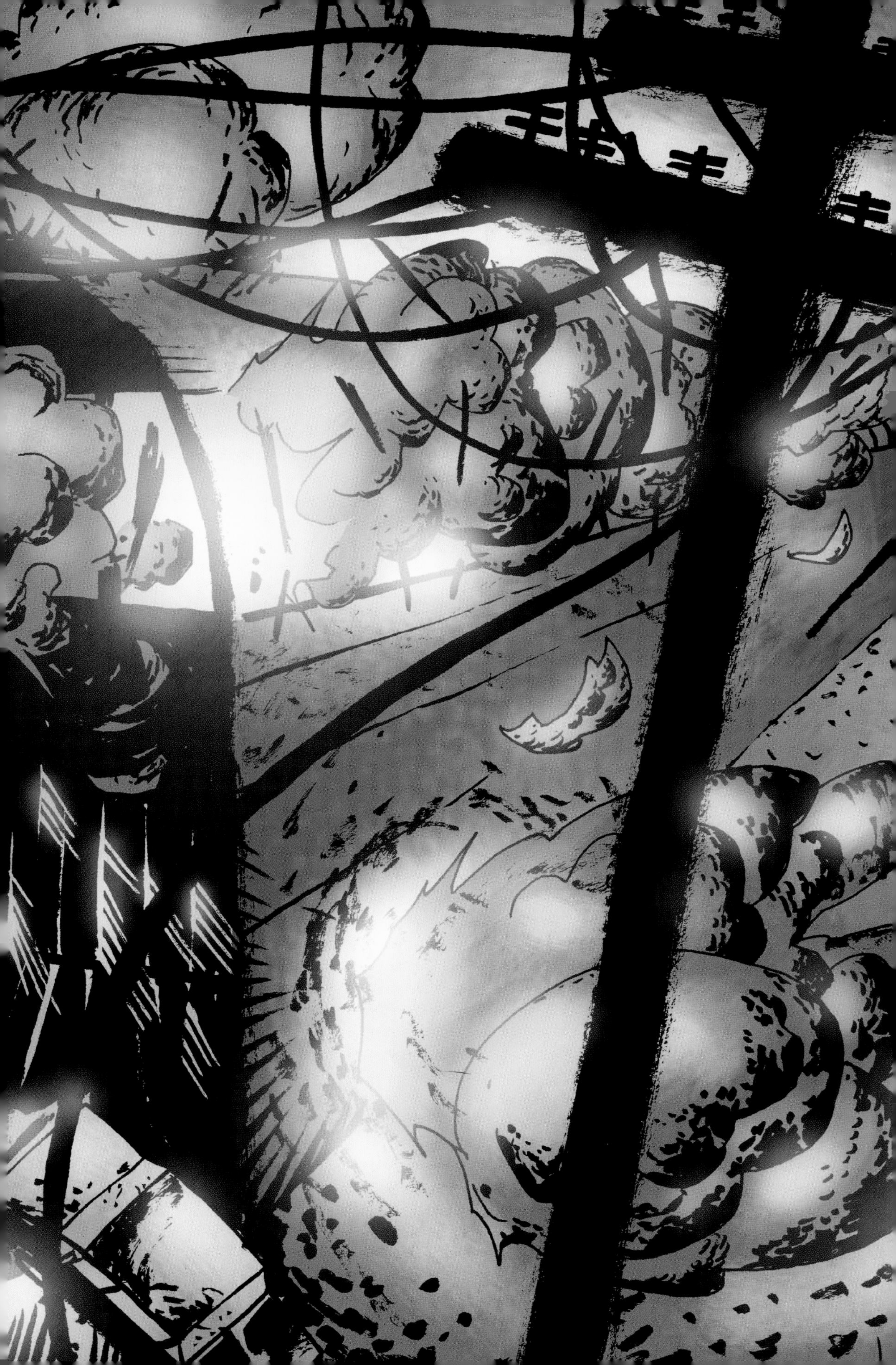

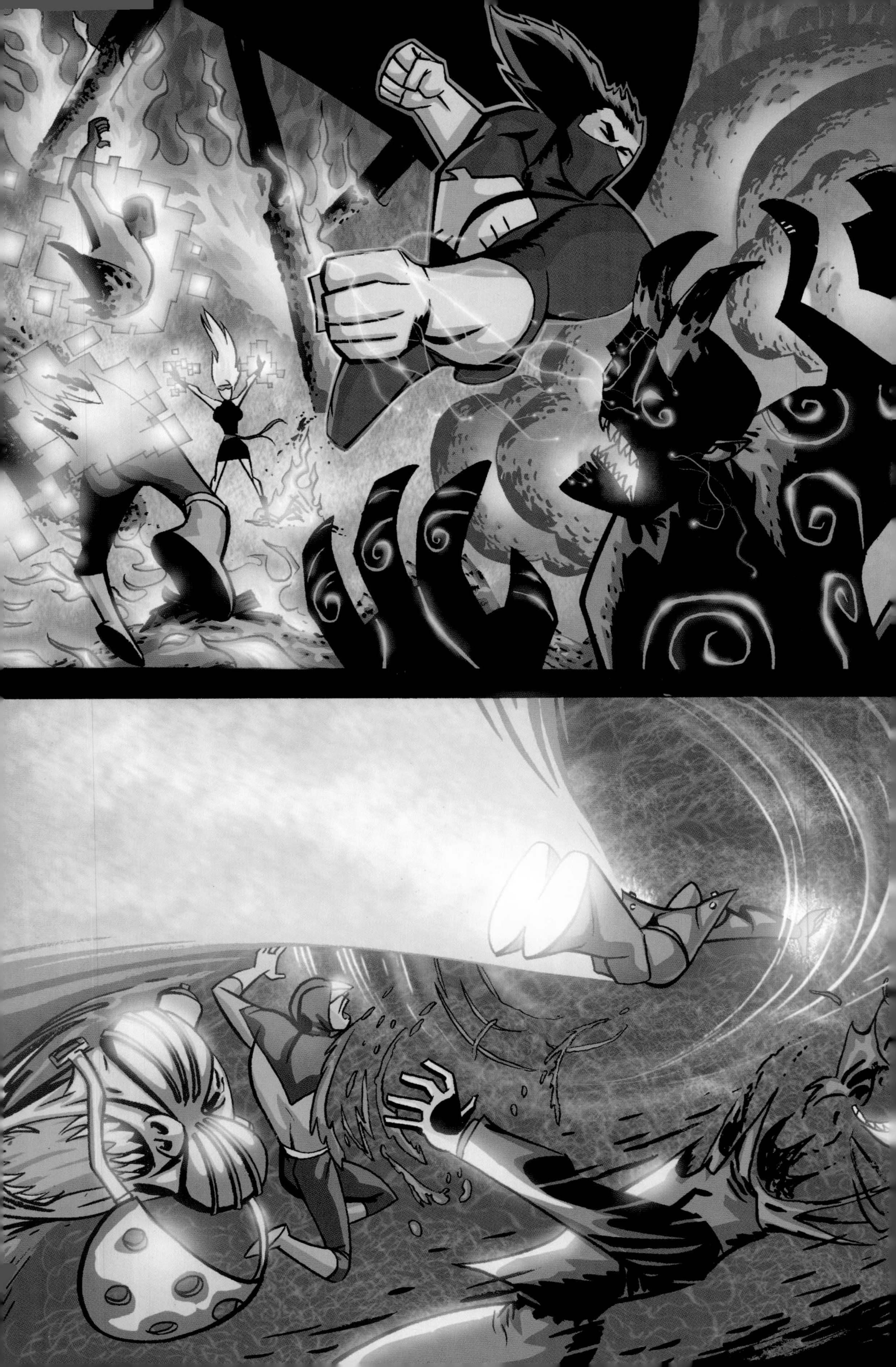

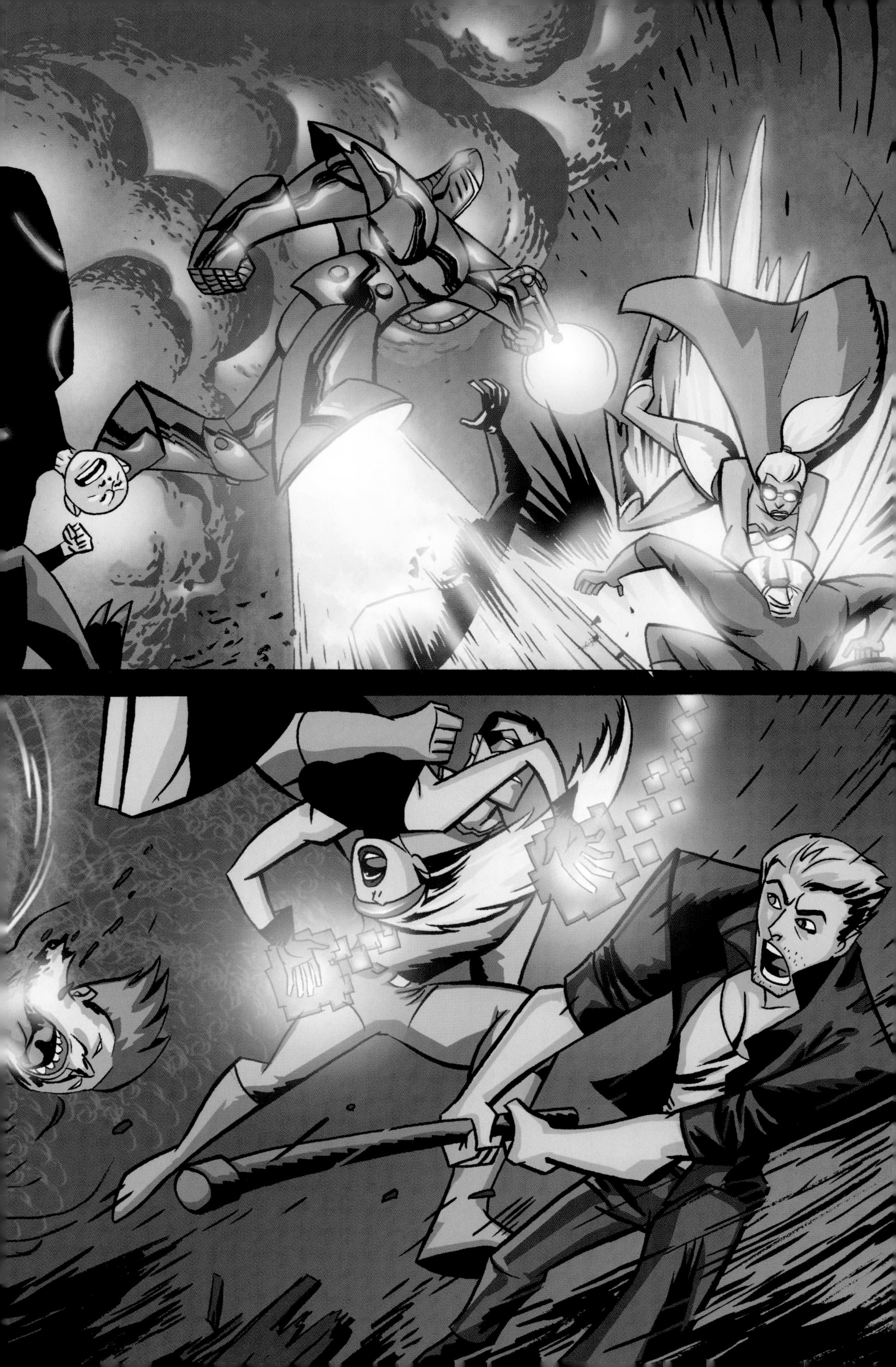

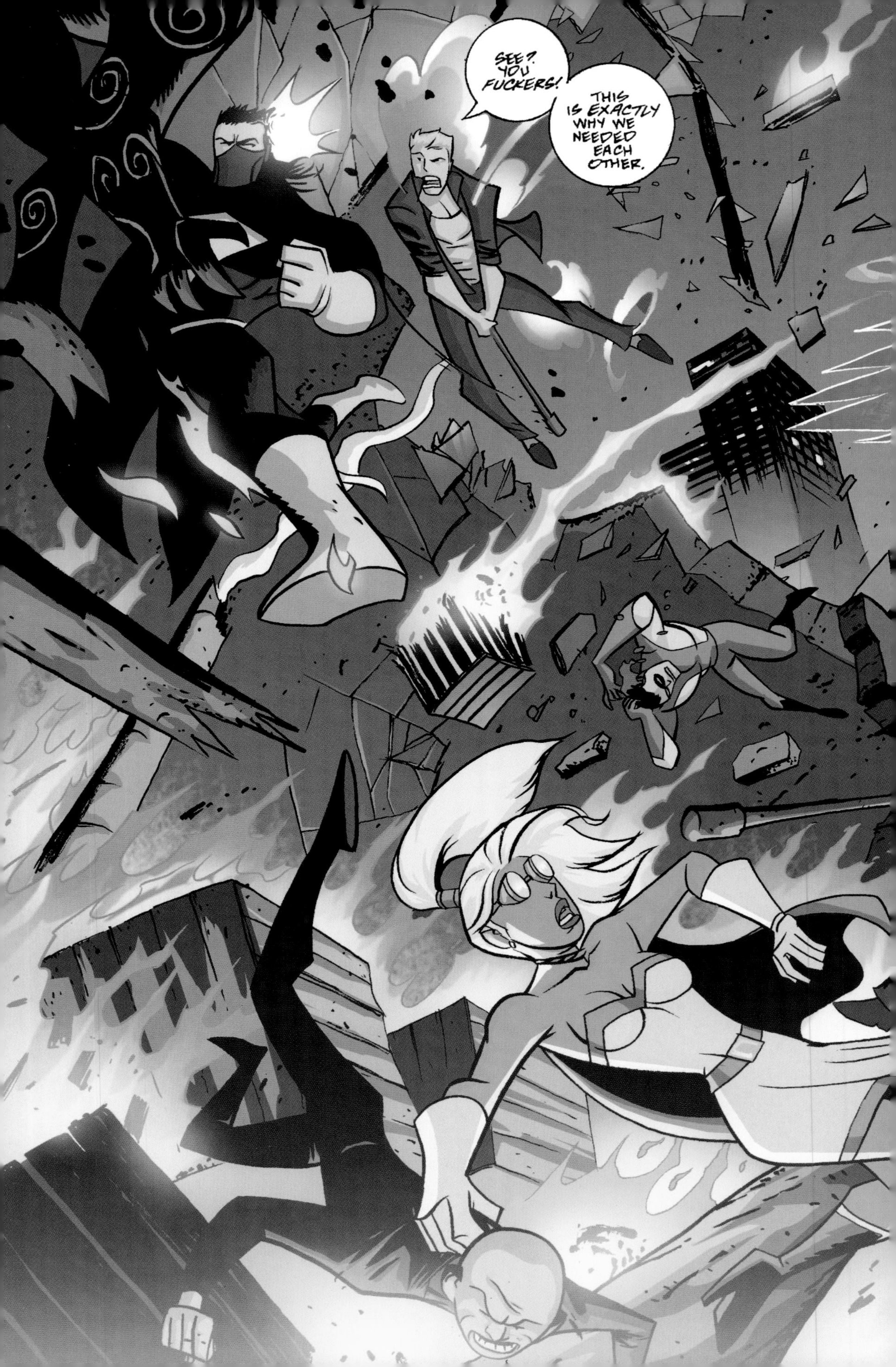
SEE? YOU FUCKERS!
THIS IS EXACTLY WHY WE NEEDED EACH OTHER.

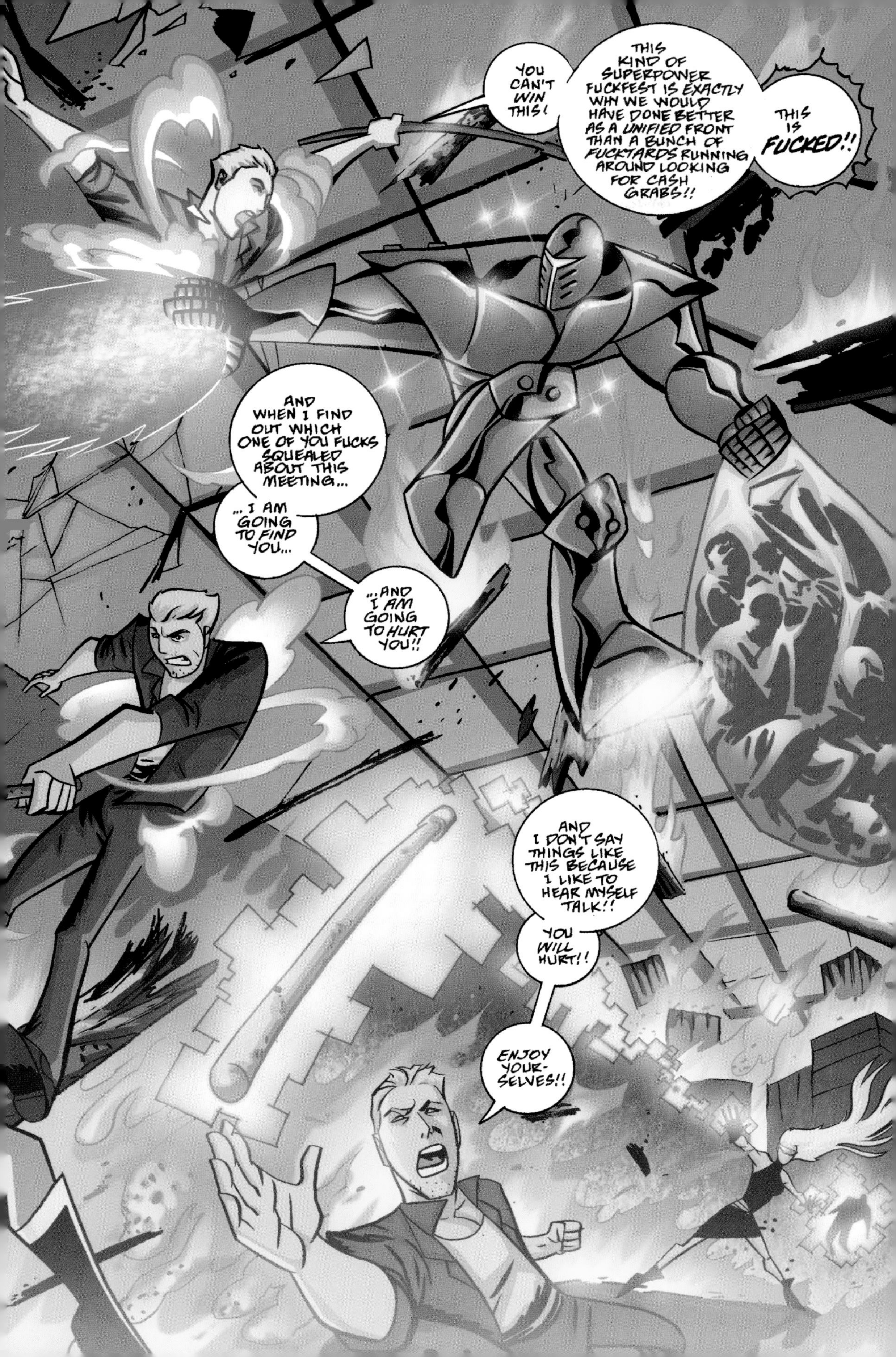
YOU CAN'T WIN THIS!
THIS KIND OF SUPERPOWER FUCKFEST IS EXACTLY WHY WE WOULD HAVE DONE BETTER AS A UNIFIED FRONT THAN A BUNCH OF FUCKTARDS RUNNING AROUND LOOKING FOR CASH GRABS!!
THIS IS FUCKED!!
AND WHEN I FIND OUT WHICH ONE OF YOU FUCKS SQUEALED ABOUT THIS MEETING...
...I AM GOING TO FIND YOU...
...AND I AM GOING TO HURT YOU!!
AND I DON'T SAY THINGS LIKE THIS BECAUSE I LIKE TO HEAR MYSELF TALK!!
YOU WILL HURT!!
ENJOY YOUR-SELVES!!

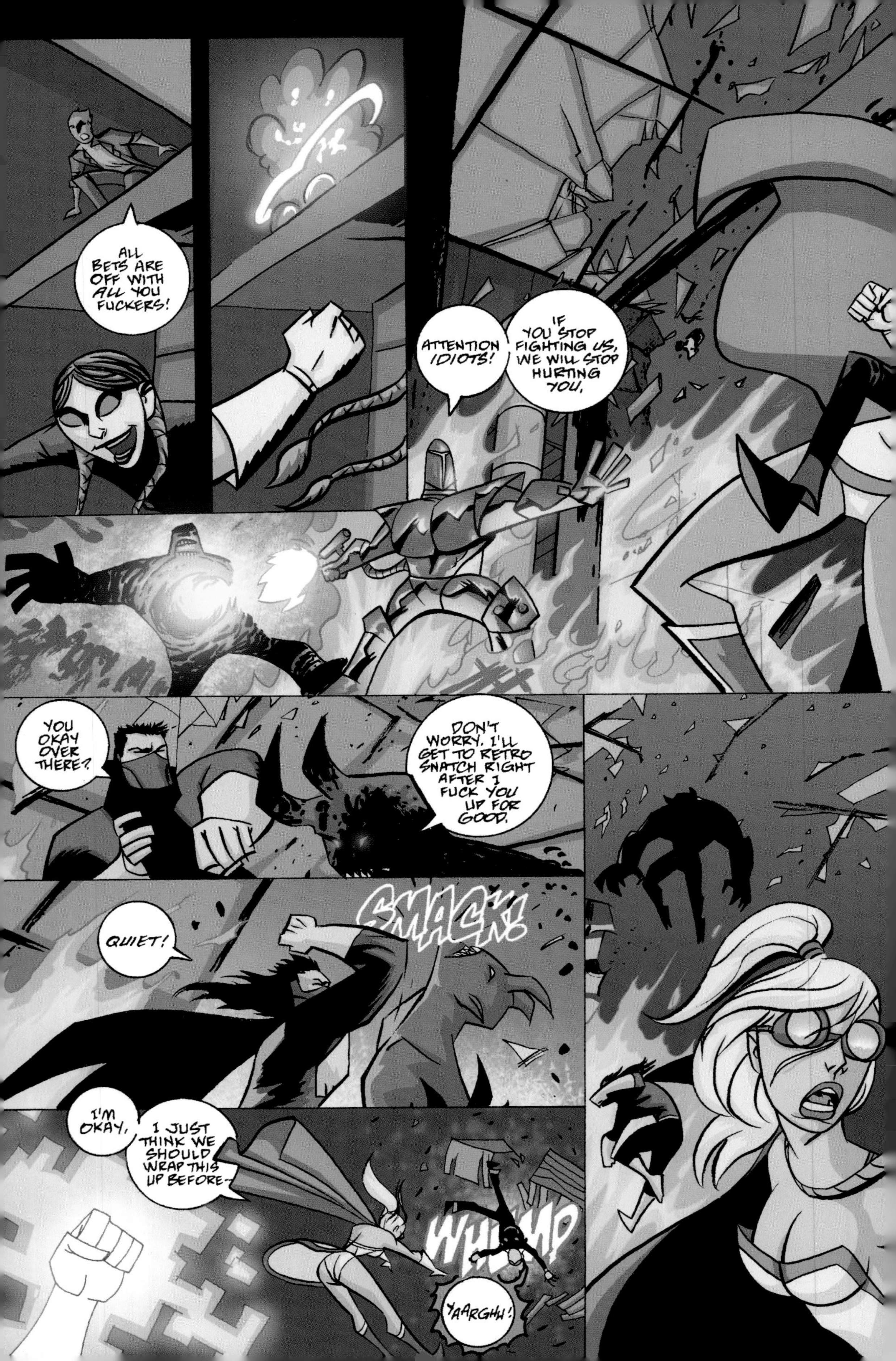
ALL BETS ARE OFF WITH ALL YOU FUCKERS!
ATTENTION IDIOTS!
IF YOU STOP FIGHTING US, WE WILL STOP HURTING YOU.
YOU OKAY OVER THERE?
DON'T WORRY. I'LL GET TO RETRO SNATCH RIGHT AFTER I FUCK YOU UP FOR GOOD.
SMACK!
QUIET!
I'M OKAY.
I JUST THINK WE SHOULD WRAP THIS UP BEFORE--
YAARGHH!

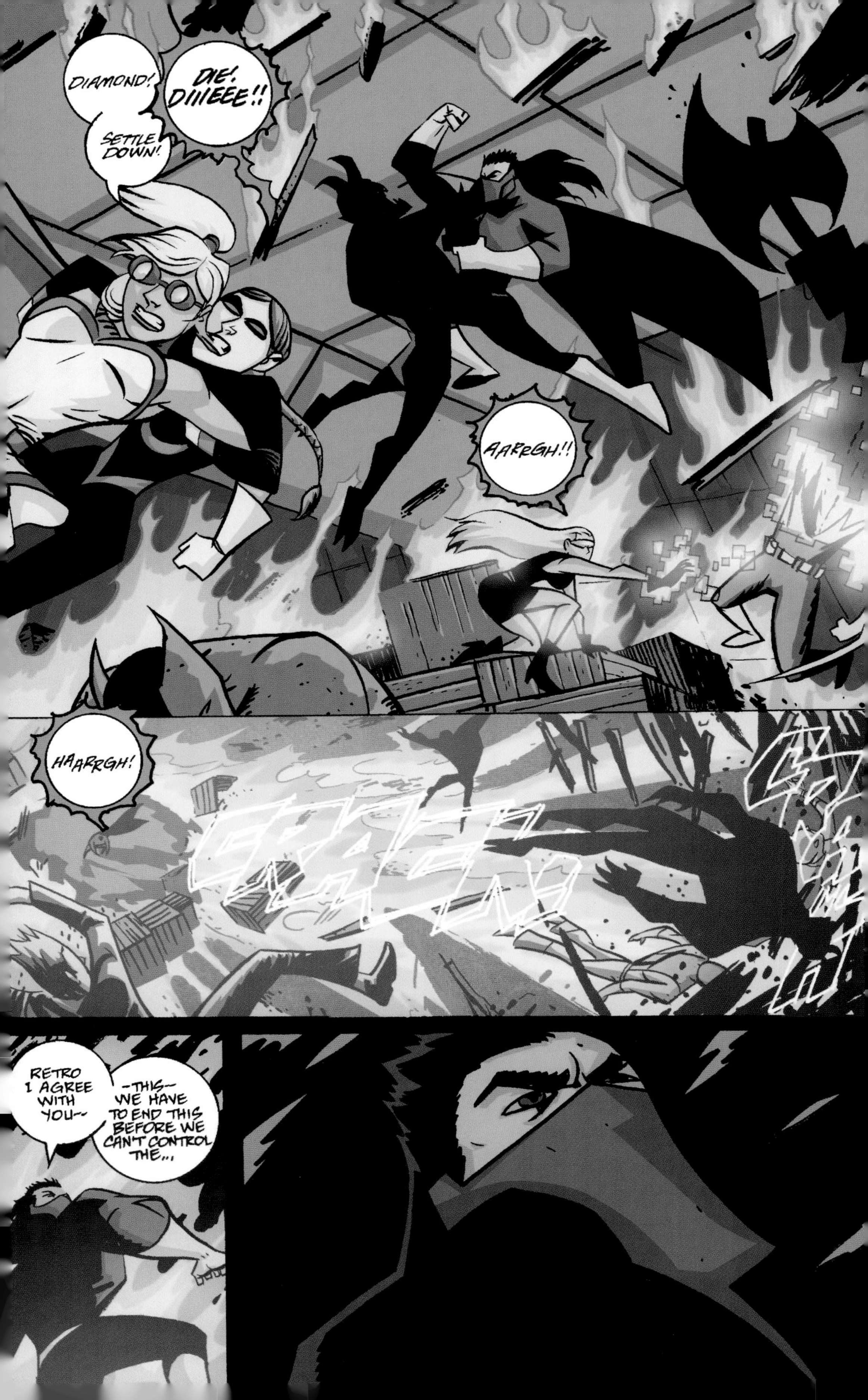
DIAMOND!
SETTLE DOWN!
DIE! DIIIEEE!!
AARRGH!!
HAARRGH!
RETRO I AGREE WITH YOU--
--THIS-- WE HAVE TO END THIS BEFORE WE CAN'T CONTROL THE...

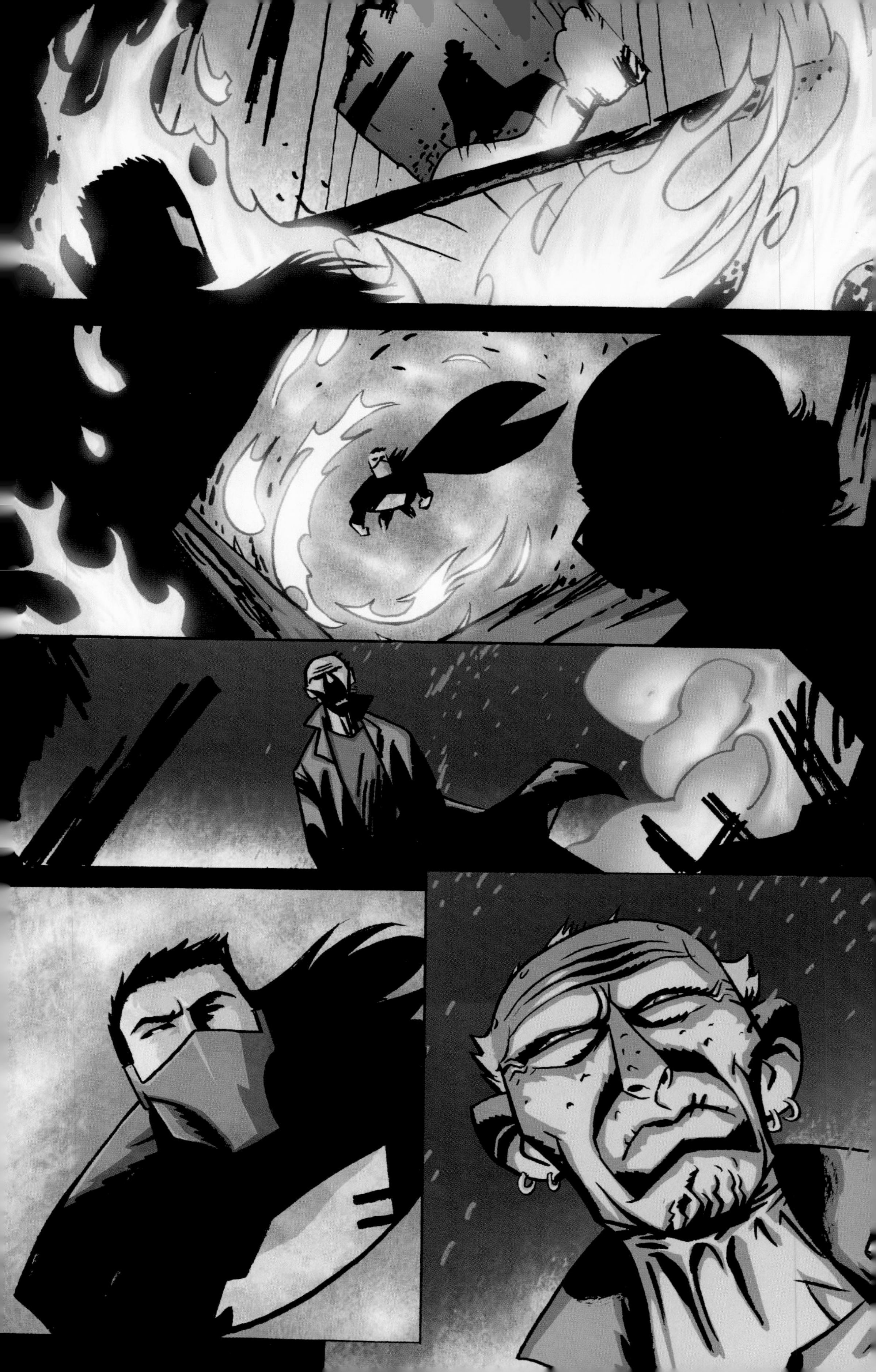

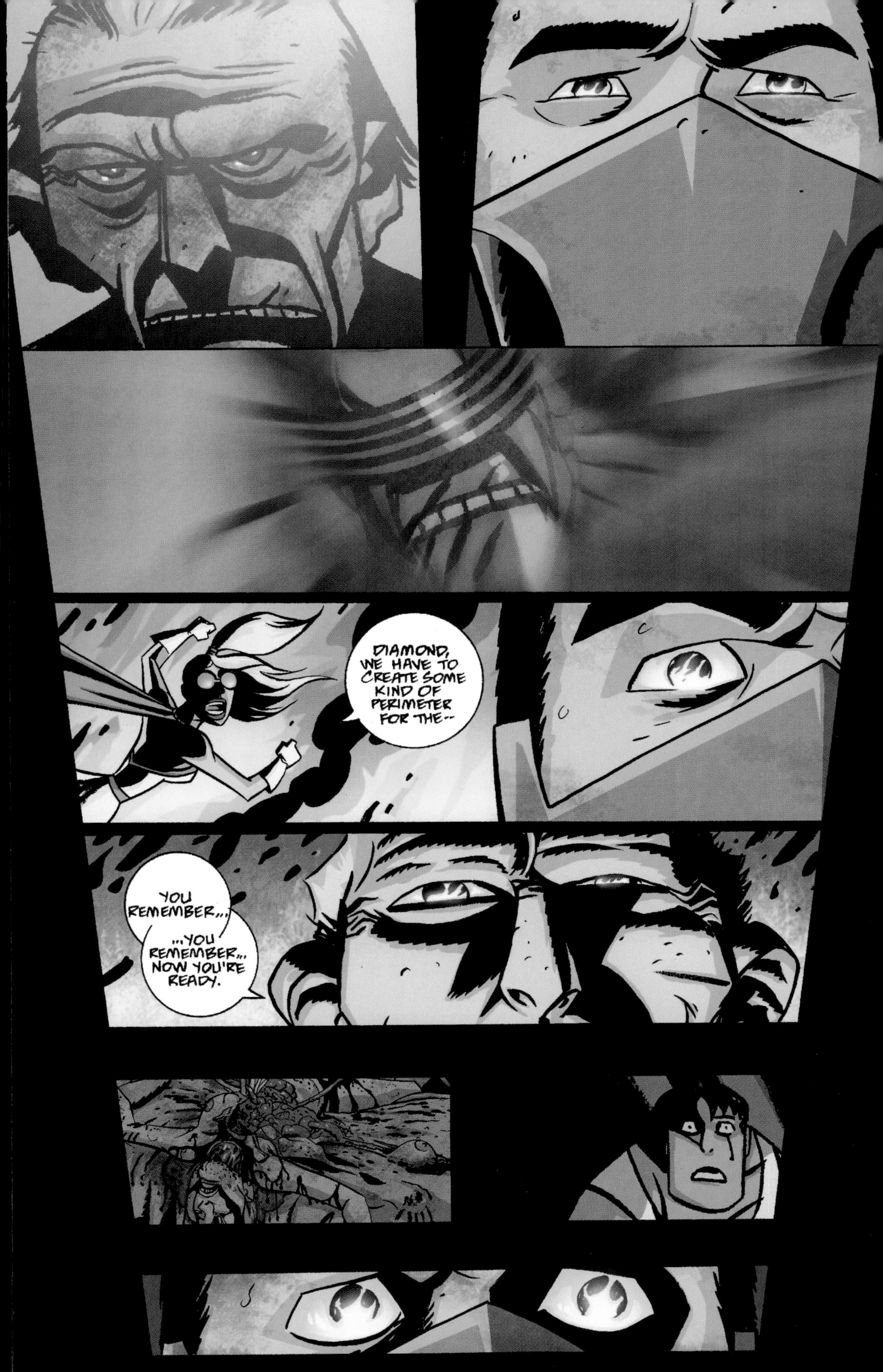
DIAMOND, WE HAVE TO CREATE SOME KIND OF PERIMETER FOR THE--
YOU REMEMBER...
...YOU REMEMBER... NOW YOU'RE READY.

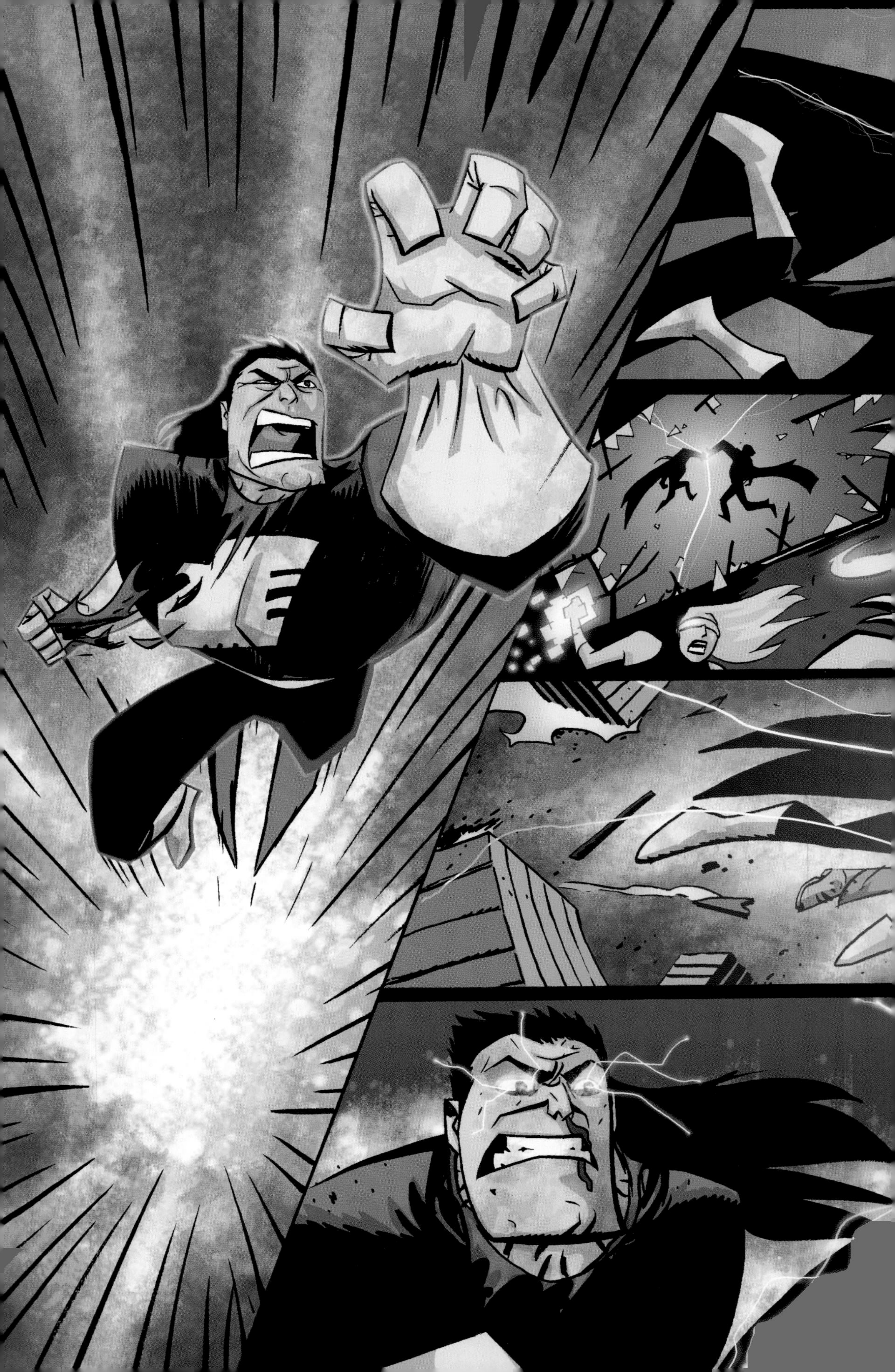

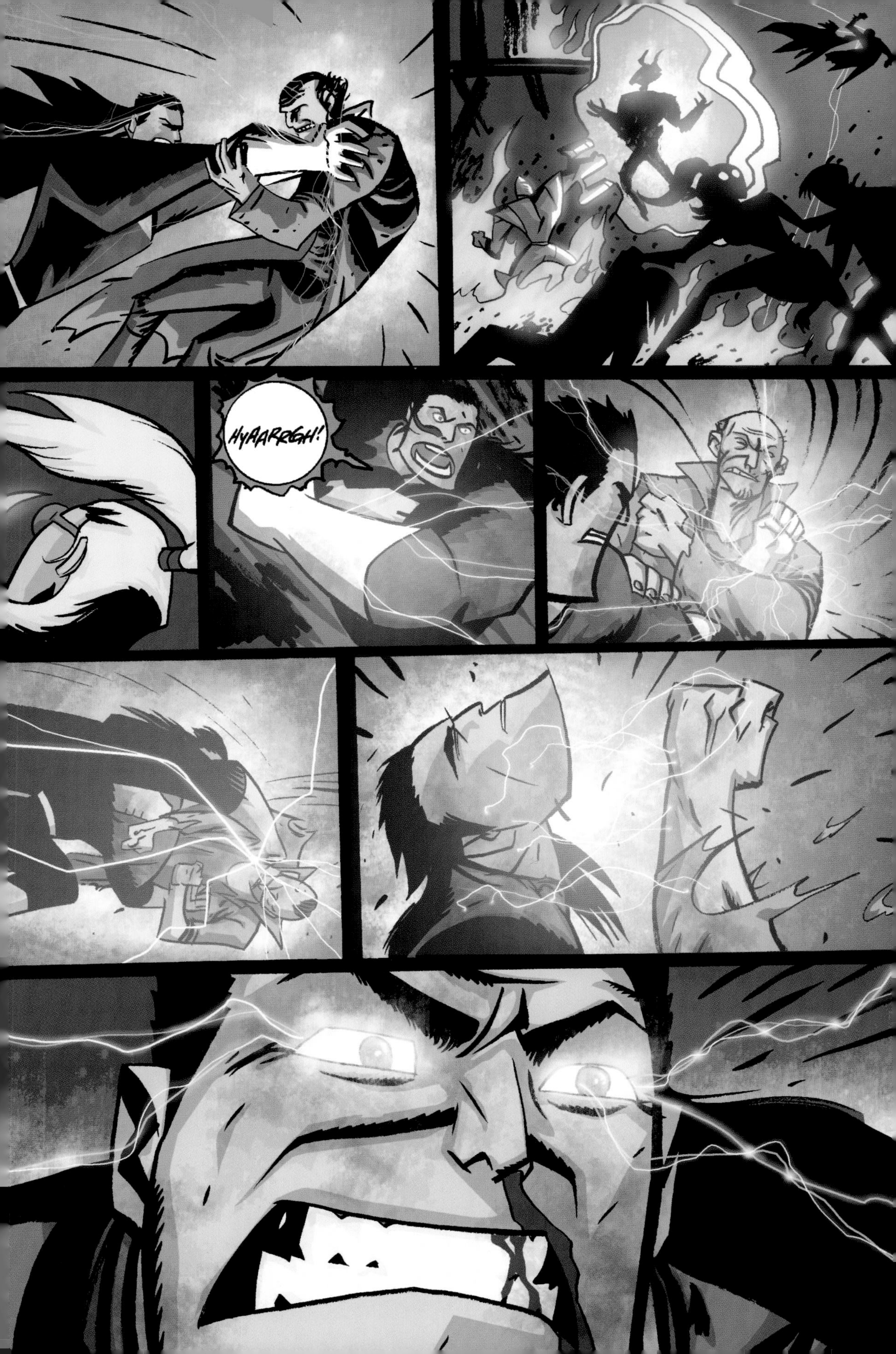
HYAARRGH!

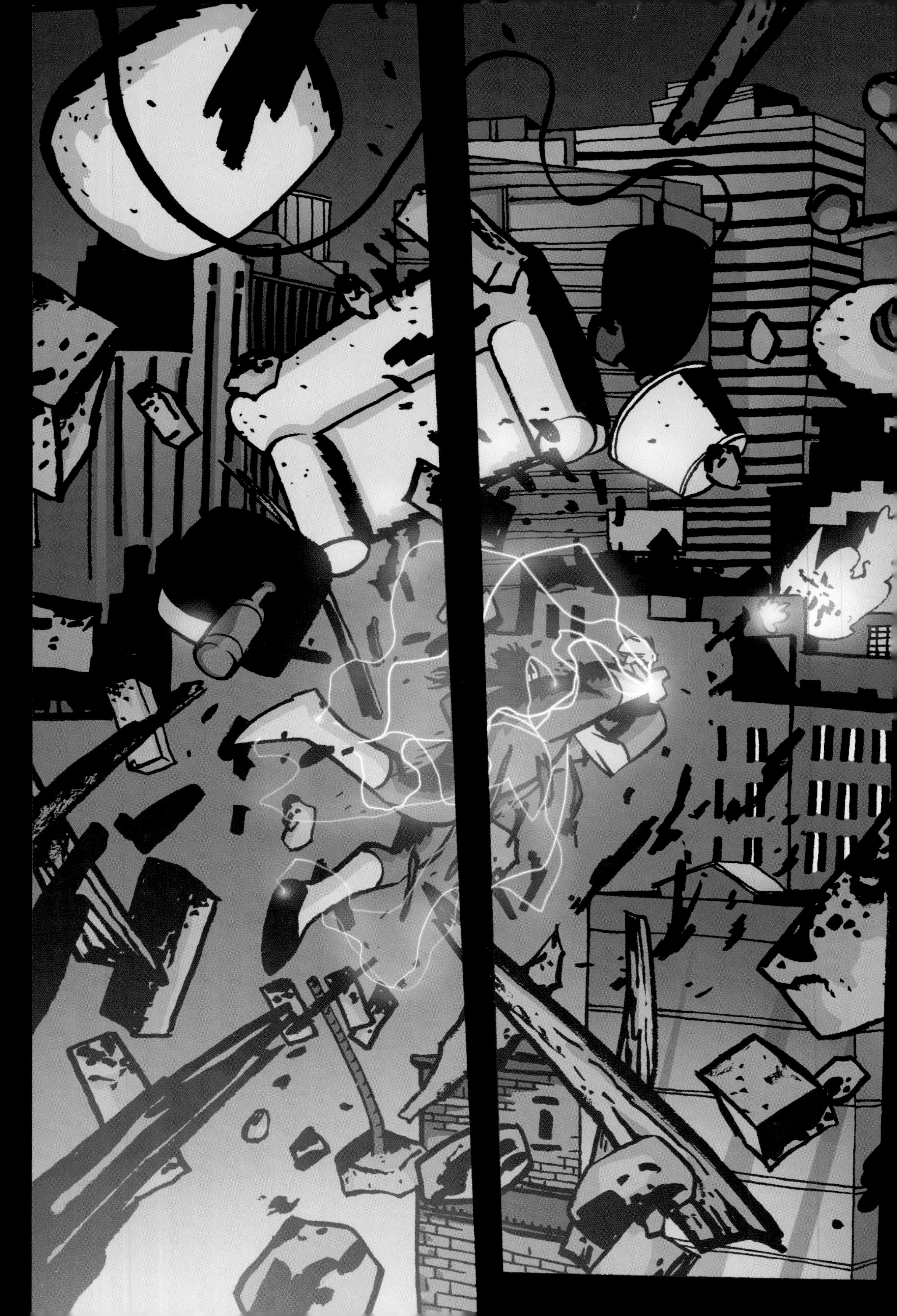

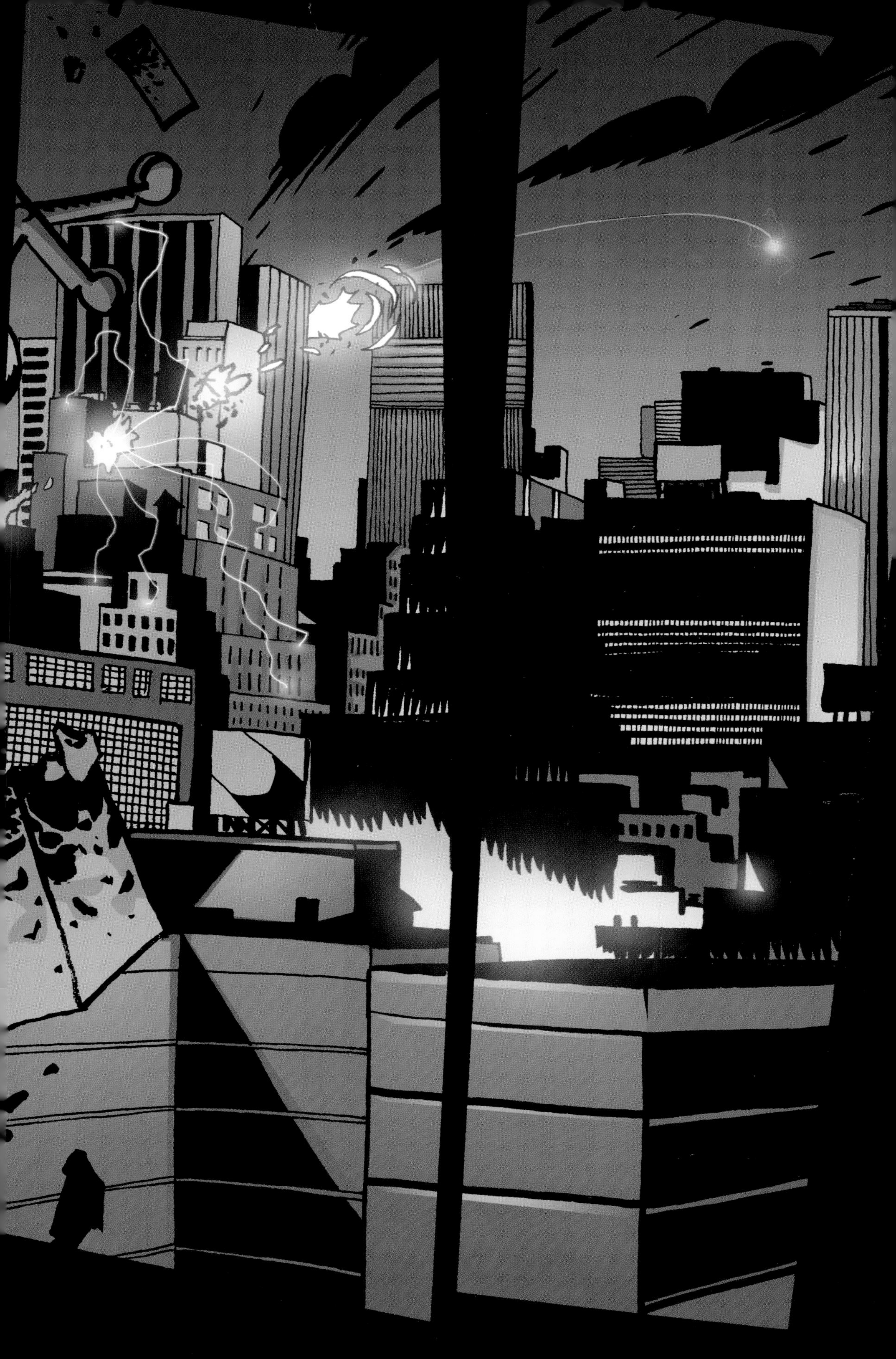

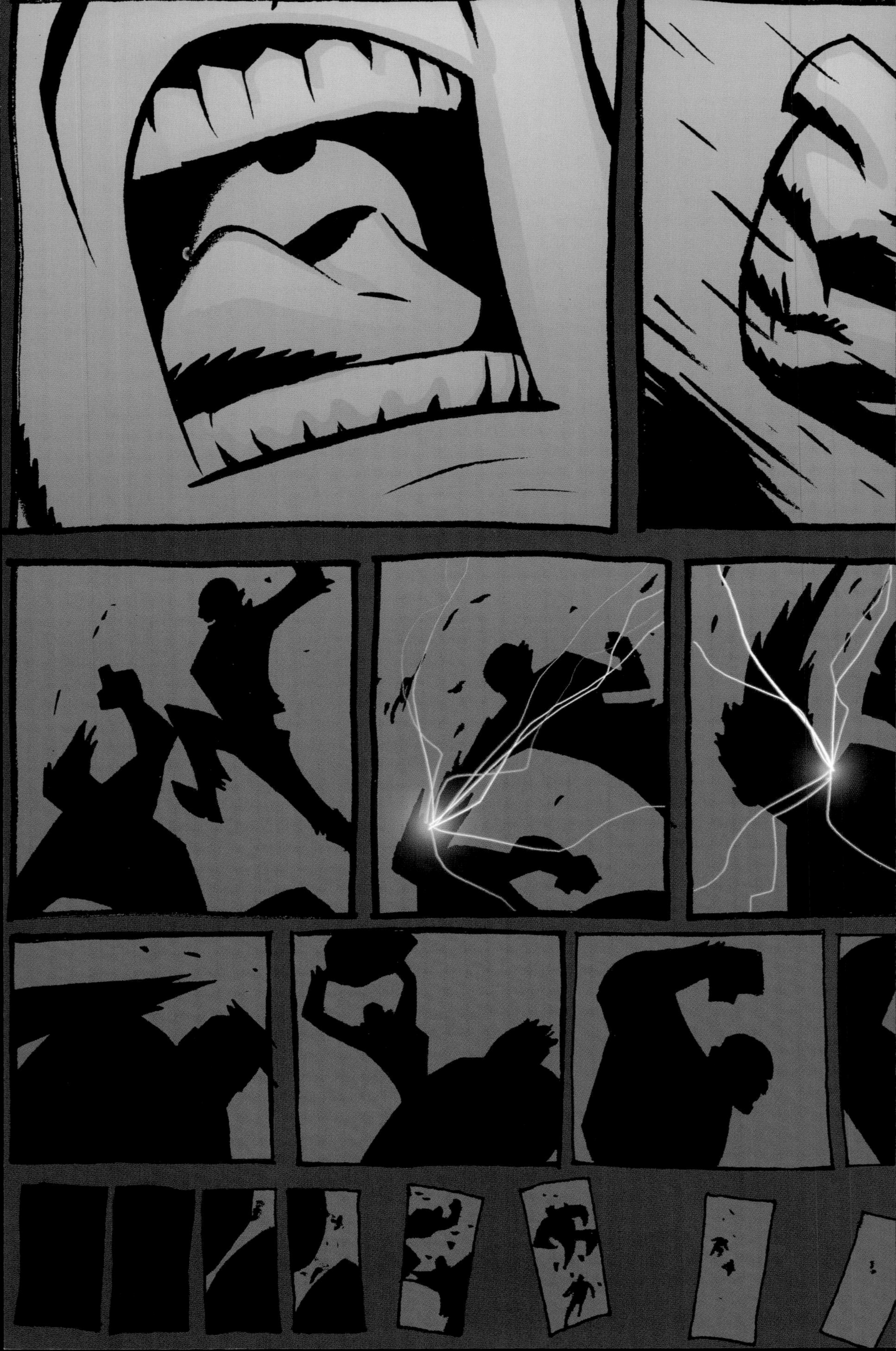

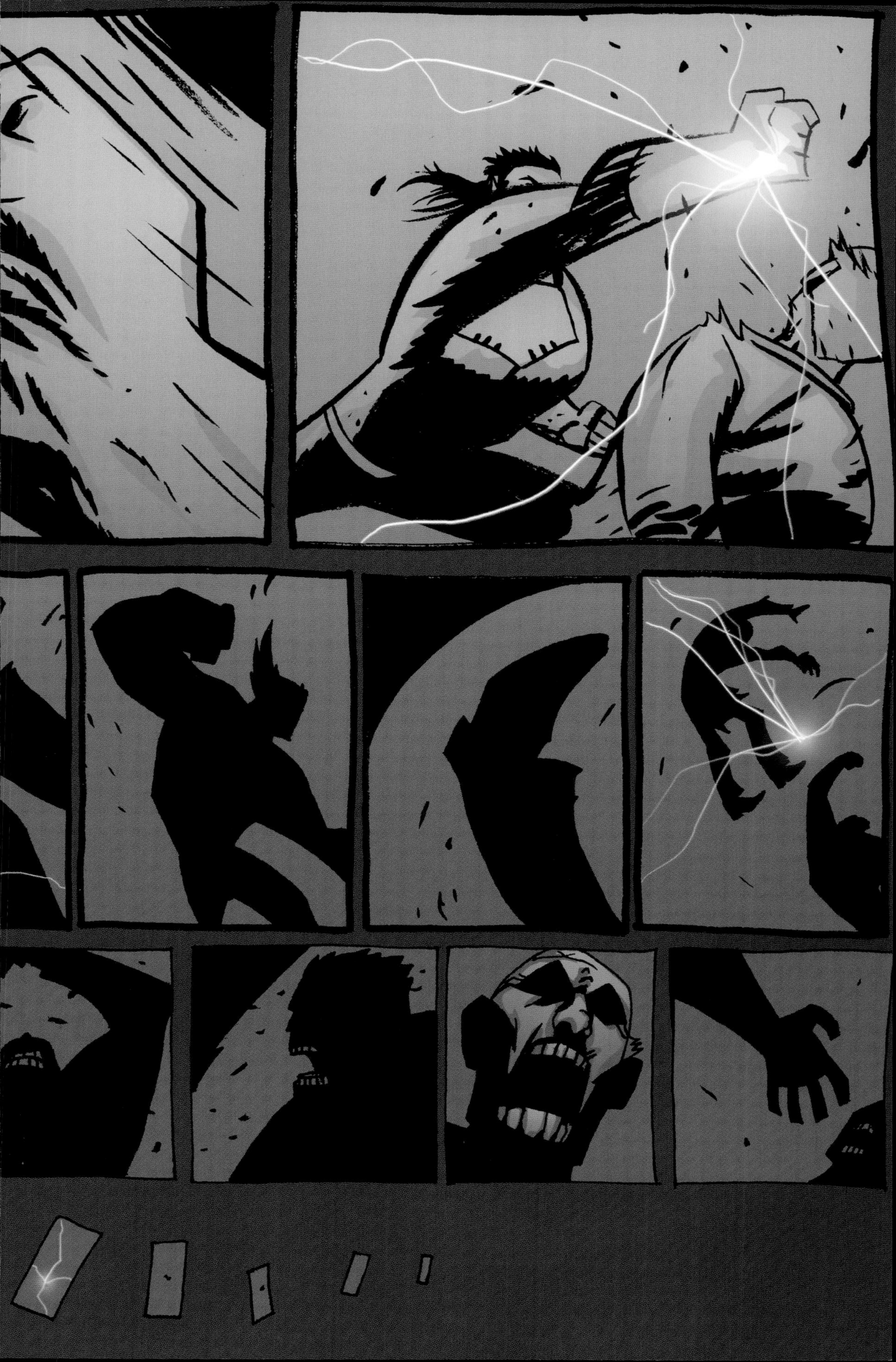

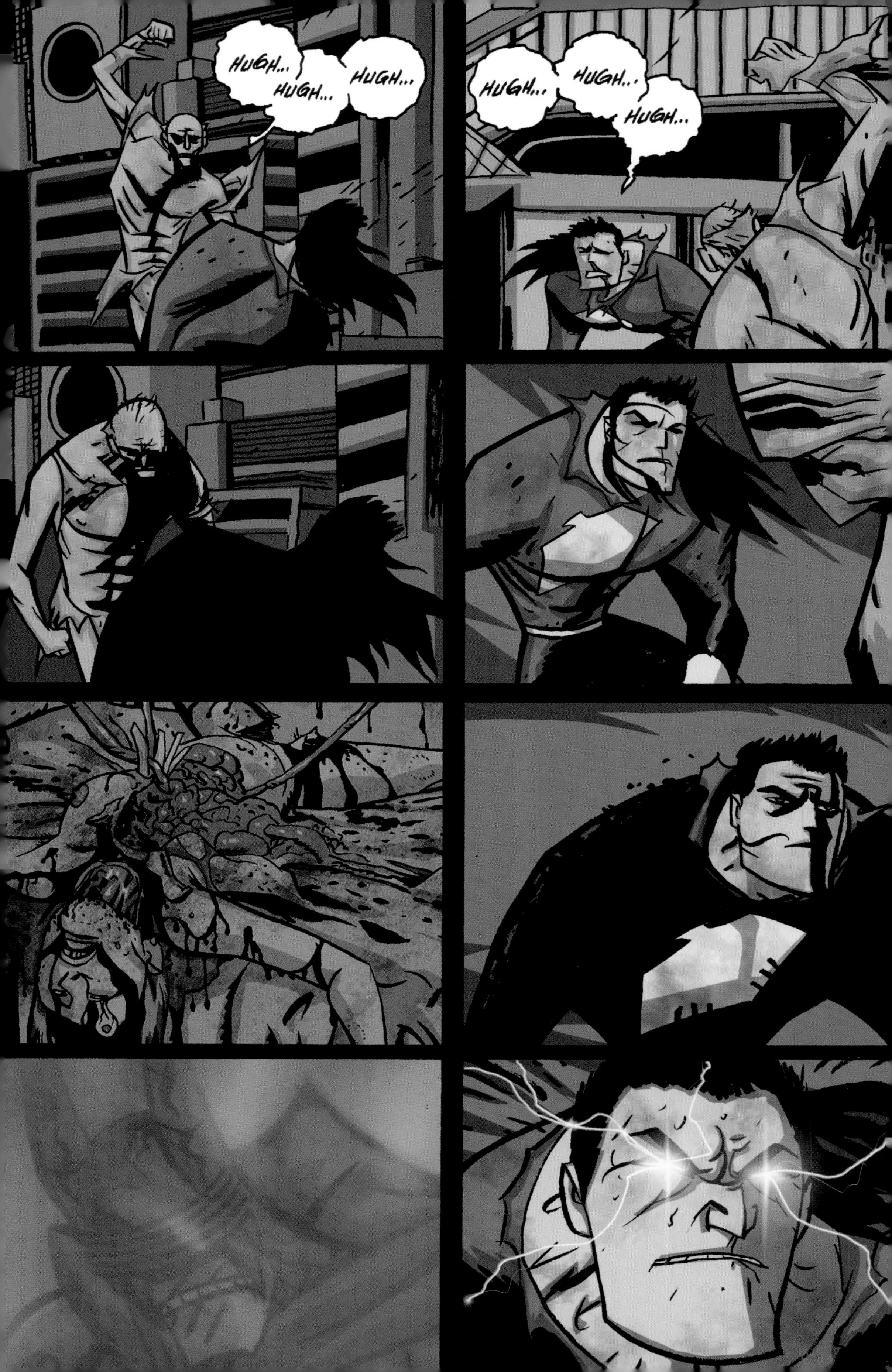
HUGH...
HUGH...
HUGH...
HUGH...
HUGH...
HUGH...

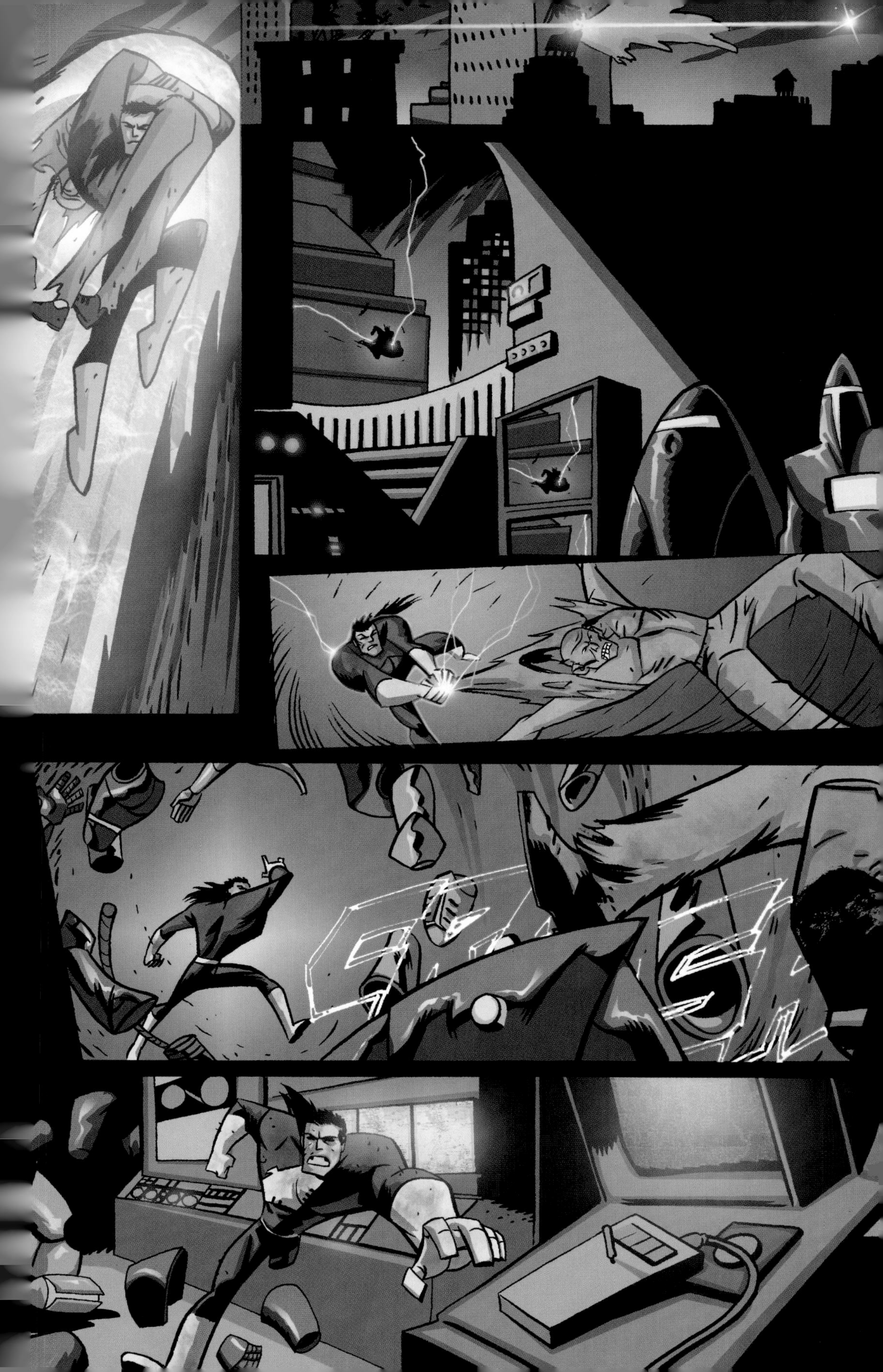

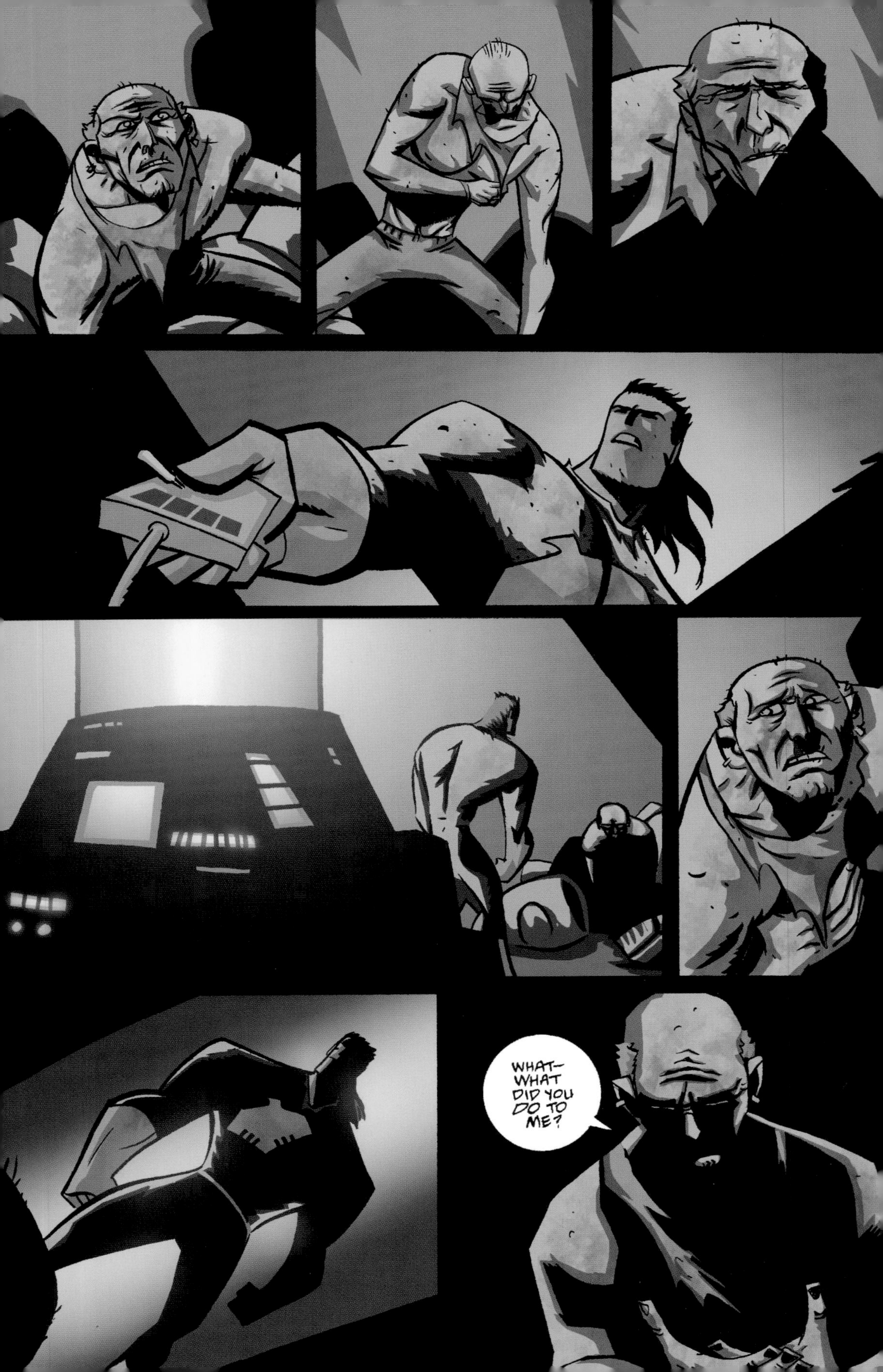
WHAT— WHAT DID YOU DO TO ME?

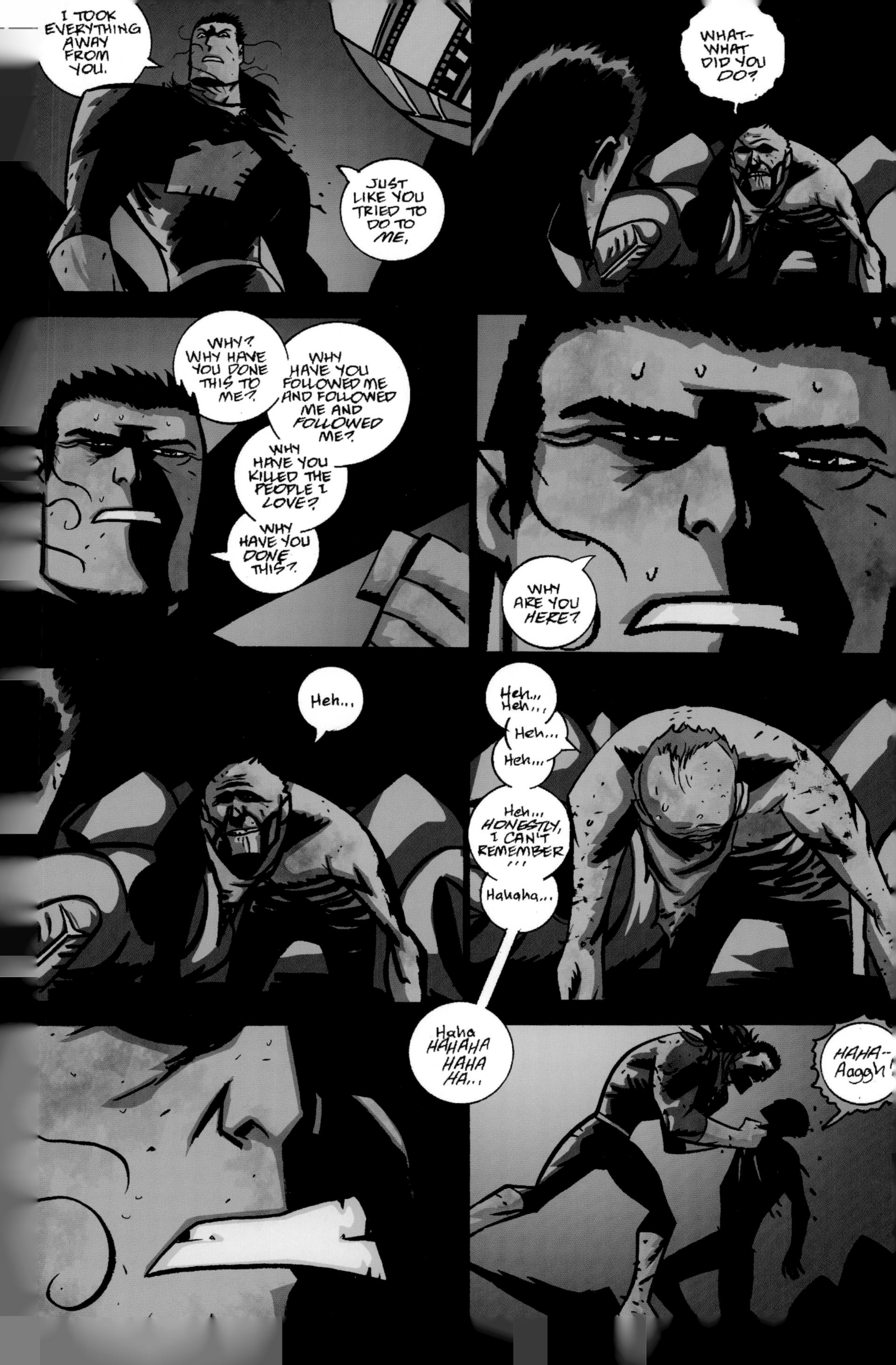
I TOOK EVERYTHING AWAY FROM YOU.
JUST LIKE YOU TRIED TO DO TO ME.
WHAT-- WHAT DID YOU DO?
WHY? WHY HAVE YOU DONE THIS TO ME?
WHY HAVE YOU FOLLOWED ME AND FOLLOWED ME AND FOLLOWED ME?
WHY HAVE YOU KILLED THE PEOPLE I LOVE?
WHY HAVE YOU DONE THIS?
WHY ARE YOU HERE?
Heh...
Heh... Heh...
Heh...
Heh...
Heh... HONESTLY, I CAN'T REMEMBER...
Hahaha...
Haha HAHAHA HAHA HA...
HAHA-- Aaggh!

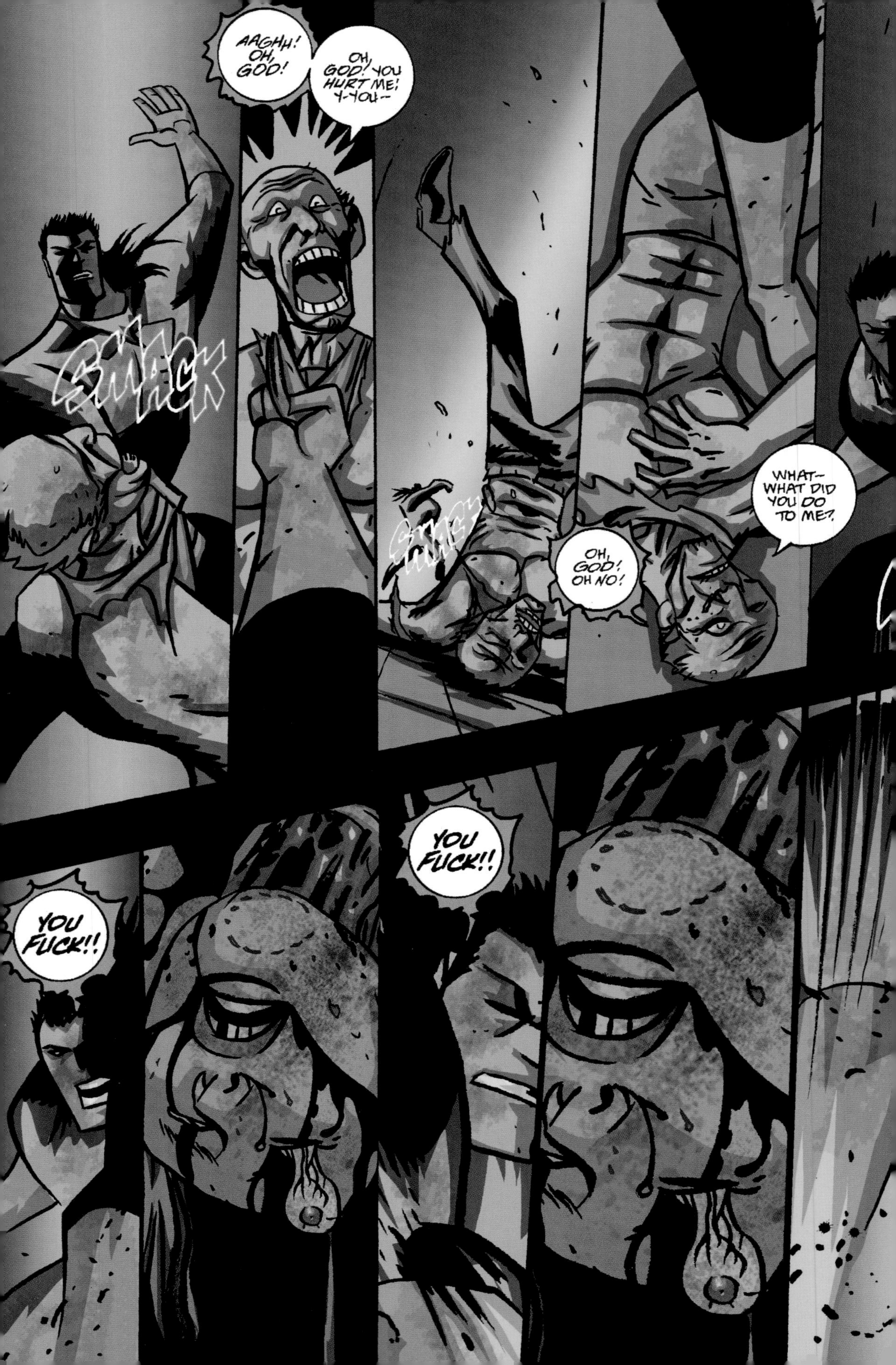
AAGHH! OH, GOD!
SMACK
OH, GOD! YOU HURT ME! Y-YOU--
OH, GOD! OH NO!
WHAT-- WHAT DID YOU DO TO ME?
YOU FUCK!!
YOU FUCK!!

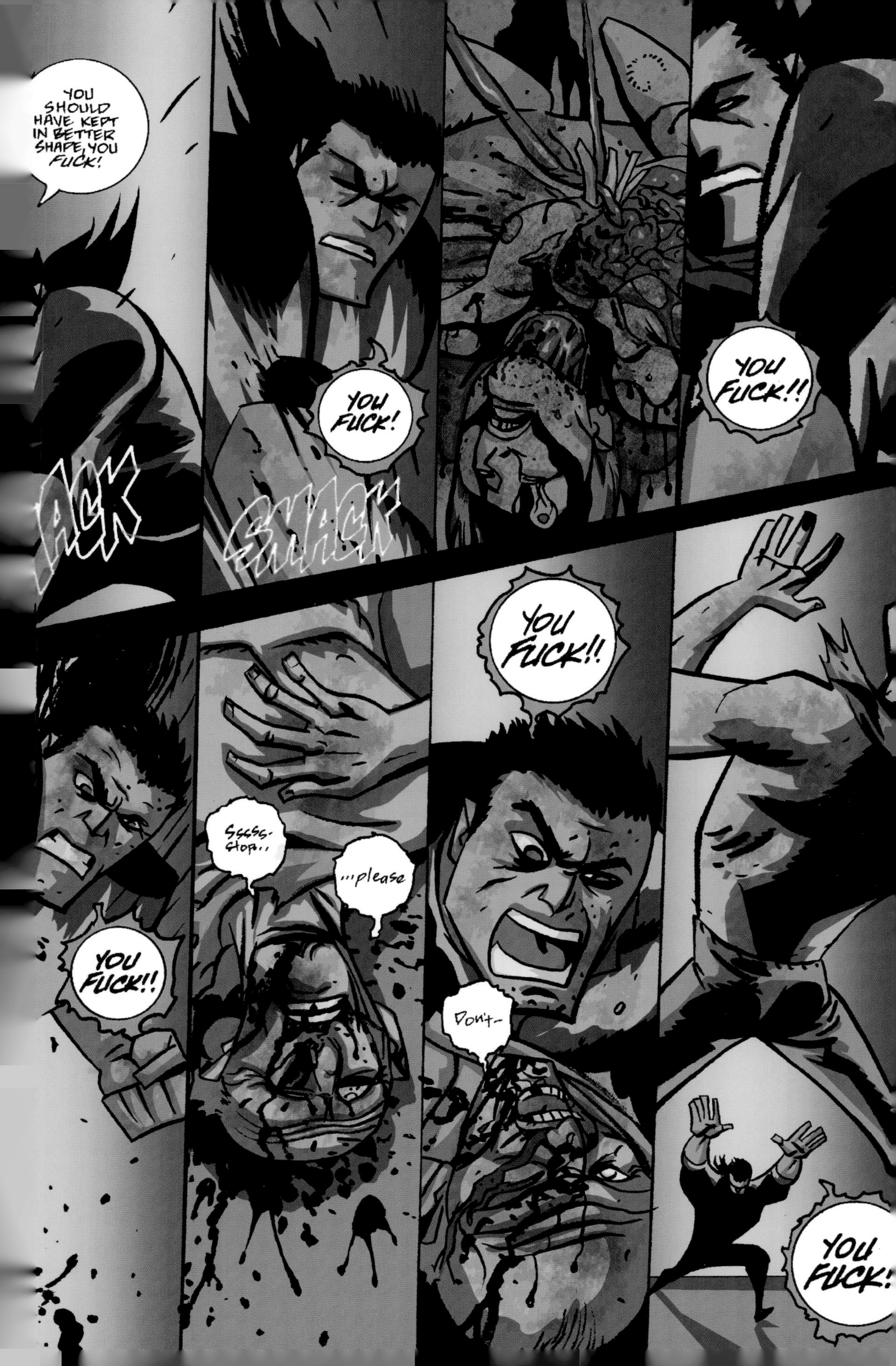

YOU SHOULD HAVE KEPT IN BETTER SHAPE, YOU FUCK!
ACK
YOU FUCK!
SMACK
YOU FUCK!!
YOU FUCK!!
YOU FUCK!!
Ssssss-stop..
...please
Don't-
YOU FUCK!

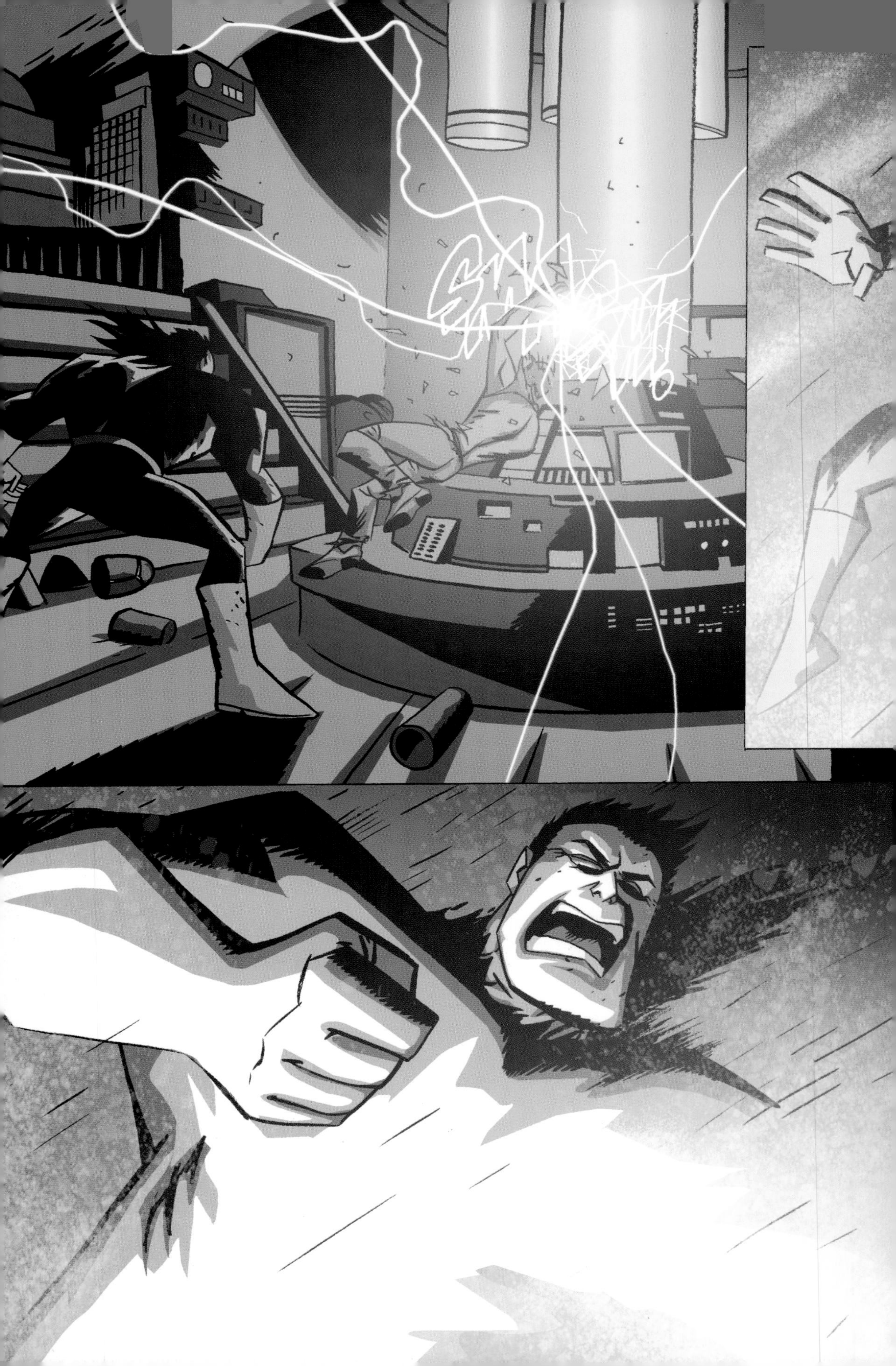

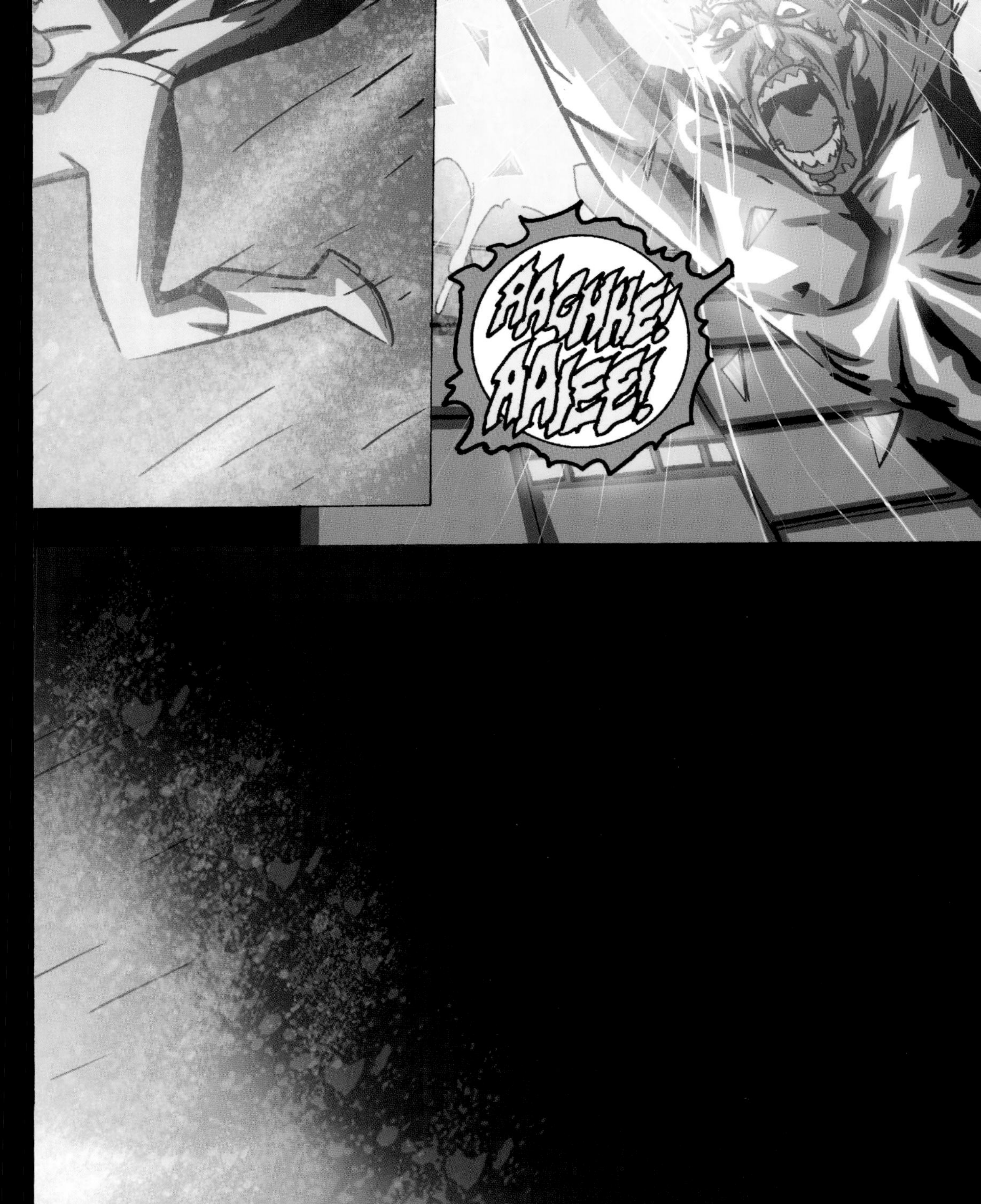
AAGHHE! AAIEE!

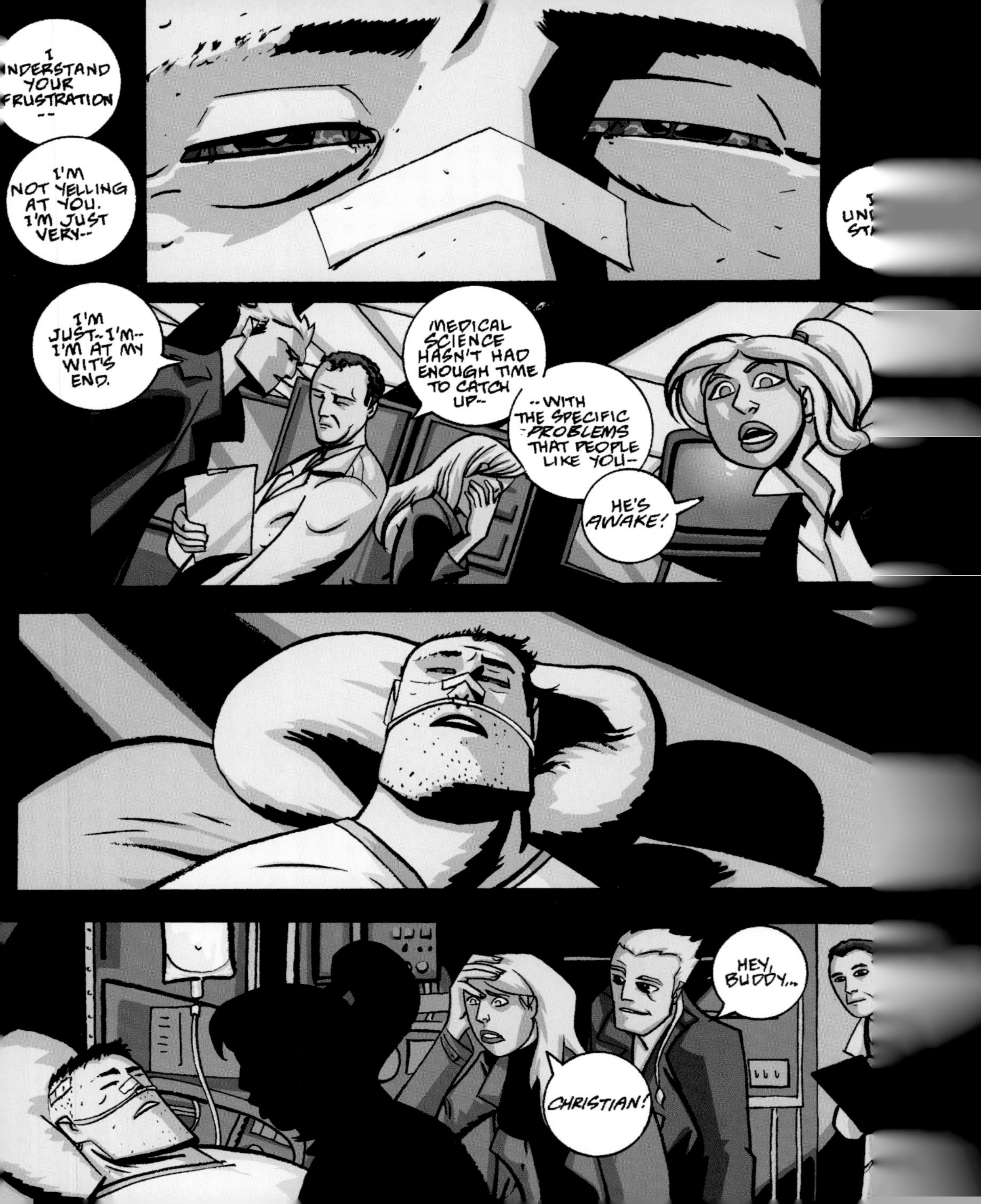
I NDERSTAND YOUR FRUSTRATION --
I'M NOT YELLING AT YOU. I'M JUST VERY--
I'M JUST-- I'M-- I'M AT MY WIT'S END.
MEDICAL SCIENCE HASN'T HAD ENOUGH TIME TO CATCH UP--
--WITH THE SPECIFIC PROBLEMS THAT PEOPLE LIKE YOU--
HE'S AWAKE!
HEY, BUDDY...
CHRISTIAN!

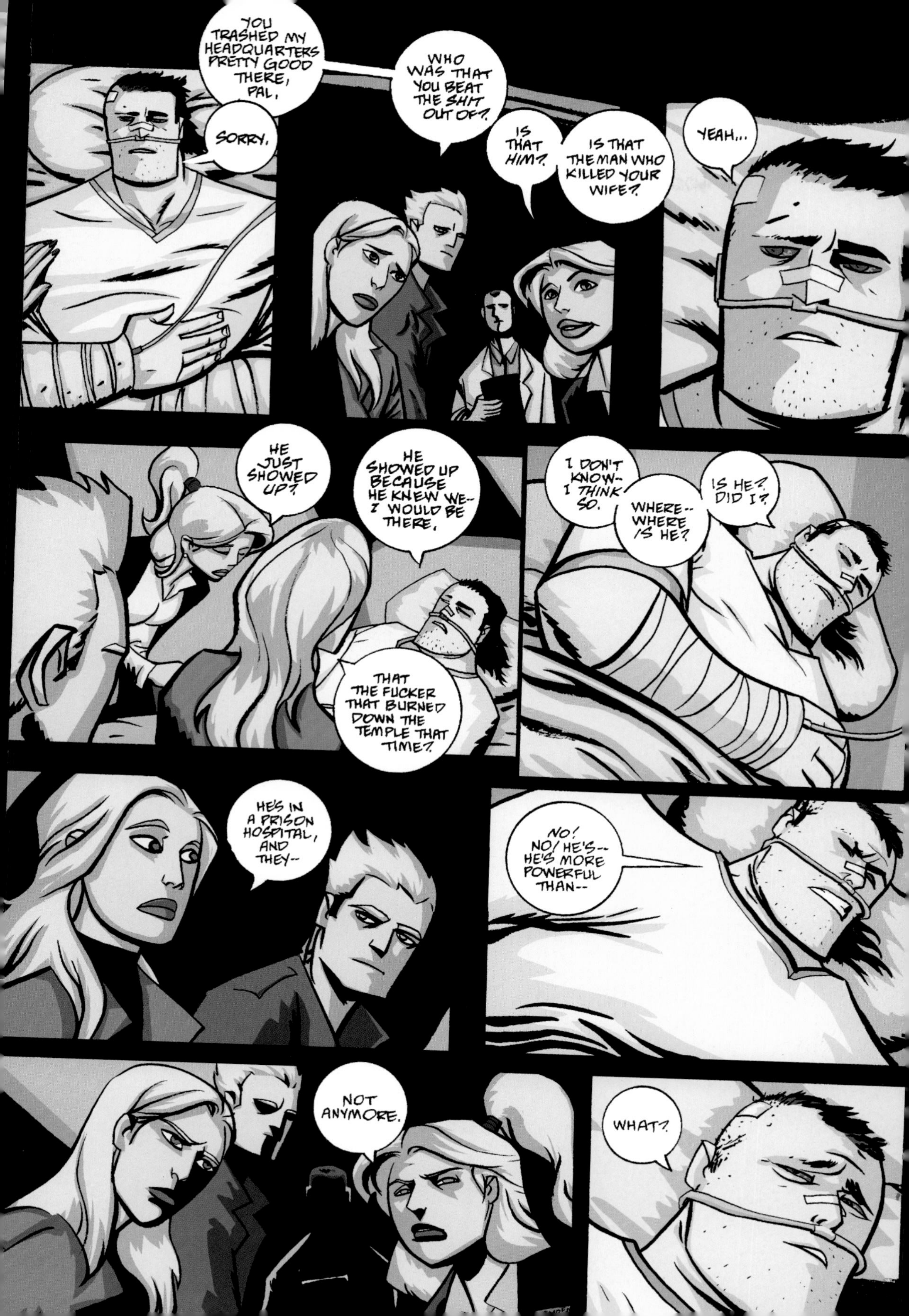
YOU TRASHED MY HEADQUARTERS PRETTY GOOD THERE, PAL.
SORRY.
WHO WAS THAT YOU BEAT THE SHIT OUT OF?
IS THAT HIM?
IS THAT THE MAN WHO KILLED YOUR WIFE?
YEAH...
HE JUST SHOWED UP?
HE SHOWED UP BECAUSE HE KNEW WE-- I WOULD BE THERE.
THAT THE FUCKER THAT BURNED DOWN THE TEMPLE THAT TIME?
I DON'T KNOW-- I THINK SO.
WHERE-- WHERE IS HE?
IS HE? DID I?
HE'S IN A PRISON HOSPITAL, AND THEY--
NO! NO! HE'S-- HE'S MORE POWERFUL THAN--
NOT ANYMORE.
WHAT?

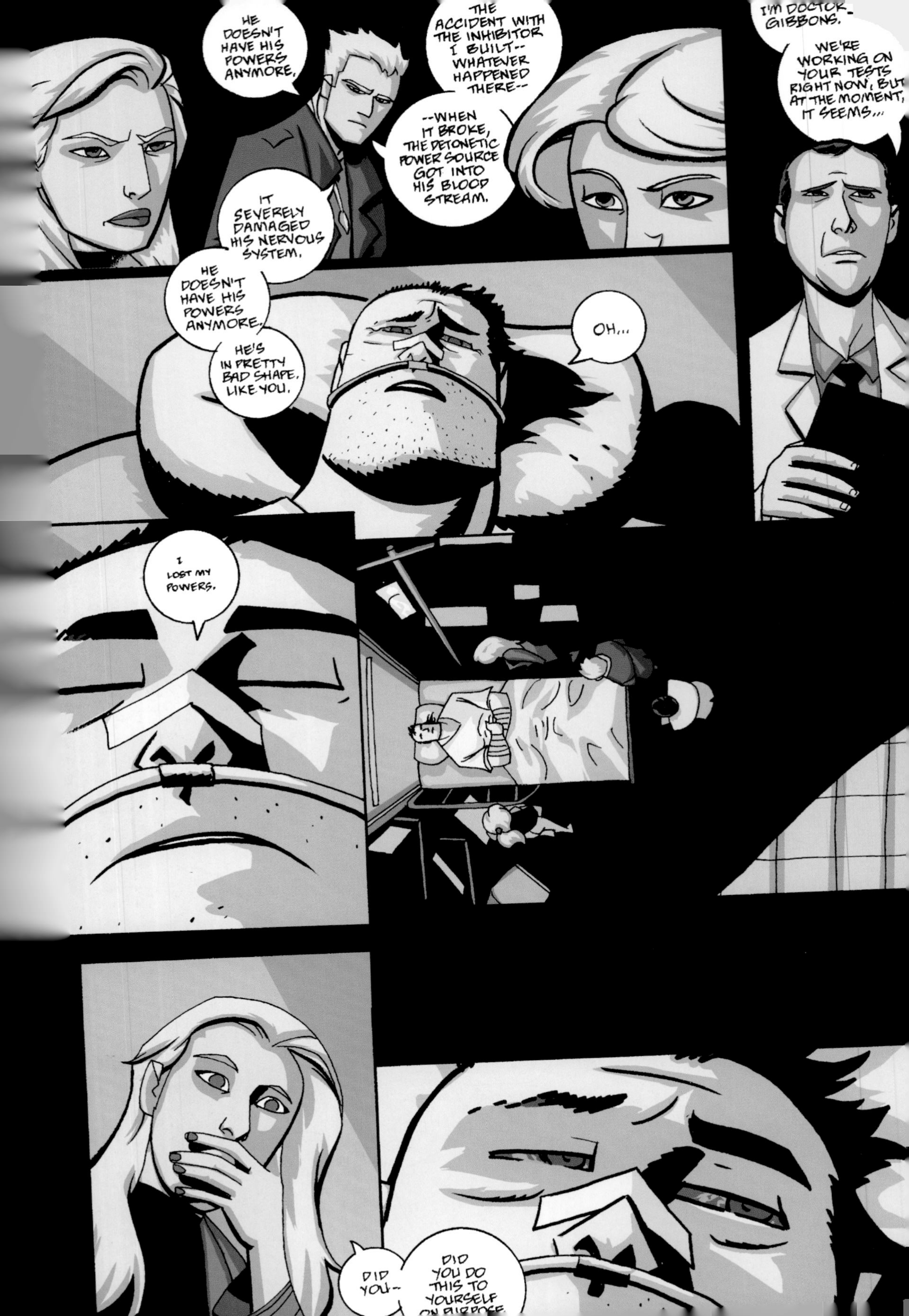
HE DOESN'T HAVE HIS POWERS ANYMORE.
THE ACCIDENT WITH THE INHIBITOR I BUILT-- WHATEVER HAPPENED THERE--
--WHEN IT BROKE, THE DETONETIC POWER SOURCE GOT INTO HIS BLOOD STREAM.
IT SEVERELY DAMAGED HIS NERVOUS SYSTEM.
I'M DOCTOR GIBBONS.
WE'RE WORKING ON YOUR TESTS RIGHT NOW, BUT AT THE MOMENT, IT SEEMS...
HE DOESN'T HAVE HIS POWERS ANYMORE.
HE'S IN PRETTY BAD SHAPE. LIKE YOU.
OH...
I LOST MY POWERS.
DID YOU--
DID YOU DO THIS TO YOURSELF

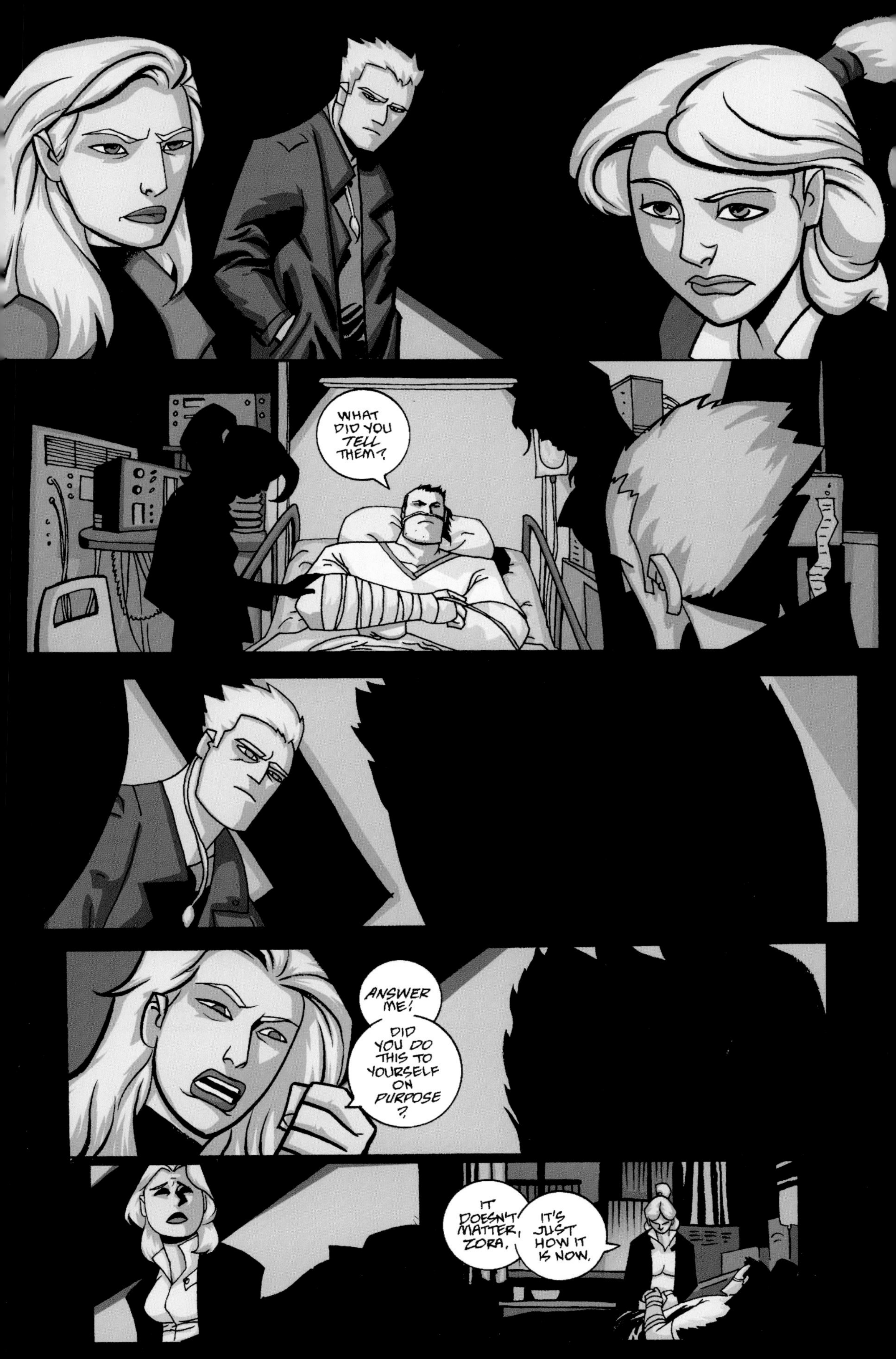
WHAT DID YOU TELL THEM?
ANSWER ME!
DID YOU DO THIS TO YOURSELF ON PURPOSE?
IT DOESN'T MATTER, ZORA,
IT'S JUST HOW IT IS NOW.

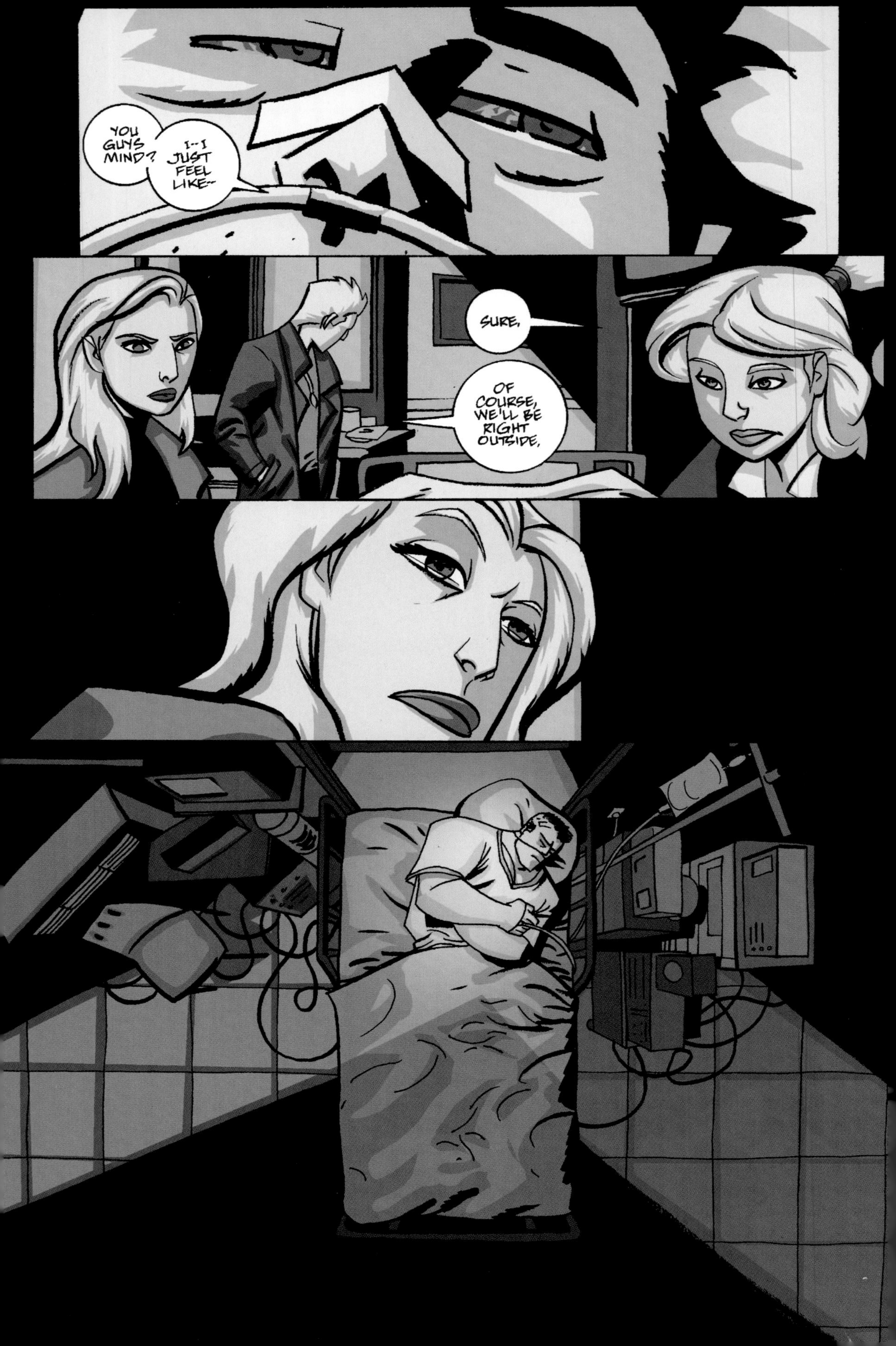
YOU GUYS MIND?
I--I JUST FEEL LIKE--
SURE.
OF COURSE. WE'LL BE RIGHT OUTSIDE.

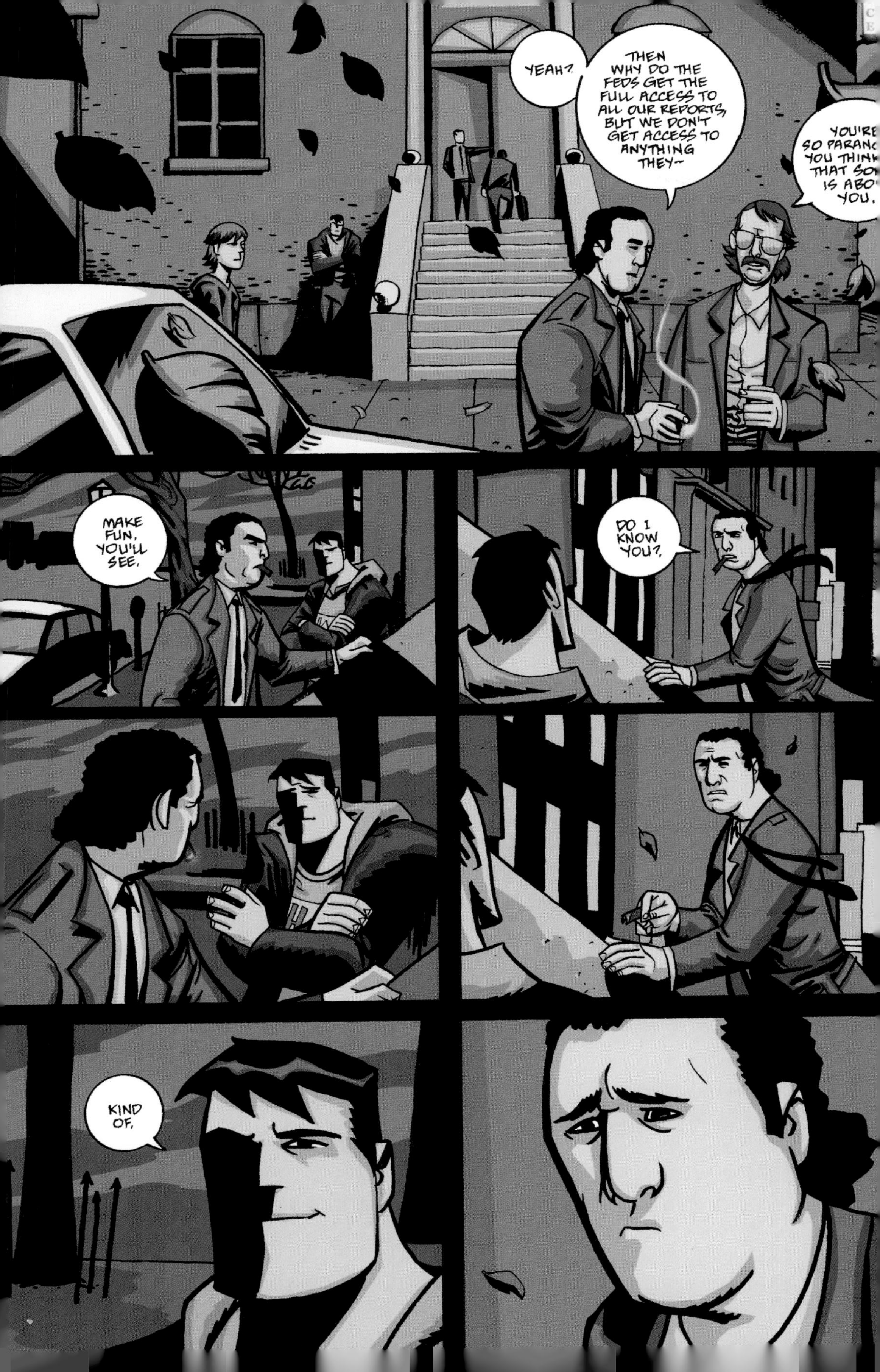
YEAH?
THEN WHY DO THE FEDS GET THE FULL ACCESS TO ALL OUR REPORTS, BUT WE DON'T GET ACCESS TO ANYTHING THEY--
MAKE FUN, YOU'LL SEE.
DO I KNOW YOU?
KIND OF.

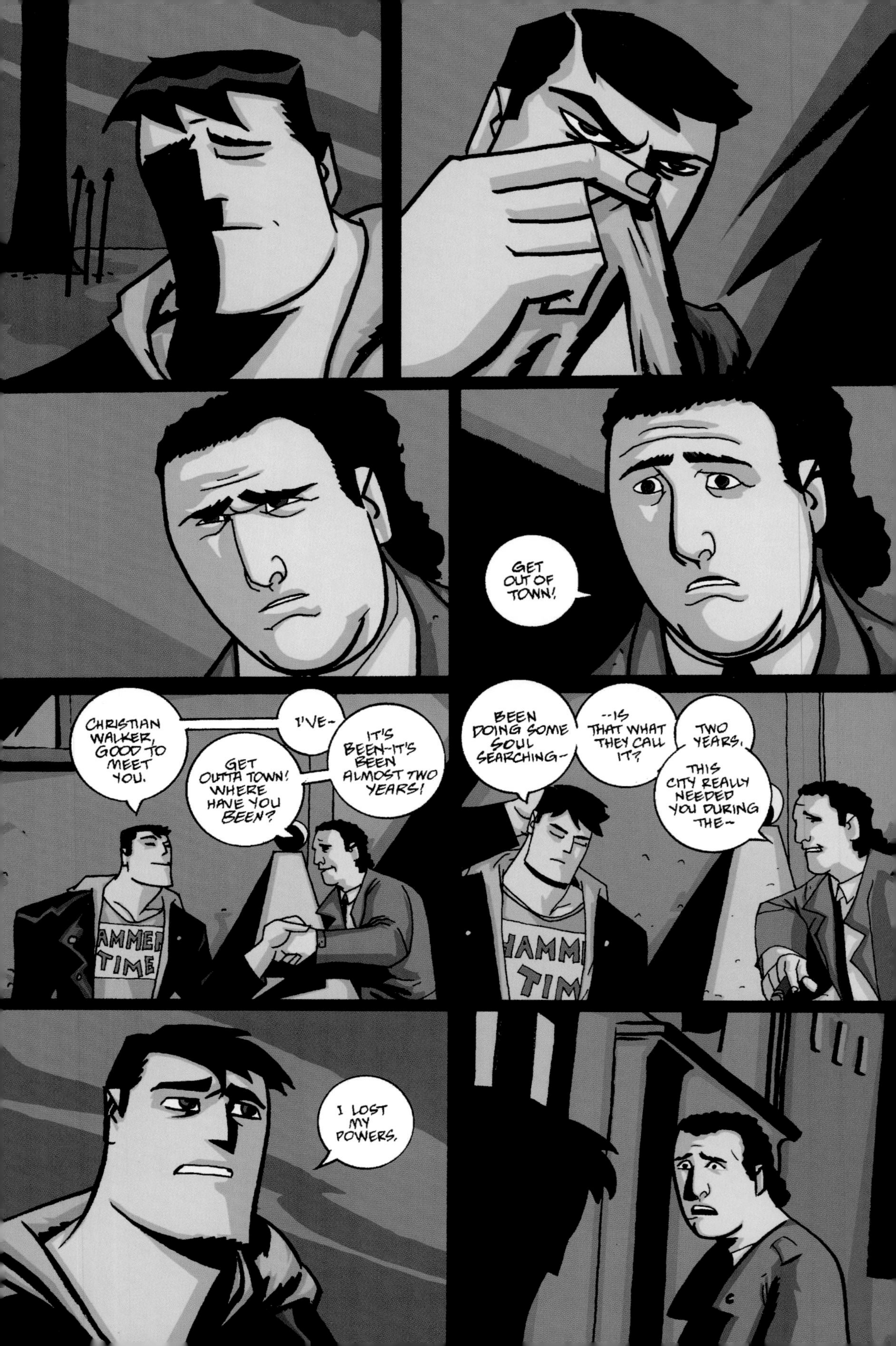
GET OUT OF TOWN!
CHRISTIAN WALKER, GOOD TO MEET YOU.
I'VE-
GET OUTTA TOWN! WHERE HAVE YOU BEEN?
IT'S BEEN--IT'S BEEN ALMOST TWO YEARS!
HAMMER TIME
BEEN DOING SOME SOUL SEARCHING-
--IS THAT WHAT THEY CALL IT?
TWO YEARS.
THIS CITY REALLY NEEDED YOU DURING THE-
I LOST MY POWERS.

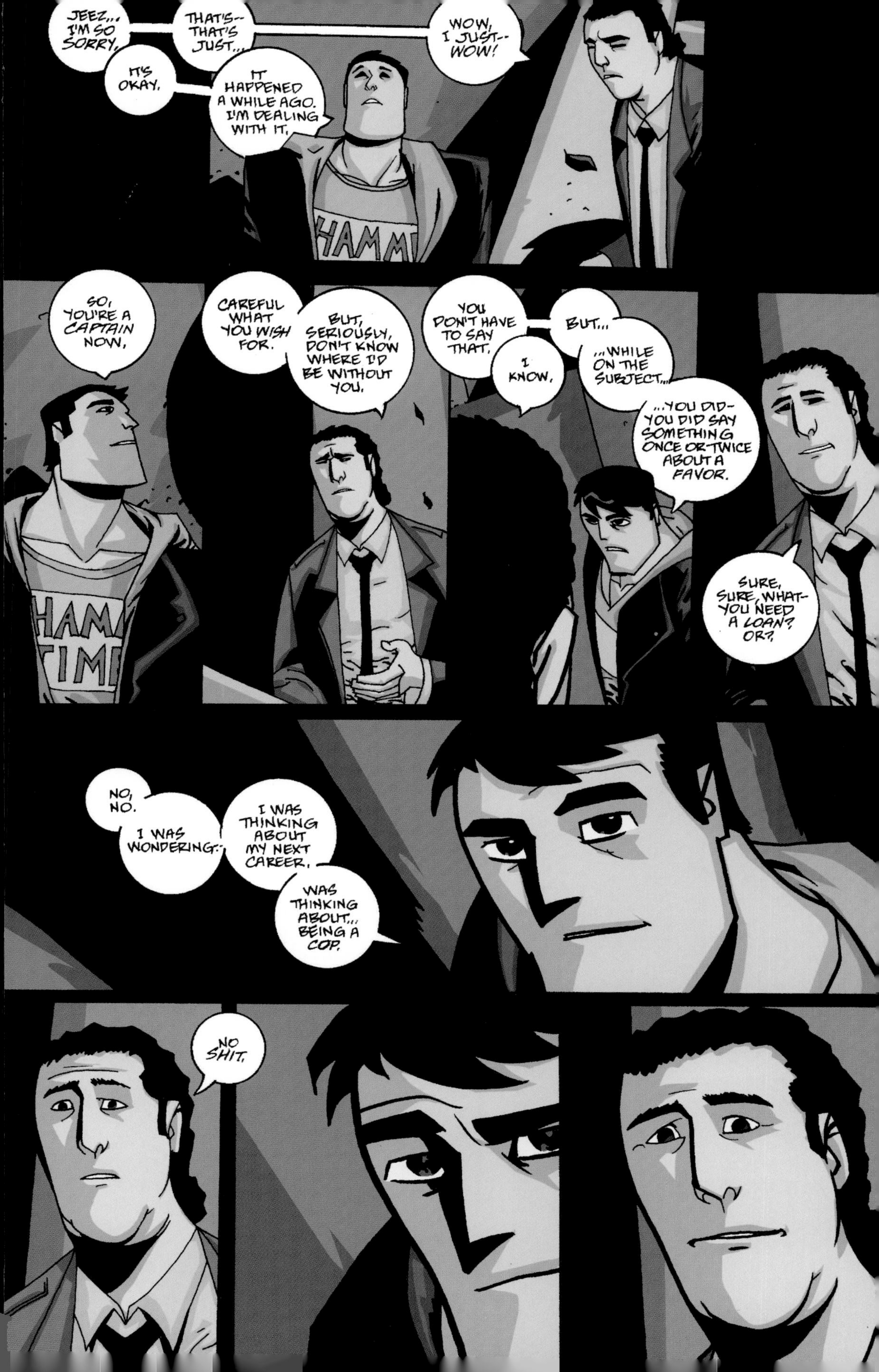
JEEZ... I'M SO SORRY.
THAT'S-- THAT'S JUST...
WOW, I JUST-- WOW!
IT'S OKAY.
IT HAPPENED A WHILE AGO. I'M DEALING WITH IT.
HAMM
SO, YOU'RE A CAPTAIN NOW.
CAREFUL WHAT YOU WISH FOR.
BUT, SERIOUSLY, DON'T KNOW WHERE I'D BE WITHOUT YOU.
YOU DON'T HAVE TO SAY THAT.
BUT...
I KNOW.
...WHILE ON THE SUBJECT...
...YOU DID-YOU DID SAY SOMETHING ONCE OR TWICE ABOUT A FAVOR.
SURE, SURE, WHAT-YOU NEED A LOAN? OR?
NO, NO.
I WAS WONDERING--
I WAS THINKING ABOUT MY NEXT CAREER.
WAS THINKING ABOUT... BEING A COP.
NO SHIT.

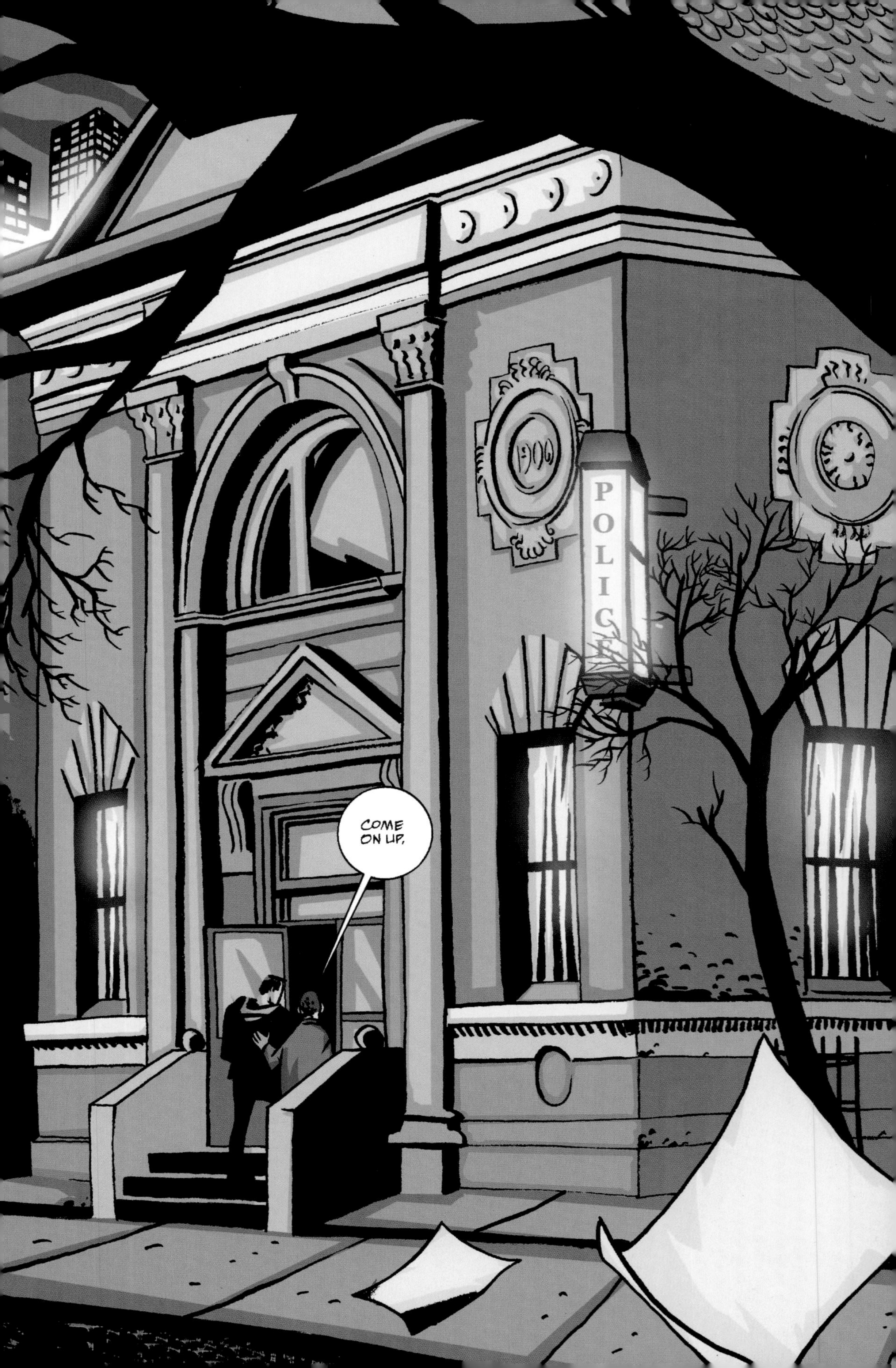
1906
POLICE
COME ON UP.

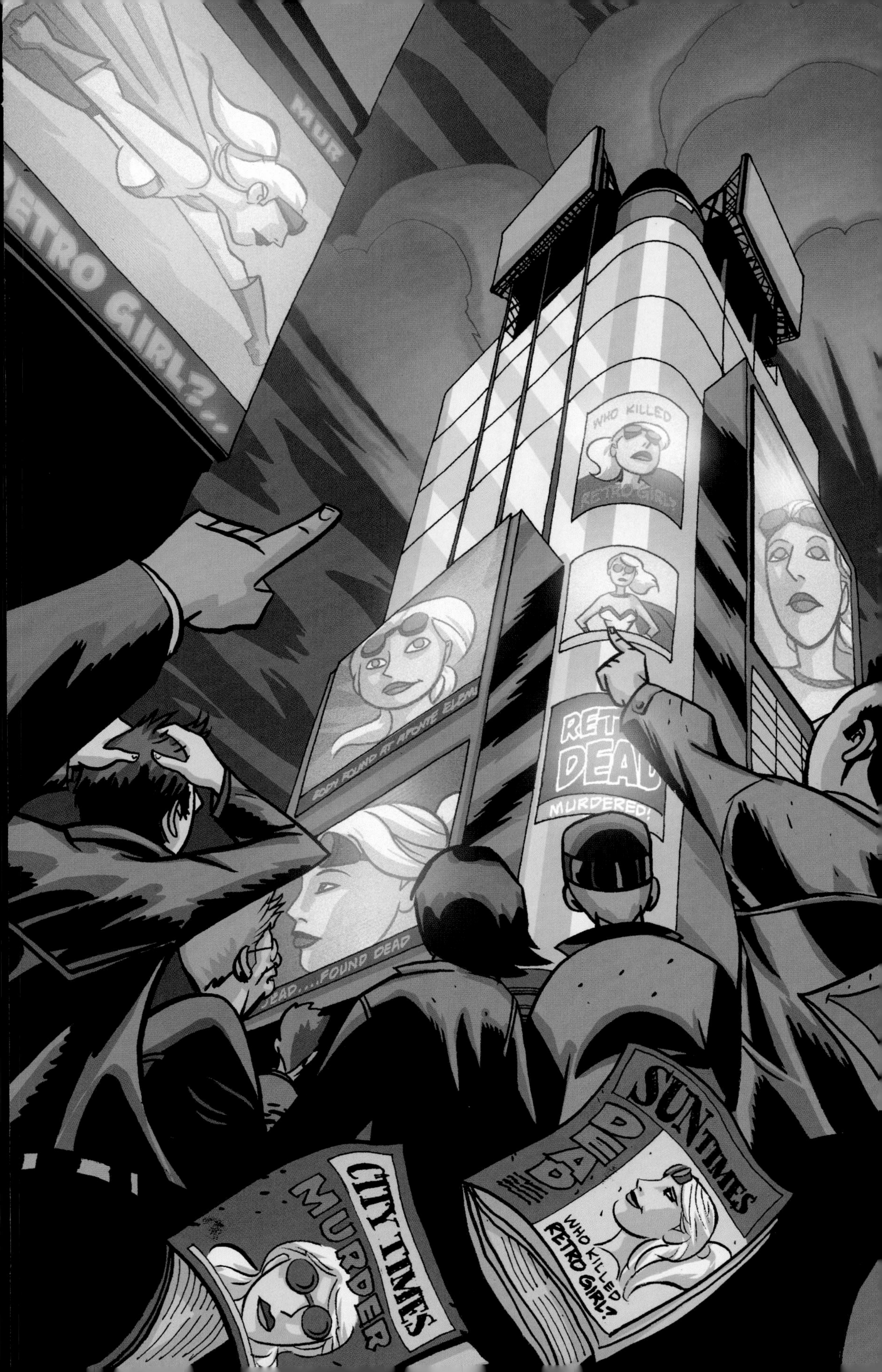
RETRO GIRL?..
MUR
WHO KILLED
RETRO GIRL
BODY FOUND AT APONTE
RET
DEAD
MURDERED!
DEAD....FOUND DEAD
CITY TIMES
MURDER
SUN TIMES
DEAD
WHO KILLED
RETRO GIRL?

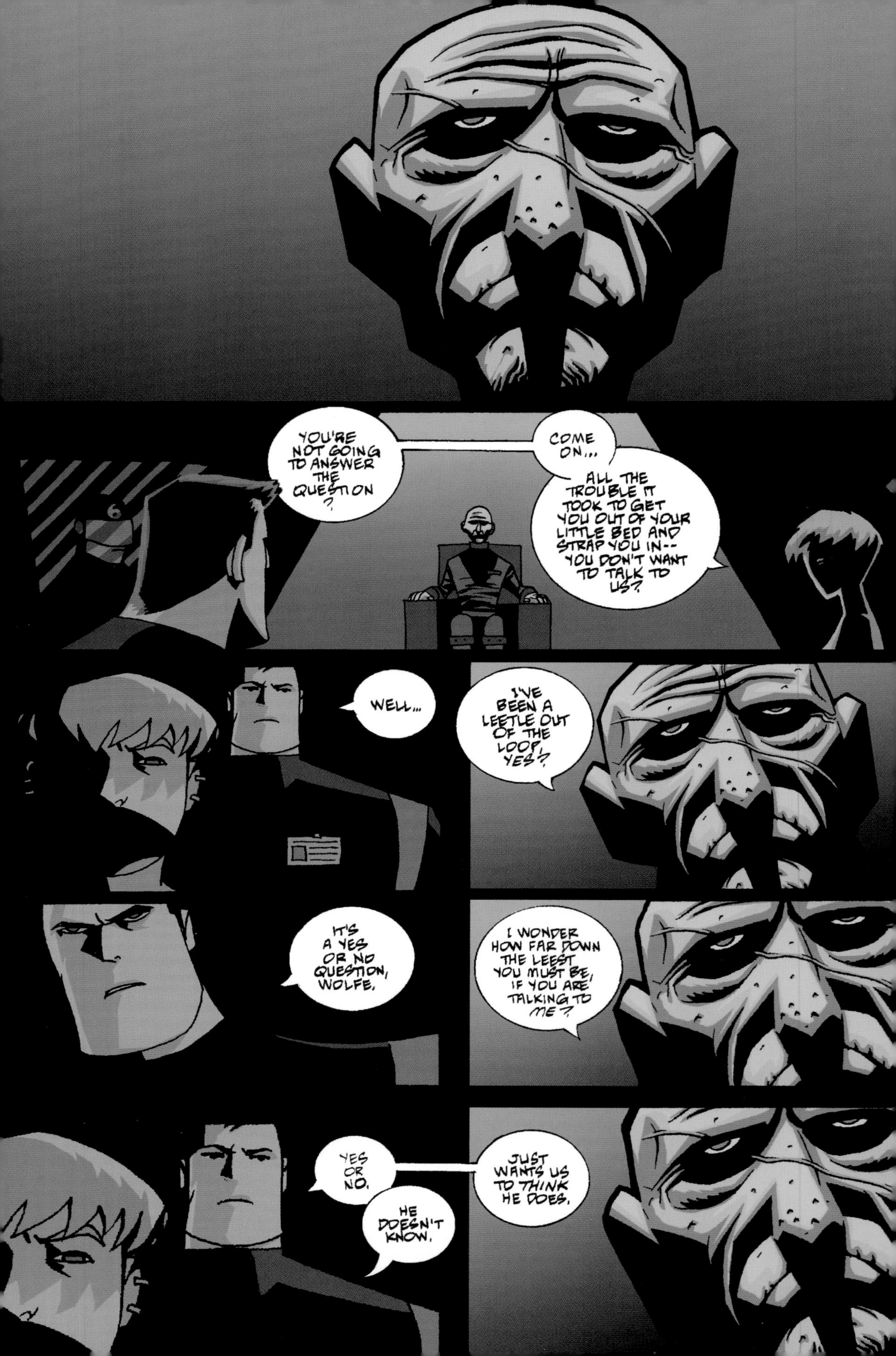
YOU'RE NOT GOING TO ANSWER THE QUESTION ?
COME ON...
ALL THE TROUBLE IT TOOK TO GET YOU OUT OF YOUR LITTLE BED AND STRAP YOU IN-- YOU DON'T WANT TO TALK TO US?
WELL...
I'VE BEEN A LEETLE OUT OF THE LOOP, YES?
IT'S A YES OR NO QUESTION, WOLFE.
I WONDER HOW FAR DOWN THE LEEST YOU MUST BE, IF YOU ARE TALKING TO ME?
YES OR NO.
HE DOESN'T KNOW.
JUST WANTS US TO THINK HE DOES.

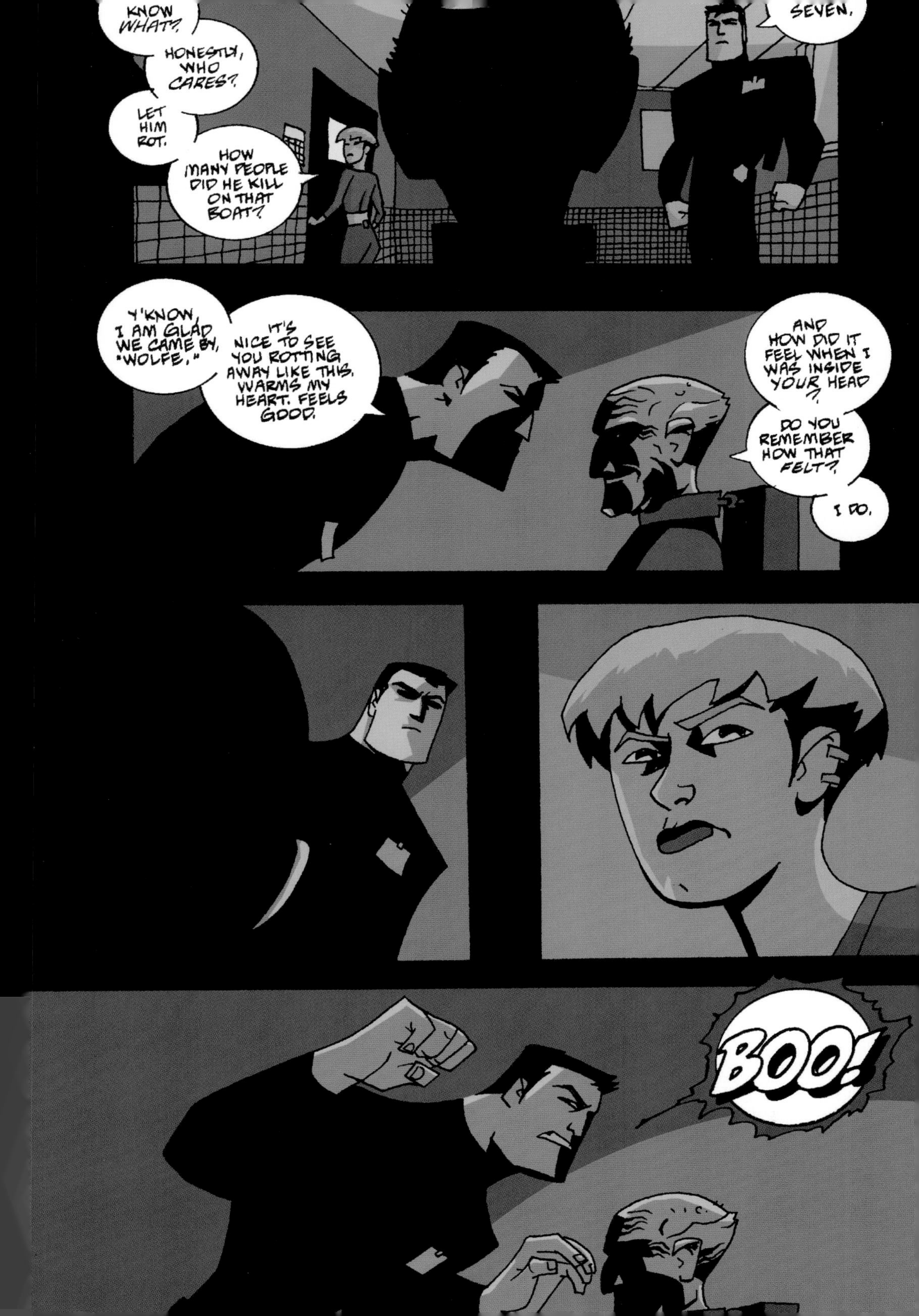
KNOW WHAT?
HONESTLY, WHO CARES?
LET HIM ROT.
HOW MANY PEOPLE DID HE KILL ON THAT BOAT?
SEVEN.
Y'KNOW, I AM GLAD WE CAME BY, "WOLFE."
IT'S NICE TO SEE YOU ROTTING AWAY LIKE THIS. WARMS MY HEART. FEELS GOOD.
AND HOW DID IT FEEL WHEN I WAS INSIDE YOUR HEAD?
DO YOU REMEMBER HOW THAT FELT?
I DO.
BOOM!

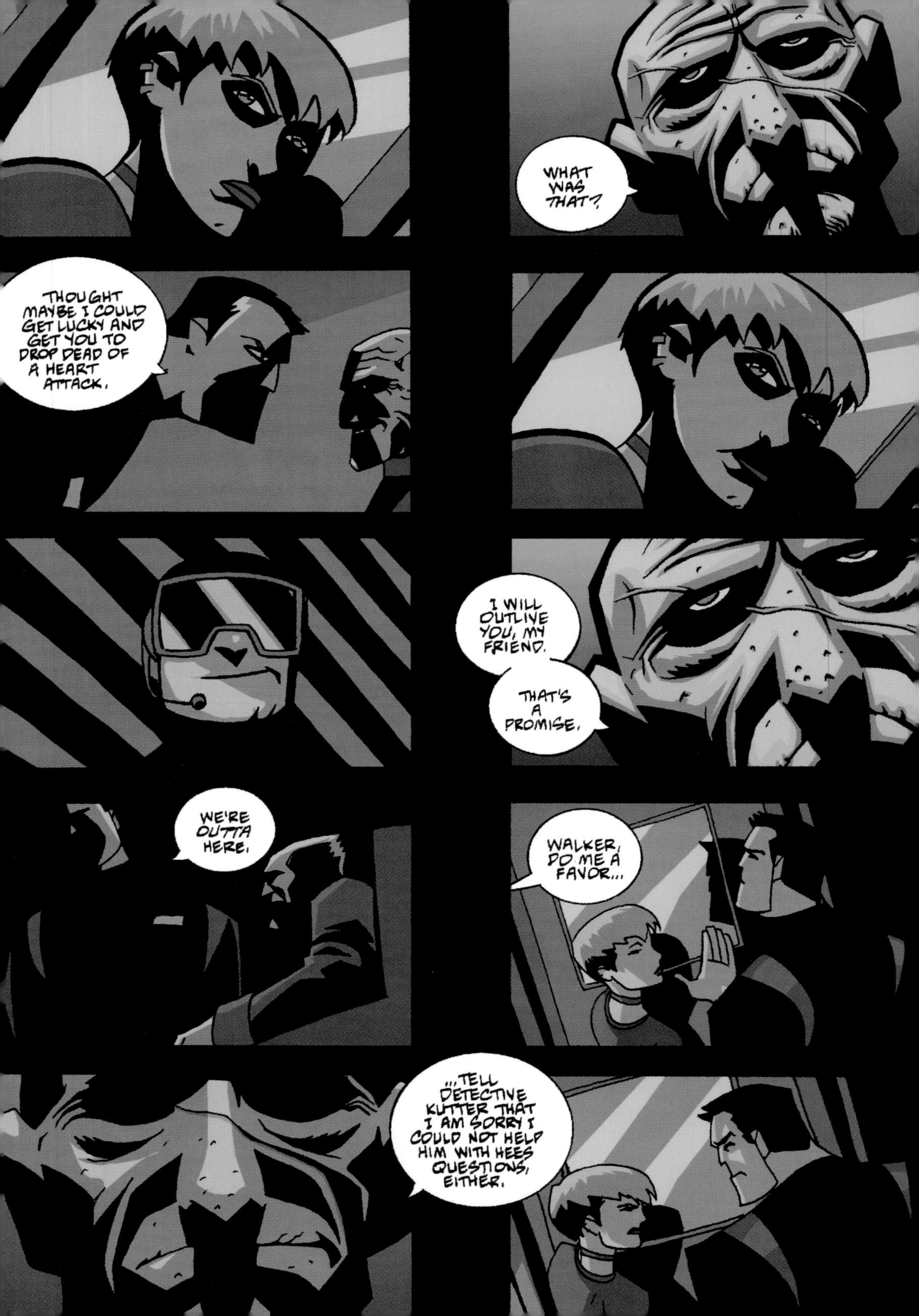
WHAT WAS THAT?
THOUGHT MAYBE I COULD GET LUCKY AND GET YOU TO DROP DEAD OF A HEART ATTACK.
I WILL OUTLIVE YOU, MY FRIEND.
THAT'S A PROMISE.
WE'RE OUTTA HERE.
WALKER, DO ME A FAVOR...
...TELL DETECTIVE KUTTER THAT I AM SORRY I COULD NOT HELP HIM WITH HEES QUESTIONS, EITHER.

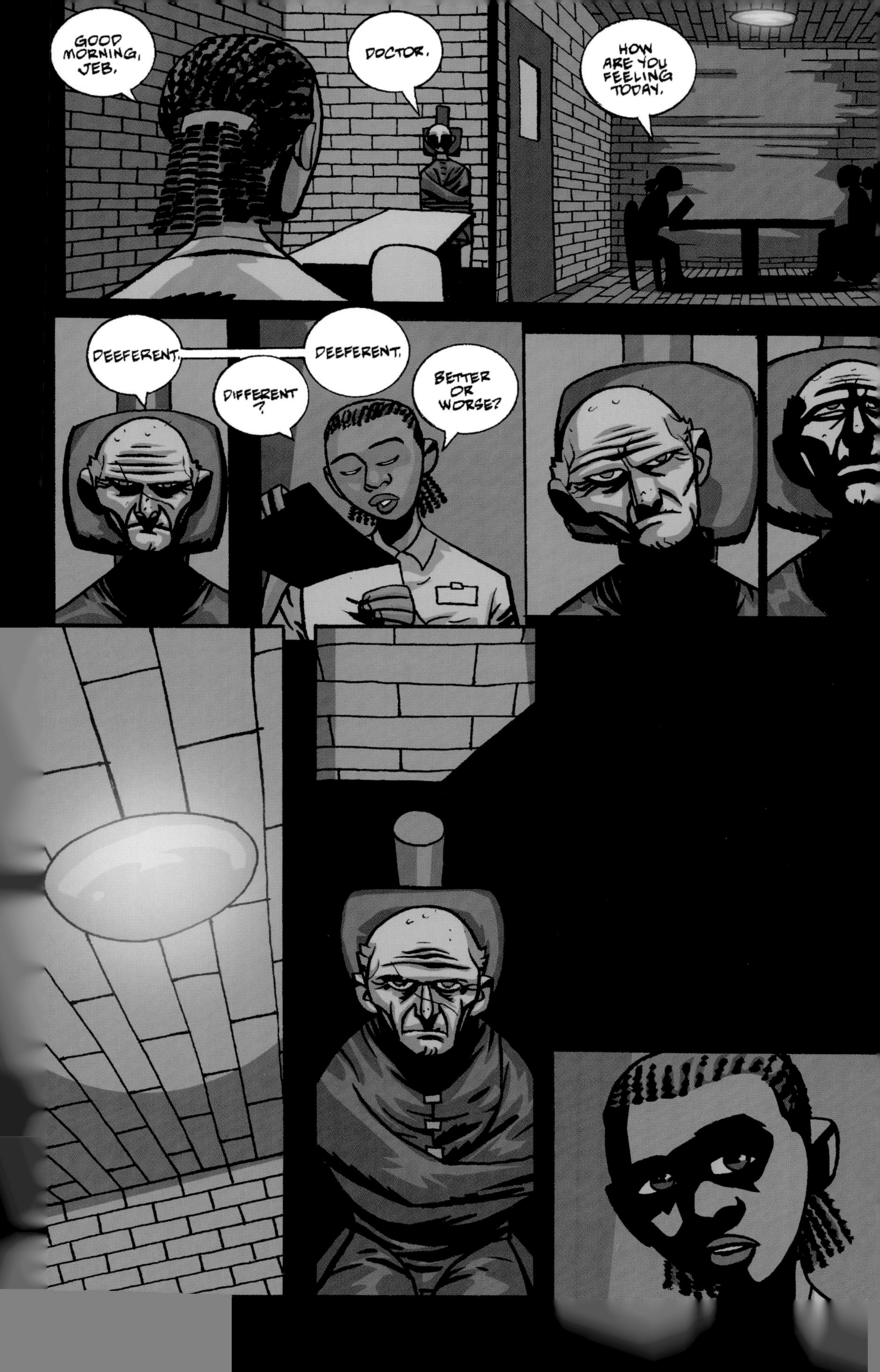
GOOD MORNING, JEB.
DOCTOR.
HOW ARE YOU FEELING TODAY.
DEEFERENT.
DIFFERENT?
DEEFERENT.
BETTER OR WORSE?

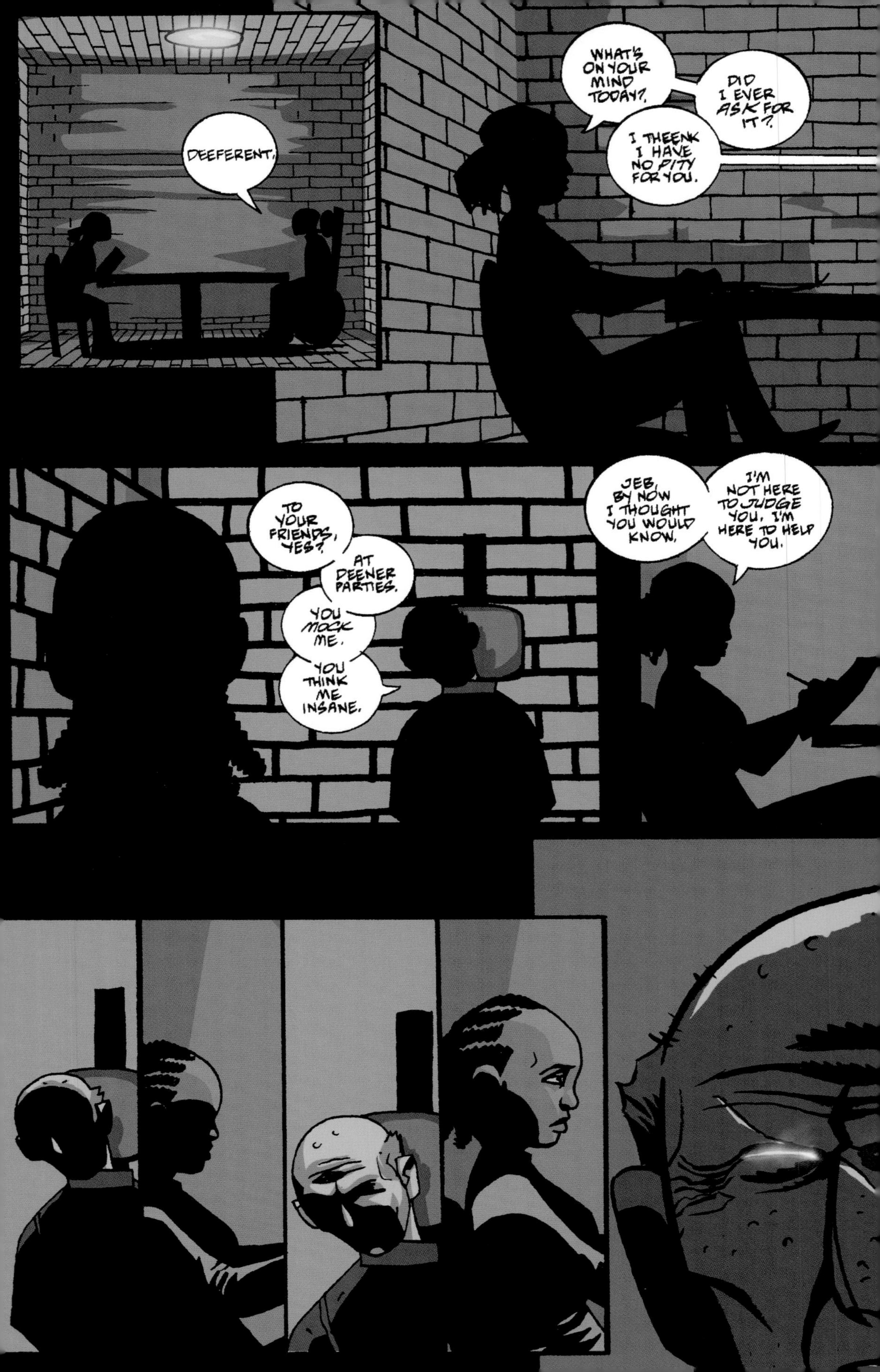
DEEFERENT.
WHAT'S ON YOUR MIND TODAY?
DID I EVER ASK FOR IT?
I THEENK I HAVE NO PITY FOR YOU.
TO YOUR FRIENDS, YES?
AT DEENER PARTIES.
YOU MOCK ME.
YOU THINK ME INSANE.
JEB, BY NOW I THOUGHT YOU WOULD KNOW.
I'M NOT HERE TO JUDGE YOU. I'M HERE TO HELP YOU.

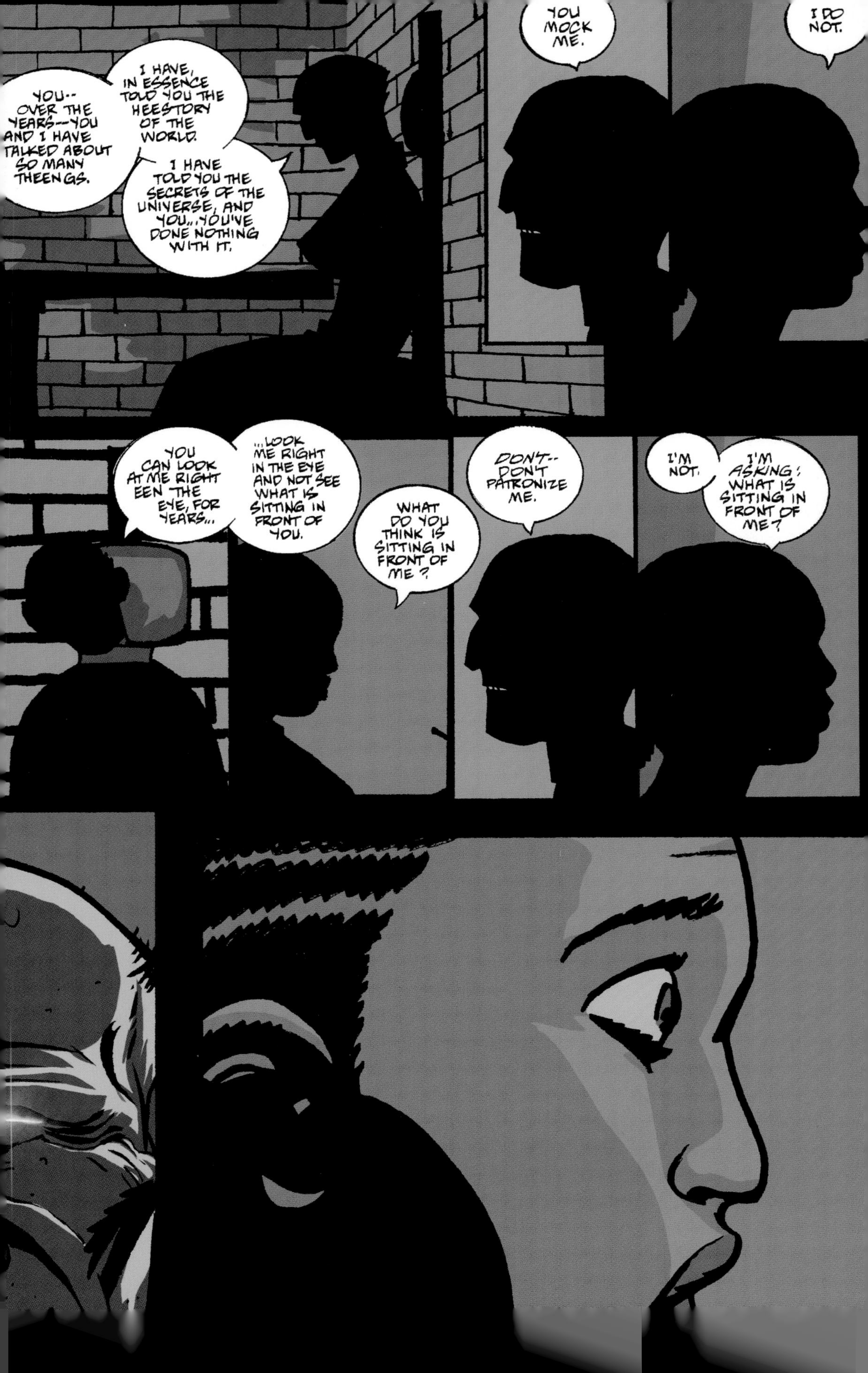
YOU-- OVER THE YEARS--YOU AND I HAVE TALKED ABOUT SO MANY THEENGS.
I HAVE, IN ESSENCE TOLD YOU THE HEESTORY OF THE WORLD.
I HAVE TOLD YOU THE SECRETS OF THE UNIVERSE, AND YOU... YOU'VE DONE NOTHING WITH IT.
YOU MOCK ME.
I DO NOT.
YOU CAN LOOK AT ME RIGHT EEN THE EYE, FOR YEARS...
...LOOK ME RIGHT IN THE EYE AND NOT SEE WHAT IS SITTING IN FRONT OF YOU.
WHAT DO YOU THINK IS SITTING IN FRONT OF ME?
DON'T-- DON'T PATRONIZE ME.
I'M NOT.
I'M ASKING: WHAT IS SITTING IN FRONT OF ME?

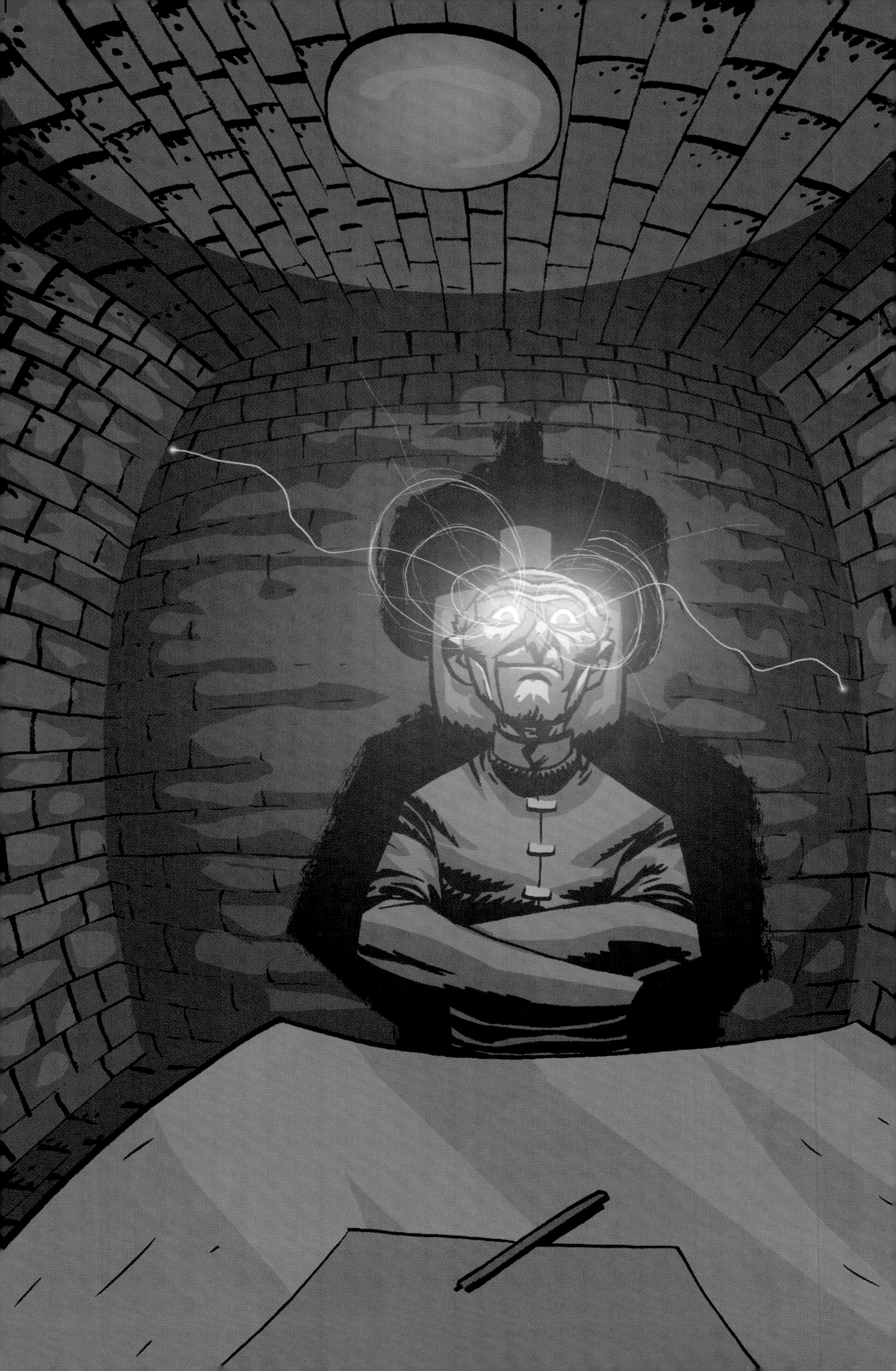

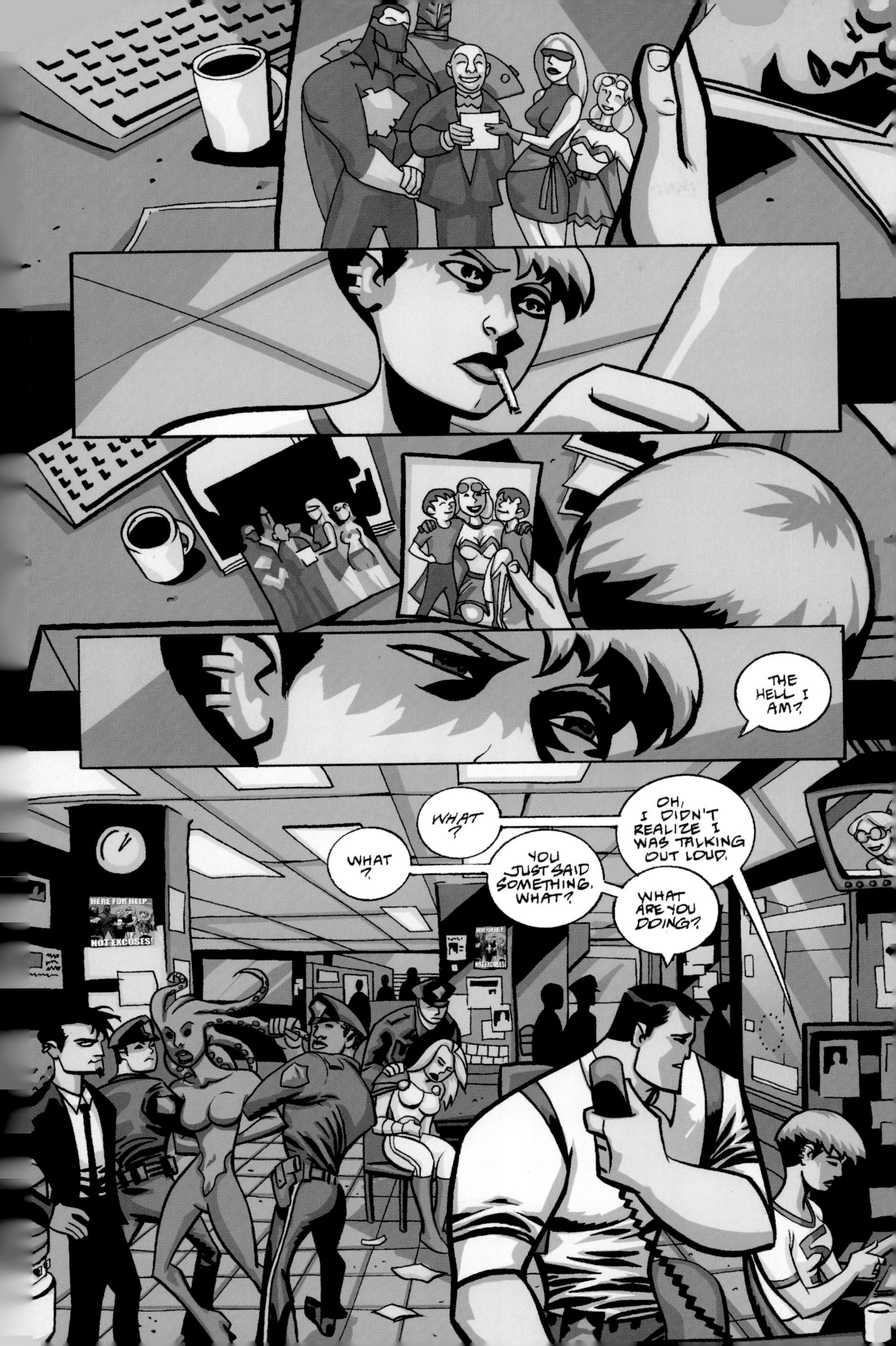
THE HELL I AM?
HERE FOR HELP... NOT EXCUSES!
HERE FOR HELP... NOT EXCUSES!
WHAT ?
YOU JUST SAID SOMETHING. WHAT?
WHAT ?
WHAT ARE YOU DOING?
OH, I DIDN'T REALIZE I WAS TALKING OUT LOUD.

GOING THROUGH THE RETRO GIRL PHOTO FILE AGAIN.

LOOKING TO SEE IF ANYONE KEEPS POPPING UP IN THE BACKGROUND, Y'KNOW?

THE CASE IS CLOSED.

NOT TO MY SATISFACTION.

IT'S CLOSED. IT'S DONE.

IT'S DONE.

THING IS, MAN, I DIDN'T EVEN KNOW HER AND I THINK THIS CASE ENDED SHIT.

YOU KNEW HER, AND--

--YOU KNEW HER, AND YOU'RE ALL--

IT'S DONE.

IT WAS YOUR FIRST CASE. FIRST CASES ALWAYS EAT AT YOU.

DON'T KNOW WHY. THEY JUST DO. IT'S DONE.

AND NOTHING ABOUT THIS IS STICKING IN YOUR GUT? LIKE--

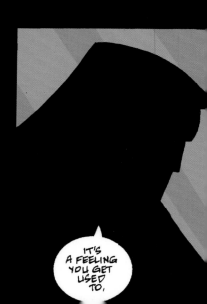

IT'S A FEELING YOU GET USED TO.

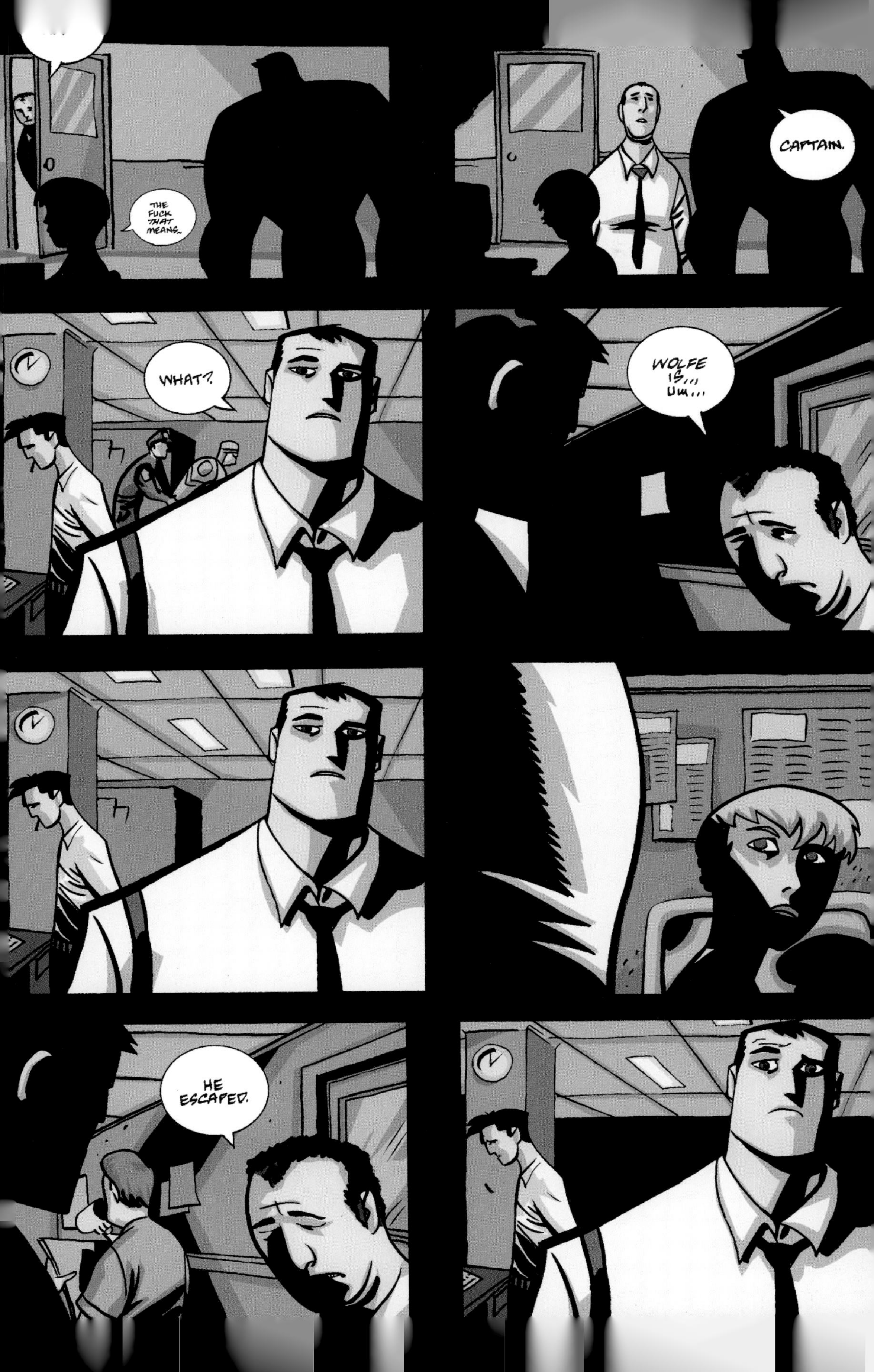
THE FUCK THAT MEANS...
CAPTAIN.
WHAT?
WOLFE IS... UM...
HE ESCAPED.

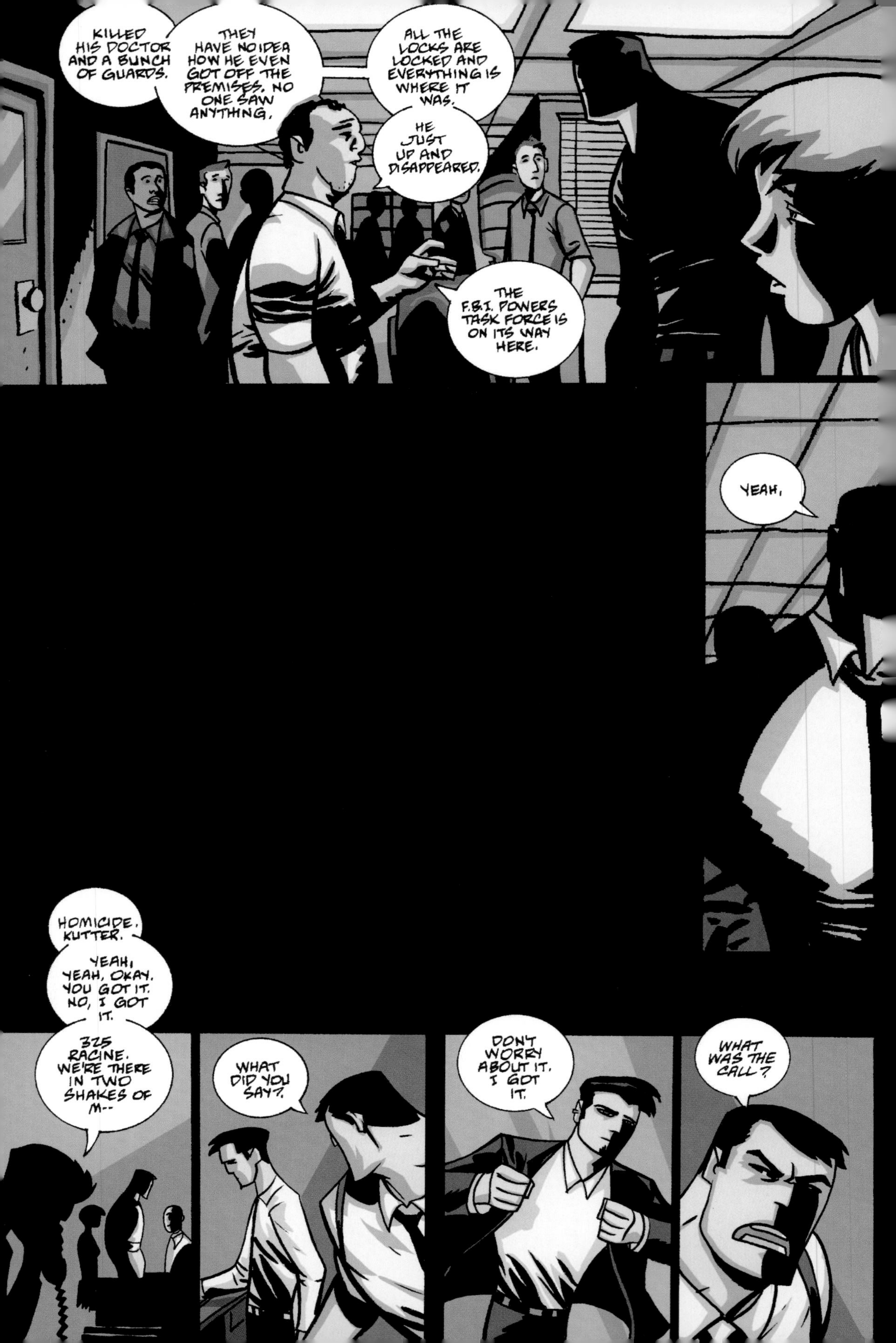
KILLED HIS DOCTOR AND A BUNCH OF GUARDS.
THEY HAVE NO IDEA HOW HE EVEN GOT OFF THE PREMISES. NO ONE SAW ANYTHING.
ALL THE LOCKS ARE LOCKED AND EVERYTHING IS WHERE IT WAS.
HE JUST UP AND DISAPPEARED.
THE F.B.I. POWERS TASK FORCE IS ON ITS WAY HERE.
YEAH.
HOMICIDE. KUTTER.
YEAH, YEAH, OKAY. YOU GOT IT. NO, I GOT IT.
325 RACINE. WE'RE THERE IN TWO SHAKES OF M--
WHAT DID YOU SAY?
DON'T WORRY ABOUT IT. I GOT IT.
WHAT WAS THE CALL?

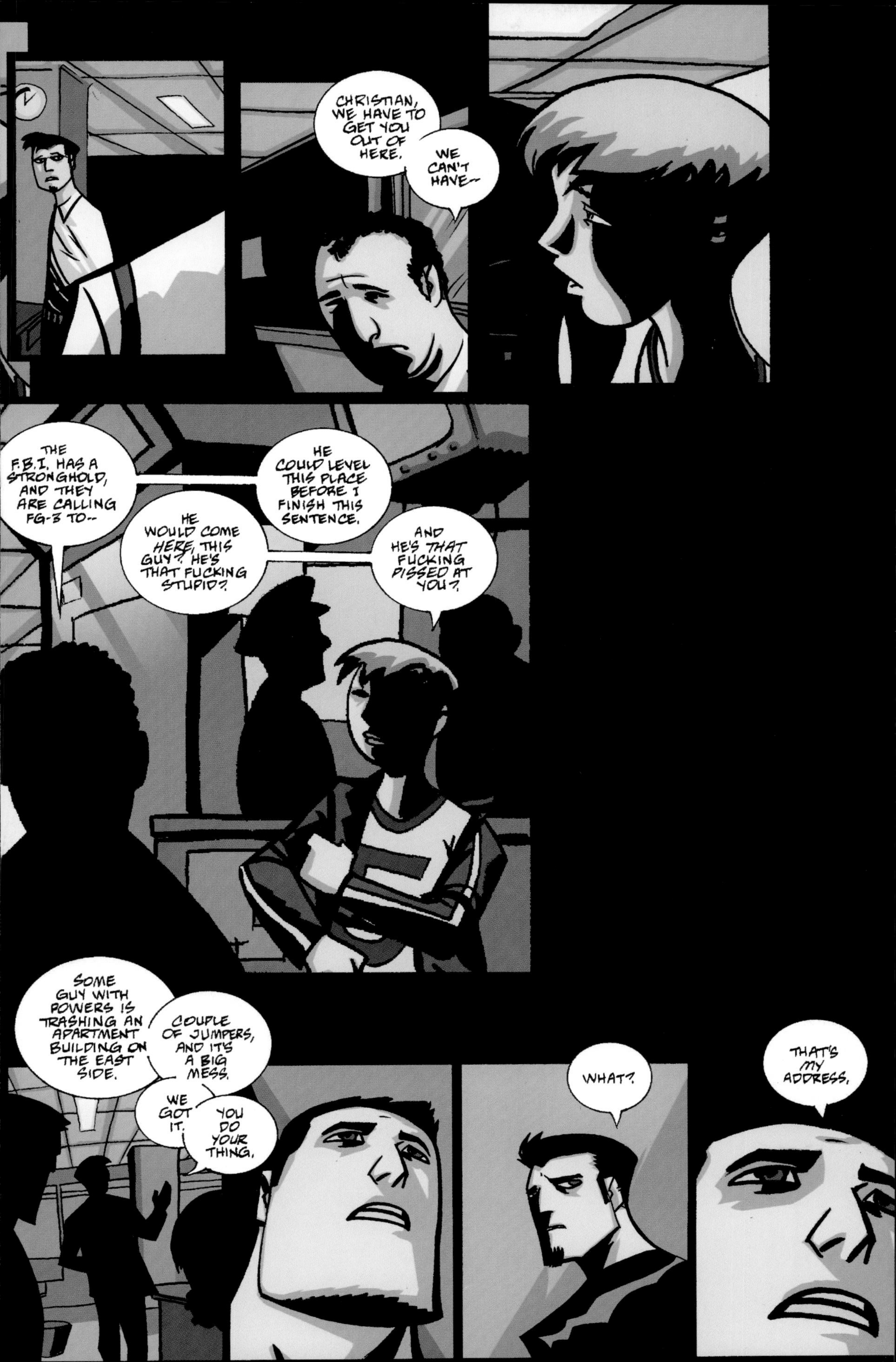
CHRISTIAN, WE HAVE TO GET YOU OUT OF HERE.
WE CAN'T HAVE--
THE F.B.I. HAS A STRONGHOLD, AND THEY ARE CALLING FG-3 TO--
HE COULD LEVEL THIS PLACE BEFORE I FINISH THIS SENTENCE.
HE WOULD COME HERE, THIS GUY? HE'S THAT FUCKING STUPID?
AND HE'S THAT FUCKING PISSED AT YOU?
SOME GUY WITH POWERS IS TRASHING AN APARTMENT BUILDING ON THE EAST SIDE.
COUPLE OF JUMPERS, AND IT'S A BIG MESS.
WE GOT IT.
YOU DO YOUR THING.
WHAT?
THAT'S MY ADDRESS.

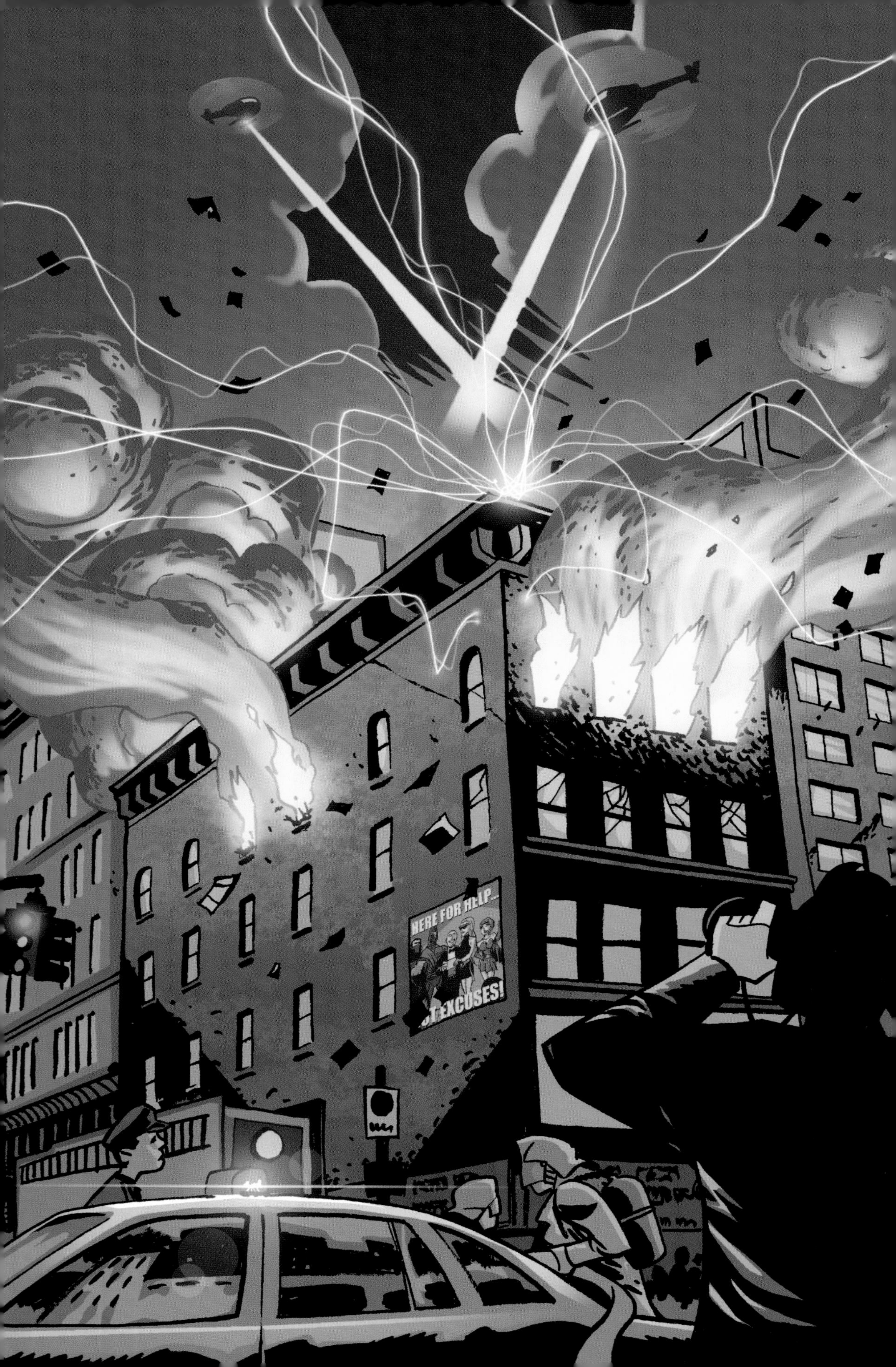
HERE FOR HELP...
T EXCUSES!

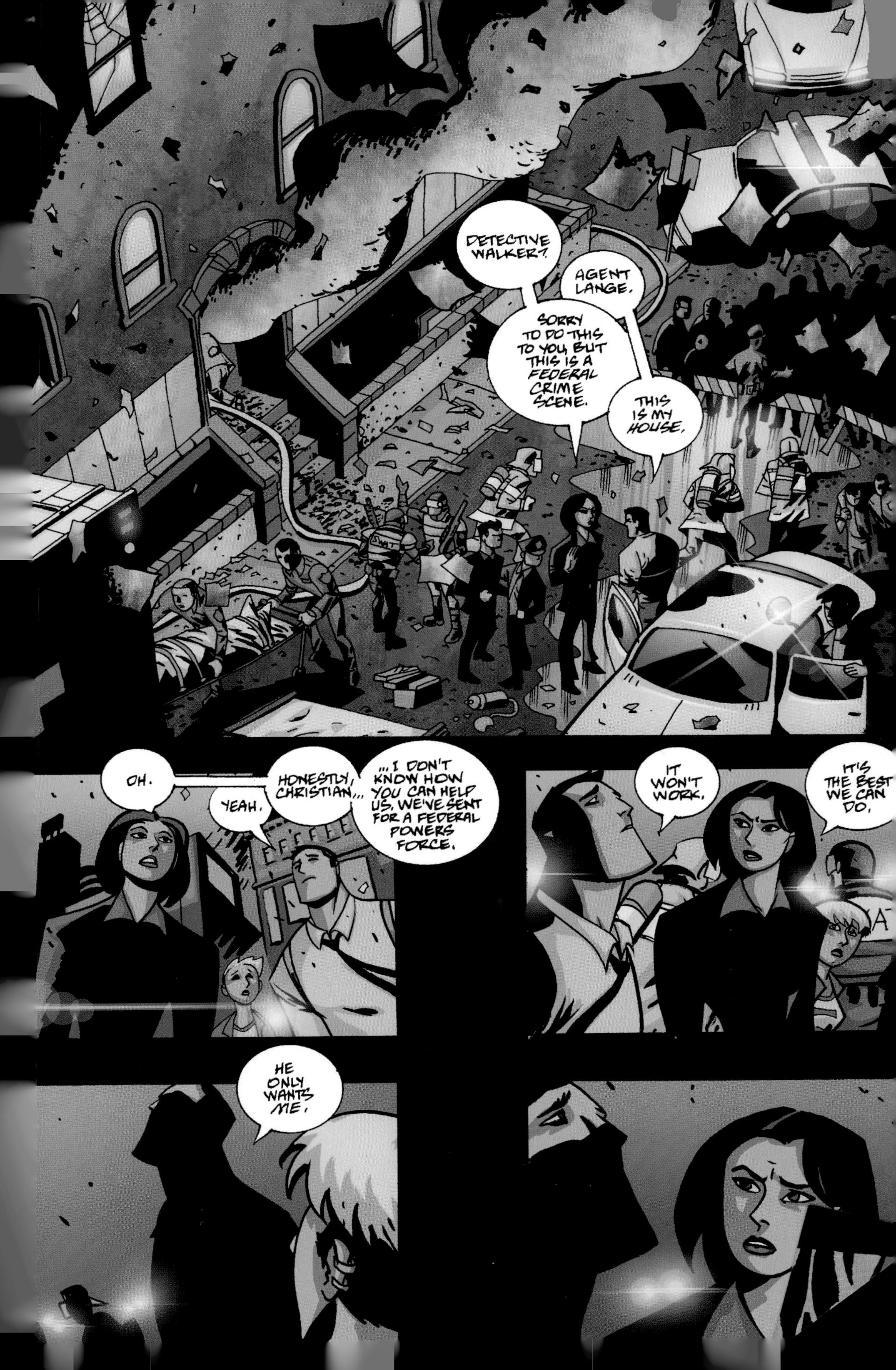
DETECTIVE WALKER?
AGENT LANGE.
SORRY TO DO THIS TO YOU, BUT THIS IS A FEDERAL CRIME SCENE.
THIS IS MY HOUSE.
OH.
YEAH.
HONESTLY, CHRISTIAN...
...I DON'T KNOW HOW YOU CAN HELP US. WE'VE SENT FOR A FEDERAL POWERS FORCE.
IT WON'T WORK.
IT'S THE BEST WE CAN DO.
HE ONLY WANTS ME.

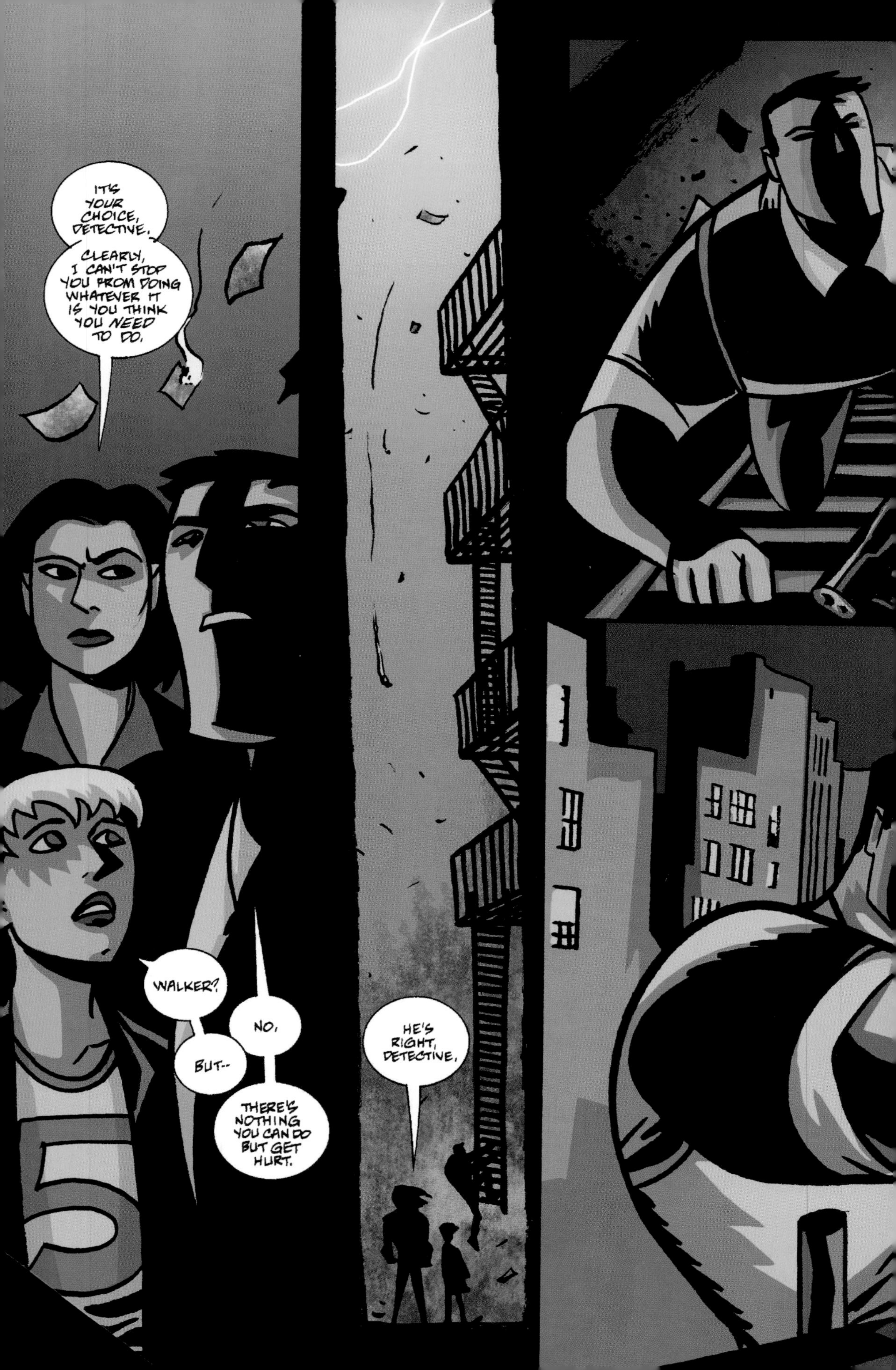
IT'S YOUR CHOICE, DETECTIVE.
CLEARLY, I CAN'T STOP YOU FROM DOING WHATEVER IT IS YOU THINK YOU NEED TO DO.
WALKER?
NO,
BUT--
THERE'S NOTHING YOU CAN DO BUT GET HURT.
HE'S RIGHT, DETECTIVE.

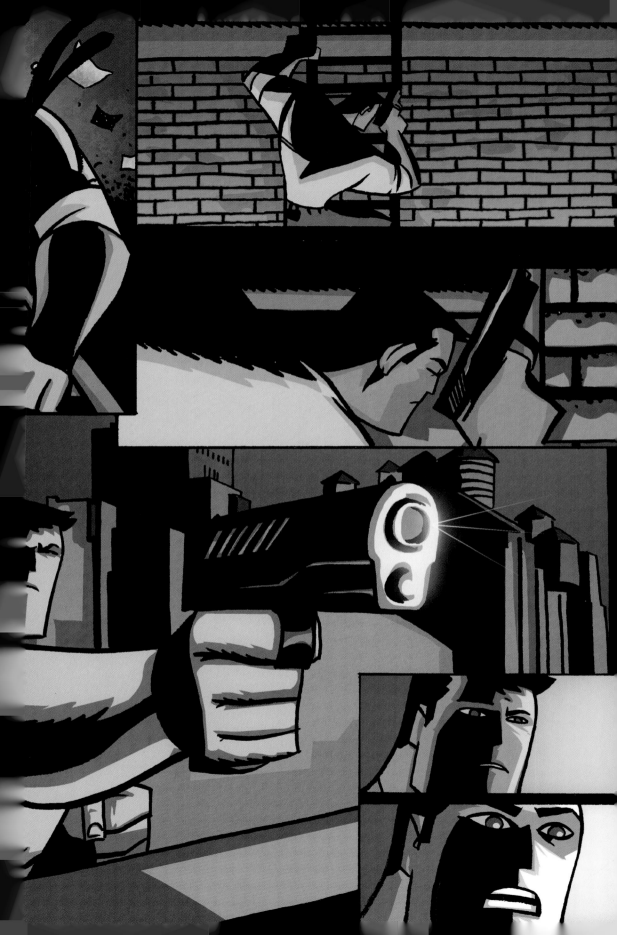

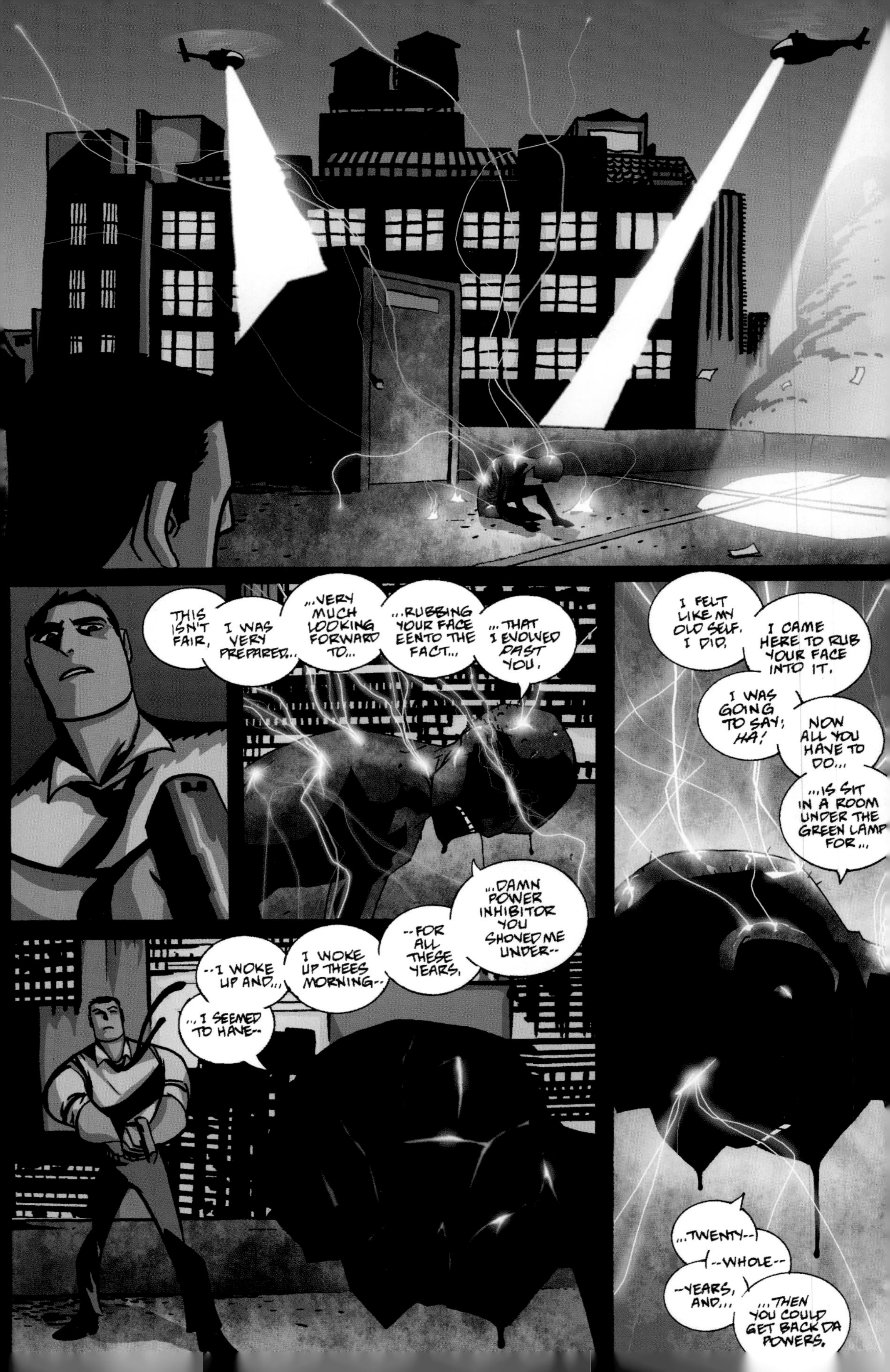
THIS ISN'T FAIR,
I WAS VERY PREPARED...
...VERY MUCH LOOKING FORWARD TO...
...RUBBING YOUR FACE EENTO THE FACT...
...THAT I EVOLVED PAST YOU.
I FELT LIKE MY OLD SELF. I DID.
I CAME HERE TO RUB YOUR FACE INTO IT.
I WAS GOING TO SAY; HA!
NOW ALL YOU HAVE TO DO...
...IS SIT IN A ROOM UNDER THE GREEN LAMP FOR...
--I WOKE UP AND...
I WOKE UP THEES MORNING--
--FOR ALL THESE YEARS.
...DAMN POWER INHIBITOR YOU SHOVED ME UNDER--
...I SEEMED TO HAVE--
...TWENTY--
--WHOLE--
--YEARS, AND...
...THEN YOU COULD GET BACK DA POWERS.

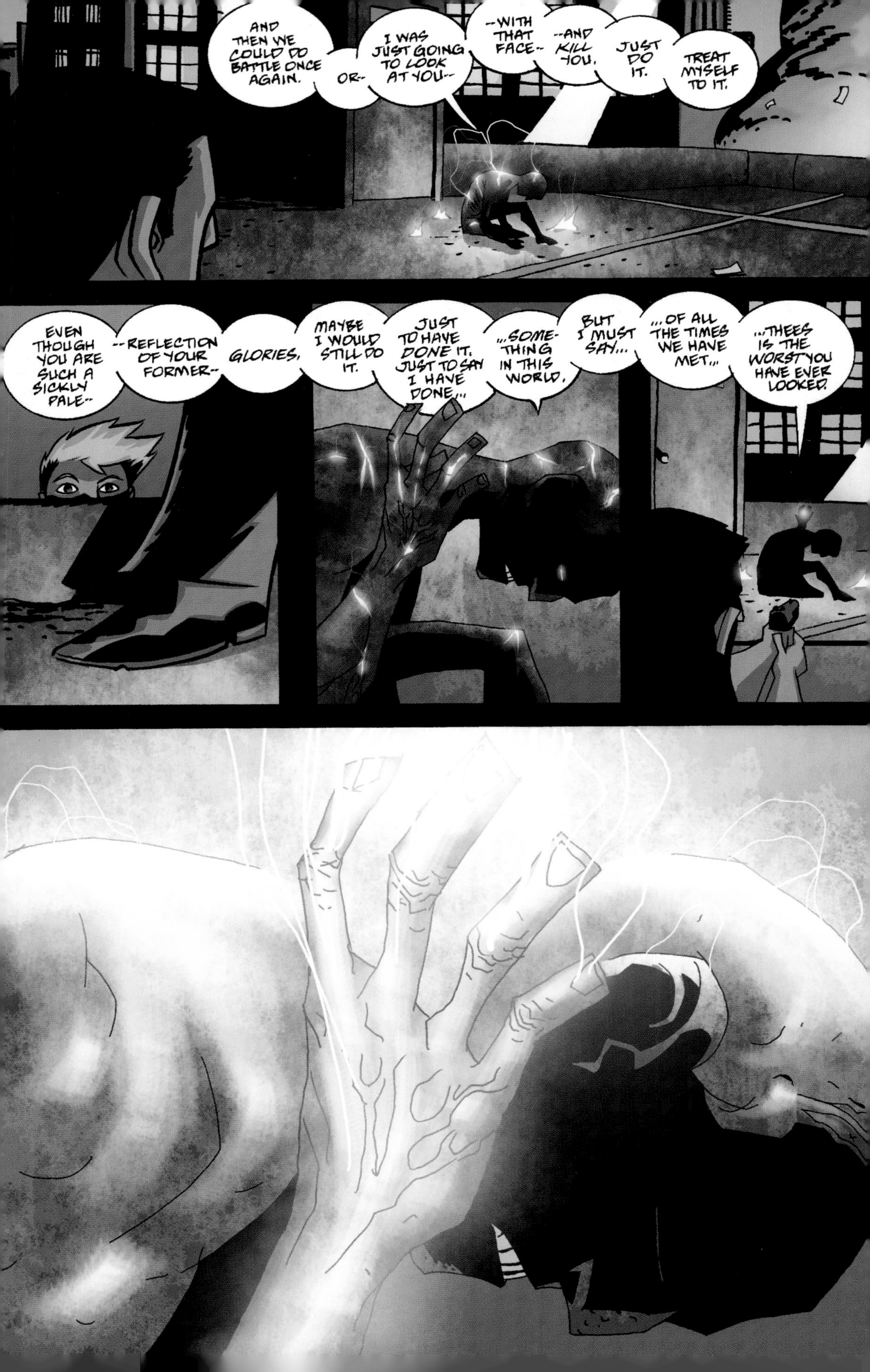

AND THEN WE COULD DO BATTLE ONCE AGAIN.
OR--
I WAS JUST GOING TO LOOK AT YOU--
--WITH THAT FACE--
--AND KILL YOU.
JUST DO IT.
TREAT MYSELF TO IT.
EVEN THOUGH YOU ARE SUCH A SICKLY PALE--
--REFLECTION OF YOUR FORMER--
GLORIES,
MAYBE I WOULD STILL DO IT.
JUST TO HAVE DONE IT. JUST TO SAY I HAVE DONE...
...SOMETHING IN THIS WORLD.
BUT I MUST SAY...
...OF ALL THE TIMES WE HAVE MET...
...THEES IS THE WORST YOU HAVE EVER LOOKED.

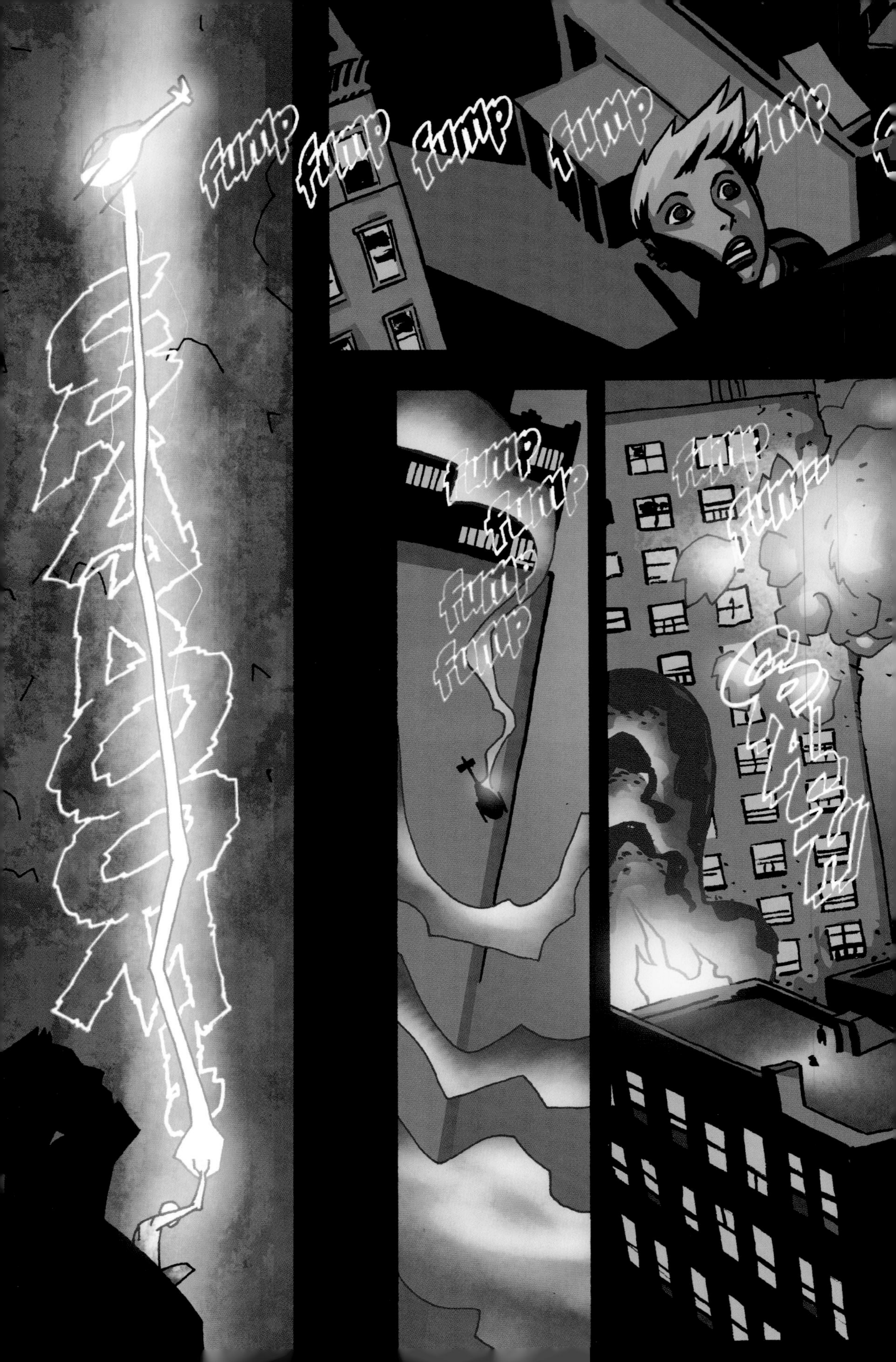
fump
fump
fump
fump
fump
fump
fump
fump
fump
fump
fump

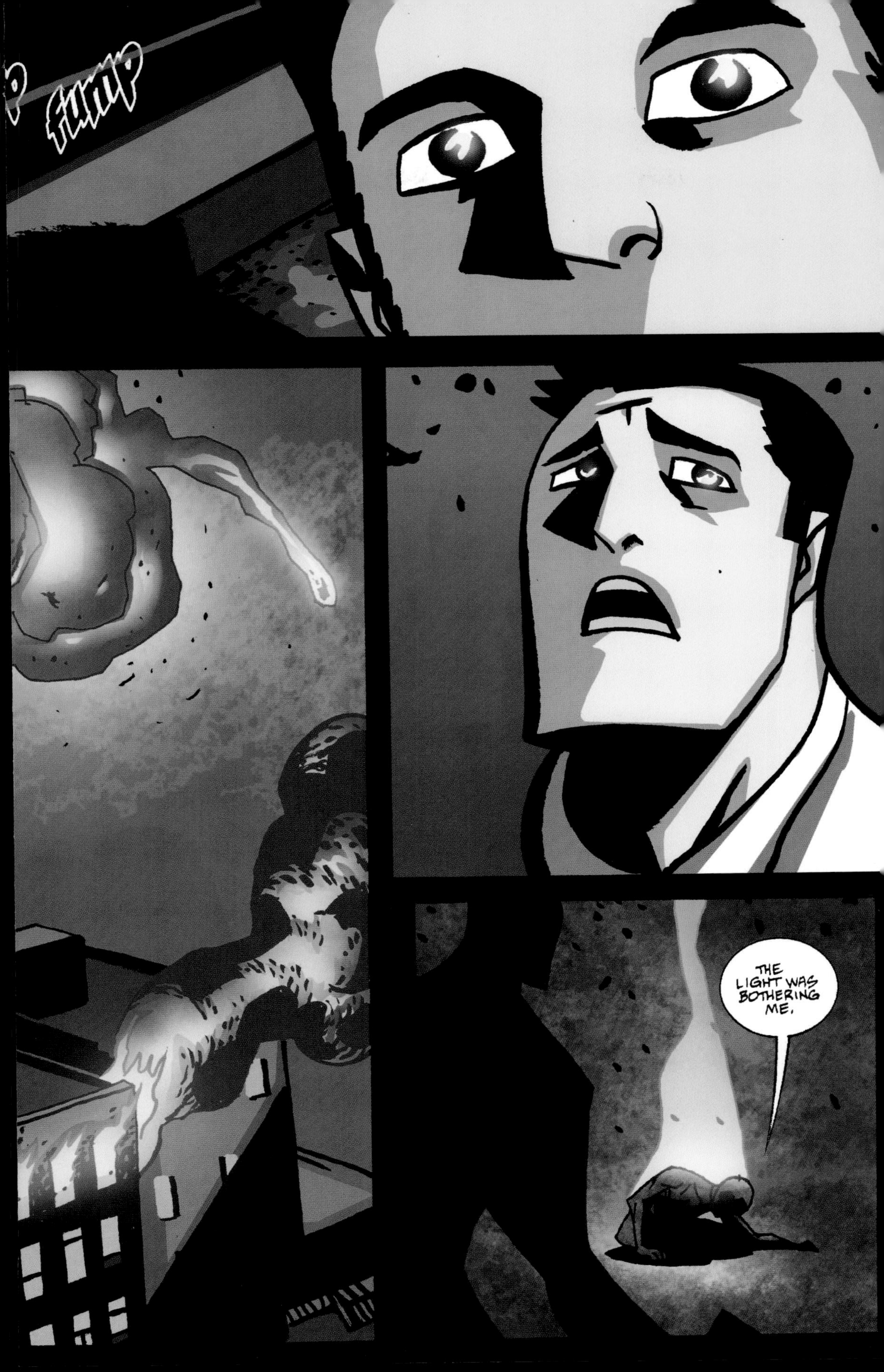
FUMP
THE LIGHT WAS BOTHERING ME.

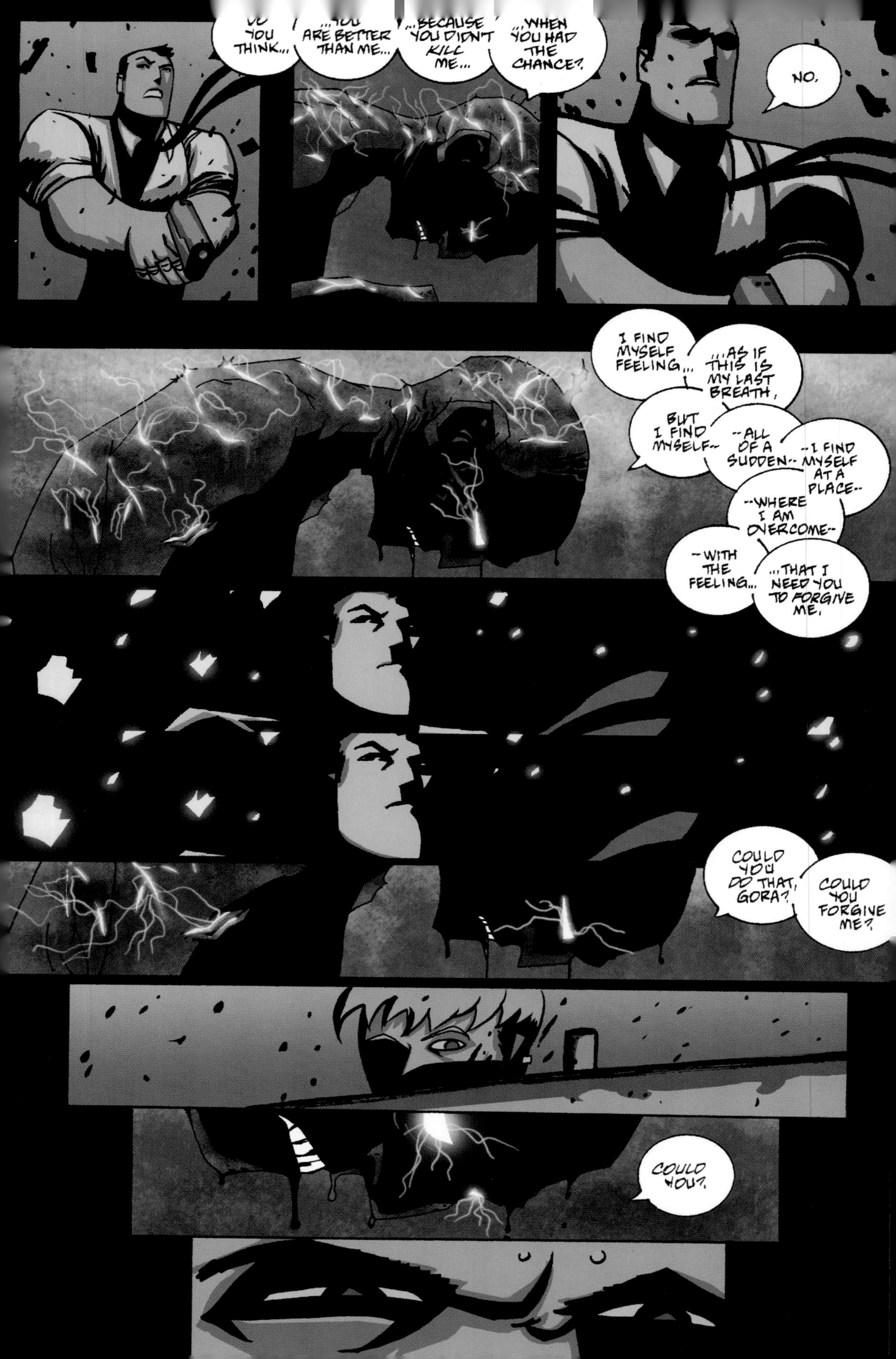
YOU THINK...
...YOU ARE BETTER THAN ME...
...BECAUSE YOU DIDN'T KILL ME...
...WHEN YOU HAD THE CHANCE?
NO.
I FIND MYSELF FEELING...
...AS IF THIS IS MY LAST BREATH,
BUT I FIND MYSELF--
--ALL OF A SUDDEN--
--I FIND MYSELF AT A PLACE--
--WHERE I AM OVERCOME--
--WITH THE FEELING...
...THAT I NEED YOU TO FORGIVE ME.
COULD YOU DO THAT, GORA?
COULD YOU FORGIVE ME?
COULD YOU?

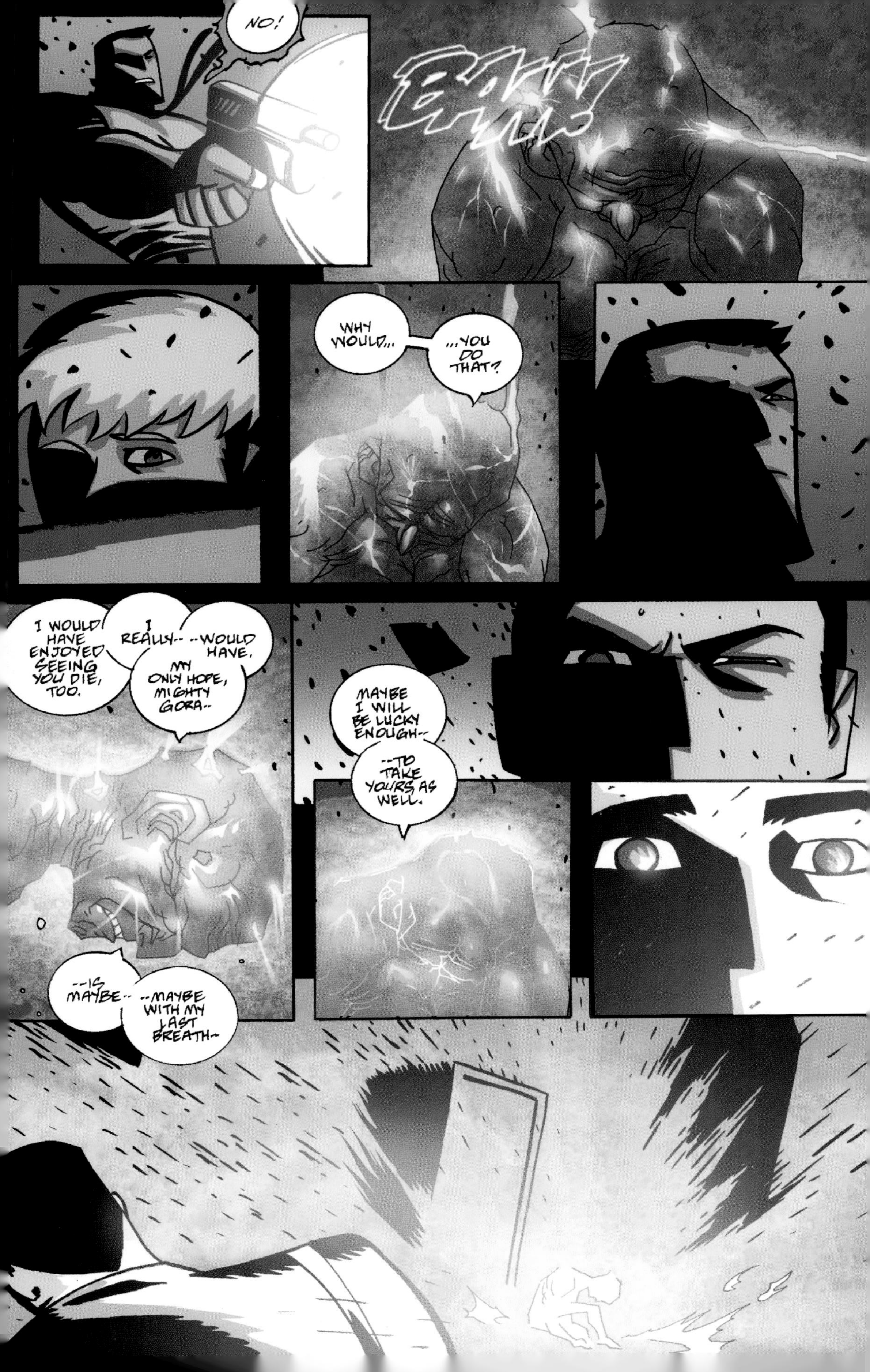
NO!
BAM
WHY WOULD...
...YOU DO THAT?
I WOULD HAVE ENJOYED SEEING YOU DIE, TOO.
I REALLY--
--WOULD HAVE.
MY ONLY HOPE, MIGHTY GORA--
MAYBE I WILL BE LUCKY ENOUGH--
--TO TAKE YOURS AS WELL.
--IS MAYBE--
--MAYBE WITH MY LAST BREATH--

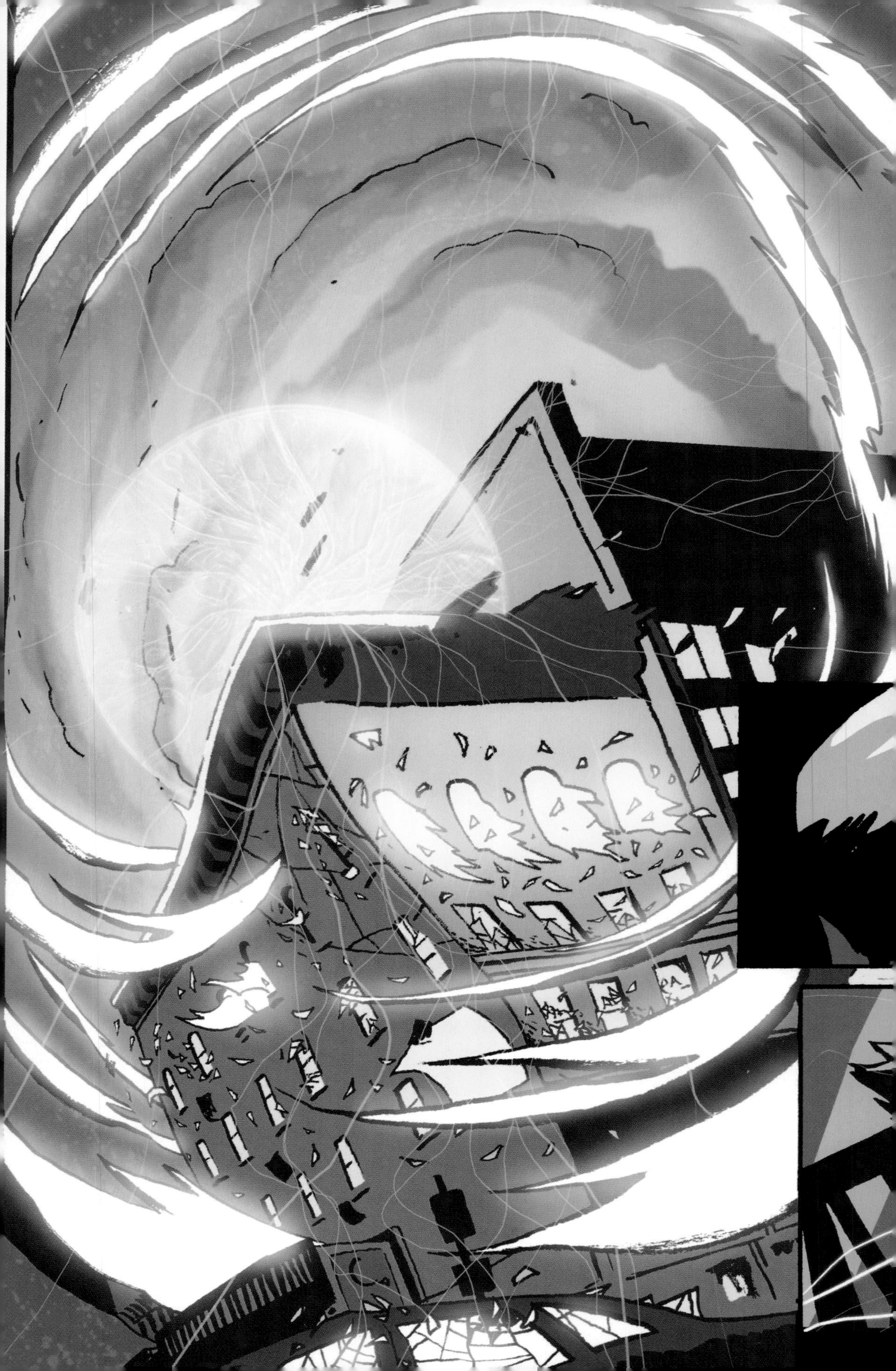

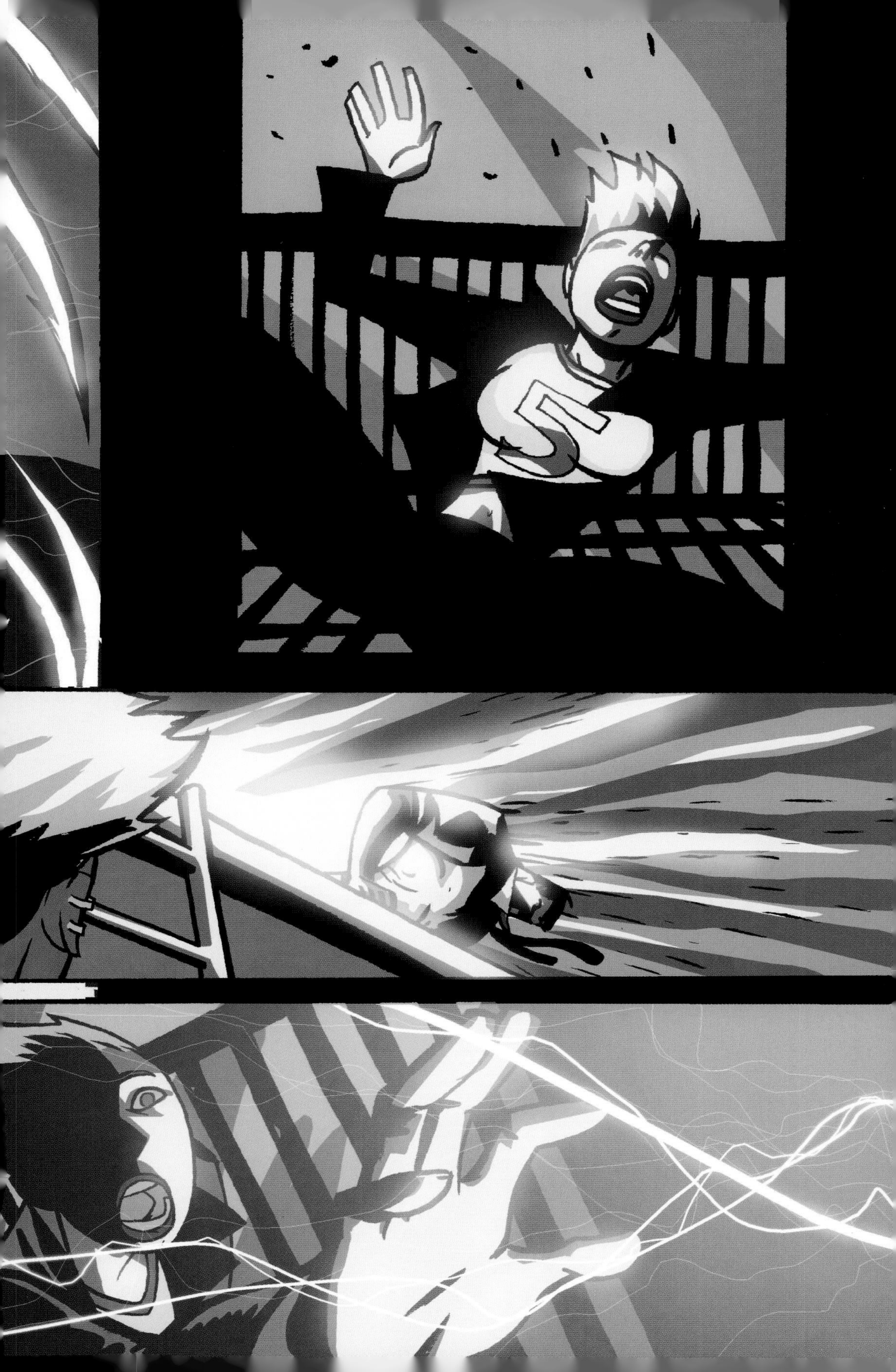

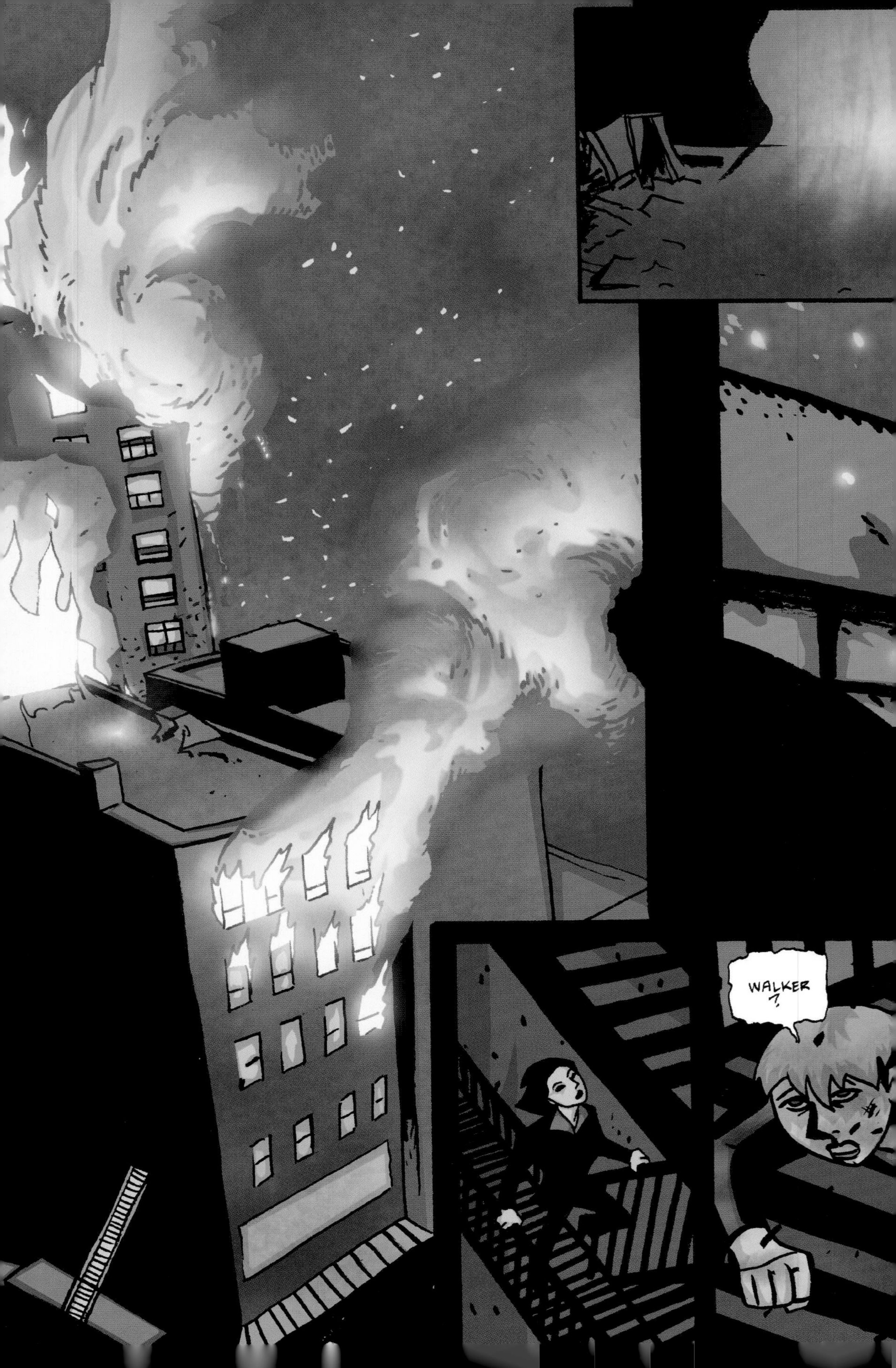
WALKER?

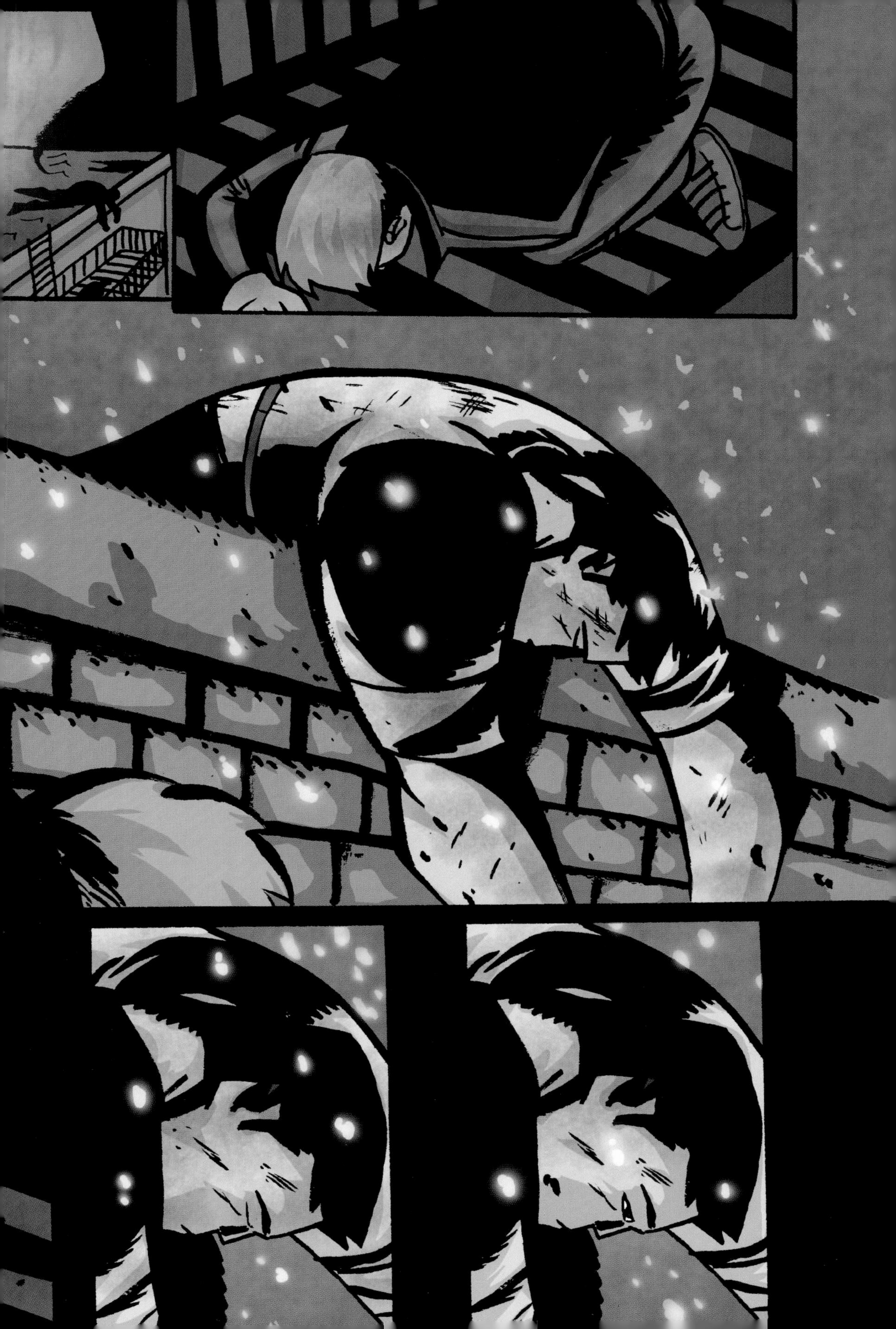

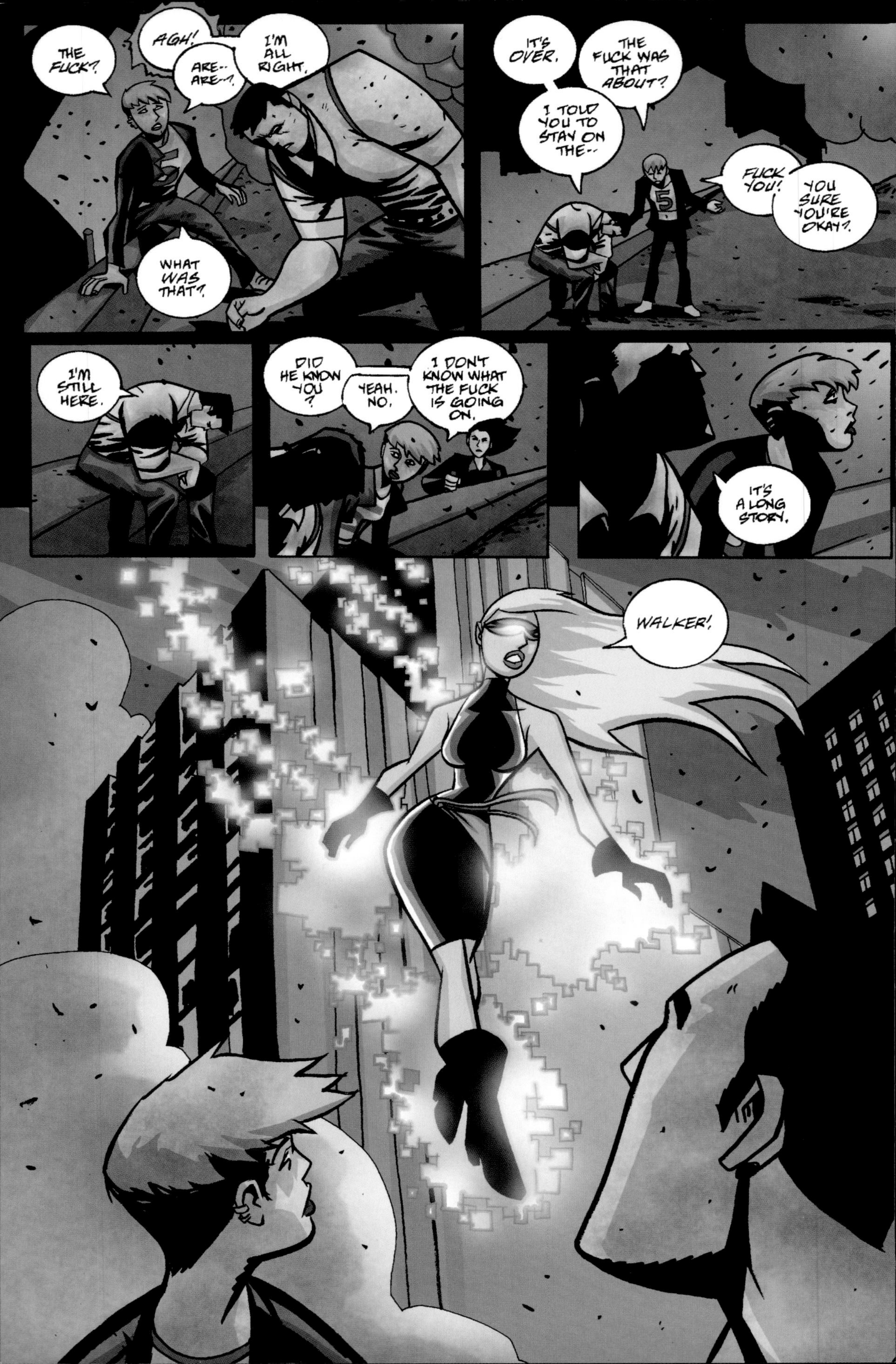
THE FUCK?
AGH!
ARE-- ARE--?
I'M ALL RIGHT.
WHAT WAS THAT?
IT'S OVER.
THE FUCK WAS THAT ABOUT?
I TOLD YOU TO STAY ON THE--
FUCK YOU!
YOU SURE YOU'RE OKAY?
I'M STILL HERE.
DID HE KNOW YOU?
YEAH. NO.
I DON'T KNOW WHAT THE FUCK IS GOING ON.
IT'S A LONG STORY.
WALKER!

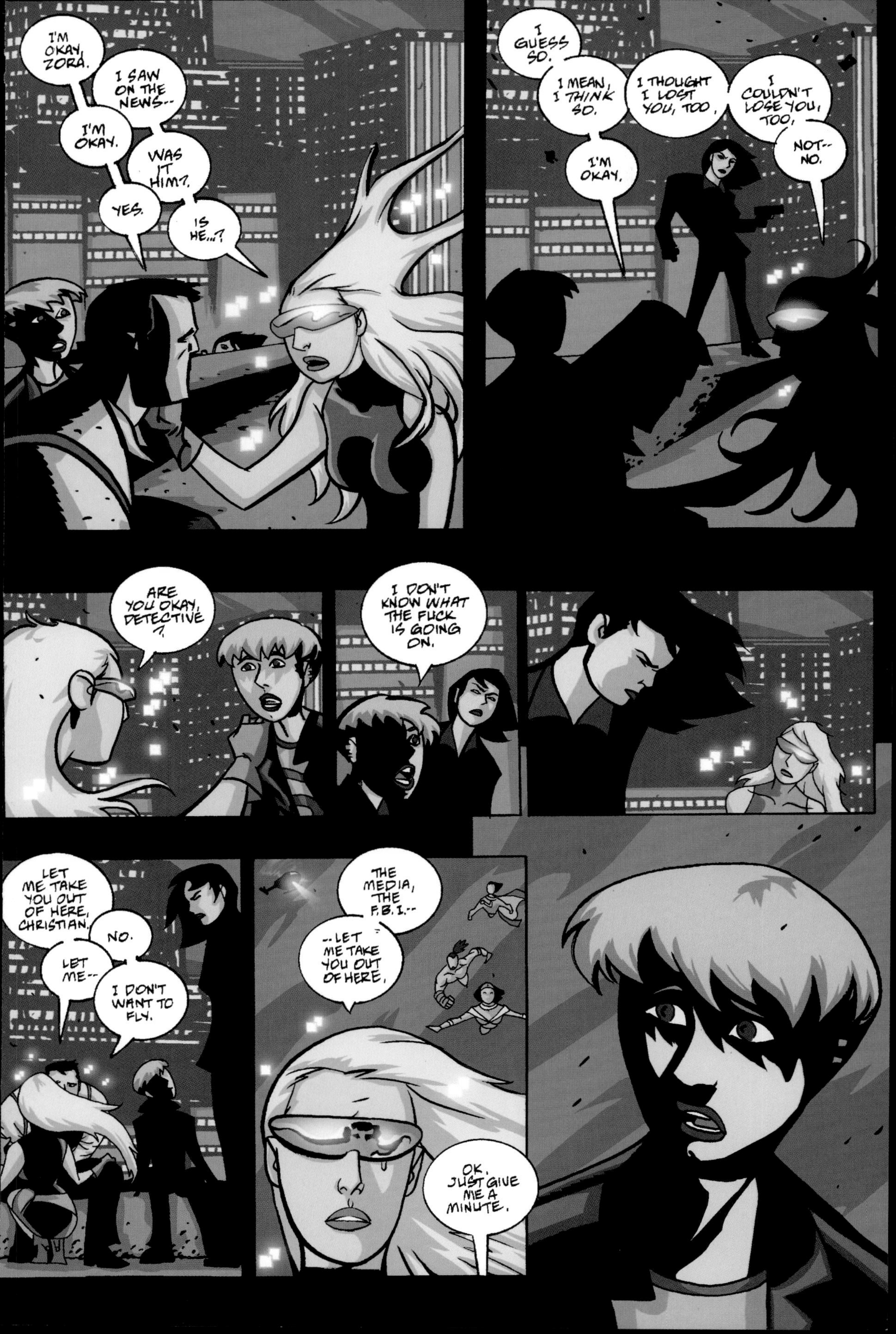
I'M OKAY, ZORA.
I SAW ON THE NEWS--
I'M OKAY.
WAS IT HIM?.
YES.
IS HE...?
I GUESS SO.
I MEAN, I THINK SO.
I'M OKAY.
I THOUGHT I LOST YOU, TOO.
I COULDN'T LOSE YOU, TOO.
NOT-- NO.
ARE YOU OKAY, DETECTIVE?
I DON'T KNOW WHAT THE FUCK IS GOING ON.
LET ME TAKE YOU OUT OF HERE, CHRISTIAN.
NO.
LET ME--
I DON'T WANT TO FLY.
THE MEDIA, THE F.B.I.--
--LET ME TAKE YOU OUT OF HERE.
OK. JUST GIVE ME A MINUTE.

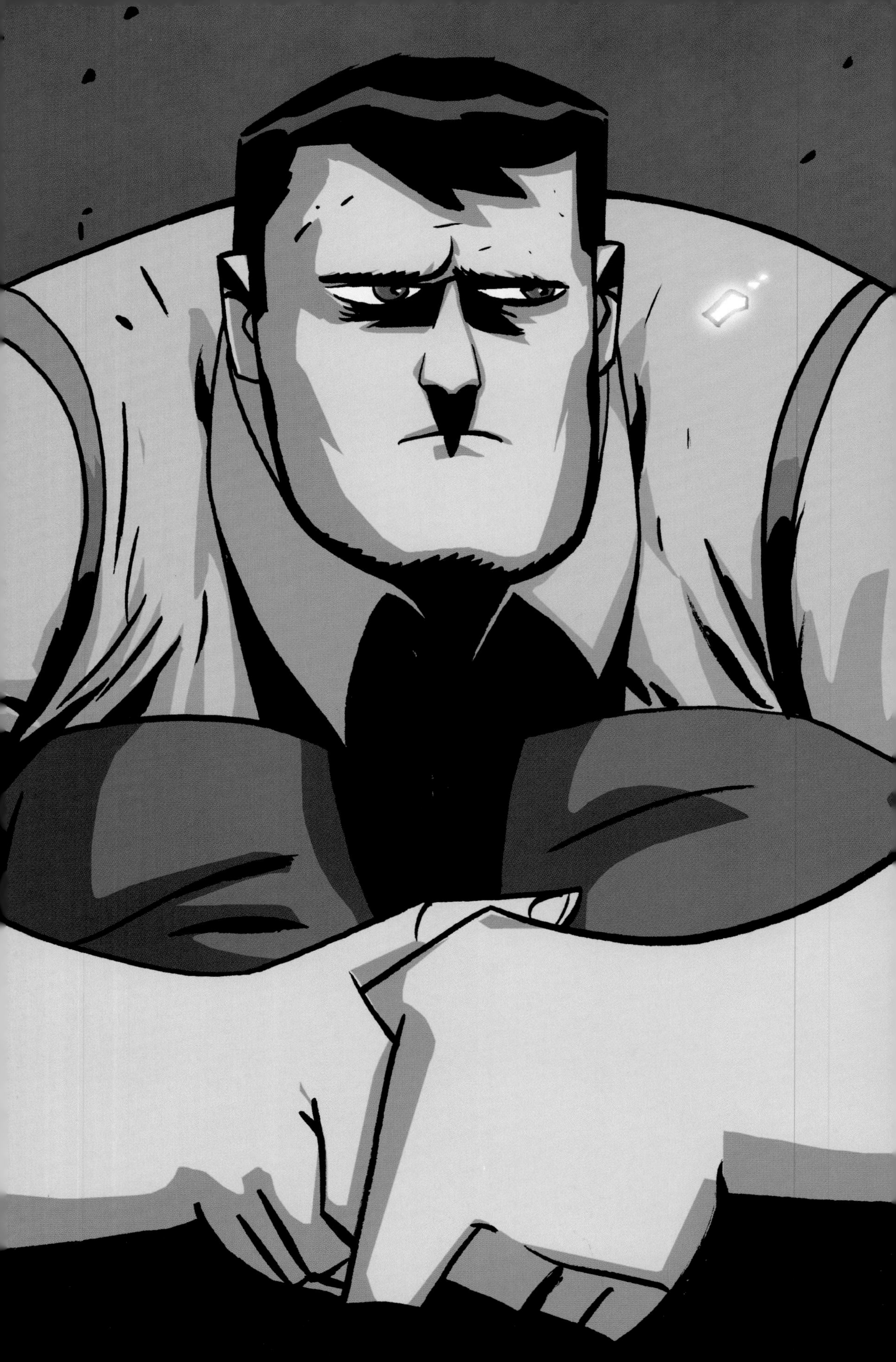

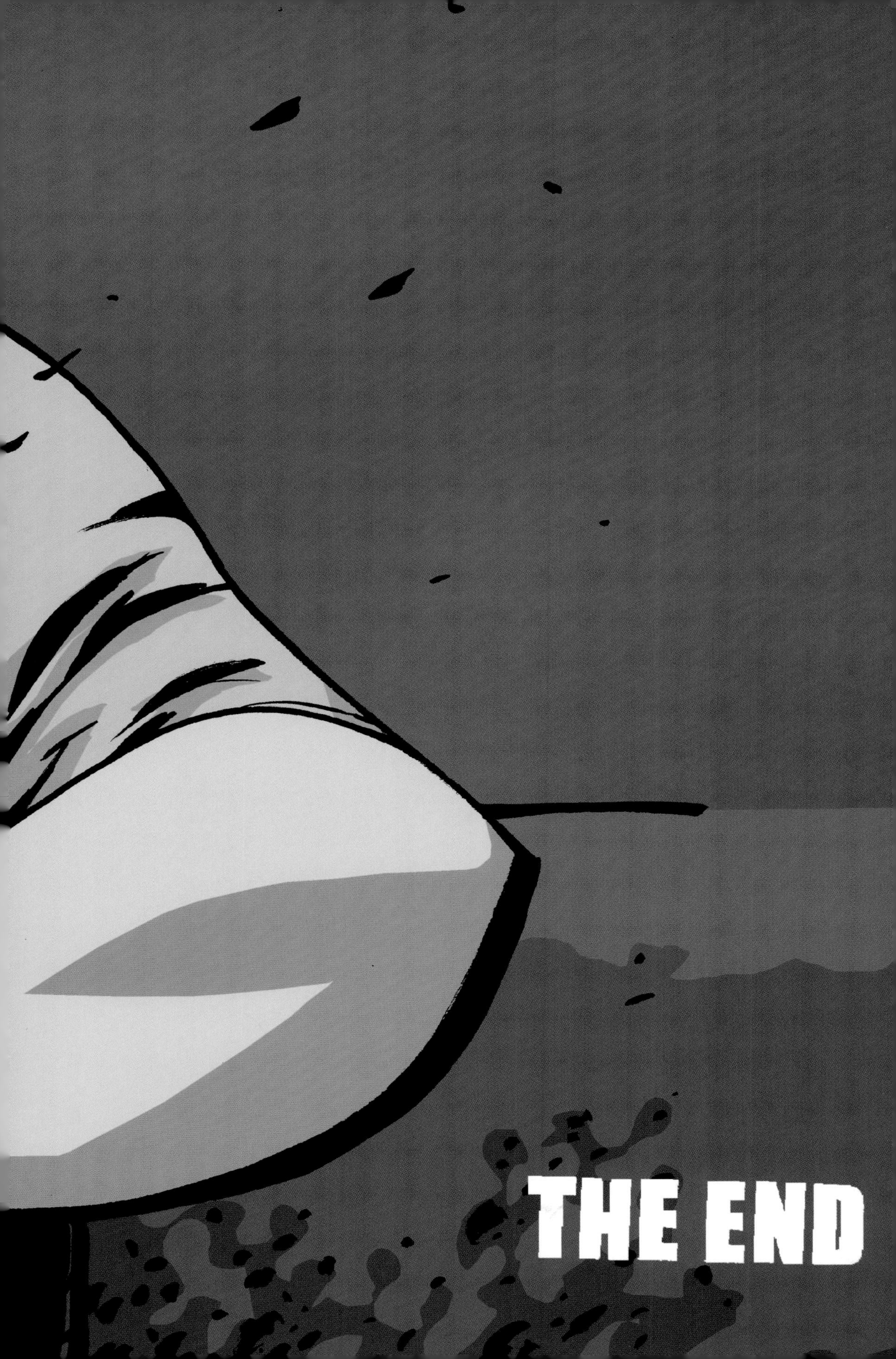
THE END

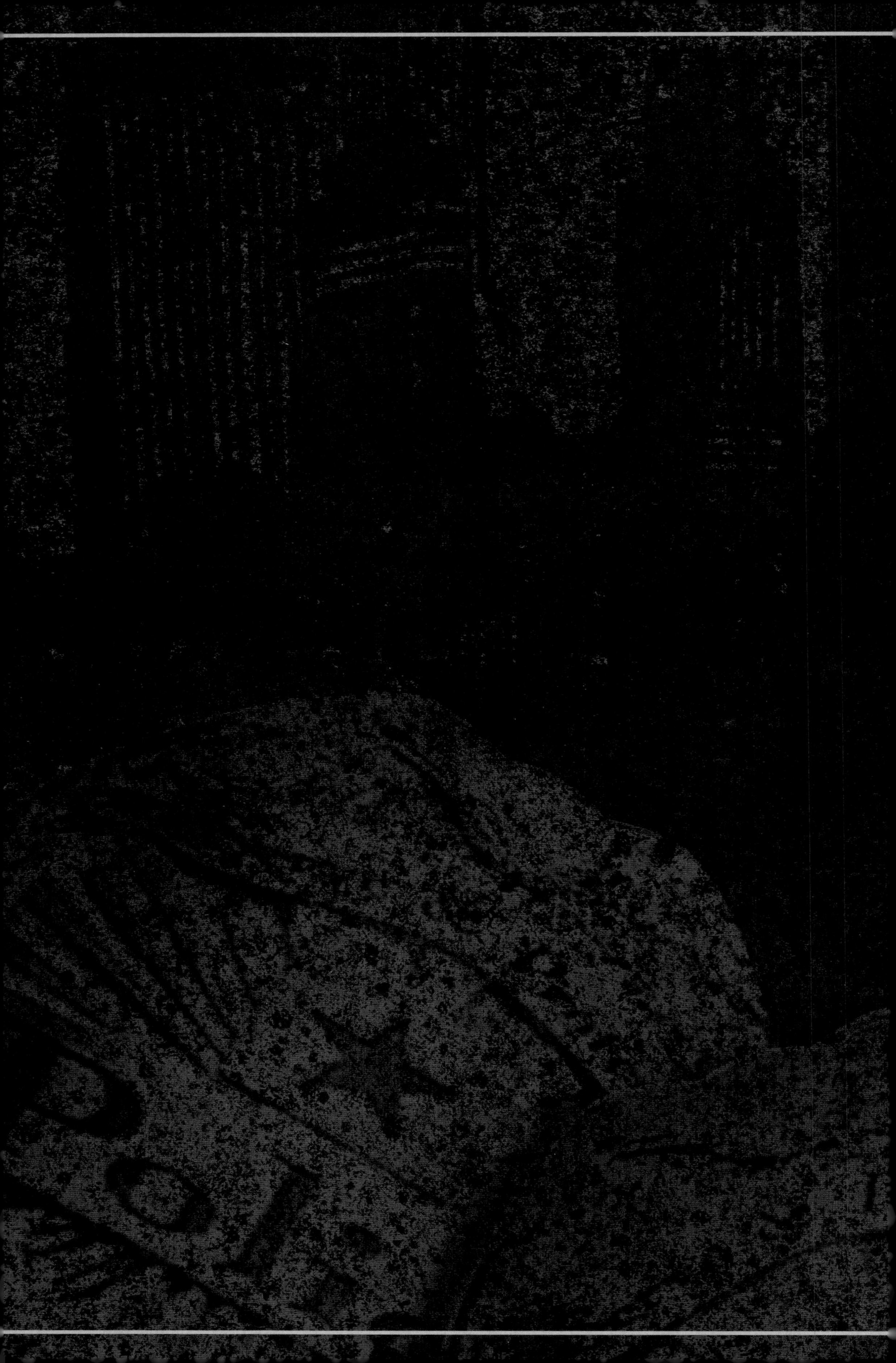

# THE SCRIPT

## Ah. The infamous monkey issue.

I think the phone call I made to Mike Oeming after writing this issue was: "Hey, Mike, I think I just killed our book. This might be the beginning of the end."

Yeah, yeah. We had this grand vision for this giant mythological story of ours and we knew this is how we wanted to open the story. With a big fucking nod to Stanley Kubrick and a real in your face "we're not fucking around with this" attitude, but we also knew that a lot of people buy this comic for some superhero homicide detective fiction and this ain't that.

And its one thing to think about writing something li this, it's another thing to have done it and realize ho whacked out this might seem at first. See you guys g to read this story in one sitting, the monthly POWE readers had to wait six weeks to get a clue to what w actually happening.

But we had a story to tell and a way we wanted to t it, so we bit our lip and got on with it.

But, boy, I didn't think I was going to be getting monk fucker jokes via email to this DAY. Alright already! I' heard them!

You should have seen my AOL account the fir two months after this issue shipped. Every subje header was:

MONKEY FUCKER
MONKEY ASS
MONKEY TAINT
MONKEY CUM
MONKEY ANAL
MONKEY LOVE WITH HOWARD STERN
MONKEY SMEGMA

And on and on it went. I am sure my account g flagged. It looked like I was running some kind monkey porn ring or something.

But gratefully most everyone hung in with the bo and got into the ride, but because this issue was closely scrutinized and because now that you've re the entire story you might appreciate what went i this on another level, or just to show you that, yes actually wrote a script for this issue, we are presenti the full script to issue 31.

## The monkey fucker issue.

Enjoy.

Or whatever.

POWERS
BY BRIAN MICHAEL BENDIS
AND MICHAEL AVON OEMING
ISSUE THIRTY ONE
FOREVER MAN PART ONE

Ok. So...

This story arc is about the first two superheroes ever.

And they are reincarnated souls whose grudge match battle to the death takes centuries and centuries. One of them will know they are reincarnated and the other will not.

Each chapter will take place in a different time period. With different feelings and tones to them.

This first chapter is the dawn of man. Please reference the opening of 2001 for tone and look. This is a direct, bold homage to that part of the film but we will gradually build on it.

The ape man figures are really dense black fur figures against the bland, bleached out, minimal backgrounds.

The color tone is oranges. Monochromatic.

The font clearly identifies to the reader that vocalizing hurts. As if the vocal chords aren't fully formed.

Page 1-

Full page image

Wide shot of a desolate, almost desert plane, a couple of badly formed hills and mountains. No greenery. No brush. Just the earth in its earliest days.

The hazy sun is setting in the distance miles away.

White Times Roman Type reads: The dawn of man

Page 2- 3

Double page spread

Another incredibly wide shot of the desolate desert earth. As if the camera in page one, shifted over to the right to show even more of this incredibly desolate world.

But in the middle of page 3 a half dozen ape men are hovering around a water hole.

For reference- here is some of my research on this that I think will help your artwork.

About 3 million year ago, the earth was populated with deer, giraffes, hyenas, cattle, sheep, goats, antelope, gazelles, horses, elephants, rhinoceroses, camels, ground squirrels, beavers, cave lions, ants, termites, porpoises, whales, dogs with huge teeth, and sabre toothed tigers! Giant sharks, about 42 feet long, were plentiful.

There were all kinds of birds and plants and fish, similar to birds, plants and fish today. (Dinosaurs died out about 65 million years ago. They were long gone.)

About this Same time in history, around 3 million years ago, the higher primates, including apes and early man, first appeared. There was a difference between

the apes and man. Human-like hominids could stand upright. Apes could not. Their hands were different, too. Ape hands were made for climbing and clinging.

Early man's hands were jointed differently, which allowed them to not only use tools, but to make tools. No one knows if they actually made tools, but remains of polished bones have been found in South Africa, which suggests they might have made simple digging tools from bone!

Their diet was mostly vegetarian, along with some meat, probably obtained by scavenging.

**Page 4-**

1- Mid shot of the six ape man hovering around the shallow watering hole. Drinking water out of their hands or putting their lips lightly to the water.

In the foreground, a small dead reptilian animal behind them they killed and ate a reptile and are now drinking. There are also some berry branches stripped of their fruit.

The man-apes were starving to death. What little food they could find consisted of only a few bugs, roots and if they were lucky enough to find one before the tapirs got to it, maybe a grub or two.

Obviously they are on the brink of extinction as evidenced by the "humanoid" bones lying around We are beginning to see slight difference in the apemen.

One is a woman. And two are a bit larger that all the rest.

Of the larger, one has a white shock in his hair like the bride of Frankenstein. He is White Stripe.

The other is a bit larger than the all the others and he has a big Red Stripe across his eyes and back. Almost like a mask.

The other three are normal black furry ape men with no features.

2- White Stripe lifts his face from the water. He has a content look on his face. He is a peaceful soul.

WHITE STRIPE
Ggrrrpprrr...

3- The woman ape lazily drips water on her chest without realizing anyone cares. Seduction.

WOMAN APE
Gggsskkk!!

4- Red Stripe watches The woman ape and honks his approval.

RED STRIPE

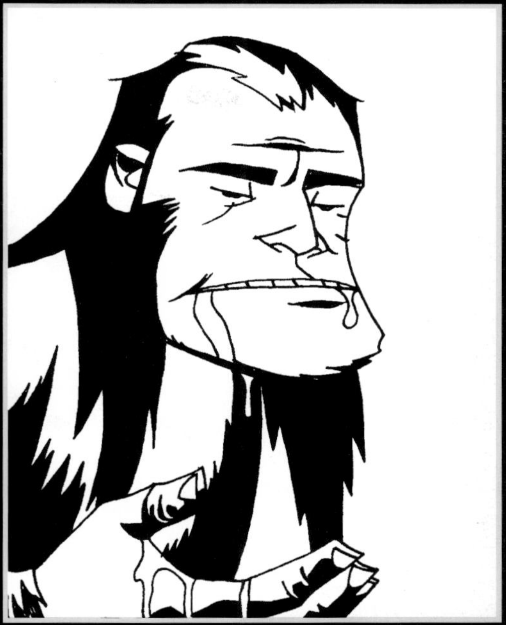

Groonkkkhhl!

5- The woman ape glares at Red Stripe with contempt.

WOMAN APE
Fftt!

6- Red Stripe grimaces at the insult.

RED STRIPE
Snort!

7- From behind Red Stripe, The woman turns away and goes back to the water. She is ignoring him.

**Page 5-**

1- Red Stripe gives her a glaringly evil look.

2- From behind the White Stripe. White Stripe watches her quietly as she drinks. In the background, Red Stripe watches the two of them.

3- The woman honks approvingly at White Stripe as water dribbles from her mouth.

WOMAN APE
Hoffkk!!

4- White Stripe honks back. They are flirting.

WHITE STRIPE
Ghhonkkk!!

5- The woman sticks her little ass in the air as she goes back to drinking.

6- White Stripe looks at her ass sticking up. He is feeling randy.

7- White Stripe's p.o.v. Tight on the ass.

8- Tighter on White Stripe looking at the ass longingly.

**Page 6-**

1- From behind Red Stripe, White Stripe mounts the woman and starts going at it.

> WHITE STRIPE
> Gruunk!

> WOMAN
> Hugh!

> WHITE STRIPE
> Gruunk!

2- The Red Stripe watches this from across the small pond, he ain't happy.

> WHITE STRIPE
> Gruunk!
> WOMAN
> Hugh!

> WHITE STRIPE
> Gruunk!

3- The two go at it. They do not notice Red Stripe.

> WHITE STRIPE
> Gruunk!

> WOMAN
> Hugh!

> WHITE STRIPE
> Gruunk!

4- The woman drinks as he humps her.

> WHITE STRIPE
> Gruunk!

> WOMAN
> Hugh!

> WHITE STRIPE
> Gruunk!

5- The other apes seem agitated and excited. One starts to whack it and doesn't even know why.

> WHITE STRIPE
> Gruunk!

> WOMAN
> Hugh!

> WHITE STRIPE
> Gruunk!

> APE
> Gahh!!

> APE
> Faap!!

> APE
> Gfaapp!!

> APE
> Raaffggh!

**Page 7-**

1- White Stripe barks at the sky. His entire face curled into a childlike smile of glee. He is finishing.

> WHITE STRIPE
> Hhaarrgghh!!

2- From behind the Red Stripe, White Stripe keeps fucking the woman and barks back.

> WHITE STRIPE
> Yyaarrggff!!!

> WOMAN
> Hagh huagh huagh

> WHITE STRIPE
> Yyaarrggff!!!

> WOMAN
> Hagh huagh huagh

> WHITE STRIPE
> Yyaarrggff!!!

3- Tight on the woman panting into the water, water dripping from her mouth.

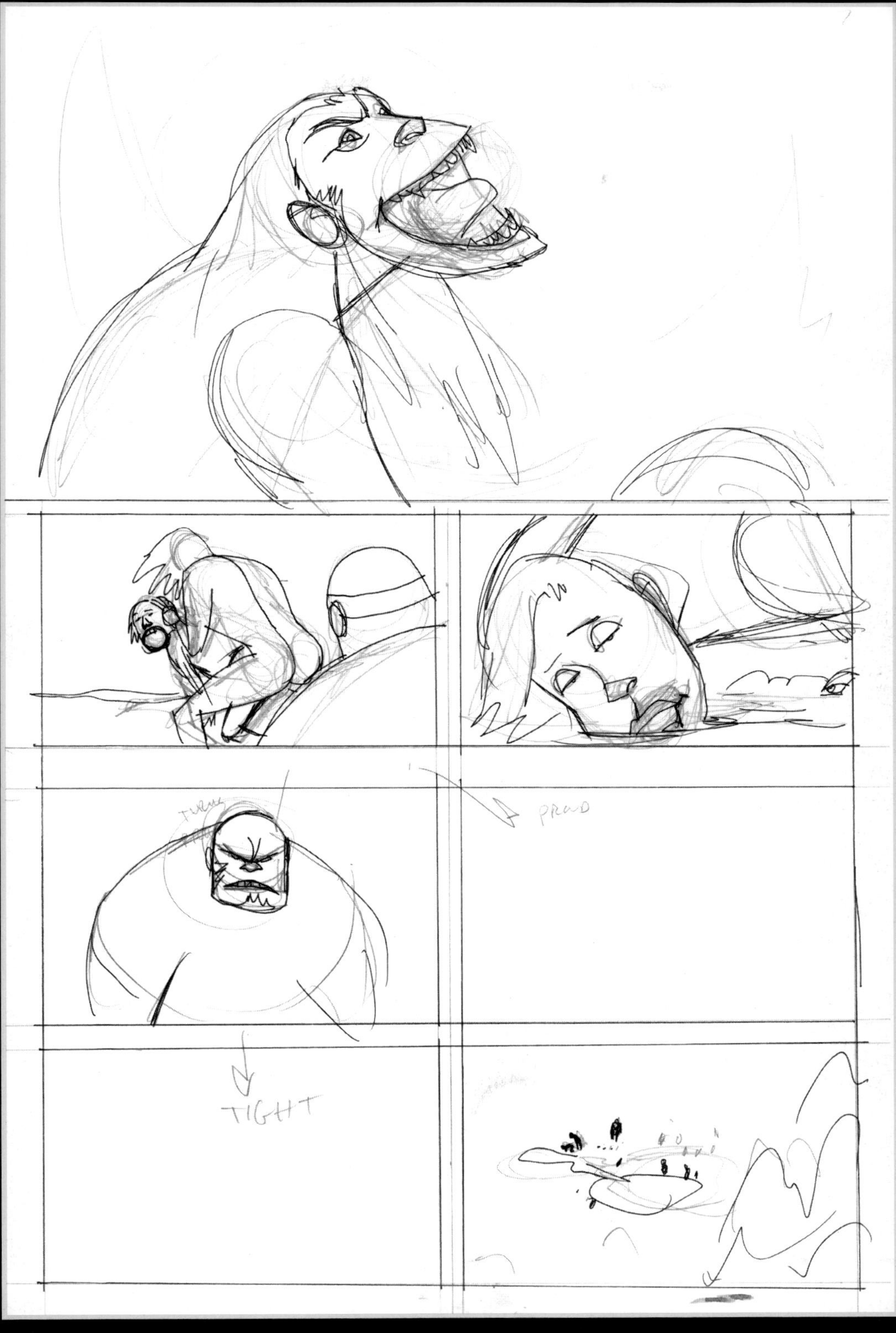
PROD
TIGHT

WOMAN
Hagh huagh huagh

4- Red Stripe glares at the scene.

RED STRIPE
Hoggnnk!

5- White Stripe looks at Red Stripe for the first time since the act began.

Its a satisfied look that is being mistaken for an arrogant look of conquest.

6- Same as 4, but tighter.

7- Mid wide of the small pond. Red Stripe is walking away as the rest continue to drink.

Page 8-

1- Ext. Cave- night

Its a crevice inside a badly formed mountain side in this barren wasteland. The crevice is a crooked, slanted triangle if an opening.

It is pouring. A monstrous amount of night rain.

2- Int. Cave- Same

The apes all sleep up against the wall of the cave. White Stripe sleeping next to woman ape. All the other apes asleep on her other side. White Stripe sleeping closest to the cave opening. Everyone huddled.

3- Sitting across from the rest of the apes is the Red Stripe. He is sitting and hugging himself. He is wide awake, staring at the White Stripe.

4- Red Stripe's p.o.v. The White Stripe is sleeping.

5- Same, The White Stripe opens his eyes and looks at

the Red Stripe sitting across from him.

6- Tight on the Red Stripe staring back.

7- Same as 4,

8- Same as 5.

Page 9-

1- Ext. Desert- day

Big panel. Action!

The man-apes are running towards us in a furious panic. They are being attacked by a hungry leopard who is nipping at their heels. Everyone is running away from the leopard with a panic and desperation.

They are running across a mostly open desert plane. Mountains behind them. a young tree here and there. Nothing to climb up.

This day is very blanche. Almost yellow, white, hot. Sunny but hazy.

WOMAN
Gyyaaarrgghhh!!!

2- White Stripe is running and looking around in a panic for somewhere to hide.

WHITE STRIPE
Huf hufgh hufgh!!

3- White Stripe finds a steep cliff to scamper up in the distance and yells for everyone to follow him.

WHITE STRIPE
Hugh  Hyaauugghh!!

4- Profile, silhouette of the incline. The others follow his lead as the leopard is just about to get to them.

5- The woman ape is climbing and crying, she looks back at...

WOMAN APE
Hyyiii!!

6- Woman ape's p.o.v. High looking down. The leopard barks and leaps. He can't follow them up the incline.

LEOPARD
Rrraagghhrr!!

Page 10-

1- The Red Stripe climbs up past White Stripe. Both are stronger and climb much faster than the others.

WHITE STRIPE
Huh huh huh!!!

2- Wide of the incline hillside. All the apes are scampering. The leopard can't reach them.

> APE
>
> Ffttt!!

> APE
>
> ggaap!!

> APE
>
> aapp!!

> APE
>
> Raaffggh!

3- The White Stripe reaches down to pull the woman ape up.

> WHITE STRIPE
>
> Gruunk!

> WOMAN
>
> Hugh!

4- High looking down. The leopard leers quiet, menacing, looking for his chance.

5- Low looking up. Past the leopard looking up at The apes mocking him. Hanging off the rocks and mocking him. The littlest apes closest to the leopard.

> WHITE STRIPE
>
> Gruunk!

> WOMAN
>
> Hugh!

> WHITE STRIPE
>
> Gruunk!

> APE
>
> Gahh!!

> APE
>
> Faap!!

> APE
>
> Gfaapp!!

> APE
>
> Raaffggh!

6- High looking down, The leopard jumps.

> LEOPARD
>
> Aarrgghh!!

Page 11-

1- Profile. The leopard leaps and grabs one o smaller apes by the foot. Pulling him down.

> APE
>
> Aaiiiasaaee!!

2- Low looking up. The other apes all react in s and climb higher.

> WHITE STRIPE
>
> Aaeegghhk!

> WOMAN
>
> Hugh!

> WHITE STRIPE
>
> Aakktt!

> APE
>
> Gahh!!

> APE
>
> Eeeaaa!!

3- The leopard viciously eats the young ape Holding him down on the ground firmly with a p the chest and is Tearing him up.

> APE
>
> Aaaaiirrgghhaarrgghh!!

4- The Red Stripe, panicked, wide eyed, grabs a off the ledge.

> APE
> (off panel)
>
> Aaaiiee!!!

5- The Red Stripe throws the rock down to the gr

> RED STRIPE
>
> Hurugh!!

6- High looking down. The rock misses and bo as the leopard continues to eat the ape, now

> LEOPARD
>
> Ggggg....

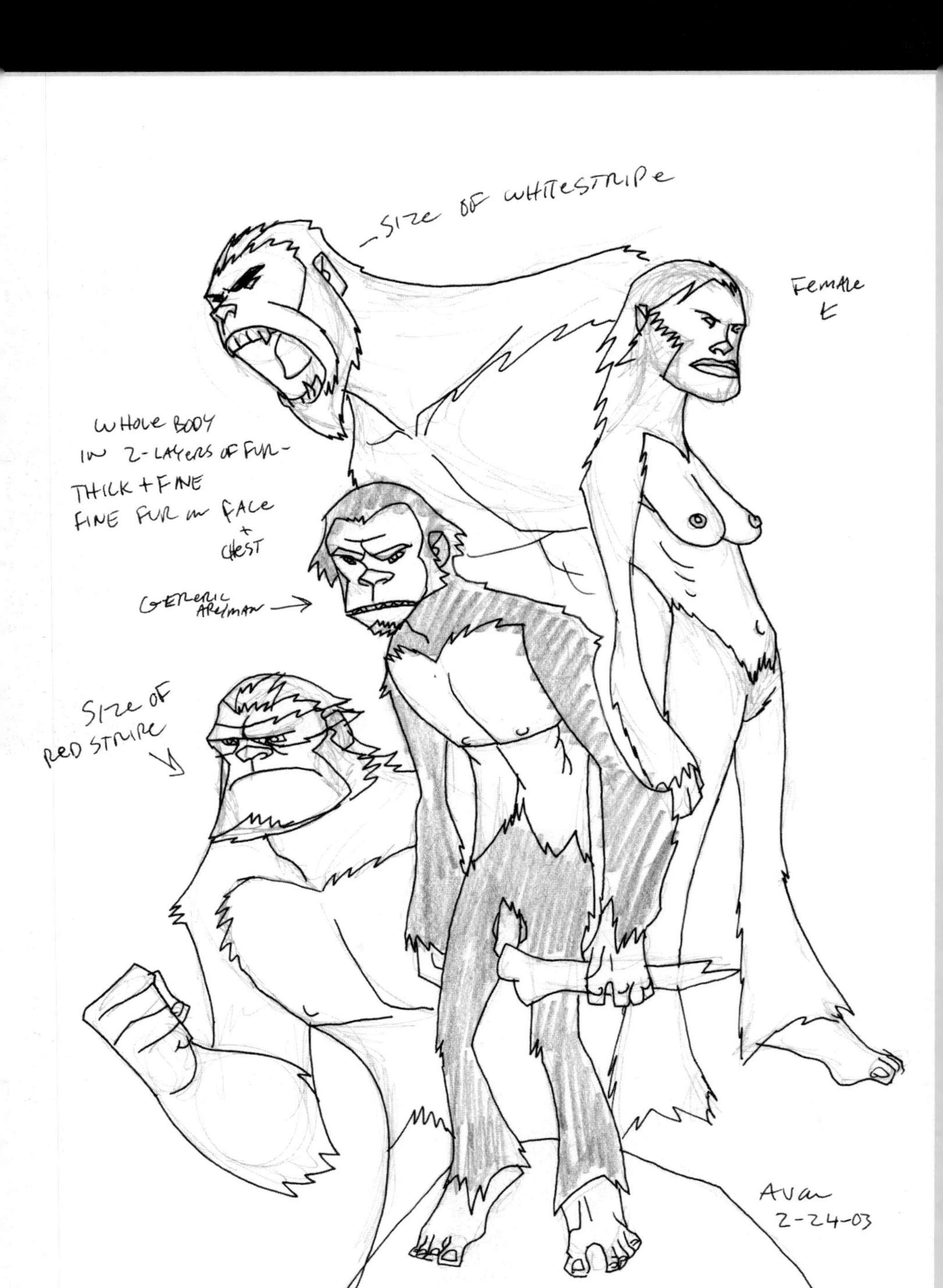
SIZE OF WHITESTRIPE
FEMALE
WHOLE BODY IN 2-LAYERS OF FUR-
THICK + FINE
FINE FUR ON FACE + CHEST
GENERIC APE/MAN
SIZE OF RED STRIPE
AVON
2-24-03

Spx: thump

- The Red Stripe grabs another rock, this time
determined to do something.

- The Red Stripe throws the rock down to the ground.

### RED STRIPE
Hurugh!!

**Page 12-**

- Mid shot of the leopard. The rock bashes him on the
head.

Spx: bonk

### LEOPARD
Aeeiii

- The woman and the White Stripe watching this.

- The leopard is hurt. Dazed and bleeding from the
head.

- The White Stripe also grabs a rock and throws it too.

- The new rock hits the leopard. The leopard has killed
his little ape.

Spx: bonk

### LEOPARD
Aeeiii

- The Red Stripe digs at the ledge to grab a big rock...

**Page 13-**

- Mid wide, full figure, profile.

Red Stripe slips off the ledge trying to throw it. He is

falling backwards, totally shocked and confused by
predicament.

### RED STRIPE
Yip!!

2- From behind the Red Stripe, Red Stripe falls on
back right in front of the bleeding leopard.

Spx: whump

### RED STRIPE
Ooff!!

3- The Red Stripe's p.o.v. The leopard immedia
turns and hunches, ready to pounce.

4- Red Stripe gets a hold of himself, realizing what
of deep shit he is in. He is lying right next to
bleeding, dead carcass of his little friend.

5- The leopard lunges for the kill, teeth out.

### LEOPARD
Raaarrgghh!!

6- White Stripe and the woman ape's faces dro
horror as they watch this horrible scene.

**Page 14-**

1- Big panel, profile. Red Stripe, still lying on his b
kicks the leopard in the face And snaps his n

Spx: crack snap

### RED STRIPE
Aagghh!!

### LEOPARD
Iiee!!

2- The leopard falls a few feet away- its head ba
hanging on. Dust billows.

Spx: whump

3- Close up on the leopard's face. Eyes open. Bl

He is Dead.

4- The Red Stripe is stunned and confused by this. Its a quiet moment after all the craziness. His foot still half up.

5- The others, still on the cliff are stunned. The smaller apes are stunned. Confused. They can't register how this worked.

**Page 15-**

1- The Red Stripe slowly gets up. He can't take his eyes off the dead carcass of the leopard lying in the foreground.

2- The Red Stripe yells at it.

RED STRIPE
Hyhyaaghg raarr!! ffaarrggh!!

3- Red Stripe gently, nervously approaches the dead carcass with his hand out. He wants to touch it but he is scared to.

4- Red Stripe's hand is close to touching the leopard...

5- White Stripe and the woman ape's faces are frozen with eyes wide open.

6- Red Stripe touches the carcass shoving it a little...

7- Red Stripe spills back, afraid that he has woken up the leopard.

RED STRIPE
Ffaasggh!!

8- Red Stripe's p.o.v. The leopard lies dead.

**Page 16-**

1- High looking down. The others start to tentatively climb down the ledge/ cliff. The leopard lies dead below them. Red Stripe still looks at it.

2- Red Stripe Looks down at his own foot with first curiosity. Considering what he did.

3- Red Stripe's p.o.v. His hairy foot.

4- Red Stripe kicks the leopard again viciously- with confidence. Its guts plop out from a superpowered force. The others bark back in shock.

RED STRIPE
Hyyaaggh!!

Spx: whump

Spx: splat

5- The others all bark back in shock.

WHITE STRIPE
Aaeegghhk!

WOMAN
Hugh!

WHITE STRIPE
Aakktt!

APE
Gahh!!

APE
Eeeaaa!!

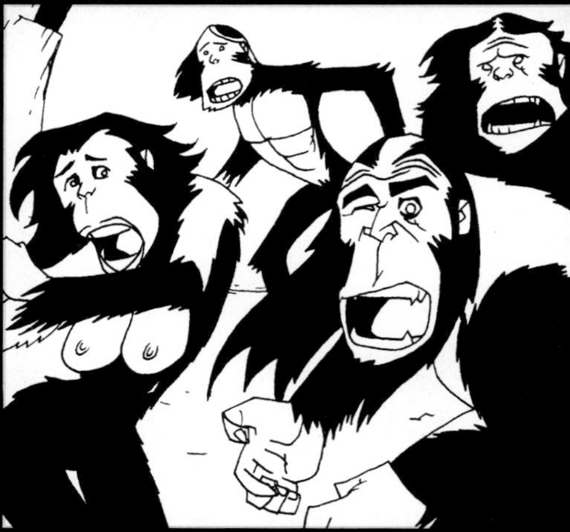

6- Low looking up. Red Stripe howls in triumph. His new found power and confidence.

RED STRIPE
Hhaaaooooaaaaa!!!!

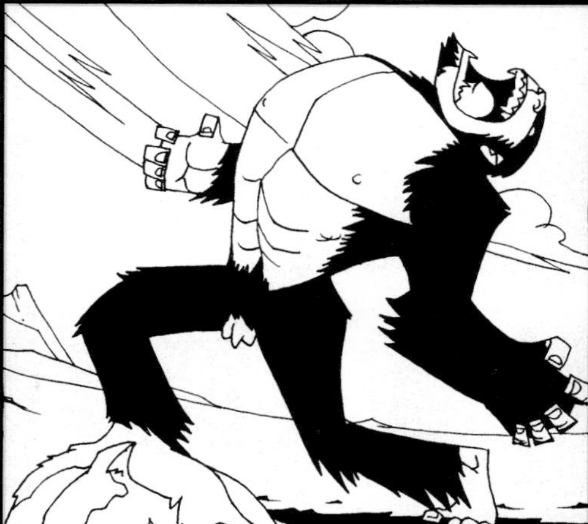

**Page 17-**

1- Ext. Pond. Dusk

Similar scene to the beginning of the issue, but the sky is almost red. There's something in the air. Its the end of the day.

Mid shot of the now five ape man hovering around the watering hole. Drinking water out of their hands or putting their lips to the water.

In the foreground, the dead leopard has been gutted and eaten raw. They ate him and are now drinking.

2- White Stripe lifts his face from the water. He has a content look on his face.

> WHITE STRIPE
> Ggrrrpprrr...

3- The woman lazily drips water on her chest without realizing anyone cares. The seduction begins again.

> WOMAN APE
> Gggsskkk!!

4- Red Stripe, with a new sense of self worth, watches and honks his approval.

> RED STRIPE
> Groonkkkhh1!

5- The woman looks back at him with a new found curiosity.

6- Red Stripe looks at her with new found assurance. He looks at her like he owns her.

> RED STRIPE
> Frunk.

7- From behind Red Stripe, The woman turns away and goes back to the water. She is ignoring him again. The White Stripe is getting ready to jump her.

8- Same as six, but tighter.

9- Tight on the Red Stripe's foot stepping forward into the water.

Spx: splumk

**Page 18-**

1- Red Stripe shoves White Stripe to the ground with a dismissive elbow and mounts the woman ape, to her surprise, and starts going at it.

The White Stripe has lost his footing and is shocked by this new development.

> RED STRIPE
> Gruunk!

> WOMAN APE
> Hugh!

> WHITE STRIPE
> Unk!

2- The Red Stripe really goes for it. Quick and hard.

> RED STRIPE
> Gruunk!

> WOMAN APE
> Hugh!

> RED STRIPE
> Gruunk!

3- The White Stripe scrambles to his feet and tries to stop the rape.
The other monkey's are watching this.

> WHITE STRIPE
> Gruunk!

> WOMAN
> Hugh!

> WHITE STRIPE
> Gruunk!

4- The Red Stripe, without missing a stroke, viciously back hands White Stripe.

> RED STRIPE
> Gruunk!

Spx: ftunk

> WHITE STRIPE
> Gunk!

5- White Stripe goes flying backwards into the other apes.

> WOMAN
> Hugh!

> WHITE STRIPE
> Gruunk!

> APE
> Aaaiicckk!!

> APE
> Wwaaiiggh!!

**Page 19-**

1- The White Stripe gets up, shocked by the violence and watching this turn of events. The other apes seem agitated and excited.

> WHITE STRIPE
> Gruunk!

APE

Gahh!!

APE

Faap!!

APE

Gfaapp!!

APE

Raaffggh!

2- From behind the White Stripe, the Red Stripe keeps his violent rape going. The woman's face is half in the water.

RED STRIPE

Gruunk!
Gruunk!
Gruunk!

WOMAN APE

Hugh!

RED STRIPE

Gruunk!
Gruunk!

3- White Stripe barks at the sky in internal pain. His entire face curled into a childlike anger.

WHITE STRIPE

Hhaarrgghh!!

4- From behind the Red Stripe, White Stripe lunges towards him.

WHITE STRIPE

Yyaarrggff!!!

RED STRIPE

Gruunk!
Gruunk!

5- The White Stripe knocks the Red Stripe off of the woman and into the water. They both tumble into the water.

RED STRIPE

Hoggnnk!

Spx: spalash

Page 20- 21

Double page spread

1- In the shallow water, the White Stripe pounds at the Red Stripe with both fists. Water splashes.

Behind them the woman rolls on the ground in pain.

RED STRIPE

Huaaggh!

WHITE STRIPE

Hugh hugh hugh!!

Spx: thump thump

2- The smaller apes jump up and down in irritation. The violence incites them.

APE

Aaagghh!!

APE

Eeeii!!

3- Profile. The Red Stripe swipes the White Stripe with a wide back arm and the White Stripe goes flying up out of the water and over the woman.
Spx: whump

4- The White Stripe lands on his face and stomach hard, stirring up dust, pebbles, and dirt from the force of the impact. Quite a few yards from the scene at the pond behind him.

Spx: thump

WHITE STRIPE

Gumph!

5- From behind the Red Stripe, The woman ape takes this moment to viciously attack the Red Stripe. She lunges and claws at his chest, crying and howling.

WOMAN APE

Aaaoohhh!! Aagghhooohhh!!

6- The Red Stripe grabs her arms and stops her attack but she is still thrashing.

WOMAN APE

Aaaoohhh!! Aagghhooohhh!!

7- From behind the Red Stripe, the woman ape is over powered by his grip but she is not giving up.

WOMAN APE

Aaaoohhh!! Aagghhooohhh!!

RED STRIPE

Huuaarrgh!

8- Same as 6, but tighter, Red Stripe yells at her to stop. His eyes turning black. Black liquid.

WOMAN APE

Aaaoohhh!!

RED STRIPE

Hhyyuuaarrgghh!!

9- Same but seven, tight on the woman apes mouth as

she screams in pain and horror at her attacker.

WOMAN APE
Aaaoohhh!! Aagghhooohhh!!

10- Same as 6, but tighter. a red swirl pours into the black liquid of his eyes.

11- Same as 9, but tighter. Her mouth goes from pain to shock, something is happening to her and her tongue sticks out a little in shock.

**Page 22-23**

Double page spread

1- Big panel, from behind the Red Stripe, the woman ape is melting.

She melts into thick black goo. Almost as if she is decomposing into waste. The black hair turns to tar.

Her face starts to slide off her head shape.

Her one good eye looks up in pain and sadness. She is dead.

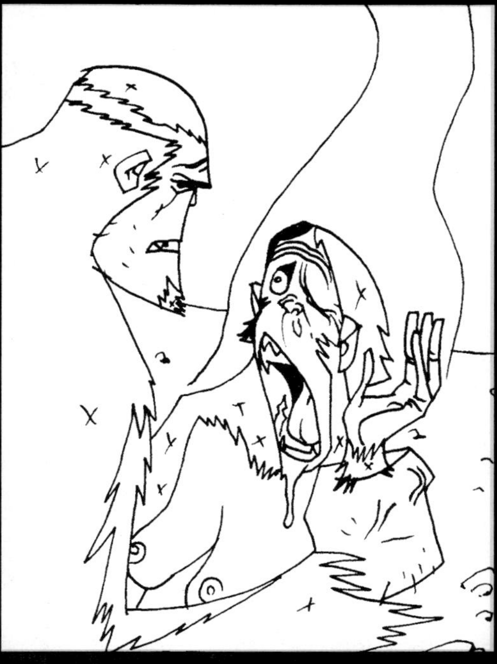

2- The smaller apes all calm down and stare.

3- Mid shot, the Red Stripe in confused that the woman in his arms has now totally turned to liquid and is pouring through his hairy fingers.

4- Wide. The smaller apes run away as fast as they can. Scared shitless. This tribe is officially broken u are running and not turning back.

The Red Stripe doesn't even notice them go.

APE
Aakk!!

APE
Eek!!

APE
Aaiiee!!

5- 3/4's view of the Red Stripe looking at his har the black puddle at his feet, he is confuse surprisingly calm. Melancholy.

6- Same, the camera turning slightly as he ho one of his hands and sniffs it.

7- Same, the camera keeps turning, the Red Stri faces us straight, but we reveal that standing behind him is a pissed off and very determined Stripe.

They will fight.

8- Tight on the White Stripe, he is stunned. Co his woman is gone.

9- The White Stripe's p.o.v. The Red Stripe's ba is still hunched over the puddle of black goo, tr figure it out.

10- Same as 8, but the White Stripe shakes sadness and is ready to fight.

WHITE STRIPE
Hyuunnk!

**Page 24-**

1- The White Stripe rushes toward the Red Strip intense passion to kill.

WHITE STRIPE
Hyyaarrgghh!!

2- The Red Stripe turns to face his attacker.

3- The White Stripe punches at him, more like his entire arm, not a very practiced move. None moves here will be graceful.

WHITE STRIPE
Hyyaagghh!!

Spx: whuuummm

4- The Red Stripe catches the punch clumsily. that surprises them both.

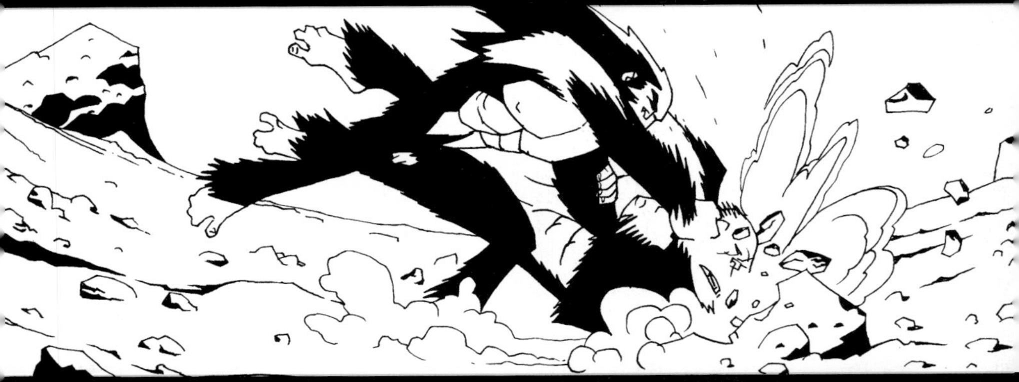

ɔx: smack

RED STRIPE
Hur!

The White Stripe whips around and hits him with s other arm. The Red Stripe really takes the hit.

ɔx: smunk

WHITE STRIPE
Aarrggh!!

**age 25-**

From behind The White Stripe, the Red Stripe is ınched over from the hit but he raises his head a bit. ıe Red Stripe took the punch. It didn't hurt.

The Red Stripe swings up and punches the White tripe in the jaw.

ɔx: smack

From behind The Red Stripe, The White Stripe umbles back a step but is surprised to see he could ıke the punch as well.

The White Stripe regains his wits and hits the Red tripe hard.

WHITE STRIPE
Hhaaggh!!

ɔx: crack

Unhurt, The Red Stripe punches the White Stripe in ıe neck.

RED STRIPE
Guh!

ɔx: whump

The Red Stripe growls at him as his eyes turns black ıd red again. He is using his powers to destroy his attacker.

RED STRIPE
Hhyyaagghhh!!

7- The White Stripe's surprised eyes burn yellow anc a bubble or two pops out. The White Stripe is instinctively fighting back with his own powers. This is officially the first superhero fight scene eve

WHITE STRIPE
Hugh hugh huguh!

8- Small panel. The Red Stripe is surprised. His eyes pool back towards normal.

RED STRIPE
Gy?

9- Small panel. The White Stripe is confused by all o this. His eyes also pool back to normal.

WHITE STRIPE
Fftt.

**Page 26-27**

Double page spread

This is the first super powered battle.

This is a double page montage of a fight that will neve end.

They are evenly matched. And evenly determined t win. Its a cave man boxing match that will never finish

Each panel is the Same angle. Two shot, mid shot. O the cave man hitting each other, each taking a turn each trying to choke the other, one flipping the other One dodging the other.

The figures are silhouette mostly. Two black figures in a violent dance. In my head they take on almost a Harvey Kurtzman fluidity. Very dramatic, expressive figure work.

To accentuate the never ending aspect each row has more and more panels. The panels getting smaller and smaller.

The first row has five widescreen panels.

The second row has seven. The third row has 9, the forth row has 11, the fifth has 11, the sixth has 13, by the time we are towards the bottom rows of the spread the panels and figures are so small that it is just stick figures hitting each other.

The background color over the piece graduates from top row to bottom row- red to orange. One gradation across the entire spread.

**Page 28-**

1- From behind The White Stripe, The Red Stripe with an almost sleepy exhaustion in his eyes, holds up his arm to punch down, but doesn't have the energy to keep it up.

The fight is ending.

> RED STRIPE
> Hugh...
>
> Hugh...
>
> Hugh...

2- From behind The Red Stripe, The White Stripe is equally tired but will not back down.

He sees that The Red Stripe is wavering and is curious to see what will happen next.

> WHITE STRIPE
> Hugh...
>
> Hugh...
>
> Hugh...

3- Similar to 1, The Red Stripe has no more steam, the arm is coming down.

> RED STRIPE
> Hugh...
>
> Hugh...

4- Wide of the pond area, the two of them stand feet apart, both totally exhausted.

5- Tight on the White Stripe. He is exhausted, sad and exhausted. His fur matted down by sweat. No fight left.

6- The Red Stripe looks disgusted with the whole thing, the significance lost on him.
His eyes droopy. Tired.

**Page 29-**

Full page image

Identical to page one. But its getting dark, deep red sky.

Wide shot of a desolate, almost desert plane, a couple of badly formed hills and mountains. No greenery. No brush. Just the earth in its earliest days.

The two ape men walk away from each other in opposite directions. They are already yards away. Both hunched over and exhausted. The fight over... For now.

White Times Roman Type reads: To be continued.

# THE GALLERY

As fanciful an idea as a time spanning story like this is, it's a lot easier for me to type up than it is for Mike to draw. Mike literally had to design an entire new cast of characters, a new setting, new costumes. All new research. All new studies for every single issue.

Every issue is an entirely new illustration project.

(But I knew he could do it. )

The following are the works in progress. And every time he sent one I said, "Ooh! Save it for the trade!"

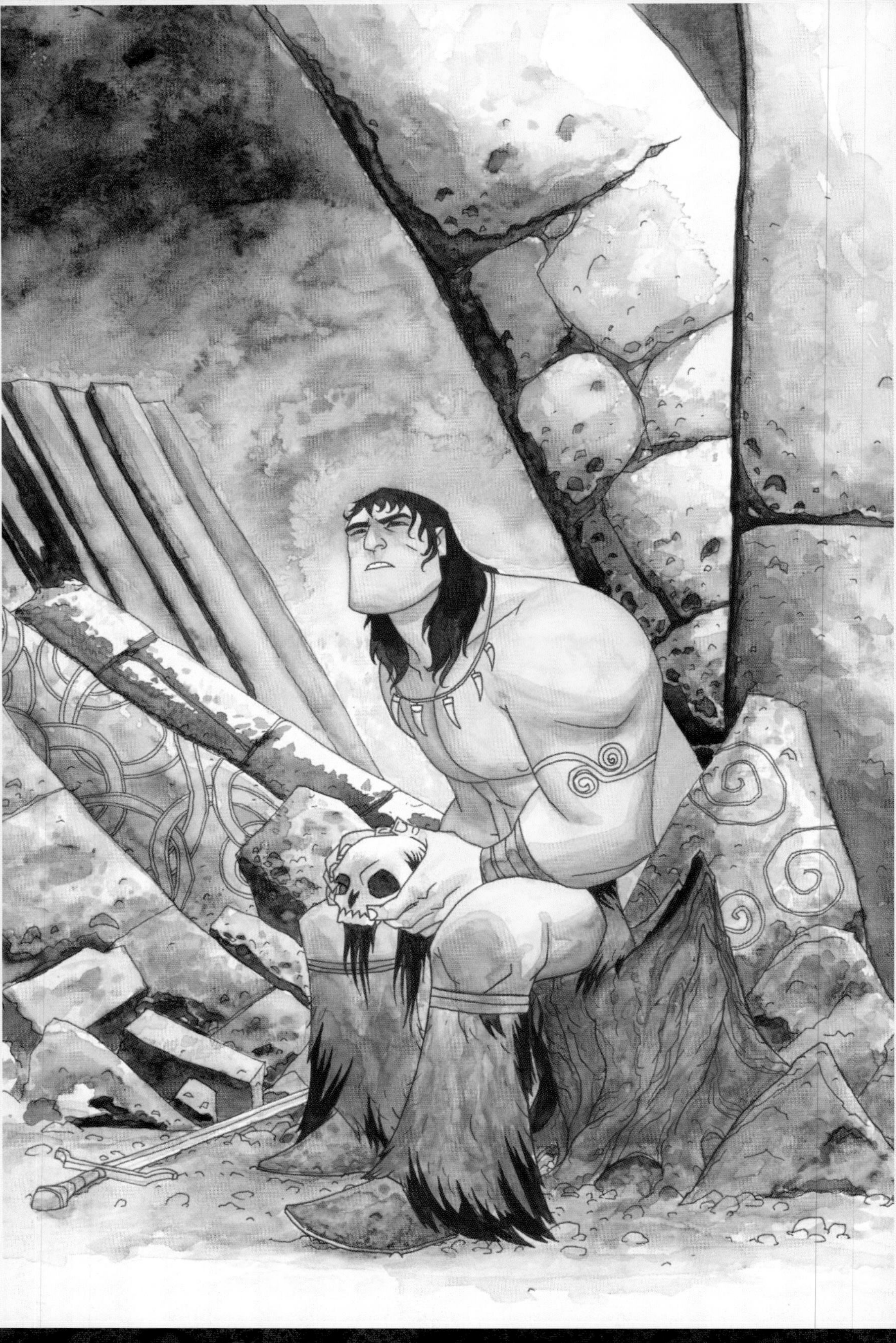

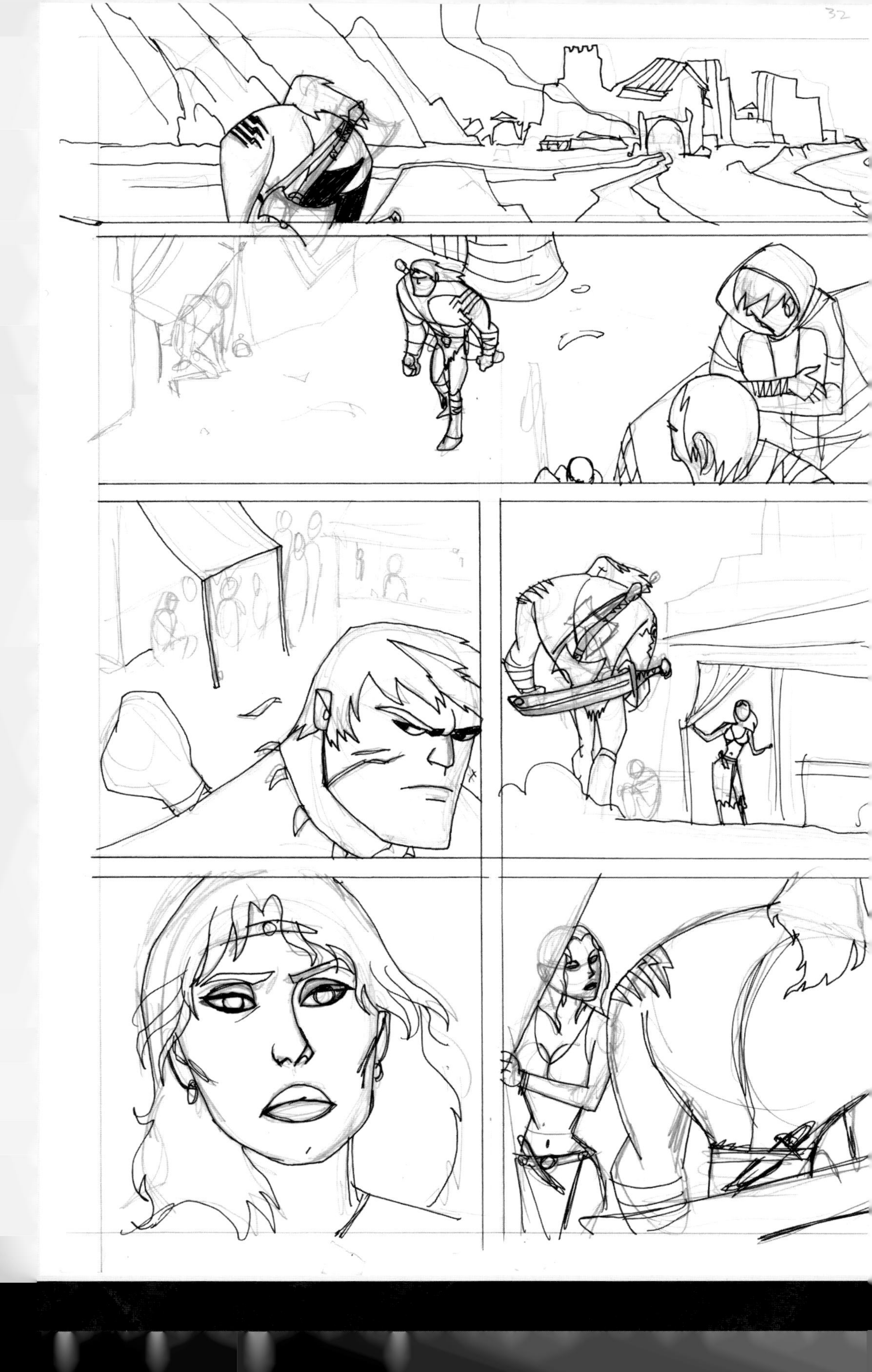

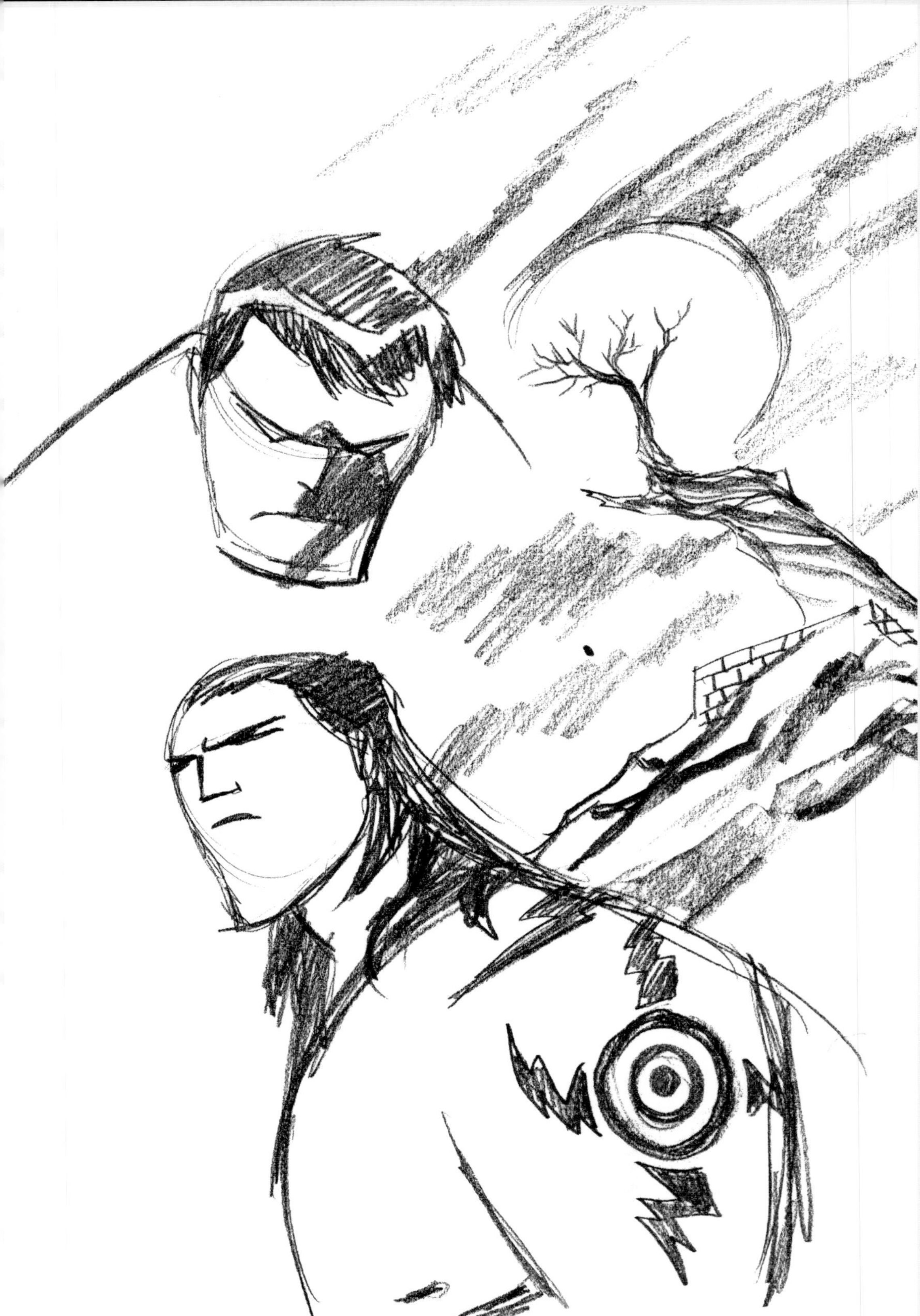

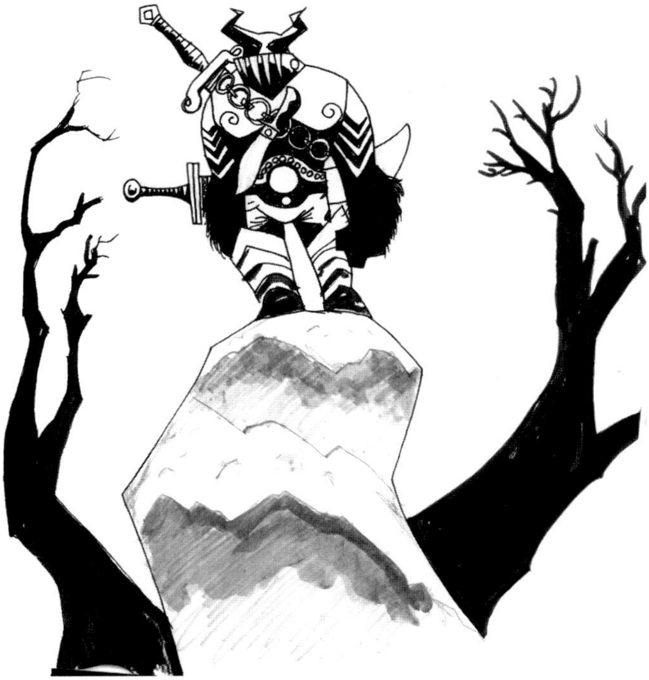

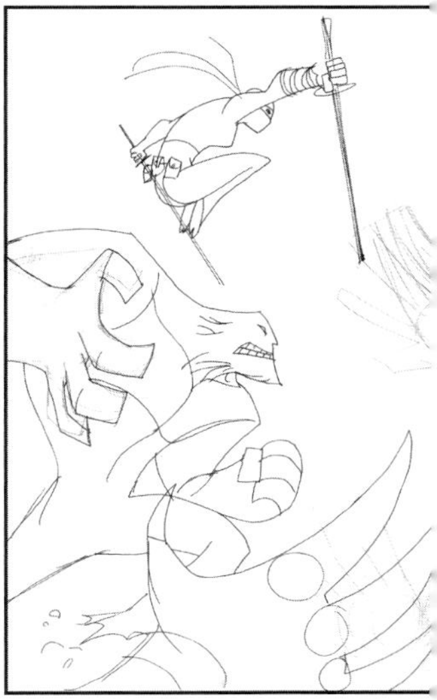

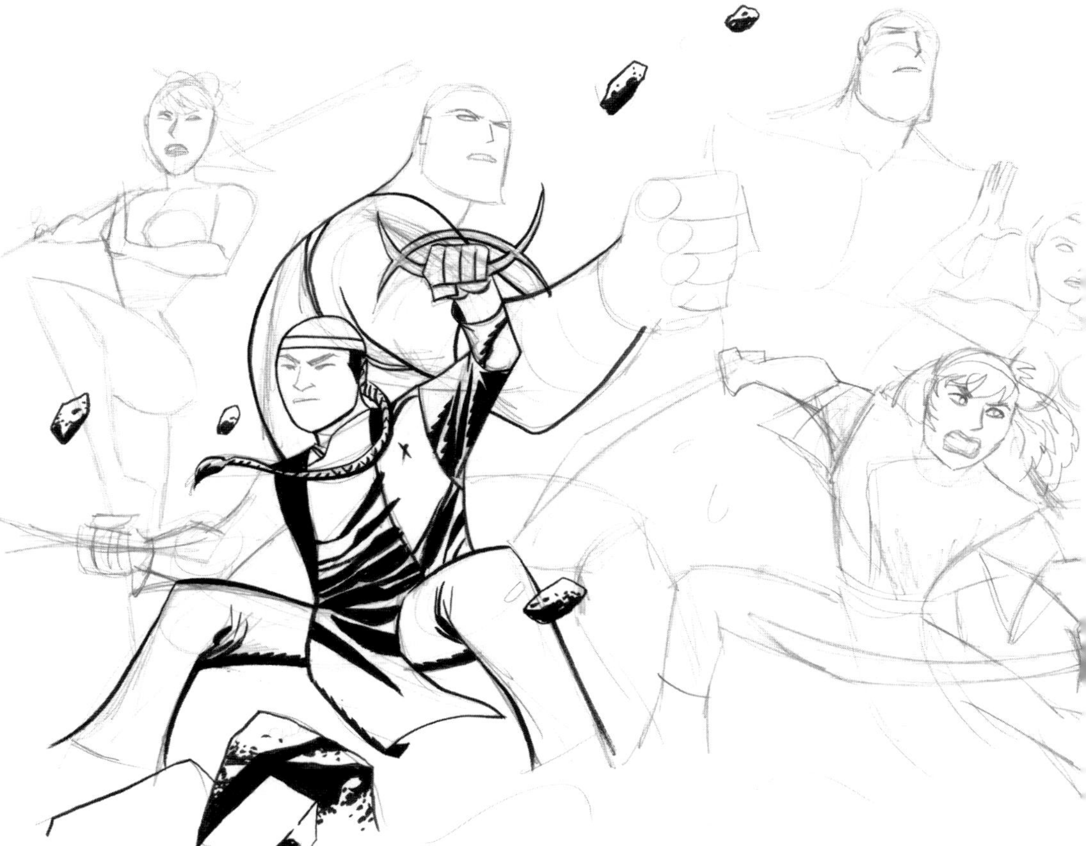

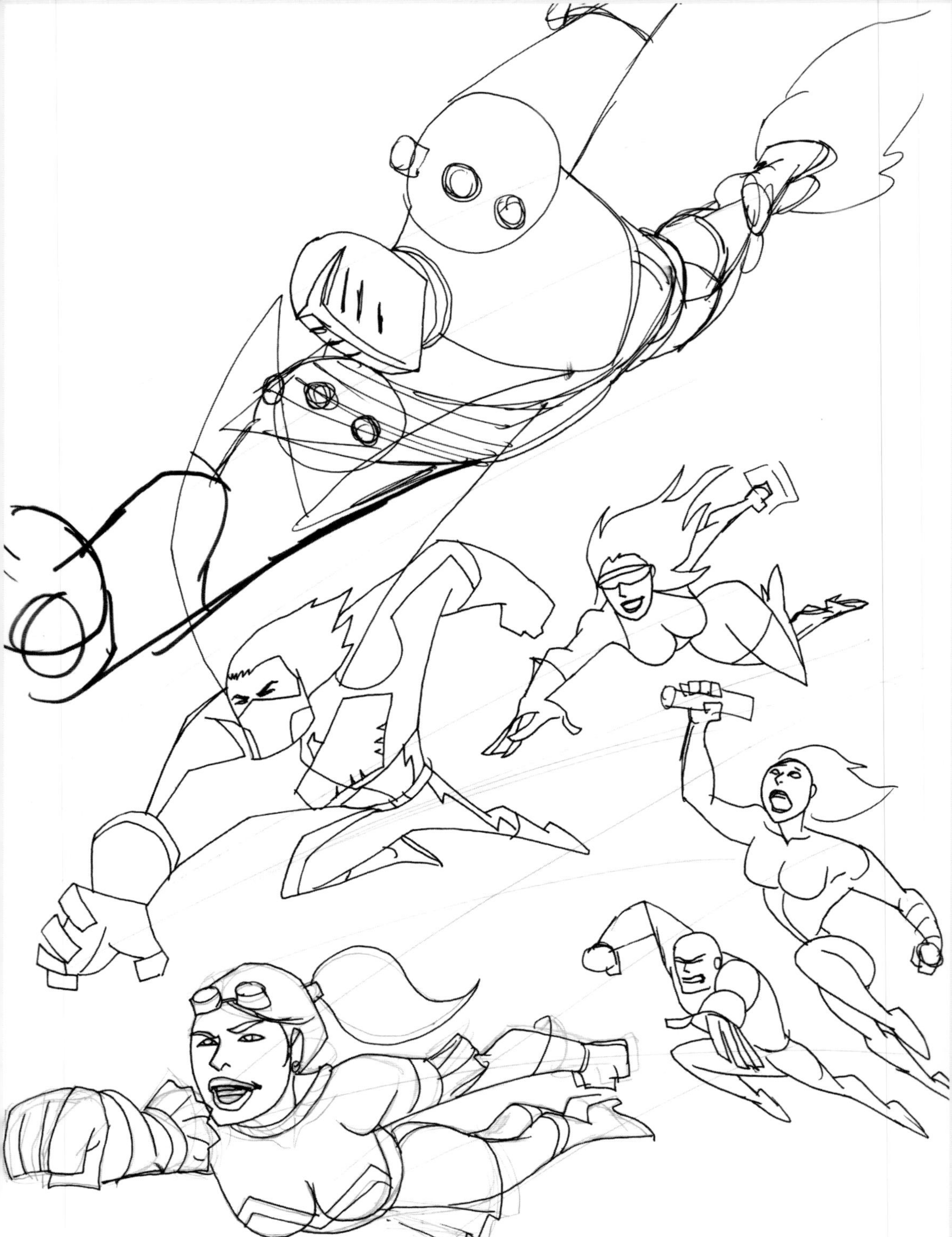

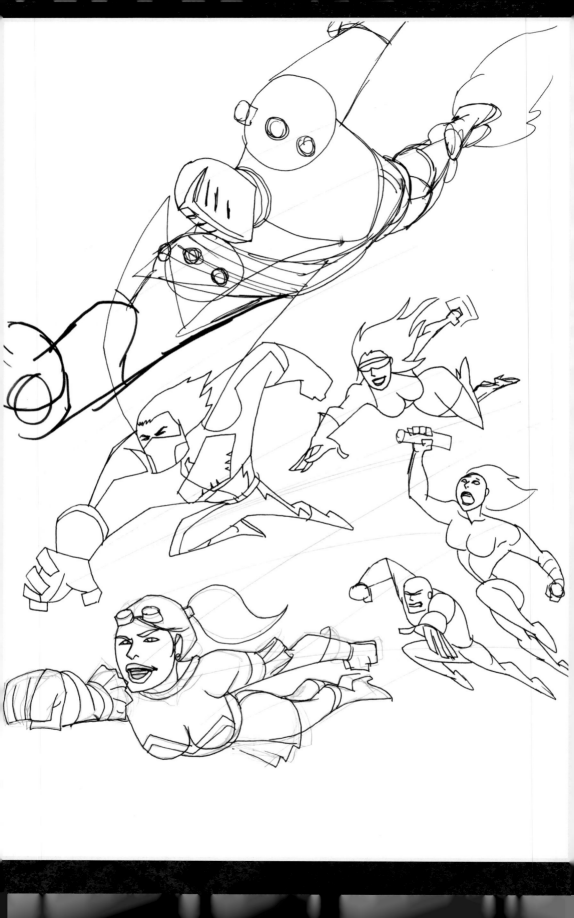

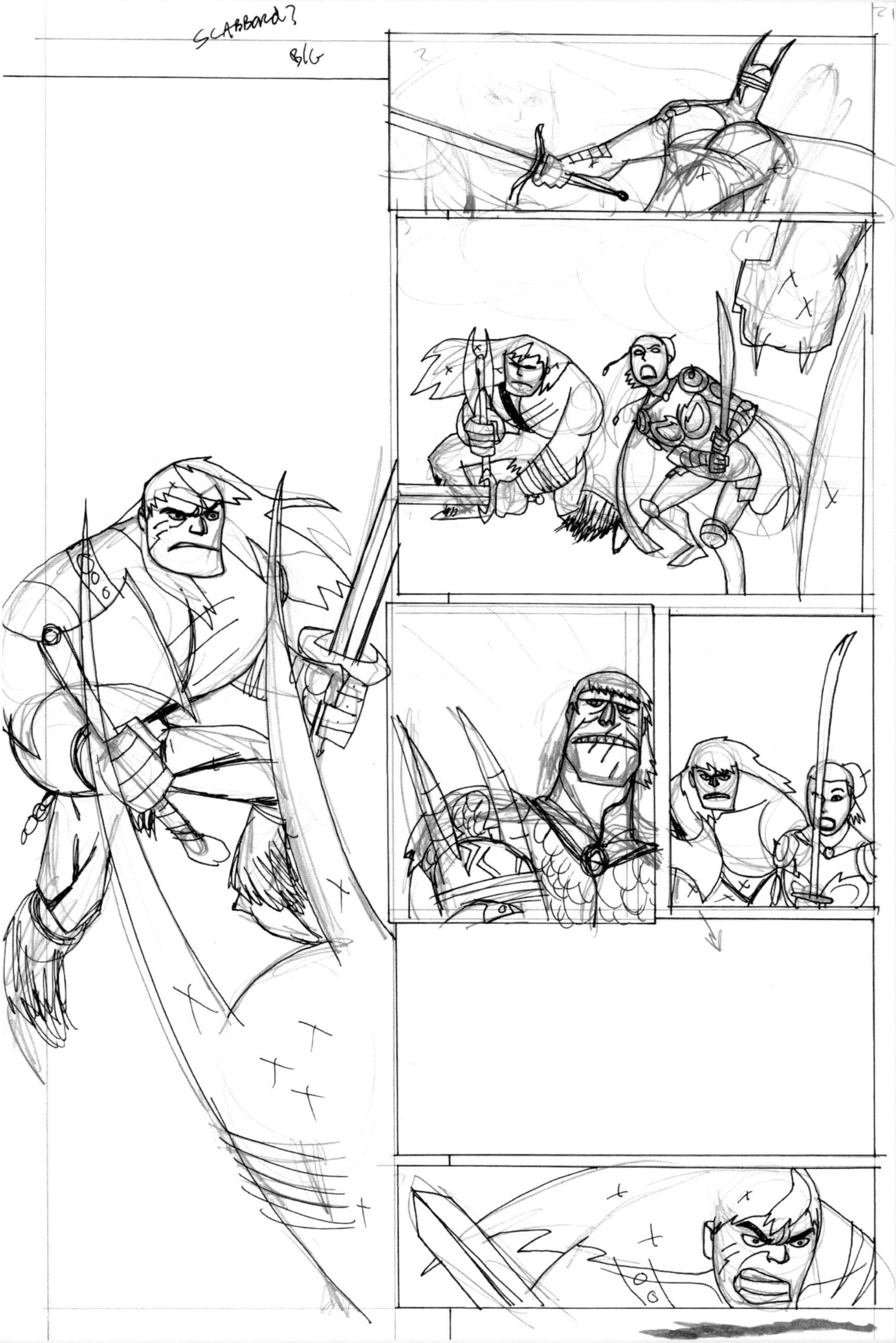
SCABBARD?
B/G
21

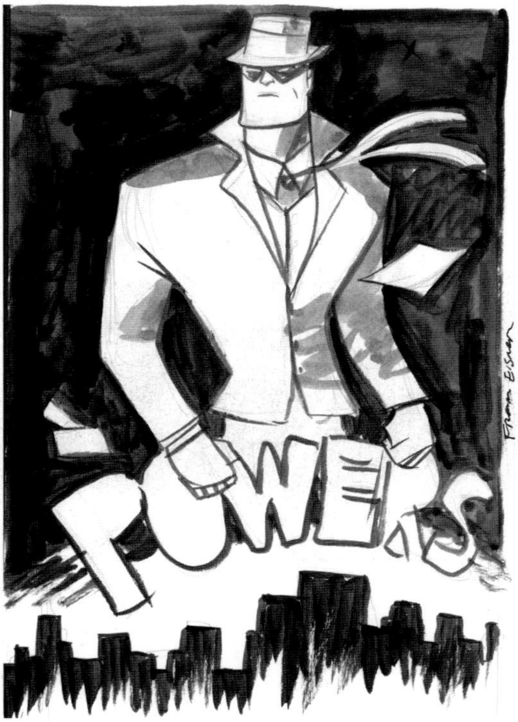
POWERS
From Eisner

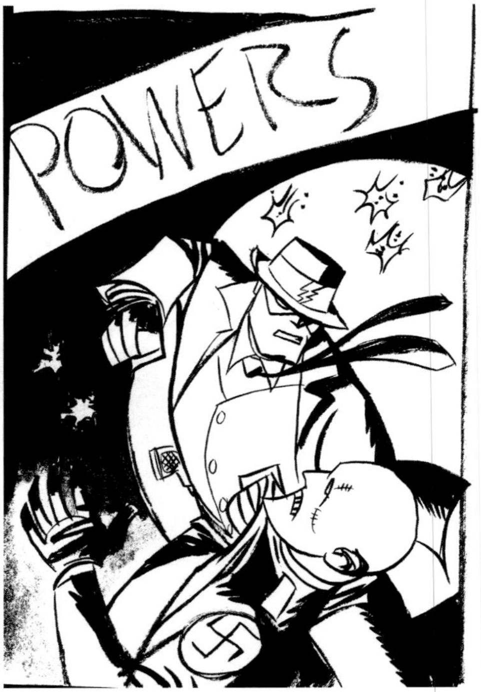
POWERS

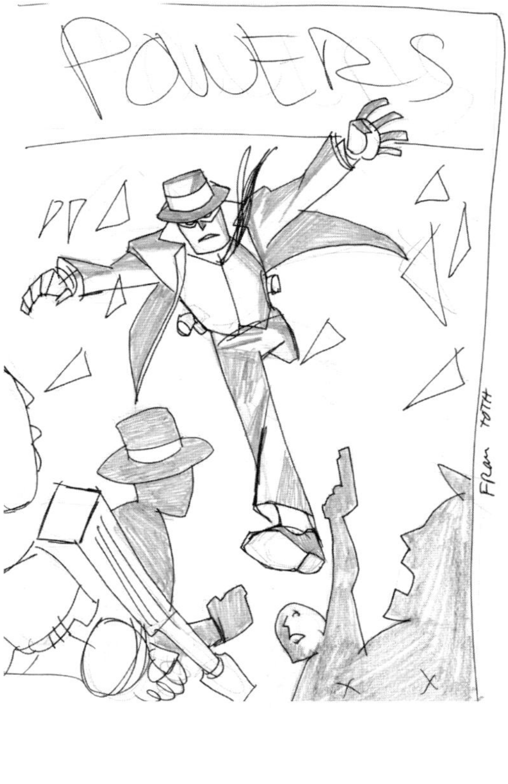
POWERS
Fran Toth

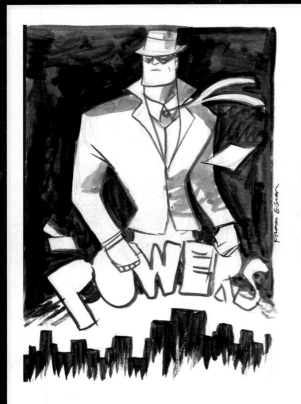

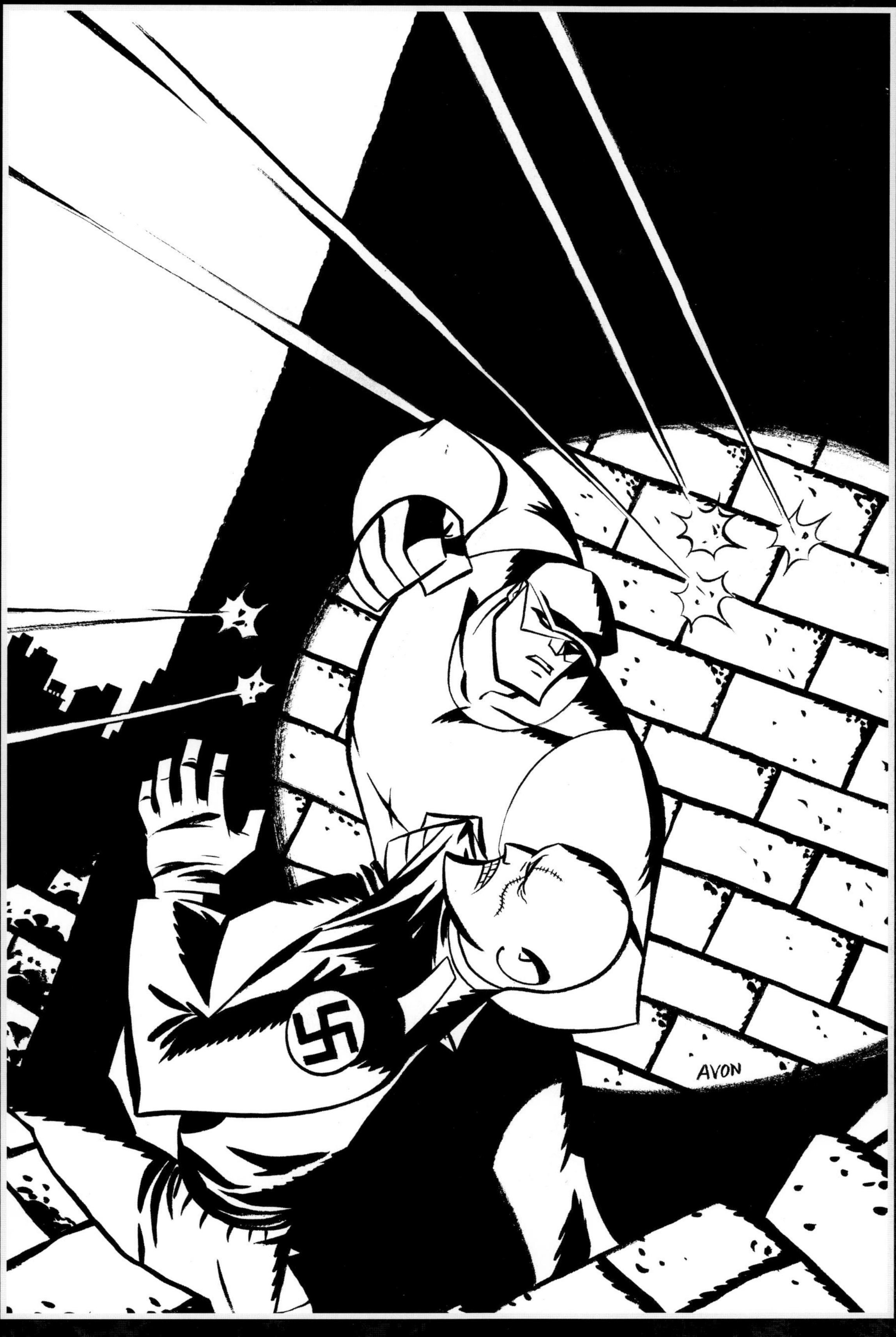
AVON

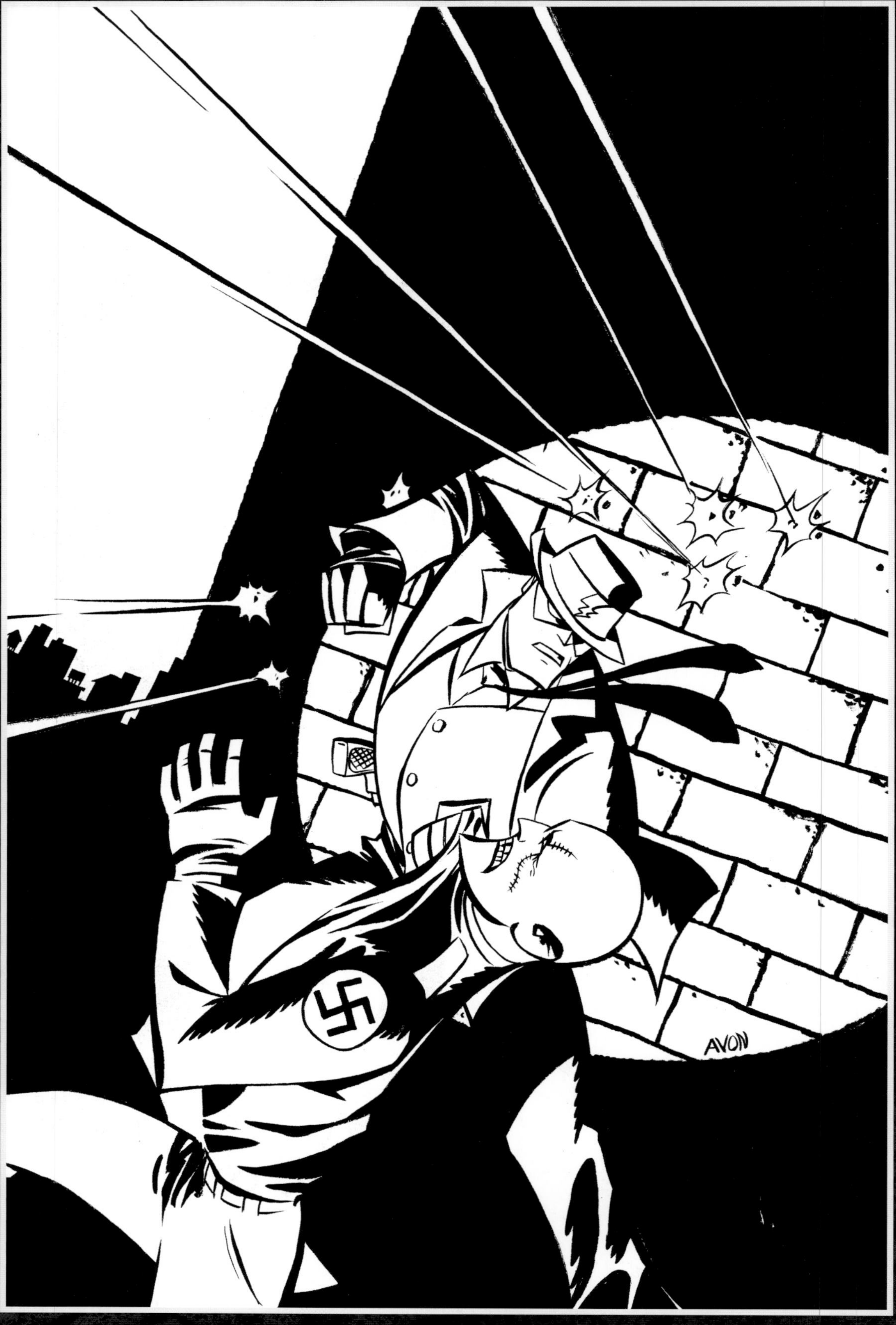
AVON

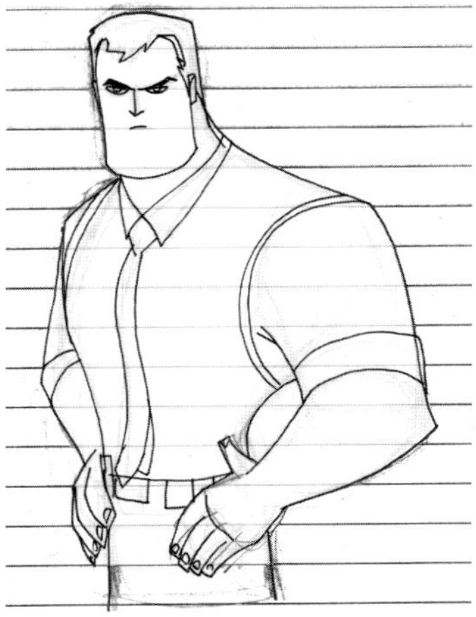

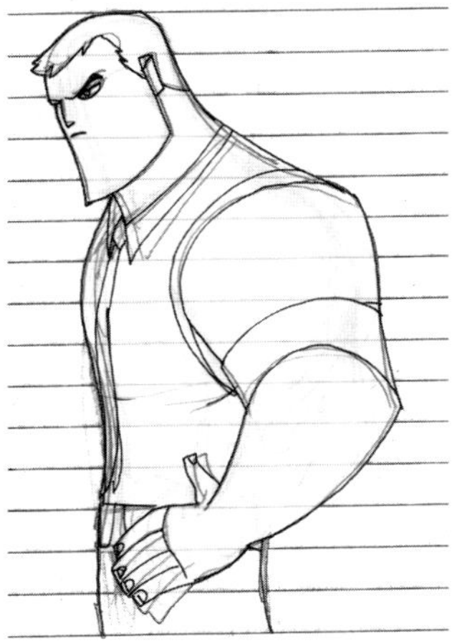

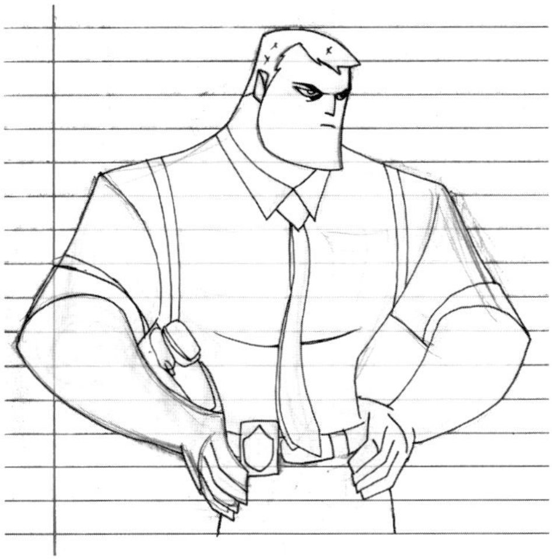

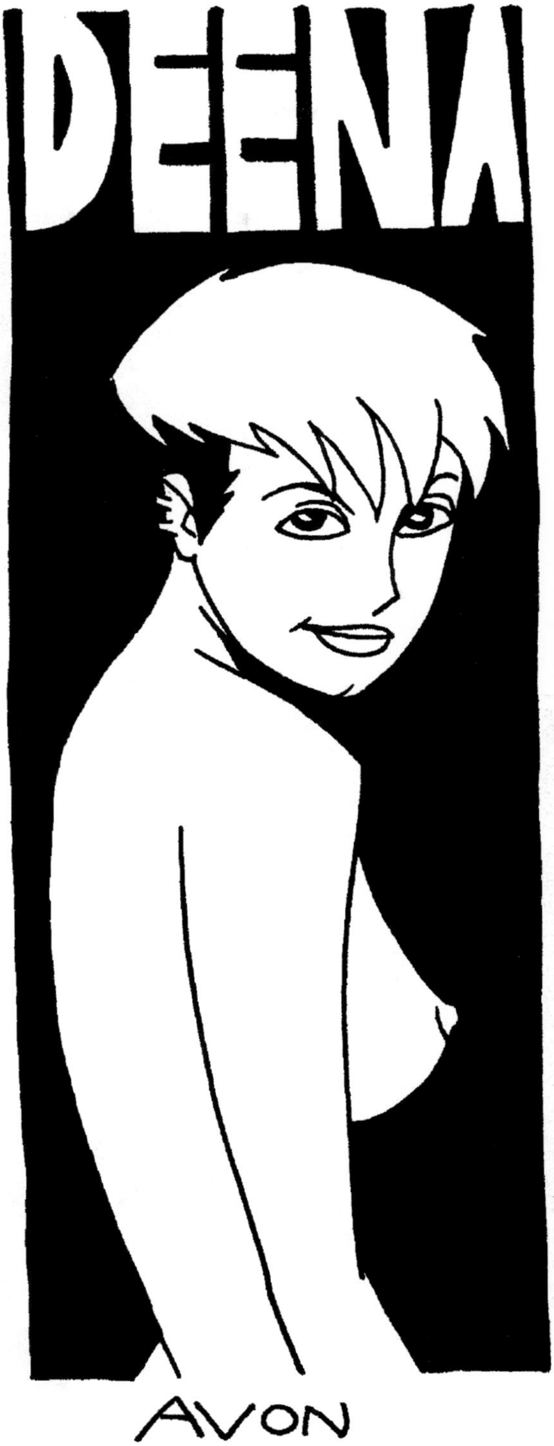
DEENA
AVON

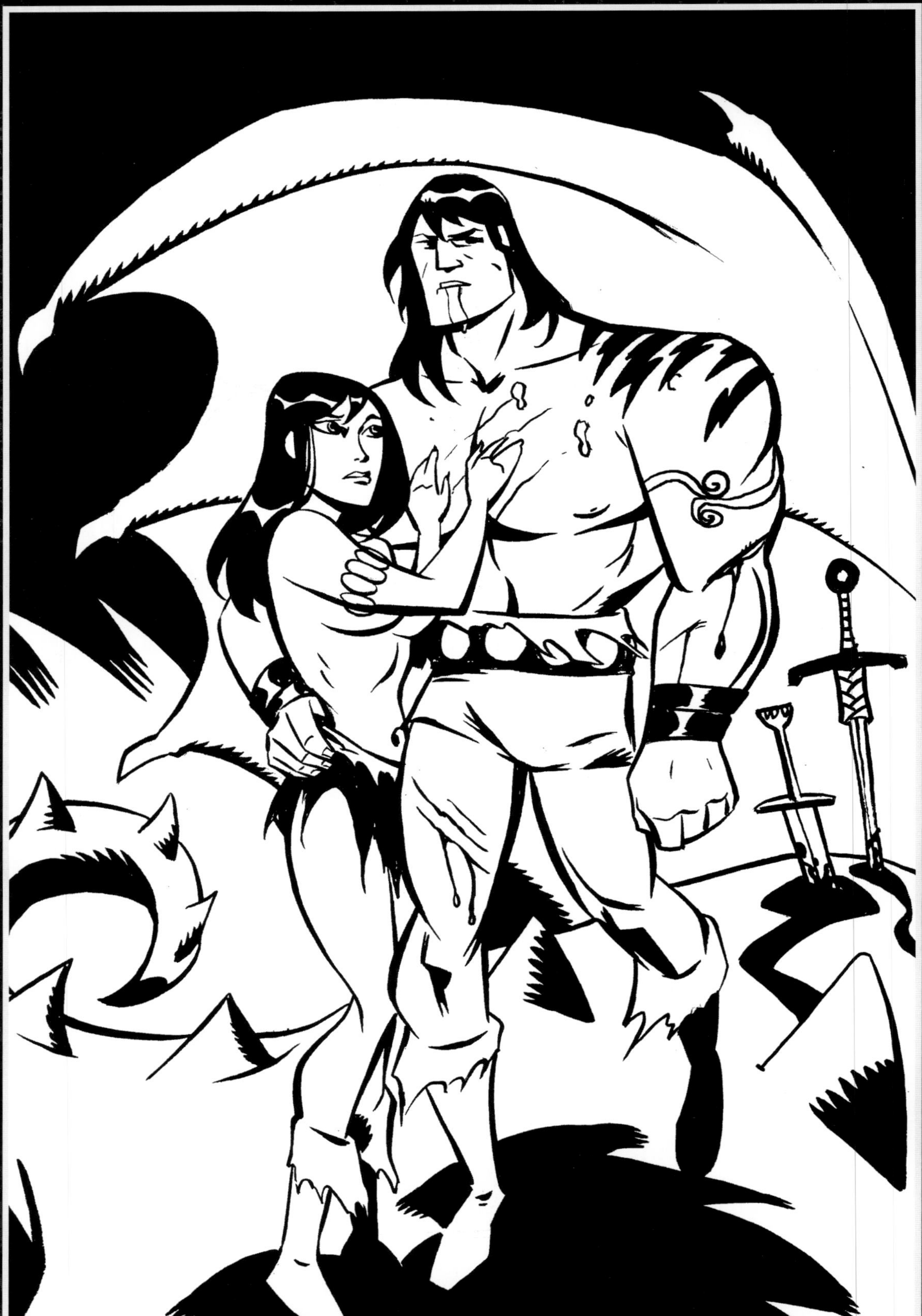

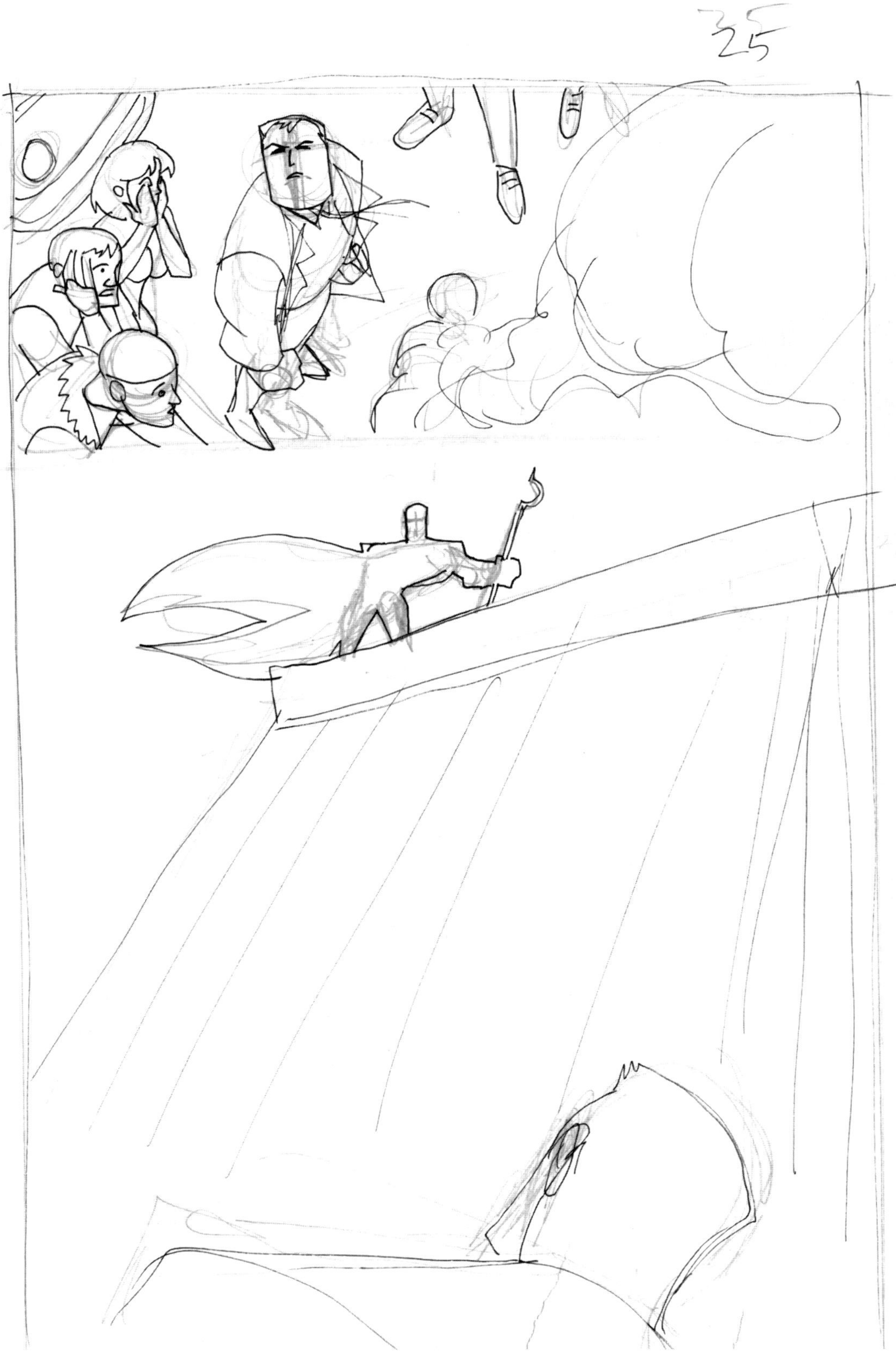
25

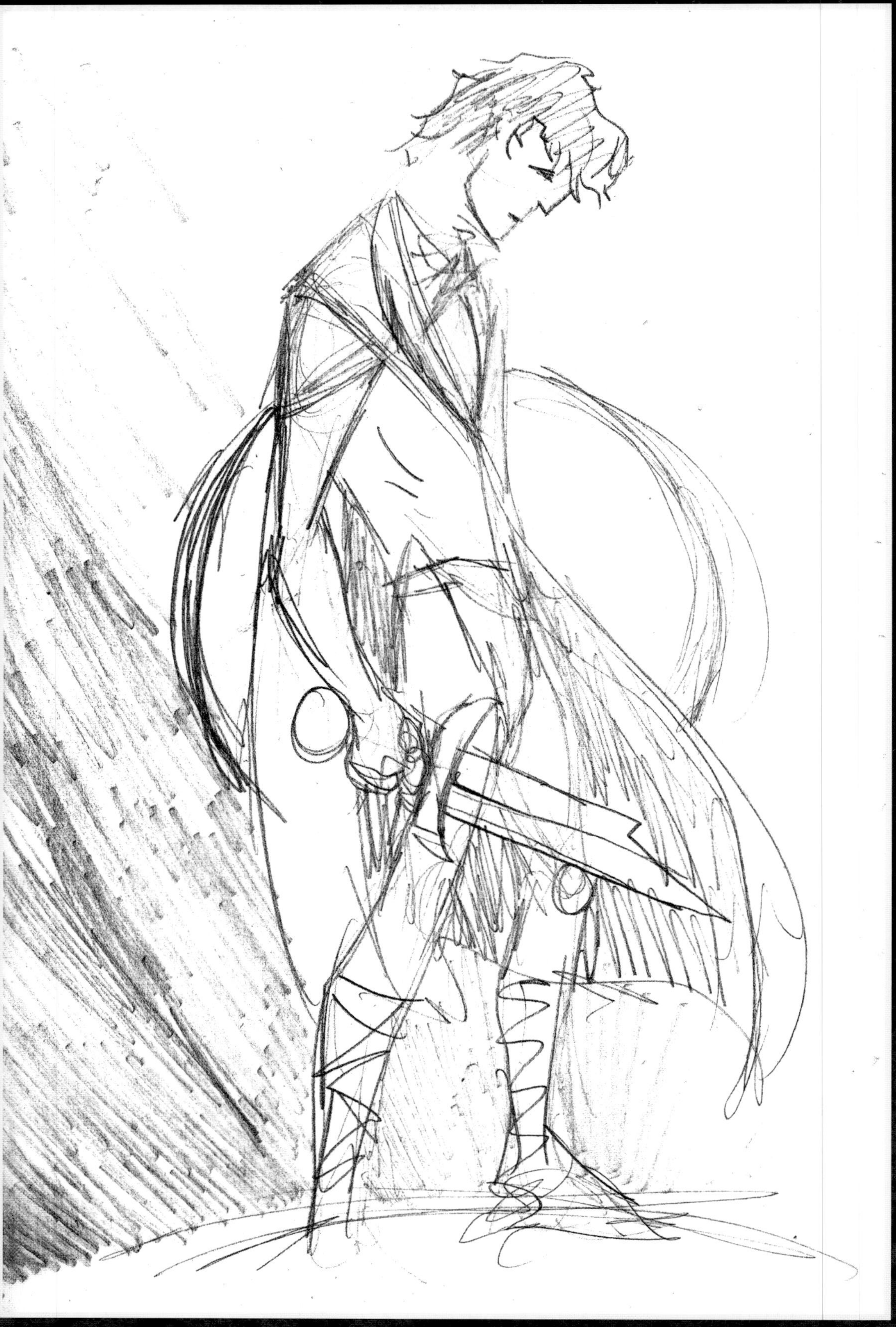

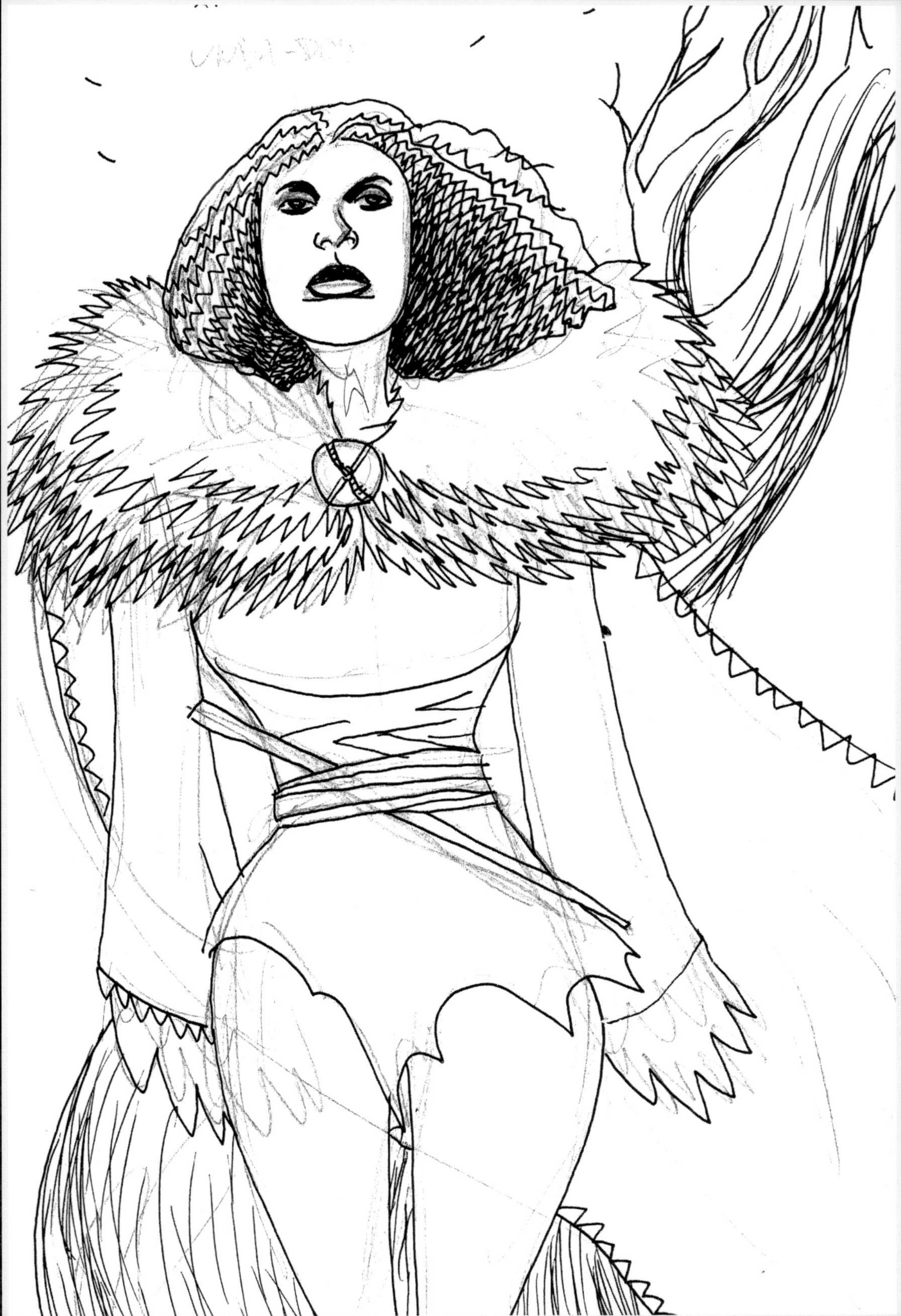

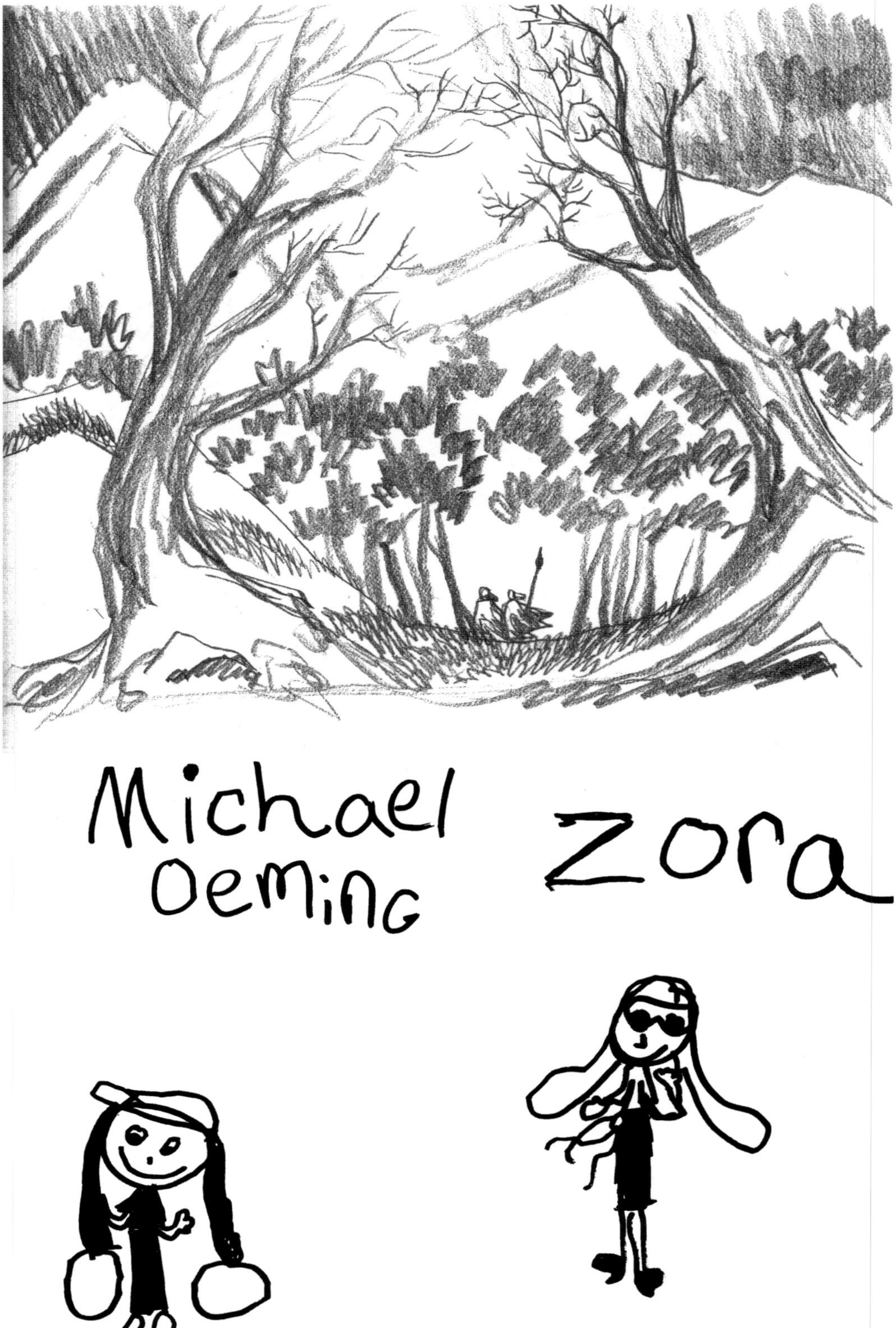
Michael Oeming
Zora

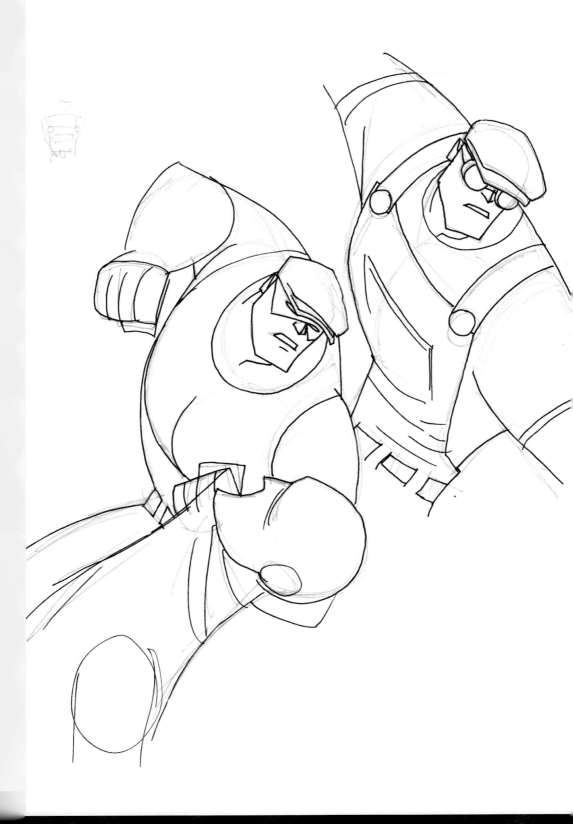

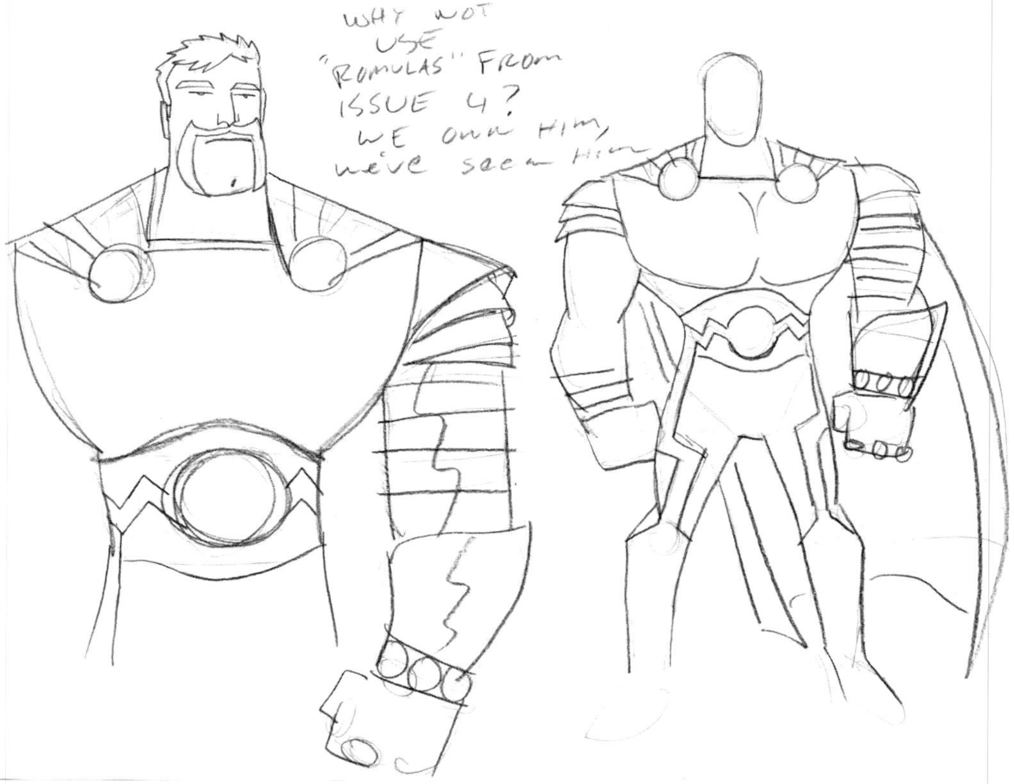
WHY NOT USE "ROMULAS" FROM ISSUE 4? WE OWN HIM, WE'VE SEEN HIM

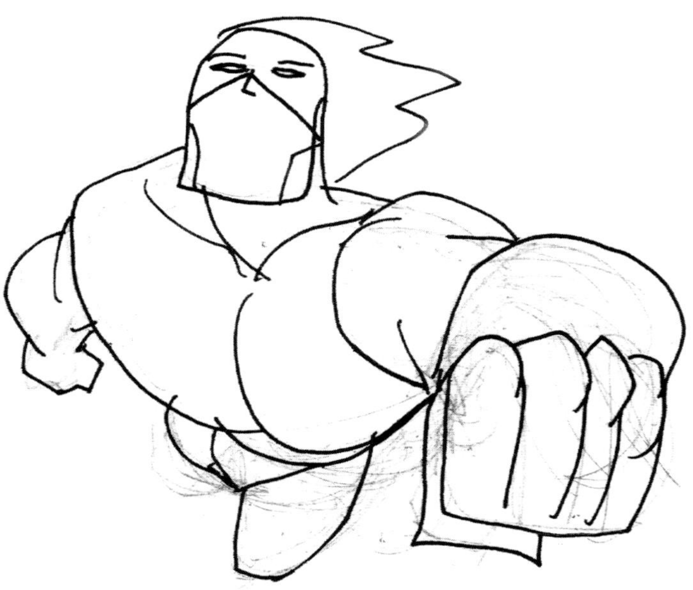

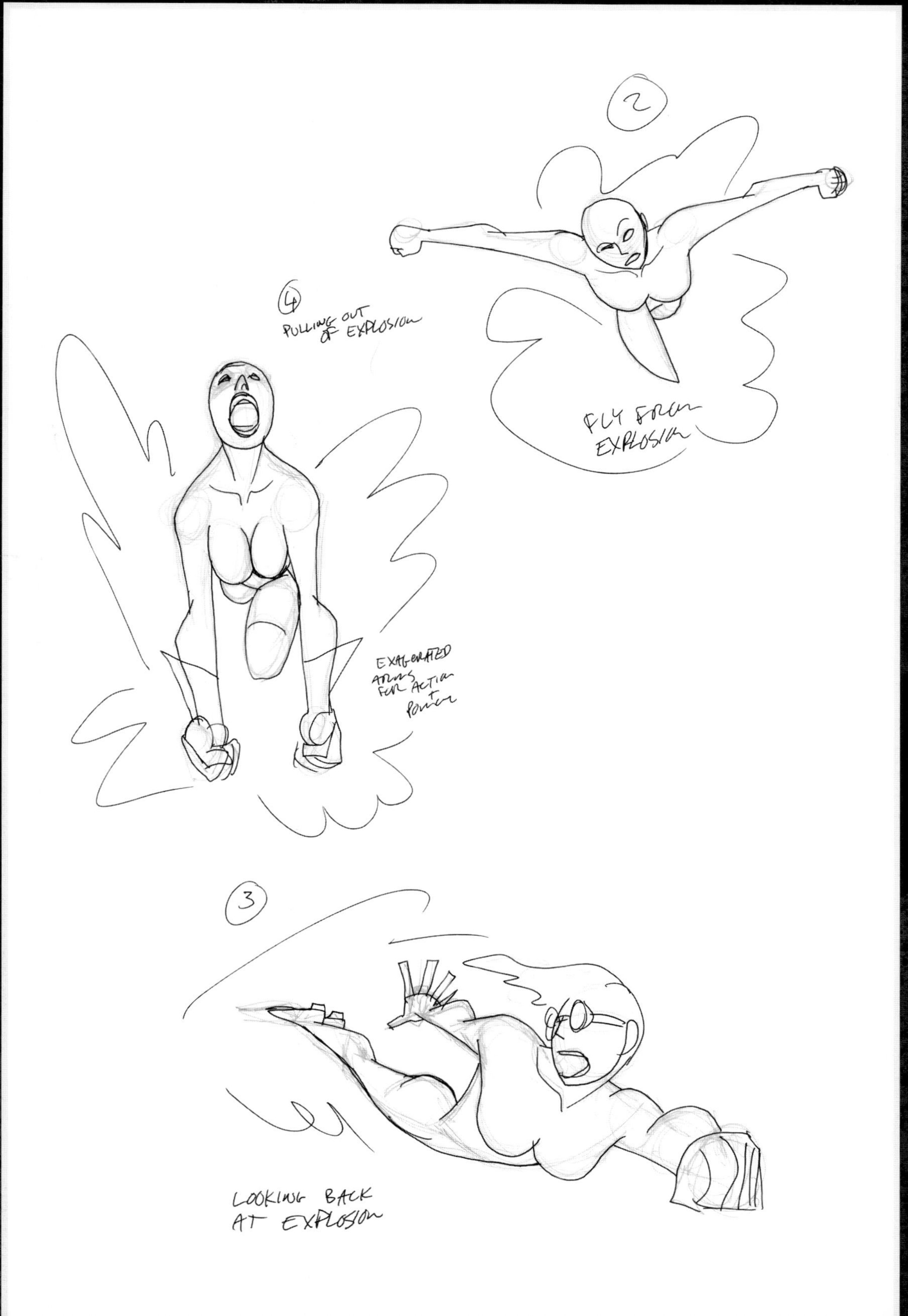

2
FLY FROM EXPLOSION
4
PULLING OUT OF EXPLOSION
EXAGERATED ARMS FOR ACTION + POWER
3
LOOKING BACK AT EXPLOSION

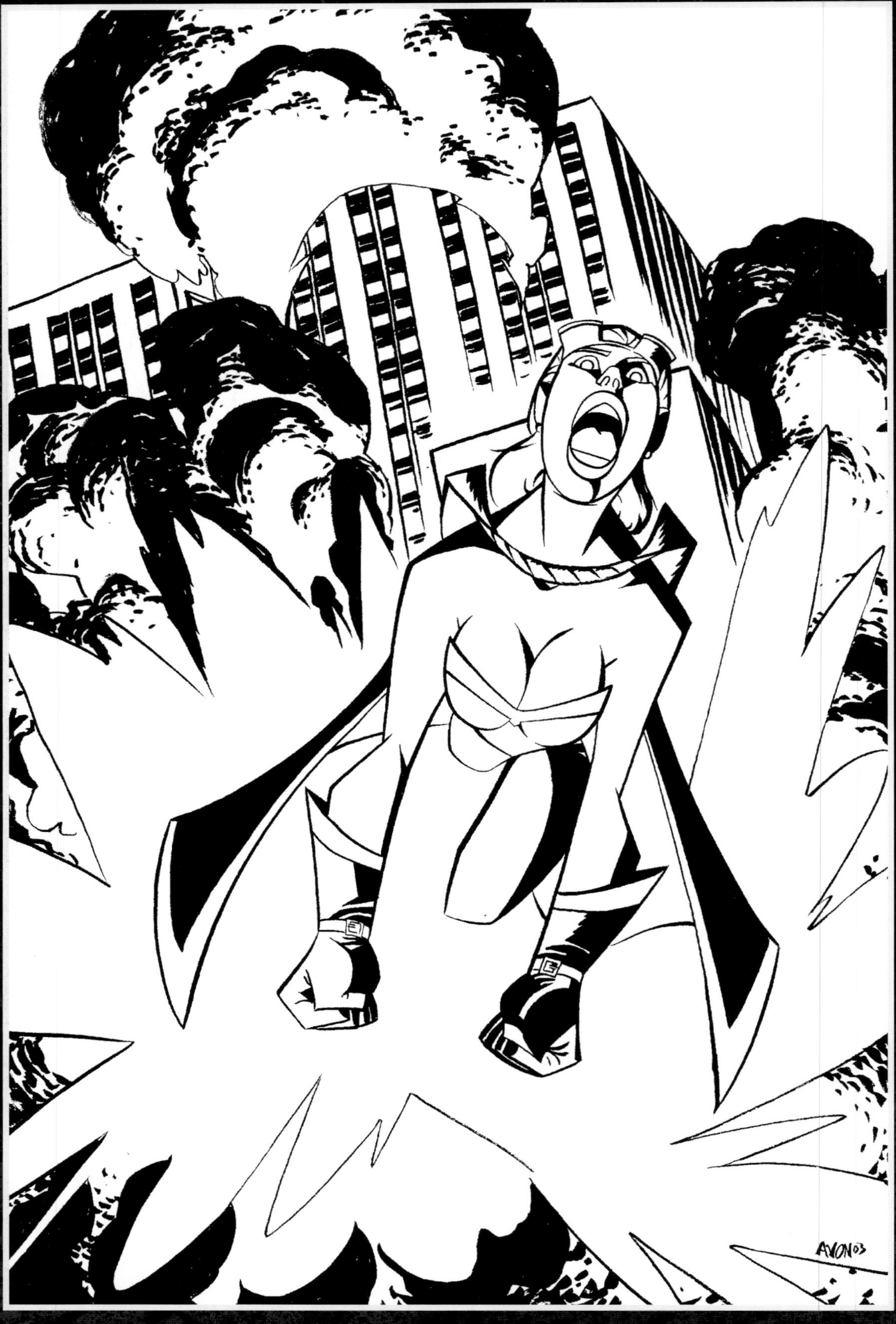
AVON03

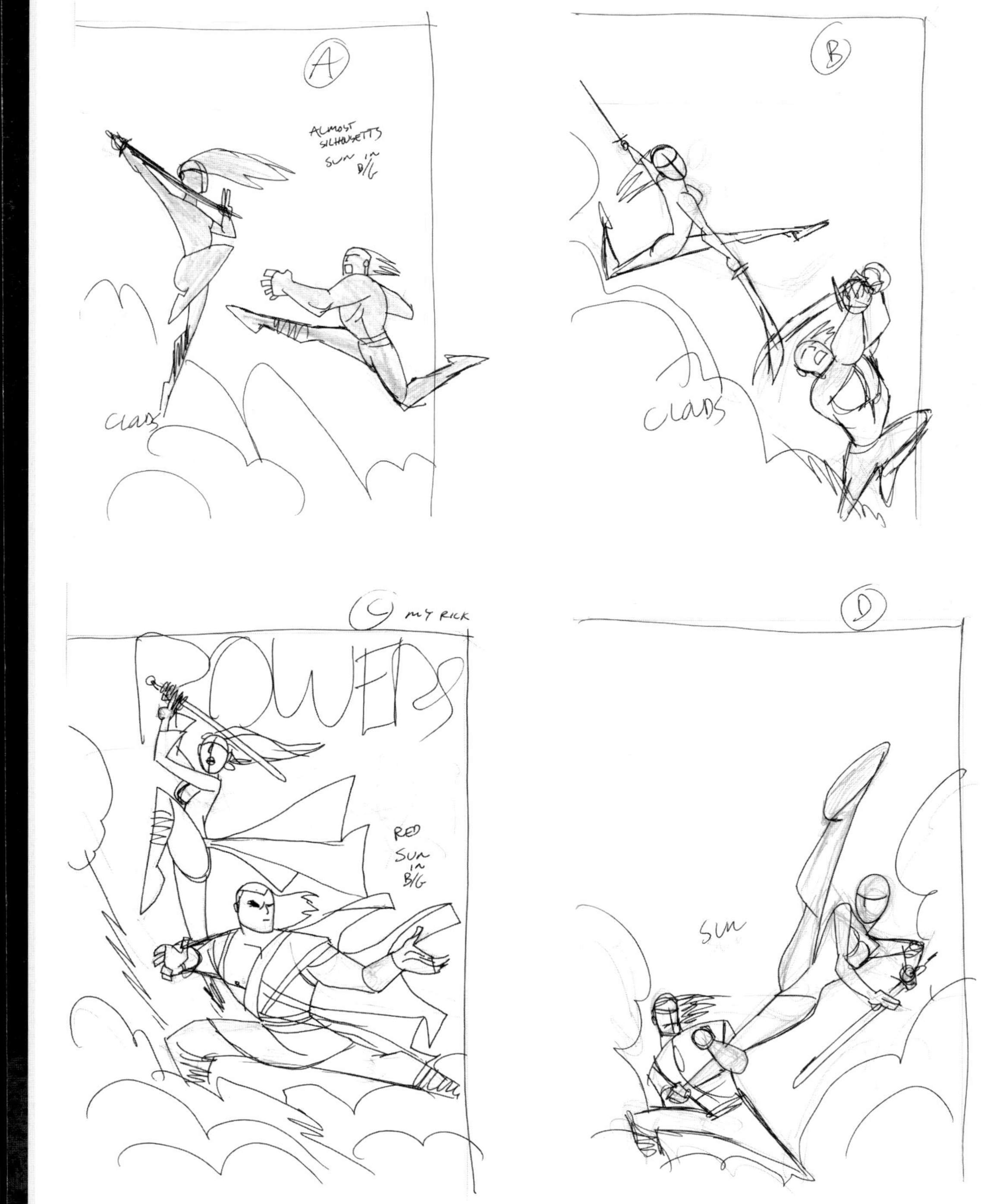
A
ALMOST SILHOUETTS
SUN IN B/G
CLADS
B
CLADS
C MY RICK
POWERS
RED SUN IN B/G
D
SUN

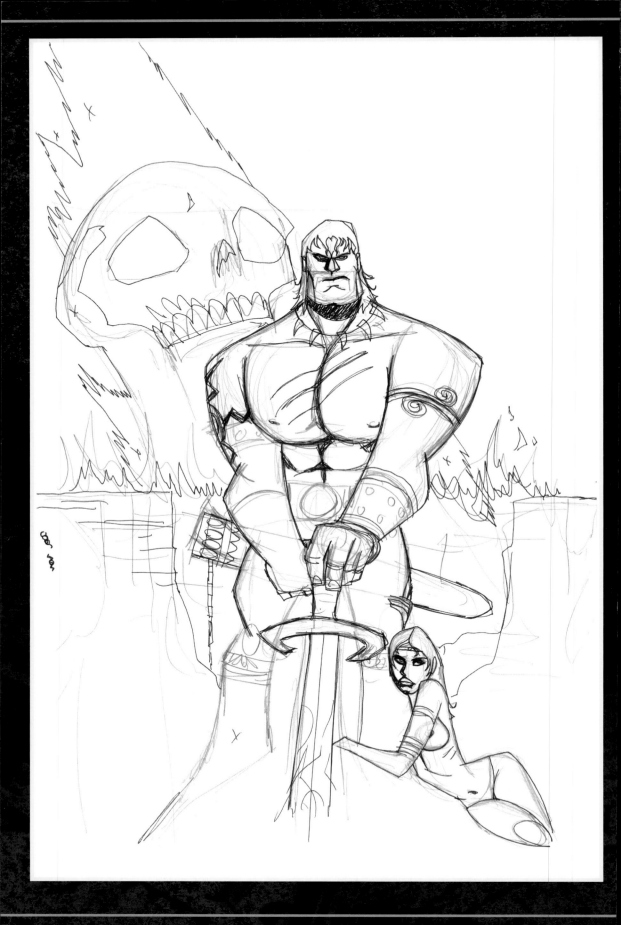

# POWERS
## COVER GALLERY

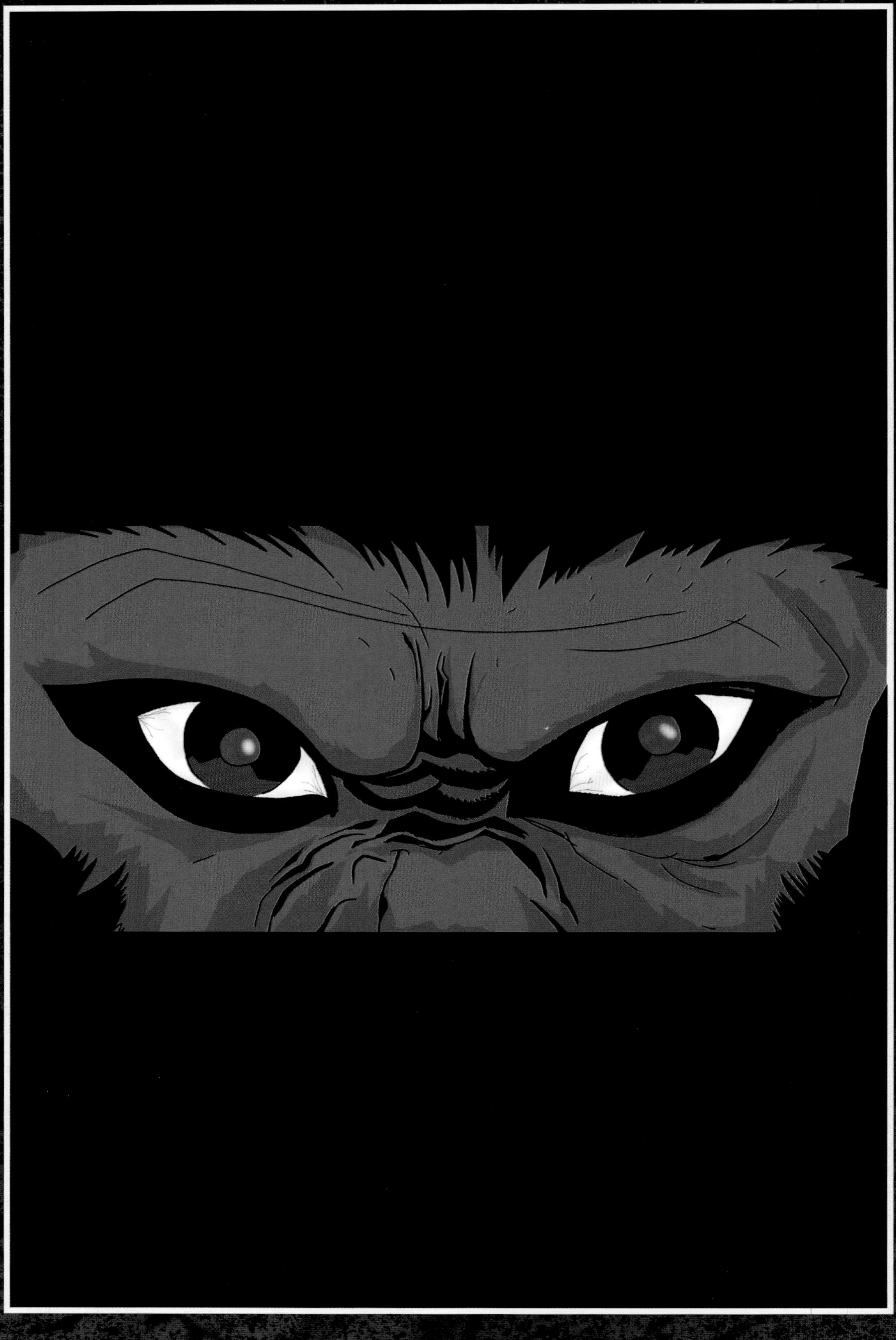

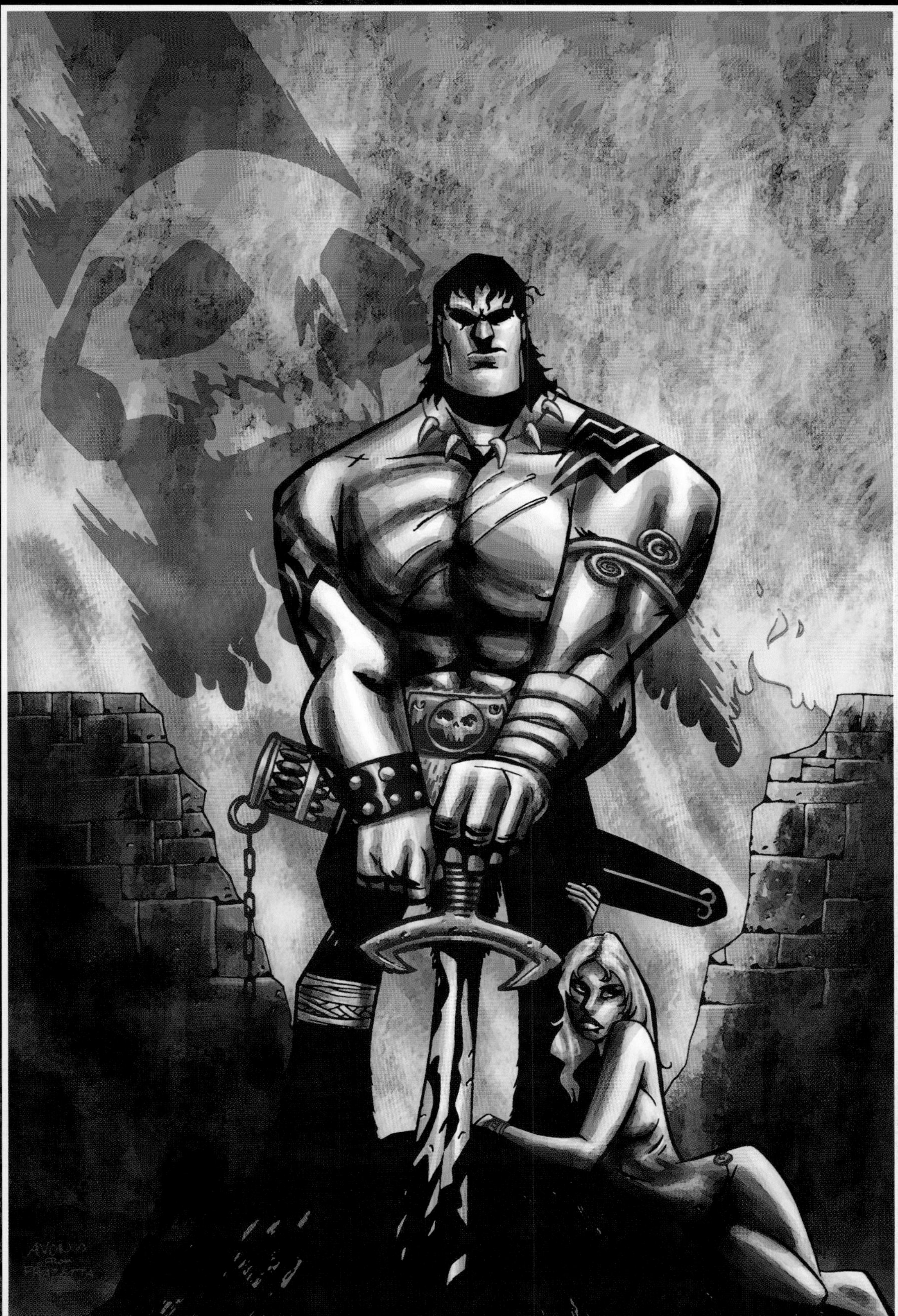

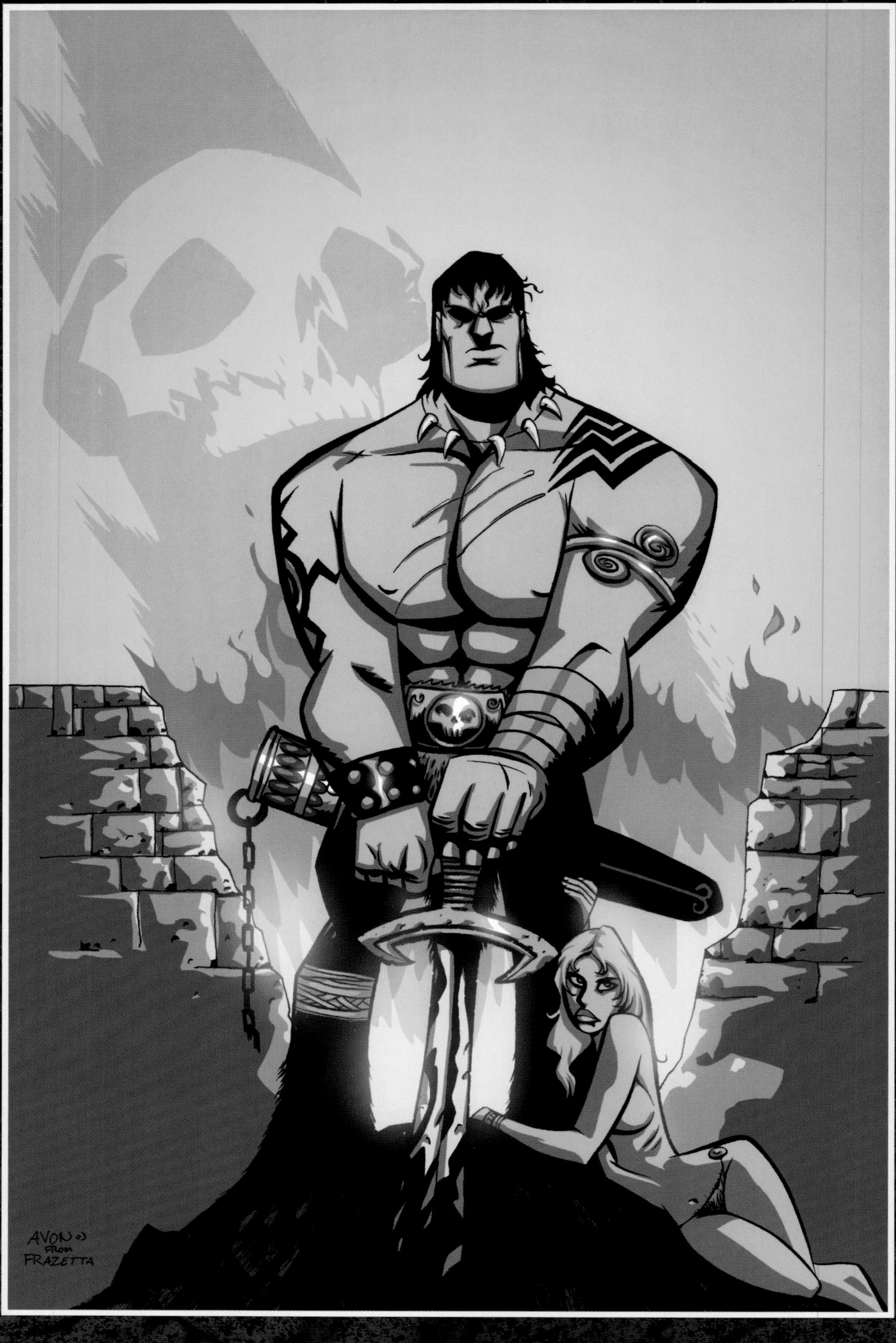
AVON 03 FROM FRAZETTA

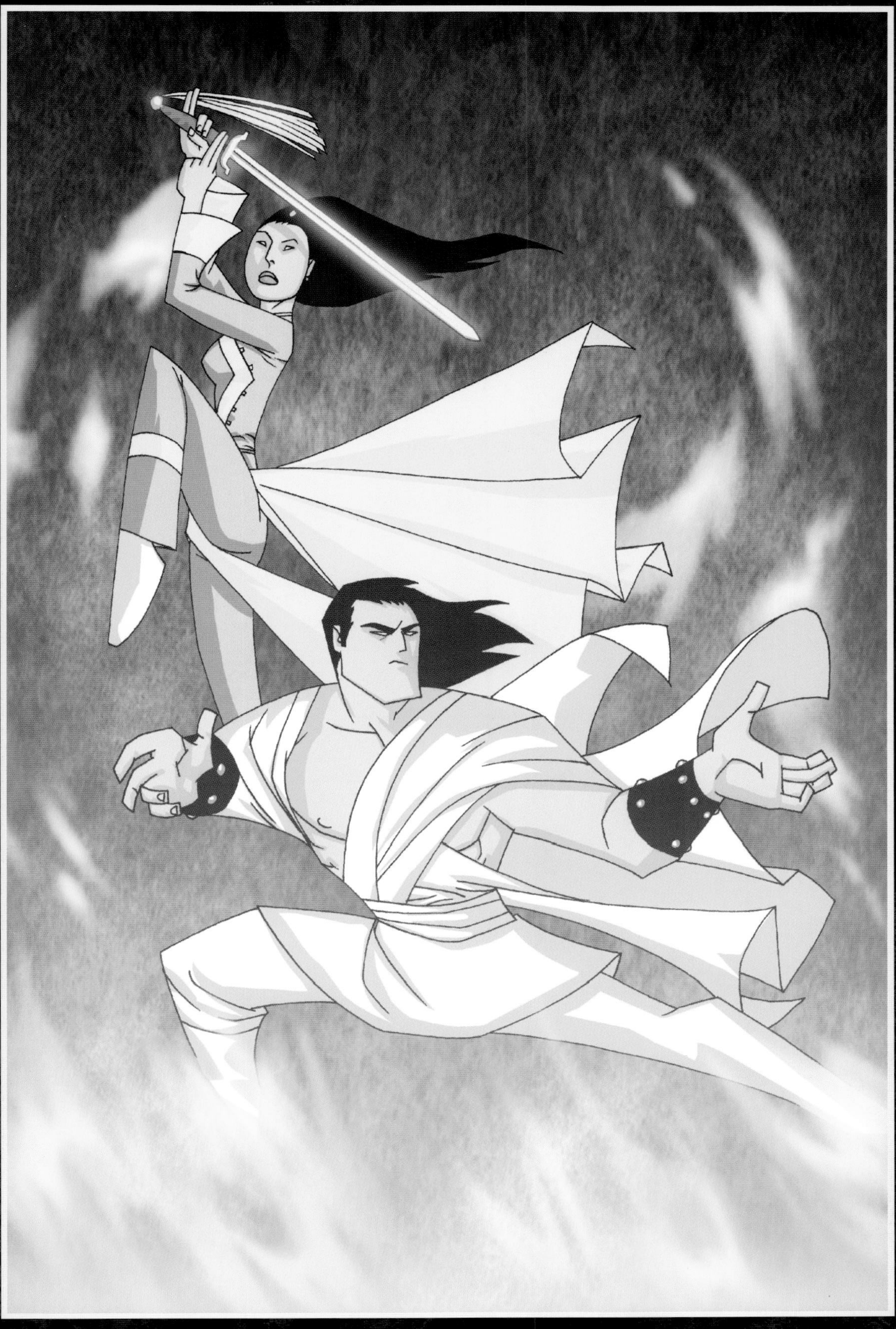

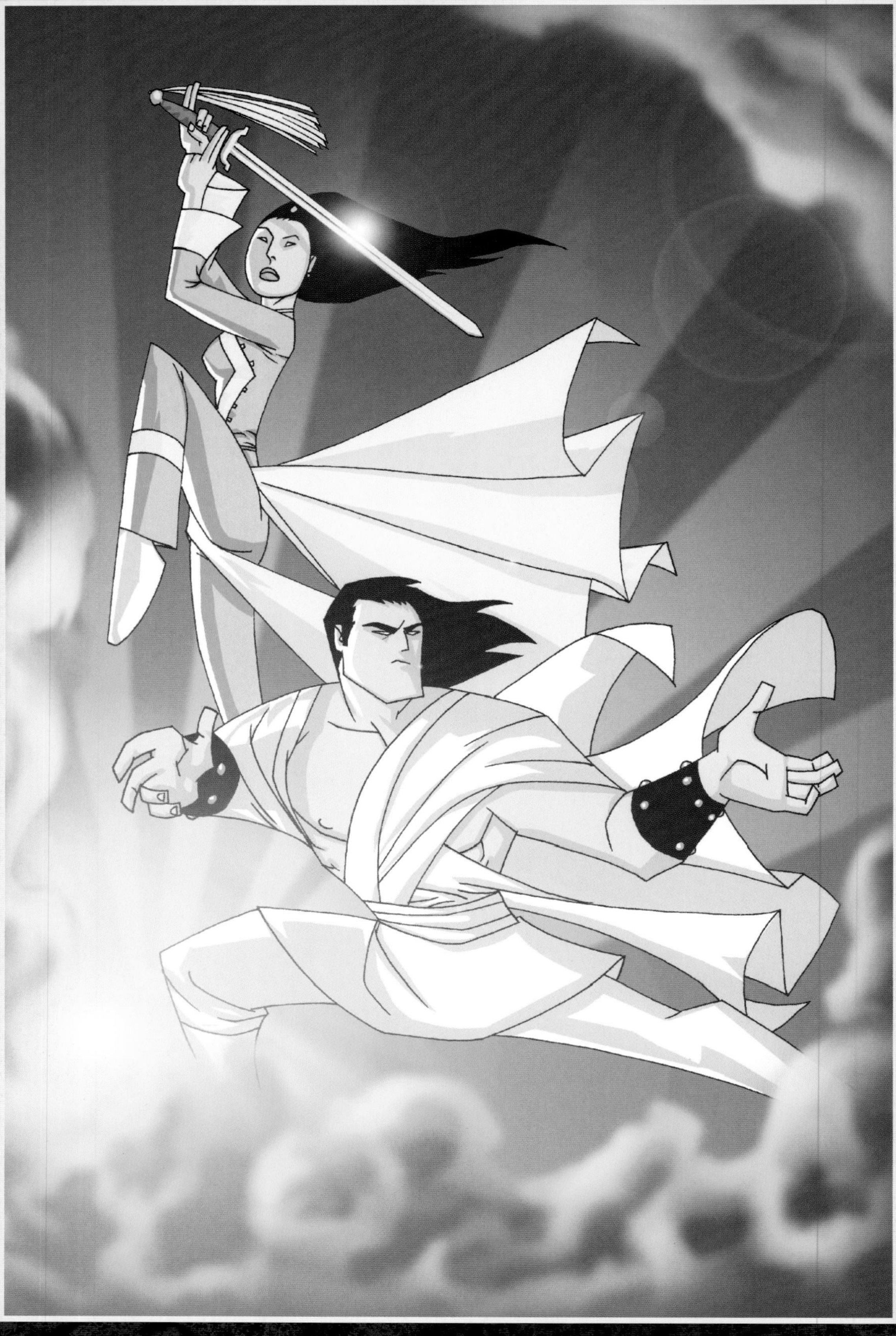

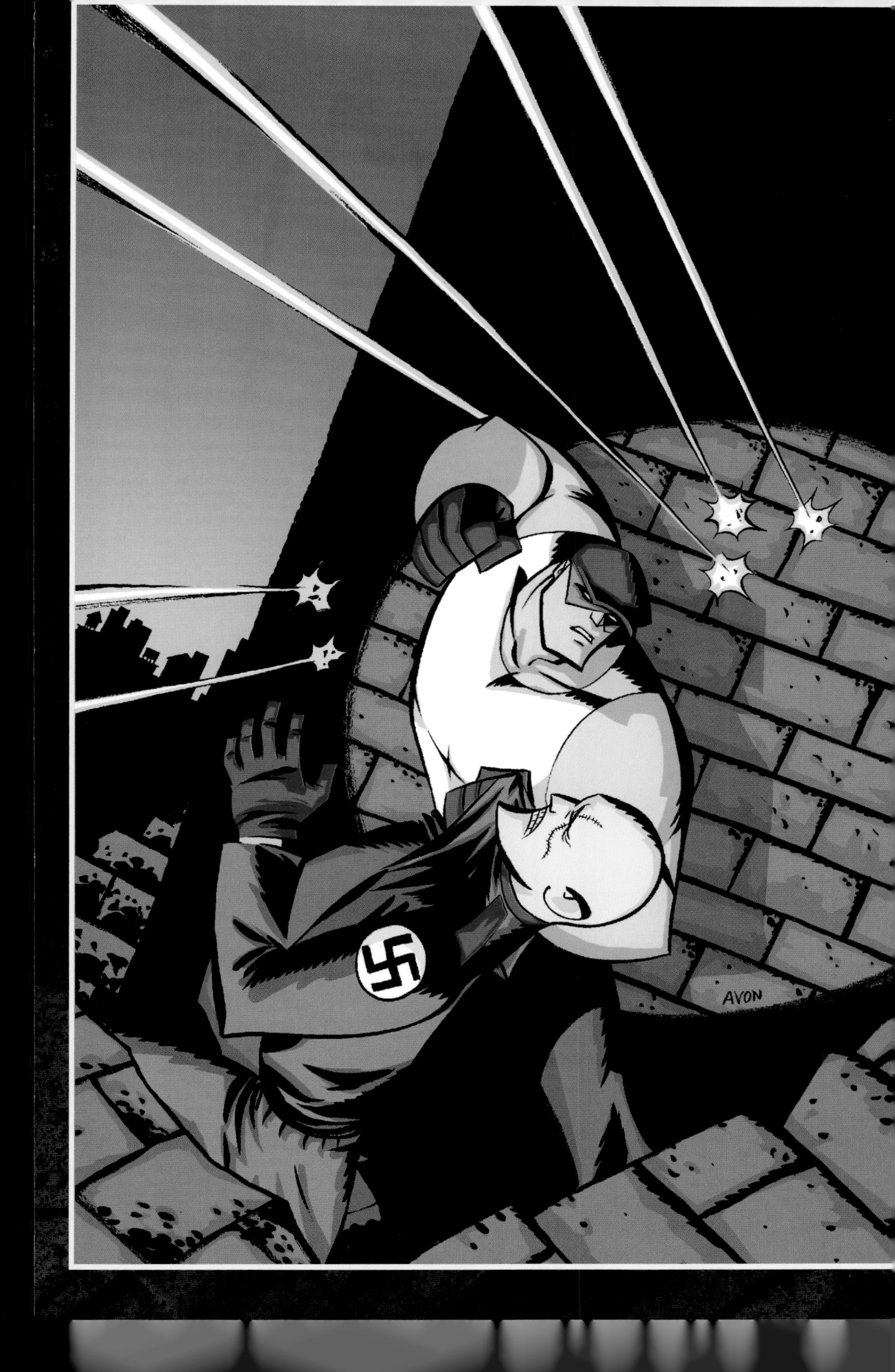
AVON

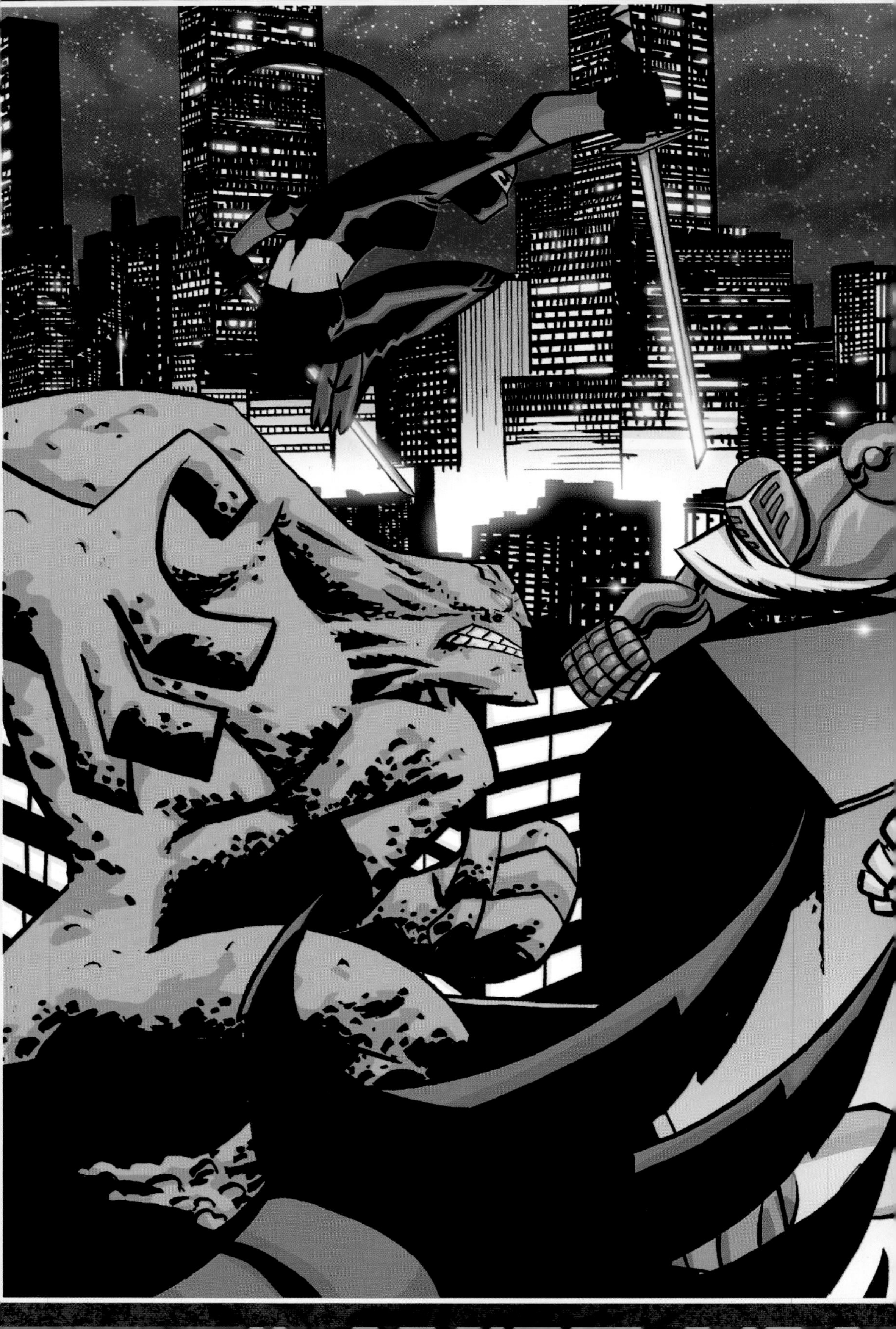

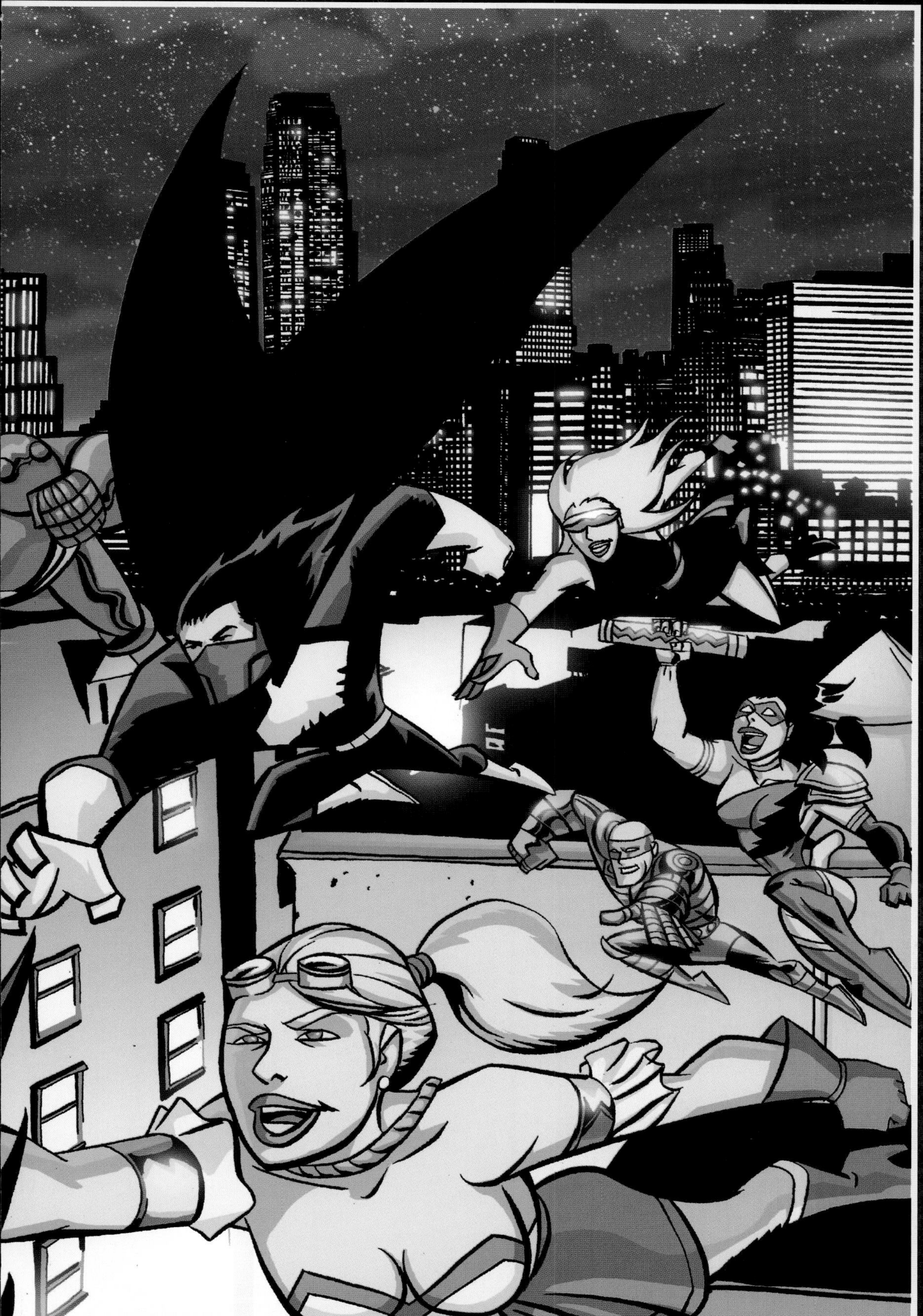

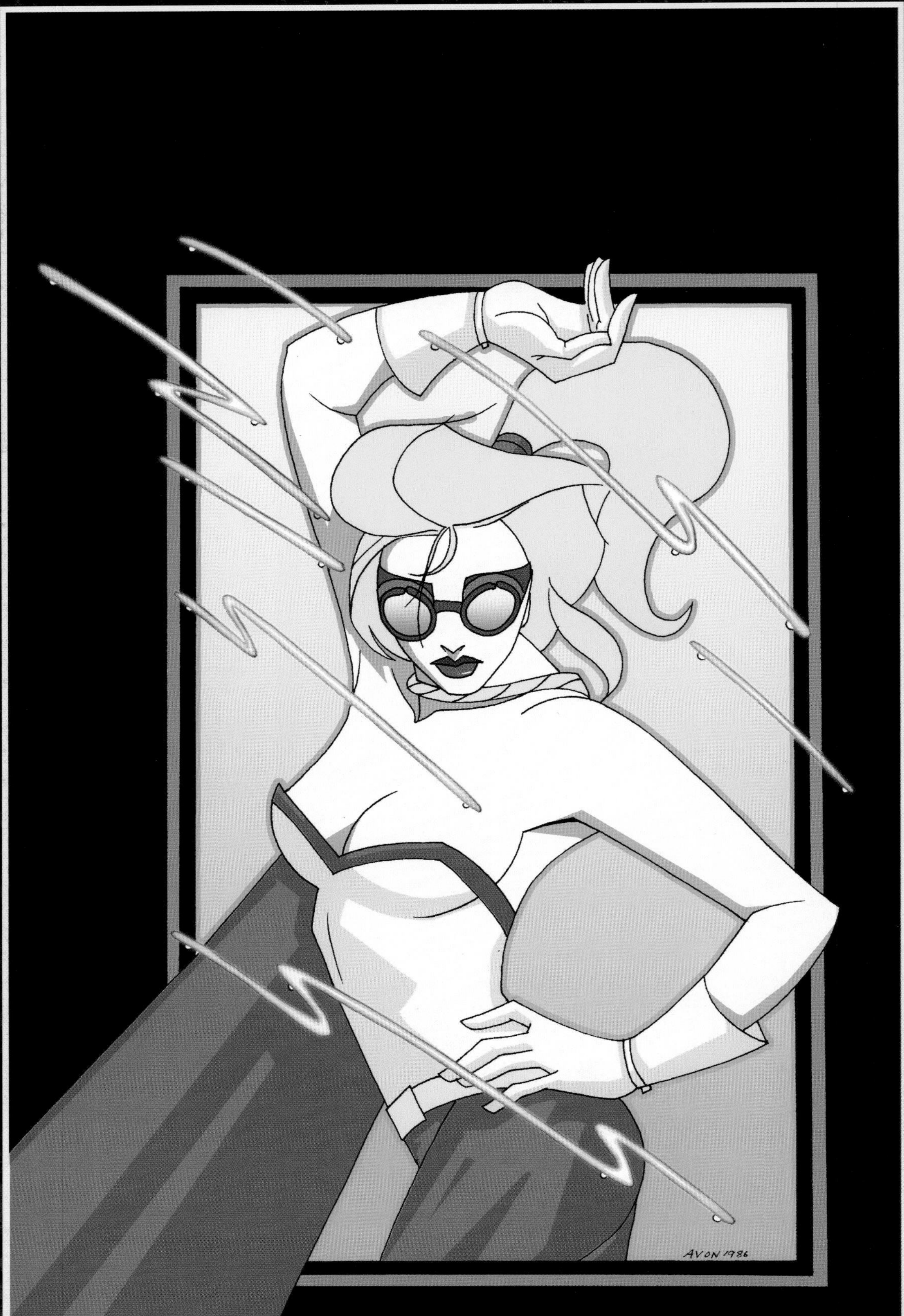
AVON 1986

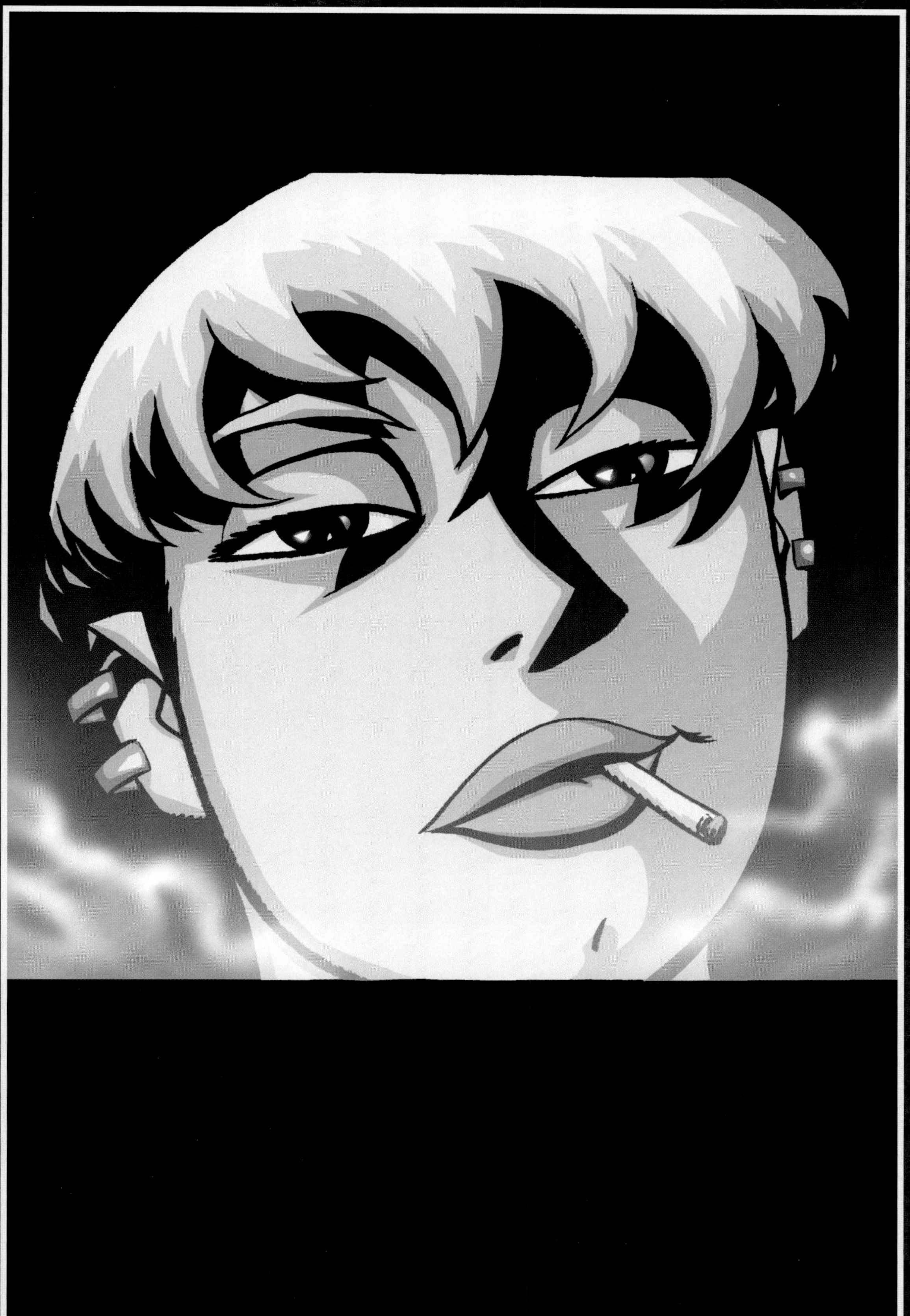

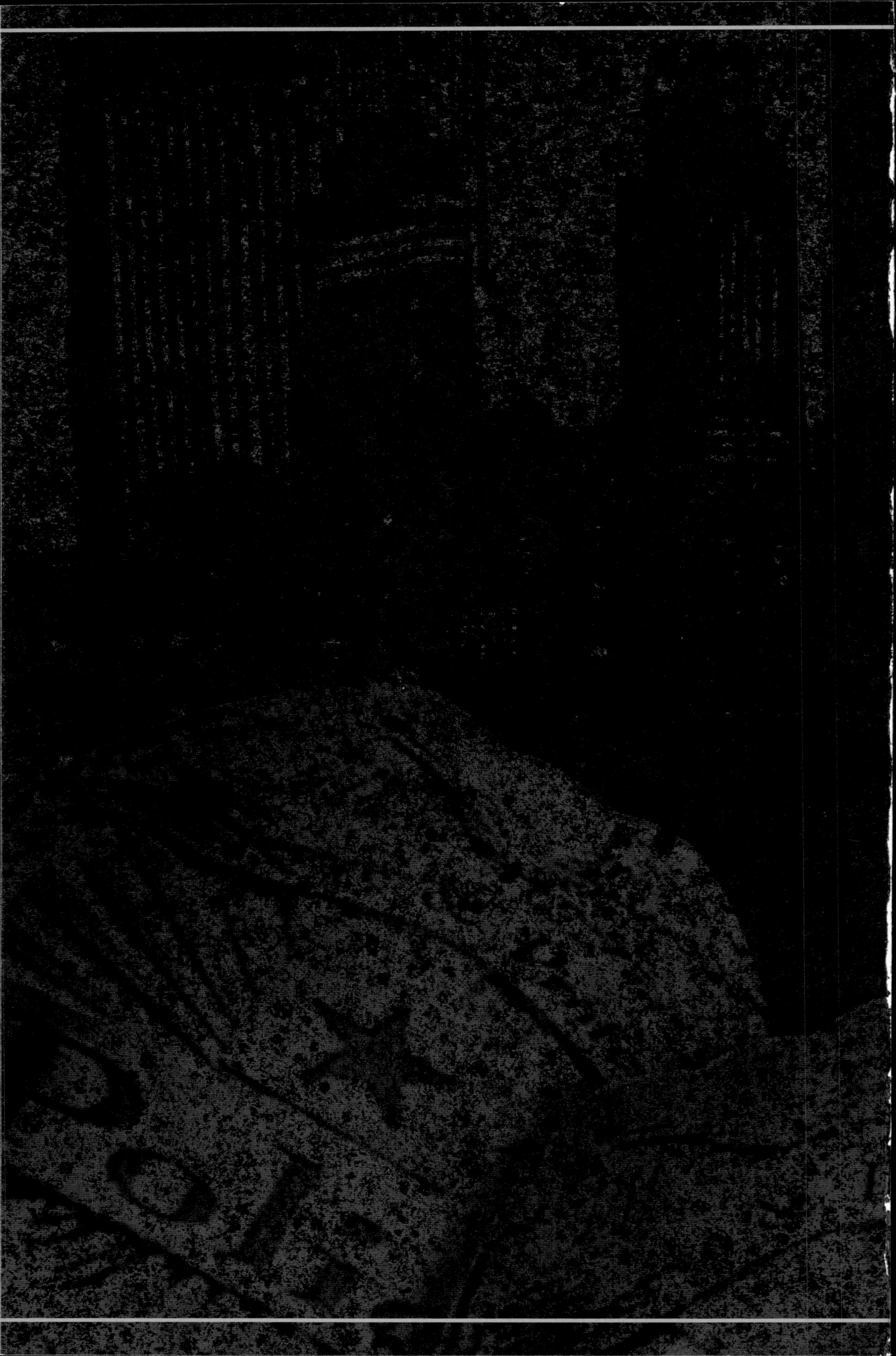